A GRAMMAR OF
NEW TESTAMENT GREEK

A GRAMMAR OF
NEW TESTAMENT GREEK
J. H. MOULTON

VOLUME III

SYNTAX

NIGEL TURNER

T&T CLARK
EDINBURGH

T&T CLARK LTD
59 GEORGE STREET
EDINBURGH EH2 2LQ
SCOTLAND

First published 1963
Latest impression 1998

ISBN 0 567 01013 9

British Library Cataloguing-in-Publication Data
A catalogue record for this book is available from the British Library

Printed in Great Britain by Page Bros, Norwich
Bound by Bookcraft Ltd, Avon

PREFACE

THIS volume on Syntax has been doomed to be delayed. Perhaps providentially, for after the revolution in Biblical studies during the first half of this century the time is most opportune to make a detailed survey of New Testament idiom. It is now over fifty years since the first edition of the Prolegomena appeared, and Dr. Moulton had perished at sea before completing Volume II. His pupil, Dr. W. F. Howard, saw that volume through the press in parts, from 1919 to 1929, but before he had opportunity to lay many plans for Volume III he himself died in 1952; and then, on condition that he had the assistance of someone who would collect the necessary material, Dr. H. G. Meecham assumed responsibility for the Syntax. It was on Dr. G. D. Kilpatrick's suggestion that I was permitted to help at this point, and we had done no more than compile a provisional bibliography when Dr. Meecham died in 1955. By the kind invitation of the publishers I then worked alone and broke the spell by living to complete Volume III. It was a privilege for me, both to bring Dr. Moulton's task to fruition in a new age, and to be associated with the distinguished name of Messrs. T. and T. Clark.

My care has been lightened by the publishers' trust in me, their generosity and wise guidance; and I am grateful to the specialist printers who, faced with many typographical problems, so promptly achieved such excellent craftsmanship.

NIGEL TURNER.

Hitchin, *Corpus Christi*, 1962.

CHRONOLOGICAL BIBLIOGRAPHY

General works on syntax. See separate chapters for detailed bibliography.

1. G. Pasor, *Grammatica Graeca Sacra Novi Testamenti Domini nostri Jesu Christi*, Amsterdam 1655 (the first NT Grammar; wise use is made of the LXX).
2. G. B. Winer, *Grammatik des neutestamentlichen Sprachidioms*[7], Leipzig 1867 (1st ed. 1822; the first scientific NT Grammar).
3. A. Buttmann, *Grammatik des neutestamentlichen Sprachgebrauchs*, Berlin 1859 (Eng. tr. by Thayer 1873). Good use of LXX.
4. W. Schmid, *Der Attizismus in seinen Hauptvertretern* (4 vols. and Index), Stuttgart 1887–97.
5. J. Viteau, *Étude sur le grec du NT. Le verbe: Syntaxe des propositions*, Paris 1893.
6. E. de W. Burton, *Syntax of the Moods and Tenses in NT Greek*, Edinburgh 1894.
7. G. B. Winer, *Gramm. des nt. Spr.* (see 2): 8th ed. by P. W. Schmiedel, I.1894, II 1.1897, II 2.1898.
8. A. N. Jannaris, *An Historical Greek Grammar*, London 1897.
9. W. W. Goodwin, *Syntax of the Moods and Tenses of the Greek Verb*, London 1897.
10. J. Viteau, *Étude sur le grec du NT comparé avec celui des Septante. Sujet, complément et attribut*, Paris 1897.
11. R. Kühner, *Ausführliche Grammatik der griechischen Sprache*, I, 3rd ed. by F. Blass, Hannover 1890.
12. R. Kühner, *Ibid.*, II, vols. 1 and 2, 3rd ed. by B. Gerth, Hannover and Leipzig 1898–1904.
13. H. Reinhold, *De graecitate Patrum Apostolicorum librorumque apocryphorum Novi Test. quaestiones gramm.* (Diss.), Halle 1898.
14. B. L. Gildersleeve, *Syntax of Classical Greek from Homer to Demosthenes* (2 vols.), New York 1900, 1911.
15. K. Meisterhans, *Grammatik der att. Inschr.*, 3rd ed. by E. Schwyzer, Berlin 1900 (previous ed. referred to sometimes).

16. P. Giles, *A Short Manual of Comparative Philology*, London 1901.

17. T. Nägeli, *Der Wortschatz des Ap. Paulus*, Göttingen 1905.

18. F. E. Thompson, *A Syntax of Attic Greek*, London 1907.

19. J. M. Stahl, *Kritisch-historische Syntax des griechischen Verbums der klassischen Zeit*, Heidelberg 1907.

20. A. Boatti, *Grammatica del grec del Nuovo Testamento*[2] (2 vols.), Venice 1908–1910.

21. G. A. Deissmann, *Bible Studies* (Engl. tr., A. Grieve)[2], Edinburgh 1909.

22. H. St. J. Thackeray, *A Grammar of the OT in Greek according to the Septuagint*, I, Cambridge 1909.

23. W. Warning, *De Vettii Valentis sermone* (Diss.) Münster 1909.

24. M. Johannessohn, *Der Gebrauch der Kasus und der Präp. in der Septuaginta*, I Gebrauch der Kasus (Diss.) Berlin 1910.

25. A. Thumb, *Handbuch der neugriech. Volkssprache*[2], Strassburg 1910.

26. J. H. Moulton, *A Grammar of NT Greek: Prolegomena*, Edinburgh 1906.

27. J. H. Moulton, *Einleitung in die Sprache des NT*. Auf Grund der vom Verf. neu bearbeiteten 3 engl. Aufl. übersetzte deutsche Ausgabe, Heidelberg 1911. (This amounts to a 4th edition of the *Prolegomena*).

28. M. Arnim, *De Philonis Byzantii dicendi genere* (Diss.), Greifswald 1912.

29. H. B. Swete, *An Introduction to the OT in Greek*, rev. by R. R. Ottley, Cambridge 1914.

30. J. H. Moulton and W. F. Howard, *A Grammar of NT Greek*, vol. II, Edinburgh 1919–1929.

31. L. Radermacher, *Neutestamentliche Grammatik*[2], Tübingen 1925.

32. H. G. Liddell and R. Scott, *A Greek–English Lexicon*, 9th ed. rev. by H. S. Jones, Oxford 1925–1940.

33. M. Johannessohn, *Der Gebrauch der Präpositionen in der LXX*, Berlin 1926.

34. H. Ljungvik, *Studien zur Sprache der apokrüphen Apostelgeschichten* (Diss.), Uppsala 1926.

35. E. Mayser, *Grammatik der griechischen Papyri aus der Ptolemäerzeit*, II vol. 1, Berlin 1926; II vol. 2, 1934; II, vol. 3, 1934.

36. J. Wackernagel, *Vorlesungen über Syntax mit besonderer Berücksichtigung von Griechisch, Lateinisch und Deutsch*[2], I, Basel 1926; II, 1928.

37. P. F.-M. Abel, *Grammaire du grec biblique suivie d'un choix de papyrus*, Paris 1927.

38. H. Pernot, *Études sur la langue des Évangiles*, Paris 1927.

39. R. Helbing, *Die Kasussyntax der Verba bei den LXX*, Göttingen 1928.

40. G. Sacco, *La koinè del Nuovo Testamento e la trasmissione del sacro testo. Lezioni preliminari per lo studio del NT greco con introduzione e crestomazia*, Rome 1928.

41. A. A. Tzartzanos, Νεοελληνικὴ σύνταξις ἤτοι Συντακτικὸν τῆς νέας ἑλληνικῆς γλώσσης . . . , Athens 1928.

42. J. H. Moulton and G. Milligan, *The Vocabulary of the Greek Testament*, London 1930.

43. J. Psichari, *Essai sur le grec de la Septante*, 1930.

44. A. T. Robertson, *A Grammar of the Greek NT in the Light of Historical Research*[5], New York 1931.

45. H. Ljungvik *Beiträge zur Syntax der spätgriechischen Volkssprache*, Uppsala 1932.

46. B. F. C. Atkinson, *The Greek Language*[2], Cambridge 1933.

47. G. Kittel and G. Friedrich, *Theologisches Wörterbuch zum NT*, Stuttgart 1933—.

48. G. Bonnacorsi, *Primi saggi di philologia neotestamentaria*, I, Turin 1933.

49. M. Zerwick, *Untersuchungen zum Markus-Stil*, Rome 1937.

50. S. G. Kapsomenakis, *Voruntersuchungen zu einer Grammatik der Papyri der nachchristl. Zeit*, Munich 1938.

51. M. Soffray, *Recherches sur la syntaxe de Saint Jean Chrysostome*, Paris 1939.

52. J. Humbert, *Syntaxe grecque* (Collection de Philologie Classique), Paris 1945.

53. M. Black, *An Aramaic Approach to the Gospels and Acts*, Oxford 1946, 2nd ed. 1954.

54. M.-J. Lagrange, *S. Matthieu*, Paris, 8th ed. 1948.

55. E. Schwyzer, *Griechische Grammatik*, vol. II, Munich 1950 (based on K. Brugmann).

56. C. F. D. Moule, *The Language of the NT* (inaugr. lect.), Camb. 1952.

57. C. F. D. Moule, *An Idiom Book of NT Greek*, Cambridge 1953.

58. F. Blass and A. Debrunner, *Grammatik des nt. Griechisch*[9], Göttingen 1954.
59. M. Zerwick, S.J., *Graecitas Biblica*[3], Rome 1955
60. R. Morgenthaler, *Statistik des nt. Wortschatzes*, 1958.
61. W. Bauer, *Griechisch-Deutsches Wörterbuch zu den Schriften des NT und der übrigen urchr. Literatur*[5], Berlin 1958.

CONTENTS

INTRODUCTION

BOOK ONE: BUILDING UP THE SENTENCE: ANALYTICAL

Chapter One

PART I.—WORD-MATERIAL FOR SENTENCE-BUILDING

Chapter Two

Chapter Three

Chapter Four

Chapter Five

Chapter Six

Chapter Seven

Chapter Eight

Chapter Nine

THE VERB: MOODS: OPTATIVE

Chapter Ten

THE VERB: NOUN FORMS: INFINITIVE

Chapter Eleven

PART II.—WORD-GROUPS DEFINING A NOUN OR ADJECTIVE

Chapter Twelve

Chapter Thirteen

Chapter Fourteen

Chapter Fifteen

PART III.—WORD-MATERIAL WHICH DEFINES A VERB

Chapter Sixteen

PREDICATIVE USE OF ADJECTIVES AND ADVERBS

Chapter Seventeen

CASE ADDITIONS TO THE VERB: WITHOUT A PREPOSITION

BOOK TWO: THE SENTENCE COMPLETE:
SYNTHETIC SYNTAX

PART I.—THE ORDINARY SIMPLE SENTENCE

Chapter Twenty

SUBJECT AND PREDICATE: APPARENT ABSENCE OF SUBJECT

Chapter Twenty-one

SUBJECT AND PREDICATE: ABSENCE OF THE VERB " TO BE "

Chapter Twenty-two

CONGRUENCE OF GENDER AND NUMBER

Chapter Twenty-three

THE SUBORDINATION OF CLAUSES

Chapter Twenty-four

INCONSISTENCIES BETWEEN MAIN AND DEPENDENT CLAUSES

PART II.—CONNECTIONS BETWEEN SENTENCES

Chapter Twenty-five

CO-ORDINATING PARTICLES

Chapter Twenty-six

IRREGULARITY OF SUBORDINATION

Chapter Twenty-seven

WORD ORDER

ABBREVIATIONS

(The numbers refer to the Bibliography)

Abel: 37
anarthr. : anarthrous
Beginnings: F. J. Foakes Jackson and Kirsopp Lake, *The Beginnings of Christianity*, London 1920–33
Bibl. Greek: Biblical Greek
Black AAGA²: 53
Blass-Debr. : 58
Burton: 6
class.: classical
Expos. T. and *Exp. T.* and *E.T.*: Expository Times
Gild. or Gildersleeve:˙ 14
Goodwin: 9
Helbing DKVS: 39
Hell. Greek: Hellenistic Greek
Humbert: 52
ICC: International Critical Commentary
JBL: Journal of Biblical Literature
JThS: Journal of Theological Studies
Jannaris: 8
Johannessohn DGKPS: 24
Johannessohn DGPS: 33
K-Blass: 11
K-G: 12
Kittel WB: 47
LXX: Septuagint
Ljungvik BSSVS: 45
Ljungvik SSAA: 34
LS: 32
MGr: Modern Greek
MT: Massoretic Text
MM Vocab: 42
Mayser: 35
Meisterhans-Schwyzer: 15
Moulton Proleg.: 26
Moulton Einl.: 27
Moulton-Howard: 30
Moule: 57
NEB: New English Bible, Oxford and Cambridge 1961
NT: New Testament
NTS: New Testament Studies

O′: Septuagint
OT: Old Testament
pap.: papyri
Pernot *Études*: 38
Radermacher[2] or Rad.[2]: 31
RSV: Revised Standard Version, Nelson 1946
Schmid Attizismus: 4
Schwyzer: 55
Soffray: 51
Stahl: 19
Thackeray: *OT Gr.*: 22
Vet. Test.: Vetus Testamentum
Wackernagel: 36
Winer-Schmiedel: 7
Zerwick: 59
Zerwick *Untersuchungen*: 49

A GRAMMAR OF NEW TESTAMENT GREEK

VOLUME III

INTRODUCTION

Dr. Moulton's own plan for the Grammar was that it should be not only a learned assessment of this field but also a practical guide to the student. I have designed volume III specially for three classes of reader: first, the teacher with an interest in exegesis, or the Bible translator either in Europe or among the young native churches who wishes to know the exact significance of every construction; then, the textual critic whom characteristic differences in the author's style may help to decide between variants; and also the student of comparative philology whose concern is the relationship of Biblical Greek to classical and Hellenistic.

The plan of this work follows a natural linguistic pattern: the building up of the sentence from its independent elements right to the complicated co-ordinations and subordinations of the period. The student who likes to have all his pronouns or all his prepositions dealt with together in one chapter must console himself by making good use of the index, for he will find that the various parts of speech are treated in the appropriate place as they contribute to the construction of the sentence. His compensation will be a better understanding of syntax in the true sense and not as a mere catalogue of parts of speech.

Space is very limited, and I wish I could have treated more fully (1) the syntax and style of Paul, (2) the study of word-order, and (3) the syntactic idiosyncrasies of the various authors, as I believe that all these are of great value for illuminating textual problems and difficult exegesis. During the course of the work those points have been constantly in mind, but their fuller treatment will yield ampler rewards. Some authors repeatedly confuse εἰς and ἐν, but others keep them carefully distinct. Knowledge of this kind brings deeper insight, as also does the study of Paul's use of the adnominal genitive, whether it is largely subjective or largely objective. We will never be at home with the fourth evangelist until we observe his peculiar performance with tenses and make allowance for his love of the perfect and pluperfect. What C. H. Turner once commenced to do for Markan syntax needs completing and carrying out for other authors too. Light has been thrown on the Infancy narrative and even on the elusive Q from a careful study of Luke's characteristic style [1]. Without a complete guide to his syntactical predilections, we will never know whether a writer is true to himself or whether he is going out of his way to impress.

I have tried to expose consistently the almost complete absence of classical standards in nearly every author. A tendency to use the active voice wherever possible in place of the declining middle [2], a tendency to give to certain transitive verbs like ἄγω and στρέφω an intransitive sense [3], to give an object to some intransitive verbs (e.g. βασιλεύω, εὐαγγελίζω), and to use the present in reported speech referring to the past; [4] the retreat of the Koine imperfect before the aorist and its confusion with the aorist; [5] the disappearance of the perfect through its assumption of aoristic functions and aoristic " weak " endings; [5] the even greater departure from classical standards in moods [6], especially the optative and infinitive, where the infin. of purpose after verbs of motion and the articular infinitive are on the increase (in spite of the retreat of the infin. before ἵνα and ὅτι in other respects [7]); the less rigid connection between the mood and the conjunction, so that the subjunctive may stand more often without ἄν and conversely ἄν (including ἐάν and ὅταν) stands with the indicative; the articular neuter of the adjective for an abstract noun [8] (τὸ ἅγιον, τὰ καλά); the non-classical use of the definite article generally; fluidity in the meaning and use of prepositions; weakening of the ἵνα-construction; indifference to the case after ἀκούω; lack of distinction between ἴδιος and αὐτοῦ, εἰς and ἐν, ὅστις and ὅς—these are well-known aberrations. More subtle, but as decisive for exegesis, is the infiltration of the comparative into the old preserves of the superlative, so that the

---

[1] *NTS* 2, 100–109; *Studia Evangelica*, Berlin 1959, 223–234.
[2] Ch. 6 § 4.   [3] Ch. 6 § 2.   [4] Ch. 7 § 1.
[5] Ch. 7 § 3.   [6] Ch. 8.   [7] Ch. 10.
[8] Ch. 1.

alert translator will not lose the opportunity of translating the one as the other, if necessary, and will not forget how philological study has made it essential to look at the superlative in the elative sense of *very*, and even to suspect the comparative in this way: πυκνότερον must be *very often* and ἀκριβέστερον *very accurately*. On the other hand, it is probably a unique feature of Bibl. Greek, under Hebraic influence, to put the positive for the superlative: e.g. *greatest* (not *great*) *in the kingdom of heaven*. So also the use of παρά and ὑπέρ with the positive, which is a Hebraic survival in Modern Greek; and since the general trend of the language was towards more emphatic comparison μᾶλλον is added to the normal comparative [1]. The translator will avoid over-translating, because nearly all ancient distinctions are blurred. He will look askance at the " theology of prepositions " and will remember that Hellenistic writers much prefer to add prepositions, especially composite prepositions, to the simple case and also confuse the nice distinctions between prepositions and between the cases, so that the exegete must always look at the context [2]. It is not that Biblical Greek has no standards at all, but pains must be taken to discover them outside the sphere of classical Greek, even outside secular Greek altogether, although the living Koine must be kept in mind always. Mark at least has simple rules which he carefully observes and, to a less extent, so have the others.

Biblical and Hellenistic Greek share the non-classical tendency to omit ὦ in the vocative. With the less cultured writers in post-Christian papyri the NT also shares the tendency to supply nominative forms for the vocative [3]. The popular love of emphatic speech demands a more extended use of pronouns of all kinds, both substantival and attributive [4], in the NT and Koine. Αὐτός becomes simply *he*. Personal pronouns are inserted where they would be unnecessary in class. Greek, and the genitives follow their nouns with a consistency which points to the influence of the Hebrew suffix. Possibly on an Aramaic model, the evangelists use the proleptic pronoun followed by a resumptive noun. But it is a Hellenistic tendency to use the simple personal pronoun for a reflexive; and in the

---

[1] See ch. 3.   [2] See ch. 18.   [3] See ch. 4.
[4] See ch. 5 and 14.

LXX and illiterate papyri we find the 3rd. pers. reflexive used
for all persons in the plural, as in the NT. Indirect pronouns
are going out of use, and the direct interrogative pronouns like
τίς find themselves serving in indirect questions; Hellenistic also
is the confusion of relative and interrogative pronouns [1]. The
genitive of the pers. pronoun (μου, etc.) is preferred in the Koine
to the possessive pronoun (ἐμός, etc.). Εἷς is a post-classical
substitute for τις. Ἴδιος becomes no more than ἑαυτοῦ or even
αὐτοῦ (simple possessive); and, in the Imperial period at any
rate, the anarthrous demonstrative pronoun is not necessarily
predicative [2]. The nice distinctions between οὐ and μή in class.
Greek have gone, and μή is encroaching [3]. Bibl. Greek shares
with the Koine the tendency to misuse and extend the scope of
the gen. absolute; [4] and, aided by Semitic precedent, to insert
the personal pronoun pleonastically; [5] moreover, the popular
tendency towards forceful expression is seen in the forming of
new compound particles, and Semitic simplicity in the reduced
number and use of particles [6].

In view of the Appendix to volume II, I have not supplied
a separate chapter on "Semitisms", which raise a vexed
question bedevilled by the objection that nearly all of them
appear in the papyri; but the discussion of the influence of the
LXX and Semitic idiom arises in every chapter of the book. To
some future work I leave discussion whether this influence
supports the hypothesis of a spoken Jewish Greek. The present
work does suggest that Bibl. Greek is a unique language with a
unity and character of its own. It does not follow that if a
construction occurs as frequently in the epistles as in the gospels
it will be less likely to have a Semitic origin [7], for direct translation is not the only possible medium of Semitic influence. When
the LXX was established its idioms powerfully influenced free
compositions of Biblical Greek [8]. The idiosyncrasies of Bibl.

---

[1] See ch. 5.   [2] See ch. 14 § 1.   [3] See ch. 19.
[4] See ch. 23 § 3f.   [5] See ch. 24 § 3.   [6] See ch. 25.
[7] See *Exp. T.* LXVII, 247. As a contrast to what this writer found
in the Loeb *Select Papyri*, vol. i, concerning the repetition of prepositions,
attention should be drawn to Mayser's considered opinion on the Ptolemaic
papyri which he had examined: " In der weitaus überwiegenden Mehrzahl
der beobachteten Fälle, zumal im Stil privater Urkunden, wird bei
καί, τε . . . καί, οὐ μόνον . . . ἀλλά usw. die Präposition nur einmal gesetzt."
(II 2, 516).
[8] Moulton-Howard 478.

Greek syntax are shared in varying degrees by almost all the NT writers, whether they were translating or not. There is a family likeness among these Biblical works, setting them apart from the papyri and from contemporary literary Greek, although the books with Semitic sources may have these features to an especial degree. This is so in the relation between the independent and attributive use of ἐκεῖνος, in which colloquial usage is entirely opposed to the Biblical; it is so with the position of ἕνεκα (-εν) [1], in the Bible the reverse of that of Polybius and the papyri; and with the three broad types of construction with πᾶς.

As to verbs, there was a Hellenistic tendency to use the historic present λέγει, etc., but its popularity in the NT is considerably helped by Aramaic precedent[2]. The perfective aorist is Hebraic. Although development of the perfect tense in the NT has reached a stage closely corresponding with that in the vernacular, there are very important respects in which it is different, and the NT represents a new development. The number of resultative perfects is few indeed compared with secular literary and vernacular texts, and the use of this form is limited to a small number of verbs, except in the emphatic, solemnly strained style of the fourth evangelist. Moreover, although a few examples of εἰμί with the perfect ptc. as a periphrastic tense appear in the Ptolemaic pap., they cannot be compared with the galaxy which is apparent in the LXX and NT [3]. Mayser's exx. are very few. Even Chantraine will not dismiss the probability of Aramaic influence. The perfect tense in general is much rarer in the NT than in the popular language, and it preserves a good deal more of its old force. While the old intransitives have almost all disappeared in the Koine, ἕστηκα and γέγονα being the only living forms, in the NT we do still have a few, especially where they can be understood with a *present* meaning (e.g. the two above, and τέθνηκα, ἤγγικα, πέποιθα, ἀνέῳγα). Some perfects are still true perfects, and not aorists, in spite of the universal confusion in the Ptolemaic and Imperial pap. Even in " colloquial " Mark, a significant distinction is sometimes made (15⁴⁴), and this is true of Paul (1 Co 15³). The oft repeated γέγραπται is correctly used, and other perfects retain their true present force.

---

[1] *Vet. Test.* 5, 1955, 208.   [2] See ch. 7 § 1.   [3] See ch. 7 § 9.

The history of the optative mood in the literary and colloquial Greek of the post-classical period is first a gradual decay
and subsequently a revival of this mood; in the first place, the
revival was due to atticistic influence, but popular Greek followed
the fashion in time. Now, the period in which this mood was
least in favour in secular writers is the period of the NT and the
later books of the LXX, which contrariwise display a comparative fondness for the mood. Is it the conservatism of religion?
It might only be that atticizing scribes confused like-sounding
endings. But the old Volitive optative is admirably suited to
the pious aspiration and longing of religious books. Volitive
optatives could owe their preservation to their incidence in the
solemn diction of Christian devotion and synagogue liturgy.
They appear in the LXX, and that version became the Church's
book. It is a form of speech well fitted for pious lips.

Some characteristically Biblical prepositions hardly occur
at all in the papyri; e.g. ὀπίσω (over 300 times in LXX and 26 in
NT), ἀπέναντι and κατέναντι. And ἔμπροσθεν is extremely
rare outside Biblical Greek. The use of cases with prepositions
is not that of the Koine, or the Biblical books show a more rapid
tendency to drop one or more of the cases, e.g.

		LXX	NT	Polybius	Papyri	Herodotus
ἐπί	(g:d:a)	1·5:1:3·7	1·2:1:2	1·5:1:3	4·5:1:2·5	
παρά	(g:d:a)	2·5:1:1·5	1·6:1:1·2		22·5:1:2·5	1·8:1:3·5
πρός	(g:d:a)	·23:1:43	·16:1:116	·2:1:15	·02:1:4	2:1:6
μετά	(g:a)	3·8:1	3·6:1	1·2:1	1·6:1	

The wider use of ἐν is remarkable in Bibl. Greek, e.g.:

	LXX	NT	Papyri
ἐν : παρά	1 : ·06	1 : ·07	1 : ·43
ἐν : περί	1 : ·06	1 : ·12	1 : ·28

It is a peculiarity of Bibl. Greek, and not of the Koine, to
use the feminine for neuter in certain expressions like εἰς κρυπτήν

and ἀπὸ μιᾶς, but the variations in the gender of λιμός are shared by the Koine [1].

A distributive *singular*, in preference to the plural, is distinctly Biblical, like τὸ σῶμα ὑμῶν, although we have κατὰ γεωργόν once in the papyri. The plural *worlds* and *heaven* belongs to Bibl. Greek, and is normal Greek only poetically. The allusive plural is normal Greek, but late : of Herod it is said, *They are dead who sought the child's life*; and *the prophets* (Mt 2²³) is simply Hosea; while ὄχλοι πολλοί is one vast crowd [2].

The use of *soul* for the reflexive pronoun must be uniquely Biblical. The use of αὐτός as a demonstrative (which has significance for exegesis) is doubtfully Koine and more likely to be due to Semitic influence; so also extra-Biblical examples of οὐ . . . πᾶς are rare [3]. Biblical Greek uses παρά and ὑπέρ for comparison in place of ἤ or the genitive and is fond of the genitive of quality. The dative is beginning to decline in Hell. Greek but the popularity of ἐν in Bibl. Greek gives it a false appearance of life [4].

The NT is not in line with the Koine in the use of cases after certain verbs. It uses the dat. as well as the acc. after προσκυνέω [5], and reverts to the Attic dat. after πειθαρχέω [6]. The acc. is invariable in the LXX (except atticistic 4Km 2²⁴, Ep. Je 65), and in the NT after καταράομαι, against the dat. of secular style [7]. The only two instances of acc. after ἐπηρεάζω which I can find, occur in NT, while secular Greek has the dative [8].

A partitive expression is often used in NT and LXX as subj. or obj. of the verb, e.g. θανατώσουσιν ἐξ ὑμῶν, without the help of τινας, in Lk 21¹⁶. This plays small part indeed in the non-Biblical language [9], and clearly reflects the Hebrew מִן. In partitive expressions the Ptolemaic papyri much prefer ἀπό to ἐκ [10], but NT writers prefer ἐκ and also often use ἐν in a partitive sense which is extremely rare in the papyri [11].

---

[1] See ch. 2.   [2] See ch. 2.   [3] Ch. 14 § 1.
[4] Ch. 17.
[5] Mayser II 2. 256; MMVocab.s.v.   The dat. becomes increasingly common in LXX : Helbing DKVS 296–298.
[6] Mayser II 2, 208. Ptolemaic pap. all gen.; dat. in A.D. 260 (MMVocab.s.v.).
[7] Kittel WB I 449; Helbing DKVS 71; Bauer s.v.
[8] Mayser II 2, 265.
[9] See ch. 15 § 2,1, I b; Mayser II 2, 351.
[10] Mayser II 2, 352.   [11] Mayser II 2, 353.

The position of the attributive adjective (and participle) in relation to the noun and article is in the Ptolemaic pap. quite different from that in Bibl. Greek. There are three possible positions : I. ὁ ἀγαθὸς ἀνήρ, II. ὁ ἀνὴρ ὁ ἀγαθός, III. ἀνήρ ὁ ἀγαθός. The art. before the noun is often omitted in Hell. Greek and particularly in the papyri, but that is very rare in Bibl. Greek [1]. I can find only one instance in the first twenty chapters of Genesis, and there are very few in the NT. As to the other two possible positions, if we take as a sample of iii/B.C. papyri the Hibeh Papyri nos. 27–120, there are twenty exx. of position I and ten exx. of the repeated article. The Tebtunis Papyri nos. 5–124 will serve for ii–i/B.C. : they have the first position with over 140 exx., but only four or five exx. with repetition of the article [2]. This is not like the picture in Bibl. Greek. In the Pauline and General epistles [3] (where direct rendering of a Hebrew text is ruled out) the proportion is : position I 24, position II 23, position III one only. Clearly the tendency in the papyri of the NT period is for the second position to be practically negligible (140 : 5), while Biblical writers are fond of the usage even when there is no emphasis. In LXX Ge 1–19 the proportion between positions I and II is 18 : 56, the very reverse of the proportion in iii/B.C. papyri. In 1 Km 1–6 the proportion is 1 : 16.

The construction ἐν τῷ with infin. occurs so often in Lk-Ac that to Dr. Howard it was " one more evidence of the great influence of the LXX on the style of Luke. " [4] It occurs in the papyri occasionally [5], but this expression, like εἰς τό and τοῦ c.infin. (of which Paul and Luke are specially fond) belongs almost exclusively to Bibl. Greek through the influence of Hebrew [6]. Dr. Howard observed that the use of ἵνα " had already gained great flexibility in the Κοινή " (p. 470). If one cannot claim that its even greater flexibility of use in the NT [7] was entirely due to Semitic influence, one must at least underline the difficulty of finding anywhere but in Biblical books such a

---

[1] See ch. 13 § 1.   [2] Mayser II 2, 25ff.
[3] The first chapters of the following books have been read : Ro, 1 and 2 Co, Ga, Ph, Col, Phm, 1 and 2 Th, 1 and 2 Ti, Ti, Heb, Jas, 1 and 2 Pt, 1 Jn.
[4] See the Appendix to vol. II of this Grammar, p. 451.
[5] Mayser II 1, 328.
[6] Mayser II 1, 321ff, 330; I 3, 43.   See below ch. 10 § 2b.
[7] See e.g. Radermacher[2] 193.   See below ch. 8 § 2 B2.

wide variety in the use of ἵνα, imperatival, causal, consecutive, epexegetical, within so small a space.

Other instances of the unique character of Bibl. Greek abound in peculiarities of word-order [1], in asyndeton [2] and parataxis [3], in the use of proleptic pronouns [4], and in the pleonastic insertion of personal pronouns [5], as well as in many other smaller and less significant ways.

I do not wish to prove too much by these examples, but the strongly Semitic character of Bibl. Greek, and therefore its remarkable unity within itself, do seem to me to have contemporary significance at a time when many are finding their way back to the Bible as a living book and perhaps are pondering afresh the old question of a " Holy Ghost language ". The lapse of half a century was needed to assess the discoveries of Deissmann and Moulton and put them in right perspective. We now have to concede that not only is the subject-matter of the Scriptures unique but so also is the language in which they came to be written or translated. This much is plain for all who can see, but the further question arises, whether such a Biblical language was the creature of an hour and the *ad hoc* instrument for a particular purpose, or whether it was a spoken language as well, something more than an over-literal rendering of Semitic idioms, a permanent influence and a significant development in the language. Students of Greek await the answer with interest.

---

[1] See ch. 27.   [2] See ch. 25 § 3.   [3] See ch. 26 § 1.
[4] See ch. 5 § 2 (a) 3 ; ch. 14 § 1. 2.   [5] See ch. 24 § 3.

BOOK ONE

BUILDING UP THE SENTENCE: ANALYTICAL

The minimal form of the sentence is Subject and Predicate. The Subject is usually expressed by a noun and the Predicate by a verb; and this verb may need a direct or indirect Object. But often the Predicate too may be a noun or its substitute.

CHAPTER ONE

SUBSTITUTES FOR NOUNS IN SUBJECT, OBJECT OR PREDICATE

§ 1. The Article with Adjectives [1]

A subject, object or predicate may be expressed without using a noun. The usual substitute for it in cultured speech is a non-substantival neuter expression, but sometimes also a masculine or feminine one. We find the article with a non-predicate adjective, and used in both (a) an individual and (b) a generic sense. By this method is represented a quality *par excellence*.

(a) Of God: Jn 5⁴⁴ ὁ μόνος BW, 1 Jn 5²⁰ ὁ ἀληθινός. Of Christ: Lk 4³⁴ ὁ ἅγιος, Ac 22¹⁴ ὁ δίκαιος. Of Satan: ὁ πονηρός. Also ἡ ἔρημος. *the desert*, Jas 2⁶ τὸν πτωχόν *beggar*. Also ὁ σοφός.

(b) οἱ πλούσιοι and οἱ ἅγιοι. οἱ πολλοί either *the majority*, or *the many* previously indicated. 1 Pt 4¹⁸ ὁ δίκαιος, ὁ ἀσεβής. Mt 25⁴ αἱ φρόνιμοι. Also οἱ μαλακοί.

But the substantival expression is more usually neuter. In the pre-Christian papyri are τὸ ἅγιον, τὸ ἄξιον, τὸ δίκαιον, τὰ καλά, τὸ στρατιωτικόν *the army*, τὸ ἱππικόν, τὸ ναυτικόν, etc. (Mayser II 1, 1ff). Again we have (a) individual, (b) generic, more often; and (c), especially in Paul, the equivalent of an abstract noun; the latter is a class. idiom (Hdt. Thuc.) and higher contemporary Koine (Strabo, Joseph., I Cl.), as well as Biblical (LXX).[2] In the NT it is characteristic of Paul and Luke and not often in the Gospels. This abstract usage followed by the gen. does not appear in the papyri.

(a) Individual concrete expressions: 2 Co 8¹⁵ OT τὸ πολύ, τὸ ὀλίγον, Philem¹⁴ τὸ ἀγαθόν *a good deed*, Ro 8³ τὸ ἀδύνατον *the one thing the Law could not do*. 1 Co 3¹⁰ θεμέλιον, sc. λίθον, 7⁵ ἐκ συμφώνου. Also τὸ

---

¹ K-G I 266ff., Gild. I § 36, Mayser II 1, 1ff. Ljungvik SSAA 24f. Schmid, Attizismus IV 608.

² Also Apost. Fathers, e.g. Mart. Petri 82²⁰ τὸ παράδοξον τοῦ θεάματος, and Pass. Andr. alt. 281⁴ff.

13

καλόν. Never τὸ συνειδός for συνείδησις, but τὸ σωτήριον for ἡ σωτηρία (Lk 2³⁰ 3⁶, Ac 28²⁸, Eph 6¹⁷ all OT), and often τὸ μαρτύριον for ἡ μαρτυρία. Neut. sing. is also used collectively to denote persons: τὸ ἔλαττον . . . τοῦ κρείττονος = οἱ ἐλάττονες . . . τῶν κρειττόνων; also neut. pl. with a gen. 1 Co 1²⁷ᶠ τὰ μωρὰ τοῦ κόσμου, etc, Papyri: τὸ δυνατόν, τὸ λοιπόν, τὰ ἴδια, τὰ καλά, τὰ ὑπάρχοντα.

(b) Generic: Mt 6¹³ τοῦ πονηροῦ (but masc?), 12³⁵ = Lk 6⁴⁵ τὰ (B al om.) ἀγαθά . . . πονηρά, Lk 6⁴⁵ τὸ ἀγαθόν, Ro 3⁸ τὰ κακά, τὰ ἀγαθά 13³ τὸ ἀγαθόν good works, Gal 6¹⁰ same, Mt 13⁴⁸ τὰ καλά . . . τὰ σαπρά fish.

(c) Abstract ideas; usually with a following gen.: Ro 1¹⁹ τὸ γνωστὸν τοῦ θ. knowledge concerning God (Chrysost.) or what is known (or can be known) about God (Origen) or God in his knowableness (Kittel WB I 719), 1²⁰ τὰ ἀόρατα αὐτοῦ he the Invisible (ib.) 2⁴ τὸ χρηστὸν τοῦ θ. = χρηστότης (which precedes) or more definitely God in his kindness (ib.), 9²² τὸ δυνατὸν αὐτοῦ how powerful he is, 1 Co 4⁵ τὰ κρυπτὰ τοῦ σκότους¹ the darkness which hides, 1²⁵ τὸ μῶρον τοῦ θ. = μωρία (which precedes) or God seeming to be foolish; τὸ ἀσθενὲς τοῦ θ. similarly. 7³⁵ τὸ εὔσχημον καὶ εὐπάρεδρον τῷ κυρίῳ, 2 Co 4¹⁷ τὸ παραυτίκα ἐλαφρὸν τῆς θλ. ἡμῶν, 8⁸ τὸ τῆς . . . γνήσιον what is genuine with respect to . . . , Ph 3⁸ τὸ ὑπερέχον τῆς = ὑπεροχή, 4⁵ τὸ ἐπιεικὲς ὑμῶν, Col 1¹⁶ τὰ ὁρατὰ καὶ ἀόρατα (no gen.), Heb. 6¹⁷ τὸ ἀμετάθετον τῆς, 7¹⁸ τὸ αὐτῆς ἀσθενὲς καὶ ἀνωφελές, 1 Pet 1⁷, Jas 1³ τὸ δοκιμεῖον = something tested (Deiss. BS 259ff. Mayser 1² 3, 52). Cp. Strabo's τὸ εὐμεταχείριστον τῆς θήρας. LXX. 2 Mac 4⁴ τὸ χαλεπὸν τῆς, 3¹⁶ τὸ τῆς . . . παρηλλαγμένον, 2³¹ τὸ σύντομον τῆς . . . , τὸ ἐξεργαστικὸν τῆς, 4 Mac 6¹³ ἐν θαυμαστῷ τῆς , 18⁸ τὰ ἀγνὰ τῆς.

§ 2. The Article with (1) Attributive Adverbs

This is like the class. τὰ εἰς τὸν πόλεμον things belonging to war. Thus in pre-Christian papyri: πᾶν τὸ ἑξῆς all other contributions, τὸ ἐφαύριον, ἐν τῷ μεταξύ, ἀπὸ τοῦ νῦν, ἕως . . . , μέχρι . . . , τὸ πρότερον, τὸ πρωΐ, τὰ ἄνω, τὰ ἐνταῦθα, τὰ ἐπάνω, εἰς τὰ μάλιστα, ἐκ τοῦ ὀπίσω (Mayser II, 1, 13). In the NT: εἰς τὸ μέσον, ἐν τῷ μέσῳ, ἐκ τοῦ μέσου (without art., if a gen. follows), Lk 16²⁶ οἱ (S*BD om.) ἐκεῖθεν, Mt 24²¹ ἕως τοῦ νῦν, 23²⁶ τὸ ἐντός, Jn 8²³, 1 Co 14¹⁶ τὸ ἀμήν, 2 Co 1²⁰ τὸ ναί, τὸ ἀμήν, Rev 3¹⁴ ὁ ἀμήν, Col 3¹ᶠ τὰ κάτω, τὰ ἄνω, 2 Co 1¹⁷ Jas 5¹² τὸ ναί, τὸ οὔ. Sometimes the noun so formed is used as an adverbial accusative: τὸ πρωΐ, τὸ ἑπτάκις Lk 17⁴D, τὸ ἀνὰ δηνάριον Mt 20¹⁰ SCLNZ everyone a penny.

The Article with (2) prepositional phrases. Mayser II 1, 9–13: τὰ ἐκ τῆς γῆς offspring or product, hence Ro 12¹⁸ τὸ ἐξ ὑμῶν so far as it originates from you; papyri τὸ κατ' ἄνδρα distributive, hence pap. and NT τὸ καθ' ἡμέραν daily; but also in pap., Ac and Paul τὰ κατά τι expresses general relationship, so τὸ κατὰ σάρκα

¹ Cp. Ex Actis Andr. 45²⁶ᶠ τὸ κρυπτόμενον αὐτοῦ τῆς φύσεως.

Ro 9⁵ = *as far as the material side is concerned*; Ph 1¹² Col 4⁷ τὰ·κατ' ἐμέ = *what concerns me*; but the same phrase Ac 25¹⁴ τὰ κατὰ Παῦλον is obviously *Paul's case* in the courts and this may be the correct interpretation in Ph and Col (*my lawsuit*); so Ac 16³⁹ D τὰ καθ' ὑμᾶς = *we acted amiss at your trial in court* (πρᾶγμα). But 2 Co 10⁷ τὰ κατὰ πρόσωπον = *what is in front of you* (spatial); Ro 12⁵ τὸ καθ' εἷς a stereotyped adv. Ac 28⁷ τὰ περὶ τὸν τόπον ἐκεῖνον (local), Herm V iii 3¹ τὰ περὶ τὸν πύργον. Local in the papyri, but sometimes of general relationship like κατά; hence probably *my circumstances* in Ph 2²³ τὰ περὶ ἐμέ, and not *my surroundings*. The gen. τὰ περί τινος is frequ. in pap. and in Luke and Paul, e.g. Lk 24²⁷ τὰ περὶ ἑαυτοῦ, Ac 18²⁵ τὰ περὶ τοῦ 'Ι. Mk 5²⁷ (but τά om. by SᶜAC²DLW al) *things concerning . . . .* With παρά: Mk 5²⁶ δαπανήσασα τὰ παρ' (παρ' om. DW) ἑαυτῆς class., Lk 10⁷ πίνοντες τὰ παρ' αὐτῶν, Ph 4¹⁸ δεξάμενος . . . τὰ παρ' ὑμῶν. In the pap. τὸ παρά τινος (sing.) is a sum of money to be paid by someone, esp. taxes due (Mayser II 1, 12), but τὰ παρά τινος (pl.) is something sent, an answer, a mandate, an errand, an ordinance. With Ph 4¹⁸ cp. P. Alexandr. 4, 15 (iii/B.C.) εἴλεφεν τὰ παρὰ σοῦ = *he received what you sent*, but P. Teb. I 12, 23 (118 B.C.) ἀποδέχομαι τὰ παρὰ σοῦ = *your instructions*. Cp. Jos. BJ. 2, 124, Ant. 8, 175.

These were all neuter but we have masc. and fem. also with prepositional phrases: Mayser II 1, 14–20 ἀπό, διά g., ἐκ, εἰς, ἐν, ἐπί g., κατά acc., μετά g., παρά g. acc., περί acc., πρό, πρός dat., ὑπό acc. ἀπό: Heb 13²⁴ οἱ ἀπὸ τῆς 'Ιτ. *Italians.* Inscr. 60 B.C. (Preis. Samm. 4980, 6) οἱ ἀπὸ τῆς πόλεως. Pap. i/B.C. (ib. 5216, 11) οἱ ἀπὸ 'Αλεξανδρείας, etc., very frequ. to represent a person's home or extraction. In the pap. also to denote a class: οἱ ἀπὸ τῆς τραπέζης are *bank officials* PSI IV 383, 8 (248 B.C.), like Ac 12¹ οἱ ἀπὸ τῆς ἐκκλησίας *church folk*, 15⁵ οἱ ἀπὸ τῆς αἱρέσεως.

ἐκ: very frequ. in Paul as we use *-ists* of members of a sect or persuasion: Ro 3²⁶ οἱ ἐκ πίστεως 'Ι. *believers in J.*, 4¹⁴· ¹⁶ οἱ ἐκ νόμου *who live by the Law*, ὁ ἐκ πίστεως 'Α. *who shares A.'s faith* (a persuasion), Ac 6⁹ οἱ ἐκ τῆς συναγωγῆς (a sect). Class. use of a country: Isocr. 4⁸² οἱ ἐκ τῆς 'Ασίας *Asians.* Papyri of descendants, members of a family or class, residents (like ἀπό); members of a family in Ro 16¹¹οἱ ἐκ τῶν Ναρκίσσου.

εἰς: Mk 13¹⁶ ὁ εἰς τὸν ἀγρόν. Ac 2³⁹ οἱ εἰς μακράν local.

ἐν: Mk 13¹⁴ οἱ ἐν τῇ 'Ι. local.

ἐπί: Mk 13¹⁵ ὁ ἐπὶ τοῦ δώματος local.

κατά: Ac 25²³ οἱ κατ' ἐξοχήν *eminent men.* Eph 5³³ οἱ καθ' ἕνα *as individuals.*

παρά g. : in class. Gk. *those sent out by.* In pap. usually someone's *agent* or assistant, a *proxy,* but less often of relatives and friends (as Mk 3²¹) W. Chr. 10, 6 (130 B.C.) etc., esp. ἡ μήτηρ καὶ οἱ παρ' ἡμῶν πάντες in a private letter BGU VI 1300, 4 (iii–ii/B.C.), 1 Cl. 12⁴ *king's messengers,* 1 Esd 1¹⁵ 1 Mac 2¹⁵ *a king's proxy,* Mk 3²¹ (see J. Moulton in *ET* 20, 1909, 476) οἱ παρ' αὐτοῦ but not DW and Lat. *his kinsfolk,* LXX Su³³ *her family and friends,* 1 Mac 9⁴⁴ vl⁵⁸ *his men.* Cf. Jos. Ant. 1, 193.

περί: Mk 4¹⁰ Lk 22⁴⁹ οἱ περὶ αὐτόν *his disciples; J. and his disciples* is impossible. Ac 13¹³ 21⁸TR οἱ περὶ (τὸν) Π. *Paul and his party* (class.); *the escorts alone* is impossible. Later than class. οἱ περί τινα was often a periphrasis for the person alone: Plu. Pyrrh. 20, 1 οἱ περὶ Φαβρίκιον = *Fabricius;* Tiber. Gracch. 2, 3 οἱ περὶ Δροῦσον = *Drusus;* so in Polyb. 4, 36; 6, 21; 11, 2; Diod. Sic. 1, 16; 1, 37; 19, 19; Ep. Arist. 51; Philo vi cont. 15; Jos. Ant. 13, 187; 15, 370; c. Ap. 1, 17. Probably we have this in NT: Jn 11¹⁹ τὰς περὶ M. καὶ M. = *Martha and Mary* only (p⁴⁵ AΘ al.). There is little if any support in the pap., unless P. Flind. Petr. I 29, 4 τὰ περὶ τὴν ἀναδενδράδα (Radermacher 2, 118).

The Article with (3) *genitives of Nouns.* In the pre- Christian papyri this neuter expression denotes (a) residence, possessions, property, house or home of the person in the genitive (Mayser II 1, 8) ; (b) with impers. genitive the phrase is largely periphrastic : τὰ τῆς γεωργίας = *field work.*

(*a*) *personal*: Lk 20²⁵ τὰ Καίσαρος, τὰ τοῦ θεοῦ *property of,* 1 Co. 1¹¹ ὑπὸ τῶν Χλόης (strictly ὑπὸ τῶν τῶν Χλόης *by them of Chloe's house*).

(*b*) *impersonal.* Nothing more subtle than periphrasis is involved : Mt 21²¹ τὸ τῆς συκῆς *the fig tree,* Ro 14¹⁹ τὰ τῆς εἰρήνης *peace,* Jas 4¹⁴ τὸ (τὰ A) τῆς αὔριον *tomorrow,* 2 Pt 2²² τὸ τῆς ἀληθοῦς παροιμίας *the true proverb.*

§ 3. The Ellipse of Various Nouns

The absence of the noun (although its idea is quite necessary, in contrast to § 1 above) occurs in adjectival and other kinds of attributes (pronominal, participial, adverbial), and the context supplies its lack [1].

Certain nouns are liable to ellipse in this way in NT and contemporary Greek. So ὁδός is to be supplied in the papyri as in Lk 3⁵ OT εἰς εὐθείας, 5¹⁹ ποίας, 19⁴ ἐκείνης, and also γῆ or χωρά very frequently: Mt 3⁵ etc. ἡ περίχωρος (Plut. LXX), 23¹⁵ ἡ ξηρά (Xen. LXX), Mk 15³⁹ ἐξ ἐναντίας (D substitutes ἐκεῖ and W omits), Lk 1³⁹· ⁶⁵ ἡ ὀρεινή, ἡ ἔρημος, ἡ

---

[1] K-G I 265ff. Gild. I §§ 32–35. Mayser II 1, 20ff.

οἰκουμένη (world; class., pap., MGr.), 17²⁴ or better scil. μερίδος (T. Levi 18⁴), Heb 11²⁹ DᶜKLP διὰ ξηρᾶς (but SAD*E p¹³ p⁴⁶ supply γῆς).

In dates in the pap. ἡμέρα is almost always omitted: Mt 11²³ etc. μέχρι τῆς σήμερον (elsewhere with ἡμέρα), Mt 27⁶² (Mk, Lk, Jn, Jas) τῇ (ἐπ) αὔριον like P. Hamb. I no. 27, 4 (250 B.C.) τῆι ἐφαύριον. Lk 13³² Ac 27¹⁹ τῇ τρίτῃ (elsewhere τῇ τρ. ἡμ.) like P. Eleph. 5, 17 (284 B.C.) τρίτηι. Lk–Ac τῇ ἑξῆς. Lk 13³³ τῇ ἐχομένη, cp. P. Hal. 1, 30 (iii/B.C.) τῆι ἐπομένηι, but in Ac 21²⁶ with no ellipse of ἡμ. Ac 16¹¹ 20¹⁵ 21¹⁸ τῇ ἐπιούσῃ, like P. Petr. III 56(b) 12 (260 B.C.), but no ellipse of ἡμ. in Ac 7²⁶. Ac 20⁷ etc. τῇ μιᾷ τῶν σαββάτων. Heb 4⁴ ἡ ἑβδόμη, but same verse has ἡμ. Herm. S. VI 5³ (Clem. Hom. IX.1) πρὸ μιᾶς. Possibly ἀφ᾽ ἧς (Ac 24¹¹ 2 Pt 3⁴ 1 Mac 1¹¹: since)¹, is an ellipse of ἡμ. (or ὥρα in Lk 7⁴⁵). There is no ellipse of ἡμ. at Col 1⁶· ⁹ Herm. M. IV 4³, but the phrase is virtually a conjunction.

Χείρ is frequ. omitted in phrases like ἡ δεξιά, ἡ ἀριστερά Mt 6³ etc., ἐν δεξιᾷ Ro 8³⁴ etc. (unless we assume ἐνδέξια, class., in view of the fact that NT writers have ἐκ δεξιῶν, not ἐν δ.). Herm. S. IX 12⁸ has δεξιά and εὐώνυμα. MGr. also. Ptolemaic pap.: δεξιάν P. Petr. II 45 (248 B.C.), but χείρ is inserted also in pap.

It is probable that we should supply περίοδος with -μηνος and -ήμερος ending adjectives. For νυχθήμερος see Blass-Debr. § 121. Hdt 2, 124 ἡ τρίμηνος. Polyb. VI 34³ ἡ δίμηνος, XXVII 7² ἡ ἕκμηνος. LXX Ez 39¹⁴ τὴν ἑπτάμηνον. 4 Mac 16⁷ ἑπτὰ δεκάμηνοι. Jg 19²A 20⁴⁷A τετράμηνος anarthrous. Ditt. Syll³ 410⁴· ²⁴ (c 274 B.C.), 442³· ¹⁷ (c 250 B.C.). In pre-Christian papyri: Petr. III 78, 13 (iii/B.C.) etc. ἡ πενθήμερος. PSI IV 380, 6 (249 B.C.) ἡ δίμηνος. 408, 9 (iii/B.C.) ἡ τετράμηνος (Mayser II 1, 23). Jn 4³⁵ τετράμηνος anarthrous (-νον HW al). Heb 11²³ OT τρίμηνον (= Ex 2² μῆνας τρεῖς) (-ος p⁴⁶).

The ellipse of ὥρα is probable in other similar examples (e.g. PSI IV 391, 4 (241 B.C.) τῆι δευτέραι τῆς νυκτός): ἐξαυτῆς at once. Not class. are πρωΐα and ὀψία in Mt Mk Jn Herm. Mk 11¹¹B ὀψίας οὔσης (other MSS either add τῆς ὥρας or substitute ὀψέ), with which cp. BU II 380³ (iii/A.D.) ὀψ(ε)ίας τῆς ὥρας, P. Ox. III 475¹⁶ (A.D. 182) ὀψίας.

Other less frequ. noun-ellipses are the following:

Ἄνεμος: Ac 27¹⁵ τῷ πνέοντι (Western).

Ἄγαλμα: 19³⁵ τὸ διοπετές.

Αὔρα: 27⁴⁰ τῇ πνεούσῃ (indicated by Arrian ep. ad Traj. 5 ταῖς αὔραις ταῖς ... πνεούσαις). Lucian Herm. 28, Char. 3 τῷ πνέοντι.

Γλῶσσα: Rev 9¹¹ ἐν τῇ ἑλληνικῇ (S ἑλληνιδι), or supply διάλεκτος or φωνή LXX.

Δραχμή: Ac 19¹⁹ ἀργυρίου (sc. δραχμῶν, but we would expect ἀργυρίων). Ἱμάτιον: Mt 11⁸ ἐν μαλακοῖς. Jn 20¹² Herm. V. IV 2¹ ἐν λευκοῖς. Rev 18¹²· ¹⁶ βυσσίνου, πορφύρας etc. Pap. (Mayser II 1, 26).

Μέρος: not class. but pre-Chr. pap (τὸ τρίτον, τέταρτον passim) Rev: τὸ τρίτον, τέταρτον, δέκατον. Mk 16⁵? ἐν τοῖς δεξιοῖς.

---

¹ And in weak variants in Herm. S. VIII 14A (but read ἄφες with P. Mich. See below p. 94.) 6⁶A (but read ἀφότε with P. Mich.).

Πληγή: Lk 12⁴⁷ᶠ δαρήσεται πολλάς . . . ὀλίγας. 2 Co 11²⁴ τεσσεράκοντα παρὰ μίαν.

Πύλη: Jn 5² but this could not be supplied by the general reader without local knowledge; it is suspect, being om. by Syr^cur. pesh.

'Ράβδος: Heb 5⁷ ἱκετηρίας (or sc. ἐλαία). Büchsel in Kittel WB III 297f traces the origin to the olive branches of the suppliant, whence after Isocr. the adj. came to mean *earnest supplication*.

"Ὕδωρ: Mt 10⁴² ψυχροῦ. Jas 3¹¹ τὸ γλυκὺ καὶ τὸ πικρόν. Aristoph. Nub. and pap: θερμόν (Gild. I § 38).

'Ὑετόν: Jas 5⁷ πρότμον καὶ ὄψιμον (S)B.

'Ελαία: Ro 11²⁴ ἡ ἀγριέλαιος, καλλιέλαιος. "Ελαιον supplied in papyri (Mayser II 1, 24).

It remains only to notice under this head some stereotyped phrases where there is noun-ellipse:

'Απὸ μιᾶς: Lk 14¹⁸ sc. γνώμη or ὁρμή or φωνή, or more probably γλῶσσα in view of Philo V 170⁸ ἀπὸ μιᾶς καὶ τῆς αὐτῆς γνώμης = with one mind or voice. And some would supply φορά *impetus*. It may be Aramaism rather than ellipse (*min chʼdā*) = at once, but it occurs in secular PSI II 286²² (iii–iv/A.D.) = *at once*, and Wilcken. Chrest. 46, 15 (A.D. 338) μίαν ἐκ μιᾶς (sc. ἡμέρα), and in MGr. Lagrange (*S. Luc* 404) suggests that ὁδός or φωνή or preferably γνώμη be understood.

Κατὰ μόνας: There is no knowing what noun to supply. Mk 4¹⁰ Lk 9¹⁸, LXX Ge 32¹⁶ Ps 4⁹ Je 15¹⁷ 1 Mac 12³⁶. Thuc. I 32.5. Xen. Mem. 3.7.4. Menander. Polyb. 4.15.11. Diod. Sic. 4.51.16. Jos. BJ 6, 326; Ant. 17, 336, etc. Herm. M. XI 8. MGr καταμόναχο. BGU III 813, 15 (ii/A.D.).

Κατ' ἰδίαν: Mt 14¹³·²³, 17¹·¹⁹, 20¹⁷, 24³, Mk 4³⁴ 6³¹ᶠ 7³³ 9²·²⁸ 13³, Lk 9¹⁰ 10²³, Ac 23¹⁹, Ga 2². 2 Mac 4⁵ 14²¹. Ign Sm. 7². Hellenistic, not class.: Plut. 2, 120d. Polyb. 1, 71, 1; 4, 84, 8. Diod. Sic. 1, 21. Philo sacr. Abel. 136. Jos. BJ. 2, 199. Pap: P. Or. gr. 51, 9 (239 B.C.); 737, 7 (ii/B.C.). Insc: Dit. Syll³. 1157, 10, and see L.S. s.v. ἴδιος. Uncertain what noun to supply.

'Ιδίᾳ: the class. equivalent of the last. 1 Co 12¹¹ PSI IV 434¹² (261 B.C.).

Δημοσίᾳ: Ac 16³⁷ etc. = *openly*. Dit. Syll. 807⁹ (A.D. 138) = *publicly*. Vettius Valens p. 71²² *publicly*. Different meaning in class. Attic: *at the public expense* or *by public consent*.

PART I

WORD-MATERIAL FOR SENTENCE-BUILDING

CHAPTER TWO

THE GENDER AND NUMBER OF NOUNS

§ 1. The Gender of Nouns [1]

As in class. Greek [2] the neuter gender may refer to a person
(e.g. τὸ γεγεννημένον Jn 3⁶ 1 Jn 5⁴, cp. masc. 5¹), provided that
the emphasis is less on the individual than on some outstanding
general quality like *foolishness*; [3] πᾶν is often added to make this
clear (1 Jn 5⁴, Jn 17² πᾶν ὅ like Heb. בֹּל אֲשֶׁר, 6³⁷ πᾶν ὅ resolves
itself into τὸν ἐρχόμενον. Ga 3²² τὰ πάντα but τοὺς πάντας
in Ro 11³². Jn 12³² πάντα S*D p⁶⁶ lat Aug; rest masc.)

Mt 12⁶ μεῖζον *something greater?* 12⁴¹f πλεῖον. Lk 1³⁵ τὸ γεννώμενον
(was τὸ τέκνον in mind?). Jn 17²⁴ the gift is depicted first in its unity=ὅ,
then individually = κάκεῖνος. 1 Co 1²⁷f τὰ μῶρα . . . τὰ ἀσθενῆ . . . τὰ
ἰσχυρά, pl. not to confuse with sing. in 1²⁵. 2 Th 2⁶ neut. synonymous
with ὁ κατέχων 2⁷. 1 Co 11⁵ she is one and the same as if (ἓν καὶ τὸ αὐτό).
Heb 7⁷ τὸ ἔλαττον 9⁵ χερουβείν as neut. pl. (or sing. AP). See Bauer
s.v. for discussion and bibliography. Neut. pl. used adverbially Ph 2⁶
τὸ εἶναι ἴσα θεῷ (ἴσα Thuc. III 14. Abel § 41a).

A direct Hebraism is fem. for neut. [4]: Mt 21⁴² LXX =
Mk 12¹¹ = Ps 117 (118)²³ αὕτη = זֹאת i.e. τοῦτο. LXX Ps 27³. 4
32⁶ 74¹⁸ 102¹⁹ 119⁵⁰. ⁵⁶ αὕτη. 1 Km 4⁷ τοιαύτη. Etc.

Perhaps an Aramaism is Lk 11³³ εἰς κρυπτήν, where fem.
pass. ptc. = a neuter, *hidden*; Bauer on the other hand takes the
view = εἰς κρύπτην (see s.v.).

Note also the use of fem. to form adv. phrases: Lk 14¹⁸ ἀπὸ
μιᾶς (see ch. 1). Mk 4¹⁰ κατὰ μόνας (ch. 1). LXX Jg 7⁵.

A masc. for a fem. is Mk 5¹⁵ λεγιών (because demon's name).
A fem. for a masc. is ἡ βάαλ.

Note the variation in the gender of λιμός Lk 4²⁵; Lk 15¹⁴
Ac 11²⁸; same variation in a papyrus ii/B.C.

---

[1] K-Blass I 358ff. Schwyzer II 27–38. Mayser II 1, 28–34. R.
Meister, " Genus bei den LXX " (Wien Stud. 34, 77ff). H. Roensch,
Itala und Vulgata, 1869, 452.
[2] Examples in K-G I 14,
[3] M. J. Lagrange, *S. Matthieu*, Paris 1948, 233, on Mt 12⁶.
[4] P. Katz, *Philo's Bible*, Cambridge 1950, 25f. Swete Intr.³ 307.

Inscriptions give a parallel for ἡ θεός and ἡ θεά Ac 19²⁷.
Also papyri: θεοί . . . πᾶσαι P. Eleph. 23¹³ (223 B.C.). SB 3444
(iii/B.C.). Or. gr. 132¹² (130 B.C.). θεὰς πάσας P. Grad. = SB
5680 (229 B.C.). Attic θεός was common gender, but later -α
indicated a fem. deity ¹.

Sometimes a pl. masc. noun covers masc. and fem. subjects:
Lk 2⁴¹ οἱ γονεῖς. To 10¹² B τοὺς πενθερούς. So οἱ ἀδελφοί,
οἱ παῖδες. Thus οἱ κύριοι (Lk 19³³ Ac 16¹⁶. ¹⁹) may cover a
man and woman owner ².

The form πέτρος (Mt 16¹⁸ σὺ εἶ πέτρος καὶ ἐπὶ ταύτῃ τῇ
πέτρᾳ) which is usually masc. (but in Hell. period also fem.,
probably in accordance with λίθος) means a *boulder*, a *stone*, and
as a simplex it is restricted on the whole to poetic and elevated
diction. On the other hand, the generally preferred πέτρα
means chiefly *rock*; it is also a kind of collective or augmentative
to πέτρος, and later it takes also the meaning a *fragment of rock*,
a *stone*. The name of the apostle Πέτρος, if it actually means *rock*
and corresponds to Aram. Κηφᾶς, cannot be connected directly
with πέτρος, since this was out of general use; it does not mean
rock but is a masculinizing of πέτρα (Wackernagel op. cit. 14f).

§ 2. The Number of Nouns ³

SINGULAR: (1) In LXX and pre-Christian papyri, a generic
sing. may appear with persons or races, and in the pap. with
numbers (like our *six foot*). The usage is not unclass., especially
in the historians, and dates from Homer (Schw. II 41): with
ὁ Ἰουδαῖος Ro 3¹ (*the Jew* as a Jew) cp. ὁ Συρακόσιος and
ὁ Ἀθηναῖος Thuc. 6, 78, 1, ὁ Χαλκιδεύς 6, 84, 3, ὁ Ἕλλην Hdt 1,
69, and the proverb *Romanus sedendo vincit*, etc. With ὁ ἀγαθὸς
ἄνθρωπος and ὁ πονηρὸς ἄ. Mt 12³⁵, ὁ ἀσθενῶν Ro 14¹, τὸ ἀγαθὸν
ἔργον 13³, and ὁ δίκαιος and ὁ ἀσεβής 1 Pt 4¹⁸, cp. ὁ δικαστής
Lycurg. 79. Generic also are the class. κέραμος Thuc. 2, 4, 2
and ἄμπελος 4, 90, 2. With class. ἡ ἵππος Hdt 1, 80, cp. LXX
Ge 14¹¹ *cavalry*, Ex 8⁶ ἀνεβιβάσθη (ὁ)ἡ βάτραχος *frogs*. 1 Pt
2²⁴ LXX τῷ μώλωπι ἰάθητε Rev. 11⁸ πτῶμα αὐτῶν.

---

¹ Wackernagel II², 25.
² So Souter in *Expos.* VIII, 1914, 94f; IX, 1915, 94f.
³ K-G I, 13–20. Schwyzer II 38–46. Gild. I §§ 37, 42–59. Mayser II
1, 34–45. Wackernagel I 73–105. U. Holzmeister, " De ' plurali
categoriae ' in Novo Testamento et a Patribus adhibito," *Biblica* 14,
1933, 68–95.

It is not possible to classify here ὁ πτῶχος Jas 2⁶ or ὁ δίκαιος 5⁶; these refer to an individual example (e.g. 2²).

We demur also at 1 Co 6⁵ ἀνὰ μέσον τοῦ ἀδελφοῦ αὐτοῦ: it is less likely to be generic than a combined result of Semitic influence and abbreviation thereof (full: *between brother and brother*), because in LXX we find e.g. ἀ.μ. ὕδατος καὶ ὕδατος Ge 1⁶ and ἀ.μ. ποίμνης καὶ ποίμνης 32¹⁶. It is not a great step to omit the repeated noun.

(2) Contrary to normal Greek and Latin practice, the NT sometimes follows the Aram. and Heb. preference for a distributive sing. Something belonging to each person in a group of people is placed in the sing.: as τὸ σῶμα ὑμῶν 1 Co 6¹⁹, ἐν τῇ καρδίᾳ αὐτῶν Lk 1⁶⁶. On the other hand, NT does frequ. exhibit the pl., e.g. καρδίαι Mt 9⁴.

	καρδία sing. of a group (Sem.)		Pl. of a group (normal)
Mt. Mk.	Mt 13¹⁵ LXX 15⁸ LXX = Mk 7⁶. Mk 3⁵ 6⁵² 7²¹ 8¹⁷		Mt 9⁴ 18³⁵ (sing. Syr. Copt^bo) Mk 2⁶. ⁸ (sing. Syr^pe. Copt^bo 2MSS)
Lk. Ac	Lk 1⁵¹. ⁶⁶ 8¹². ¹⁵ 9⁴⁷ 12³⁴ 24³². ³⁸ Ac 2³⁷ 28²⁷ LXX bis		Lk 1¹⁷ 3¹⁵ 5²² 16¹⁵ 21¹⁴. ³⁴ Ac 7³⁹. ⁵¹ vl⁵⁴ 14¹⁷ 15⁹
Jn	12⁴⁰ LXX 14¹. ²⁷ 16⁶. ²²		
Paul	Ro 1²¹ 2 Co 3¹⁵ 6¹¹ LXX Eph 1¹⁸ 4¹⁸ 5¹⁹ 6⁵ Ph 1⁷ Col 3¹⁶ D^cEKL		Ro 1²⁴ 2¹⁵ 5⁵ 16¹⁸ 2 Co 1²² 3² 4⁶ 7³ Ga 4⁶ Eph 3¹⁷ 6²² Ph 4⁷ Col 2² 3¹⁵. ¹⁶ 4⁸ 1 Th2⁴ LXX 3¹³ 2 Th 2¹⁷ 3⁵
Heb	8¹⁰ LXX vl.		3⁸LXX ¹⁵LXX 4⁷LXX 8¹⁰ LXX vl. 10¹⁶ LXX ²²
Jas	3¹⁴		4⁸ 5⁵. ⁸
Jn. Epp	1 Jn 3¹⁹ vl. ²⁰bis ²¹		3¹⁹ S lat Syr^h
Pet.			1 Pt 3¹⁵ 2 Pt 1¹⁹
Rev			17¹⁷

κεφαλή sing. of a group		Pl. as normal
Mt. Mk.	Mt 10^{30} = Lk 12^7	Mt 27^{29} = Mk 15^{29}
Lk. Ac	Lk 12^7 = Mt 10^{30} Lk 21^{18} Ac 18^6 21^{24}	Lk 21^{28}
Rev		4^4 $9^{7.17.19}$ 18^{19}
LXX	Ps $21(22)^7$ 37^4 Je 14^4 18^{16} Ziegler La 2^{15} etc.	Ps $108(109)^{25}$ etc.

ὀσφύς sing. of a group		Pl. as normal
Lk. Ac		Lk 12^{35}
Paul	Eph 6^{14}	
1 Pt		1^{13}

σῶμα sing. of a group		Pl. as normal
Mt. Lk	6^{25} = Lk 12^{22}	
Paul	Ro 8^{23} 1 Co $6^{19.20}$ 2 Co 4^{10}	1 Co 6^{15} Eph 5^{28}
Jas	3^3	

χείρ with preposition (metaph.) εἰς, ἐκ, ἐπί, διά		Plural
Mt. Mk		Mt 17^{22} = Mk 9^{31} = Lk 9^{44} Mt 26^{45} = Mk 14^{41} = Lk 24^7
Lk. Ac	Lk $1^{71.74}$ Ac 2^{23} (but C³EP pl) 15^{23}	Ac 5^{12} 14^3 24^7 vl 28^{17}
Jn	10^{39}	
Rev	13^{16} 20^4	

In addition we find ἀπὸ προσώπου and similar Semitisms always sing.: Lk 2³¹ Ac 3¹⁸· ²¹ 7⁴⁵; κατὰ πρ. Lk 2³¹; διὰ στόματος Lk 1⁷⁰ Ac 3¹⁸· ²¹ Eph 4²⁹ Col 3⁸ Rev 11⁵. We find distrib. sing. τύπον 1 Th 1⁷ (see Milligan's note) 2 Th 3⁹; στολὴ λευκή Rev 6¹¹. Distrib. sing. also in papyri: κατὰ γεωργόν (Mayser II 1, 45 n. 6).

PLURAL: Exceptionally the pl. may be used in the NT for one person or thing in both a Semitic and a normal Greek manner [1].

(1) *Semitic.* עוֹלָמִים is behind αἰῶνες[2], which means both *world* (Heb 1² 11³ 1 Ti 1¹⁷? 1 Cl 35³ 55⁶ 61² To 13⁷·¹¹) and *eternity* (Sext. Emp. phys. 1, 62. Orac. Sib. 3, 767. Barn 18² To 13² Si 18¹ Da 6²⁷Θ Lk 1³³ Ga 1⁵ Eph 2⁷ 3¹¹ Jude²⁵ Rev 14¹¹, and often), esp. in εἰς τοὺς αἰῶνας (Ps 60⁵ 76⁸ 88⁵³ Mt 6¹³ vl Lk 1³³ Ro 1²⁵ 9⁵ 11³⁶ 2 Co 11³¹ Heb 13⁸), εἰς πάντας . . . (To 13⁴ Da 3⁵² Enoch 9⁴ Or. Sib. 3⁵⁰ Jude ²⁵), and εἰς τοὺς αἰῶνας τῶν αἰώνων (Ps 83⁵ ZP 4, 1038, 22b 15, Ro 16²⁷ Ga 1⁵ Ph 4²⁰ 1 Ti 1¹⁷ 2 Ti 4¹⁸ Heb 13²¹ 1 Pt 4¹¹ 5¹¹ Rev 4⁹ᶠ 10⁶ 15⁷ 19³ 20¹⁰ 22⁵, 1 Cl 20¹² 32⁴ 38⁴ 43⁶). Thus we have *end of the world* τὰ τέλη τῶν αἰώνων in 1 Co. 10¹¹, as in T. Levi 14¹, but it may be the normal pl. of αἰών: *the fulfilment of the ages* or *the frontiers of the ages* (i.e. the limits dividing one of the seven *ages* from the ensuing one); Or. Sib. 8³¹¹ τέλος αἰώνων *end of time.*

שָׁמַיִם is behind οὐρανοί: but here again, following a Jewish idea, the pl. of seven heavens may be intended, esp. in 2 Co 12² Eph 4¹⁰. In the material sense of *sky* the sing. predominates: the exceptional plurals are Mt 24³¹ (contrast Mk 13²⁷, LXX De 30⁴), 3¹⁶·¹⁷ = Mk 1¹⁰·¹¹ (but Lk has sing.), Ac 7⁵⁶. In the less common figurative sense of *heaven* as God's abode the pl. predominates, as Mt 5¹⁶·⁴⁵ 6¹ etc.: the exceptional singulars (like ὁ μέγας ἐν οὐρανῷ Ζεύς Plat. Phaed. 246E) are Lk 10²⁰D (rest pl) 11¹³ (exc. p⁴⁵) Eph 6⁹S (rest pl) Col 4¹S* BAC (rest pl) 1 Pt 14S (rest pl), everywhere in Jn and Rev (exc. 12¹² LXX) Did 8². Taken as a whole, the sing. is more normal Greek, and scribes would correct to the sing. There is a significant variant at Mk 13²⁷: pl. is found in some MSS and some Old Latin, which is perhaps original in view of the tendency of scribes. In LXX the sing. is normal (Ge 1¹ 14¹⁹·²² To 7¹⁷BA Da Bel⁵ 1 Mac 2³⁷ al), with pl. in poetic passages (Jth 9¹², esp. Pss). For the LXX see P. Katz, *Philo's Bible* 141–146; H. Traub in Kittel WB V 510f.

(2) *Normal Greek but late.* Class. poetic sometimes: ἅρματα of one only (K–G I 18, n. 2). The allusive pl. is sometimes used when a class or variety rather than number is stressed. This is so in post-class. Greek and always the importance of the individual's action appears to be emphasized, not that of a group: Mt 2²⁰ τεθνήκασιν οἱ ζητοῦντες

---

[1] Kummerer. *Über den Gebrauch des Plur. statt des Sing. bei Soph. und Eur.*, 1869. Wackernagel I 97ff.

[2] H. Sasse in Kittel WB I 197–208 (αἰῶνες).

(Herod), Ostr. Berol. P. 10987 = SB 4631 (106 B.C.) τῶν οἴνων *the wine*,
P. Hib. 54, 23 (245 B.C.) *send us the cheese* (τυρούς). P. Petr. II 20
col. 2, 5 πλήθη σίτου *a quantity of corn* (250 B.C.). PSI VI 584, 30 (iii/B.C.)
γράψον μοι . . . ἀντίγραφα *an answer* (Mayser II 1, 34f, 39).
A difficult pl. which may be explained in this way is Mt 2²³ *prophets*:
the reference is to one prophet only. Zerwick calls it *pluralis
categoriae* (§ 4a) and he further suggests it as an explanation of Mt 27⁴⁴
(after Jerome, Aug., Ambrose): both robbers are said to reproach Jesus
whereas it was only one, and we need not call in another tradition to
help us out. Other difficulties are thus solved: Mt 14⁹ Mk 6²⁶ ὅρκους
oath (Xen. Hell 5, 4, 54. 2 Mac 4³⁴ 7²⁴ 14³². Ep. Arist. 126. Jos. Ant.
3, 272; 7, 294; see J. Schneider in Kittel WB V 458–467). Mt 21⁷
ἐπεκάθισεν ἐπάνω αὐτῶν (scribes soften the harshness), 22⁷ *army*, Mk 4¹⁰
parable, 7³⁷ *deaf* . . . *dumb* (sing.), Lk 5²¹ βλασφημίας sing, Jn 6¹⁴ σημεῖα
B al. Old Lat a boh, 6²⁶ σημεῖα 8²⁴ *sin*, 9¹⁶ *sign*, 10²¹ *blind man*. Zerwick
(§ 4b) suggests that the women of Mt 28⁹ is a pl. of category referring
only to Magdalene, in view of Jn 20¹⁴⁻¹⁸. Abel suggests (§ 41d) that
this pl. of species is used in Ac 21²⁸ Ἕλληνας = only Trophimus!
19³⁸ ἀνθύπατοί εἰσιν too, because there was but one proconsul. Matthew
uses the pl. of ὄχλος where we do not find the word at all in Mark:
5¹ 7²⁸ 9⁸·³³ 12⁴⁶ 13³⁴·³⁶ 14¹⁵. In this respect he is supported by Luke
in Mt 11⁷ 12²³ 14¹³. In addition, Matthew has ὄχλοι πολλοί 4²⁵ 8¹·¹⁸
vl 13² 15³⁰ 19². It seems that ὄχλοι πολλοί means no more than ὄχλος
or ὄχλος πολύς (or πλεῖστος) or πολὺ πλῆθος (Mk 3⁷), and is not intended
to be understood of separate groups, in view of the Mk and Lk parallels.
Therefore πολλοί must be taken in the unusual sense (as with χρόνοι) of
great (= ἱκανοί or μεγάλοι). The usage is not quite confined to Mt (see
Lk 5¹⁵ 14²⁵). But the motive for using the pl. of ὄχλος is not clear;
it is confined to Mt Lk and Ac 1–17 (apart from a vl in Mk and Jn, and
Rev 17¹⁵ where more than one crowd is meant). Probably it betrays
the influence of the later Greek meaning of the pl., i.e. *the masses*.

(3) *Classical*. The directions *north, south*, etc. are pl. Mt 2¹ 24²⁷
Lk 13²⁹ ἀπο ἀνατολῶν. Pl. also in Diod. Sic II 43, Dio Cass. 987. 32,
Jos. c. Ap. 1, 77, Philo spec. leg. 3, 187, Lucian peregr. 39, 1 Cl. 10⁴,
LXX Ge 13¹⁴ Nu 23⁷. But sometimes sing. in NT: Mt 2²·⁹ ἐν τῇ ἀνατολῇ
(or is the sing. astronomical rather than geographical? See Bauer
s.v. = *rising*). Rev 7², 16¹² ἀνατολῆς (-ῶν A). 21¹³ ἀνατολῆς (even
alongside pl. δυσμῶν; but Bʳ ἀνατολῶν). Dit. Syll³ 1112, 25. Jos. Ant.
1, 37 al. Herm. V. I 4, 1.3. Also δυσμαί *west*, which is sing. in LXX,
Enoch, Philo, Jos., Or. Sib., but generally pl. in Biblical Greek: BGU
1049, 8. LXX Ps 106³. T. Jud 5². Mt 8¹¹ 24²⁷ Lk 13²⁹ 12⁵⁴ Rev 21¹³.
In MGr some place-names exist in the pl., referring to the region around;
thus Ἀνατολάς = various parts of Asia Minor (Thumb Handbook² 27f);
it may be that here we have a clue to the pl. ἀπὸ ἀνατολῶν Mt 2¹ (also
LXX Ge 11²).

Right and *left* are pl., but also (as class.) sometimes sing: Ro 8³⁴
Eph 1²⁰ etc. *District* is pl. τὰ μέρη Mt 2²² etc., and *beyond* ἐπέκεινα
Ac 7⁴³ LXX Am 5²⁷ probably (better vl ἐπὶ τὰ μέρη D*). Names of

festivals are formed on the class. principle, as in the papyri (Mayser
II 1, 39): Mt 14⁶ Mk 6²¹ Jn 10²². *Sabbath* pl. for sing.: Zen. P. Cairo
762.6 (iii/B.C.), Plu. mor. 169c, Mt 12¹·⁵ 28¹ Mk 1²¹ Lk 4¹⁶ Ac 13¹⁴ 16¹³
Col 2¹⁶, LXX Ex 20¹⁰ Le 23³², Philo Abr. 28, Jos. Ant. 1, 33, Diog. 4, 3.
That is unless we take σάββατα as a sing. (formed from שַׁבָּת with -α added
to make it easier Greek). Other pl. festivals: τὰ ἄζυμα Mt 26¹⁷ Lk 22¹
Ac 12³ etc. Mk 14¹ (D om); οἱ γάμοι *wedding* (feast) poet. class., frequent
in papyri (where sing. = *wedlock*, as sing. in Heb 13⁴): Preisigke s.v.
(ii/A.D.), P. Ox I 111 (iii/A.D.), BGU III 909.3 (A.D. 359); also Diog. L.
3.2; it is suggested that the pl. is a Latinism from *nuptiae*; Mt 22² 25¹⁰
etc., Est 2¹⁸ 9²². Sing.: Mt 22⁸ Jn 2¹ᶠ and LXX. To 6¹³ 8¹⁹ 1 Mac 9³⁷
10⁵⁸. Τὰ πάσχα Mt 26¹⁸W may be a mistake for τὸ πάσχα. Τὰ γενέσια
(γενέθλια class. papyri; Mayser II 1, 39) Mt 14⁶ Mk 6²¹. Τὰ ἐγκαίνια
LXX and Jn 10²².

Further class. plurals: πύλαι Mt 16¹⁸ only Wi 16¹³ (elsewhere sing.
for one gate); θύραι in NT of one door in fixed idioms only, ἐπὶ θύραις
Mt 24³³ = Mk 13²⁹, πρὸ τῶν θ. fig. Jas 5⁹, πρὸ τῆς θ. lit. Ac 12⁶, else-
where several doors Jn 20¹⁹·²⁶ Ac 5¹⁹ 16²⁶ 21³⁰ (5²³ sing. or pl.?); κόλποι
Hell. Lk16²³ (sing.²²); αἵματα¹ shed blood of several persons, LXX
Hab 2⁸ etc. Rev 16⁶S (sing. BACP) 18²⁴B (sing. p⁴⁷ SACP), ancestral
Jn 1¹³ (of husband *and* wife); ὕδατα Mt 14²⁸ᶠ Jn 3²³ Rev 1¹⁵ 14² 17¹·¹⁵ etc.

Less usual in class. Greek: ἀργύρια Mt 26¹⁵ 27⁵ 28¹²; ὀψώνια Hell.
LXX pap. (sing. and pl. iii/B.C.; Mayser II 1, 37) Lk 3¹⁴ Ro 6²³ etc.,
sing. 2 Co 11⁸; κέντρα². Hell. Ac 9⁵ TR 26¹⁴ (perhaps pl. because the
goad was double-pointed); ἱμάτια *upper garment* Jn 13⁴ 19²³ Ac 18⁶·⁷
(but *clothes* pl. Mk 5³⁰ et al.); χιτῶνες Mk 14⁶³; τὰ ἅγια *temple*, or part
of, LXX, e.g. 3 Km 8⁶ Jdt 4¹² 16²⁰ 1 Mac 3⁴³ etc. Or. Sib. 3³⁰⁸ Heb 8²
9²·³·²⁴ᶠ 13¹¹ Philo Jos.; αἱ κριθαί Rev 6⁶ SACP (sing. B), sing. in post-cl.
and LXX (Bauer s.v.; Mayser II 1, 35, several papyri iii/B.C.); αἱ διαθῆκαι
Eph 2¹² Ro 9⁴ SCK (sing. p⁴⁶ BDE), sing. elsewhere in LXX NT; names
of towns, Φίλιπποι, Ἀθῆναι, Πάταρα, Ἱεροσόλυμα (P. Zen. 259 B.C.), To
AB, 1 Esd A (see Abel § 41); αἱ ἐπιστολαί 1 Co 16³?; ἡμέραι Mk 2²⁰ (and
one day in same verse) but probably a Hebraism; καιροί *period* Rosetta
stone 20 (196 B.C.) P. Petr. II 45 (246 B.C.) PSI IV 432, 5 (iii/B.C.), P. Par.
46, 7 (153 B.C.) etc. Mt 16³ this (*end-*) *period*, 21⁴¹ Lk 21²⁴ (T. Naphth. 7¹),
Ac 1⁷ 17²⁶ *the allotted span*, Ac 3¹⁹ Messianic *period* (so 1 Th. 5¹ 1 Ti 4¹);
χρόνοι Lk 8²⁷ TR (rest sing.) 20⁹ 23⁸ Ac 1⁷ Ro 16²⁵ 1 Th 5¹ 2 Ti 1⁹
Ti 1² 1 Pt 1²⁰ Jude¹⁸ Pol 1², not quite *years*, as in much later Greek,
but advancing that way, certainly *period*, as in τῶν ἐπάνω χρόνων (*the
earlier period*) P. Hib. 96, 6.23 (259 B.C.), Mayser II 1, 38, 2 Cl. 19⁴ οἱ
νῦν χρ. = *the present period*, Herm. S. IX 20, 4 οἱ πρότεροι χρ. = *the
earlier period*, M. Pol. XVI 2 οἱ καθ' ἡμᾶς χρ. = *our own period*.

Sometimes NT uses the Pluralis Poeticus for abstract subjects in a
class. way³: e.g. φόνοι P. Teb I 5, 5 (118 B.C.), μοιχεῖαι, πορνεῖαι,

---

¹ See Behm in Kittel WB I 172 n. 6.
² See K. L. Schmidt in Kittel WB III 664, 18ff.
³ E.g. θρόνοι μάχαιραι σκῆπτρα in the tragedians: Menge, *De
poetarum scaenic. Graec. sermone*, Göttingen 1905, 32ff.

κλοπαί Mt 15¹⁹ Mk 7²¹ᶠ; ἔρεις, ζῆλοι (vl in 2 Co 12²⁰) Ga 5²⁰ᶠ, with several other abstract nouns; ὑποκρίσεις 1 Pt 2¹ vl, with other abstracts, 4³, 1 Co 7² Jas 2¹ Jude¹³. These plurals may imply *cases of* . . . (Katz, op. cit. 112). In 2 Co 11²³ 2 Co 1¹⁰ (p⁴⁶ Syr) θάνατοι may imply ways of dying, i.e. *deadly perils*. Similar examples are μεθοδεῖαι Eph 6¹¹ *astuteness*; οἰκτιρμοί Ro 12¹ etc. (Hebrew), sing. Col 3¹² (K pl.); ἄναγκαι 2 Co 6⁴ 12¹⁰; θελήματα *that which (I) wish* Ac 13²² Eph 2³; μάχαι 2 Co 7⁵ Ti 3⁹; φόβοι 2 Co 7⁵ Xen. hier. 6, 5. Behind these plurals may be the thought of the diversity of words or expressions involved, although the Atticists resorted to the pl. to avoid hiatus.

The Pluralis Sociativus, or letter writer's plural (or *modestiae* or *auctoris*), is frequent in Paul especially with personal and possessive pronoun, but mainly where he seems to be writing on behalf of a group: Col 1³ (but sing. Eph 1¹⁵ᶠ) Ro 1⁵. See also Mk 4³⁰ Heb 5¹¹ 6¹·³·⁹·¹¹ 13¹⁸ᶠ·²²ᶠ 1 Jn 1⁴. This is common enough in all periods of Greek from Homer onwards and does not call for much comment. One can safely judge only by the context what number the writer really intends, since sing. and pl. alternate as capriciously in Paul as in contemporary letters. In 1 Jn the writer seems to identify himself very closely with other members of the fellowship; hence *we*.[1]

---

[1] On this subject see K. Dick, *Der schriftst. Pl. bei Paulus*, Halle 1900, Wackernagel I 98f, Stauffer in Kittel WB II 341A, 354f, Moule 118f.

CHAPTER THREE

THE COMPARISON OF ADJECTIVES AND ADVERBS

Comparison in Biblical Greek [1] is affected by the double influence of Semitic usages and the general trend of the Greek language. This resulted in more ˙ emphatic comparison, the positive adjective with παρά (= Heb. adj. and מן), a levelling of comparative and superlative, and a moving down one stage in the use of each of the three degrees. The disappearance of the Dual number is in line with this popular inability to distinguish between comparative and superlative (Zerwick § 112).

§ 1. Heightening of Comparison

As in the papyri the genuine comparative is still in wide use but the opportunity is frequently taken to heighten comparison by the addition to the comparative of particles like ἔτι and adverbs like πολύ and πολλῷ and even accumulations like πολλῷ μᾶλλον much more than in class. Greek [2]. Note also the comparative form of a comparative: 3 Jn[4] and Archiv f. Pap. (Wilcken) iii 173 (iv/A.D.) μειζοτέραν.

Πολύ or πολλῷ: PSI IV 435, 19 (258 B.C.), Ros. stone 31 (196 B.C.), Jn 4[41] 2 Co 8[22]; πολλῷ μᾶλλον P Par 26, 48 (163 B.C.) Ph 1[23] *much more better*!; μᾶλλον: 1 Cl 48[6], Herm. S. IX 28[4], 2 Co 7[13]; μᾶλλον περισσότερον Mk 7[36]; πολὺ μᾶλλον: P. Tor. VIII 65 (119 B.C.), inscr. Preiss. Samm. 5827, 17 (69 B.C.); ἔτι: P. Petr. II 13(18b)11 (255 B.C.), Ph 1[9] *still more* greatly, Heb 7[15] *still more* manifest.

§ 2. Comparative for True Superlative

Mt 8[12] τὸ σκότος τὸ ἐξώτερον, 11[11], 18[1. 4] ὁ μείζων (or elative: *very*). In Apollodorus, of Odysseus tied under the *largest* ram: τῷ μείζονι (Radermacher[2] 68); μέγιστος is almost obsolete by this time, but appears

---

[1] K-G I 20ff, II 301ff. Schwyzer II 183–185. Gild. §§ 28–39. Mayser II 1, 45–54. Jannaris 315–317. Radermacher[2] ch. VII. M. Zerwick S.J., *Graecitas Biblica*[3], Rome 1955, §§ 107–116. Otto Schwab, *Historische Syntax der griechischen Comparation in der klassischen Litteratur* (Beitr. zur histor. Syntax der griech. Spr. herausg. v. M. Schanz, IV 1–3), 1893–95.

[2] Hesiod Erga 127 πολὺ χειρότερον.

in Atticistic 2 Peter. Mk 9³⁴ τίς μείζων, Lk 7²⁸ ὁ μικρότερος *the least*, 9⁴⁸ ὁ μικρότερος ἐν πᾶσιν ὑμῖν, 1 Co 12²³ Heb 8¹¹, LXX 1 Km 17¹³A ¹⁴A Jg 6¹⁵, Barn 12² ὑψηλότερος πάντων *highest of all*.

§ 3. Comparative for Elative Superlative

In many instances where the comp. form indicates an unusually high degree of comparison in the NT and papyri (but not in Hermas), one may speak of an *elative* sense which normally belongs to the superlative. This is not class. usage and is characteristic of the inferior popular speech (Mayser II 1, 49f).

Add to Mayser's examples: P Teb. 33 (ii/B.C.) ἐν μίζονι ἀξιώματι, BU II 417, 28 (ii–iii/A.D.), 451, 11 (i–ii/A.D.), 615, 9.28 (ii/A.D.) ταχύτερον Ac 24²⁶ πυκνότερον *very often* or *so much the more often*, 2 Cl 17³ *as often as possible*, also Clem. Hom. ep. ad Jac 9, Ga 4¹³ τὸ πρότερον = τὸ πρῶτον *originally* (but the true compar. sense is possible: *the first time*), Ac 27¹³ ἆσσον *as near as possible* (or read θᾶσσον), 24²² ἀκριβέστερον *very accurately*, 18²⁶ 23¹⁵·²⁰ same, P Petr. II 16.13 (iii/B.C.), PSI IV 444, 11 (iii/B.C.), Epict. I 24, 10, Herm. V. III 10¹⁰, Philo, Jos., BU II 388 II 41 (ii–iii/A.D.), Ac 25¹⁰ κάλλιον *very well* (or merely pos.), 2 Ti 1¹⁸ βέλτιον same (Ac 10²⁸D), Ac 4¹⁶D φανερότερον *extremely obvious*, 17²² δεισιδαιμονεστέρους not class. *rather* but probably popular elative *extremely god-fearing* (strengthened by ὡς), 2 Co 8¹⁷ σπουδαιότερος *very zealous*, Ph 2²⁸ adv., Clem. Hom. 1¹⁴ τάχιον *as quickly as possible*, 11¹³ same (distinguish from 9²³). But in some instances these might well be comp. for pos.

§ 4. Comparative for Positive

Especially τάχιον *quickly*: Jn 13²⁷ (but could be elative) 1 Ti 3¹⁴ SKL 0142 (WH ἐν τάχει) 2 Ti 4⁹ I 33 (rest τάχεως or ἐν τάχει) Heb 13¹⁹ (but prob. a true comp.) 13²³ *soon* Herm. M.X 1, 6.

Other examples are νεώτερος and καινότερος, often positive however in class. Greek; so in NT πρεσβύτερος is simply a religious official; Ac 17²¹ καινότερον *something new* (but possibly an Atticistic refinement: *newer*), 25¹⁰ κάλλιον (but perhaps under § 3), Ro 15¹⁵ τολμηρότερον *boldly*; PSI V 484, 7 (258 B.C.) πρεσβύτεροι = no longer young, *old* (older than they used to be, not older than others); Mayser II 1, 47f; Or. gr. 48, 15 (iii/B.C.) οἱ νεώτεροι *the young*, P. Petr. I 21 (237 B.C.) μείζω more than normally *large*; very often in Ptolemaic papyri πλείονες = *many, more than one*: Lk 11⁵⁴ περὶ πλειόνων (vulg. *de multis*), 1 Co 9¹⁹ 10⁵ 15⁶ Ac 19³² β-text 27¹² 2 Co 2⁶ 4¹⁵ 9² Ph 1¹⁴ Heb 7²³ (RSV *many in number*); Ac 2⁴⁰ ἑτέροις τε λόγοις πλείοσιν and M. Pol. 12¹ ταῦτα καὶ ἕτερα πλείονα exclude *majority* and *more* (it must be *many* or *several*);

P. Madg. 21, 6 (222 B.C.) τοῖς φυλακίταις καὶ ἄλλοις πλέοσιν *many others*. We suggest *many* for all the above NT examples of πλείονες, rather than the class. *more* or *the majority of*.

§ 5. Elative Superlative

Not so prominent in pre-Christian papyri as in NT and Christian texts: αἱ πλεῖσται Mt 11²⁰ *very numerous* Ac 19³²D *very many*; ὁ πλεῖστος ὄχλος Mt 21⁸ Mk 4¹ *very large*; σὺν ἄλλοις πλείστοις = *with very many others* P. Teb I 45, 17; 46, 14; 47, 11 (113 B.C.). Τιμιώτατος *most rare* Rev 18¹² 21¹¹ Jos. Ant. 17, 225. Κράτιστε *Most Excellent* Lk 1³ Ac 26²⁵ Dion. Hal. opusc. I 3, 6. Ἐλάχιστος *very small* Mt 5¹⁹ 25⁴⁰· ⁴⁵ Lk 12²⁶ 16¹⁰ 19¹⁷ 1 Co 4³ Jas 3⁴. Ἥδιστα Ac 13⁸D. Ἱλαρώτεραι Herm. S. IX 10, 7. The elative superlative may be intensified by the addition of ὡς, ὅτι, ᾗ, οἷος, and sometimes ἐν τοῖς (sc. δύνασθαι or οἷος ἦν): e.g. ὡς τάχιστα Ac 17¹⁵, culminating in MGr ὅσον τὸ (τὰ) μπορεῖς γληγορύτερα *as quickly as you can*. On the other hand the true superlative, less frequent now but still active enough in the less uncultured papyri (Mayser II, 1, 51), is virtually dead in NT through Semitic influence. But see Ac 26⁵ ἀκριβεστάτην, Eph 3⁸ ἐλαχιστότερος (a compar. superlative: *less than least*). Mk 12²⁸ πρώτη πάντων. Mt 2⁶ 5¹⁹ 1 Co 6² 15⁹ ἐλάχιστος. 1 Co 14²⁷ τὸ πλεῖστον *at most*.

§ 6. Positive for Superlative

We have no NT example of repetition of the positive, as in pre-Christian papyri, but the positive itself is used in a superlative sense under Hebraic influence (although there are class. poet. examples with gen.: κακὰ κακῶν, K–G I 21, 339): Mt 22³⁶ μεγάλη *greatest* (not *the great one*; equivalent to πρώτη πάντων in the parallel Mk 12²⁸, 5¹⁹ Jn 2¹⁰ τὸν καλὸν οἶνον *best*, Lk 9⁴⁸ μέγας *greatest*, Lk 1⁴² εὐλογημένη σὺ ἐν γυναιξίν, LXX Ca 1⁸ ἡ καλὴ ἐν γυναιξίν, Heb 9²ᶠ LXX τὰ ἅγια c. gen. *holiest*.

§ 7. Positive for Comparative

Mk 9⁴² καλὸν . . . μᾶλλον *better*. Lk 5³⁹ ὁ παλαιὸς χρηστός ἐστιν *is better*. Then the frequent οἱ πολλοί which is class., the *majority*, even without οἱ (as a vl) in Mk 6² 9²⁶. Then Mt 20²⁸D ἔτι κάτω = κατώτερον, cp. MGr κόμ (= ἔτι) καλός *better*. Where comparison is introduced by ᾗ, μᾶλλον (ᾗ), παρά or ὑπέρ (or ἀπό LXX) on the Semitic pattern, the adj. may be positive as well as comparative (although the adj. with μᾶλλον and μάλιστα had already occurred in Ionic prose and Attic poetry to a small extent): Ac 20³⁵ μακάριον . . . μᾶλλον . . . ᾗ *happier than*, Ga 4²⁷ LXX πολλὰ . . . μᾶλλον ᾗ *more than*, 1 Co 12²² πολλῷ μᾶλλον . . . ἀναγκαῖα *much more necessary*, Lk 13² ἁμαρτωλοί παρά *more sinful than*, 18¹⁴ SLB δεδικαιωμένος παρά (D adds μᾶλλον) (ᾗ in W Θ, like LXX Ge 38²⁶ δεδικαίωται . . . ᾗ ἐγώ); Mt 18⁸ᶠ Mk 9⁴³· ⁴⁵· ⁴⁷ 1 Cl 51³ καλὸν ᾗ *better than*; Mk 10²⁵ Clem. Alx. εὐκόλως . . . ᾗ (it is suggested that this

is the true pre-MSS text which was amended to εὐκοπώτερον) ; Ap. Const. 4³
μακάριος ἥπερ; LXX Ge 49¹² λευκοὶ ἤ; Ex 18¹¹ μέγας παρά (Philostr.
Ap. III 19), Nu 12³ πραΰς παρά, 1 Km 1⁸ Ec 2⁹ 9⁴ ἀγαθὸς ὑπέρ, Hag 2⁹
μέγας ὑπέρ. The pos. with παρά is also MGr: see Pernot *Études* 75,
who sees in this the ultimate influence of Hebrew on MGr. Germane
to this is the frequent reduction of μᾶλλον ἤ to simple ἤ or παρά: LXX
Ps 45(44)⁸ ἔχρισεν . . . παρά, Lk 15⁷ χαρὰ ἔσται . . . ἤ; 1 Co 14¹⁹, Just.
Ap. 15⁸, BU III 846¹⁵ (ii/A.D.), Epict. III 22 θέλω . . . ἤ; Lk 17² To 3⁶
λυσιτελεῖ . . . ἤ; Mk 3⁴ ἔξεστιν ἤ; LXX Nu 22⁶ ἰσχύει . . . ἤ; 2 Mac
14⁴² θέλω ἥπερ (but βούλομαι ἤ in Homer and often); it is a Semitism
but there are some class. parallels : Andoc. 1, 125 λυσιτελεῖν ἤ, Hdt 9, 26
δικαῖόν ἐστιν . . . ἥπερ (K–G II 303), Aesop 121 συμφέρει ἤ. Even
without ἤ in Mt 5²⁹· ³⁰ συμφέρει σοι . . . καὶ μή.

§ 8. Superlative for Comparative

To complete the picture, πρῶτος and ἔσχατος must be mentioned
here. Πρῶτος = πρότερος Aelian Anim. II 38; VIII 12, P. LPw
(ii–iii/B.C.), Plut. Cat. min § 18, IG XII 5, 590, Kaibel Epigr. 642, 10
(iii–iv/A.D.), Mt 21²⁸· ³¹ *elder*, Jn 1¹⁵· ³⁰ *superior to* or *before me*, 15¹⁸
before us. Πρῶτος meaning *former* and ἔσχατος meaning *latter* occur in
Mt 27⁶⁴. Thus πρῶτος in Ac 1¹ is ambiguous: either Luke is guilty of a
popular Hellenistic mannerism or he intended to write three volumes.
Similarly difficult is Lk 2² αὕτη ἡ ἀπογραφὴ πρώτη. It is the first census
of a series (if class. Greek) ; or first of two (if Hellenistic). And if Hellenistic it could mean either *the first census of the two made by Quirinius*, or
the census before the (greater) census made by Quirinius; see Lagrange
S. Luc in loc.

With this popular Hellenistic failure to appreciate the significance
of the Dual, we may compare the confusion of ἄλλος and ἕτερος, τίς
and πότερος (Mt 9⁵ τί γάρ ἐστιν εὐκοπώτερον), and the use of ἀμφότεροι
for more than two. See below, ch. 14 § 2.

CHAPTER FOUR

VOCATIVES [1]

§ 1. The use of ὦ

Whereas in class. Greek it was only exceptionally that ὦ was omitted, the reverse is now the case. Semitic and Koine influences once again united in their effect upon the NT, for in the Hell. period ὦ was reserved for emotional or stilted speech. " So erscheint ὦ bei Epiktet neben Eigennamen nur da, wo es sich um Grössen der Vergangenheit handelt " (Johann. DGKPS 13). In pre-Christian papyri it apparently occurs nowhere for certain except in an Artemis curse of iv/B.C. (Mayser II 1, 55). In Luke and Paul it occurs with only four out of seventeen vocatives. There will therefore be some special reason for each occurrence in the NT. Surprisingly we never find it used in prayer invoking the deity; but its use is confined to

(a) the beginning of a sentence where emotion is expressed: Mt 15²⁸ (not D) ὦ γύναι, μεγάλη (emph. position, increasing the emotion) σου ἡ πίστις (contrast γύναι alone: Lk 22⁵⁷ Jn 2⁴ 4²¹ etc.); Mt 17¹⁷ Mk 9¹⁹ ὦ γενεὰ ἄπιστος (great emotion); Lk 24²⁵ ὦ ἀνόητοι (exasperation); Ac 3¹⁰ ὦ πλήρης (indignation); Ga 3¹ ὦ ἀνόητοι Γάλαται (anger); 1 Ti 6²⁰ ὦ Τιμόθεε (affection). But there is no great emotion in: Ro 2¹·³ 9²⁰ Jas 2²⁰, and in fact simple ἄνθρωπε is found Lk 12¹⁴ 22⁵⁸·⁶⁰. Never ὦ πάτερ in NT, but in Josephus and Corpus Hermeticum. See Schrenk in Kittel WB V 985, n. 251;

(b) exclamations (= ὤ): Ro 11³³ ὦ βάθος;

(c) Acts, the only NT book where ὦ cannot be said to involve some emotion: 18¹⁴ ὦ Ἰουδαῖοι (not the first word, but correct position of the vocative in Attic style), 27²¹ ὦ ἄνδρες same. (Without ὦ: ἄνδρες ἀδελφοί 1¹⁶ 13²⁶ etc.; ἄνδ. Ἰσραηλεῖται 3¹²; ἄνδρες 7²⁶ etc.; ἄνδ. Ἰουδαῖοι 2¹⁴; βασιλεῦ 26⁷). There is no emotion, and everything that is classically correct, even to position after the first main verb, about ὦ Θεόφιλε 1¹; and yet Luke relapses into κράτιστε Θ. in Lk 1³, perhaps by a Latinism; cp. Dion. Hal. Orac. Vett. 1 ὦ κράτιστε Ἀμμαῖε. See Schwyzer op. cit. on this subject. The only other Biblical book which has unemphatic or unemotional ὦ (i.e. not corresponding to Heb. exclam. הוֹי) is 4 Mac.; see Johanness. DGKPS 8–13.

---

[1] K-G I 47ff. Schwyzer II 59–64. Gild. I §§ 14–25. Humbert §§ 417–424. Wackernagel I 305–312. Mayser II 1, 55ff. Johannessohn DGKPS 7–15. Moulton Einl. 108ff. Abel § 42. Zerwick §§ 22–24.

§ 2. Nominative form instead of Vocative

Although there is no certain example in the pre-Christian papyri, yet in the less educated writers of the post-Christian papyri there is a tendency for nominative forms to usurp the vocative. In the NT generally, when adjectives are used alone, it is the nominative form: Ac 13¹⁰ ὦ πλήρης; Lk 12²⁰ 1 Co 15³⁶ ἄφρων (vl. ἄφρον). In class. Attic the articular nominative of a single noun sometimes accompanied rather harsh address to inferiors, somewhat impersonally and with particular definiteness (almost pointing): ὁ παῖς, ἀκολούθει Aristoph. Ra. 521.

There is no vocative of the article in Greek, and so if the article was required the nom. form was used, the noun taking the nom. ending, if this was different, in sympathy with the article: Ga 4²¹ οἱ ὑπὸ νόμου θέλοντες εἶναι, Col 3⁵ τὰ μέλη *members, mortify earthly things*, 3¹⁸ff αἱ γυναῖκες, ... οἱ ἄνδρες, ... τὰ τέκνα, etc., 4¹ οἱ κύριοι, Eph 5¹⁴ ὁ καθεύδων. Some NT examples owe themselves to Hebraic influence, the Semitic vocative being constituted by articular nominative; thus LXX Ps 21² Lk 18¹¹ ὁ θεός, cp. ὁ πατήρ, etc., Lk 8⁵⁴ ἡ παῖς, ἔγειρε, Mk 5⁴¹ τὸ κοράσιον (= Aramaic emphatic state טְלִיתָא), Mt 11²⁶ Mk 14³⁶ Ro 8¹⁵ Ga 4⁶ ᾿Αββα, ὁ πατήρ (Aram.), Jn 17²¹ πατήρ (anarthr.), Jas 5¹ οἱ πλούσιοι, Jn 13¹³ ὁ διδάσκαλος καὶ ὁ κύριος, 20²⁸ ὁ κύριός μου καὶ ὁ θεός μου perhaps because the vocative form κύριε is lightly used in the Gospels as almost *sir*[1]; hence the emphatic form here takes its place, *my Lord*; 19³ χαῖρε, ὁ βασιλεύς (S βασιλεῦ) (where Mt 27²⁹ BD Mk 15¹⁸ SBD have χαῖρε, βασιλεῦ ...) said by Moulton to be due to "the writer's imperfect sensibility to the more delicate shades of Greek idiom"; actually it is an artist's stroke, the def. article pointing the finger of scorn; Rev 15³ ὁ βασιλεύς (S βασιλεῦ) τῶν ἐθνῶν (but Ac 26⁷ etc. βασιλεῦ, which, Moulton felt, admitted the royal prerogative whereas ὁ βασιλεύς in the mocking of Jesus does not); Lk 18¹¹ Heb 10⁷ OT etc. ὁ θεός (in Heb 1⁸ it is only just conceivable that ὁ θεός is nom. = *thy throne IS God*); Rev 11¹⁷ 15³ OT κύριε ὁ θεός (but Mt 27⁴⁶ θεέ μου, and seldom articular in LXX[2]), cp. Epict. II 16, 13 κύριε ὁ θεός which is from Jewish–Hellenistic magic; Rev 6¹⁰ ὁ Δεσπότης ὁ ἅγιος; Lk 12³² Mk 9²⁵ Rev 18⁴ ὁ λαός μου: Mt 9²⁷ 20³⁰. ³¹ (p⁴⁵ υἱέ) υἱὸς Δαυίδ, anarthr. because of Heb. construct state (but Mk 10⁴⁷ υἱὲ Δαυίδ); Ac 7⁴² οἶκος ᾿Ισραήλ anarthr. because of construct state (LXX

---

[1] Κύριε of Jesus: Mk 7²⁸ 10⁵¹; Mt 7²¹f 8². ⁶. ⁸. ²¹. ²⁵ 14²⁸. ³⁰ 15²². ²⁵. ²⁷ 16²² 17⁴. ¹⁵ 18²¹ 20³⁰f. ³³ 25³⁷. ⁴⁴ 26²²; Lk 5⁸. ¹² 6⁴⁶ 7⁶ 9⁵⁴. ⁵⁹ vl 6¹ 10¹⁷. ⁴⁰ 11¹ 12⁴¹ 13²³. ²⁵ 14²² 17³⁷ 18⁴¹ 19⁸ 22³³. ³⁸. ⁴⁹; Jn 4¹¹. ¹⁵. ¹⁹. ⁴⁹ 5⁷ 6³⁴. ⁶⁸ 9³⁶. ³⁸ 11³. ¹². ²¹. ²⁷. ³². ³⁴. ³⁹ 13⁶. ⁹. ²⁵. ³⁶. ³⁷ 14⁵. ⁸. ²² 21¹⁵. ¹⁶. ¹⁷. ²⁰. ²¹. Of others: Mt 11²⁵ 13²⁷ 21²⁹ 25¹¹. ²⁰. ²². ²⁴ 27⁶³; Lk 10²¹ 13⁸. ²⁵ 14²¹ 19¹⁶. ²⁰. ²⁵; Jn 12²¹. ³⁸ 20¹⁵.

[2] Helbing DKVS 34. Thackeray OT Gr. § 10, 10. Katz, *Philo's Bible* 59f, 152f.

Am 5²⁵); Jn 17¹¹B ²¹BDW ²⁴· ²⁵AB πατήρ; Jn 12¹⁵ABDW OT Lk 8⁴⁸
BKLW Mt 9²² DGLW Mk 5³⁴ BDW LXX Ru 2²² ABL Jg 11³⁵ B, etc.
θυγάτηρ anarthr. How are we to explain the anarthrous nominatives
among the above? They probably never had the article, but scribes fell
into the contemporary way of substituting nom. forms in the 3rd declen.
for the special forms of the vocative. E.g. BGU II 423.11 (ii/A.D.)
κύριέ μου πατήρ, P. Ross. Georg. III 2, vol. 27 (iii/A.D.) μήτηρ.

Moreover the nominative is common, as in class. Greek to a less
extent, when additions other than an adjectival epithet, and especially
participles, are made to the vocative, including a second or a third
vocative: Mk 9¹⁹ D Lk 9⁴¹ D ὦ γενεά ἄπιστε (but other MSS and
Mt 17¹⁷ ἄπιστος), Jn 17¹¹ πάτερ ἅγιε, Lk 11³⁹ ὑμεῖς οἱ Φαρισαῖοι, Mt
6⁹ πάτερ ἡμῶν ὁ ἐν τοῖς οὐρανοῖς, Lk 6²⁵ ὑμῖν, οἱ ἐμπεπλησμένοι, Ac 13¹⁶
ἄνδ. Ἰσρ. καὶ οἱ φοβούμενοι τὸν θεόν; cp. Xen. Cyr. III 3, 20 ὦ Κῦρε
καὶ οἱ ἄλλοι Πέρσαι, Ro 2¹· ³ ὦ ἄνθρωπε ὁ κρίνων, Rev 12¹² οὐρανοὶ καὶ οἱ
ἐν αὐτοῖς σκηνοῦντες, 18²⁰ οὐρανὲ καὶ οἱ ἅγιοι καὶ οἱ ἀπόστολοι, 19⁵
αἴνετε . . ., πάντες οἱ δοῦλοι αὐτοῦ, LXX Hag 2⁴ Sach 3⁸ Ἰησοῦ ὁ ἱερεὺς
ὁ μέγας. Zerwick (§ 23) suggests that the speech of Elisabeth in Lk 1⁴⁵
becomes more intelligible if we understand ἡ πιστεύσασα as a vocative,
as implied in the Vulgate's 2nd person: *Blessed are you because you
have believed.* The difficulty is the αὐτῇ which soon follows, making
the whole into 3rd person; of course, Vulg. alters this. Artemis pap. 1
·(iv/B.C.) θεοὶ οἱ μετὰ Ὀσεράπιος καθήμενοι, P. Par. 51.39 (159 B.C.)
εὐφράνεσθαι (= εὐφραίνεσθε), οἱ παρ' ἐμοῦ πάντες, J. Chrysostom *Hom.
Stat.* 467, 17 (387 A.D.) ὁ θεός, ὁ μὴ θέλων τὸν θάνατον τοῦ ἁμαρτωλοῦ.
" Cette construction devint fréquente à l'époque romaine, si bien que le
nominatif avec l'article a fini par être l'équivalent du vocatif (σύ)."[1]

---

[1] Soffray p. 1.

CHAPTER FIVE

SUBSTANTIVAL ARTICLE AND PRONOUN

§ 1. Substantival Article[1]

The def. art. has always preserved its demonstrative force; this is apparent even in MGr. in τὸ καὶ τό, τὰ καὶ τά *this and that* and πρὸ τοῦ *previously*. In the beginning the def. art. grew out of the old demonstrative pronoun in Homer: *this one, he*. It separates some from others, individualizing something as this and not that. Considering the total use of the article, it is true that the higher the type of Greek above ordinary speech the less prolific is the use of the article, so that whereas Atticistic style keeps fairly close to the norm established by Attic prose popular speech uses the article freely. However this does not apply to the special use of the article considered in this section, the pronominal use, that is, the substantival use as opposed to the adjectival; this is much reduced in the NT. Only in Ac 17²⁸, a quotation, does τοῦ = τούτου, and there is no trace of καὶ τόν *and him*, τὸν καὶ τόν *such and such a one*, or πρὸ τοῦ *before this*. All we have is occasional occurrences of ὁ μὲν ... ὁ δέ *the one ... the other* and indefinite *one ... another*, and ὁ δέ *but he*, and ὁ μὲν οὖν *now he*.

(a) ὁ μὲν ... ὁ δέ: Ptol. pap. very rare (Mayser II 1, 56f); 1 Co 7⁷ (ὃς ... ὃς p⁴⁷ SᶜKL), Eph 4¹¹, Heb 7²⁰ᶠ· ²³ᶠ 12¹⁰. Lk 85ᶠ ὁ μὲν ... καὶ ἕτερος, Mt 13²³ ὁ μὲν ... ὁ δὲ ... ὁ δέ (but accent ὅ neut., cp.⁸). Mt 22⁵ C² X, Mk 4⁴ W τὸ μέν. Jn 7¹² οἱ μὲν ... ἄλλοι δέ. Its place is usually taken by a non-class. use of the relative: Lk 23³³ ὃν μὲν ... ὃν δέ, Mt 13⁴ ἃ μὲν ... ἄλλα δέ (D ἃ δέ) 13⁸ 16¹⁴ οἱ μὲν ... ἄλλοι δὲ ... ἕτεροι δέ, 21³⁵ 22⁵ 25¹⁵, Mk 4⁴ 12⁵ Lk 8⁵ Ac 14⁴ 17¹⁸ (τινὲς ... οἱ δέ) 27⁴⁴ 28²⁴, Ro 9²¹ 14² ὃς μὲν ... ὁ (ὅς FG) δέ, 14⁵, 1 Co 11²¹ 12⁸· ²⁸ 2 Co 2¹⁶ Ph 1¹⁶, 2 Ti 2²⁰, Jude ²²ᶠ. Papyri: P. Teb. I 61(b) 29 (118 B.C.) τὴν μὲν ... ἣν δέ, P. Ox. IX 1189, 7 (c. A.D. 117) ἣν μὲν ... ἣν δέ). There are also Semitic substitutes: ὁ εἷς ... ὁ ἕτερος Mt 6²⁴ Lk 16¹³, εἷς ... καὶ εἷς Mt 20²¹ 24⁴⁰· ⁴¹ Mk 10³⁷. Even Luke has ὁ εἷς ... ὁ ἕτερος.

---

[1] K-G I 583–588. Gild. II §§ 515ff. Schwyzer II 19–27. F. Völker, *Syntax d. griech. Papyri* I. Der Artikel, Münster 1903, § 1. Winer-Schmiedel § 17. Moulton Einl. 129.

(b) ὁ δέ, ἡ δέ, οἱ δέ. In class. Attic ὁ δέ rarely refers to the subject of the preceding sentence (Gild. II § 518). It occurs frequently in NT to continue a narrative, even in Jn where it occurs least often: 5¹¹ ὁ δὲ ἀπεκρίθη SC*GKL (ὃς δέ AB, as Mk 15²³ SD and P. Ryl. II 144, 14 (A.D. 38), P. Soc. It. IV 313, 8 (iii–iv/A.D.) ὃς δέ). Mt 26⁶⁷ 28¹⁷ οἱ δέ. It usually marks a change of subject for the new sentence, as in Attic (e.g. Mk 1⁴⁵ and throughout Mk). In Mk 10³² where οἱ δέ does not mark a change of subject the reading is probably to be rejected in favour of καί. On its rare appearances in papyri it is sometimes followed by a participle.

(c) ὁ μὲν οὖν. Acts only: 5⁴¹. With ptc. 1⁶ 2⁴¹ 8⁴ 11¹⁹ 15³·³⁰ 23¹⁸ 28⁵.

There is no instance of the article as a relative pronoun in the NT.

§ 2. Substantival Pronouns ¹

(a) *Personal.* These are very frequent in the NT.

1. The nominatives ἐγώ σύ ἡμεῖς ὑμεῖς were usually not employed in class. Greek except for emphasis or antithesis; this principle is not strictly observed in NT and papyri (Mayser II 1, 63), e.g. the stock phrases in letters ὡς ἐγὼ θέλω, ὡς ἐγὼ ἀκούω, etc., cp. Tit 1⁵ ὡς ἐγώ σοι διεταξάμην. But in the following examples at least there is some sort of emphasis or antithesis:

ἐγώ Mk 14²⁹ Lk 11¹⁹ Jn 10³⁰ Ro 7¹⁷ 1 Co 7¹² Eph 4¹ (but prob. simply to carry an apposition) 2 Ti 4⁶; if ἐγώ occurs in the papyri it is usually emphatic. Σύ Mt 6¹⁷ 26⁶⁴ 27¹¹ Jn 2¹⁰ (cp. with πᾶς ἄνθρωπος) 4⁹ (but simply to carry a phrase in apposition, rather than emphatic: also 10³³ Lk 1⁷⁶ Ac 1²⁴ Ro 14⁴) 4¹⁰ 18³⁷ (*you have said it, not me*) 21²², Ac 10¹⁵ 11¹⁴, 2 Ti 4⁵ Jas 2³. Ἡμεῖς Mt 6¹² 17¹⁹ Ac 15¹⁰ Ga 2⁹. Ὑμεῖς Mk 6³⁷.

Without much emphasis are the following: Mk 13⁹ βλέπετε δὲ ὑμεῖς ἑαυτούς, ²³ ὑμεῖς δὲ βλέπετε, Lk 1¹⁸ ἐγὼ γάρ εἰμι πρεσβύτης, 9⁹ ἐγώ, Jn 1³⁰ (c Syrᶜ om ἐγώ), 18³⁸ superfluous ἐγώ, 1 Co 2³ κἀγώ, 11²³ ἐγώ, Ph 4¹¹ ἐγώ. Mt 11²³ σύ, 27¹¹ σύ, Jn 1⁴² σύ, 6³⁰ τί οὖν ποιεῖς σὺ σημεῖον; 18³³ σὺ εἶ ὁ βασιλεύς; Ro 2³ σύ. Ac 4⁷ τοῦτο ὑμεῖς are together stylistically but it is fanciful to suppose the meaning is *people like YOU doing a miracle like THIS*; the simple question was angry, not subtle. Jn 5³⁸·³⁹·⁴⁴ (some correctors have om. ὑμεῖς). Eph 5³² (it is straining things to say that ἐγώ = *I as an apostle*; the corresponding phrase in

---

¹ K-G I 555f. Gild. I §§ 68ff. Schwyzer II 186–207. Wackernagel II 84–101. Mayser II 1, 62–73. Winer-Schmiedel § 22. Moulton Einl. 135. G. Dronke, " Beiträge zur Lehre vom griech. Pron. aus Apollonius Dyscolus," *Rh. M.* 9, 107ff.

1 Co 1¹² is simply λέγω δέ). Lk 10²³ᶠ (there cannot be any difference between ἃ βλέπετε and ἃ ὑμεῖς βλέπετε standing side by side). 2 Co 11²⁹ (the sudden insertion of ἐγώ is gratuitous and meaningless in τίς ἀσθενεῖ καὶ οὐκ ἀσθενῶ; τίς σκανδαλίζεται καὶ οὐκ ἐγώ πυροῦμαι;). Mt 10¹⁶ 11¹⁰ ἰδού ἐγώ is the Heb. הִנְנִי, but the Aram. 'ᵃnāh is used unemphatically, especially with the participle. Thus there are no grounds for thinking that scribes have inserted the pronouns; we should retain them in the variant readings.

2. The difference between the enclitic and the accented forms of pers. pronouns in the oblique cases, like μου and ἐμοῦ, is once again the fact that the accented form tends to mark a contrast, as in class. Greek: P. Rein. 18, 5 (108 B.C.) γραψαμένου ἐμοῦ τε καὶ τῆς μητρός. But in Biblical Greek, and particularly the LXX (Johannessohn DGPS 369ff) there is a large number of these accented and enclitic forms, especially in the genitive, occurring without emphasis; clearly this is due in some part to Semitic influence and the resultant tendency to attach pronouns like suffixes to substantival and verbal forms with a liberality and casualness which offends classical taste. So the redundancy in the NT also is obviously a Semitism (Lagrange, *S. Matth.* XCVI); Hebrew and Aramaic employ this pronoun so often in the form of a suffix that it would be surprising if Jewish writers did not carry the habit into their Greek. The MSS show many variants but we do well to prefer the reading which retains the superfluous αὐτοῦ, etc. The general tendency of the language was certainly in this direction, and unliterary Gentiles indulge in the repetition of μου, σου, αὐτοῦ and the other oblique cases (Moulton-Howard 431f), but this will not explain the 34 instances of αὐτοῦ in Lk 1 where the Semitic background is so obvious, and the Semitic Matthew's usage is no more abundant than Mark's or Luke's. His extreme ἀποκριθεὶς δὲ ὁ κύριος αὐτοῦ εἶπεν αὐτῷ (25²⁶) is in line with the rest of NT. Of course, the writers vary in the degree to which they depart from the Greek norm of economy in this respect, some equipping every verb with a pronoun when it can be readily inferred from the context.

Very close to the Greek norm: Jn 8³⁸ παρὰ τῷ πατρί (SD add μου) and ὁ πατήρ often in Jn without pronoun, unless he means simply *the Father*. Mt 27²⁴ ἀπενίψατο τὰς χεῖρας, 15² τὰς χεῖρας (αὐτῶν add CDEF). Ac 7⁵⁸ τὰ ἱμάτια HPS (viii–xi/A.D. uncials; but rest have pronoun), 16¹⁵ παρεκάλεσεν λέγουσα, 13³ ἐπιθέντες τὰς χεῖρας αὐτοῖς ἀπέλυσαν, Mk 6⁵ ἐπιθ. τ. χεῖρας. Ph 1⁶ ἐπιτελέσει (sc. αὐτό). Eph 5¹¹ (sc. αὐτά). 1 Ti 6² (sc. αὐτούς). Jn 10²⁹ (sc. αὐτούς). Lk 14⁴ (sc. αὐτόν).

Less Greek: Lk 24³¹ αὐτῶν δὲ διηνοίχθησαν οἱ ὀφθαλμοί, Herm. S.V 7, 3 αὐτοῦ γάρ ἐστιν πᾶσα ἐξουσία A, VIII 7, 1 ἄκουε καὶ περὶ αὐτῶν. Ac 7²¹ superfluous αὐτόν bis, as scribal activity indicates. Mt 6³ superfl. σου. Mt 8¹ vl Mk 5² superfl. αὐτῷ; and same kind of repetition occurs in Mt 4¹⁶ OT 5⁴⁰ 8¹ 26⁷¹ Col 2¹³ Ph 1⁷ Jas 4¹⁷ Rev 6⁴. On the other hand, such repetition is not unknown in class. authors (K–G II 579, n. 2 and 3) where the first pronoun forms part of a preceding participial clause: eg. Mk 10¹⁶, ἐναγκαλισάμενος αὐτὰ κατευλόγει τιθεὶς τὰς χεῖρας ἐπ' αὐτά, and 9²⁸ Lk 1⁶² Ac 7²¹ 2 Pt 3¹⁶ and especially in Rev; see also Acta Thomae 198¹⁷ ἀνθρώποις ὑμῖν οὖσιν ὥσπερ τοῖς ἀλόγοις ζώοις ἐπιτιθέασιν ὑμῖν φόρτους (Ljungvik SSAA 27 gives further examples from apocryphal Acts). The question of rhythm may play some part in the repetition, e.g. Mt 22³⁷ (as in Engl.: *with all thy heart and with all thy soul and with all thy strength*), Rev 9²¹ οὐ . . . αὐτῶν οὔτε . . . αὐτῶν οὔτε . . . αὐτῶν. And there is insertion for emphasis, e.g. P. Oxy. VIII. 1162 (iv/A.D.). τὸν ἀδελφὸν ἡμῶν ᾿Αμμώνιον παραγινόμενον πρὸς ὑμᾶς συνδέξασθαι (=σθε) αὐτὸν ἐν ἰρήνη; Passio Barth. 141³¹ τούτους πάντας τοὺς κατακειμένους ἐνθάδε ἀπὸ βαρέων νοσημάτων τίς ἐστιν ὁ καταβλάπτων αὐτούς; Jn 18¹¹ τὸ ποτήριον . . . οὐ μὴ πίω αὐτό; Mt 6⁴ ὁ πατήρ σου . . . ἀποδώσει σοι, 1 Pt 5¹⁰ PHL ὁ καλέσας ὑμᾶς . . . καταρτίσαι ὑμᾶς, Rev. 21⁶ 046 ἐγὼ τῷ διψῶντι δώσω αὐτῷ.

For accus. and infin. instead of plain infin., see pp. 147f.

For superfluous αὐτοῦ etc. after a relative, see p. 325.

See also Lk 12⁴⁸ Jn 6³⁹ 15².

It is usual to find that the accented forms of 1st p. sing. pronoun in oblique cases are used for special emphasis in the NT, especially after a preposition (with the notable exception of πρός: e.g. Mt 25³⁶ πρός με (S ἐμέ), Mk 9¹⁹ πρός με (p⁴⁵ S ἐμέ), Ac 22⁸ (S*AB ἐμέ)¹⁰, even emphatically Mt 3¹⁴ σὺ ἔρχῃ πρός με; however nearly all MSS read πρὸς ἐμέ in Jn 6³⁷ first time, and SE al the second time; inscr. from Magnesia 19¹⁰ πρὸς ἐμέ, 22⁵ πρός με, PSI IV 326, 4 πρὸς ἐμέ (261 B.C.), P. Hib. 63, 3 πρός με (265 B.C.)).

Quite in keeping with the animated style of Paul's letters is the usage of ἐγώ and σύ (all cases) which is first found in the late class. Greek of Demosthenes and which is actually more a matter of rhetoric than syntax. Paul instances both himself and his reader in a vivid way to illustrate a point, not intending to apply what is said literally to himself or his reader: Ro 2¹⁷ 7⁷ff. 9f 8²

11¹⁷ 14⁴ etc. 1 Co 10³⁰ Ga 2¹⁸.   We must refer to Bauer s.v. ἐγώ (end); Stauffer in Kittel WB II 355ff.

Normal in secular Greek is the sense-construction with pronouns: Ac 8⁵ *Samaria* foll. by αὐτοῖς, similarly Mt 4²³ 9³⁵ 11¹ Lk 4¹⁵ Ac 16¹⁰ 20² 2 Co 2¹²ᶠ Ga 2² 1 Th 1⁹ etc.; Jn 8⁴⁴ αὐτοῦ can only refer to a general conception like *falsehood* which has been no more than implied (it is unhelpful to translate *his father*; this needs at least a change of subject just before, as RVᵐᵍ, and the whole thing becomes confused at once; it might refer to a mythological *devil's father*, but even this author could scarcely be so credulous); Ro 2²⁶ αὐτοῦ has no expressed antecedent but again is vague in reference; Eph 5¹² αὐτῶν too has but a general reference which must be drawn from σκότος just before; Theodoret I 914 τοῦτο τῆς ἀποστολικῆς χάριτος ἴδιον· αὐτοῖς γάρ (ἀποστόλοις must be inferred); 2 Co 5¹⁹ αὐτοῖς after κόσμος; Mt 1²¹ αὐτῶν after λαός; Jn 17² αὐτοῖς after πᾶν (but S*W correct to αὐτῷ); Mt 14¹⁴ Mk 6⁴⁵ αὐτοῖς after ὄχλος; 3 Jn⁹ αὐτῶν after ἐκκλησία; Mt 28¹⁹ Rev 19¹⁵ LXX Ex 23²⁷ Dt 4²⁷ 18¹⁴ al Ac 15¹⁷ OT ἔθνη foll. by αὐτούς; Ro 2¹⁴ by οὗτοι, Ac 16¹⁷ OT by οὕς; Lk 23⁵⁰ᶠ αὐτῶν of members of Council, inferred; LXX Jon 1³ εὗρε πλοῖον βαδίζον εἰς Θαρσίς . . . καὶ ἀνέβη εἰς αὐτὸ τοῦ πλεῦσαι μετ' αὐτῶν; Mt 8⁴ Mk 1⁴⁴ Lk 5¹⁴ αὐτοῖς after ἱερεύς, unless it is a general ref., not to the priests but to the public; Mt 14¹¹ Mk 6²⁸ αὐτῆς after κοράσιον; Mk 5²³ αὐτῇ after θυγάτριον (p⁴⁵ AK correct to αὐτῷ); Lk 2²¹ᶠ αὐτόν after παιδίου: Col 2¹⁵ αὐτούς after ἀρχάς, ἐξουσίας; Rev 17¹⁶ after κέρατα, θηρίον. This is fairly common in class. Greek and very common in LXX: Dt 21⁸, 1 Km 14³⁴ Wis 16²⁰ αὐτοῖς after λαός; Jdt 5³ αὐτῶν after λαός; Wis 16³ αὐτοί after λαός, Si 16⁸ αὐτῶν after παροικίας.

3. In MGr αὐτός has become the pers. pronoun *he* (not *himself*). The beginnings of this development appear already in pre-Christian papyri (Mayser II 1, 64), in LXX (e.g. Ge 12¹²), and in NT especially in Luke; e.g. 1¹⁷ αὐτὸς προελεύσεται αὐτοῦ,²² καὶ αὐτός, 2²⁸ καὶ αὐτὸς ἐδέξατο αὐτό,⁵⁰ καὶ αὐτοί, 3²³, 4¹⁵ καὶ αὐτός, 6³⁵ 7⁵, 9³⁶ καὶ αὐτοί, 11¹⁴ καὶ αὐτό, 16²³ 24²¹. It is possible to argue that the emphasis is still present even in the NT examples, but even here in place of αὐτός a class. Attic writer would use ἐκεῖνος. The LXX appear to use αὐτός without emphasis but not αὐτή or αὐτό; perhaps Lk 11¹⁴ shows αὐτό so used, if καὶ αὐτὸ ἦν is genuine; as to αὐτή, the editors of the NT text are divided in preference for αὐτή and αὕτη (Lk 2³⁷ 7¹² 8⁴² Heb 11¹¹). The text is uncertain in Lk 4¹⁵ καὶ αὐτὸς ἐδίδασκεν (Ae om. αὐτός), 5¹⁷ 19².

It is not easy to decide, but probably the pronoun has some emphasis in all the following: Mt 1²¹ Col 1¹⁷ *he* and no other, Mt 8¹⁷ (Isa 53⁴)

αὐτὸς . . . ἔλαβεν *he himself carried,* 12⁵⁰, Mk 1⁸, 2²⁵ *he |himself,* 5⁴⁰ αὐτὸς
δέ (ὁ δὲ AMW), 14⁴⁴ αὐτός ἐστιν *he* is the man, Lk 5³⁷ 6⁴² 10¹ 18³⁹,
Jn 4² 6⁶ 9²¹ 16²⁷, Ac 3¹⁰ αὐτός (BDEP οὗτος), 14¹² 18¹⁹ Ro 8²³ 16² καὶ γὰρ
αὐτή *she herself,* 1 Co 3¹⁵, 1 Th 3¹¹ 4¹⁶ 5²³, 2 Th 2¹⁶ 3¹⁶, Col 1¹⁸ καὶ αὐτός
ἐστιν ἡ κεφαλή . . . *he himself* (alone).

The proleptic pronoun followed by resumptive noun is an
Aramaic peculiarity [1] : Mt 3⁴ αὐτὸς δὲ ὁ (ὁ om. D) ᾿Ιωάννης *he,*
i.e. John ; Mk 2²¹ (see below under partitive ἀπό), 6¹⁷ αὐτὸς γὰρ ὁ
(ὁ om. D) ῾Ηρ. *he, i.e. Herod,* ²²AC τῆς θυγατρὸς αὐτῆς τῆς
῾Ηρωδιάδος *her daughter, i.e. Herodias's,* Jn 9¹³ ἄγουσιν αὐτὸν
πρὸς τοὺς Φαρισαίους, τόν ποτε τυφλόν.   Probably also: Mk
6¹⁷. ¹⁸. ²² 12³⁶. ³⁷.   It appears particularly in codex Bezae [2] :
Mt 12⁴⁵ D αὐτοῦ τοῦ ἀνθρώπου ἐκείνου; Mk 5¹⁵ᶠ D καὶ
θεωροῦσιν αὐτὸν τὸν δαιμονιζόμενον . . . διηγήσαντο δὲ πῶς
ἐγένετο αὐτῷ τῷ δαιμονιζομένῳ; 6¹⁸ D αὐτὴν γυναῖκα τοῦ
ἀδελφοῦ σου. Ac 3² D (but mistake for παρὰ τῶν?). This
hypothesis of Aramaic influence could explain the apparent use
of αὐτός = οὗτος in a demonstrative sense: see p. 194.

(*b*) *Reflexive.* These pronouns do not share in the general
increase in the use of pronouns in Hell. Greek. In the NT and
pre-Christian papyri as in Hellenistic generally, even in the old
colloquial Attic (but not class. Attic), the simple personal
pronoun often serves as a reflexive; otherwise the regular
reflexive is a formation of αὐτός like ἐμαυτοῦ, σεαυτοῦ, ἑαυτοῦ,
αὐτοὺς ἡμᾶς (2 Th 1⁴), ὑμῶν αὐτῶν (e.g. Ac 20³⁰ 1 Co 5¹³ OT),
ἑαυτῶν. In the NT sometimes αυτον may be αὐτόν, but if so,
it is difficult to see why this abbreviated form should be used
instead of ἑαυτόν when it obviously causes confusion with αὐτόν.
The contracted form is dying out in Hell. Greek (Blass-Debr.
§ 64.1) and in the NT period αὑτοῦ is virtually dead. It is
therefore precarious to read αὑτοῦ where the uncials have
ΑΥΤΟΥ, and so with αὑτόν and αὑτούς (Lk 23¹² Jn 2²⁴ Ac 14¹⁷
Ph 3²¹).

1. *Direct reflexives.* Used as a direct complement of the
verb (Jn 14²¹ ἐμφανίσω αὐτῷ ἐμαυτόν) referring back to the
subject, we have in the NT usually these compound -αὐτός

---

[1] C. F. Burney, *The Aramaic Origin of the Fourth Gospel,* Oxford 1922,
85ff. Moulton-Howard 431.
[2] M. Black, *An Aramaic Approach to the Gospels and Acts* [2], Oxford
1953, 70–74.

forms, but sometimes the simple pronoun (e.g. Mt 6¹⁹ᶠ θησαυρίζετε ὑμῖν (for ἑαυτοῖς) θησαυρούς; 17²⁷ ἀντὶ ἐμοῦ καὶ σοῦ (Aram. influence for ἐμαυτοῦ?): Ac 26⁹ ἔδοξα ἐμαυτῷ (= class. μοι), 1 Co 4⁴ ἐμαυτῷ σύνοιδα. Pre-Christian papyri exhibit examples of both emphatic and unemphatic reflexives formed from αὐτός (Mayser II 1, 66). But although personal pronouns have greatly increased in number in Biblical Greek, reflexive pronouns are retreating. The process is held up by the fact that the disappearance of ἐμός and σός often calls for the substitute of a refl. pronoun. In Luke ἑαυτοῦ is more frequent (60 times) than in Matthew (31). Note that Luke has altered Matthew's θησαυρίζετε ὑμῖν (6¹⁹ᶠ) to ποιήσατε ἑαυτοῖς (12³³). Instead of the reflexive, Mt has ἔλεγξον . . . μεταξύ σοῦ καὶ αὐτοῦ (18¹⁵) and δὸς ἀντὶ ἐμοῦ καὶ σοῦ (17²⁷). But Luke uses the reflexive gen. without emphasis (ἑαυτοῦ 15²⁰, Ac 14¹⁴). The confusion has a Semitic explanation, in that Hebrew-Aramaic pronominal suffixes allow no distinction between personal and reflexive (Zerwick § 156).

Another development in the LXX, NT and illiterate papyri is the use of the 3rd person reflexive in place of 1st or 2nd person. In the plural we have e.g. for 2nd pers.: Jn 12⁸ μεθ' ἑαυτῶν, Lk 17³ προσέχετε ἑαυτοῖς, Ph 2¹², Heb 10²⁵ ἑαυτῶν, Mt 3⁹ ἐν ἑαυτοῖς, 23³¹ ἑαυτοῖς, Ac 13⁴⁶, Heb 3¹³ ἑαυτούς, Mt 25⁹ Ro 6¹³ 1 Jn 5²¹. 1st pers.: Ro 8²³ ἐν ἑαυτοῖς, 1 Co 11³¹ ἑαυτούς, 2 Co 1⁹ ἐν ἑαυτοῖς, Ac 23¹⁴ 2 Co 10¹² ἑαυτούς. In the sing. the substitution is even more commonly found; for 2nd pers.: Mt 23³⁷ Lk 1⁴⁵ 13³⁴ Mk 12³¹ vl ὡς ἑαυτόν, Jn 18³⁴ ἀφ' ἑαυτοῦ σύ . . . , corr. to ἀπὸ σεαυτοῦ by SBC*L, Ro 13⁹ FGLP, Ga 5¹⁴ FGLN*P (OT) ὡς ἑαυτόν (but σεαυτόν, as in Mt 22³⁹ LXX, is prob. to be preferred), Ac 25²¹ αὐτόν for σαυτόν. For 1st pers.: Herm. V IV 1⁵ ἠρξάμην λέγειν ἐν ἑαυτῷ S*a s (corr. to ἐμαυτῷ by Sᶜ), Herm. S. II 1 τί σὺ ἐν ἑαυτῷ ζητεῖς, IX 2⁵, Clem. Hom. XIV 10, XVII 18 ἑαυτοῦ, BU 86 (ii/A.D.) ἑαυτοῦ.

Although after a preposition we find ἑαυτοῦ etc. (as Jn 8¹⁸ ἐγώ εἰμι ὁ μαρτυρῶν περὶ ἐμαυτοῦ), yet often in NT and Koine a simple personal pronoun will be used, and this is certainly so in Mt: 5²⁹ᶠ 18⁸ᶠ βάλε ἀπὸ σοῦ, 6² μὴ σαλπίσῃς ἔμπροσθέν σου, 11²⁹ *take my yoke* ἐφ' ὑμᾶς, 18¹⁶ παράλαβε μετὰ τοῦ BDIW (but σεαυτοῦ SKLM); and especially where two pronouns are connected: 18¹⁵ μεταξὺ σοῦ καὶ αὐτοῦ, 17²⁷ δὸς ἀντὶ ἐμοῦ καὶ σοῦ. But even Mt has the reflexive form too: 9³. ²¹ εἶπον ἐν ἑαυτοῖς, 12²⁵ *divided* καθ' ἑαυτῆς, 15³⁰ ἔχοντες μεθ' ἑαυτῶν. P. Petr. II 40(a) 27 (223 B.C.) περὶ ὑμῶν ἐντείνεσθε, PSI IV 443, 19 (iii/B.C.) ὑμᾶς παρεξόμεθα, etc. (Mayser II 1, 67). Ph 2²³ τὰ περὶ ἐμέ, Eph 2¹⁶ ἐν αὐτῷ either *by himself* or *by it* (the cross): similar ambiguity Col 1²⁰, 1 Jn 5¹⁰, Jas 5²⁰.

There is the Semitic periphrasis for reflexive pronoun ¹ by means of נֶפֶשׁ, e.g. Lk 9²⁴ ἀπολέσῃ τὴν ψυχὴν αὐτοῦ is the same as ²⁵ ἑαυτὸν δὲ ἀπολέσας ἢ ζημιωθείς, and cp. Mt 20²⁸ (Mk 10⁴⁵) with 1 Ti 2⁶. Mt 16²⁵ᶠ (Mk 8³⁵⁻³⁷) in this sense: at least, Luke seems to have understood it so, for he writes ἑαυτὸν δὲ ἀπολέσας 9²⁵. So also OT quotations: Mt 12¹⁸ ἡ ψυχή μου (= ἐγὼ αὐτός), Ac 2²⁷ Heb 10³⁸. But clearly the contexts intend us to feel the force of the double meaning of נֶפֶשׁ as *soul* and *life* which cannot be rendered so neatly in Greek.

2. *Indirect reflexives.* There are NT examples, though comparatively few, of the use of the reflexive pronoun where there is little or no dependence on the verb, because of the intervention of a noun or a phrase: Mt 12⁴⁵ πονηρότερα ἑαυτοῦ (DE*W αυτου), Mk 5²⁶ τὰ παρ' ἑαυτῆς (ABL αυτης), 8³⁵ τὴν ψυχὴν ἑαυτοῦ σῶσαι (first time) B Orig. D², (second time) C³ WXYΘ fam¹³ (the rest correct to αὐτοῦ), Lk 11²¹ τὴν ἑαυτοῦ αὐλήν, 13³⁴ τὴν ἑαυτῆς νοσσιάν (D αὐτῆς), 14²⁶ τὸν πατέρα ἑαυτοῦ B, τὴν ψυχὴν ἑαυτοῦ, ³³τοῖς ἑαυτοῦ ὑπάρχουσιν (DW correct to αὐτοῦ), 16⁸ τὴν γενεὰν τὴν ἑαυτῶν, 24²⁷ τὰ περὶ ἑαυτοῦ (DEL αυτου); often in Paul, e.g. Ro 4¹⁹ 5⁸ 16⁴· ¹⁸, 1 Co 10²⁹ συνείδησιν δὲ λέγω οὐχὶ τὴν ἑαυτοῦ (emph. and contrast),³³ τὸ ἐμαυτοῦ συμφέρον; Heb 10²⁵ τὴν ἐπισυναγωγὴν ἑαυτῶν (= ἡμῶν). This is quite common in the papyri (Mayser II 1, 67ff). The use of the simple pers. pronoun is more common in the NT.

(c) *Reciprocal pronouns.* As in the papyri and to some extent in earlier Greek, ἑαυτῶν serves for ἀλλήλων in NT.: P. Petr. II 45 (246 B.C.), P. Par. 46, 12 (153 B.C.), etc.; 1 Co 6⁷ having lawsuits μεθ' ἑαυτῶν, Eph 5¹⁹ speaking ἑαυτοῖς, Col 3¹⁶ admonishing ἑαυτούς, 1 Th 5¹³ be at peace ἐν ἑαυτοῖς (SD*FGP αυτοις, clearly = αὐτοῖς); but Mk 9⁵⁰ εἰρ. ἐν ἀλλήλοις. Often side by side with ἀλλ. for variety: Lk 23¹² μετ' ἀλλήλων . . . πρὸς

---

¹ Schwyzer II 192 n.   Huber 67.   Mayser II 1, 65–72; II 2, 65–74. Winer-Schmiedel § 22, 18b.   Lagrange, *S. Matth.* XCVII.   Zerwick § 160.

ἑαυτούς (SBLT αυτους, clearly = αὐτούς), Col 3¹³; Ph 2³ is precise: ἀλλήλους ἡγούμενοι ὑπερεχόντας ἑαυτῶν; so Mk 9⁵⁰ ἔχετε ἐν ἑαυτοῖς ἅλα καὶ εἰρηνεύετε ἐν ἀλλήλοις. Other alternatives for ἀλλ.: Ac 2¹² ἄλλος πρὸς ἄλλον (ἄλλος ἄλλον in Mayser II 1, § 26 n.2). For "Semitic" εἷς τὸν ἕνα, see p. 187.

(d) *Demonstrative pronouns.* On the article as demonstr. pronoun, see pp. 34, 36f. The usual pronouns are οὗτος, ἐκεῖνος, less often ὅδε.

1. Ὅδε, fading rapidly in the Koine and lacking in the i/B.C. papyri (Mayser II 1, 73f), especially in its substantival use, in the NT it is almost confined to τάδε λέγει Ac 21¹¹ Rev 2¹. 8. 12. 18 3¹. 7. 14, P. Giss. I 36, 10 (135 B.C.), 37 II 11 (134 B.C.), etc. It is commoner in LXX, especially in the more literary parts (Thackeray OT Gr. 11). It tends to belong to official writing and not to living literature. See also Lk 10³⁹ καὶ τῇδε ἦν ἀδελφή not = ταύτῃ but *behold there was*, as LXX use τῇδε to render הִנֵּה Ge 25²⁴ = 38²⁷ καὶ τῇδε ἦν δίδυμα *behold there were*, 50¹⁸ οἵδε ἡμεῖς σοι οἰκέται *behold we are*, Ex 8²⁹⁽²⁵⁾ ὅδε ἐγὼ ἐξελεύσομαι *behold I go*, Je 3²² οἵδε ἡμεῖς ἐσόμεθά σοι *behold we shall be*.[1] See also, in this light, Lk 16²⁵ fam¹ Marc. ὅδε = *this man* (not *he . . . here*; it was misunderstood by very early scribes as Hellenistic for *here* and therefore corrected to ὧδε, in the same way as in LXX ὅδε is corrupted to ὧδε Ex 8²⁹⁽²⁵⁾ Le 10¹⁶ DaΘ 3⁹²⁽²⁵⁾, and οἵδε to ὧδε, ἴδε, etc. Num 14⁴⁰).

2. Οὗτος is very frequent in papyri and NT and as in earlier Greek refers to someone actually present (often contemptuously Lk 15³⁰ ὁ υἱός σου οὗτος, 18¹¹ οὗτος ὁ τελώνης; also Mt 26⁶¹. ⁷¹ Mk 2⁷ Jn 6⁴² 9²⁴ 12³⁴ Ac 5²⁸ 7⁴⁰ 17¹⁸), not necessarily referring to the noun which is nearest, but to the noun which is most vividly in the writer's mind (deictic). Mt 3¹⁷ οὗτός ἐστιν ὁ υἱός μου, Ac 4¹¹ οὗτος Jesus (although *God* is the nearest noun), 8²⁶ αὕτη ἐστὶν ἔρημος the road (not Gaza, though G. is the nearer noun), Mt 3³ οὗτος (refers right back to ¹), 1 Jn 5²⁰ (God, not Christ, is the true God). It often refers back to a previous description or introduction of a person (anaphoric): Mt 27⁵⁷ᶠ

---

[1] J. Ziegler's conclusion; the MSS nearest to this are Marchalianus and Venetus (ιδου οιδε). but the great uncials (SB) have a corrupted text (ιδου δουλοι) which bears no relation to הִנְנִי אֲנ̇ונ לִי. See *Beiträge zur Ieremias-Septuaginta*, Göttingen 1958, 38–39.

ἄνθρωπος . . . οὗτος προσελθών, etc., Lk 23⁵⁰ᶠ ἀνήρ . . . οὗτος οὐκ
ἦν, Ac 1¹⁶ᶠᶠ 'Ιούδα . . . οὗτος, Heb 7¹.

Indeed οὗτος in the apodosis referring back to the protasis is a
favourite usage in various NT writers (but Luke often gets rid of it):
Mt 10²² 24¹³ ὁ δὲ ὑπομείνας . . . οὗτος σωθήσεται = Mk 13¹³ (Lk alters),
Mk 12⁴⁰ = Lk 20⁴⁷ κατέσθοντες τὰς οἰκίας . . . οὗτοι λήμψονται, Jn
6⁴⁶ ὁ ὢν παρὰ τοῦ θεοῦ οὗτος ἑώρακεν, 7¹⁸ ὁ δὲ ζητῶν τὴν δόξαν . . . οὗτος
ἀληθής ἐστιν, 15⁵ ὁ μείνων ἐν ἐμοὶ . . . οὗτος φέρει καρπόν, Mt 5¹⁹ ὃς δ' ἂν
ποιήσῃ . . . οὗτος μέγας κληθήσεται, 2 Jn⁹ ὁ μένων . . . οὗτος . . . Mt 21⁴²
= Mk 12¹⁰, Mt 13²⁰. ³⁸ 15¹¹ 18⁴ 26²³, Mk 3³⁵ 6¹⁶ Lk 9²⁴ Ro 7¹⁵ ὃ μισῶ
τοῦτο ποιῶ, Jas 3² εἴ τις . . . οὗτος . . .

A characteristic usage in Paul and John is οὗτος in the
preceding clause with ἵνα, ὅτι, or infin. or a noun to follow:
Lk 1⁴³, Jn 3¹⁹ αὕτη . . . ὅτι, 8⁴⁷ etc. διὰ τοῦτο . . . ὅτι, 13³⁵,
1 Jn 2³ ἐν τούτῳ γινώσκομεν . . . ἐάν, 3¹¹, 5² ἐν τούτῳ ὅταν,
2 Jn⁶, 1 Co 7³⁷ τοῦτο κέκρικεν . . . infin., 2 Co 2¹ ἔκρινα ἐμαυτῷ
τοῦτο, τὸ μὴ . . . ἐλθεῖν, 13⁹ τοῦτο καὶ εὐχόμεθα, τὴν ὑμῶν
κατάρτισιν, 1 Ti 1⁹ εἰδὼς τοῦτο, ὅτι . . . , Heb 2¹⁵ ἀπαλλάξῃ
τούτους, ὅσοι . . . (examples in Pernot Études 50f, 62, 119,
144f), P. Petr. II 13 (19) (252 B.C.) τοῦτο . . . ὅτι, P. Par. 63
(165 B.C.) τοῦτο . . . ὅτι, PSI V 495, 23 (258 B.C.) same. Antecedent of a relative: Mt 11¹⁰ οὗτος περὶ οὗ, Jn 7⁴⁹ Ac 7⁴⁰ οὗτος ὅς,
Ph 2⁵ τοῦτο . . . ὅ. We find various adverbial usages: αὐτὸ
τοῦτο = Pauline *just this* Ro 9¹⁷ OT 13⁶ Ph 1⁶ 2 Pt 1⁵; τοῦτο
αὐτό = *just for this reason* 2 Co 2³. See Bauer s.v. αὐτός 1 h.
In Attic and literary Koine there is τοῦτο μέν . . . τοῦτο δέ *on
the one hand . . . on the other* Heb 10³³. καὶ τοῦτο = *and indeed*
Ro 13¹¹ 1 Co 6⁶· ⁸ Eph 2⁸; pl. class. Heb 11¹². τοῦτ' ἐστιν is
formal and literary, mostly in Ac, Paul, Heb (besides Mt 27⁴⁶
Mk 7²).

3. 'Εκεῖνος, which in its substantive use is almost never
found in pre-Christian papyri, refers to the remoter person or
thing, and is rarer in NT than οὗτος (except in John), with
which it is practically interchangable; it very seldom marks an
opposition to οὗτος, as it does in Herm. M. III 5: ἐκεῖνα (*the past*)
. . . ταῦτα (*the present*), but there is Lk 18¹⁴ οὗτος . . . παρ' ἐκεῖνον,
Jas 4¹⁵ τοῦτο ἢ ἐκεῖνο, Jn 5³⁸ ὃν ἀπέστειλεν ἐκεῖνος, τούτῳ . . . .
However, in Jn 21²³ οὗτος and ἐκεῖνος are not so much for contrast as for variety. 'Εκεῖνος denotes persons in their absence
deictically: ἐκεῖνοι opposed to ὑμεῖς Mt 13¹¹ Mk 4¹¹ Jn 5³⁹ Ac 3¹³

2 Co 8¹⁴; opposed to ἐγώ or ἡμεῖς Jn 3²⁸. ³⁰ 1 Co 9²⁵ 10¹¹ 15¹¹.
As οὗτος was seen to represent the person nearest to the author's
mind, so ἐκεῖνος represents the remoter person, e.g. Jn 1⁶ᶠᶠ:
οὗτος (John) ἦλθεν . . . ἵνα πάντες πιστεύσωσιν δι' αὐτοῦ;
Jesus has now been mentioned and John becomes in thought
the remoter person; hence οὐκ ἦν ἐκεῖνος τὸ φῶς. 7⁴⁵ the
officers (who were away from the scene of action) came to the
priests καὶ εἶπον αὐτοῖς ἐκεῖνοι. 13²⁴ᶠ νεύει τούτῳ (*John*) . . .
περὶ οὗ λέγει (*Jesus* subject) . . . ἐκεῖνος (*John*, the remoter
person, now Jesus has been introduced). Contemptuously like
οὗτος: Jn 7¹¹ 9²⁸ 19²¹ *this fellow*. More often anaphorically, in
the apodosis like οὗτος: Mk 7²⁰ τὸ . . . πορευόμενον, ἐκεῖνο
κοινοῖ τὸν ἄνθρωπον, Jn 1³³ ὁ πέμψας . . . ἐκεῖνος, 5¹¹, 9³⁷ ὁ λαλῶν
μετὰ σου ἐκεῖνός ἐστιν, 10¹ ὁ μὴ εἰσερχόμενος . . . ἐκεῖνος . . . ,
14²¹ ὁ ἔχων . . . ἐκεῖνος . . . , Ro 14¹⁴ τῷ λογιζομένῳ . . . ἐκείνῳ
κοινόν, 2 Co 10¹⁸ οὐ γὰρ ὁ ἑαυτὸν συνιστάνων, ἐκεῖνος . . . , Xen.
Cyr. 6, 2, 33 ὁ . . . ἀκούων, ἐκεῖνος . . . , Herm. M. VII 5. It is
dependent on the personal whim of the writer whether οὗτος or
ἐκεῖνος is used in this anaphoric way, Matthew preferring οὗτος,
John liking both. 'Εκεῖνος is even, like οὗτος, used in the
protasis with resumptive ὅτι, relative pronoun, etc.: Mt 24⁴³
ἐκεῖνο δὲ γινώσκετε ὅτι, Jn 13²⁶ ἐκεῖνός ἐστιν ᾧ ἐγὼ βάψω
(Judas was not even absent, and by any rule we would expect
οὗτος, as in Mt's parallel), Ro 14¹⁵ ἐκεῖνον . . . ὑπὲρ οὗ, Heb 11¹⁵
ἐκείνης ἀφ' ἧς. Thus, like οὗτος, its meaning is often weakened
(especially in Jn) to *he* or *they*: Mk 16¹⁰. ¹³. ²⁰ Jn 10⁶ *they* (S* om),
5³⁷ 8⁴⁴ 9⁹. ¹¹. ²⁵. ³⁶ 11²⁹ 12⁴⁸ 14²¹. ²⁶ 16¹⁴ etc. So it is inadvis-
able to build any theories of authorship on the notorious ἐκεῖνος
(= *he*, the eye-witness) in Jn 19³⁵.

4. Τοιοῦτος and τοσοῦτος are several times used substantivally in the pre-Christian papyri, especially with the article
(Mayser II 1, 76), as also in the NT: τοιοῦτος Lk 9⁹ anarthr.;
Mt 19¹⁴ Ac 19²⁵ Ro 1³² 1 Co 7²⁸ 2 Co 10¹¹ etc. articular. Τοσοῦτος
Ac 5⁸ Ga 3⁴ Heb 1⁴ etc. anarthr.; none articular. Articular
τοιοῦτος may be weakened into a more indefinite term for οὗτος:
1 Co 5⁵ 2 Co 2⁶. ⁷ 12². ³. ⁵. In correlative clauses we have Ac 26²⁹
τοιούτους . . . ὁποῖος *qualiscunque*; Heb 1⁴ τοσούτῳ . . . ὅσῳ.

Other less class. (more popular and Semitic) uses of correlatives
include: Mk 9³ οἷος . . . οὕτως; 13¹⁹ οἵα . . . τοιαύτη; Rev 12⁶. ¹⁴ ὅπου
. . . ἐκεῖ; 16¹⁸ οἷος . . . τηλικοῦτος; 17⁹ ὅπου . . . ἐπ' αὐτῶν. We can

best explain Ro 9⁶ (οὐχ οἷον δὲ ὅτι ἐκπέπτωκεν) as a mixture of οὐχ οἷον (Hell. for οὐ δήπου Phryn. 372) and οὐχ ὅτι (see p. 298).

(e) *Relative pronouns.* Already in the Koine the distinction between the relative pronoun of individual and definite reference (ὅς and ὅσος) and that of general and indeterminate reference (ὅστις and ὁπόσος) has become almost completely blurred. Indeed in general relative clauses ὅς is the rule, and although ὅστις is still used occasionally in its proper sense of *whoever*, it is nearly always misused, by Attic standards, of a definite and particular person (Mayser II 1, 76. Pernot *Études* 150–180). Moreover the use of ὅστις for ὅς is very old in Ionic Greek (e.g. Hdt II 99).

The same development proceeds in the NT. Complete indifference to the distinction is shown by Matthew who writes ἀνθρώπῳ βασιλεῖ ὅς in one place (18²³) and ἀνθρώπῳ βασιλεῖ ὅστις in another (22²) after exactly the same phrase; and by Luke who writes πόλιν Δαυὶδ ἥτις καλεῖται Βηθλέεμ (2⁴) where to translate *utpote quae* (class.) is obviously wrong. Ὅστις is almost limited to the nominative in all writers, though least of all in John who uses ὅς (sing. and pl.) nom. 16, acc. 50, gen. 6; dat. 2 times. Ὅσος is restricted, except in Hebrews, to nom. and acc. In LXX ὅστις is confined to nom. and accus. In Luke the indef. forms are restricted to ἥτις οἵτινες αἵτινες; this may have been a general rule (perhaps to avoid confusion with the article) since we note the following interchange in Heb 9² ἐν ᾗ . . . ἥτις,⁹ ἥτις . . . καθ'ἥν, 13⁷ οἵτινες . . . ὧν, Eph 5⁵ ὅς (ὅ vl) becoming in Col 3⁵ ἥτις, Ro 4¹⁶ ὅς ἐστιν πατήρ becoming in Ga 4²⁶ᶠ ἥτις ἐστὶν μήτηρ. Heb 11³³ οἵ is the sole exception in that book. Cadbury¹ explains the few exceptions to this rule in Lucan writings as due in part to doubtful readings, in part to Luke having drawn some of his material from Mark (e.g. Lk 8¹³ = Mk 4¹⁶), and in part to euphonic considerations for avoiding a clash with a previous τινες (e.g. Lk 8² γυναῖκές τινες αἵ ἦσαν . . .). The rule is effective for Paul too, except that he has ἅτινα for ἅ: Ro 16³ᶠᶠ is particularly revealing, viz. οἵτινες . . . οἷς . . . ὅς . . . ἥτις . . . οἵτινες . . . (οἵ in ⁷, but notice the vl ὅς p⁴⁶ and τοῖς DG) . . . ἥτις. It is effective for John, except that he has ὅ τι and ἅτινα; and except for ὅστις 8⁵³ (D ὅ τι),

---

¹ *JBL* 42 (1923) 150–157.

where however it might be excused by class. standards (Zerwick
§ 165). As to Matthew, in general relative clauses he observes
the rule in respect of ὅς in 10¹⁴ 23¹⁶· ¹⁸, but not in respect of ὅστις
in 5³⁹· ⁴¹ 7¹⁵· ²⁴ 10³³ etc. ¹, nor πᾶς ὅστις 7²⁴ 10³² 19²⁹. He
breaks the rule with πᾶν ῥῆμα ἀργὸν ὅ 12³⁶, πᾶσα φυτεία ἥν 15¹³.
The Ptolemaic pap. follow the same rule, irrespective of general
or individual reference. The conclusion is that we must not in
exegesis read into ὅστις any shade of meaning like *quippe qui*
(*because*); e.g. Ac 17¹¹ they were not more noble *because* they
received the message, but simply *who* received the message,
whatever the context or theology may demand. Care must be
taken also not to read in too much of consecutive (Mt 2⁶) or
concessive (Lk 1²⁰) meaning.

῞Οσπερ, which still flourishes a little in pre-Christian papyri (Mayser
II 1, 77) has been abandoned in NT, except for Mk 15⁶ CΘEFG, and
Jn 10¹⁶ ἅπερ p⁴⁵.

῞Ο ἐστιν = *i.e.* Mt 1²³ 27³³ Mk 3¹⁷ 5⁴¹ 7¹¹· ³⁴ 12⁴² 15¹⁶· ⁴² Col 1²⁴
Heb 7² Rev 20²· ¹² 21¹⁷; P. Petr II 13 (17) 4 (258 B.C.), W. Chr. 167, 21
(131 B.C.), P. Goodsp. 6, 5 (129 B.C.), P. Lond. III no. 879 (p. 9) 21
(123 B.C.).

(*f*) *Interrogative pronouns* ². (The adjectival use is also,
for convenience, discussed here.)

1. The direct interrog. pronouns τίς ποῖος πόσος ποταπός
now find themselves used in indirect questions, since the indirect
pronouns are going out of use. The confusion was not unknown
in class. Greek, but the interchange is much more freely employed
in the Koine.

Indirect use: P. Hib. 29, 41 (265 B.C.) γράφων τι ὀφείλεται, P. Eleph.
13, 7 (223 B.C.) γράφειν τί . . ., PSI IV 425, 28 (iii/B.C.) εἰδήσωμεν τίνες
οὐκ εἰλήφασιν, P. Par. 34, 9 (157 B.C.) ἠρώτησάν με ἐν ποίῳ καταλύματι
. . . (= ἐν τίνι), P. Par. 60, 4 (154 B.C.) ἀπόστιλόν μοι πόσον ἔχει καὶ
ὑπὸ ποίου χρόνου (= τίνος). For ποῖος = τίς cp. also Dit. Syll³ 344,
59 (303 B.C.) ἐκ ποίας πόλεως, Ac 23³⁴ ἐπερωτήσας ἐκ ποίας ἐπαρχείας
(= τίνος), 1 Pt 1¹¹ ἐραυνῶντες εἰς τίνα ἢ ποῖον καιρόν (tautologous
for emphasis), Lk 7³⁹ ἐγίνωσκεν ἂν τίς καὶ ποταπὴ ἡ γυνή . . ., 2 Pt 3¹¹
ποταποὺς δεῖ . . ., P. Oxy. XIV 1678, 16 (iii/A.D.) γράψον μοι ποταπὸν
θέλεις.

---

¹ In 7¹⁵ in fact the class. meaning *utpote qui* is quite appropriate
(οἵτινες ἔρχονται . . . ἐν ἐνδύμασι προβάτων).
² K-G II 515ff, Schwyzer II 212ff. Wackernagel II 110–125.
Mayser II 1, 78–80. Winer-Schm. § 25. W. Petersen, " Greek pronominal adjectives of the type ποῖος," *Trans. and Proc. Amer. Philol.
Assoc.* XLVI. 59.

2. Confusion of relative and interrogative pronouns is usual in Hellenistic Greek, although sometimes Luke appears to be correcting Matthew.

(α) In the same sentence both types of pronoun may occur: P. Par. 62, 2, 6 (ii/B.C.) ὅσα ... ἐστιν καὶ τίνες ... καὶ ὅσας, 1 Ti 1⁷ μήτε ἃ ... μήτε περὶ τίνων, 2 Cl 1² πόθεν ... ὑπὸ τίνος ... εἰς ὃν τόπον ... ὅσα.

(β) The relative pronoun was used in indirect questions and after verbs of knowing, sometimes even in class. Greek (K–G II 438f), and frequently in the Koine: P. Goodsp. 3 (iii/B.C.) ὅπως εἰδῆις ὃν τρόπον οἱ θεοί σε οἴδασιν, P. Petr. II 11 (1) (iii/B.C.) ἵνα εἰδῶμεν ἐν οἷς εἶ, etc. ..., Mt 6⁸ οἶδεν ... ὧν χρείαν ἔχετε (see Bauer s.v. οἶδα 1 f.g.). But ὅστις ἥτις ὅ, τι hardly ever occur in this way in the Koine or NT as they did in class. Greek: Jn 5²⁷ κρίσιν ποιεῖν ὅ, τι υἱὸς ἀνθρώπου ἐστιν to judge what a man is (? or read as ὅτι), Ac 9⁶ ὅ τι SBAC (but vl. τί), Herm. S. VIII 1, 4 δηλωθήσεται σοι ὅ, τι ἐστίν (A τό τί). We do however find ὁποῖος: 1 Co 3¹³ Ga 2⁶ 1Th 1⁹ Jas 1²⁴. Οἷος may occur: Lk 9⁵⁵ οἴου πνεύματος (but ποίου D 700 al; p⁴⁵ W al om the whole). ῞Οπως Lk 24²⁰.

(γ) Τίς = ὅστις or ὅς as a relative (perhaps as old as Sophocles) is Hellenistic: Athen. X 438 fin τίνι ἡ τύχη δίδωσι, λαβέτω (saying of Ptolemy Euergetes); Ptol. pap.: five exx. in Mayser II 1, 80, a papyrus (Cnidus ii–i/B.C.) ὅτι τί θέλ(ε)ις πράξω that I will do what you want, BU III 822, 4 (iii/A.D.) εὗρον γεωργὸν τίς αὐτὰ ἐλκύσῃ, LXX Le 21¹⁷, Mt 10¹⁹ δοθήσεται τί λαλήσητε (= διδάξει ὑμᾶς ἃ δεῖ εἰπεῖν in Lk 12¹²), 15³² οὐκ ἔχουσιν τί φάγωσιν, 26⁶², Mk 2²⁵ οὐδέποτε ἀνέγνωτε τί ἐποίησεν Δαυίδ (= Lk 6³ ὅ), 14³⁶ οὐ τί ἐγὼ θέλω, ἀλλὰ τί σύ (D corrects to οὐχ ὅ ... ἀλλ᾿ ὅ ...), 60 οὐδὲν ἀποκρίνῃ τί (= ὅ) οὗτοί σου καταμαρτυροῦσιν (but this involves understanding πρός before οὐδέν; we must therefore divide into two sentences οὐδὲν ἀποκρίνῃ; τί οὗτοι ...;), Lk 17⁸ ἑτοίμασον τί δειπνήσω, Ac 13²⁵ τίνα με ὑπονοεῖτε εἶναι, οὐκ εἰμι ἐγώ p⁴⁵? CD (τί ἐμέ SAB), Jas 3¹³ (but probably interrog.), Ign. Rom. 5³ τί μοι συμφέρει, ἐγὼ γινώσκω, BU III 948, 13 (iv–v/A.D.) οὐδὲν ἔχω τί ποιήσω σοι.

(δ) The confusion goes to extreme lengths in NT when we find ὅστις introducing direct questions, unless we are to understand ὅ, τι why as an abbreviation of τί (ἐστιν) ὅτι: Mt 16⁷ ὅτι ἄρτους οὐκ ἐλάβομεν, Mk 2¹⁶ ὅτι μετὰ τῶν τελωνῶν ... ἐσθίει; BL 33 (AC correct to τί ὅτι, and SDW harmonize with Mt and Lk διατί), 9¹¹ ἐπηρώτων αὐτὸν λέγοντες· ὅτι λέγουσιν οἱ γραμματεῖς ... (W harm. with Mt τί οὖν); this could be ὅτι after λέγοντες, but the parallel Mt 17¹⁰ has the question τί οὖν; and the Lat. vns. have quare and quia; 9²⁸ ἐπηρώτων αὐτόν· ὅτι ἡμεῖς οὐκ ἠδυνήθημεν (ADHII διατί, harm. with Mt); Jn 8²⁵ τὴν ἀρχὴν ὅτι καὶ λαλῶ ὑμῖν (Bodmer p⁶⁶ ειπον υμιν την αρχην is simply an insertion to make things easier) why do I speak to you at all? (class. τὴν ἀρχήν = ὅλως Hdt 4, 25; Dem. 23, 93; Lucian Eunuch. 6; P. Oxy. 472, 17 (A.D. 130); Philo spec. leg. 3, 121; Jos. Ant. 1, 100 etc.; Philostr. 1, 356, 17; Hom. Clem. 6¹¹ τί καὶ τὴν ἀρχὴν ... διαλέγομαι, 19⁶ ἐπεὶ τί καὶ τὴν ἀρχὴν ζητεῖ;); LXX Ge 18¹³ A ὅτι (τί ὅτι DM), 2 Km 7⁷ B ὅτι (Luc. τί ὅτι), 12⁹, 4Km 8¹⁴ AB ὅτι *why* (rest τί), 1 Ch 17⁶ ὅτι *why*, Barn. 8⁵ ὅτι δέ (presumably same meaning as διατί δέ in ⁴· ⁶), 10¹ ὅτι δὲ Μωϋσῆς εἶπεν Gr. Enoch 3¹ δι' ὅτι *why*?

It may not be too bold to go a step further and claim interrogative status ¹ for ὅ in the notorious ἑταῖρε ἐφ' ὃ πάρει Mt 26⁵⁰ *what have you come for*? (vulg. *ad quid*). Certainly the gen. of ὅστις occurs in this way in eccles. Greek e.g. ἀνθ' ὅτου dir. question (Jannaris § 2038), and so also of ὅς, e.g. ὧν ἕνεκα Euseb. Praep. Ev. VI 7 p. 257d (Usener, *Der hl. Tychon*, 50); possibly Arr. Epict. IV 1, 120 ἦν δοκεῖς; the abbott Arsenius asks himself 'Αρσένιε, δι' ὃ ἐξῆλθες; (Migne PG 65, 105c. Zerwick § 169).

(g) Interrogative pronouns used as exclamations. Whereas class. Greek employs the relatives οἷος, ὅσος, ἡλικός, etc. in this way (K-G II 100f), as the NT also employs οἷος in 1 Th 1⁵ 2 Ti 3¹¹ and ἡλίκος in Col 2¹ (possibly ὅσα in Ac 9¹⁶ 14²⁷) ², yet in the NT the interrogatives are used as exclamations just as they are used in indirect questions (see p. 49):

Mt 27¹³ (B*ὅσα), Mk 15⁴ ἴδε πόσα . . . Ac 21²⁰, Ga 6¹¹ ἴδετε πηλίκοις (p⁴⁶ B corr. to ἡλίκοις), 2 Co 7¹¹ (direct), Heb 7⁴; Acta Phil 62⁹ σὺ ἀγαπητὲ τοῦ θεοῦ 'Ιωάννη, πόσα αὐτοῖς διελέξω καὶ οὐχ ὑπηκούσθης, 59¹²·¹⁷; Acta Thom. 235⁸; Acta Joh. 170¹²ᶠ; Mart. Petri et Pauli 158¹⁷ᶠ πόσων καλὸν πραγμάτων τε καὶ σημείων ὑπ' ἐμοῦ σοι δεικνυμένων θαυμάζω πῶς ἀμφισβητεῖς. The usage is not generally recognized as pre-Hellenistic, in spite of the contention of O. Lagercrantz, *Eranos* 18, 1918, 26–113.

On the whole then two points are notable in the NT and contemporary use of pronouns: 1. a great increase, to the extent of redundancy, and 2. " subtiliorum distinctionum abolitio " (Zerwick §§ 146, 161–169, who rightly insists that, for correct interpretation of the NT text, canons of classical and literary taste must be laid aside).

---

¹ Other interpretations, making ὅ a relative: (1) the ὅ refers to the kiss; paraphrase. " Friendly? You give me a kiss, for *which* I presume you have come here? " (2) Wellhausen has to supply too much, i.e. " By this kiss you are accomplishing the purpose for which you are here." (3) More simply, supply a verb, e.g. " *Do* that for which you are here." (E. C. E. Owen in *JThS* 29, 1928, 384–386; and Klostermann, *Zschr. f. nt. Wiss.* 29, 1930, 311, who adduces ἐγὼ δὲ ἐφ' ὃ πάρειμι, sc. ποιήσω). (4) Supply a ref. to the kiss: " *Is this* the reason why you are here? " (Radermacher² 78). (5) Emend to ἑταῖρε, αἶρε " *Take* what you have come for " (Blass).

² In Lk 5³D, Heb 10³⁷, Philitas 7D, ὅσον ὅσον = ὀλίγον ὀλίγον (Hesychius) *very little* or *how little!*

CHAPTER SIX

THE VERB: VOICE [1]

§ 1. Absolute Verbs (Mayser II 1, 80ff)

Many transitive verbs are used in an absolute sense, apparently as intransitive, the object understood from the context:

Mk 10¹⁹ μὴ ἀποστερήσῃς, P. Par. 26, 35 (163 B.C.) ἀποστεροῦσιν = *they deprive* a person, 1 Co 6⁸ ἀδικεῖτε καὶ ἀποστερεῖτε (MM Vocab. s.v.); Col 2¹⁵ ἐδειγμάτισεν (unless we take the previous object), cp. PSI IV 442, 18 (iii/B.C.) *arranged an inspection*, Mk 13¹⁷ ἐν γαστρὶ ἔχειν, P. Magd. 4, 6 (222 B.C.) ὄν λευκὴν ἐν γαστρὶ ἔχουσαν *be pregnant*; Mt 23¹⁶·¹⁸ ὀφείλει: Semitic חָיָב is not needed to explain this absol. use, as we have Rev L. 5, 1 (259 B.C.).

§ 2. Transitive and Intransitive Verbs (Mayser II 1, 82–87)

Transitive verbs have a noun-object either in the accus. or in an oblique case; in intransitive verbs the verbal idea is entirely realized in the subject itself.

(*a*) Hellenistic Greek extensively gives to trans. verbs an intrans. sense and substitutes a reflexive idea for the object. The most frequent instance of this in the Koine is ἄγω and βάλλ᾽ with their compounds, compounds of στρέφω, and less often ἀνακάμπτω, κλίνω, λύω- and ἔχω- compounds.

ἄγω: Mt 26⁴⁶ etc. ἄγωμεν *let us go*, class. phrase ἄγε *come!*; παράγω *pass by* Mt 9²⁷ 20³⁰ Mk 15²¹ etc., Polyb. V 18, 4, P. Tebt. I 17, 4 (114 B.C.); *disappear* 1 Co 7³¹; περιάγω *go about, traverse* (not cl.) Mt 4²³ Ac 13¹¹; ἐπανάγω *return* Mt 21¹⁸ Xen. etc., P. Vat. A 15 (168 B.C.); in P. Par. 12, 20 (157 B.C.) = *return home*, but Lk 5³·⁴ *put out to sea* sc. boat; προάγω *go forward* 2 Jn⁹ vl, P. Lond. I no. 21 (p. 13) 15 (162 B.C.); *to go before* (τινα) Mt 2⁹ and *passim*, 1 Ti 1¹⁸ Heb 7¹⁸, P. Tor. I 8, 21 (116 B.C.); ptc. = *previous*; προσάγω *draw near* Ac 27²⁷ Xen. Hellenistic; σύναγε ἔτι ἄνω *move up* (but *assemble* in Or. gr. 130, 5 (146–116 B.C.) Mt 20²⁸ D; ὑπάγω Jn 3⁸ (and esp. often in Jn) = simplex as in MGr, especially in imperative, and only in pres. tense, P. Par. 15 (p. 225) 4 (121 B.C.) bis.

---

[1] K-G I 89–259. Gild. I 61–190. Schwyzer II 216ff. J. M. Stahl, *Kritisch-historische Syntax des griechischen Verbums der klassischen Zeit*, Heidelberg 1907. Jannaris 356–364. Wackernagel I 105–294. Mayser II 1, 80–130.

αἴρω: Ac 27¹³ *set sail*; μεταίρω *depart* Mt 13⁵³ 19¹, Aqu. Ge 12⁹.

βάλλω: Ac 27¹⁴ ἔβαλεν . . . ἄνεμος *rushed*; Mayser gives no parallels but there are Aesch., Eurip., Aeschin., and Enoch 18⁶, and ῥίπτω in the same sense (Radermacher², 23); Mk 4³⁷ class. ἐπιβάλλω *rush upon*; Lk 15¹², P. Lille 3, 64/5 (241 B.C.) τὸ ἐπιβάλλον μέρος; P. Grenf. I 33, 33 (103 B.C.) ἡ ἐπιβάλλουσα μερίς a fixed formula *belonging to* (Mayser II 1, 84); Mk 14⁷² ἐπιβαλὼν ἔκλαιεν is controversial: *begin* is possible in later Greek (Migne PG 93, 1708) supported by DΘ 565 ἤρξατο κλαίειν, gloss of Theophylact and Euthymius ἀρξάμενος; Diog. Laert. VI 27 ἐπέβαλε *begin*; P. Tebt. I 50, 12 (112 B.C.) ἐπιβαλὼν συνέχωσεν, exx. in Mayser II 1, 84 meaning *set to work and*; but *consider* is also possible (Marc. Ant. X 30 ἐπιβάλλων τούτῳ sc. νοῦν *consider this*).

βρέχω: Mt 5⁴⁵ Jas 5¹⁷ = ὕειν (class.) as in vernacular.

ἐγείρω: Lk 8⁵⁴ ἔγειρε (= ἐγέρθητι 7¹⁴) *be roused*.

ἔχω: Ac 21¹³ 2 Co 12¹⁴ etc. *to be* in a certain condition (class.), often in pap. letters with καλῶς *be well*, like Mk 16¹⁸; ἀπέχω *be distant* Lk 15²⁰ etc. (pp. 291, 336 for impers. use); ἐνέχω Mk 6¹⁹ Lk 11⁵³ *hate, persecute*; ἐπέχω *tarry* Ac 19²², P. Rev. L. 4, 2; 17, 6 (259 B.C.); προσ- *listen to* Ac 8⁶ 16⁴ Heb 2¹ 2 Pt 1¹⁹ pap. (τὸν νοῦν no longer inserted, as in class. Attic); *stands written* 1 Pt 2⁶ περιέχει ἐν γραφῇ ¹; Jos. Ant. 11, 104 ἐν αὐτῇ περιέχει; ὑπερ- *excel* Ro 13¹ 1 Pt 2¹³ Ph 2³ 3⁸ Wis 6⁶ (Johannessohn DGKPS 69: 2 Mac 11²² ἡ δὲ τοῦ βασιλέως ἐντολὴ περιεῖχεν οὕτως).

ἀνακάμπτω: *return* Mt 2¹² Lk 10⁶ Ac 18²¹ Heb 11¹⁵; often in papyri (Mayser and MM Vocab.).

κλίνω: *decline* Lk 9¹² 24²⁹, Hell., Polyb. P. Hib. 38, 8 (252 B.C.), MGr.; ἐκκλίνω *turn aside* Ro 16¹⁷ etc., P. Tor. I 2, 17 (116 B.C.).

προκόπτω: Ro 13¹² Hell.

ἀναλύω: *go home* Lk 12³⁶ Ph 1²³, P. Par. 22, 29 (165 B.C.) etc. See Bauer s.v. and Büchsel in Kittel WB IV 338.

ἀπορίπτω: Ac 27⁴³, class. poet., Hell.

στρέφω: *turn* intr. Ac 3¹⁹ 7⁴²? 1 Pt 2²⁵ C (rest pass.), Jn 12⁴⁰ LXX WKLMX (rest pass.), Polyb.; ἐπιστρέφω *turn round*, P. Par. (Mayser II 1, 87), but the Bibl. context requires *be converted*; ἀναστρέφω *return* Ac 5²² 15¹⁶, P. Strass. II 111, 23 (iii/B.C.); ἀποστρέφω *return* Ac 3²⁶ P. Magd. 29, 9 (219 B.C.).

καταπαύω *take rest* Heb 4⁴· ¹⁰ LXX (Ge 2² Ex 31¹⁸ etc.), Com. Att. fragm. III no. 110⁸ p. 425 Kock (see Helbing DKVS 169f), but largely trans. in class.

ἐπιφαίνω: *show oneself* (of stars) Lk 1⁷⁹ Ac 27²⁰, Hell.

(*b*) Sometimes a causative sense is given to intrans. verbs, so that they may have an object. Thus in LXX βασιλεύω = *cause to reign*, ἐξαμαρτάνω = *cause to sin*, and some translators, esp. Lamentations, have gone very far in this direction ², but the

---

¹ The reading of C corrects it and makes it transitive again: ἡ γραφή.
² Thackeray OT Gr. 24; J. Ziegler, *Beiträge zur Ieremias-Septuaginta*, Gött. 1958, 53.

process is advanced also in NT: ἀνατέλλω *cause to rise* Mt 5⁴⁵
(but intr. oft.) class. poet. Ionic, LXX Ge 3¹⁸ (Helbing DKVS 78)
1 Cl 2⁴, Diog. 12¹, Ev Naas.²; ἀναφαίνω *cause to appear* (a Hell.
peculiarity) Ac 21³ SB*, Lucian dial. mar. X 1 ἀνάφηνον;
εὐαγγελίζω Ac 16¹⁷ D* Rev 10⁷ 14⁶ (but p⁴⁷S have middle, as
elsewhere in NT), Hell. (see Friedrich in Kittel WB II 708, 710);
μαθητεύω *make a disciple of* (for *be a disc.*, as Mt 27⁵⁷, Plut.)
Ac 14²¹; κατακληρονομέω Ac 13¹⁹ OT *cause to inherit*; θριαμβεύω
lead in triumph (for *celebrate a triumph*; class. intr.) 2 Co 2¹⁴, Plut.,
MGr τονὲ σπουδάζω *I make him study*, τονὲ ζῶ *I make him live*,
μὲ πέθανε *he has caused me to die* (see Psichari 185).

§ 3. The Active Voice (Mayser II 1, 89ff. Jannaris 356 ff. Abel § 52)

The intransitive active is used in a passive sense with παρά
and ὑπό c. gen., e.g. ἀποθνήσκω ὑπὸ τῆς λύπης *died in grief* P.
Par 23, 12 (165 B.C.). It was the rule in Attic Greek, and the pass.
of ἀποκτείνω was τελευτάω or ἀποθνήσκω, as in NT, although
we find the pass. form ἀπεκτάνθη in Mk 9³¹ etc. Hdt 6, 92
ἐτελεύτησαν ὑπ' 'Αθηναίων. The pass. of (εὖ, κακῶς) ποιέω was
(εὖ, κακῶς) πάσχω, as in Ga 3⁵ ἐπάθετε εἰκῇ, and we find in
Mt 17¹² an excellent example of act. and pass. together: ἐποίησαν
ἐν αὐτῇ . . . μέλλει πάσχειν ὑπ' αὐτῶν (see P. Amh. 78, 4 βίαν
πάσχων . . . ὑπὸ 'Εκύσεως). See Ac 27¹⁷· ²⁶· ²⁹ for ἐκπίπτω as
pass. of ἐκβάλλω (in Ptolemaic papyri πίπτω as pass. of ἐπι-,
προβάλλω; Mayser II 1, 90). The intr. ἕστηκα *I still stand* (= I
have been placed), pass. in meaning though act. in form, is well
established in class. Greek, as also ἔστην, intr. but active in form
(*stand*). The simply conceived expressions ἐξεληλύθει Lk 8²
(as pass. of ἐκβάλλω) and τὸν ἀναβάντα πρῶτον ἰχθύν Mt 17²⁷,
may be due to Aramaic influence (Wellhausen Einl.² 19), but
they are not foreign to Koine ways of speech either: e.g. P. Giss.
I 39, 9 (130 B.C.) ἐὰν δέ τις ὅρκος ἢ τεκμήριον . . . ὑπὲρ τοῦ δικαίου
πέσηι (sc. εἴς σε) *be imposed* (*on you*). The use of 3rd. p. pl.
act. instead of pass. will be discussed pp. 292f.

§ 4. The Middle Voice (Mayser II 1, 91–116; Abel § 53)

MGr retains merely an active and a passive-deponent voice.
The trend of the language in our period may have moved only

very slightly away from the class. norm but it was in this
direction: where class. writers preferred the middle voice to
express a somewhat loose connection between the subject and
the action of the verb, in Hell. Greek the active voice is preferred.
The forms of the middle and passive voices are tending to merge.
The fut. and aor. tenses of the middle are declining; they alone
anyway remained distinct from the passive in form even during
the class. period.   Now deponent verbs prefer passive forms, and
ἀπεκρίθη in the NT is used (about 195 times) in place of
ἀπεκρίνατο, while ἐγενήθημεν (*we were*, not *we were made*)
displaces ἐγενόμεθα.   Moreover, where there was formerly a
fut. act. with a fut. mid. form, very often it conforms now with
the active (e.g. ἀκούσω for ἀκούσομαι).

(*a*) The middle voice has sometimes been described as
reflexive, and there are many instances of this in pre-Christian
papyri (Mayser II 1, 94–105), but Hell. Greek will as soon use
the active with a reflexive or personal pronoun in order to express a reflexive idea.   Theoretically the middle involves the
whole subject in the verb's action and expresses the subject in
some special relationship to himself; e.g. 1 Co 6¹¹ ἀπελούσασθε
you were washed, i.e. got yourselves washed.   But in our period
there is not always any significance in the writer's choice of
middle or active, and the reflexive middle in the NT is relatively
rare: Mt 6¹⁷ ἄλειψαί σου τὴν κεφαλήν, 27⁵ ἀπήγξατο, Mk 14⁵⁴
θερμαινόμενος, Jn 19²⁴ OT διαμερίσαντο ... ἑαυτοῖς, 2 Pt 2²²
ὅς λουσαμένη (Radermacher² 147).   The reciprocal middle is
even rarer: perhaps Mt 26⁴, Jn 12¹⁰ *took counsel with one another*.

(*b*) There is much confusion in the use of middle and active in
NT.   Of some verbs there is the middle form only, no active,
both in Hell. and earlier Greek (e.g. αἰσθάνομαι); but of others the
middle form is often used where we expect the active in spite of
what has been noted as to the tendency of the language to allow
the middle to disappear.   There was enough deadening of
linguistic sensitivity to make this possible.   So much so that in
the papyri and NT we can find even the active and middle of the
same verb together in the same phrase; some distinction may
have been intended, but none is apparent.   E.g.:

1. αἰτέω *and* αἰτέομαι: an attempt was often made by exegetes to
distinguish these in the NT, the active being described as a simple
requesting and the middle an asking for what is due by contract.   It is

true that the middle has a commercial or contractual flavour where the
active serves for requests to God. "Commercial": Mt 27²⁰· ⁵⁸ etc.
(mid.), Mk 6²² (act., but mid. in SW), ²³ (act.), ²⁴ (mid.), ²⁵ (mid.).
Simple requests of a beggar or son: Mt 7⁹ᶠ Ac 3² 16²⁹ (act.) 1 Co 1²²
(act.). But, although in the pre-Christian papyri the middle prevails in
the official style (Mayser II 1, 109f), there is often no principle either
here or in the NT. For instance, prayer to God can be middle: Mt 18¹⁹
etc., Ac 13²¹ LXX 1 Km 8⁵. And yet "contractual" requests can be
active or, rather, even vary in the same context: Mt 20²⁰ (act.), ²² (mid.),
Mk 10³⁵ (act.), ³⁸ (mid.). No rule applies to that or the following:
Jas 4²ᶠ οὐκ ἔχετε διὰ τὸ μὴ αἰτεῖσθαι ὑμᾶς· αἰτεῖτε καὶ οὐ λαμβάνετε διότι
κακῶς αἰτεῖσθε, 1 Jn 5¹⁴ᶠ αἰτώμεθα . . . ὃ ἐὰν αἰτώμεθα, οἴδαμεν ὅτι ἔχομεν
. . . ἃ ᾐτήκαμεν. The change may have significance, but what? For the
papyri see Mayser II 1, 109 n. 3, who quotes the ancient grammarian
Ammonius to the effect that the active is used of requesting without
reference to repayment, whereas the middle is to request with a view to
using the thing requested and repaying it. But this hardly illuminates
NT usage.

2. καρποφορέω and καρποφορέομαι: can there be significance in the
contrast between the active in Col 1¹⁰ and middle καρποφορούμενον in
1⁶? The middle is rare, but there seems to be no difference (see Bauer
s.v., but also Lightfoot in loc.).

3. *Some other verbs* appear in the middle where one expects active,
since they have a transitive sense: the mid. of τίθημι in an act. sense
has some class. precedent (e.g. Demosth. 56, 4 θέσθαι ἐν φυλακῇ like
Ac 4³), 1 Co 12²⁸ οὓς μὲν ἔθετο, 1 Th 5⁹ ἔθετο ἡμᾶς; for pap. see Mayser
II 1, 111; in view of Koine parallels, σπασάμενος in Mk 14⁴⁷ can easily
be changed to act. in Mt 26⁵¹ ἀπέσπασεν; further the following appear
in the NT in the middle with apparently the same meaning as the active:
ἀμύνω *aid* (see Bauer), ἀπείλω, ἐπιδεικνύω, ἀπεκδύομαι Col 2¹⁵ (ICC in
loc.) *strip* or *spoil*, but *divesting oneself* is the more usual meaning for
mid., συνκαλέομαι Lk 9¹ 15⁶ DF ⁹ ADEGW 23¹³, Ac 10²⁴ 28¹⁷, ἐμβάπτομαι
Mk 14²⁰ (Mt alters to act.), ἐπιδείκνυμαι *display* Ac 9³⁹, ἐπιτελέομαι
pay in full 1 Pt 5⁹ P. Teb. 61 (b) 35 (118 B.C.) (ἐὰν μὴ ἐπιτελῶνται οἱ
γεωργοὶ τὰ ἐκφόρια), ζηλόομαι Ga 4¹⁸ (or passive? Moule 25f), φανερόω
Eph 5¹³ *that which illuminates*, or pass.?, φυλάσσομαι *observe* Mk 10²⁰
(parallels make it act.) LXX Ge 26⁵ Le 20⁸. Πληρόω is controversial:
it appears in the act. Eph 4¹⁰ *fill*, but is this the same as the mid. in 1²³?
AV and RV take it so, but some take it as pass., of Christ's being filled.
Other words never appear in the act. in the NT but have an act. in the
earlier Attic: προβλέπομαι Heb 11⁴⁰ *foresee*, περιβλέπομαι Mk 9⁸ etc.
(mainly Mk, except for Lk 6¹⁰) *look around*, ἁρμόζομαι 2 Co 11² (no direct
parallel, but see Moulton Pr. 160, MM Vocab. s.v.), ἐκδίδομαι Mt 21³³· ⁴¹
Mk 12¹ Lk 20⁹ (here Mt retains Mk's mid.) frequ. in pap.: P. Giss. I 1
col. 1, 8 (173 B.C.), καταλαμβάνομαι Ac 4¹³ 10³⁴ 25²⁵ Eph 3¹⁸ *apprehend*
mentally, Dion. Halic. etc., παρατηρέομαι *watch closely* Lk 6⁷ 14¹ Ac 9²⁴,
observe scrupulously Ga 4¹⁰. 'Εκλέγομαι *choose* Mk 13²⁰ Lk 10⁴² (11 times
in Lk-Ac) Jn 6⁷⁰ (4 times) Eph 1⁴ 1 Co 1²⁷· ²⁸ Jas 2⁵, P. Magd. 29, 4

(221 B.C.) ἐγλεξάμενος τὸν βέλτιστον τόπον. The following middles are active with intrans. sense, and also have an active form in NT: ἀπορέομαι *be in doubt* Lk 24⁴ Jn 13²² Ac 25²⁰ Ga 4²⁰ 2 Co 4⁸; ὑστερέομαι *be inferior* 1 Co 12²⁴; ἐνεργέομαι Ro 7⁵ (8 times Paul) Jas 5¹⁶ *operate* (in act reserved for God or divine δυνάμεις in NT); see Lightfoot Gal. 204f., Milligan Thess. 28f., Mayor Jas. 177ff; but πολύ might be object in Jas 5¹⁶, thus making the verb trans. προέχομαι Ro 3⁹ (see Field Notes 152f., ICC in loc., Vaughan in loc.).

The evidence makes it difficult to claim, as Zerwick does (§ 178), that many of the above instances display a special use of the middle voice in which the subject is indicated as acting " ex se ipso ", much less that ἔθετο in Ac 12⁴ indicates that Herod locked Peter up *very carefully*, i.e. for himself. The general lack of nice distinctions in use of the middle rules it out.

(c) On the other hand, some verbs appear in the active where we would expect the middle in class. Greek. The context supplies all that is required in the way of a reflexive idea. This is notably true of ποιέω with a verbal noun.

The middle of ποιέω is so rare in NT that its few (mainly Lucan) examples are worth studying (see Abel § 53 e) : it is followed by ἀναβολήν, λόγον, μνείαν, πορείαν, σπουδήν; Lk 5³³ δεήσεις ποιοῦνται, 13²² πορείαν ποιούμενος, Ac 1¹ λόγον ἐποιησάμην (class., not same usage in pap.), 20²⁴ οὐδενὸς λόγον ποιοῦμαι τὴν ψυχήν, 25¹⁷ ἀναβολὴν μηδεμίαν ποιησάμενος, P. Amh. 34(c) 6 (157 B.C.), Ac 27¹⁸ ἐκβολὴν ἐποιοῦντο (techn.). The middle was the rule in class. Greek, and in some instances there is a variant correcting to the middle of ποιέω where the active appears in the stronger text: Mk 3⁶ συμβούλιον (mid. W), Jn 14²³ μονήν (mid. vl.), Ac 8² κοπετόν (mid. EHP), 23¹³ HP συνωμοσίαν (mid. vl). But the active, unchallenged, appears where we expect the middle: Mk 2²³ ὁδόν, 3⁶ συμβούλιον, Lk 1⁷² 10³⁷ ἔλεος (Hebraism; LXX Ge 24¹²), 18⁷· ⁸ ἐκδίκησιν, Ac 8² κοπετόν, 23¹² συστροφήν, 25³? ἐνέδραν; Jn 5²⁷ Jude ¹⁵ κρίσιν, Rev 11⁷ etc. πόλεμον.

This is true too of (κατα-) δουλόω : Ac 7⁶ OT 1 Co 9¹⁹ 2 Co 11²⁰ Ga 2⁴ 2 Pt 2¹⁹; and of εὑρίσκω *obtain* (where Attic prose had middle) : Mt 10³⁹ 11²⁹ Lk 1³⁰ Ac 7⁴⁶ 2 Ti 1¹⁸ etc. Attic poets. See also Mt 26⁵¹ ἀπέσπασεν τὴν μάχαιραν (but correctly σπασάμενος Mk 14⁴⁷ Ac 16²⁷), 18²³⁽²⁴⁾ 25¹⁹ συναίρω λόγον (Moulton Pr. 160), 26⁶⁵ διέρρηξεν τὰ ἱμάτια, Ac 7³³ OT λῦσον (mid. LXX), 16¹⁶ παρεῖχεν ἐργασίαν (mid. C), 19²⁴ A* DE (mid. vl), 28² παρεῖχον φιλανθρωπίαν, ³ καθῆψεν (mid. C). See Deissmann NB 81ff; Moule 24–26. The middle is on its way out.

(d) Other verbs are passive in form but with middle or deponent meaning (middle-passive). These are also in the papyri: αἰσχύνομαι ᾐσχυνήθην, γίνομαι ἐγενήθην, δύναμαι ἠδυνήθην, ἀποκρίνομαι ἀπεκρίθην, ὀργίζομαι ὠργίσθην, φοβέομαι ἐφοβήθην, ἀνάγομαι ἀνήχθην, ἐνθυμέομαι ἐνεθυμήθην.

This is all part of the general Hellenistic tendency to substitute either the passive or active forms for the declining middle. The confusion of ἐβαπτίσθην and ἐβαπτισάμην has long puzzled expositors, but there is no mystery; both the middle and passive are now being used in the sense of *to allow oneself to be* . . . , and both voices become at times virtually an intransitive active : cp. ἀναστὰς ἐβαπτίσθη Ac 9¹⁸. In the variant readings therefore there is no prima facie evidence either way : Lk 11³⁸ 1 Co 10². The development is fairly advanced in NT, where ἠγέρθη for instance is passive only in form and is used of the resurrection with a very active nuance: Mk 14²⁸ 16⁶ Mt 27⁶⁴ etc. There is simply no difference between this and ἀνέστη, where the action of the Father is assumed no more and no less (Zerwick § 175). No one *placed* the Pharisee in the Temple in Lk 18¹¹ or Paul on Mar's Hill in Ac 17²²; although σταθείς is used, they *stood* there. Translate *stand* also in Mt 18¹⁶ Ac 5²⁰ Ro 14⁴ Col. 4¹².

The following also are intrans. active in idea, rather than passive or middle: ἀπογράφομαι Lk 2¹·³·⁵ *register*; κείρασθαι, ξύρασθαι 1 Co 11⁶ *cut her hair*; ὄφελον καὶ ἀποκόψονται Ga 5¹² (MM Vocab. s.v.); ἀδικέομαι *submit to fraud*, ἀποστερέομαι *submit to loss* 1 Co 6⁷; δογματίζομαι Col 2²⁰ *submit to rules*; γαμίζομαι Mt 22³⁰ 1 Co 7³⁸ etc. *get married*; συσχηματίζομαι Ro 12² *conform*; ἱλάσθητι Lk 18¹³ *be merciful*; ἁγνισθῆναι Ac 21²⁴·²⁶ *purify oneself*.

§ 5. The Passive Voice (Mayser II 1, 116–130; Abel § 54)

(a) In common with class. Attic, when NT authors transfer certain verbs with a genitive or dative object to the passive, the indirect object becomes the subject of the verb; there may also be an impersonal indirect object in the accusative, and this remains so. E.g. :

With dative: ἐγκαλέομαι *be accused* Ac 19⁴⁰ etc., P. Magd. 21, 6 (1 B.C.) τοὺς ἐγκεκλημένους, also 33, 11 (221 B.C.) etc. (Mayser II 1, 120); διακονέομαι *be served* Mt 20²⁸ Mk 10⁴⁵; μαρτυρέομαι *be well spoken of* Ac 6³ 1 Ti 5¹⁰ Heb 7⁸ etc. (Deissmann NB 93); but this construction is not followed in 3 Jn¹² Δημητρίῳ μεμαρτύρηται, Dion. Hal. de Thuc. 8); πιστεύομαι *be entrusted with* Ro 3² etc. Polyb. etc.; *find belief, be believed in* 1 Ti 3¹⁶ of Christ, 2 Th 1¹⁰ of his witness; χρηματίζομαι *be warned* Mt 2¹² etc. Lk 2²⁶ D (different construction in the rest: ἦν αὐτῷ κεχρηματισμένον); εὐαρεστέομαι *be pleased* Heb 13¹⁶, Diodor., Diog. Laert.; ἀρκέομαι Lk 3¹⁴

1 Ti 6⁸ He 13⁵ 1 Cl 2¹, Ign. Pol. 5¹, P. Par. 22, 20 (165 B.C.), 38, 11
(160 B.C.), BGU VI 1247, 13 (149 B.C.) etc.; ἐπιτρέπομαι *be permitted*
Ac 26¹ 28¹⁶ 1 Co 14³⁴, Thuc. 3, 22 (οἷς ἐτέτακτο παραβοηθεῖν), P. Magd.
27, 6 (220 B.C.), but here the verb becomes impersonal when it is passive
and the object of the act. remains still in the dative.

With genitive: καταγινώσκω *stand condemned* Ga 2¹¹ (Field Notes
188f) Diodor., M. Aurel.; κατηγορέομαι *be accused* Mt 27¹² Ac 22³⁰ 25¹⁶;
πληρόομαι Jn 18⁹.

(*b*) Many trans. deponent verbs may be used with passive
sense (see K-G I 120, 4; Stahl 73, 3) in both class. and later
Greek. In the Koine this extends to all tenses with certain
verbs, like βιάζομαι, ἐργάζομαι, λογίζομαι, but the pres. tense
is rare, as in class. and NT.

Aorist: these passives are easy to detect as the two voices differ in
form in the aorist (and future). κατειργάσθην 2 Co 12¹² *be performed*,
several pap. (Mayser II, 1, 121); ἐλογίσθην λογισθήσεται *be reckoned*
Lk 22³⁷ Ac 19²⁷ Ro 2²⁶ 4³ etc., pap.; ἰάθην ἰαθήσεται Mt 8⁸ etc.;
ἀπαρνηθήσεται Lk 12⁹; ἐχαρίσθην Ac 3¹⁴ etc.; ἐρρύσθην Lk 1⁷⁴ etc.;
ἐμνήσθην *be remembered* Ac 10³¹ Rev 16¹⁹ LXX, not class. or pap. See
A. Prévot, *L'aoriste grec en* -θην, Paris 1935, 148–153.

Perfect: ἴαται Mk 5²⁹; ἐσμὲν εὐηγγελισμένοι Heb 4²; ἐπήγγελται
Ga 3¹⁹ 1 Cl 35⁴, LXX 2 Mac 4²⁷; ἐπιλελησμένον Lk 12⁶.

Present: rare in NT, class. λόγίζομαι Ro 4⁴· ⁵· ²⁴ 9⁸; εὐαγγελίζομαι
Mt 11⁵ Lk 7²² 16¹⁶; βιάζομαι Mt 11¹² (not Lk 16¹⁶), P. Tebt. I 6, 32
(140 B.C.), Stahl 73, 3; ἰάομαι Ac 5¹⁶ D Barn 8⁶.

(*c*) The passives of verbs like ὁράω ὀπτάνω φαίνω γινώσκω
εὑρίσκω may attach the person concerned by means of the dative,
rather than ὑπό c. gen., and then they have an intransitive meaning:

ὀφθῆναι c. dat. P. Cair. Zen. 28, 3 (255 B.C.), P. Par. 63, 11, 56
(165 B.C.), Mt 17³ Mk 9⁴ Lk 1¹¹ 22⁴³ etc.; ὀπτάνομαι Ac 1³, Eurip. Bacch.
914 (ὄφθητί μοι), P. Par. 49, 33 (160 B.C.); φαίνομαι Mt 2⁷ Lk 9⁸
Ph 2¹⁵ Heb 11³·etc., frequ. in pap. (Mayser II 1, 122) *appear*; γινώσκομαι
become known Ac 9²⁴ etc., Eurip. Cycl. 567, Xen. Cyr. 7, 1, 44 (but with
ὑπό 1 Co 8³); εὑρίσκομαι¹ Ro 10²⁰ LXX (vl. ἐν), Ac 8⁴⁰ ε. εἰς "Αζωτον
2 Co 12²⁰ *come to* (Heb. infl.), LXX Est 1⁵, Herm S. IX 13, 2; = *in
regnum dei venire* (vet. lat.); Acta Thom. 175²ᶠ; also 116⁴ᶠ πῶς νῦν
εὑρέθης ὧδε; Acta Andr. et Matth. 90⁹ᶠ πῶς εὑρέθης ἐνταῦθα; *what are
you doing here*? or *how have you got in here*? (Wright II, p. 103); Gesta
Pil. 12²; see de Boor's index to Theophanes: P. Ox. I 131 (vi–vii/A.D.);
Acta Xanth. 76³²ᶠᶠ ἡ δὲ Πολυξένη ἐξελθοῦσα τῆς πόλεως καὶ μὴ ἐπισταμένη
διὰ ποίας ὁδεύσῃ ὁδοῦ, εὑρέθη εἰς ἐρήμους τόπους ὀρέω (a striking parallel
to Ac 8⁴⁰); Migne PG 65, 377c; MGr μοῦ εὑρέθη εἰς τὴν ἀνάγκην μου *he
came to me in my need*; θεάομαι Mt 6¹ 23⁵ *appear*; σταθῆναι see Blass-Debr.
§§ 97, 1; 191.

---

¹ See Sophocles Lexicon s.v. for its use in later Greek in this sense.

CHAPTER SEVEN

THE VERB: ASPECT AND TENSE [1]

IN SOME places in the NT interpretation is affected by a consideration which is important for understanding the verb. Originally in Indo-Germanic speech the tense-stems of the verb were not intended to indicate kinds of *time*, e.g. present, past or future. That came later, and incidentally can usually be assumed in Greek; but essentially the tense in Greek expresses the kind of *action*, not time, which the speaker has in view and the *state* of the subject, or, as the Germans say, the *Aspekt*. In short, the tense-stems indicate the point of view from which the action or state is regarded. The word *Aktionsart* (kind of action) has been taken over in all countries to express this essential idea. The chief kinds of action are: (1) continuous, which grammarians call *linear*, and (2) instantaneous, which they call *punctiliar*. By their very meaning some verbs can express only either one or the other *Aktionsart*, but the majority may be used in both ways. The aorist stem expresses punctiliar, and the present expresses linear action. Sometimes however the aorist will not even express momentary or punctiliar action but will be noncommittal; it regards the action as a whole without respect to its duration; time is irrelevant to it. Now the augment (ἐ-) is a different matter. It was this which in Greek indicated the time as distinct from the *Aktionsart*, and the augment was added to both present (which becomes imperfect) and aorist action-stems

---

[1] K-G I 129–200. Gild. I 79–143. Stahl 74–220. Schwyzer II 246–269. Wackernagel I 149–210. Jannaris 433–444. W. W. Goodwin, *Syntax of the Moods and Tenses of the Greek Verb*, Lond. 1897. E. W. Burton, *Syntax of the Moods and Tenses in New Testament Greek*[4], Chicago 1909. A. Svensson, *Zum Gebrauch der erzählenden Tempora im Griech*, Lund 1930, J. Holt, *Études d'Aspect*, Copenhagen 1943 (a hist. of *Aspekt*-theories). J. W. Carpenter, *The Aktionsart of the Aorist in Acts* (Diss. of S. Baptist Theol. Sem.) 1943. Gildersleeve, *AJP* 23, 1902, 241–53. E. Purdie, " The Perfective *Aktionsart* in Polybius." *IF* 9, 1898, 63–153. Moulton Einl. 176–237. O. E. Johnson, *Tense Significance as the Time of Action*, Language Diss. no. 21, 1936. J. Humbert, " Verbal Aspect: Has it evolved from Ancient to Modern Greek? " *The Link*, Oxford 1938, 1, 21–28. Zerwick §§ 180–214a. Moulton Proleg. ch. VI.

to show that the time had passed, from the speaker's standpoint. If there is no augment to the stem we may assume that the speaker refers either to some contemporary action or else that he is not concerned with the time as such at all. Besides the augment, the future tense too indicates a temporal relationship with the speaker and considerations of *Aktionsart* do not often intrude.

§ 1. Present Indicative

It normally expresses linear action and, until the augment has transferred this tense to the imperfect, the linear action is understood as taking place at the same time as the speech. The equivalent in English might be the periphrastic present: *I am walking*. There is however a complication, because Greek has no present stem with a punctiliar root. In order to say *I walk* without reference to time, English can be unambiguous; not so Greek. It must use the indicative of the present, with all the disadvantages of ambiguity arising from its linear stem; if the aor. indic. were used it would but confuse still more by bringing in the augment which indicates past time. Thus in Greek one seldom knows apart from the context whether the pres. indic. means *I walk* or *I am walking*. In other moods than indic., of course, the problem does not arise, there being no complicating augment, and so the aorist stem is freely used to indicate punctiliar action in *present* time. One must always bear that in mind for exegesis.

(*a*) The *Historic Present* is common to cultured and unliterary speech, to class. Greek, the papyri, LXX, Josephus, and MGr., especially in vivid narrative where the speaker imagines himself present [1]. In spite of the present being the tense of linear action, the hist. present is an instance where *Aktionsart* and tense-forms do not coincide; this present usually has punctiliar action. Mark and John are particularly fond of it, and their narrative is made vivid thereby. Mk has 151 exx. (72 verbs of speaking: λέγει and pl., and φησίν); Mt has 93 exx. (68 verbs of speaking); Lk only 9, and the Hellenistic 2 Maccabees only two (14¹⁶ συμμίσγει, 15⁵ φησίν). Luke markedly

---

[1] K. Eriksson, *Das Praesens Historicum in der nachclassischen griechischen Historiographie*, Diss. of Lund, 1943. Wackernagel I 162ff. Zerwick *Untersuchungen*, 49–57. Hawkins Hor. Syn.² 143f, 213ff.

tries to avoid it, as vulgar if used to excess.　Were it not for the
universal precedent in Greek we would be tempted to allege
that the influence of the Aramaic participle accounts for this
(see Moulton-Howard 456f).　As Lagrange points out (*S. Matth.*
XCII), it is Aramaic to use λέγει or pl. at the beginning without
connecting particle: " en grec on dirait ἔφη, après un mot quel-
conque."　In Daniel we have ענה ואמר, and this appears already
in Pap. Eleph. 45 1. 16, but one also finds in these papyri the
asyndetic אמר at the beginning.　Mt has this λέγει 17 times:
8⁷ 16¹⁵ 17²⁵ 18²² 19⁸. ¹⁸. ²⁰. ²¹ ΒΘ 20⁷. ²¹. ²³ 21³¹. ⁴² 22⁴³ 26²⁵. ³⁵. ⁶⁴
27²². Jn extensively uses it and varies it with the aorist quite
naturally, sometimes keeping the main events in the present and
the incidentals in the aorist (e.g. 1²⁹⁻⁴³).　In all speech, especially
the least educated, forms like λέγει and φησίν appear in
reports of conversation: Mt Mk Jn prefer the former, Lk the
latter.　Sometimes it indicates that an event took place simul-
taneously with, or immediately after, a point of time already
given: e.g. Mt 2¹³ Mk 14¹⁷, Herm. V. I 1³, but the hist. pres. is
so universal that it is impossible to theorize.　We can only say
that in post-class. Greek there is an increasing tendency to find
it with λέγει and verbs of speaking, with verbs of seeing (this is
frequent in the LXX Pent.), and with verbs of motion, especially
coming and going (also frequ. in LXX later historical books).
Thus there are 1145 pages in the eleven books of the Archaeology
of Dionysius of Halicarnassus and 1000 historic presents—almost
one each page (Eriksson op. cit. 39).　And at its most frequent
in Josephus we find: Ant. 5 (245/68 pp.), 6 (280/82 pp.), 18
(273/71 pp.), BJ 1 (379/140 pp.) (Eriksson op. cit. 76).　The
proportion in Arrian's *Anabasis* is 162/100 pp., as compared with
Xenophon's *Anabasis* 165/100 pp. (Eriksson op. cit. 83).　But
doubtless the frequence of the picturesque participle in Heb.
narrative, which tended to be translated by the present indic.,
contributed to its popularity in Biblical Greek.

It occurs about 337 times in LXX, of which 232 are in 1–4 Kms
(Horae Synopticae², 213).　Here, according to Thackeray (Schweich
Lectures p. 21), it introduces a new scene in dramatic narrative, especially
a new character or change of locality or a turning-point.　" Even the
colloquial λέγει . . . may be brought under the same head.　It is the
loquitur introducing a new speaker.　It marks the exact point where
oratia recta begins, the past tense being retained even in the verb immediately preceding; ' he answer*ed* and saith,' ἀποκριθεὶς λέγει in St. Mark,

ὑπολαβὼν λέγει in Job LXX. The main function is this, I maintain,
to introduce a date, a new scene, a new character, occasionally a new
speaker; in other words, a fresh paragraph in the narrative." In what
Thackeray called Early Reigns "the clearest instance of the date-
registering use is the present βασιλεύει, which, along with θάπτεται,
is constant in the recurrent decease-and-accession formula " in 3 Kms.
" With this mannerism of the Alexandrian translators we should contrast
the later fourth book, where the formula consistently runs ἐκοιμήθη—
ἐτάφη—ἐβασίλευσεν." Thackeray suggested that the presents in Mark
(except λέγει) were used in a similar way for new scenes and characters
(p. 22). " They generally coincide with chapter-openings in the capitu-
lary system in Codex Alexandrinus." But the very fact that Thackeray's
later translator does not observe this canon is overwhelming evidence
that if there was such a rule it was not universally observed. At most,
it may be a tendency.

Mayser divides the use of hist. pres. in the pre-Christian
pap. into three : (a) the dramatic : and a typical example is given,
showing the variation with the aorist, in the same way as in Mk
and Jn : P. Par 23, 9ff (165 B.C.) (II 1, 131), (b) in reports of
dreams, obviously for drama and vividness, and (c) in making
records, especially on letters and documents.

(b) The *Perfective Present* is rare.

It occurs in NT with ἀδικέω Ac 25¹¹ (Mt 20¹³ is the usual sense of
pres.) almost = *be worthy of death, be in the wrong,* P. Tebt. I 22, 11
(112 B.C.) γράφον ἡμῖν τίς ἀδικεῖ.—Ἥκω Lk 15²⁷ Jn 8⁴² etc. *be here,*
Or. gr. 186, 6 (58 B.C.) ἥκω καὶ πεποίηκα τὸ προσκύνημα.—Ἀπέχω Mt
6² etc. (Deissmann L. v. 0⁴· 88) = ἀπείληφα or ἔσχηκα, v. frequ. in the
Koine (Mayser II 1, 132f).—Ἀκούω Lk 9⁹ 1 Co 11¹⁸ 2 Th 3¹¹, class. Xen.
Mem. 3, 5, 26, P. Hal. 1, 167, 177 (250 B.C.), P. Amh. II 37, 8 (ii/B.C.)
etc. *have heard.*—Νικάω Ro 12²¹ Rev 2⁷ 15² etc., class. *be a conqueror.*
Πάρεισιν Ac 17⁶ *have come* (Burton 10).—Πειθόμεθα Heb. 13¹⁸ (corr. to
perf. in SᶜCᶜDᵇᶜ IK).—Κεῖται Mt 3¹⁰.—Πάρεστιν Jn 11²⁸—Ἥττωνται
2 Pt 2²⁰.

(c) The Present which indicates the continuance of an
action during the past and up to the moment of speaking is
virtually the same as Perfective, the only difference being that
the action is conceived as still in progress (Burton § 17). It is
frequent in the NT : Lk 2⁴⁸ 13⁷ (ἰδοὺ τρία ἔτη ἀφ' οὗ ἔρχεται)
15²⁹ (τοσαῦτα ἔτη δουλεύω σοι, and I still do), Jn 5⁶ 8⁵⁸ (εἰμί)
14⁹ (μεθ' ὑμῶν εἰμί) 15²⁷ (ἐστέ), Ac 15²¹ (Μ. γὰρ ἐκ γενεῶν ἀρχαίων
κατὰ πόλιν τοὺς κηρύσσοντας αὐτὸν ἔχει, and still has) 26³¹
(πράσσει, his manner of life still continues), 2 Co 12¹⁹, 2 Ti 3¹⁵
(οἶδας), 2 Pt 3⁴, 1 Jn 2⁹ 3⁸.

(d) Concerning the *Futuristic* use of the *Present*, Moulton [1] suggested that these presents differed from the future tense "mainly in the tone of assurance which is imparted"; they are confident assertions intended to arrest attention with a vivid and realistic tone or else with imminent fulfilment in mind, and they are mainly restricted to the vernacular. In English it would be *I am to* . . . or *I am about to* . . . . It is oracular sometimes in class. Greek (e.g. Hdt 8, 140) and so it is not surprising that it is used so much in the NT of the Coming One, with the verb ἔρχομαι: Mt 11³ ὁ ἐρχόμενος *the Messiah*, 17¹¹ Ἠλίας ἔρχεται, Jn 14³ ἔρχομαι (immediately foll. by a verb in the fut.), Lk 12⁵⁴ᶠ same, 1 Co 16⁵ᶠ ἐλεύσομαι . . . διέρχομαι (*I am going through* . . .) . . . διαμενῶ; but in other languages too verbs of going employ a futuristic present (Wackernagel I 161).

In a prophetic or oracular sense other verbs too: Mk 9³¹ παραδίδοται (periphr. fut. in Mt-parallel) foll. by fut. καὶ ἀποκτενοῦσιν, Mt 26² παραδίδοται, 27⁶³ ἐγείρομαι, Jn 11⁴⁸ ἐλεύσονται καὶ αἰτοῦσιν p⁴⁵ (Θ ἔρουσιν; rest fut.), 20²³ ἀφίενται WΘ eschat. fut.? (J. Jeremias in Kittel WB III 753), Lk 13³² ἐκβάλλω . . . ἀποτελῶ . . . τελειοῦμαι, 1 Co 15³² OT ἀποθνήσκομεν. In other senses: Mt 2⁴ γεννᾶται *is to be born* or *about to be born*, 24⁴³ Jn 4³⁵ ἔρχεται, Mt 26² γίνεται, P. Par. 51, 39 (159 B.C.) [ἀφ']εσίς μοι γίνεται ταχύ, Mt 20¹⁸ Jn 20¹⁷ ἀναβαίνομεν, P. Par. 47 (153 B.C.) ἀναβαίν⟨ει⟩αὔριον, O. P. 1157, 25f (iii/A.D.), largely rhetorical and poet. in class. Greek, Lk 14¹⁹ Jn 14². ¹². Ac 20²² πορεύομαι. This use appears in the papyri; it is not always easy to decide whether there is futurity, e.g. in wills καταλείπω *I leave*, as in English (Mayser II 1, 134). See also: Mt 18¹² ζητεῖ (alongside a fut.), 26¹⁸ ποιῶ τὸ πασχα *I am about to celebrate*, Lk 3⁹ ἐκκόπτεται καὶ βάλλεται, 19⁸ δίδωμι καὶ ἀποδίδωμι, Jn 10¹⁵ τίθημι, 21²³ οὐκ ἀποθνήσκει, 1 Co 15²⁶ καταργεῖται, Rev 9⁶ φεύγει. See K–G I 137, 5. Stahl 88, 4. Wackernagel I 159, 161f.

(e) A *Conative Present*, having the same nuance as the imperfect, is conceivable where there is the notion of incompleteness and attempt: Jn 10³² *do they want to stone me?* 13⁶ *are you trying to wash* . . .? Ro 2⁴ *try to lead* or *tend to lead*, Ga 5⁴ *try to be justified*, 6¹² *try to compel*, Jn 13²⁷ *what you want to do*, Ac 26²⁸ *you try to persuade me*, 2 Co 5¹¹ Ga 2¹⁴. Incohative (*begin*): Mk 11²³ 4¹⁷.

(f) Burton (12) discusses a *Gnomic Present* used in generalizations or proverbs: Mt 7¹⁷ Jn 7⁵² 2 Co 9⁷ Jas 1¹³⁻¹⁵.

---

[1] *Einleitung*, 196.

(g) The *Aktionsart* is often difficult to determine in the present because of the lack of a punctiliar stem in the indic. which does not indicate past time. As already explained, the Greek pres. indic. must serve for *I walk* as well as *I am walking*. The following however are thought to be punctiliar actions taking place at the moment of speaking (Burton 9): Mt 5²². ²⁸ etc. *I tell you*, 14⁸, 26⁶³, Mk 2⁵ Mt 9² *sins receive forgiveness herewith*, Lk 7⁸ *off he goes*, 12⁴⁴, Jn 5³⁴, 9²⁵, Ac 8²³, 9³⁴ ἰᾶταί σε *he heals you* (not *is healing you*) or ἴαται perf.?, 16¹⁸ παραγγέλλω σοι herewith *I bid you*, 26¹ ἐπιτρέπεται almost = *herewith receive permission*.

(h) Present in reported speech referring to the past. Not only after verbs of speaking, but also perception and belief, the NT prefers the pres. tense in indirect discourse reported in the past; class. Greek has it only when the point of view of the original speaker (not the narrator) is adopted.

Mt 2²² ἀκούσας ὅτι ᾽Α. βασιλεύει, 18²⁵ πάντα ὅσα ἔχει B Orig. (rest εἶχεν), 21⁴⁵ ὅτι περὶ αὐτῶν λέγει (but past in Mk-parallel 12¹²), Mk 8¹⁶ διελογίζοντο ὅτι ἄρτους οὐκ ἔχουσιν p⁴⁵ B (D corrects to εἶχαν), but rest make it orat. recta, Ac 22² ἀκούσαντες ὅτι προσφωνεῖ DEH (rest. corr. to προσεφώνει). Exceptions in NT, conforming to class. precedent: Mk 12¹² ἔγνωσαν ὅτι τὴν παραβολὴν εἶπεν (see Mt-parallel above), Jn 16¹⁹ ἔγνω ὅτι ἤθελον (vl. ἤμελλον) αὐτὸν ἐρωτᾶν.

§ 2. Imperfect

The contrast between the indicatives of the imperfect and aorist illustrates the difference between linear and punctiliar *Aktionsart* in its most acute form, for the imperfect is the tense of incomplete action, duration and continuity; the presence of the augment indicates that all this is in past time. Although imperfects are retreating before aorists in the Koine, they are still in wide use and the class. distinctions are still being observed. There is a certain interplay between the tenses; indeed we can find no difference between ἔλεγεν and εἶπεν in the NT. Although it is usual to distinguish various kinds of imperfect, and for convenience we preserve these divisions, the classification is not inelastic and the chief determining factor for translators will be the context itself.

1. Behind its use with verbs of asking, requesting, and commanding is the idea of incomplete action in the past. It is

close to the conative idea. Such verbs, in their very nature
" imperfect ", await a fulfilment in a further action by another
agent: ἀξιόω, κελεύω, παρακελεύομαι, (ἐπ-)ερωτάω, πέμπω,
ἀποστέλλω, πυνθάνομαι, etc.; and in the Koine also ἀπαιτέω,
λέγω, προσμαρτυρέω, προσφέρομαι.

Mt 2⁴ ἐπυνθάνετο; so also Lk 15²⁶ 18³⁶ Ac 4⁷ 10¹⁸ (BC aor) 21³³
23¹⁹. Mk 8⁵ ἠρώτα; so Ac 3³ 16³⁹. Mk 8²³· ²⁷· ²⁹ ἐπηρώτα. Mt 8²
προσεκύνει = request; so 9¹⁸ 15²⁵ S*BDM, as distinct from the aorist
which means worship (Mt 2¹¹ 14³³ etc.), but Mt 18²⁶ προσεκύνει could
mean prostrated, and this is its usual meaning in NT. Lk 8²⁹ παρήγγελλεν
the unclean spirit to come out (aor. is expected). Ac 15³⁸ ἠξίου requested
not to take with them, cp. P. Tor. I 4, 73 (116 B.C.): it may mean that
Paul's suggestion about Mark was only tentative at first. Ac 16²²
ἐκέλευον to beat them (breaks the rule about unfulfilled action, as
magistrates would be certain their command would be obeyed: vulg.
iusserunt). Ac 27³³ παρεκάλει to take food (but Iterative?). Where
the aorist is found the request is usually peremptory, demanding obedience (see Zerwick § 202 on the difference between Mk 5¹⁰: " rogatio
vana est, ideo imperfectum ": and 5¹² request successful and therefore
aorist. Vulg. neglects the distinction): Ac 10⁴⁸ προσέταξεν to be baptized (essential), 23¹⁸ ἠρώτησεν (-αν) me to bring this young man to
you (demand), Mt 8³⁴ παρεκάλεσαν to go away, 18² begged, 26⁵³ demanded,
Mk 9¹⁶ (merely a dir. question, but by Jesus), Lk 8³⁷ insisted, Ac 8³¹
he made Ph. come up (not invited), 16¹⁵ insisted (παρεβιάσατο shows how
insistent he was). In Jn 4⁵² ἐπύθετο is merely a question, but an urgent
one, and the answer known.

2. A *Conative* or *Desiderative* imperfect [1], of incomplete or
interrupted action, which sometimes softens the harshness of a
remark or makes it more diffident, is discernible in NT but rare
in the Koine. Mt 3¹⁴ Mk 9³⁸ (vl. aor.) Lk 9⁴⁹ p⁴⁵ SBL *wished to
hinder*, Lk 1⁵⁹ *wished to name him* Z. (Abel cites Xen.), Ac 7²⁶
tried to reconcile them, 25²² ἐβουλόμην ... ἀκοῦσαι *would like to
listen*, 26¹¹ ἠνάγκαζον *tried to make them blaspheme* (2 Mac 6¹⁸
ἠναγκάζετο *the attempt was made to force him to eat*), where to
misinterpret this tense with AV is serious, 27⁴¹ ἐλύετο *the surf
seemed to be trying to break up the prow* (or Incohative), Ro 9³
ηὐχόμην γὰρ ἀνάθεμα εἶναι *I could almost pray*, Ga 4²⁰
ἤθελον ... παρεῖναι, Phm¹³ ἐβουλόμην, Heb 11¹⁷ *tried to offer*,
Mk 15²³ *tried to give*, Ac 18⁴ *tried to persuade*.

3. An impf. with a linear *Aktionsart* is used in descriptions
in narrative to portray and set in relief the manner of the action;

---

[1] K-G I 141. Stahl 100, 3. Mayser II 1, 135f. Burton § 23.

it is common in the Koine of the Imperial period, less so in the
Ptolemaic (Gild. I 93 ; Mayser II 1, 136). It seems to represent a
past event as still taking place at the time when an event in the
aorist suddenly intervenes to cap it. In fact, the aorist ad-
vances the bare story and the imperfect supplies the picture's
details, when the two tenses are woven together in narrative.
On the other hand, sometimes the change of tense is prompted by
no other motive than avoidance of monotony, as when Mt
changes Mk's οὐχ ηὕρισκον into οὐχ εὗρον (Mt 26⁶⁰ Mk 14⁵⁵).
There is a papyrus parallel to Mk's two imperfects : P. Hamb.
no. 27, 4 (250 B.C.) ἐπεζήτουν καὶ οὐχ ηὕρισκον, but by capping
it with an aor. Mt is probably more stylistically correct : they
were seeking a long time and in spite of that there was no sudden
solution. So in Lk 7⁶ ὁ δὲ 'Ιησοῦς ἐπορεύετο *he was going when*
ἔπεμψεν *the centurion sent friends.* Correct too is Ac 21²⁰
ἐδόξαζον τὸν θεόν, εἶπόν τε, *they kept praising God and finally
said,* 5²⁷ᶠ ἦγεν αὐτοὺς . . . ἀγαγόντες δὲ αὐτοὺς ἔστησαν; the
impf. indicates action which proceeded until finally they were
presented to the Sanhedrin, 21³ (*we kept on our course to Syria*
[impf.] *and finally landed at Tyre* [aor.]), 21³⁰ they were in process
of dragging P. out of the Temple (impf.) when suddenly the gates
were shut (aor.), Mt 8²⁴ ἐκάθευδεν he kept on sleeping till
finally ἤγειραν αὐτόν, 26⁶³ ἐσιώπα Jesus kept silent till the
High Priest εἶπεν, 3⁴ John's dress (impf.), ⁵ his audience (impf.),
⁶ his baptizing (impf.) : all contributes to a vivid picture against
the background of which John utters his rebukes (⁷ aor.),
Mk 5³² περιεβλέπετο Jesus was looking around him until the
woman came ἦλθεν, 9²⁰ᶠ ἐκυλίετο he kept rolling about, and presumably they watched him awhile until Jesus spoke ἐπερώτησεν.
There are many instances of descriptive impf., however, without
a finalizing aorist to follow. These apparently are intended to
make the narrative interesting and continuous until some action
is expected in the aor. to give point to the whole description;
but more often than not the description is left without climax :
Mk 14³⁵ ἔπιπτεν καὶ προσηύχετο (vivid details of Gethsemane),
Mt 7²⁸ ἐξεπλήσσοντο, 26⁵⁸ ἠκολούθει καὶ ἐκάθητο, Lk 2⁴⁷
ἐξίσταντο, 16¹⁹ ἐνεδιδύσκετο, 15¹⁶ ἐπεθύμει . . . καὶ οὐδεὶς ἐδίδου,
17²⁷ describing Noah's times, 24¹⁴ ὡμίλουν, ²¹ ἠλπίζομεν Jn 11³⁶
ἐφίλει, 19³ ἤρχοντο, Ac 5⁴¹ ἐπορεύοντο, 15³ διήρχοντο . . .
ἐποίουν, 14¹⁹ ἔσυρον, 18¹⁹ D διελέγετο (rest aor.), 21²⁹ ἐνόμιζον.

But how to account for Mt 4¹¹ ἄγγελοι προσῆλθον (aor.)
καὶ ‘διηκόνουν (impf.), 13⁸ the seed ἔπεσεν (aor.) and yet it
ἐδίδου (impf.) καρπόν, 25⁵ the maids ἐνύσταξαν (aor.) and yet
ἐκάθευδον (impf.), 1 Co 10⁴ in the same verse and context ἔπιον
and ἔπινον, 10⁶·¹¹ in the same context ταῦτα τύποι ἡμῶν
ἐγενήθησαν (aor.) and ταῦτα τυπικῶς συνέβαινεν (impf.)? Is it
anything more subtle than a desire for variety? If the impfs. are
descriptive, so must the aorists be, in these particular contexts.
The most we can say is that the aor. records the action without
stressing its execution, e.g. *angels, who had come, ministered to
him; the seed, which had fallen, bore fruit.*

4. The *Iterative* or customary imperfect represents interrupted continuance or repetition, rather than an action that was
done once and for all. In Mk 6⁴¹ Lk 9¹⁶ Jesus gives thanks and
breaks the bread (punctiliar), but the next verb ἐδίδου reveals
that the disciples kept returning to Jesus for more food (linear
iterative).

Mk 1³¹ διηκόνει *began to wait on them*, 5¹³ ἐπνίγοντο, 7²⁶ ἠρώτα
αὐτόν, 12⁴¹ ἔβαλλον (or Descriptive?), 15⁶ ἀπέλυεν, Lk 21³⁷ ηὐλίζετο
he used to spend the night, 2⁴¹ ἐπορεύοντο κατ’ ἔτος, 8²⁹ ἐδεσμεύετο . . .
ἠλαύνετο, Jn 4³¹ ἠρώτων, Ac 2⁴⁵ ἐπίπρασκον καὶ διεμέριζον (often
but spasmodic), 4³⁴ ἔφερον . . . καὶ ἐτίθουν, 18⁸ ἐπίστευον καὶ ἐβαπτίζοντο.
But the Markan use of this impf. is full of uncertainty. Mark keeps his
aorists in proper use, but does he his imperfects? Very often he uses
the periphrastic tense for the customary imperfect, and therefore in 1⁷
ἐκήρυσσεν λέγων the reference may be to some definite occasion and
actual saying. 14⁶⁰·⁶¹, where ἐπήρωτα = ἐπηρώτησεν confirms this
view.

5. The impf. often occurs where in English we would use the
pluperfect: that is, to express past time relative to the time of
the main action after verbs of perception and belief. Greek
tenses do not so much express relative time, which emerges from
the context, as indicate *Aktionsart*. If punctiliar action is
intended, it will be aorist. Mk 6¹⁸ ἔλεγεν γὰρ ὁ Ἰωάννης *John
had been saying*, 11³² *that John had been a prophet*, Lk 8²⁹
παρήγγελλεν *he had been commanding*, Jn 6²² *had been there*, 9¹⁸
that he had been blind and made to see (the latter aor., because
punctiliar action), Mk 9⁶ Θ οὐ γὰρ ᾔδει τί ἐλάλει *what he had
said*. Papyri: Mayser II 1, 137 (f).

6. Habit rather than logical principle appears to govern the
choice of impf. or aor. with verbs of speaking. In the papyri

ἔλεγον *I said* is found in close conjunction with a series of verbs in the aorist, even εἶπα P. Par. 51, 9 and 17–21 (159 B.C.).   In the NT ἔλεγεν occurs in Mk 4 [21. 24. 26. 30] 7[9. 20] Lk 5[36] 6[5] 9[23] etc., in contexts where εἶπεν performs exactly the same function in Lk 6[39] 15[11] etc.   MGr has this variation (Thumb *ThLZ* 1903, 422f; Schwyzer II 277f).   It is too much to claim any difference in *Aktionsart*, so that εἶπεν would be for simple reference to an utterance already made while ἔλεγεν introduced the detailed content of a speech.   In Jn 11[36f] there is no perceptible difference between ἔλεγον οὖν οἱ Ἰουδαῖοι and τινὲς δὲ ἐξ αὐτῶν εἶπαν: each introduces speech in the same way, and indeed scribes have standardized the εἶπαν to ἔλεγον (AK II).   The general practice too was to use λέγων, not εἰπών, after another verb of saying. For imperfect in conditional clauses see pp. 91f.

§ 3. Aorist Indicative

See previous section for the relationship between impf. and aorist.

(*a*) The "Aoristic Perfect" and the boundary between aorist and perfect.   The choice between perfective aorist and perfect seems to have become a matter of the personal feeling of the writer, depending on whether, in a past action, its fulfilment in the present was to be more or less prominently expressed. In the Hellenistic period, as Chantraine demonstrates (see below, pp. 81f.), the perfect increasingly trespassed on the sphere of the aorist as a narrative tense (aoristic perfect), and thereby committed suicide.   By listing together the instances where both tenses occur side by side Mayser (II 1, 139ff) shows for the uneducated Koine that the perfect at first represented an action or phenomenon with great emphasis on the fact that it was past and with clear reference to its fulfilment in the present; and yet at the same time he gives plenty of evidence that decadence soon set in and that both tenses were used "promiscuously". This is true especially of papyri in the Imperial period (Moulton Prol. 143).   We have to ask whether NT usage is in line with the uncultured mass of the papyri rather than with the educated in this respect.   The "promiscuous" use increased in the first three cc. A.D., and the aorist was used increasingly for the perfect, as well as vice versa, to such an extent that eventually in iv/A.D. the perfect as a distinct tense is altogether eclipsed.   Its doom had already been written in iv or iii/B.C. when the perfect left its first estate to become an active conjugation alongside that of the present and aorist, whereas it had originally been entirely intransitive. Such a climax led directly to its ruin, since it could not compete in the popular language with the pres. and aor. which now seemed to fulfil all its functions. Spoken language tends to eliminate superfluous elements, and having ceased to express *the state arrived at* and having assumed an active force as well it made itself redundant by sharing the meaning of the aorist. Its reduplicated stems had no chance against the simpler formations of the aorist. In MGr it has disappeared and a periphrasis takes its place. Although in Byzantine texts it is no longer distinguishable from the aorist in meaning, care must still be taken to ascertain whether the mingling in the NT is not by design, with the distinctions correctly observed. What is taken for "aoristic perfect" is often a true resultative perfect denoting a past action of which the results still vividly survive.

1. Mark is very careful when Pilate marvels that Jesus *is already dead* τέθνηκεν; Pilate then enquires when *he died* ἀπέθανεν (15⁴⁴ᶠ). So is Paul: 1 Co 15³ *Christ died* ἀπέθανεν *and was buried* ἐτάφη *and has risen again* ἐγήγερται. Mt 9²² *your faith has made you whole* σέσωκεν; *from that very hour received her wholeness* ἐσώθη. Mk 5¹⁹ *what the Lord has done* πεποίηκεν *and that he showed mercy* ἐλέησεν. Ac 21²⁸ *he brought in* εἰσήγαγεν *and has defiled* κεκοίνωκεν. There are many instances of such careful distinction in the pre-Christian papyri (Mayser II 1, 139f), e.g. *he did us no wrong* οὐθὲν ἡμῖν κακὸν ἐπόησεν, *but has always taken care of us* ἀλλ᾽ ἐκ τῶν ἐναντίων ἐπιμεμέληται P. Grenf. II 36 (95 B.C.).

2. But undoubtedly there are exx. in NT where, either alone or in conjunction with another verb in the aorist, a verb in the perfect functions in a clearly aoristic sense in narrative; and often the perfect stem assumes aoristic endings in the papyri and NT—a disguise which helped it to survive a little longer:

(α) Narrative perfect with an aorist: Rev 5⁷ ἦλθεν καὶ εἴληφεν, (Dan O' 4³⁰ᵇ εἴληφα) 8⁵ εἴληφεν . . . καὶ ἐγέμισεν, 7¹⁴ εἴρηκα (Β εἶπον) . . . καὶ εἶπεν (having no visible reduplication, the forms of εἴληφα and εἴρηκα may have appeared to the uneducated like aorists), 3³ εἴληφας καὶ ἤκουσας, 11¹⁷ εἴληφας . . . καὶ ἐβασίλευσας, Mt 25²⁰ ὁ τὰ πέντε

τάλαντα λαβών, and yet [24] ὁ τὸ ἓν τάλαντον εἰληφώς, Jn 12⁴⁰ τετύφλωκεν
. . . καὶ ἐπώρωσεν AB*Θ fam¹³ (corr. to perf. by BᶜΔ fam¹) or ἐπήρωσεν
Bodm. pap. SW (LXX Isa 53⁵ ἐτραυματίσθη καὶ μεμαλάκισται, 57¹⁸
ἑώρακα καὶ ἰασάμην, 66⁸ ἤκουσεν . . . καὶ ἑόρακεν, Ex 5²² ἐκάκωσας . . .
ἀπέσταλκας, ²³ πεπόρευμαι . . . ἐκάκωσεν, 6⁴ παρῴκηκασιν . . . παρῴκησαν
(all in first part of Exodus), Col 1¹⁶ ἐν αὐτῷ ἐκτίσθη τὰ πάντα . . . καὶ
εἰς αὐτὸν ἔκτισται (any subtle distinction here is doubtful, but the
exegete could hardly be blamed for suspecting it), P. Oxy. III 482, 1–2
(ii/A.D.) ἀπεγραψάμην καὶ πέπρακα (and see Moulton Prol. 143), Mt 13⁴⁶
πέπρακεν (perhaps because there is no aor. from the same root?) . . .
καὶ ἠγόρασεν, Jn 1³ χωρὶς αὐτοῦ ἐγένετο οὐδὲ ἕν· ὃ γέγονεν, 2 Co 12¹⁷
ἀπέσταλκα . . . ἐπλεονέκτησα (DE corr. to ἔπεμψα, some cursives to
ἀπέστειλα), 11²⁵ νυχθήμερον ἐν τῷ βυθῷ πεποίηκα, after a succession
of aors., 1 Co 2⁸ ἔγνωκεν . . . ἔγνωσαν, Ac 7³⁵ κατέστησεν . . . ἀπέσταλκεν
(CHP corr. to -στειλεν), 22¹⁵ ἑώρακας καὶ ἤκουσας, Jn 3³² ὃ ἑώρακεν καὶ
ἤκουσεν, 17² ἔδωκας . . . δέδωκας, 18²⁰ᶠ λελάληκα (corr. to aor. by C³ΔΓ)
. . . ἐδίδαξα . . . ἐλάλησα. 1 Jn 4¹⁰· ¹⁴ ἀπέστειλεν . . . ἀπέσταλκεν, Justin
M. Ap. I 22 πεποιηκέναι . . . ἀνεγεῖραι, also 32 ἐκάθισε καὶ εἰσελήλυθεν
(Moulton Prol. 143).

(β) Isolated narrative perfects: the MSS show that there was a
certain indeterminateness in the use of the two tenses which dates from
an early period in textual transmission. Mk 11² κεκάθικεν A(W)XY
ΠΦD (rest corr. to aor. like Lk 19³⁰), 14⁴⁴ δεδώκει (Mt. aor.), Rev 2²⁸
εἴληφα, 8⁵ εἴληφεν, 19³ εἴρηκαν (aor. termination), 2 Co 11²¹ ἠσθενήκαμεν
p⁴⁶ SB (corr. to aor. by DGIᵛⁱᵈ), 2¹³ ἔσχηκα, 7⁵ ἔσχηκεν (p⁴⁶ BFGK
corr. to ἔσχεν), 1⁹, Ro 5² ἐσχήκαμεν (a true pf., as we still possess it?),
Mk 5¹⁵ τὸν ἐσχηκότα τὸν λεγιῶνα, 3 Mac 5²⁰ ἔσχηκα, Lives Proph. Mal. 2
καλὸν βίον ἔσχηκε *he led a good life*. Moulton's view of ἔσχηκα was that
it took the place of a constative aor. of ἔχω, which is lacking since ἔσχον
is almost exclusively the ingressive aor. = *got, received* (Prol. 145). It
is also very like the aors. ἔθηκα and ἀφῆκα. For secular use of pres.
ἔσχηκα see Schmid II 53; for Polybius see Schoy 75–77.

The pf. γέγονα is commonly in the Gospels = γίνομαι or ἐγενόμην.
For aor.: Mt 1²² 21⁴ (see Jn 19³⁶ ἐγένετο), 24²¹ BLWZ (but corr. to
ἐγένετο by SDΘ 700 e Geo¹ Eus Hipp², while the rest harm. with Mk),
26⁵⁶, Mk 5³³ 9²¹ 13¹⁹ οὔπω γέγονεν (corr. to aor. by D 299 565 184 *b* Old
Lat. vulg. Aug Arm), 14⁴ (but om γέγονεν D 64 Old Lat (*a ff i*) Syrˢ, to
harm. with Mt 26⁸), Dan 12¹ Θ οὐ γέγονεν (Ο' οὐκ ἐγενήθη), Lives Proph.
Jer. 13f, Dan 6, Nah. 2, Elisha 2 (pap. exx. in Moulton Prol. 146).

Lk 9³⁶ ἑώρακαν, Jn 13¹⁵ δέδωκα S fam¹ fam¹³ (rest aor.), 13³ 6³²
δέδωκεν vl, 13¹ ἐλήλυθα EFG (vl. aor.), Ga 3¹⁸ κεχάρισται ὁ θεός,
4²³ γεγέννηται, Heb 7⁶ δεδεκάτωκεν . . . εὐλόγηκεν, ⁹δεδεκάτωται,
8⁵ κεχρημάτισται.

LXX evidence: Ge 16⁵ δέδωκα τὴν παιδίσκην, 24³⁰ οὕτως λελάληκέν
μοι, 26²⁸ ἑωράκαμεν (cp. Lk 9³⁶ Jn 3³²), 29³⁴ A τέτοκα, 31¹ εἴληφεν,
38²³ ἀπέσταλκα, 41⁵⁵ ἐκέκραξεν, 42³⁰ λελάληκεν, and some dubious
ones. Isai 3⁹ βεβούλευνται, 13⁴ ἐντέταλται, 20³ πεπόρευται, 22³
πέφευγασιν, 48¹⁰ πέπρακα, ¹⁷ δέδειχα, 48¹⁶ SAQΓ ἀπέσταλκεν (B aor.),

49⁶ δέδωκα, 51²² εἴληφα, 54⁶ κέκληκεν, 60¹ ἀνατέταλκεν, 61¹ ἀπέσταλκεν, 66⁹ δέδωκα, ¹⁹ ἀκηκόασιν . . . ἑορακασιν. Dan O' (all corr. to aor. or impf. in Θ): 2⁸ ἑωράκατε, ³¹. ³⁴. ⁴¹. ⁴⁵ ἑώρακας.

Chantraine ¹ argues that the pf. in Mt is puristic, but cp. ἡλίκος οὐδείς πω γέγονεν Demosth. 1, 9, similarly Isocr. 15, 30.

In view of the evidence from the Koine and LXX we cannot claim that the confusion of aor. and pf. is due to Latin influence. We find it also to a small extent in Polyb. (3, 10, 1; 4, 1, 1: δεδηλώκαμεν and ἐδηλώσαμεν) and more so in Diodorus (16, 1, 6) and Strabo 2, 5 p. 133 γέγονε = ἦν) who are further from the class. model.

(b) The *Aktionsarten* of the aorist. The rules concerning this which we have already described (above, pp. 59f.) must be viewed with great caution; the rules appear to collapse with the " linear " aorists in Ac 1²¹ (συνελθόντων, εἰσῆλθεν καὶ ἐξῆλθεν) and with Lk 9³² διαγρηγορήσαντες, Mt 27⁸ ἐκλήθη . . . ἕως τῆς σήμερον (perhaps praegnans: *was called* [and kept the name] *until to-day*). Nevertheless, assuming as a working hypothesis the essential punctiliar and momentary meaning of the aorist stem, one will find various ways of using the indicative. They depend largely on the meaning of the verb itself and vary according to whether the preliminaries (Ingressive) or consequences (Perfective) of an action or state are chiefly in mind when the verb is used; or indeed whether the action is conceived on its own without reference to its progress and result (Constative). There are the following ways, and yet there is fundamentally but one kind of aorist action or aspect and that is punctiliar.

1. The *Ingressive* (Incohative) aorist ² or *Inceptive* aorist may be found with verbs expressing a state or condition; it indicates the point of entrance into such a state: βασιλεύω *became a king*, δουλεύω *became a slave*, πιστεύω *put his trust*, etc. The tense is to be distinguished from presents in -σκω, which indicate not so much the beginning of a state but are linear and indicate a gradual becoming, to become *more and more*; which is different from *began to be silent, a hush came upon it* (ἐσίγησεν Ac 15¹²), he ceased to be rich and *became poor* (ἐπτώχευσεν 2 Co 8⁹), *he sprang to life* (νεκρὸς ἦν καὶ ἔζησεν Lk 15³²; the same translation in Ro 14⁹ Rev 2⁸ 13¹⁴ 20⁴), they did not cease to be ignorant or *begin to recognise* (οὐκ ἔγνωσαν Jn 1¹⁰ 16³), *he burst into*

---

¹ *Histoire du Parfait Grec*, Paris 1907, 235f.
² K-G I 155, 5. Stahl 137, 3. Goodwin 16. Moulton Einl. 177ff. Zerwick §§ 185f. M. W. Humphreys, " The Ingressive Second Aorist ", *Transactions and Proceedings, Amer. Philol. Association*, 23, 62.

tears ἔκλαυσεν Lk 19⁴¹, ἐδάκρυσεν Jn 11³⁵), *they said no more*
(ἐσίγησαν Lk 20²⁶, ἡσύχασαν Ac 11¹⁸). Sometimes this aor.
will vitally distinguish the meanings of a word : ἁμαρτάνω *be a*
sinner, but ἥμαρτον *commit a sin,* and so the apparent conflict
between 1 Jn 2¹ and 3⁹ can be reasonably explained (Zerwick
§ 186), cp. Ro 6¹ with 6¹⁵.

Other exx. of Ingressive are probably : Mt 5¹⁶ λαμψάτω, 2¹⁶ ἐθυμώθη,
2¹¹ ἤγγισαν, 22⁷ ὠργίσθη, Mk 10²¹ ἠγάπησεν, Lk 6²² μισήσωσιν, 8²³
ἀφύπνωσεν, Jn 4⁵² κομψότερον ἔσχεν *started to mend,* Ac 7⁶⁰ ἐκοιμήθη
fell asleep, 1 Co 4⁸ ἐβασιλεύσατε *become kings,* 2 Co 7⁹ ἐλυπήθητε,
8⁹ ἐπτώχευσεν *became poor,* πλουτήσητε, Heb 6¹⁸ κρατῆσαι (cp. pres.
4¹⁴), papyri Mayser II 1, 142. Possibly also : Mk 1¹¹ ἐν σοὶ εὐδόκησα
joy comes at thought of you (but may be infl. of Heb. stative pf.), Lk 12³²
it was his happy inspiration to give you, Mt 13²⁶ ἐποίησεν.

2. *Perfective* (or effective, or resultative) aorist (Stahl 128,
2), in which the emphasis is all on the conclusion or results of an
action. Again the meaning of the verb makes this clear (e.g.
shut, persuade, hide, fall, hinder, learn, save, escape). It is the
reverse of the Conative impf. Mt 23² ἐπὶ τῆς Μ. καθέδρας
ἐκάθισαν they took their seat and still sit (another explanation
in Moulton-Howard 458) but it may be a Hebraism (perfective),
27²⁰ *they succeeded in persuading* (cp. the Conative pres. infin. in
Ac 13⁴³ where Paul and Barn. could only *urge,* not succeed in
persuading), Mt 27⁴⁶ Mk 15³⁴ (LXX Ps 21²) ἐγκατέλιπες, the
present results of the action are much in mind, Mt 28¹⁵ διεφημίσθη
. . . μεχρὶ τῆς σήμερον ἡμέρας, Ac 27⁴³ *succeeded in preventing,*
28¹⁴ *we were prevailed upon.*

3. *Constative* (summary) or *Complexive* aorist conceives the
idea as a whole without reference to the beginning, progress, or
end ; it is a total yet punctiliar aspect, for it must not be supposed
that punctiliar *Aktionsart* necessarily involves a brief space of
time. The action is represented as complete, an assumption
which must be made from the context, which indicates that no
further action of the same kind is contemplated. E.g. Jn 7⁹
ἔμεινεν, Ac 14³ ἱκανὸν χρόνον διέτριψαν, 18¹¹ ἐκάθισεν, the
limits of the action being defined by *eighteen months,* 28³⁰ ἐνέμεινεν
two whole years, 10³⁸ διῆλθεν, Ro 15² ἤρεσεν constantly, 2 Co 11²⁵
ἐραβδίσθην. Infin. Ac 11²⁶ ; imper. Mt 6³⁴.

4. The aorist in *Epistolary* style (as in Latin) is logical,
since the action so described will be past at the time the letter

is read (Schwyzer II 281).   Ac 23³⁰ etc. ἔπεμψα (ἀπέστειλα in
the papyri, Mayser II 1, 144), Eph 6²² Ph 2²⁸ Col 4⁸ Phm¹².   It is
notable, however, that one never finds ἔγραψα (Koine) but always
γράφω, and always ἀσπάζεται.   1 Co 5⁹ ἔγραψα probably refers to
an earlier letter; 1 Co 5¹¹ Ro 15¹⁵ to an earlier place in the same
letter.   In Ga 6¹¹ it might be taken either way: if epistolary,
the picture is of P. taking his pen and finishing the letter himself.
Note that he does not use the epistolary aor. in 2 Co 13¹⁰ (γράφω).
It may be epistolary in 2 Co 8¹⁷·¹⁸·²² 9³·⁵.   In 1 Jn 2¹²·¹⁴
γράφω occurs three times, then ἔγραψα three times (perhaps for
the sake of variety; the author of Jn is fond of varying his
tenses) which may refer back to some earlier writing.

   5. *Gnomic* aorist ¹ is a timeless and almost futuristic aorist,
expressing axioms which avail for all time.   The explanation
may be that, the present stem in Greek being linear, it would not
be suitable for expressing generalities; the timeless tense is
therefore used, but the augment denoting past time cannot be
jettisoned and has to go with it.   We must look rather to the
stem than the augment.   This is more likely to be the correct
assumption than that the writer had in mind a single specific
instance after the manner of fables and parables (" a certain man
went . . . ").   It is true however that in the NT the Gnomic
aorist is found almost only in conjunction with comparisons
(perfect with similar meaning: Mt 13⁴⁶ Jas 1²⁴).   Mt 13⁴⁴·⁴⁶·⁴⁸
(but these could well be ordinary aorists; see Moule p. 13), 18¹⁵
(vulg. fut.), 5²⁸, Mk 11²⁴ ἐλάβετε SBCLW (AN pres.; D fut.),
Lk 7³⁵ ἐδικαιώθη *wisdom is justified* (general statement), Jn 1⁵,
15⁶ ἐβλήθη ἔξω . . . καὶ ἐξηράνθη (the latter aor. may suggest the
immediacy of the result of excision), ⁸, Ga 5⁴, 1 Pt 1²⁴ (LXX
Isai 40⁷) ἐξηράνθη ὁ χόρτος, καὶ τὸ ἄνθος ἐξέπεσεν, Jas 1¹¹
ἀνέτειλεν γὰρ ὁ ἥλιος . . . καὶ ἐξήρανεν τὸν χόρτον . . .; these
may incidentally be Gnomic but they also would render the Heb.
perfect too literally, unless we see in the aoristic punctiliar
Aktionsart a graphic picture of the fading of the grass and flower;
Moule includes also Jas 1²⁴ κατενόησεν . . . ἐπελάθετο *no sooner
has he looked . . . than he has gone away and . . . forgotten* (p. 12)
and aptly quotes Ign. Eph. 5³ ἑαυτὸν διέκρινεν forthwith

   ¹ K-G I 161.   Schwyzer II 286.   Zerwick § 191.   H. C. Elmer, "A
Note on the Origin and Force of the Gnomic Aorist ", *Trans. and Proceedings, Amer. Philol. Association*, 25, 59–63 (1894).   Wackernagel I 181.

excommunicates himself; Herm. V. III 12, 3; 13, 2; M. III 2;
S. IX 26, 2; Epict. IV 10, 27 (aor. and pres. together: ὅταν θέλῃς,
ἐξῆλθες καὶ οὐ καπνίζῃ). See Jannaris § 1852 for MGr. The
aorists in the Magnificat may be Gnomic (Lk 1[51-53]); they possibly also help to explain the popularity of this kind of aorist in
Biblical Greek—what God did in the past is evidence of what he
will always do. Lk 16[4] ἔγνων τί ποιήσω may be Gnomic, or
merely an example of the way Greek more exactly interprets the
Aktionsart: *the idea occurred to me, what to do.*

6. *Proleptic* aorist looks like a future, taking place after
some actual or implied condition, e.g. Jn 15[6] if a man will not
abide in Christ ἐβλήθη ἔξω . . . καὶ ἐξηράνθη *he will be cut off
and withered*, 15[8] ἐδοξάσθη *he will be glorified if you bear fruit.*
The timeless aor. is a suitable tense to express this projection
of the future into the present as if some event had already
occurred. Ga 5[4] if you are going to be justified by the Law
κατηργήθητε ἀπὸ Χριστοῦ *you will be severed from Christ*; see
also 1 Co 7[28].

§ 4. Moods of Present and Aorist in relation to their Time and Aktionsarten.

(a) Present and aorist Imperative and prohibitive Subjunctive [1]

The same distinction holds in the imperative as in the
indicative; the present is durative or incomplete or iterative and
the aorist punctiliar or constative. It affects commands in
this way, that the aorist imper. is more or less restricted to
precepts concerning conduct in specific cases; and this applies
also to prohibitions, which in the aorist are subjunctive. Somewhat peremptory and categorical, they tend to be ingressive,
giving either a command to commence some action or a prohibition against commencing it. On the other hand, present
imperatives give a command to do something constantly, to

---

[1] K-G I 189C. Gild. I §§ 401–422. Stahl 148–152, 363. Schwyzer II
339–344. Mayser II 1, 145–150. Moulton Einl. 198ff, 271ff. Zerwick
§§ 181–183, 189. Georges Cuendet, *L'impératif dans le texte grec et dans
les versions gotique arménienne et vieux slave des Évangiles*, Paris 1924.
E. Kieckers, *Zum Gebrauch des Imperativus Aoristi und Praesentis*, Idg.
Forsch. XXIV, 1909, 10–16. F. W. Mozley, " Use of the Present and
Aorist Imperative ", *JThS* 4, 1903, 279ff. L. A. Post, " Dramatic Uses of
the Greek Imperative ", *AJP* 59, 1938, 31ff. W. Heidt, " Translating
New Testament Imperatives ", *Catholic Biblical Quarterly*, 13, 1951, 253ff.

continue to do it; or else a prohibition against its continuance,
an interruption of an action already begun. But they are less
pressing, less rude, less ruthless, than the aorist. Requests to the
deity are regularly aorist, for they aim to gain a hearing for
specific matters rather than to bind continually. These distinctions are broadly observed in all periods and even in MGr. On
the other hand there are passages which do not conform: in
2 Co 13¹¹· ¹² after a chain of *present* imperatives we find the aor.
ἀσπάσασθε without being aware of anything significant in the
change. The problem of the *Aktionsarten* of the tenses is by no
means solved as yet for the NT, and possibly John gives a clue
when he seems to vary the tense according to the verb he is
using. Why is the same prohibition, however, μὴ ὀμόσῃς in
Mt 5³⁶ and μὴ ὀμνύετε in Jas 5¹²?

1. *Present Imperative:*

(α) *Positive.* Mt 26³⁸ Mk 14³⁴ do not go away (aor.) but
be on guard always (γρηγορεῖτε). Lk 22⁴⁰· ⁴⁶ Heb 13¹⁸ *keep
praying* προσεύχεσθε. Pres. of περιπατέω and στοιχέω *go on
walking*: 1 Co 7¹⁷ Ga 5¹⁶· ²⁵ Eph 4¹⁷ 5²· ⁸ Ph 3¹⁶ Col 2⁶ 4⁵
1 Th 4¹². See Lk 11⁹ αἰτεῖτε, ζητεῖτε, κρούετε: *petite per-
severanter . . . quaerite indefesse . . . pulsate iterum atque iterum*
(Zerwick § 181). But ἔρχου and ἐλθέ do not seem to conform,
for the pres. = *start to come* Jn 1⁴⁷ ἔρχου καὶ ἴδε, while the aor.
ἐλθάτω = *continue to come* Mt 6¹⁰ (the Kingdom being present
already as a grain of seed). In Mt 14²⁹ however ἐλθέ conforms:
either ingressive *start to come!* or perfective *come here!* 1 Co 7³⁶
let him go on doing what he wants ποιείτω. But except for Jn 21¹⁰
ἐνέγκατε, we find always φέρε, φέρετε, whatever the context.
Mt 5²⁴ *first be reconciled* (aor.) *and then come and offer as many
gifts as you like* πρόσφερε (but 8⁴ προσένεγκε τὸ δῶρον). Another
exception is ἔγειρε, ὕπαγε, πορεύου and pl., which are used
perhaps for politeness, as less peremptory, regardless of the
Aktionsart: Ac 22¹⁰ πορεύου where the rule demands aor.
Mt 2²⁰ 25⁹ Lk 5²⁴ also. But πορεύθητι correctly Mt 8⁹ *be off!*
We usually find πιστεύω in the pres. also: Mk 1¹⁵ *persevere in
repentance* μετανοεῖτε *and belief* πιστεύετε, 5³⁶ *stop being
frightened* μὴ φοβοῦ, but *go on having faith* πίστευε (perhaps
corrected in Lk 8⁵⁰: *start to have faith* πίστευσον). In Mk the
command is to continue to have as much faith as before; in Lk,

it is to begin having faith, or to have a better faith than before
the child died.   Perhaps Luke felt the subtle difference.

(β) *Negative.*   Mt 6¹⁹ *stop laying up* μὴ θησαυρίζετε,²⁵
cease being anxious μὴ μεριμνᾶτε (but ³⁴ *never be anxious* μὴ
μεριμνήσητε).   Mk 5³⁶ 6⁵⁰ etc. Lk 1¹³· ³⁰ 2¹⁰ 5¹⁰ 8⁵⁰ etc. *stop
being frightened!* μὴ φοβοῦ and pl.   Lk 8⁵² they were weeping, and
he said *Weep not* (or *Stop weeping*) μὴ κλαίετε.   Jn 2¹⁶ μὴ ποιεῖτε
stop making, 5⁴⁵ μὴ δοκεῖτε *cease to imagine,* 19²¹ μὴ γράφε *stop
writing,* i.e. *alter what you have written,* 20¹⁷ μή μου ἅπτου *stop
touching me!* 6⁴³ μὴ γογγύζετε.   Ro 6¹² μὴ βασιλευέτω *continue
to reign,* ¹³ *do not continue yielding your members to sin* μὴ
παριστάνετε, *but start yielding yourselves to God* παραστήσατε.
2 Co 6¹⁷ μὴ ἅπτεσθε (SAQ in LXX Isai 52¹¹, B aor.).   Eph 4²⁶
μὴ ἁμαρτάνετε, 5¹⁸ μὴ μεθύσκεσθε, Col 3⁹ μὴ ψεύδεσθε.   Jas 1⁷
he must stop thinking μὴ οἰέσθω, 5¹² μὴ ὀμνύετε (aor. Mt 5³⁶).
1 Pt 4¹⁵ *let none of you ever suffer* πασχέτω; the writer prefers
pres. to aor. imper.; we might expect aor. at 1¹³· ¹⁵· ¹⁷· ²²
2²· ¹³· ¹⁷ 3¹⁰· ¹¹· ¹⁴· ¹⁵ 4⁷ 5². ⁵· ⁶· ⁸· ⁹.   See also Mt 6¹⁶ 1 Ti 4¹⁴ 5²².
PSI IV 353, 16 (254 B.C.) μὴ ἐπιλανθάνου ἡμῶν *do not forget us in
future.*   P. Tebt. I 6, 43 (140 B.C.) μηθενὶ ἐπιτρέπετε πράσσειν
τι τῶν προδεδηλωμένων *stop allowing anyone to do what we have
ordered previously.*

2. *Aorist imperative or Prohibitive subjunctive.*

(α) *Positive.*   Important for exegesis is the aor. imper. in
1 Co 7²¹ μᾶλλον χρῆσαι; the Corinthian Christians are urged to
make use once and for all of the opportunity to be free; only
with a pres. imper. ought the interpretation to be *use your
present state* to the glory of God.   Mt's χαίρετε in 5¹² is altered by
Luke to aor. because he adds *in that day.*   Mt 5⁴² δός of a definite
occasion and person, where Lk 6³⁰ δίδου to *anyone* who asks.
Mt 6²⁸ καταμάθετε is a command now, once and for all, to look at
the lilies, probably during a walk in the fields, Lk. 9²³ ἀρνησάσθω
ἑαυτὸν καὶ ἀράτω τὸν σταυρὸν αὐτοῦ (aor.) καὶ ἀκολουθείτω μοι
(pres.); the self-denying is a decision, once and for all (om. the
harmonizing vl. καθ᾽ ἡμέραν), but the *following* is a continuous
discipline.   12⁵⁸ δός ἐργασίαν.   19³⁰ λύσαντες αὐτὸν ἀγάγετε.
14²³ ἔξελθε.   Jn 2¹⁹ λύσατε.   4¹⁶· ³⁵.   Ro 13¹³ *now let us walk*
περιπατήσωμεν.   Jas 4⁹ *start to be wretched and mourn and weep*
ταλαιπωρήσατε πενθήσατε κλαύσατε, ¹⁰ *start to humble yourselves*

ταπεινώθητε, 5⁷· ⁸ *be patient* (as a precept) μακροθυμήσατε.
Mt 26⁴⁸ κρατήσατε *arrest him!* (but 2 Th 2¹⁵ κρατεῖτε *go on
preserving*; Rev 2²⁵ aor. misused).   Aorists for precepts until the
coming of Christ: Mt 5³⁹ στρέψον, 6⁶, 1 Ti 6¹²· ¹⁴· ²⁰, 2 Ti 4². ⁵
1¹⁴ 2². ³· ¹⁵.   1 Pt 1¹³· ¹⁷· ²² 2¹⁷ 5², 1 Jn 5²¹, 2 Cl 8⁶.   Prayer:
Mt 6¹⁰ δός (aor. because Mt adds *this day*) Lk 11³ δίδου *continue
to give* because *day by day* is added (SD harm. with Mt); aor. in
all petitions of Lord's Prayer (ἁγιασθήτω γενηθήτω δός ἄφες),
and in prayer in papyri (Mayser II 1, 145f).   Greetings:
ἀσπάσασθε, but also pres. in papyri, against NT usage.

(β) *Negative*.   Mt 5¹⁷ μὴ νομίσητε *never think!* 6² μὴ σαλπίσης
never sound!   Categorical prohibitions: Mt 7⁶ μὴ δῶτε, 6³⁴ μὴ
μεριμνήσητε, Jn 3⁷ μὴ θαυμάσης.   In 3rd. pers. prohibitions
occur in aor. imper. and occasionally in the form μή τις with aor.
subjunctive: 1 Co 16¹¹ 2 Co 11¹⁶ 2 Th 2³.

But there are exceptions to what seems a fairly definite
principle: Jn 3⁷ has μὴ θαυμάσης, which sounds unnatural as
cease to marvel (but perhaps like our *Never marvel!*).   In Mt 1²⁰
10²⁶ we expect *stop fearing* (pres.) instead of μὴ φοβηθῇς and
pl. = *never fear*.   We have some aorists too in prayer to the
deity: Mt 6¹³ Lk 11⁴ μὴ εἰσενέγκης, Ac 7⁶⁰ μὴ στήσης, but a
suggested reason has already been given.   In general, some
writers prefer the pres. (Paul) and others the aor. (1 Pt) imper.

3. Difference in *Aktionsart* is best seen when both tenses lie
together.

Ac 12⁸ *put your cloak on* περιβαλοῦ (punctiliar) *and keep
behind me* ἀκολούθει (linear).   Jn 5⁸ ἆρον (ingressive) . . . καὶ
περιπάτει (linear), 9⁷ ὕπαγε (exclam. and invariable) καὶ νίψαι,
2⁵⁻⁸ φέρετε alongside ποιήσατε γεμίσατε ἀντλήσατε (see above
for invariable φέρετε), 2¹⁶ ἄρατε ταῦτα ἐντεῦθεν *get these things
out of here!* μὴ ποιεῖτε *stop making* . . . .   Ro 6¹³ *do not continue*
παριστάνετε, *but once and for all* παραστήσατε.   Mt 26³⁸ Mk 14³⁴
do not go away μείνατε ὧδε (constative), but *continue to watch*
γρηγορεῖτε, Lk 10⁴ *cease carrying* μὴ βαστάζετε, *never salute*
ἀσπάσησθε, 17⁸ ἑτοίμασον τί δειπνήσω *get something ready*,
περιζωσάμενος διακόνει μοι *continue to wait*.   P. Petr. II 40(a)
12 μὴ ὀλιγοψυχήσητε *stop being faint-hearted*, ἀλλ' ἀνδρίζεσθε
continue to be brave (223 B.C.).

To Moulton the general agreement of Mt and Lk in the use
of tense in their parallel passages showed " how delicately the

distinction of tenses was observed " [1]. That is not the only possible conclusion to be drawn, and Moulton seems to many today to be a little over confident in the rules of *Aktionsart* [2]. There is a case for Luke having known Mt and having followed his use of tenses. In any case the NT use of tenses is not so strikingly standardized or logical.

Before the prohibitive aor. subjunctive we often find in the NT ὅρα ὅρατε βλέπετε, which do not, however, affect the construction: Mt 8⁴ 18¹⁰ Mk 1⁴⁴ 1 Th 5¹⁵.

The prohibitive aor. imperative is later than the NT: Horn quotes the first as iii/A.D.

(b) *Infinitive of Present and Aorist* [3]

In general the same distinction holds. When the infin. indicates a direct command, which is rare in the NT, though very frequent in the papyri (and χρή or δεῖ may perhaps be assumed), the tense is always present: [4] Lk 9³ μηδὲν αἴρετε . . . μήτε ἂν δύο χιτῶνας ἔχειν [5]; Ac 15²³ 23²⁶ Jas 1¹ (χαίρειν, the wish-infin. of epistolary style), Ro 12¹⁵ (χαίρειν, κλαίειν), Ph 3¹⁶ (στοίχειν), 2 Ti 2¹⁴ (μὴ λογομαχεῖν, which may however depend on διαμαρτυρόμενος; AC* λογομάχει); aor. Ign. Eph. 11¹.

The consecutive, final and epexegetical infin. maintains the same distinctions in the pap. and NT (Mayser II 1, 151f); *pres.*: Mk 3¹⁴ to proclaim continually, Ac 20²⁸ to shepherd continually; more often with *aor* (see below p. 136). In sentences with πρίν, πρὶν ἤ, πρὸ τοῦ the infin. again indicates *Aktionsart* rather than time; *aor.* Mt 1¹⁸ *before ever they came together*, 26³⁴ *before the cock start to crow*. Kind of action rather than of time is also differentiated by the independent articular infin. The distinction holds after verbs of which the meaning requires punctiliar action in the dependent infin.; they are θέλω, βούλομαι, αἱρέομαι, δοκεῖ, κρίνω, δύναμαι, δυνατός, κελεύω and verbs which concentrate on the fulfilment of the desired course. There are exceptions in the Koine: Jn 9²⁷ pres. with θέλω, Ac 16²² with κελεύω, in

---

[1] *Einleitung* 274.

[2] But the brilliant ch. VI of the Prolegomena is still vitally important for the student of tenses.

[3] K-G I 192ff. Stahl 180ff. Mayser II 1, 150–168. Moulton Proleg. 204.

[4] Unless, as seems likely, κηρυχθῆναι Lk 24⁴⁷ is imperatival.

[5] An alternation of imperat. and infin. which is paralleled in the papyri, but always 3rd pers.: Mayser II 1, 303f.

pap. with βούλομαι (but proportion of 2 : 1 for aor.) and θέλω, κρίνω, δεῖ.

With μέλλω the fut. infin. was most frequent in class. Greek, but is restricted to Ac in NT; in the more official language as well as in the colloquial speech of the pap. there is the aor., and occasionally the fut. in official style, but in the less educated and in the NT the pres. prevails [1]. NT has 3 fut., 5 aor., 84 pres. Aorist: Lk 20[36] D Marc., Ac 12[6] AB, Ro 8[18] Ga 3[23] Rev 3[2. 16] 12[4]. Fut. infin. also for ἐλπίζω in NT, although class. fut. is found in papyri (Mayer II 1, 216). Note the subtle nuance in 1 Co 7[9] κρεῖττον γάρ ἐστιν γαμεῖν ἢ πυροῦσθαι *to be in a married state* (not *to marry*). Note also that when Barnabas wished to take Mark (παραλαβεῖν), all Paul may have objected to was παραλαμβάνειν (Mark's being with them throughout the journey) Ac 15[37f].

(c) Participle of Present and Aorist [2]

Like the infin., the ptc. had originally no temporal function but simply indicated the kind of action [3]. The *time* of action was inferred from the context. But eventually the aorist ptc. came to denote a time which was past in relation to the main verb, and the present ptc. time which was contemporaneous (Mayser II 1, 175f). The reason for this may have been the difficulty of thinking of an act as a simple event (aor. ptc.) without also conceiving of it as taking place in the (immediate) past. The pre-position or post-position of the ptc. has little to do with this: Mk 1[31] ἤγειρεν αὐτὴν κρατήσας τῆς χειρός (relative past time in spite of post-position). Yet in spite of that development there are numerous examples of the aor. ptc. denoting coincident action [4], where the time of the action is not antecedent to that of the main verb; there is the common phrase ἀποκριθεὶς εἶπεν which is the same as ἀπεκρίθη εἰπών,

---

[1] K-G I 177n. 4.   Stahl 195.   Moulton Einl. 184, 2.   Mayser II 1, 166.
[2] K-G I 197.   Stahl 209ff.   Gild. I §§ 329ff.   Mayser II 1, 168–176. Schwyzer II 385–409.   Moulton Einl. 211ff.   C. D. Chambers, "A Use of the Aorist Participle in some Hellenistic Writers," *JThS* 24, 1923, 183ff. A. T. Robertson, " The Aorist Participle for Purpose in the Κοινή," *JThS* 25, 1924, 286ff.
[3] Zerwick § 184 goes so far as to distinguish ὁ ἀκούων (he who hears with lasting effect) from ὁ ἀκούσας (who hears ineffectively and momentarily): Lk 6[47–49].
[4] For the pre-Christian papyri, see Mayser II 1, 173f.

and also Ac 1²⁴ προσευξάμενοι εἶπαν and its reverse Mk 14³⁹ προσεύξατο . . . εἰπών. The meaning of the ptc. is not always that of the main verb : Mt 27⁴ ἥμαρτον παραδούς, Ac 10³³ καλῶς ἐποίησας παραγενόμενος, 18²⁷ προτρεψάμενοι οἱ ἀδελφοὶ ἔγραψαν, Lk 15²³ φαγόντες εὐφρανθῶμεν; Heb 2¹⁰ ἀγαγόντα is more suitably interpreted of coincident action (by bringing in). So 1 Ti 1¹² Heb 6¹³. Usually the main verb is aorist, but some-times future: Lk 9²⁵ 3 Jn⁶; sometimes pres. and impf. Mk 8²⁹; sometimes perf. Ac 13³³.

Even time which is future to the main action seems to be denoted by the aor. ptc. ¹ : Mt 10⁴ Judas who was to betray him ὁ καὶ παραδοὺς αὐτόν, Jn 11² Mary who was to anoint ² ἡ ἀλείψασα, Ac 16⁶ διῆλθον . . . κωλυθέντες (= ἐκωλύθησαν δέ?), 25¹³ κατήντη-σαν . . . ἀσπασάμενοι = καταντήσαντες . . . ἠσπάσαντο (vl ἀσπασό-μενοι to correct this anomaly) but we might by straining this make it an aor. of coincident action, the arrival and greeting being timed together! Wilcken Chr. 26 II³² (A.D. 156), LXX 1 Mac 15²⁸ ἀπέστειλε . . . ἕνα . . . κοινολογησάμενον (Lucianic; rest fut.).

Equally unexpected is the pres. ptc. expressing action relatively future in time. It is characteristic of Jn, e.g. 5⁴⁵ ἐστὶν ὁ κατηγορῶν ὑμῶν Μωϋσῆς (where the parallel κατηγορήσω just before makes it inevitable that this ptc. has future sense).

Ac 14²¹ᶠ ὑπέστρεψαν . . . ἐπιστηρίζοντες they returned . . . to strengthen, 15²⁷ ἀπεστάλκαμεν ἀπαγγέλλοντας we have sent . . . who will tell you, 18²³ ἐξῆλθεν διερχόμενος τὴν Γαλατικὴν χώραν he went from A. to go through, 21¹⁶ συνῆλθον . . . ἄγοντες went with us . . . in order to bring us. Pre-Christian papyri, Mayser II 1, 170. Post-Christian also, e.g. P. Oxy. I 120 11 (iv/A.D.) ἀπόστιλόν μοι τινα . . . παραμένοντά μοι.

It is debatable whether we may go so far as to see in the pres. ptc. an indication of time prior to the time of the main

---

¹ See Chambers, op. cit., for passages in support; also W. F. Howard ibid. 403–6; and per contra A. T. Robertson op. cit. For another explana-tion see Zerwick § 198: " fortasse potest intellegi de actione simpliciter subsequente (loco καί cum verbo coordinato : κατήντησαν καὶ ἠσπάσαντο)." There may be analogous cases in Ac, which Z. admits to be doubtful, but we are in danger, according to some grammarians, of making nonsense of grammar if we see fut. action in the aor. ptc. Nevertheless Z. draws a good example of ἐλθών of posterior action from Philostr. vit. Ap. I 22.

² Unless a previous anointing is referred to, viz. Lk 7³⁸, in which case Mary of Bethany is identified with the sinful woman from the street. The aor. ptc. is usually explained however of time past in relation not to the events described but to the time of writing.

verb [1]. Mayser gives some possibilities from the papyri and there are instances in class. Greek. The prior action which is thus indicated is usually continued action, so that the ptc. amounts to an impf.:

> Mt 2²⁰ *they who were seeking* 23¹³ *those who were entering* (trying to enter?) τοὺς εἰσερχομένους, 27⁴⁰ *you who were trying to destroy* ὁ καταλύων . . . *and rebuild* οἰκοδομῶν, Jn 9²⁵ *I was blind* τυφλὸς ὤν *but now I see*, 12¹⁷ *the crowd that was with him* ὁ ὤν, Ac 4³⁴ *they sold* πωλοῦντες, Ga 1²³ *who persecuted* ὁ διώκων, Eph 4²⁸ *who stole* ὁ κλέπτων, Rev 20¹⁰ *who deceived them* ὁ πλανῶν αὐτούς, 2 Jn ⁷ ἐξῆλθον . . . οἱ μὴ ὁμολογοῦντες. Pres. and aor. together: Lk 2⁴² ἀναβαινόντων αὐτῶν . . . καὶ τελειωσάντων.

§ 5. Perfect Indicative [2]

The following are the significant trends of the Hellenistic period, as they are exemplified in the NT probably better than in any other single text of the time.

(1) By extending its sphere to cover the functions of the aorist, the perfect tends eventually to disappear and be confused with the aorist (see above under Aoristic Perfect). There is, particularly in the less cultured papyri, a tendency to emphasize the connection of a past action with the present, and in consequence to favour the perf. tense.

(2) The confusion is well illustrated by the introduction into the perf. system of the " weak " endings of the aorist.

(3) The perf. participle middle is developed and gradually assumes the strength of an adjective.

(4) A periphrastic conjugation becomes established.

In common with the Koine generally the NT and Ptolemaic papyri significantly extend their use of the perfect to a greater extent than do the literary writers of the period. They allow it to trespass seriously on the territory of the aorist. The *Aktionsart* belonging properly to the tense is either fulfilment in the present of a process begun in the past or else the contemplation of an event having taken place in the past with an interval

---

[1] H. G. Meecham, " The Present Participle of Antecedent Action. Some N.T. Instances." *Exp. T.* 64, June 1953, 285. Mayser II 1, 170f.

[2] K-G I 146–150.   Stahl 107–119.   Gild. I §§ 226–34.   Schwyzer II 286–288. Mayser II 1, 176–207. P. Chantraine, *Histoire du Parfait Grec*, Paris 1907. Moulton Einl. 220ff. Zerwick §§ 209–212. J. E. Harry, " The Perfect Forms in later Greek from Aristotle to Justinian," *Proc., Amer. Philol. Association* XXXVII 53. H. J. Cadbury, "A Possible Perfect in Acts ix, 34," *JThS* 49, 1948, 57ff. M. S. Enslin, " Perfect Tense," *JBL* 55, 121–31.

intervening, whereas the English perfect is used when no interval
intervenes. It is therefore a combining of the *Aktionsarten* of
aorist and present. Originally it had no resultative force but
simply expressed the subject's state; this had been arrived at by
some previous activity, but the state arrived at was represented
by the perfect as so permanent that the perfect can be said from
long before the NT period to have present meaning [1]. Several
examples of this present perfect have survived in the Ptolemaic
papyri (Mayser II 1, 177f) and NT: οἶδα, ἕστηκα, πέποιθα *trust*,
κεῖμαι, μέμνημαι, τέθνηκα *be dead*, πέπεισμαι *be sure*, ἤλπικα
hope, ἤγημαι *believe* (cl.), κέκραγα, ὅλωλα, πέφηνα, εἴωθα. They
have in fact become independent presents, each one divorced
from its own present stem. Among these ἀπόλωλα was disappearing (Mt has 2, Lk 5), the popular style of Mk being innocent
of it and the " literary " Luke having most; it was giving way to
ἀπολλύω. Τέθνηκα is still *to be dead* but its distinction from
ἀπέθανον is disappearing. 'Ανέῳγα survives at Jn 15¹¹ 1 Co 16⁹
2 Co 6¹¹ but is already being displaced by ἀνέῳγμαι in cl. Attic,
and Paul falls back on ἀνεῳγμένης 2 Co 2¹². Πέποιθα Gospels:
Mt has 2, Lk 3, Mk 10²⁴ τοὺς πεποιθότας ἐπὶ (τοῖς) χρήμασιν DAΘ
fam¹ fam¹³ lat syr bo (but SBW *k* sa om), Paul. "Εστηκα Gospels:
Mt has 13, Lk 10, Jn 16, Mk ptc. only ἑστηκώς 9¹ 11⁵ (vl ἑστώτων)
13¹⁴ (vll. ἑστός and στῆκον), ἑστώς 3³¹ (vl στήκοντες), and usually
in NT, but a new pres. form is being coined from this perf. i.e. στήκω
(8 times, and in variants for ἕστηκα). Οἶδα the old pres. pf., is preserved. 'Εγρήγορα is archaic, but a new verb γρηγορέω has been
built on it. "Ηγγικα *to be here* appears as well as ἐγγίζω Mk 1¹⁵ 14⁴²
(SC aor.); conceivably it is a true pf. *to have drawn near*. "Ηκα Mk
8³ (vl εἰσίν) Atticistic correction? Εἴωθα Mk 10¹ εἰώθει = impf.

But not all these intrans. perfects became independent presents.
Some of them still survive with their resultative force in the Koine and
Bibl. Greek: ἀκήκοα, κεκάθικα, ἠκολούθηκα, κέκραγα, εἴωθα, διαμεμένηκα,
συμβέβηκα, τετελεύτηκα, μεμαρτύρηκα, κεκοπίακα, πεπίστευκα, σέσηπα,
πέπονθα, εἴληφα, τέτυχα.

Four books from LXX: Ge (παρ-) ἕστηκα 18²² 24¹³· ³⁰· ³¹· ⁴³ 45¹;
γέγονα 3²² 18¹² 44²⁸ 47⁹ : κεκόπακα 8⁷· ⁸· ¹¹; προβέβηκα 18¹¹ 24¹; γεγήρακα
18¹³ 27²; συνῴκηκα 20³; προσώχθεικα 27⁴⁶A; παρεμβέβληκα 32¹;
ἐκπεπόρνευκα 38²⁴; ἧκα 42⁷ 45¹⁶ 47³; συμβέβηκα 42²⁹ AD; ἡμάρτηκα
43⁹; ἐκλέλοιπα 47¹⁵· ¹⁸; τέθνηκα 50¹⁵.

---

[1] For ἔσχηκα, πέπονθα, and πεποίηκα in a present sense in Polyb., see
A. Schoy, *De perfecti usu Polybiano*, Bonn 1913, 75f.

Ex (παρ-) (συν-) ἕστηκα 3⁵ 7¹⁹ 17⁶. ⁹ 24¹⁰ 33⁸. ¹⁰ 9³¹ 18¹³. ¹⁴ 20²¹
24¹³; οἶδα 3⁷. ¹⁹ 5² 10²⁶ 32¹. ²². ²³ 33¹². ¹⁷ 23⁹; τέθνηκα 4¹⁹ 14³⁰ 21³⁵;
κέκραγα 5⁸; γέγονα 8¹⁵ 9¹⁸. ²⁴ 10⁶. ¹⁴ 11⁶ 32¹. ²³ 34¹⁰; ἡμάρτηκα 9²⁷
10¹⁶; πέφευγα 14⁵; καταβέβηκα 19¹⁸; τετέλευκα 21³⁴ 22¹; πέπτωκα
23⁵; κεχρόνικα 32¹.

Isa (συν-)πέπτωκα 3⁸ 9¹⁰ 21⁹ 23¹³; (ἀφ-) (παρ-) ἕστηκα 6² 5²⁹
17⁵ 59¹¹. ¹⁴; πέπτωκα 9¹⁰ 21⁹ 23¹³; πέφευγα 22³; γέγονα 23²; ἀπόλωλα
23¹⁴; πέποιθα 30¹⁵. ³² 33² 36⁷ 37¹⁰ 50¹⁰ 59⁴; κεκόπιακα 47¹³ ἤγγικα 56¹;
ἀνατέταλκα 60¹; ἧκα 60⁴; παραβέβηκα 66²⁴.

Dan O′ ἕστηκα and compounds 2³¹ 3⁹¹ 7¹⁰ 8³. ⁶ 10¹³ 11² 12¹. ⁵;
ἠγνόηκα 9¹⁵.

Thus the old intrans. perfect was giving way before the
active, transitive and resultative pf.   The resultative was already popular in the Attic orators and continued to be so in the
literary texts of the Hellenistic period, and subsequently in
Atticistic texts.   Many *new* perfects of a resultative kind appear.
The vernacular shows the same tendency, and by iii/B.C. the
verbal balance between the intrans. and resultative is reached.
The decline of the resultative perfect did eventually set in (see
above, pp. 68f.) and by i/A.D. as revealed by the NT the number of
such perfects has shrunk, except in the literary traditions; its
form is limited to only a few verbs (cp. the variety in the LXX
books just examined) and its meaning is difficult to distinguish
from the aorist.   There is an instructive exception: in the
Johannine writings, by contrast especially to the Synoptists and
Paul, the resultative pf. is frequent.   There are 77 examples;
Mk has only 8, Lk 14, and Mt 7.   The intrans. perfects are not
less frequent: there are still 100 in the Joh. writings.   We may
ascribe this to the peculiar style of the Fourth Gospel, its love of
emphasis and solemnity, its stress on the abiding significance of
everything.   Generally, however, the NT writers use only a
perfect which is already well established by tradition, the same
verbs being employed repeatedly.   Let us take Mk as an
example: 5¹⁵ ἐσχηκότα (om D 17* 27 Old Lat. vulgᵖˡ syrˢ bo),
5³⁴ 10⁵² σέσωκεν, 14⁴⁴ δεδώκει, δέδωκεν Θ (aor. in D *ackr*¹ vulg¹:
scribes did not like the " Latin " plupf. in Greek), 15¹⁰ παραδ-
εδώκεισαν (aor. DWΘ fam¹³ fam¹ 700 *a c* vulg¹), 5¹⁹ πεποίηκεν
(aor. DΚΦ fam¹ 517 565 700), 7³⁷ πεποίηκεν, 11¹⁷ πεποιήκατε
BLΔΨ 892 1342 orig (aor. rest), 15⁷ pf. or plupf., 5³³ διὸ πεποιήκει
λάθρᾳ DΘ28 565 700 *a ff* geo arm (but neither διό nor λάθρᾳ is
Marcan!).   In Mt εἴρηκα occurs twice, but the following only

once : ἔγνωκα, ἡτοίμακα, εἴληφα, πέπρακα, σέσωκα. Lk (who is
more flexible) has : δέδωκα, συνήρπακα, συνείληφα, σέσωκα once ;
ἀπέσταλκα, κέκληκα, ἑώρακα, πεποίηκα 2.   1 Co κέκρικα, εἴληφα,
μεμέρικα, ἑώρακα once, κέκληκα 2, ἔγνωκα 3.   The resultative
pf. is however often used with what seems to be aoristic force.
So the MSS show many variations with the aorist.   Although
the resultative pf. is so frequent in Jn the same verb occurs over
and over again : ἤντληκα, βέβληκα, βέβρωκα, ἐλήλακα, τεθέαμαι,
πεπλήρωκα, τετύφλωκα, πεφίληκα once ; ἀκήκοα, γέγραφα,
μεμίσηκα twice ; ἀπέσταλκα, εὕρηκα, τετήρηκα 3 ; ἔγνωκα,
πεποίηκα 4 ; εἴρηκα, μεμαρτύρηκα 5 ; λελάληκα 10 ; δέδωκα
14 ; ἑώρακα 17.

To a slightly less degree, as we have seen, there is the same limitation
in the LXX.   Thus, Ge κεκόπακα 3; δέδωκα (NT) 5; τέθεικα, πέπρακα
(NT), ἀνενήνοχα, ἐκπεπόρνευκα, ἐκλέλοιπα, σέσωκα (NT), λελάληκα
(NT) once; εἴληφα (NT) 3; πεποίηκα (NT) 5; (ἐπ-) ἀκήκοα 4; τέτοκα 3;
ἔωρακα (NT) 4; εἴρηκα (NT) 3; ἀπέσταλκα (NT) 3; εὕρηκα 3.   Εx
καταλέλοιπα, ἐμπέπαιχα, συνκέκλεικα, λελάληκα (NT), ἠγάπηκα,
κέκραξα, προσκεκύνηκα, ἦσαν πεποιηκότες once; (εἰσ-) ἀκήκοα 3;
ἑώρακα (NT) 5; ἀπέσταλκα (NT) 5; δέδωκα (NT) 2; εἴρηκα (NT) 4;
παρῴκηκα 2; πεποίηκα (NT) 2; ἡμάρτηκα 3; εὕρηκα 4.   Isa συνῆκα,
ἀποβέβληκα, πεπότικα, ἔσπαρκα, ἐζωγράφηκα, εἴληφα (NT), κέκληκα
(NT), πεποίηκα (NT), ἐγκαταλέλοιπα, ἀκήκοα, κέκληκα once; ἀπέσταλκα
(NT) 3; λελάληκα (NT) 2; ἀπολώλεκα 2; ἑόρακα (NT) 2; δέδωκα (NT) 4,
πέπρακα (NT) 2.   Dan ἑώρακα (NT) 8; εὕρηκα, σέσωκα (NT), εἴρηκα
(NT) once.   This is enough to show that the resultative pf. was becoming
lifeless, fossilized in a few verbs only.   Comparing the situation, for
instance, in Thucydides book II we find only εἴρηκα and δέδωκα among
the resultatives which are so common in LXX and NT, and hardly any
of the resultatives in that book are repetitions of the same verb.   By
iii and iv/A.D. the perfect has greatly declined, and in the collection of
Christian papyri of this date by G. Ghedini [1] we find only εὕρηκα,
ἐνήνοχα, (παρα-)δέδωκα, ἐπέσταλκα, προστέθεικα, ἠπάντηκα, εἴρηκα.

We may glance at some exegetically interesting examples of
the perfect in the NT.   It expresses a present state in πέπεισμαι
I am persuaded, but it may not be simply a pres. pf., as the
processes involved are important, as well as the resultant state ;
and the same is true of ἤλπικα.   But truly present are τέθνηκα
and ἥγημαι.   Illustrative of a tense which expresses action
begun in the past but fulfilled in the present is the series of
resultative perfects in 2 Ti 4[7] : *I have fought* ἠγώνισμαι, *I have*

---

[1] *Lettere cristiane dai papiri greci del III e IV secolo,* Milan 1923.

finished τετέλεκα, *I have kept* τετήρηκα, i.e. until now. It is remarkable that ἑώρακα occurs so often in the NT and ἀκήκοα comparatively seldom; but to explain the aor. of the latter side by side with the perf. of the former by the theory that to have seen the Lord was a more abiding experience than merely to have heard him, is utterly fantastic (Jn 3³² Ac 22¹⁵ Clem. Hom. 1⁹). Of the two perfects used by Pilate (Jn 19²² ὃ γέγραφα γέγραφα) the first must be simply for euphony, as it is aoristic.

Although a very large number of perfects in the NT cannot fairly be distinguished from aorists, there are still some which retain true resultative, and some a present, meaning.

§ 6. Other Moods of the Perfect in relation to Time [1]

(a) Of perfects with present meaning there are in NT and Koine the *imperatives* ἔρρωσο, ἔρρωσθε (Ac 15²⁹ 23³⁰ SELHP) and the periphrasis with ἴσθι. In Eph 5⁵ τοῦτο ἴστε γινώσκοντες may be a Hebraism (cp. γινώσκων οἶδεν LXX 1 Km 20³, and ἴστε γινώσκοντες Sym Je 49(42)²²). In Jas 1¹⁹ ἴστε may be imper. or indic. (S* ἴστω); so also Heb 12¹⁷. In Mk 4³⁹ (as opposed to φιμώθητι in DW, and 1²⁵ Lk 4³⁵) πεφίμωσο is probably a solemn stereotyped phrase used in adjurations.

(b) On the other hand, the *infinitive* is fairly common. In indirect speech (antecedent action): Lk 10³⁶ 22³⁴, Jn 12¹⁸. ²⁹, Ac 12¹⁴ 14¹⁹ 16²⁷ 25²⁵ 27¹³, Ro 15⁸, Col 2¹, 1 Ti 6¹⁷ 2 Ti 2¹⁸, Heb 11³. Subject or object (its time is coincident with the main verb): Lk 12⁵⁸ Ac 19³⁶ Ro 15¹⁹ Ac 26³² 2 Co 5¹¹, 1 Pt 4³ 2 Pt 2²¹. With prepositions διά εἰς μετά (antecedent action): Mk 5⁴ Lk 6⁴⁸ Ac 8¹¹ 18² 27⁹ Eph 1¹⁸ Heb 10⁹. ¹⁵ 11³ (Mayser II 1, 186ff).

(c) The *participle* also is fairly common, and its time is relative to that of the main verb, either antecedent or coincident. E.g. coincident: Jn 4⁶ 19³³ Ro 15¹⁴. Antecedent: Mt 26⁷⁵ Lk 16¹⁸ Jn 11⁴⁴ 18¹⁸ (Mayser II 1, 192ff). It is here, as well as in the indicative, that a difference from class. Greek is apparent: there was a distinct tendency in the Hellenistic period to connect very closely a past action with its present consequences. Hence Mt 5¹⁰ οἱ δεδιωγμένοι. It was preferable to say " who has been here a week " than to say " who came here a week ago." Aquila came from Italy recently (Ac 18²), but in Hellenistic they thought, " he has been here since coming from Italy recently." Hence the perfect where class. Greek would have aorist. Thus there can be no difference between preaching Christ ἐσταυρωμένον (as he has been since Good Friday) and preaching Christ σταυρωθέντα (as he was on Good Friday): the one is rather more classical than the other.

---

[1] K-G I 192β.   Stahl 152f.   Gild. I §§ 406–409.   Mayser II 1, 185–207. Moulton Einl. 277.

§ 7. Pluperfect [1]

The tense was never very frequent in the class. period—much less so than in Latin or English—and in the Ptolemaic papyri it shrank to an inconsiderable number of verbs, and was restricted largely to epistolary style. It still appears in NT, but many of the plupfs. of the Latin Bible translate the aorist: e.g. Ac 14²⁷. When it occurs it is simply the perfect placed in past time, relative to the time of speaking: Lk 16²⁰ *he lay* (we might use the impf. *he was lying*), Jn 9²² *the Jews have agreed* put into the past, 11.⁴⁴ past of *his face is swathed in a towel*.

§ 8. Future [2]

(a) *Indicative.* This is the one tense which does not express the *Aktionsart*, but simply states the time of action relative to the speaker. However, it is usually punctiliar, the periphrastic future being used when it is required to indicate linear action (Moulton Proleg. 149f), but the question is really a matter of opinion (Moule p. 10).

The future expresses a command, both in secular (Mayser II 1, 212f) and Biblical Greek. In the Mosaic Law this is particularly so, and prohibitions are formed by the addition of οὐ. All from the OT are: Mt 5²¹. ⁴³. ⁴⁸ 1 Pt 1¹⁶. Otherwise it occurs: Mt 6⁵ οὐκ ἔσεσθε, 20²⁶ οὐχ οὕτως ἔσται, 21³ ἐρεῖτε, ¹³ κληθήσεται, 27⁴ σὺ ὄψῃ (Latin?), ²⁴ ὑμεῖς ὄψεσθε (Latin?), Ac 18¹⁵ ὄψεσθε αὐτοί (Latin?); also Mk 9³⁵ Lk 1³¹; 1 Cl 60² καθαρεῖς, Herm V. II 2, 6 ἐρεῖς; several times in Barn. 19²ᶠᶠ, Herm. M. XII 3, 1, Did. 11⁷. But Jesus' own commands are imperative: Mt 5⁴⁴ ἀγαπᾶτε, 10¹³ ἐλθάτω ἡ εἰρήνη ὑμῶν ἐπ' αὐτήν (D fut). The MSS often vary between fut. ind. and imper. (Cuendet op. cit. 124), e.g.: Mt 20²⁷ Lk 17⁴.

Entirely due to Semitic influence is Rev 4⁹ᶠ καὶ ὅταν δώσουσιν τὰ ζῷα δόξαν . . . πεσοῦνται . . . καὶ προσκυνήσουσιν . . . καὶ βαλοῦσιν *when they gave glory . . . they fell . . . worshipped . . . threw*; we suspect literal rendering of the Heb. impf. which can be future under some circumstances.

Apparently Gnomic are: Ro 5⁷ *will die* = *is willing to*, 7³ χρηματίσει almost imper. *let her be called.* Deliberative: Mt 11¹⁶ *am I to compare.*

(b) *Infinitive.* It expresses time which is future in relation to the main verb; it has died out in colloquial speech, for the pap. examples are nearly all very early (Mayser II 1, 216), but it is still found in Ac and Heb: Jn 21²⁵ SBC (rest aor.) οἶμαι, Ac 11²⁸ 24¹⁵ 27¹⁰ (μέλλω), 23³⁰ (μηνύω), 26⁷ B (rest aor.) ἐλπίζω, Heb 3¹⁸ (ὄμνυμι).

(c) *Participle.* The same applies. Independent use: Lk 22⁴⁹ τὸ ἐσόμενον (D γενόμενον), Jn 6⁶⁴ παραδώσων (D pres., S μέλλων), Ac 20²² τὰ συναντήσοντά μοι, Ro 8³⁴ ὁ κατακρινῶν? 1 Co 15³⁷ τὸ σῶμα τὸ

---

[1] K-G I 151ff. Stahl 119–123. Gild. I §§ 235–237, Mayser II 1, 207–211. Moulton Einl. 232ff.
[2] K-G I 170ff. Stahl 140ff. Gild. I §§ 265–284. Mayser II 1, 211ff. Keith. " The Future in Greek," *Class. Q.*, 1912, 6, 121.

γενησόμενον, 1 Pt 3¹³ τίς ὁ κακώσων ὑμᾶς, 2 Pt 2¹³ κομιούμενοι (S*B arm ἀδικούμενοι), Heb 3⁵ τῶν λαληθησομένων. Dependent: very rare, the pres. ptc. or infin. or a clause taking its place: Mt 27⁴⁹ ἔρχεται σώσων (W σῴζων, S* σῶσαι, D καὶ σώσει), Mk 11¹³ vl ὡς εὑρήσων, Ac 8²⁷ ἐληλύθει προσκυνήσων, 22⁵ ἐπορευόμην ἄξων, 24¹¹ ἀνέβην προσκυνήσων, ¹⁷ ποιήσων . . . παρεγενόμην, Heb 13¹⁷ ὡς λόγον ἀποδώσοντες (probably genuine only in Ac and Heb). Instead, perhaps under Heb. or Aram. influence, we have the pres. ptc. for fut., e.g. ᾿Ιούδας ὁ παραδιδούς (Mt 26²⁵), ἀποδημῶν (25¹⁴), περὶ τῶν πιστευόντων (Jn 17²⁰); also Mt 20²⁰ 22¹⁶, Lk 1³⁵ 2³⁴ 14³¹ 22¹⁹ᶠ, Ac 21²ᶠ 26¹⁷. In all these, translate as a final clause or a future (Zerwick §§ 208, 208ᵃ).

§ 9. Periphrastic Tenses [1]

As Lagrange notes, it is a " construction très usitée en araméen, connue des Grecs mais surtout avec le participe au parfait." (*S. Matth.* XCI.)

(a) *Present and Imperfect* [2]. For this εἰμί serves (but never γίνομαι in Ptol. pap. and rarely in NT) with pres. ptc.   In NT it is rarely the pres. ind. of εἰμί but usually ἦν ἔσομαι εἶναι or ἴσθι. Scribes of a later age did not like the periphr. tense and altered it at e.g. Mk 1³⁹ 2⁴ 3¹ 5¹¹· ⁴⁰ 9⁴ 13²⁵ 14⁴ 15²⁶.   But the development is not far advanced in Hell. Greek, not even in the popular style of the papyri (Mayser II 1, 223f).   Due acknowledgement must therefore be given to the influence of Semitic speech [3] for the popularity of the usage in NT: so many of the examples occur in Mt, Lk, and the first part of Ac.   In Jn the ἦν cannot always be considered independently, even with a little straining: 1⁹· ²⁸ 2⁶ 3²³ 18³⁰ ἦν κακὸν ποιῶν (vl κακοποιός).   What possible distinction can there be between ἐβάπτιζεν and ἦν βαπτίζων in Jn 3²²· ²³, or between ἐν τῷ εἶναι αὐτὸν προσευχόμενον and ἐν τῷ προσεύχεσθαι αὐτόν in Lk 9¹⁸· ²⁹?   Björck (op. cit. 68f) argues against Semitic influence and (op. cit. 53f) urges that sometimes the instances are only apparently periphrastic, the ptc. being adjectival.   Indeed it is probably a supplementary predicate in Mk 1⁴ ἐγένετο ᾿Ιωάννης ὁ βαπτίζων ἐν τῇ

---

[1] K-G I 38n. 3.   Gild. I § 191. 285–290. 291. 293.   Stahl 144–147. Schwyzer II 407 (ζ).   Mayser II 1, 223ff.   Moulton Einl. 357ff.   Radermacher², 102.   Bauer s.v. εἰμί 4.   P. F. Regarde, *La Phrase Nominale dans la Langue du NT*, Paris 1919, 111–185.

[2] G. Björck, ῾Ην διδάσκων.   *Die periphr. Konstruktionem im Griech.*, Uppsala 1940.

[3] Aramaic in particular; de Zwaan in *Beginnings* II 62 mentions the Aram. imperfect.

ἐρήμῳ κηρύσσων . . . (= ἐγένετο καὶ ἐκήρυσσεν), 9³· ⁷, Mt 5²⁵, Lk 1²⁰, Ac 9⁹. No doubt in some instances the copula really means *there is* or *there are*, but not in the vast majority.

Present: Mt 1²³ 7²⁹ 19²² 27³³ etc., Mk 5⁴¹ 15²². ³⁴ Lk 6⁴³ 8³² SBD, Jn 1⁴² 5², Ac 1¹² 4³⁶ 14¹⁵ 25¹⁰, Ro 13⁶ 15⁴, 1 Co 8⁵, 2 Co 2¹⁷ 9¹² 10¹¹, Ga 1¹⁰. ²²f 4²⁴, Col 1⁶ 2⁵· ²³ 3¹, Eph 5⁵ DEKL, 1 Ti 5²⁴, Jas 1¹⁷ 3¹⁵, 2 Pt 3⁷, Rev 1¹⁸ 3¹⁷. Πρέπον ἐστιν Mt 3¹⁵ 1 Co 11¹³. Δέον ἐστιν Ac 19³⁶ 1 Cl 34². Ἐξόν (sc. ἐστιν) Ac 2²⁹ 2 Co 12⁴. Συμφέρον (sc. ἐστιν) 2 Co 12¹ p⁴⁶ SBFGP (συμφέρει DEKL).

Imperfect: in Mk there is abundance of periphr. tenses (29): 1⁶· ¹³· ²². ³³· ³⁹ 2⁴· ⁶· ¹⁸ 3¹ 4³⁸ 5⁵· ¹¹· ⁴⁰ 6⁵² 9⁴ 10²². ³²bis 14⁴· ⁴⁰· ⁴⁹· ⁵⁴ 15⁷· ²⁶· ⁴⁰· ⁴³; Mt 7²⁹ 12⁴ 14²⁴ SCE (B differs) 17³ 19²² 24³⁸ 27⁵⁵· ⁶¹ Lk 1¹⁰· ²¹· ²² 2⁸· ³³· ⁵¹ 3²³ 4²⁰· ³¹· ³³· ³⁸· ⁴⁴ 5¹⁶· ¹⁷· ²⁹ 6¹² 8³² SBD (ACEFG diff) ⁴⁰ 9³⁰· ⁵³ 11¹⁴ 13¹⁰· ¹¹ 14¹ 15¹ 19⁴⁷ 21³⁷ 23⁸· ⁵¹ 24¹³· ³²· ⁵³; Jn 1²⁸ 2⁶ 3²³ 5⁵ 10⁴⁰ 13²³ 18¹⁸· ²⁵· ³⁰ 19⁴¹ ἦν τεθειμένος SB (AD [ἐτέθη]); Ac 1¹⁰· ¹³· ¹⁴ 2²· ⁵· ⁴² 8¹· ¹³· ²⁸ 9⁹· ²⁸ 10²⁴· ³⁰ 11⁵ 12⁵· ⁶· ¹²· ²⁰ 14⁷ 16⁹· ¹² 18⁷ 19¹⁴ 21³· ⁹ 22¹⁹· ²⁰; 2 Co 5¹⁹; Ga 1²²· ²³f 2¹¹; Ph 2²⁶; Eph 2¹²; Ti 3³; 1 Pt 2²⁵; Rev 1¹⁶ 10² 17⁴ 21¹¹· ¹⁴.

(b) *Perfect and Pluperfect*. We have an illustration of the principle that when a grammatical form tends to disappear, having lost its characteristic force, the language will find a substitute; often that substitute is a periphrasis. Class. Greek furnishes numerous examples of periphrastic optative and subjunctive, and the periphrasis began to extend to other parts so that εἰμί with perf. ptc. is very common in NT. No real difference can be detected between ἐπεγέγραπτο Ac 17²³ and ἦν γεγραμμένον Jn 19¹⁹. Even in the same book within a few lines we find γεγραμμένα ἐστίν Jn 20³⁰ and ταῦτα δὲ γέγραπται 20³¹. Cp. 1 Jn 4¹² τετελειωμένη ἐστιν, 2⁵ τετελείωται; Herm. S. IX 4 ὑποδεδυκυῖαι ἦσαν alongside ὑποδεδύκεισαν. Although it may be possible occasionally to trace the presence of the class. force of *insistence*[1], as when Paul separates ἑστώς (a pres. pf.) from εἰμί with great emphasis, referring to his position as a suitor for Imperial justice (Ac 25¹⁰), yet usually there is no emphasis and the question of Semitic background is immediately raised. The same construction occurs in the early part of Acts, where there are grounds for supposing Semitic influence (5²⁵ εἰσίν . . . ἑστῶτες). Mayser does not give many exx. from secular Greek. Nevertheless, whatever its origin, the periphrastic

---

[1] Thucydides book II: 4³· ⁵ 6² 10³ 12² 49³ 78³ (often with expressive force).

perfect persisted in the mainstream of the language and is in
regular use at the present day with the force of the Latin and
English perfect.

LXX. Ge 27³³ 30³³ 40⁶ 41³⁶ 43⁹ 44³². Ex 12⁶· ³⁴ 17¹² 21²³· ³⁶
32¹⁵ 33¹³ 34³⁰ 39²³. Isa 1¹¹ 8¹⁴· ¹⁷ 9¹⁹ 10²⁰ 11⁵ bis 12² 13³· ¹⁵ 17⁷· ⁸· ⁹
20⁵· ⁶ 22³· ¹⁴· ²⁴ 27¹⁰ 28⁷ 30¹² 33¹² 36⁴· ⁵ 42²⁰ 54¹¹ 58¹⁴. Dan. 2²⁰· ⁴²
3⁵²· ⁵³· ⁵⁴· ⁵⁶ 6³ 8²⁶ 10⁹ 12⁹.

Pre-Christian papyri: 5 in iii/B.C., 11 in ii/B.C. (Mayser II 1, 224f).
NT: Mt 1²³ 9³⁶ 10³⁰ 18²⁰ 26⁴³; Mk 1⁶· ³³ 6⁵² 14²¹ D 15⁷· ²⁶· ⁴⁶;
Lk 1⁷ 2²⁶ 4¹⁶· ¹⁷ 5¹· ¹⁷· ¹⁸ 8²· ³ 9⁴⁵ 12²· ⁶ 15²⁴· ³² 18³² 20⁶ 23¹⁵· ⁵¹· ⁵³· ⁵⁵
24³⁸; Jn 1²⁴ 2¹⁷ 3²¹· ²⁴· ²⁸ 6³¹· ⁴⁵ 10³⁴ 12¹⁴· ¹⁶ 13⁵ 18¹⁸· ²⁵ 19¹¹· ¹⁹· ²⁰
20³⁰; Ac 1¹⁷ 2¹³ 4³¹ 8¹⁶ 9³³ 12⁶· ¹² 13⁴⁸ 14²⁶ 16⁹ 17²³ 18²⁵ 19³² 20⁸· ¹³
21²⁹· ³³ 22²⁰· ²⁹ 25¹⁰· ¹⁴ 26²⁶; Ro 7¹⁴ 13¹ 15¹⁴; 1 Co 1¹⁰ 5² 7²⁹ 14⁸ 15¹⁹;
2 Co 1⁹ 4³; Ga 2¹¹ 4³; Eph 2⁶· ⁸· ¹²; Col 2¹⁰; Heb 4² 7²⁰· ²³ 10¹⁰; Jas 5¹⁵;
2 Pt 3⁵· ⁷; 1 Jn 4¹²; Rev 7⁵ 17⁴ 21¹⁹.

(c) Future Perfect periphrasis is very rare too (Mayser II 1,
225): Mt 16¹⁹ 18¹⁸ Lk 12⁵² Heb 2¹³ (Isa 8¹⁷); but it takes the
place of the normal fut. pf.

(d) Periphr. Future, normally linear in *Aktionsart*, is
expressed by θέλω and μέλλω with infin. or by the fut. of εἰμί
with the ptc. Mt 10²² 24⁹ Mk 13¹³, Lk 21¹⁷ ἔσεσθε μισούμενοι,
21²⁴. Mk 13²⁵ (corr. by Mt 24²⁹) Lk 5¹⁰ 12⁵² 22⁶⁹ Ac 6⁴ D 13¹¹
1 Co 14⁹ Jude ¹⁸; Lk 1²⁰ ἔσῃ σιωπῶν. Μέλλω Mk 13⁴ Lk 7² 22²³
Jn 12⁴ Ac 18¹⁴ 20³ 28⁶.

(e) Periphrasis with aorist ptc. (= plupf.): Lk 23¹⁹ B ἦν
βληθείς (Engl. impf. or plupf.?) vl. perf., Jn 18³⁰ S*, 2 Co 5¹⁹
ἦν θέμενος. No more in NT, but in post-Christian Greek (K-G I
38f. Gild. I 125f. Radermacher², 102).

(f). Periphrasis with verbal adjectives in -τος: Lk 4²⁴ δεκτός
ἐστιν (= δέχεται), Ac 11¹⁷ ἤμην δυνατός, 28²² γνωστόν ἐστιν,
Jn 18¹⁵ ἦν γνωστός, 6⁴⁵ ἔσονται διδακτοί, Ro 1²⁵ ἐστιν εὐλογητός.

(g) Periphrasis with γίνομαι: Mk 9³ (9⁷), 2 Co 6¹⁴ Col 1¹⁸,
Heb 5¹², Rev 1¹⁸ 3² 16¹⁰, Did 3⁸, LXX Isa 30¹².

(h) Other periphrases: pres. subjunctive Eph 4¹⁴ Jas 1⁴. Perf.
subj. Lk 14⁸ Jn 3²⁷ 6⁶⁵ 16²⁴ 17¹⁹· ²³ 1 Co 1¹⁰ Ph 1¹⁰ 2 Co 1⁹ 9³ Jas 5¹⁵
1 Jn 1⁴, LXX Isa 8¹⁴ 10²⁰ 17⁸ 20⁵· ⁶. Pf. imper. Lk 12³⁵. Pf. ptc.
Eph 4¹⁸ Col 1²¹. Infin. Lk 9¹⁸ = 11¹. Imper. Mt 5²⁵ Lk 19¹⁷ Hom.
Clem. ep. ad Jac³, Mart. Pelag. 26¹⁵. Eph 5⁵?

It is well to note that in true periphrastic tenses the copula
keeps very close to the participle; there are hardly more than
four exceptions to this rule in Mark.

CHAPTER EIGHT

THE VERB: MOODS: INDICATIVE AND SUBJUNCTIVE

In the use of moods Hellenistic Greek moves further away from class. Greek than in its use of tenses. The optative mood is less used, although there is a considerable survival in the LXX and NT. The infinitive has retreated on some flanks and advanced on others.

§ 1. The Indicative [1]

1. The imperfect indicative (without ἄν), in main clauses, to express necessity really concerns only ἔδει, since χρή is not Hellenistic [2]. The time is either *past* (*it would have been necessary*, but did not happen) or else *present* (*it were necessary*, but is not happening); in English *ought* serves for both and we make the second verb carry the time-indication.

(a) *Past*: Lk 24²⁶ *would it not have been necessary* οὐχὶ ταῦτα ἔδει παθεῖν τὸν Χριστόν, Heb 9²⁶ *it would then have been necessary* ἔδει αὐτὸν πολλάκις παθεῖν. Mt 18³³ *ought you not to have pitied*, 23²³ Lk 11⁴² *ought you not to have done*, Mt 25²⁷, Lk 13¹⁶. Ptol. papyri (dates): 266, iiim, 258, 258, 258, 258, 165, 107.

(b) *Present*: Ac 24¹⁹ *they ought to be here* οὓς ἔδει ἐπί σου παρεῖναι. P. Hib. 46, 13 (258 B.C.) ἔδει πάλαι τὰ ἐνέχυρα αὐτῶν ὧδε εἶναι καὶ πεπρᾶσθαι, also iiim.

Other imperfects are used in a similar sense for the pres. in NT, but not the papyri: καθῆκεν Ac 22²² (D² καθῆκον), ἀνῆκεν Eph 5⁴ (DE τὰ οὐκ ἀνήκοντα) Col 3¹⁸, ἐδύνατο Mt 26⁹ Jn 9³³ Ac 26³², ὤφειλον 2 Co 12¹¹, καλὸν ἦν Mt 26²⁴, κρεῖττον ἦν 2 Pt 2²¹. It is not suggested that the past obligation was not lived up to; it is simply a present obligation expressed for some reason in the imperfect. The reason may be the same as that which

---

[1] K-G I 202–216. Stahl 351ff. Gild. I §§ 361–368. Schwyzer II 301–309. Mayser II 1, 226–229. R. Law, " Imperfect of Obligation in the NT ", *Exp. T.* 30, 330ff. For fut. ind. as a command, see above.

[2] In NT only Jas 3¹⁰; in LXX only Pr 25²⁷ 4 Mac 8²⁵ A. There are two uncertain examples in the Ptol. pap.: Mayser II 1, 226.

prompts the English past tense *ought* instead of present *owe*:
simply because the obligation logically conceived is anterior to
the implied fulfilment of the obligation.   What we do not find
in NT are : ἐξῆν *it were possible*, ἦν with the verbal adj. in -τέος,
ὀλίγου with aor. ind. for something that nearly happened, and
προσήκει.

2. In the same way an unfulfilled or impossible wish can be
expressed by ὤφελον or ἐβουλόμην, etc., as a regret. 1 Co 4⁸
ὄφελον (ὤφελον DᶜEL) ἐβασιλεύσατε, 2 Co 11¹ ὄφελον (ὤφ.
DᶜEFGKL) fut. ind., Rev 3¹⁵ ὄφελον (ὤφ. BP) ψυχρὸς ἦς ἢ ζεστός,
Ign. Sm. 12¹, LXX and Epict. have ὄφελον (and ὤφ.) with indic.,
Gr. Enoch 10⁶⁻¹⁰ ὄφελον subj. Nothing in papyri. In class.
Greek a wish relating to the past which can no longer be fulfilled
is expressed by εἴθε with ind.; a wish which cannot be fulfilled,
relating to past or present, by ὤφελον or εἴθε (εἰ γάρ) ὤφελον,
with inf.   But the pap. and NT have no instance of εἴθε and
εἰ γάρ used in this way.

By omitting the apodosis, a protasis with εἰ may become
a wish clause (Lk 19⁴² Ac 23⁹).

Ac 26²⁹ SᶜAB εὐξαίμην ἄν (class.), Ro 9³ ηὐχόμην ἀνάθεμα
εἶναι. Ἐβουλόμην : Arist. Ran 866, P. Flor. I 6, 7 (A.D. 210)
Ac 25²² Phm¹³. Ἤθελον: Soph. Ajax 1400, Epict. (= *I must*),
Ga 4²⁰, Clem. Hom. 1⁹, BU IV 1078⁸ (A.D. 39), P. Lond III 897²⁰
(p. 207) (A.D. 84), MGr ἤθελα.

In cl. Attic the aor. (rarely the impf.) was used with ἄν to
denote what would have happened at a past time if the attempt
had been made, and therefore what *might, could*, or *should* have
taken place.   Thus ἠβουλόμην ἄν = *I should (could) have wished*
(under other circumstances), Lat. *vellem*. But already in Attic
orators the ἄν is dispensed with (K-G I 205; Stahl 358).

3. The " unreal " indicative (impf. for what *should be* now;
aor. for what *should have been*) is found in conditional sentences;
the ἄν which is the characteristic of " unreal " usage may not
even be present.   The tenses maintain their proper *Aktionsarten*
(NB. plupf. Ac 26³² 1 Jn 2¹⁹).

(*a*) Apodosis with ἄν ¹: Mt 11²¹ εἰ . . . ἐγένοντο (*had been*

¹ Whether Mt 15⁵ Mk 7¹¹ comes here is debatable. It might be an
apodosis, with a protasis to be supplied like " if it had not been δῶρον."
Thus translate, Δῶρον *is the benefit which you would have received from me.*
But ἐάν is not elsewhere used for ἄν in " unreal " use (hence D's correction
to ἄν).

done) . . . ἄν . . . μετενόησαν (*would have repented*), Jn 18³⁰ εἰ μὴ
ἦν . . . , οὐκ (syrˡᵉʷ οὐδ') ἄν σοι παρεδώκαμεν *if he were not* . . .
we would not have, 18³⁶ (see below).   Ptol. pap : iii/B.C. (6), ii/B.C.
(1).   We have pres. indic. in the protasis in P. Par. 47 (153 B.C.)
ἰ μὴ μικρόν τι ἐντρέπομαι, οὐκ ἄν με ἴδες τὸ π⟨ο⟩ρσωπόν μου
πόποτε, which is parallel to Lk 17⁶ εἰ ἔχετε πίστιν . . . , ἐλέγετε
ἄν *if you have faith, you would say* (the " real " condition, pres.
indic., may be due to politeness, for the disciples had claimed to
have *some* faith, when they asked for it to be increased. *If you
had faith* would seem to deny this too bluntly.)

The position of ἄν: it goes back as far as possible, and often there
ĭs οὐκ ἄν; note the following: Lk 19²³ κἀγὼ ἐλθὼν σὺν τόκῳ ἂν αὐτὸ
ἔπραξα, Jn 18³⁶ οἱ ὑπηρέται ἂν οἱ ἐμοὶ ἠγωνίζοντο (B*om ἄν; SBᵐᵍ
LWX have ἠγωνίζοντο ἄν), 8¹⁹ εἰ ἐμὲ ᾔδειτε καὶ τὸν πατέρα μου ἂν
ᾔδειτε BLW (ᾔδειτε ἄν ΛΓΔ), Ga 1¹⁰ χρ.δοῦλος οὐκ ἂν ἤμην, Heb 10²
ἐπεὶ (*otherwise*) οὐκ ἂν ἐπαύσαντο.

(*b*) Apodosis without ἄν: Mk 9⁴² Lk 17² DW καλόν ἐστιν αὐτῷ
μᾶλλον εἰ περιέκειτο (vl. περίκειται) μύλος ὀνικὸς . . . καὶ ἐβλήθη
(vl. βέβληται), but the " real " indic. of the other MSS may have some
point: " If such a man as that is drowned, it is just as well!"   So also
Ga 5¹¹ εἰ . . . ἔτι κηρύσσω, τί ἔτι διώκομαι. Mt 26²⁴ Mk 14²¹ καλὸν
(ἦν) αὐτῷ εἰ οὐκ ἐγεννήθη. Jn 9³³ εἰ μὴ ἦν . . . οὐκ ἠδύνατο, 15²⁴ εἰ
τὰ ἔργα μὴ ἐποίησα .∴. ἁμαρτίαν οὐκ εἴχοσαν, 19¹¹ οὐκ εἶχες B (ἔχεις
SA) ἐξουσίαν . . . εἰ μὴ ἦν . . . , 8³⁹ εἰ τέκνα . . . ἐστε, τὰ ἔργα . . . ἐποιεῖτε
SB² ΔΓΘ fam¹³ (+ ἄν SᶜKL) (ποιεῖτε p⁶⁶ B*700 Old Lat syrˢ), Ac 26³²
ἀπολελύσθαι ἐδύνατο . . . εἰ μὴ ἐπεκέκλητο Καίσαρα, Ro 7⁷, Ga 4¹⁵
(SᶜDᶜEKLP add ἄν), 2 Cl 20⁴, Gosp. Petr. 2⁵, LXX 2 Mac 5¹⁸, 3 Mac 5³².
Ptol. pap. (dates): 141 116 2.

4. The augment-indicative with ἄν stands in dependent
clauses in an iterative sense (= class. optative).   It is certainly
found in class. Greek in *main* clauses to denote a customary
past action [1].   But in NT and simple Koine it never occurs in
main clauses; in temporal and conditional relative clauses it may
be a remnant of the class. usage [2] in main clauses.   The class.
ὃς ἄν (ὅταν) βούλοιτο ἐδύνατο becomes in later Greek ὃς ἄν
(ὅταν) ἐβούλετο ἐδύνατο.

---

[1] *He would often do it, he used to do it*; Goodwin § 162.   The only
exception seems to be Soph. Ph. 442ff. ὃς οὐκ ἂν εἵλετο (Schwyzer II
350).
[2] Burton § 26.

Again ἄν stands early, as near as possible (if not actually joined) to the conjunction or relative: Mk 3¹¹ τὰ πνεύματα, ὅταν αὐτὸν ἐθεώρουν, προσέπιπτον, 6⁵⁶ ὅπου ἐὰν (ἄν) εἰσεπορεύετο ... ἐν ταῖς ἀγοραῖς ἐτίθεσαν ..., 15⁶ ὃν ἂν ᾐτοῦντο DG rightly, Ac 2⁴⁵ 4³⁵, 1 Co 12² ὡς ἂν ἤγεσθε; LXX Ge 38⁹, Ex 33⁸ ἥνικα δ' ἄν εἰσεπορεύετο, Ps 119 (120)⁷ ὅταν ἐλάλουν αὐτοῖς ἐπολέμουν με δωρέαν each time I spoke to them, 1 Mac 13²⁰, Nu 21⁹ (A aor.): see Ottley, Introduction to OT in Greek, 1914, 306. Polybius 4, 32, 5 ὅταν ... ἐν πειρασμοῖς ἦσαν, Herm S. IX 6, 4.

The aor. is found, as well as impf. Mk 6⁵⁶ ὅσοι ἂν (SΔ om) ἥψαντο SBDLΔW (ἥπτοντο ΑΝΧΗΓΠ) αὐτοῦ, ἐσῴζοντο: von Soden accepts impf., the more normal construction, but aor. is not without precedent. Mk 11¹⁹ ὅταν SBCKL (ὅτε AD) ὀψὲ ἐγένετο, ἐξεπορεύετο ἔξω τῆς πόλεως = whenever it was evening, every evening, not as some translators take it when it was evening (of that day); by class. standards it is what Field called a " solecism " (Notes 35), but not by Hellenistic, in which it is normal iterative indic. with ἄν. Ac 3² ὃν ἐτίθουν καθ' ἡμέραν πρὸς τὴν θύραν τοῦ ἱεροῦ. It would suggest, in Rev 8¹ (ὅταν ἥνοιξεν), that the Lamb's breaking of the seals was a repetitive performance, in spite of the aor. Aor. elsewhere: Polyb. 4, 32, 6 ὅταν ... ἐτράπησαν, 13, 7, 8. 10. LXX Ge 30⁴² vl, Ez 10¹¹. Herm. S. IX 4, 5; 17, 3. Barn 12². P. Lond. IV 1394 (A.D. 709) ἀπόστειλον πρὸς ἡμᾶς εἴ τι δ' ἂν συνῆξας χρυσίου ἀπὸ τῶν αὐτῶν δημοσίων For ὅταν with indic. however in a non-iterative meaning see pp. 112f. For pres. and fut. indic. with ἄν see p. 110.

§ 2. The Subjunctive [1]

(A). MAIN CLAUSES

1. A substitute for the Imperative

The difference in meaning between pres. and aor. imper. has already been discussed (pp. 74–78); for the perfect imper. see pp. 85, 89. All that remain are the substitutionary forms of the imperative, of which we have already discussed the pres. and aor. infinitive and fut. indic. (pp. 78, 86). There remains the subjunctive, both positive and negative.

---

[1] K-G I 217–225. Gild. I §§ 369–386. Stahl 228, 364ff. Schwyzer II 309ff. Wackernagel I 230ff. F. Slotty, Der Gebrauch des Konjunktiv und Optative in den griechischen Dialekten, I. 1915.

(a) *The Jussive.* This use of 2nd and 3rd p. subjunctive in positive sentences was never acceptable to Ionic and Attic writers (K-G I 220) and probably does not appear in NT[1] although there are examples from inscriptions of v–iii/B.C. (Slotty op. cit. 22ff) and post-Christian Greek [2]. They are all aor. and so could be confused with fut. through the phonetic resemblance of -σει and -σῃ, -σομεν and -σωμεν, etc. Moreover, confusion was already apparent in Attic Greek poetry between the subjunctive and optative for wishes (K-G I 225), and all the time the opt. was generally losing ground; thus the way was prepared for the jussive use of the subjunctive in the popular Koine (exx. in Slotty op. cit. 34, Mayser II 1, 230), while the analogy of the prohibitive subjunctive was ever at hand to suggest this development.

The hortative subj. in 1st p. does however occur in NT (as in class. Greek); Jn 14³¹ Ga 5²⁶ 1 Co 11³⁴ διατάξωμαι ADEFG (-ξομαι p⁴⁶ SBC). Also, where cl. Greek used ἄγε, φέρε or δεῦρο, Hellenistic has ἄφες (ἄς with 1st and 3rd p. subj. in MGr as an imper.) and δεῦρο with 1st p.: Mt 7⁴ 27⁴⁹ Mk 15³⁶ SDV 12⁷ Lk 6⁴² Ac 7³⁴ OT Rev 17¹ 21⁹, Lk 2¹⁵ διέλθωμεν δή, Epict. 1, 9, 15 ἄφες δείξωμεν, P. Oxy. III 413, 184 (ii/A.D.).

(b) *Negative.* In prohibitions, as have seen (pp. 74–78), it depends on the *Aktionsart* of the verb whether the pres. imper. or aor. subj. with μή is used; never probably the pres. subj. in NT [3] but Herm. S. IV 5 (A pap^mich) οὐδὲν διαμάρτῃς. In neg. hortatory sentences, e.g. 1 Co 16¹¹ μή τις . . . ἐξουθενήσῃ *let no one despise,* 2 Co 11¹⁶ 2 Th 2³.

῞Οπως (ἄν) and ὅπως μή with subj. or fut. ind. occur in the Ptol. pap. like the class. ὅπως and fut. ind., but not the NT.

(c) *Imperatival* ἵνα. However the NT does display exx. of ἵνα with subj. in 2nd and 3rd p. [4] Mt 20³³ κύριε, ἵνα ἀνοιγῶσιν,

---

[1] Possible exceptions at 1 Co 7³⁹ FG γαμηθῇ (3rd p), 11³³ ἐκδέχησθε (2nd p).

[2] Reinhold, *Apost. Väter* 104; Ign. Pol 8³ διαμείνητε; Barn. 19¹ σπεύσῃ; Ljungvik BSSV 71 (ἐν νόῳ ἔχῃς ὅτι BGU II 5, ii–iii/A.D.).

[3] Possibly except Col 3⁹ p⁴⁶ μὴ ψεύδησθε.

[4] Schwyzer II 318. Horn 120ff. Radermacher[2] 170. Pernot *Études* 63, 97ff, 123, 148f. Moulton Einl. 281. C. J. Cadoux, " The Imperatival Use of ἵνα in NT," *JThS* 42, 1941, 165ff. H. G. Meecham, ibid. 43, 1942, 179f. A. R. George, ibid. 45, 1944, 56ff. (criticism of Cadoux and Meecham). H. G. Meecham *Exp. T.* 52, Aug. 1941, 437. Mayser II 1, 231f. Ljungvik SSAA 38.

Mk 5²³ ἵ̈ α . . . ἐπιθῇς (or it depends on παρακαλεῖ), 10⁵¹ ʽΡαββουνεὶ
ἵνα ἀνα[λέψω. Lk 18⁴¹. Jn 6³⁹ ἵνα . . . μὴ ἀπολέσω, 9³ ἵνα
φανερωϐ ῇ, 13¹⁸ ἵνα ἡ γραφὴ πληρωθῇ, 15²⁵. 1 Co 5² ἵνα ἀρθῇ ἐκ
μέσου ὑμῶν ὁ τὸ ἔργον τοῦτο πράξας usually taken as final, but
only imperat. ἵνα will make good sense, as RSV (but not quite
NEB), 7²⁹ ἵνα . . . ὦσιν, 2 Co 8⁷ ἵνα περισσεύητε, 9⁴ ἵνα μὴ
λέγωμεν (p⁴⁶ C*DG it λέγω) not to say, Col 4¹⁶ ἵνα . . . ἀναγνωσθῇ
see that it is read, Ga 2¹⁰ ἵνα μνημονεύωμεν we must remember,
Phm¹⁹, Eph 5³³ ἡ δὲ γυνὴ ἵνα φοβῆται τὸν ἄνδρα. 1 Ti 1³ ἵνα
παραγγείλῃς (or depends on παρεκάλεσα), 1 Jn 2¹⁹ (final in RV,
NEB) ἵνα φανερωθῶσιν they must be manifest. Doubtful in Jn 1⁸
he must bear witness, 14³¹ the world must learn, 18⁹·³² 19²⁴,
Mk 14⁴⁹ the Scripture must be fulfilled, 1 Co 7⁵·¹⁰·²⁹ 2 Co 8⁷·¹³
9⁴ Col 2⁴. None in Ac, Past, Heb, Jas, 1, 2 Pt, Rev. The use is
popular (Slotty 35), although it is found also in LXX 2 Mac 1⁹
ἵνα ἄγητε τὰς ἡμέρας τῆς σκηνοπηγίας. Note νά with 2nd
and 3rd p. subj. as imper. in MGr. Ptol. pap.: pos. iii/B.C. (2),
neg. iii/B.C. (1).

LXX displays a great many exx. because of the influence of its
Semitic background: Ge 18²¹ ἵνα γνῶ I must know, 30⁸? ἵνα εὕρη ὁ
παῖς σου χάριν, 44³⁴ ἵνα μὴ ἴδω let me not see, 47¹⁹ let me not die before
you. Ex. Le none. Nu 11¹⁵ let me not see my wretchedness, 21²⁷ let the
city be built. Dt 5¹⁴ your servant must rest. Josh 22²⁴ let not our children
say. Jg Ru Km none. 1 Ch 21³ ἵνα μὴ γένηται εἰς ἁμαρτίαν τῷ ᾽Ισραήλ
let him not be accused of sin. 1 Esd. none. 2 Es Ne. To S none. To
B 8¹² ἵνα θάψωμεν αὐτὸν καὶ μηδεὶς γνῷ (B ὅπως). Est. Jdt. none.
Ps 38⁵ ἵνα γνῶ let me know. Pr Eccl Ca Wi Si Isa Je Ba. none. Ezk
37²³ they must no longer be defiled pres. subj. Dan O' none. 2 Mac 1⁹
ἵνα ἄγητε see that ye keep. 3 4 Mac none. Jb 32¹³ (cp. Eph 5³³ Mk 5²³)
1 Mac 1⁹? Acta Petri et Pauli 209¹⁴ ἵνα γνῷς, βασιλεῦ, Acta Phil. 39¹ff
ἵνα λαλῶσιν ὁμοιότητα ἄνθρωπον (following an imperat.), 86²¹ff μὴ
καλυψάτω με . . . ἀλλ᾽ ἵνα διαπεράσω . . . Before an imperat.: Acta
Thom. 253⁶ff ἵνα . . . πέμψη . . . καὶ εὐφραινέσθωσαν . . . , 253¹⁰f ἵνα μὴ
ἀπόληται ἡ πεποίθησίς μου καὶ ἡ ἐλπίς μου ἡ ἐν σοὶ μὴ καταισχυνθῇ, 254⁶ff.

In view of this wealth and the secular poverty of examples, we may
claim the imperatival ἵνα as virtually a Semitism, illustrating the homo-
geneity of Biblical Greek and its distinction from the Koine.

2. *Emphatic Denial and Prohibition with* οὐ μή

Besides the imperatival use of the subj. in main clauses, we
have the following:

The use of οὐ μή [1] to express emphatic denial or a strong

---

[1] Which also occurs as *nonne* in questions expecting answer yes (see
below ch. 19 § 2).

prohibition [1], not so strongly as in class. Greek [2], is in NT almost restricted to quotations from LXX, to sayings of Jesus, and to Rev. The fut. ind. is also used in NT but not in Ptol. pap. The subj. is very strongly attested in the papyri, and this seems to rule out an exclusively Semitic influence. For theories on the origin of the οὐ μή construction, see Moulton Proleg. 188ff, Goodwin 389ff, Thompson *Syntax* 431–438. It was probably οὔ (*no!*)· μή (*it is not*), then punctuated οὐ μή.

(a) In Denials

1. *Aorist.* Aor. subj. occurs in class. Greek. L.S. (s.v. οὐ μή) gives exx from Aesch. Soph. Eurip. Hdt. Thucyd. Aristoph. Plato, Xen. Demosth. Post-cl.: Aelius Aristides (ii/A.D.), Diogenes; Epict. III 22, 33 οὐ μὴ ἀποθάνωσιν; Ep. Barn. 17[2] οὐ μὴ νοήσητε *you will not understand*; Ep. Clem. 27[5] καὶ οὐδὲν μὴ παρέλθῃ τῶν δεδογματισμένων ὑπ' αὐτοῦ. Ptol. Pap.: many exx., esp. Zen. P. 59084. 9 (257 B.C.) οὐ μὴ κινηθῶ *that will certainly make no impression on me*; 59396. 4 (iii/B.C.) πρὸς δέ σε οὐθὲν μὴ διενεχθῶμεν *we will certainly not quarrel with you.* Imperial: P. Oxy. 119 (ii–iii/A.D.) οὐ μὴ φάγω, οὐ μὴ πείνω. LXX: (Ge οὐ μή 15 times in 337 negs; Ex 13 in 302; Dt 33 in 499) Ge 6[3] οὐ μὴ καταμείνῃ τὸ πνεῦμά μου etc. (9), Ex (6), Le (6) Nu (11), Dt (33), Isa (88), Je α (28) β (50); also, e, g, Jb 7[9], Wi 18.SA 3[1] 6[22] 12[10]; Ps. Sol. I 5; Vit. Proph. Jer. 14. NT:—Mt 5[18. 20. 26], 15[6] οὐ μὴ τιμήσῃ E*FGK (rest fut.), 16[28] οἵτινες οὐ μὴ γεύσωνται θανάτου, 21[19], 24[2. 34. 35] οὐ μὴ παρελθῶσιν (Mk 13[31] ACD[c] a harmonization), 21 οὐδὲ οὐ μὴ γένηται, 26[29. 35] οὐ μή σε ἀπαρνήσωμαι AEGK (rest fut.), Mk 9[1. 41], 13[2] οὐ μὴ ἀφεθῇ ὧδε λίθος ἐπὶ λίθον ὃς οὐ μὴ καταλυθῇ, 19. 30, 14[25. 31] (-σωμαι SEFGK), 16[18], Lk 9[27] 12[59] o.μ. ἐξελθῇς, 13[35] o.μ. ἴδητε. 1[15] o.μ. πίῃ, 6[37a.b.], 8[17] o.μ. γνωσθῇ..., 18[7] οὐ μὴ ποιήσῃ; 17. 29f οὐχὶ μὴ ἀπολάβῃ, 21[18. 32] 22[16] οὐκέτι οὐ μή, 18. 67. 68, Jn 4[48] 6[35] (vl. fut. ind.), 8[12] (vl. fut. ind.) 51. 52. (vl. fut. ind.), 10[28], 11[26. 56], 13[8] οὐ μὴ νίψῃς (D fut. ind.), 18[11] οὐ μὴ πίω αὐτό; Ac 13[41] (LXX Hab1[5]), Ga 4[30] οὐ μή (p[46] FG om) κληρονομήσῃ ACFG (rest fut.), Ro 4[8] (Ps 31[2]) οὐ μὴ λογίσηται, 1 Co 8[13] Heb 8[12] (Je 38[34]), 13[5] οὐ μή σε ἄνω οὐδὲ p[46] (rest οὐδ' οὐ) μή σε ἐγκαταλίπω D (rest-λείπω) very emph., Rev 2[11]

---

[1] K-G I 176f, II 221–223. Jannaris § 1827. Slotty *Konj. und Opt.* 42 § 90. Gild. *AJP* 3, 1882, 202–205. C. D. Chambers, *Cl. Rev.* 10, 1896. 150–153; 11, 1897, 109–111; Wharton ibid. 10, 1896, 239; R. Whitelaw ibid. 239–244; A. Y. Cambell ibid. 57, 1943, 58–61. Mayser II 1, 233. R. Ludwig, *D. prophet. Wort* 31, 1937, 272–279. Moulton Proleg. 187–192.

[2] Very rare indeed in Hell. Greek. I read the following books without finding a single οὐ μή among 1370 negatives: Aratus *Phaenomena* (iv–iii/B.C.), Callimachus *Hymns* and *Epigrams* (iii/B.C,). Lycophron *Alexandra* (iii/B.C.), Aelian *Letters of Farmers* ii–iii/A.D.), Philostratus *Love Letters* (ii–iii/A.D.), Alciphron *Fishermen, Farmers, Parasites, Courtesans* (iv/A.D.). But in *Didache* (ii/A.D.), there were 2 out of 124 negs., and in Ep. Clem. (i/A.D.) 1 out of 95 negs.; in Eps. Ign. 1 out of 217.

οὐ μὴ ἀδικηθῇ, 3¹², 7¹⁶, 15⁴ τίς οὐ μὴ φοβηθῇ; 18²¹⁻ ²³ etc. 1 Pt 2⁶ (Isa 28¹⁶).

2. *Present.* Classical: Xen. Plato, Soph. Is. Ptol. Pap: comparatively rare, e.g. Zen. P. 59610. 21 οὐ μὴ βούλωνται φυλάσσειν (iii/B.C.), Mich. Zen. 77. 13 οὐ μὴ ἕξηις αὐτῶι ἐγκαλέσαι (iii/B.C.). No true ex. occurs in NT, a vl. only Heb 13⁵ p⁴⁶. LXX, e.g. Ge 28¹⁵ Dt 15¹¹ AF, Isa 10²⁰ οὐκέτι μὴ πεποιθότες ὦσιν, 11⁹ οὐ μὴ κακοποιήσουσιν οὐδὲ μὴ δύνωνται, 16¹² οὐ μὴ δύνηται ἐξελέσθαι αὐτόν, 24²⁰ οὐ μὴ δύνηται ἀναστῆναι 36¹⁴ οὐ μὴ δύνηται ῥύσασθαι ὑμᾶς, Je 1⁹ 15²⁰ 29¹¹ 30¹² 43⁵.

3. *Future.* Class.: Aesch. Soph. Aristoph. Xen. Aeschin. NT:— Mt 15⁶, 26³⁵, 16²² οὐ μὴ ἔσται σοι τοῦτο, Lk 21³³ οἱ δὲ λόγοι μου οὐ μὴ παρελεύσονται apparently a conflation of Mt-Mk: Mt 24³⁵ οὐ μὴ παρέλθωσιν, Mk 13³¹ οὐ παρελεύσονται. (ACDᶜ harmonize Lk with Mt; such details make it likely that Luke knew Mt.¹), Lk 10¹⁹ οὐδὲν οὐ μὴ ὑμᾶς ἀδικήσει.

Jn 4¹⁴ οὐ μὴ διψήσει, 6³⁷ οὐ μὴ ἐκβαλῶ ἔξω, 10⁵ οὐ μὴ ἀκολουθήσουσιν (vl. aor. subj.), Mk 14³¹ οὐ μή σε ἀπαρνήσομαι, Jn 20²⁵ οὐ μὴ πιστεύσω, Ga 4³⁰ οὐ γὰρ μὴ κληρονομήσει (Ge 21¹⁰), Heb 10¹⁷, Rev 9⁶ οὐ μὴ εὑρήσουσιν, 18¹⁴ οὐκέτι οὐ μὴ εὑρήσουσιν Herm. M. IX 2; IX 5; S. I 5. Barn 11¹ πῶς τὸ βάπτισμα . . . οὐ μὴ προσδέξονται, 19⁷ μήποτε οὐ μὴ φοβηθήσονται (cp. Did. 4¹⁰). LXX:— e.g. Ge 21¹⁰ A οὐ γὰρ μὴ κληρονομήσει ὁ υἱός . . . (D om μή), Nu 35³³ A (rest οὐ), Dt 4³¹ οὐκ ἐνκαταλείψει σε οὐδὲ μὴ ἐκτρίψει σε, 28³⁰ AF οὐ μὴ τρυγήσεις αὐτόν (B om μή). Isa (12), Je α (9), β (4). Enoch 98¹² 99¹⁰.

(b) In Prohibitions ²

1. *Fut. Ind.* In class. Greek "interrogative": Soph. *Tr.* 978, Eurip. *Supp.* 1066, *Andr.* 757, *El.* 982, *Hipp.* 213, Aristoph. *Ach.* 166, *Nu.* 367, *V.* 397. Editors and MSS vary between fut. ind. and aor. subj. Probably both were allowed, but subj. may have been commoner in denials and fut. ind. in prohibitions. LXX: Le 11⁴³ οὐ μὴ κοιμηθήσεται ὁ μισθὸς τοῦ μισθωτοῦ . . . Dt 1⁴² οὐκ ἀναβήσεσθε οὐδὲ μὴ πολεμήσετε (F aor. subj.), 6¹⁴ AF οὐ μὴ πορεύσεσθε (B om μή), 7¹⁶ AF οὐ μὴ λατρεύσεις τοῖς θεοῖς (B om μή), 2 Km 24¹⁴ οὐ μὴ ἐμπέσω *let me not fall*, Je 11²¹ οὐ μὴ προφητεύσεις . . . (-σης A). Mt 16²² οὐ μὴ ἔσται σοι τοῦτο. Barn 10⁴ οὐ μή, φησίν, κολληθήσῃ οὐδὲ ὁμοιωθήσῃς, 5.

2. *Aor. Subj.* LXX:—Ge 3¹ οὐ μὴ φάγητε, ³ οὐδὲ μὴ ἅψησθε, 21¹⁶ οὐ μὴ ἴδω τὸν θάνατον τοῦ παιδίου μου, Ex (7), Le (1), Nu (3), Dt (13). NT:—Mt 13¹⁴ Ac 28²⁶ (LXX Isa 6⁹) Jn 13⁸ οὐ μὴ νίψῃς μου τοὺς πόδας. Ep. Barn. 10⁶ οὐ μὴ γένῃ παιδοφθόρος οὐδὲ ὁμοιωθήσῃ,⁷⸱ ⁸ οὐ μή, φησίν, γενηθῇς τοιοῦτος, 19² οὐ μὴ ἐγκαταλίπῃς ἐντολὰς κυρίου (cp. Did. 4¹³), ⁴ οὐ μή σου ὁ λόγος τοῦ θεοῦ ἐξέλθῃ ἐν ἀκαθαρσίᾳ τινῶν, ⁵ οὐ μὴ διψυχήσῃς, ⁵ οὐ μὴ ἄρῃς τὴν χεῖρά σου ἀπὸ τοῦ υἱοῦ σου, ⁶ οὐ μὴ γένῃ

---

¹ See *Studia Evangelica* (Texte und Untersuchungen, LXXIII) 1959, pp. 223–234.
² W. W. Goodwin, *Trans. American Philol. Assocn.* 1869–70, 52. Slotty op. cit. 43. Mayser II 1, 233 (very rare in papyri, and never prs. subj. or fut. ind.).

ἐπιθυμῶν τὰ τοῦ πλησίον σου . . . οὐ μὴ γένῃ πλεονέκτης,[7] οὐ μὴ ἐπιτάξῃς δούλῳ σου (contrast Did. 4[10]).

3. A Cautious Statement.

Μή with subjunctive to express a cautious statement in a main clause [1] is rare in NT: Mt 25[9] μήποτε οὐκ ἀρκέσῃ SALΣ (μήποτε οὐ μὴ ἀρκ. BWC; D ἀρκέσει), 1 Th 5[15] ὅρατε μή τις ἀποδοῖ ἀλλά . . . διώκετε, 2 Ti 2[25] μήποτε δῷ αὐτοῖς ὁ θεός perhaps God will give. Fairly frequ. in Platonic dialogue, e.g. it would be rude μὴ ἀγροικότερον ᾖ, it would not be right μὴ οὐ θεμιτὸν ᾖ. Only rarely in Ptol. pap. (e.g. P. Par. 32, 162 B.C.) μὴ οὐκ ἀποδώσοι. It is similar to the prospective or future subj. [2] without μή.

Foreign to class. Attic, this substitute for fut. ind. emerges in later Greek (K–G I 218). It was understandable that the like-soundings -ηι and -ει should be confused in fut. and aor., but ἀφεθῇ αὐτοὺς ἡ ἁμαρτία (LXX Isa 33[24]) and εἴπω σοι (for ἐρῶ σοι)[3] go beyond that. So also Ptol. pap. UPZ 31, 7 (162 B.C.) εὐδοκῶ . . . ἐπέλθω. Exx. from post-Christian pap. in Moulton Einl. 292, 2. LXX Isa 10[16] S ἀποστείλῃ. Hom. Clem. 11[3] δυνηθῇ.

4. Deliberative Subjunctive [4].

The dubitative subj., the interrogative form of the hortatory, occurs in class. Greek (K-G. I 174, 233; Slotty 51) sometimes in 3rd p., but generally 1st p., negatived by μή and introduced immediately by βούλει, βούλεσθε, etc. Incidentally the fut. ind. (see above p. 86) is found sometimes in class. Greek (Plato Crito 50B) and NT: Lk 16[11f] τίς πιστεύσει; τίς δώσει; Mt 16[26] τί δώσει (for Mk 8[37] τί δοῖ, which p[45] ACDW harm. with Mt), Lk 22[49] εἰ πατάξομεν (-ωμεν GH), Mk 6[37] ἀγοράσωμεν . . . καὶ δώσομεν p[45] AB (-σωμεν SD fam[13] 28 565; δῶμεν WΘ fam[1]), Ro 3[5] 4[1] etc. τί ἐροῦμεν. Sometimes even pres. ind. in NT: Jn 11[47] Herm. S. IX 9, 1 τί ποιοῦμεν, 1 Jn 3[17] μένει (or μενεῖ fut.). Plato Symp. 214A πῶς ποιοῦμεν.

---

[1] K-G I 224, 7. Stahl 366, 3. Gild. I § 385. Moulton Einl. 303ff. Slotty §§ 84–86, 318, 331. Schmid Attic. III 90. Mayser I 1, 234.
[2] Schwyzer II 313f. Slotty § 130. Mayser II 1, 234–5. Moulton Einl. 292, 2. Reinhold 101–103. Sophocles Lexicon p. 45.
[3] P. Würthle, Die Monodie des Michael Psellos auf den Einsturz der Hagia Sophia, 1917, 22f.; Mayser II 1, 235.
[4] Mayser II 1, 235. Schwyzer II 318. A. W. McWhorter, "A Study of the so-called Deliberative Type of Question (τι ποιήσω;)" Trans. and Proc., Amer. Philol. Association, 41, 1910, 157ff.

Subjunctive: Mt 6²⁵ φάγητε, etc. 23³³ πῶς φύγητε: 26⁵⁴ πῶς ... πληρωθῶσιν; Mk 12¹⁴ δῶμεν ἢ μὴ δῶμεν; Lk 11⁵ ἕξει ... πορεύσεται ... καὶ εἴπῃ (AD a fut.), ⁷ κἀκεῖνος εἴπῃ (D ἐρεῖ), 23³¹ ἐν τῷ ξηρῷ τί γένηται (DK fut.); γένηται also in Epict. IV 1, 97;100. Ro 10¹⁴ᶠ ἐπικαλέσωνται (p⁴⁶ KLP -σονται), πιστεύσωσιν (vl. -σουσιν), ἀκούσωσιν SᶜA²B (L -σουσιν, S*D -σονται, p⁴⁶ -σωνται), κηρύξωσιν (vl. -ουσιν), Hom. Clem. 19² πῶς ... στήκῃ (from Mt 12²⁶), Herm. S. V 7, 3 πῶς σωθῇ A (P. Mich. -θήσεται), Pass. Perp. et Felic. 1¹ διὰ τί μὴ ... γραφῇ παραδοθῇ LXX 2 Km 23³ πῶς κραταιώσητε. In Ptol. pap. only in dependent clauses, e.g. οὐκ εἴχομεν ὅθεν αὐτῶι δῶμεν, (dates): 254 247 248 iiim (3) 257; once infin. (251); see Mayser II 1, 235f. Introduced by θέλεις, βούλεσθε etc. as in class. Greek (K-G I 221f): Mt 13²⁸ Lk 9⁵⁴ 18⁴¹ Jn 18³⁹.

(B) SUBORDINATE CLAUSES.

1. Fearing.

The subj. appears as in class. Greek after expressions of anxiety with μή or μήποτε or μήπως, e.g. P. Magd. 9, 3 (iii/B.C.) φοβουμένη μὴ συμπέσηι, MGr φοβοῦμαι μήπως. It occurs after φοβοῦμαι in Luke, Paul and Heb. as a semi-literary feature, rather than popular. Pres. subj.:—Heb 4¹ μήποτε δοκῇ, 12¹⁵ μή τις ἐνοχλῇ (after ἐπισκοπέω). Fut. ind.:— Ro 11²⁰ᶠ φοβοῦ ... μήπως οὐδὲ σοῦ φείσεται p⁴⁶ DFG (φείσηται in minusc. only; SABCP om μήπως). Aor. subj.:— Ac 23¹⁰ φ. (or εὐλαβηθείς HLP) μὴ διασπασθῇ, 27¹⁷· ²⁹ μήπως. 2 Co 11³ 12²⁰. Past indic.:—Ga 4¹¹ μήπως εἰκῇ κεκοπίακα (p⁴⁶ 1739 ἐκοπίασα).

After other words than φοβοῦμαι:—Lk 12⁵⁸ δὸς ἐργασίαν ... μήποτε κατασύρῃ σε ... καὶ παραδώσει (note change to fut. ind.), 14⁸ᶠ do not sit ... μήποτε ... ἢ κεκλημένος (D ἥξει), Ac 5³⁹ we cannot kill them μήποτε καὶ θεομάχοι εὑρεθῆτε. 2 Ti 2²⁵. Perhaps Mt 25⁹ go and buy ... μήποτε ... PSI V 495, 8 εὐλαβεῖσθε μήποτε (subj.?) (258 B.C.). P. Tebt. 43, 22 προορώμενοι μήποτε ... συκοφαντηθῶμεν (118 B.C.). P. Par. 45 προσέχων μὴ εὕρῃ (153 B.C.). Μή alone (Lat. ne): Mk 13³⁶ Col 2⁸ μή τις ἔσται (final?). Μήπως 2 Co 9⁴. Like cl. Greek, NT Greek distinguished between fear of an uncertain thing in the future (subj.) and fear regarding a present inevitable reality (indic.). Note the difference even in the same verse: Ga 2² I laid before them the Gospel μήπως εἰς κενὸν τρέχω ἢ ἔδραμον. 1 Th 3⁵ I have sent ... μήπως ἐπείρασεν ὑμᾶς ὁ πειράζων καὶ εἰς κενὸν γένηται ὁ κόπος ἡμῶν.

2. Purpose

(a) Use of ἵνα, ἵνα μή, and μή [1].

The purpose clause has increased its modes of expression in
Hell. Greek. Here we are simply concerned with ἵνα. Its
mood was always subjunctive in class. Greek (or oblique
optative), and it is generally so in the Koine, even after a secondary tense. The alleged opt. δῴη Eph 1[17] is probably a subj.
Hell. Greek also has fut. ind., and we have this in NT, especially
in Rev and Paul, quite profusely but always with evidence that
scribes have corrected to aor. subj. The addition of κἄν in two
instances (Mk 6[56] Ac 5[15]) supplies a modifying or conditional
element: so that even if.

Fut. indic.

Mt 12[10] ἵνα κατηγορήσουσιν SWX (rest corr. to -σωσιν). Lk 14[10]
ἵνα . . . ἐρεῖ (ADW corr. to εἴπῃ), 20[10] ἵνα δώσουσιν (CDW δῶσιν).
Jn 7[3] ἵνα θεωρήσουσιν (B[3] X -σῶσιν). 17[2] ἵνα δώσει (var. corr.: δώσῃ
S[c]CG; δώσω S*; δῷς W; ἔχῃ D). Ac 5[15], 21[24] ἵνα ξυρήσονται SB*D*E.
1 Co 9[15] ἵνα τις κενώσει, [18] ἵνα θήσω, [21], 13[3] ἵνα καυθήσομαι (CK -σωμαι;
p[46] SAB καυχήσωμαι), Ga 2[4] ἵνα καταδουλώσουσιν SAB* CDE (vl. subj.),
Eph 6[3], Ph 2[11] ἵνα κάμψῃ . . . ἐξομολογήσονται (ACDG -σεται). 1 Th 5[10]
ἵνα ζήσομεν A (D*E corr. to ζῶμεν; S to ζήσωμεν). 1 Pt 3[1] ἵνα . . .
κερδηθήσονται. Rev 3[9] ἵνα ἥξουσιν (B -ωσιν) καὶ προσκυνήσουσιν
(B -σωσιν), 6[4] ἵνα σφάξουσιν, [11] ἵνα ἀναπαύσονται AP 046 1 (SC -σωνται),
8[3] ἵνα δώσει (BP -σῃ), 9[4] ἵνα ἀδικήσουσιν (SP 046 1 -σωσιν), [5] ἵνα
βασανισθησονται (vl -σθῶσιν), 9[20] 13[12] ἵνα (μή) προσκυνήσουσιν (vl
-σῶσιν), 14[13] ἵνα ἀναπαήσονται (P -παυσῶνται) (ὅτι p[47]), 13[16] ἵνα
δώσει ΔΩΣ 1, 22[14] ἵνα ἔσται . . . καὶ εἰσέλθωσιν (causal ἵνα, like 14[13]?).
On causal ἵνα see below p. 102. There are instances also where, after ἵνα,
ὅπως, or μή, with subj., there follows καί with fut. ind. to indicate further
result: Mt 5[25], 13[15] OT, 20[28] D μήποτε . . . ἐπέλθῃ . . . καὶ καταισχυνθήσῃ,
Mk 5[23] A, Lk 22[30] (many vll), 12[58], Jn 12[40] OT, 15[8] ἵνα καρπὸν . . .
φέρητε καὶ γενήσεσθε (BDL corr. to γένησθε), Ac 21[24] (see above), Ro 3[4]
OT SADE, Eph 6[3] OT, Barn 4[3] S, Herm. M. VI 2[10]; S. IX 7[6], 28[5],
LXX Je 29[11] DaSu[28]. (Other exx. in Radermacher[2] p. 216).

Pres. ind.

Jn 5[20] ἵνα θαυμάζετε SL, 17[24] ἵνα θεωροῦσιν W (rest subj.),
Ga 6[12] ἵνα . . . μὴ διώκονται p[46] ACGKL (subj. BSD), Eph 1[18] FG ἵνα

---

[1] K-G II § 553. Mayser II 1, 240ff. Schwyzer II 671ff. W. B.
Curry, *The Nature and Use of the ἵνα-clause in the NT* (Diss. of S-W Bapt.
Sem., 1949). E. Stauffer in Kittel WB III, 327ff (NT in general); in
Theol. Stud. u. Krit. 102, 1930, 232–257 (purpose-ἵνα in Paul). H. Diel,
De enuntiatis finalibus apud Graecarum rerum scriptoribus posterioris aetatis,
Munich 1895.

οἴδατε, Ti 2⁴ ἵνα σωφρονίζουσιν S*AGF, Rev 16¹⁵ ἵνα βλέπουσιν p⁴⁷,
Ign Eph 4² ἵνα . . . ᾄδετε . . . μετέχετε. Very rare in Ptol. pap.: P. Par.
23, 23 εἵνα διακονεῖ (165 B.C.), Or. gr. 139, 21 ἵνα . . . ὑπάρχει (146–
116 B.C.); even these are doubtfully indicative and may be bad spelling
for subj. (Mayser II 1, 244); later BU IV 1081³ (ii–iii/A.D.) ἐχάρην ἵνα
σε ἀσπάζομαι (causal ἵνα?).

Pres. subj.

Mt none.—Mk 3⁹. ¹⁴. ¹⁴ 4¹² 6⁴¹ 8⁶.—Lk 5¹⁴ 8¹⁶ 9⁴⁰ aor.? 11³³
18⁵. ¹⁵ 22³⁰.—Jn 3¹⁵. ¹⁶ 4³⁶ 5²⁰. ²³. ⁴⁰ 6²⁸. ³⁸ (8⁶) 9³⁹ 10¹⁰. ³⁸ 13¹⁵. ¹⁹
14³. ¹⁶ 15². ¹¹. ¹⁶ 16⁴. ²⁴ ³³ 17¹¹. ¹³. ¹⁹. ²². ²³. ²³. ²⁴. ²⁶ 20³¹.—Ac 8¹⁹ 24⁴.—
Ro 9¹¹ 11²⁵ 15⁴. ⁶. ²⁰.—1 Co 1²⁷. ²⁷ 5⁷ 7³⁴ 14³¹ 15²⁸.—2 Co 1⁹. ¹⁷ 4⁷ 5¹². ¹⁵
9³. ⁸ 12⁷ 13⁷.—Ga 1¹⁶ 4¹⁷ 6¹².—Eph 4¹⁴. ²⁸ 5²⁷.—Ph 1¹⁰. ²⁶. ²⁷ 2¹⁹.—
Col 2⁴ 3²¹.—1 Th 4¹². ¹³.—1 Ti 2² 4¹⁵ 5⁷. ²⁰ 6¹.—2 Ti 3¹⁷.—Ti 1⁹. ¹³
2⁴. ⁵. ¹⁰ 3¹³. ¹⁴.—Heb 5¹ 6¹⁸ 9²⁵ 13¹⁷.—Jas 1⁴.—1 Pt 4¹¹.—1 Jn 1³. ⁴
2¹ 4¹⁷.—Phm ¹³. ¹⁴. ¹⁵.—Rev 3¹⁸ 7¹ 11⁶ 12¹⁴ 16¹⁵ (Total: = 111).

LXX Ge 6¹⁹ 21³⁰ 42² 43⁸.—Ex 11⁹ 20²⁰ 26¹³ 27²⁰ 36²⁹ 38¹⁶. ²⁷.—
Dt 5¹⁶. ²⁹ 10¹³ 16²⁰ 29⁹ 30⁶.—Jos 1⁷ 3⁴ 4⁶. ²⁴ 22²⁵. ²⁷ 23⁶.—Jg 5¹⁵ A.—
2 Esd 6¹⁰ 7²⁵.—To 14⁹ BᵇA.—Est 4¹⁷.—Pr 3⁶. ²³ 5⁹ 6⁵. ²² 26⁵ 27¹¹. ²⁶. ²⁶.
—Wi 9² 12²² 13⁹ 14¹⁷ 16³.—Si 8⁴. ¹⁵ 17⁹ 22¹³ 30²⁸. ³⁶ 35².—Isa 40²⁰
44¹⁵.—Je 39¹⁴.—Ezk 14¹¹.—1 Mac 12³⁶.—2 Mac 1¹⁸ 6¹⁵ 11³⁶.—3 Mac
2³⁰.—Jb 2⁸ 33³⁰ (Total:—62). Ptol. pap. (dates): 223 251 241 iii 255
iii 240 iii 258 241 iii 250 223 261 250 222 255 241 iii 241 258 iii 240 260
253 251 258 261 248; 153 99 163 154 113 57 165 118 ii 161 131 110 103
152 95 168 5 2 166 153 164 118 114 ii 168 115 76 117 (Total:—57).

Aor. Subj.

Mt 1²² 2¹⁵ 4¹⁴ 5²⁹. ³⁰ 7¹ 9⁶ 12¹⁰ (fut. ind.) ¹⁷ 14¹⁵ 17²⁷ 18¹⁶ 19¹³. ¹⁶
21⁴ 23²⁶ 26⁵. ⁵⁶ 27²⁶.—Mk 1³⁸ 2¹⁰ 3². ¹⁰ 4¹² (see below) ²¹. ²² 5¹². ²³
6³⁶. ⁵⁶ (ἵνα κἄν) 7⁹ 9²² 10¹³. ¹⁷ 11²⁵ 12². ¹³. ¹⁵ 14⁴⁹ 15¹¹. ¹⁵. ²⁰. ³² 16¹.—
Lk 1⁴ 5²⁴ 6⁷. ³⁴ 8¹² 9¹² 11⁵⁰. ⁵⁴ 12³⁶ 14²³. ²⁹ 15²⁹ 16⁴. ⁹. ²⁴. ²⁸ 19⁴. ¹⁵
20¹⁰. ¹⁴. ²⁰ 22⁸.—Ac 2²⁵ 4¹⁷ 5¹⁵ ἵνα . . . κἄν 9²¹ 16³⁰ 22⁵. ²⁴ 23²⁴.—Jn
1⁷. ⁸. ¹⁹. ²². ³¹ 3¹⁷. ²¹ 4⁸ 5³⁴. ³⁶ 6⁵. ¹⁵. ³⁰. ⁵⁰ 7³² 8⁵⁹ 9³⁶ 10¹⁰. ¹⁷. ³¹. ³⁸
11⁴. ¹¹. ¹⁵. ¹⁶. ¹⁹. ³¹. ⁴². ⁵². ⁵⁵ 12⁹. ²⁰. ³⁶. ³⁸. ⁴⁷. ⁴⁷ 14¹³. ²⁹. ³¹ 15¹⁶ 17¹. ¹²
18⁹. ²⁸. ³²· ³⁷ 19⁴. ¹⁶. ²⁴. ²⁸; negative: 3¹⁶. ²⁰ 4¹⁵ 5¹⁴ 6¹². ⁵⁰ 7²³
12³⁵. ⁴⁰. ⁴². ⁴⁶ 16¹ 18²⁸. ³⁶ 19³¹.—Ro 1¹¹. ¹³ 3⁸ 5²⁰. ²¹ 6¹. ⁴. ⁶ 7⁴. ¹³ 8⁴. ¹⁷
11¹¹. ¹⁹. ³¹. ³² 14⁹ 15¹⁶.—1 Co 1²⁸ 2¹² 3¹⁸ 4⁶. ⁸ 5² (imperatival?) 5 7⁵. ³⁵
9¹⁵. ¹⁹. ²⁰. ²⁰. ²². ²³. ²⁴. ²⁵ 10³³ 11¹⁹ 14⁵. ¹⁹ 16⁶. ¹¹; neg.: 1¹⁵. ¹⁷ 8¹³ 9¹² 11³².—
2 Co 1¹¹. ¹⁵ 2⁴. ⁹ 4¹⁰. ¹¹. ¹⁵ 5⁴. ¹⁰. ²¹ 7⁹ 8⁹. ¹⁴ 11⁷. ¹². ¹⁶. ¹⁶ 12⁹ 13⁷; neg.:
2³. ⁵. ¹¹ 6³ 9³. ⁴ 10⁹ 13¹⁰.—Ga 2⁵. ⁹. ¹⁶. ¹⁹ 3¹⁴. ²². ²⁴ 4⁵ 6¹³.—Eph 2⁷. ¹⁰. ¹⁵
3¹⁰. ¹⁸. ¹⁹ 4¹⁰. ²⁹ 5²⁶. ²⁷ 6³. ¹³. ²²; neg.: 2⁹.—Col 1¹⁸. ²⁸ 2² 4⁴. ⁸.—Ph
2¹⁰. ¹⁵. ²⁸. ³⁰ 3⁸; neg.: 2²⁷.—1 Th 2¹⁶ 5¹⁰.—2 Th 2¹² 3⁹. ¹⁴.—1 Ti 1¹⁶. ²⁰
3¹⁵ 5¹⁶ 6¹⁹.—2 Ti 1⁴ 2⁴. ¹⁰ 4¹⁷.—Ti 1⁵ 2⁸. ¹⁴ 3⁷; neg.: 1 Ti 3⁶. ⁷.—Heb
2¹⁴. ¹⁷ 4¹⁶ 10⁹. ³⁶ 11³⁵ 12²⁷ 13¹². ¹⁹ neg.: 3¹³ 4¹¹ 6¹² 11²⁸. ⁴⁰ 12³. ¹³.—
Jas 5⁹. ¹² 4³.—1 Pt 1⁷ 2². ¹². ²¹. ²⁴ 3¹. ⁹. ¹⁶. ¹⁸ 4⁶. ¹³ 5⁶.—2 Pt 1⁴.— 1 Jn
2²⁸ 3¹. ⁵. ⁸ 4⁹ 5¹³.—Rev 2¹⁰ 3¹¹. ¹⁸ 6² 8¹² 9¹⁵ 12⁴. ⁶. ¹⁵ 13¹⁵ 16¹² 19¹⁵. ¹⁸
21¹⁵; neg.: 3¹⁸ 8¹² 18⁴ 20³. (Total:—322).

LXX Ge 26, Ex 37, Le 7, Nu 4, Dt 43, Jos 4, Jg Ru 3, Km 8, Chr 3, 1 Esd 1, 2 Esd-Ne 2. To S 2, To B 5, Jdt 6, Est 1, Ps 6, Pr 35, Eccl. 5, Wi 23, Si 25, Jb 16, Isa 26, Je 9, Ba 2, La 1, Ezk 3, DaO′ 7, Θ 4, 1 Mac 3, 2 Mac 3, 3 Mac 1, 4 Mac 2. (Total:—112).

It is difficult to decide between telic and ecbatic force for ἵνα in the formula with πληρόω, ἀναπληρόω, τελειόω. It is probably telic, since ὅπως is occasionally substituted for ἵνα in the formula, and especially in view of the Jewish theology probably lying behind it. But in Lk 9⁴⁵ ἵνα μὴ αἴσθωνται αὐτό is probably consecutive rather than final. In Col 2⁴ ἵνα may be final: *I say this in order that* . . . , but equally possible is an imperatival sense: *Let no one* . . . . 2 Co 1¹⁷ is similarly controversial. The ἵνα in Jn 9² (τίς ἥμαρτεν . . . , ἵνα) is consecutive, but the weak variant ὅτι indicates that scribes took it for causal ἵνα. It is like Epict. III 1, 12 τί εἶδεν ἐν ἐμοὶ ὁ Ἐπίκτητος, ἵνα . . . περιίδῃ; So also the ἵνα in Mk 15³² καταβάτω ἵνα ἴδωμεν καὶ πιστεύσωμεν is obviously consecutive. For instances of ecbatic ἵνα elsewhere, see Jannaris §§ 1758, 1951; Radermacher² 191f.

The question of causal sense for some instances of ἵνα in NT has also been raised [1]. In Rev 22¹⁴ it is claimed that μακάριοι . . . ἵνα is parallel with μακάριοι ὅτι in Mt 5³ᶠᶠ; but the possibility of telic force cannot be ruled out. In Rev 14¹³ the question of imperatival ἵνα arises: *They shall rest!* The ἵνα of Mk 4¹² = Lk 8¹⁰ is transformed into causal ὅτι in the Mt-parallel, but this would not prove identity of meaning. In 1 Pt 4⁶ (ἵνα κριθῶσιν . . . καὶ ζῶσιν) it would be possible to assume that ἵνα is causal and that a second ἵνα (telic) has fallen out before ζῶσιν— or that we are to take ἵνα first as causal and then as telic. The causal as well as final use of ἵνα was acknowledged by the grammarian Apollonius Dyscolus (ii/A.D.) and no doubt this was so in NT. The causal makes excellent sense in Jn 8⁵⁶ (Abraham rejoiced *because* . . .). The real crux is Mk 4¹². The consecutive of NEB is not so good as final (OT background) or causal (good precedent and excellent sense). Lohmeyer in

---

[1] On causal ἵνα see Jannaris § 1714; Pernot *Études* 90–95; H. Windsich, " Die Verstockungsidee in Mk 4.12 und das kausale ἵνα der späteren Koine," in *ZNW* 26, 1927, 203ff; A. T. Robertson, " The Causal Use of ἵνα," *Studies in Early Christianity* 1927, 49ff; C. H. Dodd, in *JThS* 23, 1922, 62f; U. Holzmeister, in *Biblica* 17, 1936, 512ff; LS s.v.; Bauer s.v. (II2).

his commentary (Göttingen 1937, in loc) states truly " ἵνα bedeutet in der Koine . . . auch, wenngleich seltener, ' weil ' ".

Ἵνα instead of almost any infinitive [1], for epexegetic infinitive, in demands after verbs of willing and the like, and also in an ecbatic sense, marks the beginning of a process which ended in the disappearance of the infinitive and substitution of νά with subj. in MGr.

Subjunctive:

Mt 4³ εἰπὲ ἵνα . . . γένωνται, 16²⁰ ἐπετίμησεν B*D (διεστείλατο SCΘ) ἵνα . . . εἴπωσιν.—Mk 5¹⁰ παρεκάλει . . . ἵνα μὴ . . . ἀποστείλῃ, 3⁹ εἶπεν . . . ἵνα . . . προσκαρτερῇ. 6²⁵ θέλω ἵνα . . . δῷς, 9³⁰ ἤθελεν ἵνα τις γνοῖ, 10³⁵ θέλομεν ἵνα . . . ποιήσῃς, ⁵¹. Mk. command: 3⁹. ¹² 5⁴³ 6⁸. ¹² 7³⁶ 8³⁰ 9⁹ 10⁴⁸ 12¹⁹ 13³⁴ 15²¹; grant 10³⁷ 11¹⁶. ²⁸; beseech 5¹⁰. ¹⁸ 6⁵⁶ 7²⁶. ³² 8²² 9¹⁸ 14³⁵. ³⁸ 13¹⁸.—Mt 7¹² θέλητε ἵνα ποιῶσιν, 18¹⁴ θέλημα . . . ἵνα ἀπόληται, 20²¹ εἰπὲ ἵνα καθίσωσιν, ³¹ ἐπετίμησεν . . . ἵνα σιωπήσωσιν, 27³² ἠγγάρευσαν ἵνα ἄρῃ, 28¹⁰ ἀπαγγείλατε . . . ἵνα ἀπέλθωσιν, 12¹⁶ ἐπετίμησεν . . . ἵνα μὴ . . . ποιήσωσιν, 14³⁶ παρεκάλουν . . . ἵνα aor. subj., 24²⁰ 26⁴¹ προσεύχεσθε ∴. . ἵνα aor. subj., 27²⁰ ἔπεισαν . . . ἵνα aor. subj.—Lk 6³¹ θέλετε ἵνα ποιῶσιν, 14³ *whence is this to me* ἵνα ἔλθῃ; command: 4³ εἰπὲ . . . ἵνα, 10⁴⁰ εἰπὸν ἵνα, 18³⁹ ἐπετίμων . . . ἵνκ 20²⁸ ἔγραψεν . . . ἵνα; request: 7³⁶ ἠρώτα . . . ἵνα, 8³² παρεκάλεσαν . . . ἵνα, 8³¹ παρεκάλουν . . . ἵνα, 9⁴⁰ ἐδεήθην . . . ἵνα, 16²⁷ ἐρωτῶ . . . ἵνα, 21³⁶ δεόμενοι . . . ἵνα, 22³² ἐδεήθην . . . ἵνα, ⁴⁶ προσεύχεσθε . . . ἵνα; completing verbal idea 7⁶ ἱκανός . . . ἵνα, 17² *better for him* ἵνα; Ac. command: 16³⁶ ἀπέσταλκαν ∴. . ἵνα ἀπολυθῆτε, 17¹⁵ λαβόντες ἐντολὴν . . . ἵνα, 19⁴ λέγων . . . ἵνα, plot: 27⁴² βουλὴ ἐγένετο ἵνα. Jn, will: 6⁴⁰ θ·λημα . . . ἵνα . . . ἔχῃ, 17²⁴ θέλω ἵνα . . . ὦσιν, command: 11⁵⁷ δεδώκεισαν . . . ἐντολὰς ἵνα, 13²⁹, ³⁴ ἐντολὴν καινὴν δίδωμι ἵνα, 15¹² ἡ ἐντολὴ ἡ ἐμὴ ἵνα, ¹⁷ ἐντέλλομαι . . . ἵνα, 17⁴ τὸ ἔργον . . . ὃ δέδωκάς μοι ἵνκ ποιήσω, beseech: 4⁴⁷ ἠρώτα ἵνα καταβῇ, 17¹⁵. ²¹ ἐρωτῶ ἵνα, 19³¹ ἠρώτησαν ἵνα, agree: 9²² συνετέθειντο . . . ἵνα, 11⁵³ 12¹⁰ ἐβουλεύσαντο ἵνα, allow: 12⁷ ἄφες . . . ἵνα, epexegetic: 6²⁹ τοῦτό ἐστιν τὸ ἔργον τ. θεοῦ ἵνα πιστεύητε, 8⁵⁶, 12²³ 13¹ 16². ³² ἡ ὥρα ἵνα, 15⁸ ἐν τούτῳ ἐδοξάσθη . . . ἵνα καρπὸν πολὺν φέρητε, ¹³ *greater love* . . . ἵνα (= *i.e.*), 17³ *this is eternal life* ἵνα, 18³⁹ *there is a custom* ἵνα; consecutive: 9² τίς ἥμαρτεν . . . ἵνα τυφλὸς γεννηθῇ; completing verbal action 1²⁷ ἄξιος ἵνα, 2²⁵ χρείαν εἶχεν ἵνα, 4³⁴ ἐμὸν βρῶμά ἐστιν ἵνα, 5⁷ ἄνθρωπον οὐκ ἔχω ἵνα, 6⁷ οὐκ ἀρκοῦσιν αὐτοῖς ἵνα ἔκαστος βραχὺ λάβῃ, 11⁵⁰ 16⁷ συμφέρει ὑμῖν ἵνα, 13² *put it in the heart* ἵνα, 16³⁰ οὐ χρείαν ἔχεις ἵνα; *after* ποιέω 11³⁷.—Ro command 16²; pray 15³¹. ³².—1 Co 16¹⁰ βλέπετε ἵνα; seek 14¹. ¹²; say 7²⁹; epex. 4³; a small thing ἵνα 9¹⁸ (fut. ind.); beseech 1¹⁰ 14¹³ 16¹². ¹⁶; it is required 4²; 14⁵ θέλω . . . λαλεῖν . . . ἵνα προφητεύητε,

---

[1] Even subject infinitive, e.g. Jn 16⁷ συμφέρει ὑμῖν ἵνα ἐγὼ ἀπέλθω, and 1 Co 9¹⁸.

16¹² θέλημα ἵνα νῦν ἔλθῃ.—2 Co beseech 12⁸ παρεκάλεσα ἵνα; exhort 8⁶ 9⁵.—Ga consecutive 5¹⁷.—Eph pray 1¹⁷ 3¹⁶ 6¹⁹. ²⁰ δεήσει ἵνα.—Ph pray 1⁹ epex. 2² *namely* ἵνα.—Col pray 1⁹ αἰτούμενοι ἵνα 4³.¹²; βλέπε ἵνα 4¹⁷; after ποιέω 4¹⁶.—Th beseech 1 Th 4¹. ¹ 2 Th 3¹² παρακαλέομαι; pray 2 Th 1¹¹ 3¹. ²; consec. 1 Th 5⁴.—1 Ti exhort 1³. ¹⁸ 5²¹ Ti 2¹² 3⁸.— 2 Pt 3¹⁷ φυλάσσομαι.—Joh epp. command 1 Jn 3²³ 4²¹ 5¹⁶ 2 Jn ⁵. ⁶; epex. 1 Jn 1⁹ (cp. Heb 6¹⁰) faithful and just ἵνα; 2²⁷ χρείαν ἔχω ἵνα, 3¹¹ the message ἵνα, 5³ love of God ἵνα; 2 Jn ⁶ love ἵνα; 3 Jn⁴ joy ἵνα; 2 Jn⁸ βλέπετε ἵνα.—Rev command 6¹¹ 9⁴ ἐρρέθη ἵνα (fut. ind.); 9⁵ ἐδόθη αὐταῖς ... ἵνα 19⁸; 14¹³ ναὶ λέγει τὸ πνεῦμα ἵνα (fut. ind.); completing verbal action 2²¹ χρόνος ἵνα; 8⁶ prepare ἵνα; 21²³ οὐ χρείαν ἔχει ... ἵνα; epex. (or consec?) 9²⁰ repented ἵνα (fut. ind.); 13¹³ ἵνα = *i.e.*; after ποιέω (cp. Mt 24²⁴ ὥστε) 3⁹ 13¹² (fut. ind.) ¹⁵. ¹⁶. ¹⁷.

LXX: Ge 22¹⁴ consec., 24³ ἐξόρκισε σε κύριον ... ἵνα μὴ λάβῃς.—Ex 6¹¹ λαλέω.—Dt command 6² ὅσα ἐνετείλατο ἵνα φοβῆσθε κύριον; swear 4²¹.— 3 Km 6² (5¹⁷) command ἐνετείλατο ἵνα Bᵃᵇ.—1 Ch 21¹⁸ command εἰπεῖν ... ἵνα.—2 Ch 18¹⁵ adjure ὁρκίζω σε ἵνα μὴ λαλήσῃς (A fut. ind.).— 1 Esd command 4⁴⁷ ἔγραψεν ... ἵνα προπέμψωσιν, ⁵⁰ ἔγραψεν ... ἵνα ... ἀφίουσι (B pres. ind., A pres. subj.), 6³¹ προστάξαι ἵνα, 8¹⁹ προσέταξα ... ἵνα ... διδῶσιν pr. ind.; beseech 4⁴⁶ δέομαι ... ἵνα ποιήσῃς τὴν εὐχήν; care 6²⁷ ἀτενίσαι ἵνα συνποιῶσιν.—Ne 7⁶⁵ εἶπεν ... ἵνα μὴ φάγωσιν.— To S command 14⁹ ἐνυποταγήσεται ... ἵνα ὦσιν ...; beseech 6¹⁸ δεήθητε ... ἵνα ἔλεος γένηται (not B); completing verbal idea 3¹⁵ *he has no other child* ἵνα κληρονομήσῃ αὐτόν (not B), 5⁷ χρείαν ... ἔχω ἵνα βαδίσῃς (not B), ⁹ πιστὸς ... ἵνα πορευθῇ μετὰ σοῦ (B τοῦ and inf.), 6¹⁵ *they have no other son* ἵνα θάψῃ αὐτούς (not B).—To B beseech 8⁴ προσευξώμεθα ἵνα ἡμᾶς ἐλεήσῃ ὁ κύριος (S ὅπως).—Jdt 7²⁸ μαρτυρόμεθα ὑμῖν ... ἵνα μὴ ποιήσῃ.—Mal 1⁹ beseech δεήθητε ... ἵνα ἐλεήσῃ ὑμᾶς Sᶜᵃ.—Ps allow 38¹⁴ ἄνες μοι ἵνα ἀναψύξω.—Ca beseech 5¹ αἰτεῖται ... ἵνα καταβῇ S.—Wi consec. 14⁴.—Si beseech 37¹⁵ δεήθητι ... ἵνα εὐθύνῃ, 38¹⁴ δεηθήσονται ἵνα εὐοδώσῃ; promise 44¹⁸ διαθῆκαι αἰῶνος ἐτέθεσαν ... ἵνα μὴ ἐξαλειφθῇ, 45²⁴ ἐστάθη ... διαθήκη ... ἵνα ... ᾖ.—Isa command 36¹²; βουλεύομαι 42²¹.—Ba pray 1¹¹ προσεύξασθαι ... ἵνα ὦσιν.—Ezk after ποιέω 36²⁷ ἵνα ... πορεύησθε.—Da Ο' command 3¹⁰ προσέταξας καὶ ἔκρινας ἵνα πᾶς ... προσκυνήσῃ (Th. μὴ and aor. subj.), 3⁹⁶ κρίνω ἵνα ... διαμελισθήσεται fut. ind. (no ἵνα in Th), 6¹² οὐχ ὁρισμὸν ὡρίσω ἵνα πᾶς ἄνθρωπος μὴ εὔξηται εὐχήν (Th ὅπως), adjure 6¹² ὁρκίζομέν σε ... ἵνα μὴ ἀλλιώσῃς ... καὶ ... ἐλαττώσῃς (Th om); fear 1¹⁰ ἵνα μὴ ἴδῃ (Th μήποτε); request 1⁸ ἠξίωσεν ... ἵνα μὴ συμμολυνθῇ (Th ὡς οὐ μή), 2¹⁶ ἠξίωσεν ἵνα δοθῇ (Th ὅπως), 2⁴⁹ ἠξίωσεν ... κατασταθῶσιν (co-ord. in Th).—Da Θ be ready 3¹⁵ (LXX infin).—Jb command 37⁶ A.—1 Mac command 4⁵⁹ ἔστησεν ... ἵνα ἄγωνται, 11⁴¹ ἀπέστειλεν ... ἵνα ἐκβάλῃ; write 15¹⁹ γράψαι ... ἵνα μὴ συμμαχῶσιν.—2 Mac command 2² ἐνετείλατο ... ἵνα μὴ ἐπιλάθωνται; beseech 2⁸ ἠξίωσεν ἵνα καταγιασθῇ.—4 Mac beseech 16¹² οὐδ' ἵνα μὴ ἀποθάνωσιν ἐπέτρεπεν ....

In the Greek Bible the books which use ἵνα in a non-final sense at least equally as often as in a final sense are: Ch, 1 Esd, To S, Dan Ο', 1 Mac, Mt, Mk.

As to order of clauses, the ἵνα-clause generally follows the governing main clause, except where a second clause depends on the main verb; the exceptions in pre-Christian papyri are (dates): iii 244 iii 164 152 (all pre-positive).

(b) Use of ὅπως (μή), ὡς, etc.[1]

In NT ὅπως is rather strictly confined to final sentences and to its use after *beseech* (e.g. παρακαλέω). In class. Attic it was also used with fut. ind. after *strive, take care*, but that is restricted to ἵνα in NT. In both NT and Koine[2] ἵνα and ὅπως alternate for the sake of variety: Jn 11[57], 1 Co 1[29] ἵνα ... καταργήσῃ, ὅπως μὴ καυχήσηται 2 Co 8[14] ἵνα γένηται ... ὅπως γένηται; 2 Th 1[12]. John restricts himself almost entirely to ἵνα, in spite of the return of ὅπως in Hell. Greek; in the Ptol. papyri it is almost as frequent as ἵνα (302 : 260), although most exx. of ὅπως occur in official writing (Mayser II 1, 247–52, 256, 261). The figures of R. C. Horn (p. 31) corroborate Mayser:

Period	ἵνα	ὅπως	Proportion
Ptolemaic	222	200	same
Imperial	436	88	5 : 1
Byzantine	153	41	4 : 1

For class. Greek, see the figures in Goodwin, appendix III.

Ὅπως has largely lost its ἄν in NT, in spite of many instances in the early papyri and older inscriptions, especially in official writings (Mayser II 1, 254–57; II 3, 50; Meisterhans 254; Horn 31); exceptions in the NT are Lk 2[35] Ac 3[20] 9[12]vl 15[17] OT (Am 9[12] where no ἄν), Ro 3[4] (Ps 50 (51)[6]), 9[17] (Ex 9[16] where our text has no ἄν).

The only place in NT where final ὡς occurs is Ac 20[24] (vl. ὅπως). It is rare also in the Koine. R. C. Horn gives only P. Tebt. 56, 11ff (ii/B.C.), P. Prk. 5232, 35 (A.D. 14), P. Path 1 (99 B.C.), P. Prk 5357, 9 (prob. Byz.).

Other ways of expressing purpose in the later Koine are: ὑπὲρ τοῦ c. inf. (P. Giess. ii/A.D.), πρὸς τό c. inf. (P.B.M. A.D. 187,

---

[1] K-G II 375, 2; 385, 5.   Schmid Attic. IV 621.   Mayser II 1, 254–8.
[2] Mayser II 1, 245; Diogen. of On. I 8 οὐχ ἵνα ... ἀλλ᾽ ὅπως ... Cp. in 1 Clem ὅπως and εἰς τό.

P. Flor. A.D. 514, O.P. A.D. 335, P.B.M. A.D. 345). εἰς τό c. inf.
(O.P. A.D. 190, O.P. A.D. 427), ὥστε c. inf. (P. Flor. iii/A.D. bis).
See pp. 135f., 141-144. In Hellenistic colloquial speech there was
much overlapping in the use of ἵνα (or ὅπως) and ὥστε (or ὡς);
so much so that ἵνα (ὅπως) are even used with the inf. and ὥστε
with subj., with their final and consecutive rôles respectively
reversed (see Ljungvik BSSVS 46f).

Certain writers like Aristophanes, Plato and the orators,
favoured ἵνα, but Homer, Thucydides, Xenophon, Herodotus,
and Attic inscriptions of v–iv/B.C. favoured ὅπως. Polybius
always chooses ἵνα and this development is reflected in NT and
inscriptions and papyri of i/A.D., until the Atticistic revival of
ὅπως set in about iii–iv/A.D.

	ἵνα	ὅπως
Homer	9	145
Thuc. (whole)	53	156
Xen. (i–iii)	32	52
Herodotus	17	107

	ἵνα	ὅπως
Polybius (i–v)	62	0
NT	746	58
Test. Sol.	16	10
Ep. Arist.	28	17
Pap. i/A.D.	2	0
ii/A.D. *	17	3
iii–v	21	3

* From P. Bouriant, P. Lug. Bat. 1, 2, 3, P. Oslo 1, 2, 3.

Ac is the only NT book with much stylistic pretence in this
respect (as with τε). Where there is a variant, except in Ac,
we should probably accept ἵνα, e.g. Mt 6¹⁸D. However, ὅπως
seems to be preferred with verbs of *beseeching*: Mt 8³⁴ παρεκάλεσαν,
9³⁸ δεῖσθαι, Lk 7³ ἐρωτᾶν, Ac 8¹⁵ προσεύχεσθαι, Jas 5¹⁶ εὔχεσθαι.

3. *Relative clauses* [1]

A futuristic subjunctive (neg. μή) in relative clauses introduces an element of uncertainty and supposition. Sometimes

---

[1] K-G II § 559. Stahl 521ff. Meisterhans-Schw. 236f. Moulton
Einl. 259ff. Mayser II 1, 261–267. M. L. Earle, "Subjunctive of
Purpose in Relative Clauses in Attic Greek," *Trans. & Proc. American
Philol. Assocn.*, 23, 17; J. E. Harry, "The Use of οἷος, ποῖος, and
ὁποῖος,". ibid. 38, 18. A. W. Argyle, "The Causal Use of the Relative
Pronouns in the Greek N.T.", *Bible Translator* 6, 1955, 165–169 (repetition
is not a Semitism). H. J. Cadbury, "Relative Pronouns," *JBL* 42,
150–7.

the clause is the equivalent of a condition (ὃς ἄν = ἐάν τις);
sometimes of a final clause. The main verb is usually future or
an imperative, but the general idea may be timeless. These
general relative clauses almost invariably contain the particle
ἄν (even if the verb is in the indic. mood[1]), and it stands as
near to the rel. pronoun as possible, though δέ, γάρ, etc., may
intervene. Its presence was virtually essential in classical
prose and is only very rarely omitted in NT and Egyptian Koine.
Of course, the conditional particle ἐάν is gaining on ἄν from
iii/B.C. In the papyri it becomes more frequent at the end of
ii/B.C. and during i/B.C. (ἄν:—iii 130; ii–i 78. ἐάν:—iii 4;
ii–i 16). The use of pres. or aor. subj. bears little or no relation
to the *Aktionsart*. In the papyri, the difference appears to be
that the pres. indicates that the time of the subordinate clause
is coincident with that of the main (or durative action, if relatively
past), while the aor. indicates a relatively past time. To take
the half-dozen instances of pres. tense in Mt: in 7¹² the main
verb is *do so to them* and the rel. clause is *what you wish them to
do to you*, i.e. at the time when you are doing it to them; 11²⁷
the Father is known only to that man *to whom the Son has been
willing* (from time to time, durative) *to reveal him* ᾧ ἐάν βούληται;
16²⁵ 20²⁶·²⁷ *that man will lose his life who is desirous* (at that
moment) *to save it* (whereas also in 16²⁵ is the aor., meaning *who
by that time has already lost it, he will save it*); 20⁴ *I will pay you
whatever* (at that time) *is the right payment* ὃ ἐάν ᾖ δίκαιον.
By way of contrast, we discover from the more abundant
aorists in Mt that the relative action is always antecedent to the
main action: 5¹⁹ *he will be called least, who* (by that time shall
have) *relaxed*; ³² *he makes his wife an adulteress who divorces*
(i.e. has already divorced) *her*.

1. *Pres. subj.*

   (a) with ἄν: (α) coincident time, e.g., LXX Ge 39³, Mk 9³⁷ ὃς ἄν
ἐμὲ δέχηται BL 892; Jn 2⁵ ὅ τι ἄν λέγῃ *whatever he will be saying to you*:
do it at the time he is saying it (for a different explanation, making it
equivalent to universal ἄν c. subj. in conditional clauses, see Zerwick

---

[1] It is a feature of Hell. Greek that the connection between the mood
and the conjunction (e.g. subj. after ἄν) is becoming less determined, and
so we have εἰ with subj., ἐάν with indic., ὅτε with subj., ὅταν with indic.,
etc. In MGr only the fuller conjunctions ἐάν and ὅταν remain, and they
have both indic. (real) and subj. (probable).

§ 235: *whatsoever at any time he says to you.*) (β) antecedent continuous or iterative time, e.g. Mt 20²⁷ Mk 10⁴³ᶠ ὃς ἂν θέλη ... ἔσται ὑμῶν (δοῦλος).

(*b*) with ἐάν: (α) coincident, e.g. LXX Ge 6¹⁷ ὅσα ἐὰν ᾖ, 20¹⁵, 21²² (durative), 30³³, 44¹; Mt 7¹² ὅσα ἐὰν θέλητε (or continuous), 11²⁷ ᾧ ἐὰν βούληται, 20⁴ ὃ ἐὰν ᾖ δίκαιον, Mk 6²² αἴτησόν με ὃ ἐὰν θέλῃς. (β) antecedent cont. or iterat., e.g. Mt 16²⁵ 20²⁶ Mk 8³⁵ ὃς ... ἐὰν θέλη.

(*c*) without ἄν or ἐάν, e.g. Mt 10³³ ὅστις δὲ ἀρνήσηται BLW (rest ἄν).

2. *Aor. subj.*

(*a*) with ἄν: LXX Ge 2¹⁷ 3⁵ 11⁶ 12¹ 21⁶ 22² 24¹⁴. ⁴³ 26² 42³⁸ 44⁹. ¹⁰ 48⁶ AB. Mt 5¹⁹ ὃς δ' ἂν ποιήση, ²¹ φονεύση, ²² 15⁵ εἴπη, 5³¹ 19⁹ ὃς ἂν ἀπολύση (OT Dt 24¹), 10¹¹ εἰς ἣν ἂν πόλιν ... εἰσέλθητε, ¹⁴ ὃς ἂν μὴ δέξηται, ³³ ὅστις δ' ἂν ἀρνήσηται vl., 12⁵⁰ ὅστις ... ἂν ποιήση, 16²⁵ ὃς δ' ἂν ἀπολέση, 18⁶ ὃς δ' ἂν σκανδαλίση, 19⁹ ὃς ἂν ἀπολύση, (21⁴⁴ ἐφ' οὗ ἂν πέση), 23¹⁶. ¹⁸ ὃς ἂν ὀμόση, 26⁴⁸ ὃν ἂν φιλήσω. Mk 3³⁵ ὃς ἂν ποιήση, 3²⁸ ὅσα ἂν βλασφημήσωσιν SD (ὅσας ἄν AFΦ fam¹ 22 28 157 700), 3²⁹ ὃς δ' ἂν βλασφημήση, 6¹¹ ὃς ἂν (τόπος) μὴ δέξηται, 9³⁷ ὃς ἂν ... δέξηται DWΔΘ (corr. to ἐάν by 565 579 700), ⁴¹ ὃς γὰρ ἂν ποτίση (S ἐάν; ΗΓΔ Ψ 28 ποτίσει), ⁴² ὃς ἂν σκανδαλίση (ACX ἐάν), 10¹¹ ὃς ἂν ἀπολύση (ANX 700 ἐάν), ¹⁵ ὃς ἂν μὴ δέξηται (ANX 700 ἐάν), 11²³ ὃς ἂν εἴπη. 14⁴⁴ ὃν ἂν φιλήσω (LNΔΨ' ἐάν).

(*b*) with ἐάν: LXX Ge 15¹⁴ 20¹³ 21¹² 28¹⁵. ²² 31³² 34¹¹ 41⁵⁵ 42³⁸ 48⁶ (Rahlfs). Mt 5¹⁹ ὃς ἐὰν ... λύση, ³² ὃς ἐὰν ... γαμήση, 10⁴² ὃς ἐὰν (vl) ποτίση, 11⁶ ὃς ἐὰν (vl) μὴ σκανδαλισθῇ, 12³² ἐὰν (vl) εἴπη. 14⁷ ὃ ἐὰν αἰτήσηται (an apparent exception: she had not asked anything yet, but would have done so before he was able to make the gift), 15⁵ ὠφεληθῇς, WHT (rest aor. ind.), 16¹⁹ δήσης, 18⁵ δέξηται, ¹⁹ οὗ ἐὰν αἰτήσωνται ¹⁸ ὅσα ἐὰν δήσητε, 21²² ἐὰν (vl) αἰτήσητε, 22⁹ ὅσους ἐὰν εὕρητε, 23³ πάντα ... ὅσα ἐὰν εἴπωσιν.—Mk 3²⁸ ὅσα ἐὰν βλασφημήσωσιν ΒΔΘ, ὅσας ἐὰν βλ. CFΣ 33 565 892 1071, 6²³ ὅτι ἐάν με αἰτήσης ΒΔ p⁴⁵ 118 124 435, ὅτι ὃ ἐὰν μ.α. SAC Θ fam¹³ 33, 7¹¹ ὃ ἐὰν ἐξ ἐμοῦ ὠφεληθῇς (DW 28 ἄν), 8³⁸ ὃς γὰρ ἐὰν ἐπαισχυνθῇ SBC Θ p⁴⁵ (ἄν GHKSUWΠΦ fam¹· ¹³ 22 543 28 33 700 Cl. Alx D), 9³⁷ ὃς ἐὰν ἐμὲ δέξηται ACNXΓΣΦ, 10³⁵ ὃ ἐὰν αἰτήσωμεν (ἄν DW 6369 C*; αἰτήσομεν SᶜA), 13¹¹ ὃ ἐὰν δοθῇ (ἄν ADW 229 1342).

(*c*) neither ἄν nor ἐάν: Mt 10³³ BLW ὅστις δὲ ἀρνήσηται.

3. *Pres. and Aor. side by side*

Mt 16²⁵ ὃς ... ἐὰν θέλη — ὃς δ' ἂν ἀπολέση.

Thus in Mt the situation is different from that in pre-Christian papyri, and precisely the same as in LXX Ge (Rahlfs' text).

PAPYRI   MATTHEW

Present			Aorist			Present			Aorist		
ἄν	ἐάν	neither	ἄν	ἐάν	neither	ἄν	ἐάν	neither	ἄν	ἐάν	neither
118	12	3	85	8	2	1	5	–	18	14	1

LXX GE   MARK

Present			Aorist			Present			Aorist		
ἄν	ἐάν	neither	ἄν	ἐάν	neither	ἄν	ἐάν	neither	ἄν	ἐάν	neither
1	5	–	13	10	–	2	2	–	12	7	–

Also in contradistinction to the papyri [1], the NT sometimes
employs the subj. in relative clauses, in a final sense, where class.
Greek used the fut. ind.: Mk 14¹⁴ Lk 22¹¹ ποῦ ἐστιν τὸ κατάλυμα
ὅπου φάγω (D corr. to fut.), Lk 11⁶ ὃ παραθήσω αὐτῷ *something
to set before him*, 9⁵⁸ οὐκ ἔχει ποῦ τὴν κεφαλὴν κλίνῃ *nowhere to
lay*, Ac 21¹⁶ ἄγοντες παρ' ᾧ ξενισθῶμεν Μνάσωνι.   LXX Je 11⁶
ἐπικατάρατος ὁ ἄνθρωπος, ὃς . . . ἔχει . . . καὶ στηρίσει . . . καὶ
. . . ἀποστῇ.

In the papyri too, qualitative-consecutive relative sentences
employ the indicative, not the subjunctive. Like Latin, NT
sometimes uses subj.: Heb 8³ ἔχειν τι . . . ὃ προσενέγκῃ *something to offer* (but also Isocr. IV 44 ἔχειν ἐφ' οἷς φιλοτιμηθῶσιν),
1 Clem 38² ἔδωκεν δι' οὗ ἀναπληρωθῇ.

The difference between indic. and subj. in these general
relative clauses is ideally and approximately that between εἰ c.
indic. and ἐάν c. subj. in true conditional clauses. The former
indicates an assumption which is actual and realized, while the
latter points to future probabilities which may not actually be
realized. But in the papyri which concern official decrees and
statutes, as Mayser remarks, the distinction is often effaced and
in fact the two moods can be used quite promiscuously (II 1, 266).
This applies equally to the NT:

---

[1] Mayser II 1, 214, 267. But not necessarily to Hellenistic Greek
generally. See examples in Radermacher² 170.

Mt 13¹² ὅστις γάρ ἔχει (ind.), Mk 4²⁵ ὃς γάρ ἔχει AE²G ὃς ἂν ἐχῇ (subj.) DE*F ὃς ἂν ἔχει (ind.), 4²⁵ ὃς οὐκ ἔχει (ind.), E*G ὃς οὐκ ἔχῃ (subj.), Lk 8¹⁸ ὃς γάρ ἂν ἔχῃ (subj.), δοθήσεται αὐτῷ, καὶ ὃς ἂν μὴ ἔχῃ (subj.), καὶ ὃ δοκεῖ (ind.) ἔχειν, ἀρθήσεται ἀπ' αὐτοῦ.—Mt 10³² ὅστις ὁμολογήσει (ind.), ³³ ὅστις δ' [ἂν] ἀρνήσηται (subj.).—Lk 12⁸ πᾶς ὃς ἂν ὁμολογήσῃ (subj.) p⁴⁵ SΘ (B*D Mcion. harm. with Mt 10³²). Thus the moods fluctuate for no good reason, and only the context can really decide whether the rel. clause is definite or indefinite.

Very occasionally the indic. occurs with ἄν in NT and LXX (see pp. 91, 92f): Future Mk 3²⁸ ὅσας ἐὰν βλασφημήσουσιν L, 8³⁵ SBCD² ἀπολέσει (ALW -σῃ), Lk 12⁸ ὁμολογήσει AB*DR, 17³³ SAL (BDEW -σῃ), Ac 7⁷ δουλεύσουσιν ACD. LXX Le 27¹² καθότι ἂν τιμηθήσεται. Barn 11⁸ SC ὃ ἐὰν ἐξελεύσεται. Present Mt 11²⁷ LW ᾧ ἐὰν βούλεται, Rev 14⁴ ὅπου ἂν ὑπάγει.

There are a few exx. of subj. without ἄν (ἐάν) in the papyri—five, all told, in Mayser—but all the NT exx. are textually suspect: Mt 10³³ BWL, Ga 6¹⁶ p⁴⁶ ὅσοι στοιχήσωσιν, Jas 2¹⁰ SBC ὅστις . . . τηρήσῃ, 2¹⁰ SABC πταίσῃ, Herm. S. II 3 bis.

4. Temporal Clauses [1]

A special kind of relative clause, they follow the same construction with regard to relative time in the use of subj. with ἄν. As with the relative conjunction, ἄν stands as near as possible to the temporal conjunction. It is only with ἕως, and then largely in the aor., that ἄν can be omitted. In post-Christian papyri these particles have a final sense (Ljungvik BSSVS 43–46).

(a) Clauses with ἄχρι, ἕως and μέχρι.

Pres. subj. = as long as, of indefinite continuance in either past or future.

With ἄν: none in NT. Ptol. pap. (dates): 237 285.

Without ἄν: none in NT. Ptol. pap.: 140.

Pres. indic.: Mt 5²⁵ ἕως ὅτου εἶ while. Jn 9⁴ ἕως ἡμέρα ἐστιν. Ptol. pap. (dates): 223 iii 164.

We may note ἕως with pres. indic. in a futuristic sense: Mk 6⁴⁵ SBL ἕως αὐτὸς ἀπολύει (vl. ἀπολύσῃ, -σει, D αὐτὸς δὲ

---

[1] K-G II § 567. Stahl 444ff. Mayser II 1, 268ff. Meisterhans-Schwyzer 242, 9; 247, 1; 251b. Schwyzer II 648ff. A. Tschuschke, De πρίν particulae apud scriptores aetatis Augusteae prosaicos usu (Diss. of Breslau), 1913.

ἀπολύει), Jn 21²². ²³ ἕως ἔρχομαι *until I come*, also 1 Ti 4¹³. This can hardly mean *as long as*, any more than in Herm. S. IX 11, 1 ἕως ἔρχεται, V 2, 2; IX 10, 5. 6. The papyri have ἕως with pres. subj. on two occasions with possible meaning *until*, but never pres. ind., or even fut. ind. like Lk 13³⁵ vl.

Aor. subj. (ἕως and μέχρι) = *until*, of a punctiliarly conceived future event preceded in time by the action of the main clause:

with ἄν: Mt 2¹³ ἕως ἄν εἴπω, 5¹⁸ 24³⁴ ἕως ἄν πάντα γένηται, 5²⁶ ἕως ἄν ἀποδῷς, 10¹¹ ἕως ἄν ἐξέλθητε, 12²⁰ ἕως ἄν ἐκβάλῃ (Isa 42³)₄ 16²⁸ ἕως ἄν ἴδωσιν, 22⁴⁴ ἕως ἄν θῶ (Ps 110¹), 23³⁹ ἕως ἄν εἴπητε.—Mk 6¹⁰ ἕως ἄν ἐξέλθητε, 9¹ ἕως ἄν ἴδωσιν, 12³⁶ ἕως ἄν θῶ.—Lk 9²⁷ ἕως ἄν ἴδωσιν, 20⁴³ ἕως ἄν θῶ (Ps 110¹), 21³² ἕως ἄν πάντα γένηται.—Ac 2³⁵ (Ps 110¹).— 1 Co 4⁵ ἕως ἄν ἔλθῃ.—Ga 3¹⁹ ἄχρις ἄν ἔλθῃ (vl. ἄχρις οὗ).—Heb 1¹³ (Ps 110¹).—Μέχρις ἄν none.

without ἄν: Mt 10²³ ἕως ἔλθῃ, 14²² ἕως ἄν ἀπολύσῃ (-σει ΚΓ), 17⁹ ἕως οὗ ἐγερθῇ, 18³⁰ ἕως ἀποδῷ, ³⁴ ἕως οὗ ἀποδῷ, 26³⁶ ἕως οὗ . . . προσεύξωμαι *while, as long as* (fut. subj.?).—Mk 13³⁰ μέχρις οὗ . . . γένηται (Β μέχρις ὅτου; S μέχρι; W ἕως; D ἕως οὗ), 14³² (-ξομαι D).—Lk 12⁵⁰ ἕως ὅτου τελεσθῇ, ⁵⁹ ἕως ἀποδῷς 13⁸ ἕως ὅτου σκάψω, ³⁵ ἕως εἴπητε (vl.), 15⁴ ἕως εὕρῃ, ⁸ ἕως οὗ εὕρῃ, 17⁸ ἕως (+ ἄν ΑΚ) φάγω καὶ πίω *while, as long as*, 21²⁴ ἄχρι (οὗ) πληρωθῶσιν, 22¹⁶ ἕως ὅτου πληρωθῇ, ¹⁸ ἕως οὗ . . . ἔλθῃ, ³⁴ ἕως . . . ἀπαρνήσῃ, 24⁴⁹ ἕως οὗ ἐνδύσησθε.—Jn 13³⁸ ἕως οὗ ἀρνήσῃ. —Ac 23¹² ἕως οὗ ἀποκτείνωσιν, ¹⁴ -ωμεν (final, as in later papyri), ²¹ ἕως οὗ ἀνέλωσιν, 25²¹ ἕως οὗ ἀναπέμψω.—Ro 11²⁵ ἄχρι οὗ . . . εἰσέλθῃ.— 1 Co 11²⁶ ἄχρι οὗ ἔλθῃ, 15²⁵ ἄχρι οὗ θῇ (Ps 110¹).—2 Th 2⁷ ἕως (+ ἄν FG) . . . γένηται.—Heb 10¹³ ἕως τεθῶσιν.—Jas 5⁷ ἕως λάβῃ.—2 Pt 1¹⁹ ἕως οὗ . . . διαυγάσῃ.—Rev 6¹¹ ἕως πληρωθῶσιν, 7³ ἄχρι σφραγίσωμεν, 15⁸ ἄχρι τελεσθῶσιν, 17¹⁷ Β ἄχρι τελεσθῶσιν (vl τελεσθήσονται), 20³· ⁵ ἄχρι τελεσθῇ.—Ga 4¹⁹ μέχρις οὗ μορφωθῇ.—Eph 4¹³ μέχρι καταντήσωμεν.

	Present subjunctive			Aorist subjunctive					
	ἕως	ἕως ἄν	μέχρι ἄν	ἕως	ἕως ἄν	μέχρι	μέχρι ἄν	ἄχρι	ἄχρις ἄν
Ptol. pap.	1	4	1·	7	44	–	3	–	–
NT	–	–	–	28	18	3	–	9	1

In the earlier papyri ἕως ἄν predominates, but in the Imperial period ἕως is preferred.

(b) *Clauses with* ἐπάν, ὅταν, ὡς ἄν.

With pres. subj.

(1) Usually of an iterative action, indefinite, in the past or future. By far the most frequent, in secular and Biblical Greek, is ὅταν. The main clause has most often the present or future, but also the aorist. *Whenever.* See pp. 92f.

῞Οταν:—Mt 6² ὅταν οὖν ποίῃς ἐλεημοσύνην, ⁵ ὅταν προσεύχησθε, 6. 16, 10²³ 15².—Mk 11²⁵ ὅταν στήκητε BWG (ACD -κετε; S στῆτε) 13⁴. 11 14⁷. ²⁵.—Lk 11² (AWCH προσεύχεσθε), ²¹. ³⁴ 12¹¹ 14¹². ¹³ 21⁷.— Jn 7²⁷ (SHXΔ* ἔρχεται) 8⁴⁴ 9⁵ 16²¹.—Ro 2¹⁴.—1 Co 3⁴ 14²⁶.—2 Co 12¹⁰ 13⁹.—1 Th 5³.—1 Jn 5².—Rev 4⁹ SQ δώσωσιν (vl. δώσουσιν 10⁷.) ῾Ηνίκα:—2 Co 3¹⁵ ἕως σήμερον ἡνίκα ἂν ἀναγινώσκηται Μωϋσῆς.

(2) Of a definite action occurring in the future : *when.*

῞Οταν:—Mt 26²⁹.—1 Co 15²⁴.—Rev 18⁹.—Pap (A.D. 270).

῾Ως ἄν:—Ro 15²⁴ πορεύωμαι εἰς τὴν Σπανίαν. Only in Ptol. pap., not in later Koine (Horn 133). Its use in Paul (so also 1 Co 11³⁴, Ph 2²³) might be due to his familiarity with LXX; more probably he is using the spoken language of his day (Horn 136): P. Fay. I 111 16 (A.D. 95) ὡς ἐὰν βλέπῃς.

᾿Επάν *after*:—Lk 11³⁴ ἐπὰν δὲ πονηρὸς ᾖ (D ὅταν).

῞Οτε c. subj. is late (Jannaris § 1988), but see Lk 13³⁵ AD ὅτε εἴπητε.

With aor. subj.

(1) Most commonly of a definite action taking place in the future but concluded before the action of the main verb. Thus the main verb is usually fut. ind., but it may be imper. The particles are ὡς ἄν, ὅταν, and ἐπάν.

᾿Επάν:—Mt 2⁸ ἐπὰν δὲ εὕρητε ἀπαγγείλατέ μοι (D ὅταν).—Lk 11²² νικήσῃ (D ἐάν), ³⁴ ᾖ (D ὅταν). BU 523, 17 ἐπὰν ἀναβῇς *after you have been.*

῞Οταν:—Mt 5¹¹, 9¹⁵ ἐλεύσονται ἡμέραι ὅταν ἀπαρθῇ, 10¹⁹ 12⁴³ 13³² 19²⁸ 21⁴⁰ 23¹⁵ 24¹⁵. ³². ³³ 25³¹.—Mk 2²⁰ 4¹⁵. ¹⁶. ²⁹. ³¹. ³² 8³⁸ 9⁹ 12²³. ²⁵ 13⁷ ὅταν ἀκούσητε (vl. ἀκούετε), ¹⁴. ²⁸. ²⁹.—Lk 5³⁵ ὅταν ἀπαρθῇ, 6²⁶ 8¹³ 9²⁶ 13²⁸ S ἴδητε (B*DX ὄψεσθε; ABᶜᵒʳʳ W -ησθε), 16⁴. ⁹ 17¹⁰ 21⁹. ²⁰ 23⁴².—Jn 4²⁵ 5⁷ 7³¹ 8²⁸ 10⁴ 14²⁹ 15²⁶ 16⁴. ¹³. ²¹ 21¹⁸.—Ac 23³⁵ 24²².— Ro 11²⁷.—1 Co 13¹⁰ 15²⁴. ²⁴. ²⁷. ²⁸. ⁵⁴ 16². ³. ⁵. ¹².—2 Co 10⁶.—Col 3⁴ 4¹⁶.—2 Th 1¹⁰.—1 Ti 5¹¹.—Ti 3¹².—Heb 1⁶.—Jas 1².—Rev 11⁷ 12⁴ 17¹⁰ 20⁷.

῾Ως ἄν:—1 Co 11³⁴ τὰ δὲ λοιπὰ ὡς ἂν ἔλθω διατάξομαι.—Ph 2²³ ὡς ἂν ἀφίδω:—LXX Ge 12¹² ὡς ἂν ἴδωσίν σε ... ἐροῦσι.—P. Hib. I 59, 2 (247 B.C.), UPZ I 7I, 18 (152 B.C.); Horn 133, Mayser II 1, 271f, 274f.

(2). Much rarer are the instances where the action is indefinite or iterative:

'Επάν:—(= בכל־עת אשר) LXX Est 5¹³ S¹ ἐπὰν ἴδω Μαρδ. *all the while that*, Da O′ Bel¹² ἐπὰν κλεισθῇ *after it has been.*

"Οταν:—Lk 6²² 11²⁴ 12⁵⁴ 14⁸. ¹⁰ 21³⁰. ³¹.—Jn 2¹⁰.—Rev 9⁵.

'Ηνίκα:—LXX Ex 1¹⁰ καὶ ἡνίκα ἂν συμβῇ ἡμῖν πόλεμος *each time.*— Dt 7¹².—2 Co 3¹⁶ (Ex 34³⁴) ἡνίκα δὲ ἐὰν ἐπιστρέψῃ.

For ὅτε, ὅταν, and ἐπάν with indic., see pp. 92f.

	Pres. subj.		Aor. subj.				
	ὅταν	ὡς ἄν	ὅταν	ὡς ἄν	ἐπάν	ἐπειδάν	ὁπηνίκ' ἄν
Ptol. pap.	20	10	19	49	3	2	3
NT	33	1	82	2	1	–	–

(c) *Clauses with* πρίν.

Neither πρίν nor πρὶν ἄν occur with subj. in the Ptol. pap., but πρίν c. subj. occurs in papyri from ii–v/A.D. (Horn 128). Πρίν was possible without ἄν in class. Greek and it so occurs in LXX and NT. Lk 2²⁶ πρὶν ἢ ἂν ἴδῃ (S* ἕως ἂν ἴδῃ; B om ἢ; ADW om ἄν), 22³⁴ πρὶν ἢ ἀπαρνήσῃ AWΓ (SBL ἕως; K ἕως οὗ; D ἕως ὅτου). With optative Ac 25¹⁶ (see next ch.). LXX Si 11⁷ πρὶν (+ἢ SA) ἐξετάσῃς; Sym. Ps 57 (58)¹⁰ πρὶν ἤ (LXX πρὸ τοῦ c. inf.); Sym. Je 40 (47)⁵ πρὶν ἢ ἀπαλλάγω ἐγώ.—Herm. S. V 7, 3 πρὶν ἀκουσθῶσι τὰ ῥήματα.

5. *Conditional Sentences* [1]

The subjunctive occurs in the hypothetical protasis which is introduced by ἐάν. This is often written εἰάν and sometimes ἤν in the papyri, never in NT. Moreover, we find ἄν for ἐάν, as there was interchange at this time between the two particles; and this occurs six times in Jn especially in connection with τις (cp. ἄν τις ὑμῶν κακῶς ἐρεῖ in a very badly written papyrus from the Fayum, SB 5627, 11).

---

[1] K-G I § 399, 2; II § 575. Meisterhans-Schwyzer § 89. Stahl 390. Schwyzer II 682–688. Mayser II 1, 275–288. Moulton Einl. 292ff. E. B. Clapp, " Conditional Sentences in the Greek Tragedies," (*Trans. and Proc. Amer. Philol. Assn.* 22, 81). J. Sterenberg, *The Use of Conditional Sentences in the Alexandrian Version of the Pentateuch.* (Diss. of Munich, 1908.)

Parallel with relative and temporal clauses, the aor. subj. denotes a single event taking place in the future, and the pres. subj. a general or iterative occurrence which may or may not be expected to take place at any time. The pres. denotes also coincident action with the main verb, whereas the aor. is like the Latin future, and is fut. perf. in its relation with the main clause.

(a) 'Εάν *with pres. and aor. subjunctive.*

(1) *Present:* very common in Koine. In a general and iterative sense, as " condicio universalis " (Zerwick § 227c), the pres. subj. denotes a hypothesis which can occur over and over again (present *Aktionsart*). The most common example of this condition in the Ptol. pap. is stereotyped phrases in decrees and punishments, having a continual validity. In the main clause is a pres. ind. (or even optative), mainly an imperative or jussive of some kind.

Mt 5²³ ἐὰν οὖν προσφέρῃς *as often as you*, 6²². ²³, 8² ἐὰν θέλῃς, δύνασαι (how tentative, cp. with Peter's εἰ θέλεις 17⁴!), 10¹³. ¹³ 15¹⁴ 17²⁰ 21²¹.—Mk 1⁴⁰ 9⁴⁵. ⁴⁷ 14³¹ ἐὰν δέῃ . . . οὐ μή σε ἀπαρνήσομαι (S -σωμαι).—Lk 5¹² 6³³ 10⁶ 13³ ἐὰν μὴ μετανοῆτε is not distinguishable from ⁵ ἐὰν μὴ μετανοήσητε (as scribes realized, correcting to μετανοῆτε), 19³¹.—Jn 3². ²⁷ 5³¹ 6⁶². ⁶⁵ 7¹⁷ 8¹⁶. ³¹ 9³¹ 11⁹.¹⁰ 12²⁶. ²⁶ 13¹⁷. ³⁵ 14¹⁵. ²³ 15⁴. ⁴. ⁷. ¹⁴ 21²² ἐὰν αὐτὸν θέλω μένειν . . . τί πρὸς σέ; (difficult because so definite; class. would be εἰ), ²³.—Ac 5³⁸ (see Zerwick §§ 219–220: Gamaliel seems strangely biased. He says doubtfully *If it should be of men* (ἐὰν ᾖ) but confidently *If (as it seems) it is of God* (εἰ . . . ἐστιν), the one hypothetical, the other " real ". Luke has composed the speech and is giving his own conviction, not Gamaliel's), 13⁴¹ 26⁵.—Ro 2²⁵. ²⁵. ²⁶ 9²⁷ 11²². ²³ 12²⁰. ²⁰ 13⁴ 14⁸ .⁸. ⁸.—1 Co 4¹⁵ 5¹¹ 6⁴ 7³⁶ 9¹⁶. ¹⁶ vl. 11¹⁴. ¹⁵ 13¹. ² 14¹⁴. ²⁴. ²⁸ 16⁴.—Col. 3¹³.—1 Th 2⁸.—1 Ti 1⁸ 3¹⁵.— 2 Ti 2⁵.— Jas 2¹⁴. ¹⁵. ¹⁷ 4¹⁵ (vl. aor. subj.).—1 Pt 3¹³.— 1 Jn 1⁷. ⁹ 2³ γινώσκομεν . . . ἐὰν . . . τηρῶμεν (S* φυλάξωμεν), ¹⁵ 3²⁰. ²¹ 4¹².—Heb 6³ ἐάνπερ.

(2) *Aorist:* This represents a definite event as occurring only once in the future, and conceived as taking place before the time of the action of the main verb. It is expectation, but not fulfilment as yet. It is very near the meaning of ὅταν, and is often more than mere probability (see LXX Isa 24¹³ *when;* Am 7²). In the apodosis occurs fut. and pres. indic., or imper. or jussive.

Mt 4⁹ 5¹³. ²⁰. ⁴⁶. ⁴⁷ 6¹⁴. ¹⁵ 9²¹ 12¹¹. ²⁹ 16²⁸ 18³. ¹². ¹³. ¹⁵. ¹⁶. ¹⁷. ¹⁹ ἐὰν συμφωνήσωσιν (SD fut. ind.) . . . γενήσεται FGKMW, ³⁵, 21³. ²¹. ²⁵. ²⁶

22²⁴ 24²³. ²⁶. ⁴⁸ 26⁴² 28¹⁴.—Mk 3²⁴. ²⁵. ²⁷ 5²⁸ 7³. ⁴. ¹¹ 8³ 9⁴³. ⁵⁰ 10¹². ³⁰ 11³. ³¹ 12¹⁹ OT 13²¹.—Lk 4⁷ 6³⁴ 12³⁸. ⁴⁵ 14³⁴ 15⁸ 16³⁰. ³¹ 17³. ³. ⁴ 19⁴⁰ ἐὰν οὗτοι σιωπήσωσιν (SBALWR fut. ind.; D σιγήσουσιν) κράξουσιν ΓΔΘ 20⁵. ⁶. ²⁸ 22⁶⁷. ⁶⁸.—Jn 3³. ⁵. ¹² 5⁴³ 6⁵¹ 7³⁷ 8³⁶. ⁵¹. ⁵². ⁵⁴. ⁵⁵ 9²² 10⁹ 11⁴⁰. ⁴⁸ 12²⁴. ²⁴. ³². ⁴⁷ 13⁸ 14³. ¹⁴ (vl. pres. subj.), 15¹⁰ 16⁷. ⁷ 19¹² 4⁴⁸ 6⁴⁴. ⁵³ 7⁵¹ 8²⁴ 20²⁵.—Ac 15¹ 27³¹.—Ro 7². ³. ³ 10⁹. ¹⁵ 14²³ 15²⁴.—1 Co 4¹⁹ 7⁸. ¹¹. ²⁸. ³⁹. ⁴⁰ 8⁸.¹⁰ 9¹⁶ (vl. pres. subj.) 10²⁸ 12¹⁵. ¹⁶ 13³. ³ (vl. fut. ind.), 14⁶. ⁶. ⁷. ⁹. ¹¹. ¹⁶. ²³. ³⁰ 15³⁶ 16⁷. ¹⁰ (see Allo in loc., but this type of condition does not express mere probability: Zerwick § 226).—2 Co 5¹ 10⁸ ἐὰν . . . καυχήσωμαι (SLP fut. ind.) . . . οὐκ αἰσχυνθήσομαι p⁴⁶ BGH 33, 12⁶, 13².—Ga 1⁸ 5².—Col 4¹⁰.—2 Th 2³.—1 Ti 2¹⁵.—2 Ti 2⁵. ²¹.—Heb 3⁶. ⁷ OT 4⁷ 10³⁸ OT.—Jas 2² 5¹⁹.—1 Jn 1⁶. ⁸. ¹⁰ 2¹ ἐάν τις ἁμάρτῃ . . . ἔχομεν 2²⁴. ²⁸. ²⁹. 3² 4²⁰ 5¹⁶.—Rev 2⁵ 3³. ²⁰ 22¹⁸. ¹⁹.—Heb 3¹⁴ ἐάνπερ.

(b) Εἰ *with fut. indic.*

This sometimes conveys the same idea but occurs very seldom in Ptol. pap. The feeling of definiteness and actual realization accompanies it. It is almost causal. Mt 26³³ Mk 14²⁹ εἰ (καὶ) πάντες σκανδαλισθήσονται (i.e. granting the assumption: *let us suppose that all will actually be offended*).— Lk 11⁸ εἰ καὶ οὐ δώσει *although*.—1 Co 9¹¹ μέγα εἰ ἡμεῖς . . . θερίσομεν (i.e. we are in fact doing it).—1 Pt 2²⁰. ²⁰ εἰ ὑπομενεῖτε. The difficulty about this view is 2 Ti 2¹² εἰ ἀπαρνησόμεθα, where the condition was surely conceived as no more than hypothetical.

With pres. indic.

Si igitur. Mt 5²⁹ εἰ ὁ ὀφθαλμός σου σκανδαλίζει σε (altered from ἐάν c. subj. in Mk 9⁴³⁻⁴⁷), 6³⁰ εἰ . . . ὁ θεὸς οὕτως ἀμφιέννυσιν *since he clothes*, 17⁴ (a foregone conclusion for Peter). Lk 22⁴² εἰ βούλει.—Mt 19¹⁰.—Lk 6³², Jn 7⁴ εἰ ταῦτα ποιεῖς, Jn 11¹²D εἰ κοιμᾶται.—Ac 5³⁸ᶠ.—Ro 2¹⁷ᶠᶠ 7¹⁶. ²⁰ 8¹¹ 11¹⁷.—1 Co 7³⁶ εἰ δέ τις . . . νομίζει (Paul knows this is actually happening). —Ga 1⁹ 2¹⁸.—Heb 7¹⁵.

(c) 'Εάν *with pres. ind.*

This calls for some comment; it is an abnormal use in the Ptol. pap., confined to ἐὰν δεῖ and ἐὰν φαίνεται, for other exx. are of doubtful reading or capable of different explanation (Mayser II 1, 284f). But Horn quotes BGU 597 (A.D. 75). From ii/A.D. the construction makes more frequent appearance, as εἰ and ἐάν are beginning to be confused (we have exx. in ii/A.D., iii/A.D., and late Imp. period), and increases in Byzantine Greek. It seems to bear a causal sense: 1 Co 4¹⁵ ἐάν . . . ἔχετε (perhaps a half-way-house of actuality between ἐὰν ἔχητε *you may have* and εἰ ἔχετε *since you have*), 13² ἐὰν ἔχω . . . καὶ εἰδῶ?, Jn 5³¹ ἐὰν . . . μαρτυρῶ?, 1 Jn 5¹⁵ ἐὰν οἴδαμεν (S corr. to ἴδωμεν).—1 Th 3⁸ ἐὰν . . . στήκετε (S*DE corr. to -ητε).— Mk 11¹³ D (ειδειν εαν τι εστιν).

Fut. indic. too: Ac 8³¹ πῶς γὰρ ἂν δυναίμην ἐὰν μή τις ὁδηγήσει με SB*GE, Rev 2²² SA.—Herm. M. V 1, 2; IV 3, 7.

Apparent use of ἐάν with impf. (ἦν, ἦσθα, ἦσαν) in papyri and LXX (also p⁴⁶ 1 Co 7³⁶ 14²⁸) is probably an illusion, since these forms are intended as subjunctive (see Debrunner *Glotta* 11, 1920, 25f).

	ἐάν		εἰ	ἐάν
	Pres. subj.	Aor. subj.	Fut. ind.	Indic.
Ptol. pap.	246	218	9	5 ?
NT	88	159	8	6 ?

(d) Εἰ *with subjunctive.*

It appears to encroach on the province of ἐάν. This is unusual in Ptolemaic times (there are two exx. from iii/B.C.) but it becomes increasingly common in papyri from ii/A.D. onwards (see confusion mentioned in previous section): BGU (c. A.D. 100), P. Giess. (ii/A.D.), P. Ryl. (ii/A.D.), P. Lips. (A.D. 240), P. Grenf. (late iii/A.D.), P. Rein. (iv/A.D.), PSI (iv–v/A.D.), OP (v/A.D.), PR (v–vi/A.D.), OP (v–vi/A.D.), OP (A.D. 583), P. Cair. (Byz.), etc.[1]

There is therefore nothing surprising in Rev 11⁵ καὶ εἴ τις θελήσῃ SA (p⁴⁷ θελήσει; C θέλει; καὶ η in S* = κἂν?), Lk 11¹⁸ εἰ μερισθῇ p⁴⁵Γ (rést (δι)εμερίσθη). On 1 Co 14⁵ see p. 321 (ἐκτὸς εἰ μή is a fixed formula).

6. *Indirect Questions*

Greek, unlike Latin, keeps the mood and tense of *direct* speech, e.g. Mk 6⁵⁵ ὅπου ἤκουον ὅτι ἐστιν. Therefore these

---

[1] R. C. Horn op. cit. p. 31; Reinhold op. cit. 107; Jannaris §§ 1988f; Radermacher² 199.

subjunctives in indirect speech will also have been subjunctive in direct speech. Thus Mt 6²⁵ is an indir. deliberative question: μὴ μεριμνᾶτε τί φάγητε; also Mk 9⁶ οὐ γὰρ ᾔδει τί ἀποκριθῇ (according to Latin standards this would be *he did not know what he was saying*, as in the Lk-parallel 9³³ ὃ λέγει); Heb 8³ after ἔχω is ὃ προσενέγκῃ; Mk 8¹ᶠ Lk 12¹⁷; Mayser II 1, 214, 235. Mt 10¹⁹ δοθήσεται ὑμῖν τί λαλήσητε; Mk 6³⁶. We may have fut. ind. in an indir. delib. question: Ph 1²² (p⁴⁶ B subj.), or else punctuate τί αἱρήσομαι;. In relative past time (for class. optative) NT keeps subj. as a rule: Ac 4²¹ μηδὲν εὑρίσκοντες τὸ πῶς κολάσωνται αὐτούς; but see under Optative (next ch.). This is so in Hell. Greek generally (e.g. Epict. Ench. 7; Marc. Ant. 9, 3, 7).

CHAPTER NINE

THE VERB: MOODS: OPTATIVE

THE MOOD was declining [1] during the last three centuries B.C.
It is still used fairly widely to indicate a wish in the papyri,
LXX and NT, in spite of the popularity of the imperative, in
curses as well as requests.   It was probably never used much in
conversation, even in Athens; Xenophon was addicted to it but
it is scarce in Attic inscriptions.   The figures per 100 pp. are
approximately Alciphron (*Letters*) 109, Xenophon (*Mem.*) 350,
Plato (*Phaedo*) 250, Strabo 76, Polybius 37, Diodorus Siculus 13,
Callimachus 49 (in 49 pp.), Aratus 94 (in 46 pp.).   Even Dionysius
of Halicarnassus (30 B.C.) and Diodorus Siculus (i/B.C.) who
maintain the Attic tradition tend to dispense with it.   In fact,
the fut. optative, never more than a substitute in indirect speech
for the future indic., is quite extinct in Hellenistic Greek.   The
aor. opt. proved toughest, lasting until viii/A.D.   The optative
to express a wish (volitive) was the most persistent, surviving
particularly in set phrases like μὴ γένοιτο; whereas the potential
optative, in main and conditional clauses, was rare in the
Ptolemaic, and almost extinct and awkwardly used, in the

---

[1] Hilaire Vandaele, *L'Optatif Grec. Essai de Syntaxe historique*, Paris
1897.   F. G. Allinson, " On Causes Contributory to the Loss of the
Optative in Later Greek," *Studies in Honor of B.L. Gildersleeve*, Baltimore,
1902, pp. 353–356.   K. Reik, *Der Optativ bei Polybius und Philo von
Alexandria*, Leipzig 1907.   C. Mutzbauer, *Die Grundbedeutung des Kon-
junctiv und Optativ und ihre Entwicklung im Griechischen* (Ein Beitrag zur
historischen Syntax der griechischen Sprache), Leipzig-Berlin   1908.
C. Harsing, *De optativi in chartis Aegyptiis usu*, Diss. Bonn 1910.   J.
Scham, *Der Optativgebrauch bei Klemens von Alexandrien in seiner sprach-
und stilgeschichtlichen Bedeutung.   Ein Beitrag zur Geschichte des Attizismus
in der altchristl. Literatur*, Diss. Tübingen 1913.   F. Slotty, *Der Gebrauch
des Konjunktivs und Optativs in den griechischen Dialekten.   I. Teil: Der
Hauptsatz*, Göttingen 1915.   D. C. Fives, *The Use of the Optative Mood in
the Works of Theodoret, Bp. of Cyrus* (Patristic Studies of the Cath. Univ.
of America) 1937.   R. de L. Henry, *The Late Greek Optative and Its Use
in the Writings of Gregory Nazianzen* (Patr. Stud. Cath. Univ. America,
68) 1943 (on pp. 95–99 are bibliographies of LXX, NT, and Papyri).
E. L. Green, " The Optative Mood in Diodorus Siculus," *Proc. & Trans.
Amer. Philol. Assn.* 62.   Mayser II 1, 288ff.   Schwyzer II 338ff.

Imperial papyri [1]. The reason for the decline probably lies in the " syntactical weakness " (Schwyzer II 337) of the optative. No one can or could quite define its essential function. The two chief functions, volitive and potential, were too dissimilar to give a unity to the mood, and the subjunctive was always at hand for a substitute for either. Moreover, the refinements inherent in the use of the optative were beyond the powers of uneducated Greeks and most barbarians. Those later writers who sought to revive the mood found it difficult to recapture the ancient subtleties. Horn has demonstrated that the optative did gain a new lease of life in the Byzantine period, usually in set phrases or interchangeably with the subjunctive, and its revival in ii/A.D. in the vulgar texts merely followed the earlier learned reaction against its disappearance. Literary writers, especially the Atticists, affected it. Even the ii–iii/A.D. papyri follow suit and the scribes of some NT MSS favoured it. Alongside this went a growing confusion in its use, indicating that the revival was artificial; even an educated writer like Procopius of Caesarea (Schwyzer II 338) confuses it with subjunctive, uses it excessively, and in a non-Attic way.

Optatives which do occur in Hell. authors may be classified:

	MAIN			SUBORDINATE					
	Voli-tive	Potential		Condi-tion	Ob-lique	Com-parat.	Final	Tem-poral	Total
Ptol. pap.	54	127	*Total* 181	13	17				30
LXX	434	41	475	26	7	18	13		64
NT	39	3	42	8	16			2	26

The NT thus shows only a slight decrease from the LXX. There is a tendency to replace optatives with the subjunctive, and optatives occur only in Lk–Ac (28), Paul (31), 1 Pt, 2 Pt (4), Jude (2), Mk (2), Heb (1).

---

[1] Thus it is used after *primary* tenses in the main clause: A.D. 249 ἵνα τοῦτο εἰδέναι ἔχοις, ἐπιστέλλεταί σοι; iv/A.D. ὁπόταν βουληθείης; A.D. 345 ἐὰν δέ τις αὐτῶν ἀφυστερήσιεν καὶ μὴ παραστήσωμεν.

§ 1. Main Clauses

Its disappearance was slightly slower than in dependent clauses. In main clauses it has two distinct functions: to express a wish, usually in set phrases (where the mood survived longest), and to express a rather mild affirmation, generally with ἄν but occasionally without in uncultivated speech. The addition of ἄν to the latter does not infallibly distinguish the two functions, although in the papyri and NT ἄν is not usually lacking with potential optative.

(a) Wish

There is no ἄν. Gradually the subjunctive, fut. indic., and 3rd p. imperat. encroach upon this usage, but here the optative held out the longest. Even in class. times it was not easy to dissociate *wish* (opt.) from *exhortation* to others to fulfil the wish (subj.) or even from positive command (imper.). A cultured writer like auct. ad Heb. has the optative of wish only once. Radermacher (p. 160) illustrates this " struggle of the moods " by referring to a curse-table of 4 B.C. with μὴ τύχη εὐιλατου in the fourth line but μὴ τύχοι in the eighth; and to Acta Thomae 129 συντμήθεισαν καὶ γένωνται. Even in good literary texts ἠξίουν, ἤθελον, ἐβουλόμην often take the place of the older ἀξιοίην ἄν, βουλοίμην ἄν, θέλοιμι ἄν (Ac 25²² ἐβουλόμην; Ga 4²⁰ ἤθελον); and ἵνα c. subj. will now express a wish. However, the opt. εἴη occurs at all periods in the papyri and is common in Biblical Greek.

Mayser and Horn illustrate by the following occurrences the decline and revival of the wish optative in papyrus texts; it was weakest in the NT period. iv/B.C. (2), iii/B.C. (5), ii/B.C. (23), i/B.C. (1) i/A.D. (1), ii/A.D. or ii–iii/A.D. (8), iii/A.D. or iii–iv/A.D. (6), iv/A.D. (4), later (8, all γένοιτο). By contrast, let us look at their incidence in Biblical Greek:
LXX. Ge 9²⁷ 19⁹ vl. 27²⁸ 28³ 31⁴⁹. ⁵³ vl. 34¹¹ 43¹⁴. ¹⁴. ²⁹ 44⁷*¹⁷* 48¹⁶. ¹⁶ 49 ⁶. ⁶. ⁸.—Ex 15¹⁶.—Lev 5¹⁶.—Nu 5²² 6²⁴. ²⁴. ²⁵. ²⁵. ²⁶. ²⁶ 23¹⁰. ¹⁰.—Dt 27¹⁵ (same phrase in ¹⁶. ¹⁷. ¹⁸. ¹⁹. ²⁰. ²¹. ²². ²³. ²⁴. ²⁵. ²⁶ 28¹². ¹³. ²⁰. ²¹. ²². ²⁴. ²⁵. ²⁷. ²⁸. ³⁵. ³⁶ 29¹⁹(18) 33⁷. ¹⁶. ²⁷.—Jo 7²⁵ 22²². ²⁹* 24¹⁶*.—Jg 5²⁴. ²⁴. ³¹ 9¹⁹. ¹⁹. ²⁰ quat. (ter A) 13¹⁷ (not A).—Ru 1⁹. ⁹ (not A) ¹⁶. ¹⁷ 2⁴. ¹². ¹². ¹³ 3¹¹. ¹².—1 Km 1¹⁷ 2²⁰ 3¹⁷ 14⁴⁴. ⁴⁴ 20¹³. ¹³. ¹⁶ 24¹³. ¹³. ¹⁶ quat. 25²². ²². ²⁶. ³¹ 26¹⁹. ¹⁹·¹⁹A 20. ²⁴. ²⁴. ²⁴ A (B ind.)—2 Km 3⁹. ⁹. ²⁹. ³⁵. ³⁵ 7²⁶ 14⁷ 16⁴ 18³² 19¹³(15) bis 23⁴ 24²³.— 3 Km 1³⁷. ³⁷. ⁴⁷ 2²³. ²³. ³³ 8⁵⁷ ter 10⁹ 19². ² 20(21)³* 21(20)¹⁰. ¹⁰.— 4 Km 6³¹. ³¹ (Analysis:

---

* μὴ γένοιτο.

α, ββ, γγ = 41; βγ, γδ = 12).—1 Ch 12¹⁷B¹⁷B bis (S sec. ἐλέγξατο,
A sec. ἐλέγξαι, 21³ 22¹². ¹².—2 Ch 7⁴¹ 24²².—1 Esd 6³²⁽³³⁾.—2 Esd
15(5)¹³.—Ps 6¹¹ quat. (R imper.) 7⁵· ⁶· ⁶· ⁶B 11 (12) ⁴B (AR fut. ind.)
16(17)² 17(18)³⁶Rᵛⁱᵈ (B imper.) 19(20)²· ²· ³· ³B (R*ᵛⁱᵈ imper.)⁴· ⁵· ⁵B
(AR fut. ind.) 20(21)⁹· ⁹ 24(25)²· ²U (B imper.)²⁰ 30(31)²· ¹⁸ ter 32(33)²²
34 (35)⁴ B bis (SAU imper.) ¹⁹· ²⁴· ²⁵ Bᵃᵇ ²⁶· ²⁶· ²⁷· ²⁷· ²⁷ B (SAR imper.)
35 (36)¹² B (SᶜᵃR fut. ind.) 36 (37)¹⁵ B (R imper.)¹⁵ 39 (40)¹² A (B ind.)
¹⁵· ¹⁵· ¹⁵ B (R* imper.) ¹⁵· ¹⁷ 40 (41)³ ter ⁴ B (AR fut. ind.)¹⁴ 51 (52)⁶· ⁶
(R sec. indic.)⁶ Bᶜ (B ind.) 62 (63)⁶ (R ind.) 66 (67)² ter ⁷· ⁸ 67 (68)³ 68
(69)⁷· ⁷· ¹⁵· ²⁵ 69 (70)³ quat. (SR imper.)⁴ (SR imper.) 70(71)¹ 71(72)¹⁹
73 (74)²³ (Sᶜᵃ RT indic.) 84 (85)⁸ 88 (89)⁵³ 89 (90)⁵· ⁶ quat. 103 (104)³⁴· ³⁵
105 (106)⁴⁸ 108 (109)⁷· ⁷· ¹³ Sᶜᵃ T (S imper.)¹⁴· ¹⁴· ¹⁵ 112 (113)² 113¹⁶
(115⁸) ²² (115¹⁴) 118 (119)⁵· ⁴¹· ¹⁷⁰· ¹⁷² (AR* ind., T subj.) 120 (121)³
(subj?)⁷ (ART fut. ind.) 127 (128)⁵ ter (AR ind.; T subj.) 133 (134)³ A
(S fut. ind., T aor. subj.) 134 (135)¹⁸ 136 (137)⁵· ⁶ 146 (147)¹.—Pr 4²⁷ᵇ
A (B fut. ind.) 11²⁶ 24⁵² (30¹⁷· ¹⁷).—Eccl. 5⁷ B (ACSᶜᵃ ind.).—Jb 1²¹
3³· ⁴· ⁵· ⁶ quat. ⁷· ⁷· ⁸· ⁹ ter 5⁴ B (A ind.)⁴· ⁵· ¹⁴· ¹⁵· ¹⁵· ¹⁶· ¹⁶ 6¹⁰· ²⁹
12²⁵· ²⁵ 13⁵ 15⁶· ⁶ C (B fut. ind.)²⁸· ²⁸· ³⁰ B (A ind.)³³· ³³ 16⁶⁽⁵⁾· ¹⁹⁽¹⁸⁾·
21⁽²⁰⁾· ²¹ ⁽²⁰⁾ B ²² (21) 17⁸ B (A ind.) ⁹· ⁹ 18⁷· ⁷· ⁸· ·⁸ A (B pf. ind.) ⁹· ¹¹· ¹¹·
¹³· ¹⁴· ¹⁴· ¹⁷· ¹⁸ 19²⁶ 20¹⁰· ¹⁰· ¹⁵ C (B ind.) ¹⁶· ¹⁶ B (A fut. ind.) ¹⁷· ²³· ²³·
²⁴· ²⁵· ²⁵· ²⁶· ²⁶· ²⁷· ²⁷· ²⁸· ²⁸ 21²⁰· ²⁰ 22²² S* 23⁴ (Sᶜᵃ ind.) ⁵ ter 24¹⁸· ¹⁹· ²⁰· ²⁰
27⁵· ⁷ 29¹³ 30²⁴ 31⁸· ⁸· ¹⁰· ¹⁰· ²²· ²²· ²⁸· ³⁰· ³⁰· ⁴⁰ (A subj.) 24¹⁰· ¹¹ (A ind.).—
Wi 7¹⁵.—Si 22² C (A fut. ind.) 25¹⁹ ⁽²⁶⁾ 33 (36)⁴· ¹¹ 38¹⁵ 43²¹ ⁽²³⁾ S* (B
fut. ind.) 45²⁶ ⁽³¹⁾ 46¹¹ ⁽¹⁴⁾· ¹² ⁽¹⁴⁾ 49¹⁰ ⁽¹²⁾ 50²³ ⁽²⁵⁾ 51²⁹ ⁽³⁷⁾ bis.—Jdt
10⁸· ⁸ 13²⁰ ⁽²⁶⁾ 15¹¹ ⁽¹²⁾· ¹⁰ ⁽¹¹⁾ B (SA aor. ind.).—To B 3⁹· ¹¹ 5¹⁴ ⁽¹⁹⁾·
¹⁷· ⁽²²⁾· ¹⁹ ⁽²⁴⁾ 7¹⁷ ⁽²⁰⁾ 10¹² 11¹⁷ 13¹⁰ ⁽¹²⁾ bis.—To S 3⁹ 5¹⁰· ¹⁴· ¹⁴· ¹⁷ quat. ¹⁹
7⁷· ¹²· ¹⁷ 9⁶ 10¹¹· ¹¹· ¹² quat. 11¹⁴· ¹⁷ 13¹⁰· ¹⁰.—Ob¹² A.—Jon 2⁸.—Zach
3².—Isa 14²⁹ 25¹ 28²².—Je 3¹⁹ 11⁵· ²⁰ 15¹¹ 17¹⁸ ter 20¹² 36²² (29²²).—
La 1²² 2¹⁸.—Da O′ 3³⁹· ⁴⁴· ⁴⁴· ⁴⁴· ⁹⁸ (41) 4¹⁶ ⁽¹⁹⁾· ³⁴ᶜ.— Da Θ 3³⁹· ⁴⁴ ter
⁹⁸ (41) 7²⁵ ⁽²⁶⁾.—1 Mac 8²³· ²³ 9¹⁰* 13⁵*.—2 Mac 1² V (A inf.) ³· ⁴· ⁴· ⁵ ter
15²⁴.—4 Mac 6¹⁵ S (A imper.) ¹⁷· ²¹ 13⁹ A (SV subj.).

NT. Mk 11¹⁴ (vl. subj.).—Lk 1³⁸ 20¹⁶*· ¹⁶*.—Ac 8²⁰ (the only pres.
tense among the volitives).—Ro 3⁴*· ⁶*· ³¹* 6²*· ¹⁵* 7⁷*· ¹³* 9¹⁴* 11¹*· ¹¹*
15⁵· ¹³.—1 Co 6¹⁵*.—Ga 2¹⁷* 3²¹* 6¹⁴*.—1 Th 3¹¹· ¹²· ¹² 5²³.—2 Th 2¹⁷· ¹⁷
3⁵· ¹⁶.—Phm 20 ὀναίμην.—2 Ti 1¹⁶· ¹⁸ 4¹⁶.—Heb 13²¹.—1 Pt 1² 5¹⁰.—
2 Pt 1².—Jude ²· ⁹.

Ps. Sol 4⁷ ἐξάραι (or imper?) ⁸· ⁹· ¹⁶*· ¹⁸· ¹⁸· ¹⁹· ²¹ KPM (not AV)
²²· ²⁸· ²⁹* 11⁹ 12⁴· ⁴· ⁵· ⁶· ⁶· ⁸· ⁸ 17¹⁰· ²⁷· ²⁷· ⁵¹ 18⁶ (The only other opt.
in this book renders the Heb. frequentative impf.: ὁ πλοῦτος αὐτῶν
διέλθοι went forth).—Vit. Proph. (only final, after ἵνα).—T. Sol. D 6¹
βασιλεῦ Σολομῶν, χαίροις.—Clem. ad Cor. tit. 23¹ 45⁷ 54.—Ign. ad Eph.
2¹ 11²· ² 12², ad Magn. 11, ad Trall. 13³, ad Smyrn. 5³.
    Some Hell. authors: Aratus *Phaenomena* (1154 lines): 16 (χαίροιτε),
100, 154, 155, 304, 324, 460, 637, 758, 823, 824, 824, 1049, 1050, 1086,
1088, 1090.—Callimachus *Hymn* I (Zeus) 64, 68; ·II (Apollo) 113; III
(Artemis) 84, 137 (εἴην), 137; IV (Delos) 98, 162, 195, 240, 326 (χαίροι);

---

    * μὴ γένοιτο.

VI (Demeter) 116 (εἴη).—Alciphron *Letters* II 2¹ 5³ (μὴ . . . γένοιτο) 14¹
16¹ 174* 20³ 25³; III 12¹· ¹ (εἴη) ⁵ (εἴη) ⁵ 15⁴ (γένοιτο) 26² 28⁴ 32¹· ¹
35³ 37² 38³ 41; IV 3² (γένοιτο) 5¹ (εἴη) 9² (γένοιτο) 18³· ³*¹⁶· ¹⁶ 19²¹· ²¹.

It is clear then that the optative can still express a wish or
prayer, nearly always in 3rd p. and especially in the formula
μη γένοιτο (15 in NT). Only two of the NT instances are
imprecations (prayers for evil): Mk 11¹⁴ Ac 8²⁰. In fact, there
is a strong tendency to use the imperative: ἀνάθεμα ἔστω Ga 1⁸ᶠ
1 Co 16²². The author of Ac uses λαβέτω instead of LXX λάβοι
when citing the Psalms (1²⁰). In spite of this, there still remain
39 instances of wish-optative. The LXX does not contain any
more on an average per page.

(b) Potential

The opt. with ἄν indicates a potential mood; sometimes it is
described as an " urbane " or " deliberative " optative.

It frequently helped the writer to express what would
happen on the fulfilment of some supposed condition; to express,
in fact, an apodosis without a protasis. It was becoming a
luxury of speech and was beginning to disappear in favour of
the subj. or fut. ind. with ἄν. As with the volitive, it was largely
in set phrases that it survived: thus καλῶς ἂν ἔχοι. Already in
Polybius it seems to be confined to these. Careful authors use
it more frequently than the NT authors, but they are in doubt
whether to use ἄν or some other particle like ἴσως or δήπουθεν.
The vagaries of scribal transmission may be partly responsible
for the omission of ἄν, but Reinhold (*de Graecitate patrum Apost.*
p. 110) brings forward enough examples to show that there was
confusion here at the close of the Hellenistic period. In the
Attic inscriptions investigated by Meisterhans (p. 247f), opt. c.
ἄν is found only in some poetry (iv/B.C.) but in decrees, etc.,
there would be little occasion for it. In the iii/B.C. papyri
however this opt. is widespread in certain epistolary phrases:

καλῶς ἂν ποιήσαις 264. 257. 245. iii.—χαρίζοιο ἄν *be so good* 258
ter. 250 bis. iii quat.—καλῶς ἂν ἔχοι 25 times in iii/B.C.—εἴη ἂν ὡς θέλω
260. 252. 223, 257.—βούλομαι P. Petr. III.—εἴη ἂν ὡς ἡμεῖς θέλομεν
257. 256. iii–ii.—εἴη ἂν τὸ δέον. 242 ter.—Other phrases 258 (Horn).
iii (Horn). 223. 260 bis. 255.

ii/B.C.: χαρίζοιο ἄν 156.—χαρίζοι⟨ο⟩ δ' ἄν 156.—εἴη ἂν ὡς θέλω
ii (Horn). 170 (Horn). 153 (Horn).—εἴη ἂν ὡς βούλομαι 168. 153 ter.

---

* μὴ γένοιτο.

164 (cp. 2 Mac 11²⁸).—εἴη ἂν ὡς εὔχομαι BGU IV.—εἴη ἂν ὡς αἱρούμεθα Goodsp.—εἴη ἂν τὸ δέον P. Par. (156 B.C.).—Other phrases 160 (Horn). BU, P. Par. 63 (164 B.C.), 64. 64, P. Par. (156 B.C.), P. Lond. I (168 B.C.), Cairo (123 B.C.).

i/B.C.—none.

i/A.D. : εὖ ποιήσαις (no ἄν) 95.

ii/A.D. : c. 130. 167.

iii/A.D. : 274. 298. late. iii–iv.

Later: 346. iv. 591. vi–vii.

It should be said that some of the above are not a fair sample of the popular speech, but are part of the florid style of officials or the affectation of literary aspirants. The less stereotyped phrases had been dropped from the living speech by the close of iii/B.C. All that was retained thereafter were certain polite set phrases which die very hard.

Unless we include 4 Mac, this optative is not common in the LXX, although we might include the deliberative optative in questions under this head. Apart from the latter there is only 2 Mac 11²⁸ outside 4 Mac (1¹· ⁵· ⁷· ⁸ no ἄν, ¹⁰ 2⁶· ²⁴ 3⁴ S [AV ind.] 5⁶· ¹³ no ἄν, 7¹⁷· ²² 8⁶ 9⁶· ²⁴). But there are questions of a potential or deliberative or futuristic kind:

with ἄν: Ge 23¹⁵ 44⁸.—Dt 28⁶⁷· ⁶⁷.—Jb 19²³ 25⁴ 29² 31³¹ 41⁴ (5).—Pr 20¹⁸ (24).—Si 25³ (5).—Ezk 15².

without ἄν: Nu 11²⁹.—Jg 9²⁹.—2 Km 18³³ (19¹).—Ps 119 (120)³· ³. —Ca 8¹.—Jb 23³ (A ἄν) 31³⁵ 38²⁰· ²⁰.—4 Mac 8¹⁷ 14¹⁰ (Sᶜᵃ ἄν) 15⁴.

In NT there seems to be but one genuine instance which is not a question (Ac 26²⁹ ABSᶜ), and this is where in the royal presence of Agrippa, Paul employs the stilted εὐξαίμην ἄν. Luke makes the Athenians to say τί ἂν θέλοι οὗτος λέγειν; (Ac 17¹⁸), and the Ethiopian to ask *how could I?* πῶς γὰρ ἂν δυναίμην; (8³¹). Perhaps also Ac 2¹²E. It was old-fashioned in the NT age, and the writers prefer a mere future (Ro 3⁶ 1 Co 15³⁵) or other device. But we must also include here many dependent questions of a deliberative kind which are only incidentally dependent, and are still deliberative when transformed into direct speech: Lk 1⁶² 6¹¹ (not D) 9⁴⁶ 15²⁶ (vl. om ἄν).—Jn 13²⁴ vl.—Ac 5²⁴ 10¹⁷ 17²⁰ vl. 21³³ (EHLP add ἄν). But opinions may legitimately differ whether the following have opt. simply because of the class. rules of sequence: Lk 1²⁹ (but D ἄν) 8⁹ (vl. om opt.) 18³⁶ (vl. + ἄν) 22²³ (vl. ind.). In Lk 3¹⁵ (διαλογιζομένων μήποτε αὐτὸς εἴη ὁ χριστός) what they actually asked themselves may be expressed by opt. The presence of ἄν would seem to decide in favour of an original potential in these doubtful cases.

In this respect LXX and NT are much of a unity, and

because of the infrequence of this opt. the LXX should be classified with the papyri of i/B.C.–i/A.D. rather than with those of iii/B.C.

T. Sol. D 4⁴ διαπορῶν τί ἄρα ἀποκρίνοιτο.—Ign. ad Eph. 2², ad Magn 2, 12, ad Rom 5², ad Polyc. 6².

Some Hell. authors: Alciphron *Letters* I 11³ (εἴποις ἄν *you might say*), 13¹ (ἠπόρουν ὅ τι πράξαιμι *I didn't know what to do*), 14³ (πῶς ... ὑπομείναιμεν *how could we endure?*), 22¹ ἄν; II 2² (εἴπαις ἄν *you might say*), 10³ ἄν, 15² ἄν; III 2² (εἴποι τις ἄν *you might say, as it were*), 11¹ ἄν; IV 2³ ἄν, 3³ ἄν, 8¹ ἄν, 10⁴, 11⁵ ἄν, 13⁶· ⁷ ἄν, 16⁷ ἄν, 18² ἄν ². ³ ἄν, 19³ ἄν.— Callimachus *Hymns* I 15. 15. 91 κεν; II 26. 27. 31 ἄν, 35 κε; III 15. 104, 155 κεν, 177 κεν, 250; IV 25 κε, 126 κε; V 103.—Aratus *Phaenomena* 12 κε, 78 ἄν, 142 ἄν, 169, 195 κεν, 211 κεν, 451 κε, 456 ἄν, 463 κε, 495 κε, 530 κε, 559 κεν, 562 ἄν, 566 ἄν, 579 ἄν, 607 ἄν, 712 κε, 729 κε, 731, 782 κε, 793 ἄν, 797 κεν, 798 ἄν, 802 κε, 815 ἄν, 816 ἄν, 818 κε, 827 κεν, 839 κεν, 839, 850 κε, 857 ἄν, 873 κεν, 876 ἄν, 879 ἄν, 888 κε, 904, 915, 1006 κε, 1066, 1085, 1144, 1144 κε, 1145 ἄν, 1148, 1148, 1154 κεν.

§ 2. Dependent Clauses

Here is a still more rapid decline in the Hell. period, and the opt. has become almost entirely alien to the popular speech. In more artificial language it still serves in indirect speech and final and conditional clauses, whereas in class. Greek it regularly appeared in dependent clauses after a historic tense where the subj. would have appeared had the clause depended on a primary tense. The NT retains the subj. even in historic sequence, in common with popular Greek in general from the mid-ii/B.C. The class. rule is rarely observed in the Ptolemaic papyri (Mayser II 1, 288).

(a) Iterative

This is the regular class. function of the opt. in dependent clauses following a historic tense. It expresses reiteration, best rendered in English by *ever* (*whoever, whenever, if ever*). The impf. ind. or aor. ind., sometimes with ἄν (see above, Indic. Mood), was substituted for this in the later period. The LXX and NT have ὅταν and ὁπόταν with impf. or aor. ind., but Mayser can find no instance of this in the Ptolemaic papyri, while Radermacher finds one or two instances in Polybius. The iterative opt. was soon confused with the potential, and ἄν was consequently added, as is seen in Aristeas 59 (Wendland) τὴν διάθεσιν εἶχεν ὥστε, καθ' ὃ ἂν μέρος στρέφοιτο, τὴν πρόσοψιν εἶναι τὴν αὐτήν.

Clear instances of iterative opt. are found in the Ptol. pap.,
Philo, and NT, especially with εἰ τύχοι *for example* (1 Co 14¹⁰
15³⁷). Papyri:—

iv/B.C.: UPZ no. 1. 12f ⟨ὃ⟩ ς δ' ἀν[ελοι] τὰ γράμματα ταῦτα [κα] ἰ
ἀδικοῖ 'Αρτεμισίην. ὁ θεὸς αὐτῶι τὴ⟨ν⟩ δίκην ἐπιθ[είη]. This is a
potential opt. within a hypothetical relative clause, hardly distinguishable from the iterative.

iii/B.C.: Petr. II 18 (2b) 15 ἔτυπτεν αὐτὸν κατὰ τοῦ τραχήλου καὶ
εἰς ὃ μέρος τύχοι τοῦ σώματος (246). Formal language of a bill of
complaint. Magd. 42 πληγάς μοι ἐνέβαλεν καὶ πλείους εἰς ὃ τύχοι μέρος
τοῦ σώματος (221).

ii/B.C.: 162 (Horn). 118 (Horn). 117 (Horn). PSI III 167 18
(118 B.C.) formal language. Teb 24. 65 τύχοι (117 B.C.). BGU VI
1253. 10 (but Lobel's emend. does away with opt. here).

i/ A.D.: 18 (Horn)

ii/A.D.: 131 (Horn)

iii/A.D.: c 376 (Horn)

later: 409 and eleven other exx. of temporal, to viii/A.D. Stylistic
revival of opt. in Byzantine Greek: v–vi/A.D., vi/A.D., c 551. 616. In
an iterative temporal clause this revival appears to have begun already
in 2 Clem 12³ ὅταν λαλῶμεν . . . καὶ . . . εἴη.

Except for εἰ τύχοι the iterative opt. is no longer in use in
LXX and NT, having quite disappeared from the colloquial
language by this time [1]. Mark's method of filling the gap (ὅταν
with past ind.) is found elsewhere with extreme rarity [2]. More
frequently ἄν is added [3] to the indicative.

(b) *Conditional*

The reaction in favour of the opt. influenced a wider circle
than the Atticists, particularly in conditional and final clauses
in the case of non-atticizing cultured writers. After ii/A.D. the
influence spread to more popular authors. Radermacher
observes that the text Περὶ Ἑρμηνείας (prob. i/A.D., not atticistic)

---

[1] In literary writers, e.g.: Aratus *Phaenomena* 823 ὅτ' εὐδίου
κεχρημένος ἤματος εἴης *whenever you desire a fair day*, 1141 ὅτ' ὄμβρου
σήματα φαίνοι (mice build nests) *whenever Zeus shows signs of rain,—*
Callimachus *Hymns* III 136 τῶν εἴη μὲν ἐμοὶ φίλος ὅστις ἀληθής *whoever
is a true friend of mine.* VI 68 ὅσσα πάσαιτο τόσων ἔχεν ἵμερος αὖτις.

[2] Polyb. IV 32.5f.—LXX Ex 17¹¹·¹¹, Nu 11⁹ 21⁹, Jg 6³ (A ὅταν;
B ἐάν), 1 Km 17³⁴, Ps 77³⁴ 118³² 119⁷, Jb 20²² (A ὅποτε; B ὁπόταν).
NT Mk 3¹¹.

[3] LXX Le 27¹² καθότι ἄν c. fut. ind., To 7¹¹B ὅποτε ἂν εἰσεπορεύοντο.
NT Mk 6⁵⁶ ὅσοι ἂν ἥψαντο, Ac 2⁴⁵ 4³⁵ καθότι ἂν χρείαν εἶχεν. 1 Co
12² ὡς ἂν ἤγεσθε.

employs as a typical form of conditional sentence εἰ c. opt. in
the protasis and fut. indic. in the apodosis. So also Philo [1],
Herm. S. IX 12, 4 (οὐδεὶς εἰσελεύσεται, εἰ μὴ λάβοι: Harnack
λάβῃ), Theophilus ad Autolycum I 6. The atticizing influence
must have been wide. Epictetus, and Diodorus (Kapff, p.
88) use opt. after εἰ quite extensively. It is rare in LXX and
papyri (Harsing 38f; Mayser II 1, 293); none of the instances
adduced by Horn appear to be earlier than i/A.D. and the majority
are Byzantine. Radermacher notes that the Pergamum
inscriptions have but one instance and prefer ἐάν c. subj. in the
protasis and fut. ind. in the apodosis. Moreover in most examples from the Ptolemaic papyri εἰ c. opt. stands obliquely for
the direct form ἐάν c. subj., and so ought strictly to be considered as indirect speech. Besides, most of them betray the
stilted language of official letters or decrees.

Of true conditions with opt., there are only three in NT: Ac 24¹⁹
ἔδει . . . κατηγορεῖν, εἴ τι ἔχοιεν πρὸς ἐμέ, 1 Pt 3¹⁴ εἰ καὶ πάσχοιτε
. . . , μακάριοι, ¹⁷ κρεῖττον . . . , εἰ θέλοι τὸ θέλημα τοῦ θεοῦ, πάσχειν . . .
There are about 25 in LXX, which is almost the same percentage,
especially if 4 Mac is ignored: 1 Km 24²⁰. ²⁰ εἰ εὕροιτό τις τὸν ἐχθρὸν . . .
καὶ ἐκπέμψαι αὐτόν (fut. ind. in apodosis) (Α εὑρὼν . . . ἐκπέμψαι),
14⁶ εἴ τι ποιήσαι ἡμῖν Κύριος (sc. it would be well); hardly conditional:
Perhaps the Lord will.—2 Km 16¹² εἴ πως ἴδοι Κύριος: perhaps the Lord . . .
(see above).—4 Km 6²⁷ μή σε σώσαι Κύριος·πόθεν σώσω σε; Ps 138 (139)⁹
S*ᶜᵃ (BR* subj.) ἐὰν λάβοιμι τὰς πτέρυγάς μοι (apodosis fut. ind.).—
Jb 6² εἰ γάρ τις ἱστῶν στήσαι μου τὴν ὀργὴν, τὰς δὲ ὀδύναι μου ἄραι
ἐν ζυγῷ (apod. fut. ind.), 6⁸ εἰ γὰρ δῴη, καὶ ἔλθοι μου ἡ αἴτησις, καὶ τὴν
ἐλπίδα μου δῴη ὁ Κύριος (no apodosis): if only God would give me . . .!
20²³ εἴ πως πληρώσαι γαστέρα αὐτοῦ (apod. opt.), 34¹⁴ εἰ γὰρ βούλοιτο
συνέχειν (apod. fut. ind.), 38²⁰ εἰ ἀγάγοις με εἰς ὅρια αὐτῶν (a question;
not a true condition).—Isa 49¹⁵. εἰ δὲ καὶ ταῦτα ἐπιλάθοιτο γυνή (apod.
fut. ind.) (S* ind.).—2 Mac 9²⁴ Α ὅπως ἐάν τι παράδοξον ἀποβαίη (V ind.).—
4 Mac 2⁸ κἂν φιλάργυρός τις εἴη . . . , 4¹⁷ εἰ ἐπιτρέψειεν . . . (apod. aor.
ind.), ²³ εἴ τινες αὐτῶν φάνοιεν, 5³ εἰ δέ τινες μὴ θέλοιεν, ¹⁹ εἰ
μιεροφαγήσαιμεν, 6¹⁸ εἰ νῦν μεταβαλοίμεθα ¹⁹Α γενοίμεθα τοῖς νέοις
ἀσεβείας τύπος (S γενώμεθα), 8². ² εἰ μὲν μιεροφαγήσαιεν . . . εἰ δὲ
ἀντιλέγοιεν, 9² εἰ μή . . . γνώσει χρησαίμεθα, ²⁷ ὡς δ' εἰ φαγεῖν βούλοιτο,
12⁴Α εἰ μὲν μὴ πεισθείης (S πισθείς), 14¹⁷ εἰ δὲ καὶ μὴ δύναιτο κωλύειν.

The use of slightly antique language in the presence of
Felix, rather than εἴ τι ἔχουσιν, is understandable. The only
way to account for the apparently impeccable Attic of the

---

[1] K. Reik, Der Optativ bei Polybius and Philo, Leipzig 1907, 154.

Petrine optatives is to suppose them to have been abstracted
from the archaic periods of a solemn exhortation; even here the
potential clause (opt. c. ἄν) which might have been expected in a
classical apodosis does not occur, for the genius of living
speech has forcibly interposed the pres. tense since persecution
is at hand. Zerwick ascribes the opt. to the writer's tactfulness
of heart and a reluctance to mention sufferings except very
tentatively to those who were actually destined to meet them
(§ 228d). The other instances of εἰ c. opt. are not so much
real conditions as final clauses (Ac 17²⁷ 27¹²)[1], and there are
parenthetical phrases introduced by εἰ = *if possible* or *as it
were*: εἰ δυνατὸν εἴη (vl. ἦν), εἰ δύναιντο (Ac 20¹⁶ 27³⁹) and
εἰ τύχοι (1 Co 14¹⁰ 15³⁷). Other clauses introduced by εἰ and
dependent on a verb like ζητεῖν are virtually indirect questions,
a class. survival: Ac 17¹¹ 25²⁰. The LXX also uses εἰ c. opt. in
these several ways—another indication of kinship in style and
syntax with the NT. In neither LXX nor NT is there an
instance of εἰ c. opt. in the protasis and opt. c. ἄν in the apodosis; and notice εἴ πως in 2 Km 16¹² Jb 20²² Ac 27¹². However,
the LXX has εἰ c. opt. to express a wish, Hebrew אִם; Mk 8¹²
uses εἰ c. fut. ind.

The constructions of εἰ c. opt. in conditions is still common in
literary writers, but the style is very affected and poetic:
Aratus *Phaenomena* 563 ἀτὰρ εἰ νεφέεσσι μέλαιναι γίνοιτ' *if they
be dark with clouds*, 564 ἢ ὄρεος κεκρυμμένα ἀντέλλοιεν *or if they rise
hidden behind a hill*, 825 εἰ δ' αὔτως καθαρόν μιν ἔχοι *if he be so pure
again*, 826 δύνοι δ' ἀνέφελος *and if he set cloudless*, 838 εἴ γε μὲν
ἀμφοτέροις ἄμυδις κεχρημένος εἴη *if he is draped both in black and red*,
855 καὶ εἴ ποτε χείματος ὥρῃ ὠχρήσαι κατιών *if in winter his hue wax
wan at evening*, 858 εἰ δ' ὁ μὲν ἀνέφελος βάπτοι *but if cloudless he dip*,
872 εἰ μὲν κεῖναι μᾶλλον κνέφαος φορέοιντο ἀκτῖνες *the more those beams
are borne in shadow*, 874 εἰ δ' ὀλίγος τανύοιτο περὶ δνόφος ἀκτίνεσσιν
but if but faint the dust that veils his beams, 887 εἰ δὲ μὲν ἐκ βορέαο μι'
οἴη φοινίσσοιτο *but if only one shine purple to the north*, 905 εἰ δ' ὁ
μὲν ἐκ βορέω Φάτνης ἀμενηνὰ φαείνοι *if the Ass shine feebly to the north
of the Manger*.—Callimachus *Hymn* III 178 καὶ εἰ Στυμφαΐδες εἶεν *even
if they were*, IV 129 καὶ εἰ μέλλοιμι ῥοάων διψαλέην ἄμπωτιν ἔχων
even if I must wander.—Especially frequent in the atticistic Alciphron's
Letters: I 1. 5 εἰ χειμὼν ἐπιλάβοιτο *in case of bad weather*, 10, 4 ἵν' εἰ
πού τι . . . εὑρεθείη σῶμα *if any corpse is found* (oblique), 12, 2 εἰ . . .

---

[1] Ac 17²⁷ ζητεῖν τ. θεόν, εἰ ἄρα γε ψηλαφήσειαν αὐτὸν καὶ εὕροιεν, 27¹²
ἔθεντο βουλὴν ἀναχθῆναι . . . εἴ πως δύναιντο . . . παραχειμάσαι.

πύθοιτο *if he should hear* (+ fut. ind.), 13, 4; 16, 3; 20, 2: II 12; 14, 2; 15, 1; 18, 3 εἰ δὲ μάθοι *if he finds out* (+ fut. ind.); 21, 3; 28, 2; 37, 2; III 5, 2 εἰ μὴ τὸ χωρίον πρὸς τοῖς ἀργυρίοις λάβοι (says she will not bestow her favours) *unless she gets the landed estate in addition to the cash* (oblique); 5, 3; 8, 2; 10, 3. 4; 14, 3; 16, 1; 26, 4; 28, 4; 34, 1; 38, 1. 2. 3; 42, 2; IV 3, 3; 10, 3. 3; 17, 6; 19, 3. 19. 21.   Often in an oblique sense after a historic tense.

(c) *Final*

This is another atticism which is very rare in the papyri. Class. authors had used the opt. after a secondary tense, but apart from the doubtful Mk 12²S (ἵνα λάβοι) we find it neither in the NT nor Koine generally; it is almost absent from Polybius. The Atticists went so far as to use the opt. where the classical rule preferred subj.   After ii/A.D., less literary authors followed suit, e.g. Vettius Valens and some later papyri.   Radermacher finds odd examples as early as Plutarch and the apocryphal Acts of Apostles.   Attic inscriptions of the period invariably have subj. after ἵνα, although they occasionally have opt. after ὅπως. Diodorus Siculus, who is distinctly a literary man, has only about eight final optatives compared with 179 subjunctives. Epictetus, who has potential opt. four times, has it only once in a final clause.   Meisterhans shows it once in Attic inscriptions, iv/B.C. fin. (p. 247).   Examples in the Ptol. pap. are difficult to establish: there may be a fut. opt. in ii/B.C. ἠξίωσα ἵνα χρηματισθήσοιτο P. Tebt I.   There is nothing else before ii/A.D. fin.   The discarding of the final opt. in post-class. Greek represents one of the furthest departures of that Greek from the Attic model.

Opt. after ἵνα, ὅπως: percentage, as compared with subj.					
Biblical	ii/ B.C.	i/B.C.	i/A.D.	ii/A.D.	iii/A.D.
2 Mac 71% (atticist) LXX 1·7% NT nil	Polyb. 7%	Diod. Sic. 5%	Josephus 32% Plutarch 49%	Arrian 82% Appion 87%	Herodian 75%

It is safe to say that there is nothing of this atticistic elegance in NT.   It is unlikely that the pointing in Eph 1¹⁷ is δώῃ (WH

text); B has δῷ (WH mg); and in any case the ἵνα may be imperatival; final opt. does not come very well after a present
tense, except with the Atticists and much later writers, and
makes the achievement of the purpose more remote than the
author could have intended. The same δωη occurs in 2 Ti 2²⁵
(vl. δῷ) after μήποτε and balances a subj., but it must be admitted
that in the same epistle δωη cannot be anything else than an
opt. (1¹⁶· ¹⁸) ¹. There is textual uncertainty in two other places
in Eph (3¹⁶ 6¹⁹) and in Jn 15¹⁶, but the opt. always rests on
slender evidence. These optatives, like that in Mk 12², are
probably the learned corrections of atticistic scribes. In Eph 6¹⁹
moreover the ἵνα is epexegetical rather than final. It may
seem that the class. rule of sequence in oblique clauses is being
followed in Mk 14¹⁰ᶠ where παραδοῖ (as if from an -ω verb) is
used in a final and a relative clause, but we must remember that
οι and η were often confused and this may be a scribe's correction of παραδῇ. This could also be the explanation of ἵνα τις γνοῖ
Mk 9³⁰ (a correction of a corrupt γνῇ).

Kinship in syntax between LXX and NT is further indicated by the fact that, apart from 4 Mac, there is no sure
example of this optative.

LXX: Ps 37 (38)¹⁷ R* μήποτε ἐπιχαρείησάν μοι οἱ ἐχθροί μου
(B subj.).—Pr 22¹⁷ S* τὴν δὲ σὴν καρδίαν ἐπίσημον ἵνα γνοῖς (vl. subj.),
¹⁹ S* ἵνα γνώρισον τὴν ὁδόν σου (vl. subj.).—Jb 21² Α ἀκούσατε...
ἵνα μὴ εἴη μοι (B ᾖ).—4 Mac 4⁶ ὅπως ... λάβοι, ²³ ὅπως ... θάνοιεν,
5⁶ ὅπως ... σώζοιο, 6⁸ ASᶜᵃ ὅπως ἐξανισταῖτο (S* ἐξανίστατο), 8¹²
ὅπως ... πείσειεν, 10¹ ὅπως ἀπογευσάμενος σώζοιο, 12⁶ ὅπως ...
παρορμήσειεν, 12⁶ V* ὅπως ποιήσαιεν (Α ποιῆσαι), 17¹ ἵνα μὴ ψαύσειεν
τι τοῦ σώματος.

Aratus Phaen. 381. 496. 1127 (after primary tense).—Callimachus
Hymn I 34. 53, III 27. 61. 89. 108. 167.—Alciphron Letters I 15, 1 (after
primary tense), II 3, 2 (primary), III 7, 5 (primary), IV 18, 3 (primary).

(d) Indirect Statements

The Atticists took this opt. too under their special protection,
even after a primary tense; e.g. Alciphron IV 7, 5 τὰς νεφέλας
ὁπόθεν εἶεν καὶ τὶς ἀτόμους ὁποῖαι ἀγνοοῦμεν. After a secondary tense in indirect speech the opt. was employed in class.

---

¹ Moreover the argument about balance is weaker in view of 2 Mac 9²⁴
where an opt. does in fact balance a subj.

Greek but there was never any constraint about it; direct speech
was legitimate within the dependent clause. Hellenistic writers
took advantage of the concession, and, although Diodorus
Siculus uses the opt. 29 times like this, he leaves the direct
speech as it is in 475 instances [1]. Even Atticists, like Dionysius
of Halicarnassus, shared this preference. On the whole it would
not appear that the opt. in, and because of, indirect speech, even
after a secondary tense, was favoured in Hell. Greek. In the
papyri, most of the Hellenistic examples are early (9 out of 10
are iii/B.C.) and the rest are nearly all in the Byzantine period
of optative-revival (A.D. 117. 265. 336. 345. 543. 583. 583).

In the LXX and NT therefore it is a sign of atticizing style,
and only a few books display it: Jb 23³ (γινώσκειν) ὅτι εὕροιμι
αὐτὸν ἔλθοιμι εἰς τέλος.— 2 Mac 4¹ ἐκακολόγει . . . ὡς οὗτός τε
εἴη.—4 Mac 4²².—Ac 25¹⁶ ἀπεκρίθην ὅτι οὐκ ἔστιν ἔθος . . .
χαρίζεσθαι . . . πρὶν ἢ . . . ἔχοι . . . τε . . . λάβοι (but οι and η
were often confused).

Alciphron I 13, 1 ἠπόρουν ὅ τι πράξαιμι, II 5, 2 τοῦ προξένου
φήσαντος ὡς δεοίμην χρημάτων *when my sponsor said that I
needed money*, III 2, 1 κατεμέμφετο ὅτι μὴ θαμίζοιμι παρ' αὐτόν
blamed me for not coming to see him more often, 2, 2 φράσας παρ'
ὅτου καλοῖτο *told her who had invited her*.

(e) Indirect Questions

This opt. also is rare, and here too in class. Greek it was
permissible to retain the form of the direct question. Strangely,
although it had disappeared in pre-Christian times, Luke is fond
of this opt. Excluding deliberative questions, which are
incidentally indirect [2], Luke has opt. six times. Thus in Lk 9⁴⁶
τὸ τίς ἂν εἴη μείζων αὐτῶν we have an indirect question and
must not translate εἴη *might be*; it is not indefinite, deliberative,
or future, but means *was*. Only Est. and 2 Mac (A-text) betray
any traces of it in LXX, and there is sometimes the excuse of a

---

[1] See the tables in Kapff op. cit. p. 63.
[2] These probably owe their origin to a dir. delib. question: Lk 1⁶²
ἐνένευον . . . τὸ τί ἂν θέλοι, 3¹⁵ διαλογιζομένων πάντων . . . μήποτε αὐτὸς
εἴη ὁ χριστός, 6¹¹ διελάλουν πρὸς ἀλλήλους τί ἂν ποιήσαιεν τῷ Ἰησοῦ.
15²⁶ ἐπυθάνετο τί ἂν εἴη ταῦτα.—Jn 13²⁴ vl. πυθέσθαι τίς ἂν εἴη.—
Ac 5²⁴ διηπόρουν . . . τί ἂν γένοιτο τοῦτο, 10¹⁷ διηπόρει . . . τί ἂν εἴη τὸ
ὅραμα, 17²⁰ βουλόμεθα οὖν γνῶναι τί ἂν θέλοι (B τίνα θέλει ταῦτα εἶναι),
21³³ ἐπυνθάνετό τις εἴη καὶ τί ἐστιν πεποιηκώς (vl. τίς ἄν).

doubly dependent clause (Est 3³ 2 Mac 3³⁷A). The only other
examples, besides Clem ad Rom 14³, are in the papyri, mostly
in iii/b.c. ¹, and in the atticistic revival of such writers as
Alciphron ².

LXX: Est 3 (13)³ πυθομένου ... πῶς ἂν ἀχθείη τοῦτο ἐπὶ πέρας
(potential?).—2 Mac 3³⁷ A ἐπερωτήσαντος ... ποῖός τις εἴη ἐπιτήδειος
(V ἦν).—4 Mac 11¹³ πυνθανομένου τοῦ τυράννου εἰ βούλοιτο ...

NT: Lk 1²⁹ διαλογίζετο ποταπὸς εἴη ὁ ἀσπασμός, 8⁹ ἐπερώτων
... τίς αὕτη εἴη ἡ παραβολή, 18³⁶ ἐπυνθάνετο τι εἴη τοῦτο, 22²³
συνζητεῖν .. τὸ τίς ἄρα εἴη, Ac 17¹¹ ἀνακρίνοντες τὰς γράφας εἰ ἔχοι ταῦτα
οὕτως, 25²⁰ ζήτησιν ἔλεγον εἰ βούλοιτο.

It is not clear why Luke should have indulged in this galaxy of
atticisms. It lends at least some weight to the suggestion that the
Lucan writings were finally written up not earlier than the second
century.

We are led directly to a final point. Why all these optatives in Biblical Greek, if the Scriptures were written and
rendered in the language of the people? The opt. was dead, as
far as popular language was concerned, except for a few set
phrases. It would appear from our survey that all the LXX
books which have the opt. to a considerable extent must either
be dated early in the Hellenistic period or else must be supposed
to have been affected by the atticistic revival of this mood.
Job uses it extensively, and it should be remembered that this
book belongs to the Kethubim, and for a long time such works
were not regarded with the reverence accorded to those of the
first and second division of the Canon. As a translation the
Greek Job is free enough to be called a paraphrase, and much of
the Hebrew is omitted. Similar conditions apply to the Greek
Proverbs, and that book, on account of its preference of οὐδείς

---

¹ P. Petr. III 51, 9 ἐρωτώμενος, «πόσον» εἴ «η» αὐτὸς εἴη (iii/b.c.);
note that πόσον and η are added by the scribe himself and should not be
read; doubly dependent.—II 20 πυνθανομένου ... εἴ τι συντεθεικὼς
αὐτῶι εἴης (252 b.c.); doubly dependent.—BGU VI 1246, 3 πυθομένου
... εἰ δυναίμην (iii/b.c.); doubly dependent.—P. Eleph. 13, 3 ἐπυνθανόμην
... εἴ τι βούλοιτο (223/b.c.).—Wilcken Theb. Book XII 12 ὑπεδείξαμεν
ταυτὴν τὴν ὠνὴν αὐτία, εἴ πως δύναιντο προσεπιδέξασθαί τι (ii/b.c.).
—P. Par 35, 29 πυνθανομένων δ' ἡμῶν, τοῦ τίνος χάριν εἴησαν (163 b.c.).
—Insc. Magnes. 215.—An inscr. i/a.d.—BGU 347².10.—Post-Christian
papyrus a.d. 170—Harsing appears not to be able to find any post-
Christian instances: p. 31.

² I 17, 1 ἠρόμην ... ὅτου εἴη. ἠρόμην ... τίνα τρόπον ... ἀποκέοιτο.
III 17, 1 ποῖ καταχθείην ... καὶ εὐκαίρως ἐμφάγοιμι μόνος. 24, 2 εἴ πού
τι τῶν κόκκων ἐπιδράξασθαι δυνηθείη.

to οὐθείς, could not be much earlier than 100 B.C.   The opt. in
these books, therefore, is more likely to be due to the atticistic
revival than to survival from the class. usage in the early stages
of Hell. Greek.

On the other hand, it is significant that we find the quota of
optative in Comparative clauses almost exclusively in the
Pentateuch, Psalms, Proverbs, and Isaiah [1], which is an argument for grouping these books closely.   Moreover, we find
support for their early date in the fact that Mayser can only find
one instance of this construction, and this is in iii/B.C. (P. Cair.
Zen. 14, 18 κέχρηται ἡμῖν, ὡς ἂν εἴ τις ἐχθρῶι χρήσαιτο, 256 B.C.).
There is no evidence that this construction is due to atticism,
but it could well be a survival in iii/B.C. of the quite common
class. construction, aided by the similar idiom in Hebrew
(אִישׁ כַּאֲשֶׁר with impf.).

On the whole, it is more likely that the dependent optatives
in Job, Psalms, and Proverbs (Kethubim) are due to a stylistic
or atticistic influence rather than to a date in iii/B.C. or early
ii/B.C.   Isaiah, however, which has a volitive opt. and a comparative opt. once in 40 pages, and yet does not in other ways display
an atticizing influence, but is good Koine Greek, may be
supposed to date from iii/B.C. or early ii/B.C., if the use of the
opt. is any criterion, and assuming that the needs of the synagogue lectionary would demand an early translation of this
Prophetical book.   The Prophets were read in the synagogues,
in addition to the Pentateuch, and there was no distinction of
" former " and " latter " until much later; so that the optatives
in Jg, Kingdoms, Isaiah and Ezek. α might seem to be reasonably accounted for by the early date of their translation, which
in turn was due to the desire to hear them in the synagogues.

There is much to be said for the suggestion that this apparent
lingering of the indirect opt. into the NT period and beyond may
be due to scribal activity in confusing like-sounding endings,
and in addition to this, in the case of indirect questions, the
potential idea may enter into each instance far more deeply
than would appear at first; hence it is not the class. rule of
sequence which is surviving so much as the old potential opt.—

---

[1] With ἄν: Ge 33[10], Isa 66[20], Ezk 1[16].   Without ἄν: Ex 33[11] AF,
Nu 22[4. 7] (AF fut. ind.), Dt 1[31]AF (B ind.)[44] 85[B] (AF subj.) 28[29] 32[11],
Jg 16[9] (A ind.), Ps 82 (83)[15] (R fut. ind.), Pr 23[7] 25[26. 26], Isa 11[9] 21[1].

admirably suited to Christian aspiration and piety! Indeed, one must not reject too lightly the possibility that the optatives in NT owed their preservation in some measure to their incidence in the pompous and stereotyped jargon of devotion. These opt. phrases are decidedly formal (e.g. εἰ τύχοι = *e.g.*); εἴη, θέλοι and γένοιτο occur again and again. Because the LXX came to be a Church book, the same consideration should be given to the problem there. The optatives may reflect a date of translation early in the Hell. period. But if by any chance, as seems likely on other grounds, there was a new recension of some part at least of the LXX made much nearer to the Christian age, the retention of the optatives at a time when everywhere they were diminishing need not surprise us in view of their value for the liturgy, Jewish and Christian.

CHAPTER TEN

THE VERB: NOUN FORMS: INFINITIVE

IN SOME DIRECTIONS the infinitive [1] is now enlarging its sphere, especially in the infin. of purpose after verbs of motion; and, particularly in the more cultured Hell. writers, the articular infin.—a development which by chance coincides with Semitic partiality for the infin. with prepositions and thus explains its popularity in NT. In other directions the infin. is retreating, especially in face of ἵνα and ὅτι, the latter being prevalent after verbs of speaking, perceiving and believing—some of which kept very strictly to infin. in class. Greek.

§ 1. With the Function of a Dative

(a) Final-consecutive

This use with verbs of moving, sending, and giving, etc., or in loose connection with a whole clause which it supplements, has strongly increased in Hellenistic in comparison with class. prose. Malalas has especial preference for the final infin. after εἶμι, ἔρχομαι, ἵσταμαι, ὁρμάω, περιτρέχω, πέμπω, ἀπάγω, κατάγω, καλέω. In NT this development is even more pronounced. Sometimes the infin. is used alone, sometimes with ὥστε and more rarely ἐφ' ὧι.

1. The simple infin. of purpose (class. with *giving, permitting,* etc.) is used with still more verbs of motion than in class. Greek and became really popular from c. 150 B.C.:

With ἔρχομαι Mt 2² ἤλθομεν προσκυνῆσαι, 4¹ ἀνήχθη πειρασθῆναι, 5¹⁷, 11⁷ ἐξήλθατε ... θεάσασθαι, 20²⁸ ἤλθεν διακονηθῆναι, 27⁵⁵ W ἠκολούθησαν διακονῆσαι (rest ptc.), Lk 9⁵², 18¹⁰ ἀνέβησαν προσεύξασθαι,

---

[1] K-G II 3–46. Stahl 596–680. Jannaris 480–89. Wackernagel I 257–76. Meisterhans-Schwyzer § 90. Schwyzer II 357–384. Mayser II 1, 296–339. F. H. Allen, *The Infin. in Polybius compared with the use of the Infin. in Biblical Greek,* Diss. Chicago 1907. Abel §§ 69–71. Zerwick §§ 266–279ᵇ. Ljungvik SSAA 40–45. Moulton Einl. 319ff. Pernot *Études* 31ff. 69ff. 102ff. 124ff. P. Aalto, *Studien zur Geschichte des Infinitiv im Griech.,* Helsinki 1953.

Ac 10³³ πάρεσμεν ἀκοῦσαι, Jn 4⁷ ἔρχεται ... ἀντλῆσαι ὕδωρ, 14² πορεύομαι ἑτοιμάσαι τόπον, 21³ ὑπάγω ἁλιεύειν, Ro 10⁶ 1 Co 10⁷ 16³ Heb 9²⁴ Herm. S. IX 9, 1, Mart. Petr. 88, 7, Acta Petri et Pauli 186, 4. But John is very fond of parataxis with verbs of motion, rather than the infin.; e.g. ἔρχεσθε καὶ ὄψεσθε 1⁴⁰; also 1⁴⁷ 11³⁴ 14³ 19³⁸ 20¹⁹ etc. The Atticists themselves quite often used the infin.: exx. in Schmid, *Der Attizismus*, 1887–1897, II 56, III 79, IV 81, e.g. ἀφίκετο, ἀκοῦσαι. Radermacher ² (p. 152) draws several exx. from apocryphal Acts of the Apostles. Pernot is exhaustive for the Gospels, and shows (pp. 103ff) that Mt often prefers infin. after verbs when Mk does not, thus, ὁμολογέω 14⁷ (cp. Mk 6²³), θέλω 15³² (cp. Mk 8³), δίδωμι 13¹¹ (cp. Mk 4¹¹), ἑτοιμάζω 26¹⁷ (cp. Mk 14¹²); and Mt tends to substitute an infin. for Mk's final ἵνα, thus ἀποστέλλω 21³⁴ (cp. Mk 12²), ἔρχομαι 28¹ (cp. Mk 16¹); or else εἰς τό c. inf. 26² for Mk's final ἵνα (cp. Mk 15²⁰). The fut. ptc. would have been more usual in class. Attic but it is scarcely used in NT.[1] In the Ptolemaic papyri ἀναβαίνω, διαβαίνω, ἀπέρχομαι, κατάγω are followed by infin. of purpose (Mayser II 1, 297). Witkowski ep.² 38, 34 ἐὰν ἀναβῶ κἀγὼ προσκυνῆσαι.—Xenophon of Ephesus p. 393, 29 ἐληλύθει προσεύξασθαι τῷ θεῷ.—Acta Petri et Pauli 17 ἀπῄει ποιῆσαι.—Mart. Petr. VI εἰσέρχομαι ... σταυρωθῆναι.—Mart. Pauli IV ἔρχεται ... κρῖναι. In the LXX there is a marked tendency to use the infin. after verbs of coming, going, and sending: e.g. Le 14⁴⁹ 17¹¹ 21¹⁷ Isa 61¹ᶠ. It is used also with verbs like δίδωμι, ἀποστέλλω, as in class. Attic: Mt 25³⁵ ἐδώκατέ μοι φαγεῖν, Mk 3¹⁴ ἀποστέλλῃ κηρύσσειν, 7⁴ παρέλαβον κρατεῖν, Ac 12⁴ 16⁴ παραδιδόναι φυλάσσειν.—Often δίδωμι, φάγειν, or πιεῖν.—Ac 12⁴ᶠ ἐξελέξω ... λαβεῖν, 20²⁸ ἔθετο ἐπισκόπους ποιμαίνειν, Jn 6³¹ ἄρτον ... ἔδωκεν αὐτοῖς φαγεῖν (LXX Ps 78²⁴) 6⁵²; 47. ¹⁰ δός μοι πεῖν, 4³⁸ ἀπέστειλα ὑμᾶς θερίζειν. Ἔχω (cp. Byz. Greek): Jn 4³² βρῶσιν ἔχω φαγεῖν, (8⁶) 8²⁶ πολλὰ ἔχω ... λαλεῖν, 16¹². Πέμπω: Jn 1³³ ὁ πέμψας με βαπτίζειν.

The construction with ἵνα is sometimes substituted for infin. in the papyri, as in the phrase δέξασθαι τὸν υἱὸν αὐτῆς εἵνα διακονεῖ ἡμῖν (P. Par 23, 22) which comes shortly after προσλάβεσθαι τὸν υἱὸν διακονεῖν ἡμῖν (22, 25) (165 B.C.), So also in NT: 1 Co 9¹⁵ ἀποθανεῖν ἢ ... ἵνα ... κενώσῃ, 14⁵ λαλεῖν ... μᾶλλον ... ἵνα προφητεύητε. It raises a question where the MSS differ between the constructions: have scribes and commentators introduced ἵνα or have atticistic correctors preferred the shorter form with the infin.? Mt 27²⁶ Mk 15¹⁵ Jn 19¹⁶ παρέδωκεν ἵνα σταυρωθῇ, Jn 5³⁶ δέδωκεν ... ἵνα τελειώσω (Tert. corr. to τελειῶσαι), 11³¹ ὑπάγει ... ἵνα κλαύσῃ (Chrys. corr. to κλαῦσαι), ⁵⁵ ἀνέβησαν ... ἵνα ἁγνίσωσιν (Chrys. ἁγνίσαι), 12²⁰ ἀναβαινόντων ἵνα προσκυνήσωσιν (Chrys. προσκυνῆσαι).

2. The infin. of purpose is helped by ὥστε (and ὡς?) in LXX, NT, and occasionally in the papyri (Mayser II 1, 298) and Josephus; it is common after NT, down to Byzantine period;

---

[1] Ac 24¹¹ ἀνέβην προσκυνήσων. Cp. Lk 18¹⁰ Ac 8²⁷.

it helped to give the dying infin. of purpose a little longer life in this period:

Mt 10¹ ἔδωκεν ἐξουσίαν ὥστε, 27¹ συμβούλιον ἔλαβον ὥστε θανατῶσαι αὐτόν (D corr. to ἵνα θανατώσουσιν), Lk 4²⁹ ἤγαγον ... ὥστε κατακρημνίσαι (AC εἰς τό) 9⁵² εἰσῆλθον ὥστε ἑτοιμάσαι (vl. ὡς p⁴⁵ SB), 20²⁰ ἵνα ἐπιλάβωνται αὐτοῦ λόγου, ὥστε παραδοῦναι αὐτὸν τῇ ἀρχῇ τοῦ ἡγεμόνος (ΑWΓ εἰς τό), Ac 20²⁴ AHLP ὡς τελειῶσαι (E ὥστε, probably -τε has fallen out before τελ-). LXX Ge 15⁷ 1 Mac 4². ²⁸ 10³, 2 Mac 2⁶ Mart. Dasii 5 δέδοκται ... ὥστε ... προσαχθῆναι. Epict. IV 6, 8. ἐσπούδακας ... μανθάνειν ὥστε ἄλυπος εἶναι. Final ὡς: Clem. Hom 12¹.

3. Ὥστε also appears with finite verb, imperative and subjunctive (Mayser II 1, 300): Ga 2¹³ ὥστε συναπήχθη (vl. συναπηχθῆναι) Jn 3¹⁶. Ὡς with indic.: Clem. Hom. 2²⁵; ὡς with subj. 12¹⁷.

4. Ὥστε c. infin. in a consecutive sense is more widely used than in class. Attic. Class. Greek would have indic. in Ac 15³⁹ ἐγένετο παροξυσμὸς ὥστε ἀποχωρισθῆναι αὐτοὺς ἀπ' ἀλλήλων. Clem. Hom. ὡς c. inf. 8¹¹ 20¹³.

5. Infin. without ὥστε, to express result. Lk 1⁵⁴ ἀντελάβετο Ἰσραὴλ ... μνησθῆναι ἐλέους, ⁷² ποιῆσαι ἔλεος. The influence of Heb. infin. is likely in Lk 1-2 and the infin. is best rendered as a ptc. or gerundive (so also Mt 21³² Ac 7¹⁹ 15¹⁰ Ga 3¹⁰ Ph 3¹⁰).— Ac 5³ διὰ τί ἐπλήρωσεν ... τὴν καρδίαν σου ψεύσασθαί σε, Heb 6¹⁰ οὐ γὰρ ἄδικος ὁ θεὸς ἐπιλαθέσθαι, Rev 5⁵ ἐνίκησεν ... ἀνοῖξαι (Β ὁ ἀνοίγων), 16⁹ οὐ μετενόησαν δοῦναι αὐτῷ δόξαν. Class.: Hdt V 76, Xen Hell. V 1, 14. Hellenistic: Epict. IV 1, 50, P. Oxy III 526, 3 (ii/A.D.), Herm. M. VIII 2, Did 4³. For ἵνα possibly expressing result, see p. 102.

6. The so-called Infinitive Absolute (class. ὡς ἐμοὶ δοκεῖν) is literary and very rarely found in papyri or NT: PSI IV 392, 6 (242 B.C.) ὅπερ σὺν θεῶι εἰπεῖν πεπείσμεθα. Cair. Zen. 11, 7 (256 B.C.) σὺν θεοῖς ἐλπίζω σε στεφανωθήσεσθαι.—NT: Heb 7⁹ ὡς ἔπος εἰπεῖν (frequent class.).—Ign. Trall. 10; Sm 2 τὸ δοκεῖν.—Diogn. 6¹ ἁπλῶς εἰπεῖν (see Schwyzer II 379).

(b) *Imperatival Infinitive:* see above, p. 78.

§ 2. Infinitive with Various Case-functions

(a) *Without Article*

To supplement verbs of perception, belief, saying, etc., it was usual in class. Greek to have the infin. as the object, but the ptc. was also possible; and with all but verbs of believing it was also permissible to have a ὅτι construction. Very prominent in NT is the vast reduction in the use of infin. and an extension of the ὅτι construction, which now becomes usual except in the more educated writers, Luke, Paul, Hebrews. Even verbs of believing now have this construction. Ὡς is nearly confined to Luke and Paul[1], and πῶς is now being confused with ὡς. Later on, πῶς absorbs all the functions of ὅτι, ὡς, and finally drives them out altogether. The beginnings of this seem to be appearing already in NT[2]. We notice too a reluctance to use the class. indirect speech form of accusative and infinitive; even Luke prefers the direct form (Ac 1⁴ 25⁴ᶠ). For Mark, see Zerwick *Untersuchungen* 24ff. Later on, ὡς ὅτι too becomes the equivalent of ὅτι (Mayser II 3, 45 n. 1; Jannaris § 1754; Sophocles Lex. s.v. ὡς): Hom. Clem. 1⁷ 11²⁸ 14⁷ 16⁶·⁷, P. Oxy XVI 1831, 1; 1833, 1 (v/A.D.) ὡς ὅτιπερ. The beginnings of this (although without a verb of speaking to introduce it) may lie in NT use of ὡς ὅτι (*i.e.*, *viz.*, *to the effect that*), 2 Co 5¹⁹ (RV *to wit*; RSV *that is*; NEB *what I mean is, that* . . .) 11²¹, 2 Th 2².

1. *Infinitive as a Direct Object.* *Verba putandi* in strong contrast to class. Greek now commonly are followed by ὅτι in Hell. Greek (Radermacher[2] 190). But δοκέω c. accus. and infin. 1 Co 12²³ 2 Co 11¹⁶; ἡγέομαι c. accus. infin. Ph 3⁸; λογίζομαι c. inf. Ro 3²⁸ 6¹¹ 14¹⁴ 2 Co 11⁵ Ph 3¹³; νομίζω c. inf. Lk 2⁴⁴ etc. and Paul; οἴομαι c. inf. Jn 21²⁵ Ph 1¹⁷ 1 Clem 30⁴ OT 2 Clem 14²; πείθομαι c. accus. inf. Ac 26²⁶; πέποιθα and πέπεισμαι Lk 20⁶ Ro 2¹⁹ 2 Co 10⁷, Ign Trall 3²; πιστεύω c. infin. Ac 15¹¹ Ro 14²; ὑπονοέω c. accus. inf. Ac 13²⁵ 27²⁷ Herm. V. IV 1, 6. In general the infin. with these verbs is confined to Luke, Paul and Heb., as a mark of literary style (Mayser II 1, 312). Ὀμνύω ὅτι (Mt 26⁷⁴ Mk 14⁷¹ Rev 10⁶) is unclassical; see by contrast Heb 3¹⁸ (fut. infin.). With *verba volendi* and *iubendi*, in class. Greek ὥστε was often

---

[1] Mk 12²⁶ vl. πῶς, Lk 6⁴ vl. πῶς, 8⁴⁷ (D ὅτι), 23⁵⁵ 24⁶ (D ὅσα) ³⁵ (D ὅτι), Ac 10²⁸·³⁸ 20²⁰ (πῶς at ¹⁸), Ro 1⁹, Ph 1⁸, 1 Th 2¹⁰. The Hellenistic use of ὡς = ὅτι is the true explanation of Mk 14⁷² Lk 22⁶¹, not that in *Nov. Test.* 2, 1958, 272ff.

[2] Πῶς after ἀνέγνωτε Mt 12⁴ Mk 2²⁶ 12²⁶ vl.; after ἐθεώρει Mk 12⁴¹; after ἐπέχων Lk 14⁷; after ἀπαγγέλλω Ac 11¹³ 1 Th 1⁹. See also perhaps Mk 10²³ (A. Pallis, *Notes on St. Mark*, new ed. Lond., 1932, 35), and Pallis also includes Mk 10²⁴ λέγει αὐτοῖς· Τέκνα, πῶς δύσκολόν ἐστιν, which he explains as hyperbaton for λέγει πῶς (= ὅτι) δυσκ. ἐστιν, τέκνα. See also Barn. 11¹ 14⁶, 1 Clem 19³ 21³ 34⁵ 37² 50¹. Epict. IV 13, 15: δεῖξόν μοι σεαυτὸν πιστὸν . . . καὶ ὄψει ὅτι πῶς οὐκ ἀναμένω (yet ὄψει in II 12, 4).

added to the infin. or ὅπως and fut. ind. substituted, and later ἵνα which
we find often in NT except in Luke, Paul and Hebrews. Ἵνα after
ἐρωτάω is Hellenistic (Mk 7²⁶ etc., Ptol. pap. Mayser II 1, 243). The
accus. of the object with infin. after παραινέω is a mark of literary style
(only Ac 27²²). Θέλω usually has accus. and infin., as in Ptol. papyri
(Mayser II 1, 160), but ἵνα in Mt 7¹²; 1 Co 14⁵ has both (θέλω ὑμᾶς λαλεῖν
..., μᾶλλον δὲ ἵνα προφητεύητε); cp. MGr θά = θενά = θέλω ἵνα. In
Jn 8⁵⁶ ἵνα follows ἠγαλλιάσατο (was glad that he should), just as it follows
ἐχάρην in pap. BU IV 1081, 5 (ii–iii/A.D.), whereas the ptc. follows χαίρω
in Ptol. pap. - (Mayser II 1, 175, 353). Different from class. Greek is
the passive construction (as in Latin) instead of active after verba iubendi:
Mt 18²⁵ ἐκέλευσεν αὐτὸν πραθῆναι, Ac 5²¹ ἀπέστειλεν ἀχθῆναι αὐτούς
(P. Tebt. 331. 16 [A.D. 131] ἀξιῶ ἀχθῆναι αὐτούς), 23³ κελεύεις με
τύπτεσθαι, Herm. S. IX 8, 3 ἐκέλευσε διὰ τῶν παρθένων ἀπεχθῆναι
(P. Oxy I 33. col. II 14 [end ii/B.C.] ἐκέλευσεν αὐτὸν ἀπεχθῆναι, Mart.
Matth. 243, 18ff ἐκέλευσεν πλῆθος ἀνθρακίας ἐνεχθῆναι; followed by
active φέρειν δέ. Mk 6²⁷ ἐπέταξεν ἐνεχθῆναι (but SBCΔ act.: ἐνέγκαι)
τὴν κεφαλὴν αὐτοῦ (cp.³⁹), Ac 22²⁴ εἴπας μάστιξιν ἀνετάζεσθαι αὐτόν
(but act. in D* ἀνετάζειν), Mk 10⁴⁹ εἴπεν αὐτὸν φωνηθῆναι ADWX (but
in SBCLΔ corr. to direct command). But active (like class. Greek):
Ac 23¹⁰ 16²² Mk 6³⁹ ἐπέταξεν αὐτοῖς ἀνακλῖναι πάντας (SB*G ἀνακλιθῆναι,
to harm.¹ with Mt 14⁹), 5⁴³ D δοῦναι (rest δοθῆναι). There is textual
variation in Mk 8⁷ between παραθεῖναι, παρατεθῆναι, and numerous
examples of alternation in apocryphal Acts (Ljungvik SSAA 42, n. 2).
For LXX, see Bonnaccorsi 553, Abel § 309.

2. *Infin.* in looser dependence on main verb, without any apparent
case-relationship.

a. Adverbial: with *be able, know how, begin, must,* etc., the Ptolemaic
papyri and NT have only the infin.: δύναμαι, ἰσχύω, ἔχω (*must* Lk 12⁵⁰),
ἄρχομαι. The latter never occurs with ptc. in NT, as in class. Greek
(see pp. 154f); it is very frequent in the Syn. Gospels especially in a Semitic
pleonastic sense as ἤρξατο, ἤρξαντο (see *JThS* 28, 352f), as it has very
little force; in no instance must it definitely mean *begin to,* and often
it is plainly better to ignore the auxiliary; it appears to be a periphrasis
for both aor. and impf. It is liked by Mark (26 times, + 3 in D) more
than Matthew (6 times) where it may even have some point (4¹⁷ 16²¹).
Also with infin. are προλαμβάνω Mk 14⁸ (= class. φθάνω c. ptc.), κινδυνεύω
Ac 19²⁷· ⁴⁰, προσποιέομαι Lk 24²⁸, προστίθεμαι *to do more* (see p. 227);
verbs meaning to *instigate, compel* (but πείθω, ποιέω, ἀγγαρεύω also
have ἵνα); *to be on guard, be ashamed, be frightened* (but ἵνα with βλέπετε,
φυλάσσομαι, προσέχω), *to allow* (but ἀφίημι with ἵνα Mk 11¹⁶), and
there is in general a larger freedom to use the infin. in loose connection

---

¹ Nevertheless, this accus. c. infin. construction after a verb which
already has an object has ample precedent: Pass. Barth. 133, 29f σὺ
κελεύεις ἡμᾶς λυθῆναι αὐτήν; Mart. Andr. alt. 58, 14f κελεύσας τοῖς δημίοις
ἀδιατμήτους αὐτοῦ τὰς ἀγκύλας καταλειφθῆναι; also Acta Joh. 170. 29f;
Acta Thom. 218, 25ff.

with the verb perhaps under Semitic influence: e.g. *to see to cast out* (Mt 7⁵ Lk 6⁴²), *looked round to see* (Mk 5³²), *be a long time in coming* (Lk 12⁴⁵).

b. Nominal. An infin. or ἵνα will follow not only a personal verb but also an adj. or noun, or an impersonal verb.

(i) *Nouns*: the Ptolemaic papyri have infin. after ἐξουσία (NT), κήρυγμα, πρόσταγμα, σχολή, χρεία (NT), ὥρα (NT) etc. The NT has ἵνα after συνήθεια (Jn 18³⁹), ὥρα (Jn 12²³ 13¹ 16²); ὥρα followed by infin. as in class. Greek (Ro 13¹¹); καιρὸς τοῦ c. inf. (1 Pt 4¹⁷); καιρός c. inf. (Heb 11¹⁵ Rev 11¹⁸); καιρός c. ὅτε (2 Ti 4³), ὥρα c. ὅτε (Jn 4²¹· ²³ 5²⁵ 16²· ²⁵), ὥρα ἐν ᾗ (Jn 5²⁸). Apparently the use of ὥρα and καιρός with ὅτε or ἐν ᾗ is confined to definite prophecy; the inf. indicating a nearer imminence. The NT also has infin. after ἐξουσίαν ἔχω (Jn 10¹⁸ 1 Co 9⁴ᶠᶠ Heb 13¹⁰ Rev 11⁶); δίδωμι ἐξουσίαν c. infin. (Jn 1¹² Rev 13⁵), c. ὥστε (Mt 10¹), c. ἵνα (Ac 8¹⁹), and χρείαν ἔχω c. infin. (Mt 3¹⁴ etc. Jn 13¹⁰ same subject, and ἵνα where there is a new subject [1], 1 Th 4⁹ ScD*H), τοῦ c. accus. infin. (Heb 5¹²), c. ἵνα (Jn 2²⁵ 16³⁰ 1 Jn 2²⁷).

(ii) *Adjectives and adverbs.* The Ptol. pap. display ἄξιος (NT), δυνατός (NT), ἐπιτήδειος, ἕτοιμος (NT), ἑτοίμως (NT), ἱκανός (NT), πιστός, ὥριμος: all with infin. In the NT: ἱκανός c. ἵνα (Mt 8⁸ Lk 7⁶), c. infin. (elsewhere), ἄξιος c. ἵνα (Jn 1²⁷), c. infin. often, c. τοῦ and infin. (1 Co 16⁴), c. relative clause (Lk 7⁴), ἕτοιμος, ἑτοίμως ἔχω c. inf. (Ac 21¹³ 2 Co 12¹⁴ 1 Pt 4⁵), ἐν ἑτοίμῳ ἔχω c. inf. (2 Co 10⁶).

3. *The Infinitive as Subject.*

Impersonal verbs: δεῖ, συμφέρει, ἔξεστιν, ἐγένετο, γίνεται, συνέβη —usually (acc. c.) infin., but sometimes ἵνα (e.g. συμφέρει ἵνα Mt 5²⁹ᶠ 18⁶ etc., ἔδει ἵνα πάθῃ Barn 5¹³). For the Ptol. pap. Mayser II 1, 307f (infinitive).

Neuter adjectives or nouns with the copula or without: Ptol. pap. ἀναγκαῖον, δίκαιον, ἔθος, ἐπιτήδειον, etc. (Mayser II 1, 306f) mainly infinitives. NT: δυνατόν c. infin. (Ac 2²⁴), ἀρκετόν c. ἵνα (Mt 10²⁵), καλόν c. infin. (1 Co 9¹⁵), ἐλάχιστον ἵνα (1 Co 4³), βρῶμα ἵνα (Jn 4³⁴).

Preceding demonstrative pronoun: in Jn particularly, the infin. gives way to ἵνα (1 Jn 5³ αὕτη . . . ἵνα . . .), especially if the epexegesis is theory rather than fact (Jn 15⁸ ἵνα καρπὸν πολὺν φέρητε). For fact he often substitutes ὅτι (1 Jn 2³ 3¹⁶ 5²).—Infin.: Ac 15²⁸ 1 Th 4³ Eph 3⁸ Jas 1²⁷.—But ἵνα: Lk 1⁴³ (although the epexegesis is fact) Jn 6⁴⁰ 17³ 1 Jn 3¹¹· ²³ 4²¹ 2 Jn⁶.

In Hebraistic figures of speech: Lk 21¹⁴ Ac 19²¹ τιθέναι (τίθεσθαι) ἐν τῇ καρδίᾳ (τῷ πνεύματι): Hebraism. Ac 16¹⁴ ἧς διήνοιξεν τὴν καρδίαν (Hebraism) προσέχειν (cp. τοῦ inf. Lk 24⁴⁵). Lk 2¹ δόγμα . . . ἀπογράφεσθαι πᾶσαν τὴν οἰκουμένην. Ac 14⁵ ἐγένετο ὁρμή.—On the other hand we find ἵνα following: Mt 18¹⁴ etc. θέλημά ἐστιν, Jn 13³⁴ Ac 17¹⁵ ἐντολὴ ἵνα, Ac 27⁴² βουλὴ ἐγένετο, Jn 13² *put into the heart* ἵνα παραδοῖ αὐτόν.

---

[1] Hence Jn 16³⁰ the vl. of Syrˡᵉʷ is not likely to be correct, having ἵνα introducing the same subject: οὐ χρείαν ἔχεις ἵνα τινὰ ἐρωτᾷς. Nor can οὐ χρείαν ἔχετε γράφειν be correct in S*ADᶜ at 1 Th 4⁹.

4. *The Infinitive* with πρίν, πρὶν ἤ.

Πρίν occurs three times (all iii/B.C.) and πρὶν ἤ five times in Ptol. pap. in Mayser's list. In NT and Koine generally we do not find the indic. but (a) after a positive sentence, accus. c. infin.: Mt 26³⁴. ⁷⁵ (A adds ἤ) Mk 14⁷² Lk 22⁶¹ (B adds ἤ) Jn 4⁴⁹ 8⁵⁸ (not D and lat)¹ 14²⁹ Ac 2²⁰ OT (WH text); ἤ c. infin. Mt 1¹⁸ πρὶν ἤ συνελθεῖν αὐτούς, Mk 14³⁰ (SD om ἤ), Ac 2²⁰ (WHᵐᵍ) 7². (b) after a negative sentence: ἤ c. subjunctive Lk 2²⁶; ἤ c. optative Ac 25¹⁶; ἤ c. infin. Diogn. 2³. In LXX and NT πρίν is being superceded by πρὸ τοῦ, but it occurs mainly in To, Si, Isa, and 2–4 Mac.

(b) Articular Infinitive ²

Essentially the function of an article with an infin. is the same as with a noun since the infin. is probably in origin a noun, except that with the infin. the article often appears for no reason except to supply the case-ending which is lacking. The cult of the articular infinitive was promoted by the Atticists but it is already seen in Luke, Paul, Hebrews, James and Peter, and especially in the higher kinds of Koine writing ³. Votaw ⁴ shows in his thesis that in the OT translation books the anarthrous and articular infinitives are about equal in number, whereas in NT the articular is rarer. It is almost absent from the Johannine writings, but in the Ptol. pap. its use is not confined to literary or official texts (Mayser II 1, 321).

It serves the purpose of almost every kind of subordinate clause.

A. Without Preposition.

1. Τό c. infin. serves the purpose of a mere infin. comparatively rarely in the Ptol. pap. and almost exclusively in the bureaucratic style. It is hardly used in the NT outside Paul:

Mt 15²⁰ τὸ ... φαγεῖν (subject), 20²³ τὸ καθίσαι obj., Mk 9¹⁰ τὸ ἀναστῆναι (subject), 12³³ τὸ ἀγαπᾶν (subject),' Ac 25¹¹ τὸ ἀποθανεῖν, Ro 4¹³ τὸ κληρονόμον αὐτὸν εἶναι, 7¹⁸ τὸ θέλειν ... τὸ κατεργάζεσθαι, 13⁸ τὸ ... ἀγαπᾶν, 1 Co 11⁶ τὸ κείρασθαι ἤ ξύρασθαι, 14³⁹, 2 Co 8¹⁰ᶠ τὸ θέλειν, Ph 1²⁴ τὸ δὲ ἐπιμένειν τῇ σαρκί, 2⁶ 4¹⁰ τὸ ὑπὲρ ἐμοῦ φρονεῖν, Ga 4¹⁸ (SABC om τό), Heb 10³¹. 1 Co 7²⁶ 2 Co 7¹¹ 9¹ περισσόν μοι ἐστιν τὸ γράφειν, 10² δέομαι τὸ μὴ παρὼν θαρρῆσαι, Ro 14¹³ τὸ μὴ

---

¹ For πρίν without verb, used as preposition, see pp. 260, 270.

² Goodwin 315. Moulton Einl. 343. H. F. Allen, op. cit. 29ff.

³ There is but one instance of the very literary practice of adding an adj. (Heb 2¹⁵ διὰ παντὸς τοῦ ζῆν) as in 2 Mac 7⁹ ἐκ τοῦ παρόντος ζῆν, and class. Greek.

⁴ C. W. Votaw, *The Use of the Infin. in Biblical Greek*, Chicago 1896.

τιθέναι πρόσκομμα, [21], 2 Co 2[1], 1 Th 3[3] τὸ μηδένα σαίνεσθαι, 4[6] τὸ μὴ ὑπερβαίνειν, Ac 4[18] τὸ καθόλου μὴ φθέγγεσθαι (S*B om τό).—LXX 2 Esd 6[8] τὸ μὴ καταργηθῆναι.

2. Τοῦ c. infin.[1] is used often in LXX (Hebrew Infin. Construct), more rarely in the Ptol. pap.; it belongs to a higher level of the Koine, and is mainly found in Paul (13) and Luke (44) in NT, and scarcely elsewhere except in Mt and Mk [2].

(i) Epexegetical: after nouns like χρόνος (Lk 1[57] τοῦ τεκεῖν), καιρός (1 Pt 4[17]), ἐπιποθία (Ro 15[23]), ἐξουσία (Lk 10[19]), εὐκαιρία (Lk 22[6]), γνώμη (Ac 20[3]) to be of opinion that, also ἐλπίς and χρεία. See also Lk 2[6] Ac 27[20] 1 Co 9[10] Heb 5[12]. But John on the contrary sometimes introduces ἵνα instead of τοῦ c. infin. after nouns like χρεία, ὥρα, χρόνος. Rev 12[7] is possibly epexegetical or appositional ὁ Μιχαὴλ καὶ οἱ ἄγγελοι αὐτοῦ τοῦ ACP (p[47] SB om τοῦ) πολεμῆσαι; on the other hand, it is more probably a translation of Semitic imperatival לְ c. infin. (Moulton-Howard 448f); note the subjects of the infin. in the nom., which is not Greek at all; in support of imper. cp. LXX Hos 9[13] Ἐφραΐμ τοῦ ἐξαγαγεῖν Ephraim must ..., Eccl 3[15] 1 Ch 9[25]; elsewhere in Rev τοῦ c. inf. is also never sure (9[10] p[47] SAP om τοῦ; quite weak vl. 14[15]); Debrunner suggested that the author was following his tendency elsewhere to use the nom. in preference to another case, so here instead of gen. or dat.[3]—After adjectives, as class. (Xen. Anab. 7, 7, 48; Polyb. 39, 9, 12): Lk 17[1] ἀνένδεκτον ... τοῦ ... μὴ ἐλθεῖν impossible that, 24[25], Ac 23[15] ἕτοιμοί ἐσμεν τοῦ ἀνελεῖν αὐτόν, 1 Co 16[4] ἄξιον ... τοῦ πορεύεσθαι.—After verbs which in class. Greek took the gen.: Lk 1[9] ἔλαχε τοῦ θυμιᾶσαι (so LXX 1 Km 14[47]; but class. has inf. only), 2 Co 1[8] ἐξαπορηθῆναι ... τοῦ ζῆν.

(ii) Consecutive or final sense, especially Luke and Paul, and the most common type in NT; on the whole, however, Paul prefers εἰς τό or πρὸς τό for final and consec.: Mt 13[3] ἐξῆλθεν ... τοῦ σπείρειν, 2[13] ζητεῖν τοῦ ἀπολέσαι, 21[32] μετεμελήθητε τοῦ πιστεῦσαι (consec.), 3[13] 11[1] 24[45] (D om τοῦ); Lk 2[21] eight days τοῦ περιτεμνεῖν (fin. or consec.), Ro 8[12] ὀφειλέται ... τοῦ κατὰ σάρκα ζῆν, 1[24] τοῦ ἀτιμάζεσθαι (consec.), 11[8] OT ὀφθαλμοὺς τοῦ μὴ βλέπειν such as, 10 OT σκοτισθήτωσαν οἱ ὀφθ. τοῦ μὴ βλέπειν, 1 Co 10[13] τοῦ δύνασθαι, Ac 14[9] πίστιν τοῦ σωθῆναι (consec.), 9[15], 2 Co 8[11] ἡ προθυμία τοῦ θέλειν, Ph 3[21] τὴν ἐνέργειαν τοῦ δύνασθαι αὐτόν the power by which he can, Ac 3[12] Ro 7[3] Ph 3[10] Heb 10[7] OT 11[5] Hom. Clem. 9[22]. Often the consec. sense is only weak: Lk 1[73] 4[10] 5[7], 24[25] βραδεῖς τῇ καρδίᾳ τοῦ πιστεῦσαι, Ac 7[19] 18[10], Ro 6[6] 7[3]

---

[1] Schwyzer II 132. Birklein, *Entwicklungsgeschichte des substantivierten Infin.* (= Schenz, Beitr. III 1, Würzburg 1888) 55f. Moulton-Howard 448ff.

[2] But see Thuc. I 4, etc., and Tacitus *Ann.* II 59 Aegyptum proficiscitur cognoscendae antiquitatis.

[3] Blass-Debr. § 400, 8.

Ph 3¹⁰, LXX 3 Km 17²⁰.—The mere infin. already has the same final sense, but for the purpose of clarity τοῦ may be added to a second final infin. (only in writings with pretence to style, viz. Mt Lk Ac, e.g. Mt 2¹³ μέλλει γὰρ H. ζητεῖν τὸ παιδίον τοῦ ἀπολέσαι αὐτό, Lk 1⁷⁷ ἑτοιμάσαι ... τοῦ δοῦναι, 78ᶠ ἐπιφᾶναι τοῖς ἐν σκότει ... τοῦ κατευθῦναι, 2²². ²⁴ παραστῆσαι ... καὶ τοῦ δοῦναι, Ac 26¹⁷ᶠ ἀποστέλλω σε, ἀνοῖξαι ..., τοῦ ἐπιστρέψαι ..., τοῦ λαβεῖν. For τοῦ after ἐγένετο, see Ac 10²⁵.— Τοῦ μή c. inf. after verbs of hindering, ceasing, etc. (Lk and LXX) has class. precedent (Xen. Anab. 3, 5, 11), but the use goes further in NT and LXX and τοῦ μή has a consecutive sense: Lk 4⁴² 17¹ 24¹⁶ Ac 10⁴⁷ 14¹⁸ 20²⁰. ²⁷, LXX Ge 16² συνέκλεισεν τοῦ μή, 20⁶, Ps 38² 68²⁴ (Ro 11¹⁰).—Another Septuagintism, especially in Lk–Ac and Jas, is τοῦ c. inf. after verbs which in class. Greek would take the simple infin., e.g. Lk 4¹⁰ OT ἐντέλλεσθαι (Ps 90 (91)¹¹), 5⁷ κατανεύειν, 9⁵¹ στηρίζειν τὸ πρόσωπον, Ac 3¹² ποιεῖν (BU II 625, 28 πᾶν ποιεῖν τοῦ: ii–iii/A.D.), Ac 2¹ D 10²⁵ (not D) Act. Barn. 7 ἐγένετο, 15²⁰ ἐπιστεῖλαι αὐτοῖς τοῦ ἀπέχεσθαι, 21¹² παρεκαλοῦμεν ... τοῦ μὴ ἀναβαίνειν αὐτόν, 23¹⁵ ἕτοιμος, 20 συντίθεσθαι. 27¹ ἐκρίθη τοῦ it was determined to, 20³ ἐγένετο γνώμη τοῦ, Jas 5¹⁷ προσεύχεσθαι, Herm. V. III 7, 2 ἀνέβη ἐπὶ τὴν καρδίαν; LXX e.g. 3 Km 1³⁵ ἐνετειλάμην, Ezk 21¹¹ 1 Mac 5³⁹ ἕτοιμος.

3. Τῷ c. infin. is sometimes instrumental in the Koine but usually causal (Mayser II 1, 323f; II 3, 61¹⁰; Polyb.). Only once in NT and causal: 2 Co 2¹³ had no rest because τῷ μὴ εὑρεῖν με Τίτον (various corrections: DE ἐν τῷ μή; LP τὸ μή; S*C² τοῦ μή).

B. With a Preposition or Prepositional Adverb [1].

The construction was frequent enough in class. Greek, but in Hellenistic (especially NT) its frequence is proportionately far higher, particularly εἰς τό and ἐν τῷ. The prepositions occur in the following order of frequence in NT (Burton § 407): εἰς (63–72), ἐν (52–56), διά (27–31), μετά 15, πρός 12, πρό (9), ἀντί, ἐκ, ἕνεκεν, ἕως 1. In the Ptol. pap. on the other hand it is: διά 112, περί 38, μεχρί 18, πρός 16, ἐπί 15, ἕως 14, πρό 11, εἰς 10, χάριν 10, ὑπό 10, παρά, ἕνεκα 8, πρός c. dat. 7, ἐν, μετά 5, ἅμα, ἐκ 4, πλήν 3, ἄνευ 2, ἀντί 1. Conspicuous is the frequence of διά in the Koine, and of εἰς and ἐν in Biblical Greek.

1. Διά τό c. infin. almost = ὅτι or διότι, denoting cause: Mt 13⁵. ⁶ 24¹² Mk 4⁵. ⁶ Lk 2⁴ 6⁴⁸ 8⁶ 9⁷ etc., in Jn 2²⁴ διὰ τὸ αὐτὸν γινώσκειν πάντας (om. Syrˢⁱⁿ) (the preposition with art. infin. is unusual in Jn),

---

[1] Mayser II 1, 324ff. Burton §§ 406–417. Goodwin §§ 800–803. Johannessohn DGPS passim.

Ac 4² 8¹¹ etc., Ph 1⁷ (no other ex. in Paul), Heb 7²³ᶠ 10², Jas 4² (parallel with διότι in³). LXX Ge 39⁹ Ex 16⁸ 17⁷ 19¹⁸ 33³ Dt 1³⁶ 1 Mac 6⁵³ 10⁷⁷ 11² 14³⁵ 2 Mac 2¹¹ 3¹⁸. ³⁸ 4³⁰ 6¹¹ 8³⁶ 10¹³ 15¹⁷ 3 Mac 1¹¹ 5³⁰ 4 Mac 15⁴. In Mk 5⁴ it is evidential rather than causal (Burton § 408).

2. Εἰς τό c. inf. = ἵνα or ὥστε, expresses purpose or result in Xenophon and often in LXX and post-Christian Greek, and is difficult to distinguish from τοῦ c. inf.; it occurs in Heb, 1 Pt, and Jas, but especially in Paul where it expresses hardly anything but purpose (e.g. Ro 12³ εἰς τὸ σωφρονεῖν, while Luke favours τοῦ c. inf. It may also express "tendency, measure of effect, or result" (Burton § 411). In LXX: = לְ Ge 30³⁸ εἰς τὸ πιεῖν, 32⁸ εἰς τὸ σῴζεσθαι, 49¹⁵ εἰς τὸ πονεῖν, Ex 27²⁰ εἰς φῶς καῦσαι, 1 Mac 12³⁶ εἰς τὸ διαχωρίσαι, 2 Mac 1³ εἰς τὸ σέβεσθαι, 2²⁵ εἰς τὸ ... ἀναλαβεῖν, 3 Mac 6⁶ εἰς τὸ μὴ λατρεῦσαι, 7³ εἰς τὸ ... κολάζεσθαι: Johannessohn DGPS 300–2. See Mayser II 1, 331 and Moulton Proleg. 220 for papyrus exx.: here it is telic, but remoter purpose is in mind, which is just the position in NT according to Moulton. It is not strictly final.

These exx. seem to be final or very near it:

Mt 20¹⁹ εἰς τὸ ἐμπαῖξαι, 26² 27³¹.—Mk 14⁵⁵ (D ἵνα θανατώσουσιν). —Lk 5¹⁷ (not D).—Lacking in Joh. writings.—Ac 7¹⁹.—Ro 1¹¹. ²⁰ (but a causal clause follows, and so may this be; as the passage deals with divine action, however, it is better to retain the usual near-final meaning of εἰς τό, whatever theologians may say: i.e. RV text is correct against RSV and NEB), 3²⁶ (parall. to ²⁵ εἰς ἔνδειξιν), 4¹¹. ¹¹. ¹⁶. ¹⁸ 7⁴ 8²⁹, Eph 1¹², Ph 1¹⁰, 1 Th 2¹⁶ εἰς τὸ ἀναπληρῶσαι the purpose of God (final), 3⁵ in order to know, 1 Co 10⁶ 9¹⁸.—Heb 2¹⁷ 8³ (6 other exx. in Heb, all final).

These exx. may have a looser connection with what goes before. Here we are reminded of Westcott's distinction between εἰς τό and ἵνα, especially where they occur in close proximity; εἰς τό marks the remoter aim. Moulton (Proleg. 218ff) felt that in Heb. the use was uniformly telic, but Paul's use was not so uniform:—

Ro 12³, φρονεῖν εἰς τὸ σωφρονεῖν, 1 Co 8¹⁰ εἰς τὸ ἐσθίειν expresses a measure of effect (leading him to eat), 11²² μὴ γὰρ οἰκίας οὐκ ἔχετε εἰς τὸ ἐσθίειν καὶ πίνειν houses to eat and drink in, 2 Co 8⁶ εἰς τό to such a degree that, Ga 3¹⁷, 1 Th 2¹² either equivalent to simple infin. or to ἵνα after verbs of exhorting, etc., 3¹⁰ δεόμενοι εἰς τὸ ἰδεῖν = ἵνα ἰδῶμεν, 4⁹ same (epexegetic).—Heb 11³ by faith we perceive that the universe was fashioned by the word of God εἰς τὸ μὴ ἐκ φαινομένων τὸ βλεπόμενον γεγονέναι: perhaps consec. (NEB), but Westcott urged its final force because Heb always makes εἰς τό c. inf. final.—Jas 1¹⁹ ταχὺς εἰς τὸ ἀκοῦσαι the infin. simply limits an adj. as it limits a noun in Ph 1²³: τὴν ἐπιθυμίαν ἔχων εἰς τὸ ἀναλῦσαι (p⁴⁶ DEFG om εἰς in error).

3. Μετὰ τό c. inf. indicates time: after. Mt 26³², Mk 1¹⁴ 14²⁸ 16¹⁹, Lk 12⁵ 22²⁰, Ac 1³ 7⁴ 10⁴¹ 15¹³ 19²¹ 20¹, 1 Co 11²⁵, Heb 10¹⁵. ²⁶.— LXX Ge 5⁴ etc., Ru 2¹¹, 1 Km 1⁹ 5⁹, 1 Mac 1⁹. ²⁰.—For Polyb. and Diod. Sic. see Krebs, Die Präp. bei Polyb. 61.

4. Πρὸς τό c. inf. indicates purpose but is sometimes weakened to *with reference to*, and is much rarer than εἰς τό. It may express tendency and ultimate goal, rather than purpose, as in papyri.

Mt 5²⁸ ὁ βλέπων γυναῖκα πρὸς τὸ ἐπιθυμῆσαι: there is hardly any telic force, but simple accompaniment (*and*); not even consecutive 6¹ πρὸς τὸ θεαθῆναι αὐτοῖς (final), 13³⁰ 23⁵ 26¹².—Mk 13²².—Lk 18¹ πρὸς τὸ δεῖν προσεύχεσθαι *with regard to*.—Ac 3¹⁹ SB (rest εἰς).—2 Co 3¹³ final, Eph 6¹¹ (DEFG εἰς), 1 Th 2⁹, 2 Th 3⁸.—Jas 3³ TR.

LXX: Je 34¹⁰, 1 Mac 10³⁸ 12¹⁰, 2 Mac 4⁴⁵ 5²⁷, 3 Mac 4¹¹ (all final). Polyb. 1, 48, 5.—Jos. Ant. 14, 170; 15, 148, etc.

No doubt the obvious correspondence with the Heb. ל c. inf. assisted in the weakening of this expression in Bibl. Greek, till it means simply *in — ing* or is merely like a simple ptc, as in לֵאמֹר.

5. Παρὰ τό c. inf. is not NT, but 1 Clem 39⁵· ⁶ = LXX Jb 4²⁰· ²¹ *because*, Polybius, papyri. LXX: causal Ge 29²⁰ (A om) Ex 14¹¹ Dt 9²⁸ 4 Km 1³· ⁶· ¹⁶ A Ba 3²⁸ Ze 3⁶ 4 Mac 10¹⁹ Dit. Syll.³ 834¹⁰.

6. Ἀντὶ τοῦ *instead of* (original meaning): Jas 4¹⁵. But causal Ezk 29⁹ 34⁷⁻⁹ 36³, pap. 113 B.C.

7. Διὰ παντὸς τοῦ ζῆν Heb. 2¹⁵.

8. Ἐκ τοῦ 2 Co 8¹¹ ἔχειν *according to your means* (cp. καθὸ ἂν ἔχῃ ¹²).

9. Ἕνεκεν τοῦ 2 Co 7¹² φανερωθῆναι (ἕν. redundant, but analogy of ἕν. τοῦ ἀδικήσαντος just before. Ἕνεκα before τοῦ c. inf. in Joseph. Ant. 11, 293, and in papyri (Mayser II 1, 325), and LXX 1 Esd 8²¹ ἕνεκεν τοῦ μὴ γενέσθαι ὀργήν, Am 1⁶ 2⁴ etc., and Menander Fr. 425, 2.

10. Ἕως τοῦ Ac 8⁴⁰ ἐλθεῖν (founded on the analogy of πρίν, and post-class.); Polyb., Joseph., etc., pap. from iii/B.C.; LXX especially frequent with ἐλθεῖν Ge 10¹⁹ 19²² 43²⁵ 1 Mac 7⁴⁵ (without τοῦ) 16⁹; Ge 3¹⁹ 8⁷ 13¹⁰ 24³³ 28¹⁵ 33³ 1 Mac 3³³ 5¹⁹· ⁵⁴ 14⁴¹ (Johannessohn DGPS 304).

11. Μέχρι (ἄχρι) τοῦ c. inf. (class.) not Bibl. Greek.

12. Πρὸ τοῦ *before*. In all parts of LXX (usually = בטרם) but only twice in Isa, twice in 2–4 Mac, and not in Wi or Si (these books prefer πρίν): Ge 17, Ex 2, Le 1, Dt 1, Jos 1, JgRu 2, 4 Km 2, Ch 2, To 5, Jdt 2, Jb 2, Ps 6, Pr 6, MP 5, Isa 2, Je 4, Ezk 1, 2 Mac 2. With pres., Jn 17⁵ εἶναι, D γενέσθαι). With aor. Mt 6⁸, Lk 2²¹ 22¹⁵ Ac 23¹⁵ Jn 1⁴⁹ 13¹⁹, Ga 2¹² πρὸ τοῦ γὰρ ἐλθεῖν τινας. 3²³. In Ptol. pap. only aor. inf. (Mayser II 1, 327).

Of other genitive prepositions, NT has no πλήν (class. *except*) or ὑπέρ (class. final; 2 Mac 4³⁶), and no ἀπό, ἐπί, μετά, περί, ἄνευ (Am 3⁵), χωρίς or χάριν.

13. Ἐν τῷ c. infin.¹ is a marked feature of the style of Luke; in a temporal sense it occurs about 30 times in Lk, but only 5 in Ac. In its temporal sense it is a Hebraism and non-classical: it is the usual LXX rendering of ב c. infin. (Heb) and it renders כ c. infin. (Aram. Dan

---

¹ Mayser II 1. 328; Moulton-Howard 451; and see above (Introduction p. 8).

6²¹ Θ). It is doubtful whether its temporal sense occurs in Soph. *Ajax* 554 ἐν τῷ ⸌φρονεῖν γὰρ μηδὲν ἥδιστος βίος; this is still the class. meaning of *consists in*. The total instances are: Lk 34, Ac 8, Paul 4, Heb 4, Mt 3, Mk 2. Thus in NT 55, LXX 500, Xenophon 16, Thucydides 6, Plato 26.

(*a*) The usual NT meaning is temporal (*while* or *after*) though in some instances it is not impossible to trace the element of cause too. There are few, if any, class. parallels for the meaning *while, during*, for which a gen. absol. or pres. ptc. would have been used. Probably the Heb. בְּ influenced the authors of Bibl. Greek, as in LXX Ge 28⁶ 1 Km 2¹⁹ Mal 1⁷·¹². Mk 4⁴ ἐν τῷ σπείρειν αὐτόν, Mt 13⁴·²⁵ 27¹² Lk 8⁵.— Lk 1⁸ 2⁶·⁴³ (might be causal: *because they were returning*), 5¹ etc. Clearly its frequence in Lk is due to LXX influence (Zerwick § 273). Very often in Lk it is combined with ἐγένετο-constructions as a subordinate clause = וַיְהִי בְּ, e.g. 1⁸ 2⁶; Luke's imitation of LXX is particularly plain here (Zerwick § 275), e.g. Ge 11² for בְּ ἐγένετο ἐν τῷ κινῆσαι αὐτούς, 35¹⁸; for כַּאֲשֶׁר 24⁵²; for וַיְהִי הֵם מְרִיקִים שַׂקֵּיהֶם 42³⁵.— Ac 2¹ (causal, explaining why they were gathered together), 9³, 19¹ ἐγένετο.—Ro 3⁴ OT, 15¹³ ἐν τῷ πιστεύειν (DEGF om) *because you believe*.—Ga 4¹⁸. Ptol. pap. (Mayser II 1, 328f). Johannessohn, *Das biblische* ΚΑΙ ΕΓΕΝΕΤΟ *und seine Geschichte*, Göttingen 1926, 199ff.

Though Luke uses the aor. infin. he is more fond of the pres.; there are but twelve exx. of aor. in NT. It is probably not true to say quite simply that pres. infin. = *while* and aor. inf. = *after*. Aor. is timeless while pres. is durative. The context must decide relative time. Thus in Ḥeb 2⁸ we have aor.; but RSV, looking at the context, could be correct to render it *putting everything in subjection*, not *having put* (NEB *in subjecting all things*). It is, however, a rough and ready rule to suppose, as with pres. and aor. ptc., that temporal ἐν τῷ c. pres. inf. indicates contemporaneity, and ἐν τῷ c. aor. infin. indicates anterior action. This being so, we may compare Lk 10³⁵ with 19¹⁵: ἐν τῷ ἐπανέρχεσθαι (pres.) is *at my return*, but ἐν τῷ ἐπανελθεῖν αὐτόν is *after his return*. We may also compare Lk 9²⁹ with 14¹: ἐν τῷ προσεύχεσθαι αὐτόν (pres.) is *while he was praying*, but ἐγένετο ἐν τῷ ἐλθεῖν αὐτὸν εἰς οἶκον is *after he had gone into the house*. The following exx. of aor. infin. in Lk–Ac may or may not imply anterior action: Lk 2²⁷ ἐν τῷ εἰσαγαγεῖν *after they entered*, 3²¹ ἐν τῷ βαπτισθῆναι *after they were baptized*, but the context may require *while they were being baptized* (NEB *during a general baptism of the people*, because it goes on to state καὶ Ἰησοῦ βαπτισθέντος; 8⁴⁰ (SB pres), 9³⁴·³⁶ 11³⁷ 14¹ 19¹⁵ 24³⁰, Ac 11¹⁵.

LXX (= בְּ) Ge 28⁶ ἐν τῷ εὐλογεῖν αὐτόν (pres.) *while he blessed him*, Mal 1⁷·¹² ἐν τῷ λέγειν ὑμᾶς (pres.) *when you say*.—Ge 39¹⁵ = כְּ ἐν τῷ ἀκοῦσαι αὐτόν (aor.) *when he heard*, 44³¹ ἔσται ἐν ἰδεῖν αὐτόν (aor.) *when he sees*.

(*b*) It appears in the LXX in a causal sense (= בְּ): Ge 19¹⁶ ἐκράτησεν... ἐν τῷ φείσασθαι κύριον αὐτοῦ *because the Lord was merciful to him*, 1 Mac 2⁵⁴·⁵⁸ ἐν τῷ ζηλῶσαι ζῆλον *because he was deeply zealous* RSV, 2⁵⁵ ἐν τῷ πληρῶσαι λόγον *because he fulfilled the command* RSV, 2⁵⁶ ἐν τῷ ἐπιμαρτύρασθαι τῇ ἐκκλησίᾳ *because he testified in the assembly* RSV.

NT: Lk 1²¹ ἐθαύμαζον ἐν τῷ *because he delayed*, Mk 6⁴⁸ βασανιζομένους ἐν τῷ ἐλαύνειν *by the rowing*, Ac 3²⁶ ἐν τῷ ἀποστρέφειν instr. (Je 11¹⁷), 4³⁰ similar, Heb 8¹³ ἐν τῷ λέγειν *because he says*, 2⁸ ἐν τῷ ὑποτάξαι causal, or like a ptc.

It appears also in LXX in a final sense, translating ‫ל‬: 1 Km 1²⁶ ἐν τῷ προσεύξασθαι *here in order to pray*.

(c) Other uses include an epexegetical: He 3¹² ἐν τῷ ἀποστῆναι NEB (RSV consec.), 2 Co 2¹³ DE ἐν τῷ μὴ εὑρεῖν (see above p. 142) Preisigke Sammelbuch I 620, 6f (inscr. 97 B.C.) λείπεσθαι ἐν τῷ μὴ εἶναι ἄσυλον *is wanting in this, that it has no* ...; 1 Clem 10¹ πιστὸς εὑρέθη ἐν τῷ αὐτὸν ὑπήκοον γενέσθαι *in this, that* ..., Lk 12¹⁵ οὐκ ἐν τῷ περισσεύειν τινὶ ἡ ζωὴ αὐτοῦ ἐστιν.

§ 3. Cases with the Infinitive [1]

1. (a) There are few exceptions in the Koine to the class. rule that the subject of a dependent infin. is not expressed again if it is the same as the subject of the independent verb; dependence of the infin. upon a preposition makes no difference. (b) If the infin. has a nominal predicate or is connected with an apposition which defines the subject of the main verb, the apposition is not a ground for altering the construction to that of accus. and infin.; however, a nominal predicate will do this sometimes. (c) Also, if the object of the infin. is identical with the object of the main verb, there need be no repetition of the object.

Examples:—

(a) Subject of infin. not expressed: Lk 24²³ λέγουσαι ... ἑωρακέναι, Ro 1²² φάσκοντες εἶναι σοφοί, 1 Jn 2⁶·⁹ ὁ λέγων ἐν αὐτῷ μένειν ... ἐν τῷ φωτὶ εἶναι, Ti 1¹⁶ θεὸν ὁμολογοῦσιν εἰδέναι, Jas 2¹⁴. Also for θέλω, βούλομαι, ζητέω, etc. there are abundant exx.

(b) Nom. with infin.: Mt 19²¹ θέλεις τέλειος εἶναι, Jn 7⁴ WH ζητεῖ αὐτὸς ἐν παρρησίᾳ εἶναι (p⁶⁶ BW*D have αὐτό accus.; syr^cur b e om αὐτός), Ac 18¹⁵ κριτὴς ἐγὼ τούτων οὐ βούλομαι εἶναι, Ro 9³ ηὐχόμην ἀνάθεμα εἶναι αὐτὸς ἐγώ, 1²² φάσκοντες εἶναι σοφοί *claiming to be wise*, Ph 4¹¹ ἔμαθον αὐτάρχης εἶναι *learnt how to be*, 2 Co 10² δέομαι τὸ μὴ πάρων θαρρῆσαι *I beg that when I am present I may not be bold*, Heb 5¹² ὀφείλοντες εἶναι διδάσκαλοι, 11⁴ ἐμαρτυρήθη εἶναι δίκαιος *certified to be righteous*. The construction conflicts with that in Mk 14²⁸ (μετὰ τὸ

---

[1] K-G II § 475f. Schmid *Attizismus* II 57; III 81; IV 83. 620. Mayser II 1, 334ff.

ἐγερθῆναί με προάξω), Ac 5³⁶ (Θεῦδας λέγων εἶναί τινα ἑαυτόν), and Jas 4² (οὐκ ἔχετε διὰ τὸ μὴ αἰτεῖσθαι ὑμᾶς).

(c) Also if the obj. of the infin. is identical with that of the governing verb, there need be no repetition of the obj.: Ac 26²⁸ ἐν ὀλίγῳ με πείθεις Χριστιανὸν ποιῆσαι *you seek to convince me that you have made me in a moment a Christian*; a striking parallel is provided by Fridrichsen (*Coniectanea neot.* III, 1938) from Xen. Mem. I 2, 49 πείθων τοὺς συνόντας αὐτῷ σοφωτέρους ποιεῖν τῶν πατέρων (K–G II 32; Zerwick § 279ᵇ).

2. Although class. writers preferred a personal construction it was possible to make it impersonal, and on the whole the latter is preferred in NT and Koine. But δοκέω at least has personal construction in NT: Act 17¹⁸ δοκεῖ καταγγελεὺς εἶναι, 1 Co 3¹⁸ εἴ τις δοκεῖ σοφὸς εἶναι; 8² 14³⁷, Ga 2⁹ etc., Jas 1²⁶ (whereas there is impersonal δοκεῖ in Herm. M. IV 2, 2; S. IX 5, 1; Clem. Hom. 10²); and we find personal ἔδοξα ἐμαυτῷ δεῖν πρᾶξαι (Ac 26⁹) as well as impersonal ἔδοξέ μοι (Lk 1³ etc., Ac 15²⁸ etc.), and there is, even in the passive, δεδοκιμάσμεθα πιστευθῆναι (1 Th. 2⁴) *we have been approved to be entrusted with.* Adjectives like δυνατός and ἱκανός have a personal construction too. Moreover, there is the personal construction with πρέπει (Heb 7²⁶). However, there is nothing like the class. λέγομαι εἶναι.

3. Quite often in the Koine and NT, although the governing verb and the infin. have the same subject, the latter will be in the accus. This is distinct from class. Greek, which has either the nominative or no noun at all with the infin. It is a Latin construction and is reproduced in Greek inscriptional translations from the Latin but, as Moulton pointed out (Proleg. 213), this perfectly natural levelling process developed in regions untouched by Latin, and no outside influence was needed to increase the tendency towards uniformity. The reflexive pronoun, and sometimes the non-reflexive pronoun, in the accus. case, is added superfluously to the infin. In class. Greek they preferred to insert a non-reflexive referring to the subject of the main verb in the nominative; so they would probably have put αὐτὸς δέ for ἑαυτόν in Ac 25⁴ (ἀπεκρίθη τηρεῖσθαι τὸν Παῦλον, ἑαυτὸν δὲ μέλλειν . . .) where Luke may have deviated from class. usage into the accus. because he wished to co-ordinate the new subject with Παῦλον.

Reflexive pronoun:

Lk 23² λέγοντα ἑαυτὸν Χριστὸν βασιλέα εἶναι, 20²⁰ ὑποκρινομένους ἑαυτοὺς δικαίους εἶναι (D om εἶναι), Ac 5³⁶ λέγων εἶναί τινα ἑαυτόν,

8⁹ λέγων εἶναί τινα ἑαυτὸν μέγαν, Ro 2¹⁹ πέποιθας σεαυτὸν ὁδηγὸν εἶναι *you are sure that you are* (αὐτός would be class., as in fact in 9³), 6¹¹ λογίζεσθε ἑαυτοὺς εἶναι νεκρούς (hardly accus. in class. Greek), 2 Co 7¹¹ συνεστήσατε ἑαυτοὺς ἁγνοὺς εἶναι (non-reflexive with ptc. in class. Greek, Rev 2⁹ 3⁹ τῶν λεγόντων Ἰουδαίους εἶναι ἑαυτούς (gen. in class. Greek), Ph 3¹³ ἐγὼ ἐμαυτὸν οὔπω λογίζομαι κατειληφέναι (superfluous ἐμαυτόν), Heb 10³⁴ γινώσκοντες ἔχειν ἑαυτοὺς κρείσσονα ὕπαρξιν.

Non-reflexive pronouns:

Lk 20⁷ D ἀπεκρίθησαν μὴ εἰδέναι αὐτοὺς πόθεν, Ac 25²¹ ἐπικαλεσαμένου τηρηθῆναι αὐτόν, Eph 4²² ἀπόθεσθαι ὑμᾶς (but a long way from governing verb ἐδιδάχθητε).

In the Ptol. pap., on the other hand, the non-refl. predominates over the reflexive (Mayser II 1, 335f).

4. The personal pronoun and not the reflexive, is added quite often when the articular infin. is introduced by a preposition : there is but one NT instance of this without a preposition (2 Co 2¹³ τῷ μὴ εὑρεῖν με Τίτον).   Mt 26³² Mk 14²⁸ μετὰ τὸ ἐγερθῆναί με προάξω (for αὐτός), Mt 27¹² Lk 2⁴ ἀνέβη . . . διὰ τὸ εἶναι αὐτόν (superfluous pronoun), 19¹¹ 9³⁴ 10³⁵ 22¹⁵, Ac 1³ παρέστησεν ἑαυτὸν ζῶντα μετὰ τὸ παθεῖν αὐτόν, 4³⁰ 8⁴⁰ 19²¹D, Ro 1²⁰ καθορᾶται . . . εἰς τὸ εἶναι αὐτοὺς ἀναπολογήτους, 3⁴ OT, Heb 7²⁴ (superfl. αὐτόν), Jas 4² οὐκ ἔχετε διὰ τὸ μὴ αἰτεῖσθαι ὑμᾶς, Jn 2²⁴.   Frequent in Hermas (V. II 1, 3 ; M. IV 1, 7 ; S. VI 1, 5 ; VIII 2, 5. 9 ; 6, 1 ; IX 6, 8 ; 18, 3).   Papyri (Mayser II 1, 336).

5. The infin. is often used alone, where in class. Greek they would have employed the full accus. c. infin. construction.

Mt 23²³ ἔδει ποιῆσαι (sc. ὑμᾶς), Lk 2²⁶ ἦν αὐτῷ κεχρηματισμένον μὴ ἰδεῖν θάνατον (sc, αὐτόν), Ac 12¹⁵ ἡ δὲ διϊσχυρίζετο οὕτως ἔχειν (sc. ταῦτα, as in 24⁹), Ro 13⁵ ἀνάγκη ὑποτάσσεσθαι, Heb 13⁶ p⁴⁶ M ὥστε θαρροῦντας λέγειν (rest add ἡμᾶς), 1 Pt 2¹⁵ φιμοῦν (sc. ὑμᾶς?).   Mayser II 1, 336f.

6. The accus. c. infin. is restricted in use in the Koine in comparison with class. Greek, the ὅτι periphrasis having taken its place in nearly all NT writers according to the tendency of later Greek.   But there is still a place for accus. c. infin., after verbs of stating, showing, perceiving, making, allowing, and κελεύω (where the obj. is a different person from the subject). Then there is ἐγένετο and συνέβη and similar expressions like δεῖ and ἀνάγκη.   Some anomalies occur, as when the accus. inadvertently remains (as sometimes in class. Greek) even

although the infin. is replaced by ἵνα or ὅτι: Mk 1²⁴ οἶδά σε τίς εἶ,
Lk 13²⁵ οὐκ οἶδα ὑμᾶς πόθεν ἐστέ, Mk 11³² εἶχον τὸν 'Ιωάννην
ὅτι προφήτης ἦν, Jn 9²⁹ τοῦτον δὲ οὐκ οἴδαμεν πόθεν ἐστίν, Ac
3¹⁰ 4¹³ 16³ p⁴⁵DEH ᾔδεισαν τὸν πατέρα αὐτοῦ ὅτι "Ελλην
ὑπῆρχεν, 27¹⁰, 2 Th 2⁴ ἀποδεικνύντα ἑαυτὸν ὅτι ἐστὶν θεός.

7. The accus. c. inf. occurs as well as gen. or dat. c. infin.
(especially in Luke).

(a) with verbs of commanding: Mk 6²⁷ ἐπέταξεν ἐνεχθῆναι τὴν
κεφαλὴν αὐτοῦ, Ac 15² ἔταξαν ἀναβαίνειν Παῦλον, 10⁴⁸ προσέταξεν
αὐτοὺς βαπτισθῆναι. Dative:—Mk 6³⁹ etc. Ac 22¹⁰ 1 Co 5¹¹ ἔγραψα ὑμῖν
μὴ συναναμίγνυσθαι, Rev 3¹⁸ συμβουλεύω σοι ἀγοράσαι παρ' ἐμοῦ.
N.B. λέγω c. dat. Mt 5³⁴· ³⁹ Lk 12¹³ Ac 21⁴, c. accus. Mk 5⁴³ Lk 19¹⁵
Ac 22²⁴.

(b) with impers. expressions: ἔξεστιν, ἔθος ἐστίν, ἀθέμιτον
αἰσχρόν καλόν ἐστιν, συμφέρει. Accus.:—Jn 18¹⁴ συμφέρει ἕνα
ἄνθρωπον ἀποθανεῖν, Mt 17⁴ Mk 9⁵ Lk 9³³ καλόν ἐστιν ἡμᾶς ὧδε εἶναι,
Ro 13¹¹ ὥρα ἡμᾶς ἐγερθῆναι (ἡμῖν class.), Mk 9⁴⁵ καλόν ἐστίν σε εἰσελθεῖν
... χωλόν, Mk 9⁴³· ⁴⁷ (vl. σοι and σε), Mt 18⁸· ⁹ σοι. Dative:—
Lk 2²⁶ ἦν αὐτῷ κεχρηματισμένον μὴ ἰδεῖν θάνατον, Ac 5⁹ συνεφωνήθη ὑμῖν
πειράσαι. Wavering:— Mt 3¹⁵ πρέπον ἐστιν ἡμῖν πληρῶσαι (S* ἡμᾶς),
Mk 2²⁶ ἔξεστιν c. accus. SBL (c. dat. ACDW), Lk 6⁴ ἔξεστιν c. accus.
(D dat., like Mt 12⁴), 20²² ἔξεστιν c. accus. (CDW dat.), [Mk 10² ἔξεστιν
dat.] [P. Lille 26⁶ (iii/B.C.) ἔξεστιν accus.], 1 Co 11¹³ πρέπον ἐστιν accus.,
papyri Mayser II 1, 338.

(c) With ἐγένετο ¹ often: e.g. Ac 9³ ἐγ. αὐτόν ἐγγίζειν, 16¹⁶ ἐγ.
δὲ ... παιδίσκην τινὰ ὑπαντῆσαι ἡμῖν, and even after a dat.: 22⁶
ἐγένετο δέ μοι ... περιαστράψαι φῶς. This is sometimes so, even
when the person in the dat. is the same as in the accus.: 22¹⁷ ἐγ. μοι
... γενέσθαι με, Ga 6¹⁴ p⁴⁶ ἐμοὶ δὲ μὴ γένοιτό με καυχᾶσθαι (rest
om με).

(d) With verbs of asking, etc. (ἐρωτάω, παρακαλέω, αἰτέομαι,
ἀξιόω, παραινέω) the accus. c. inf. may follow: Ac 13²⁸ ᾐτήσαντο Πειλᾶτον
ἀναιρεθῆναι αὐτόν, 1 Th 5²⁷ ὁρκίζω ὑμᾶς ἀναγνωσθῆναι τὴν ἐπιστολήν,
Ac 21¹² παρεκαλοῦμεν τοῦ μὴ ἀναβαίνειν αὐτόν. But with δέομαι the
gen. follows: Lk 9³⁸ δέομαί σου ἐπιβλέψαι, Ac 26³ (δέομαι ἡμᾶς is class.).

(e) Often there is accus. c. inf., although it stands in apposition
to a pronoun in the gen. or dat.: e.g. Lk 1⁷³ᶠ τοῦ δοῦναι ἡμῖν ... ῥυσθέντας
λατρεύειν, Ac 15²²· ²⁵ (ABL dat.) etc., Ga 6¹⁴ p⁴⁶, Heb 2¹⁰ [2 Pt 2²¹
κρεῖττον ἦν αὐτοῖς μὴ ἐπεγνωκέναι ... ἢ ἐπιγνοῦσιν ὑποστρέψαι is
classically correct; Lk 9⁵⁹ (but accus. in DΘ), Ac 27³ SAB (but accus.
in HLP)].

¹ But the dat. and infin. is more usual with ἐγένετο: Ac 11²⁶ ἐγένετο
αὐτοῖς διδάξαι, 20¹⁶, Ga 6¹⁴, P. Par. 26 (163 B.C.) ὑμῖν γίνοιτο κρατεῖν.

CHAPTER ELEVEN

THE VERB: ADJECTIVE-FORMS: PARTICIPLE

THE USE OF the participle [1] is more lavish in Greek than in Latin. We are here discussing its substantival, adverbial, attributive, and predicative uses, leaving the genitive and accusative absolute for a later chapter. The predicative use (e.g. παύομαι λέγων), which supplements the main verbal idea, is on its way out. The adverbial use (e.g. 1 Ti 1¹³ ἀγνοῶν ἐποίησα) is still strong, and so are the attributive and substantival. As far as forms go, the fut. is in eclipse (see pp. 86f, 135). For *Aktionsart*, see above pp. 86f. For periphrastic conjugation, see above p. 89.

The participle is not so much a mood, as an adjective, and so its modal function will be apparent only from the context. The ptc. standing independently as a main verb may be like an indicative or an imperative, but the NT and papyri instances are not difficult to explain as true participles (see p. 343).

§ 1. Substantival Participle

The neuter ptc., usually with article (as class.), is often used in the Koine to designate an abstract or concrete noun, whether individually or collectively. It is also used with masc. or fem. article of a person. The neuter is not so frequent as in class. Greek. For papyri, Mayser II 1, 346ff.

(a) *Personal*. Articular: these have pres. tense where we expect aor., esp. Mk 5¹⁵. ¹⁶ ὁ δαιμονιζόμενος even after his healing; action (time or variety) is irrelevant and the ptc. has become a proper name,

---

[1] K-G I 197–200; II 46–113. Stahl 680–761. Schwyzer II 384ff. Moulton Einl. 284–288; 352–368. Mayser II 1, 339–357. Jannaris 489–506. Wackernagel I 281–294. Radermacher² 205–210. H. Balser, *De linguae Graecae participio in neutro genere substantive posito²*, Leipzig 1878. C. B. Williams, *The Participle in the Book of Acts*, Diss. Chicago 1909. H. B. Robinson, *Syntax of the Participle in the Apostolic Fathers*, Chicago 1915. C. O. Gillis, *Greek Participles in the Doctrinal Epistles of Paul*, Diss. of S-W. Bapt. Sem., 1937. W. K. Pritchett, "Μή with the Participle," *AJP* 79, 1958, 392ff.

it may be under Hebraic influence, insofar as the Heb. ptc. is also time-less and is equally applicable to past, pres. and fut. So also Heb 7⁹ ὁ δεκάτας λαμβάνων, Ph 3⁶ διώκων τὴν ἐκκλησίαν. Sometimes the pres. has its proper durative force, e.g. 1 Th 1¹⁰ ὁ ῥυόμενος ἡμᾶς (Jesus' work is durative), 2¹² (5²⁴) ὁ καλῶν ὑμᾶς, 4⁸ ὁ διδοὺς τὸ πν. αὐτοῦ. ... Virtually a proper name: ὁ ἐρχόμενος (fut), Mt 26⁴⁶ ὁ παραδιδούς με (my betrayer), Mk 1⁴ 6¹⁴. ²⁴ ὁ βαπτίζων (the Baptizer), Jn 8¹⁸ ἐγώ εἰμι ὁ μαρτυρῶν, 6⁶³, Ac 17¹⁷ τοὺς παρατυγχάνοντας (casual passers-by NEB), Ro 2¹ ὁ κρίνων (you the judge), Ro 8³⁴ τίς ὁ κατακρινῶν, Eph 4²⁸ ὁ κλέπτων (generic), LXX 1 Km 16⁴ ὁ βλέπων (gen.), Si 28¹ ὁ ἐκδικῶν (gen.). This ptc. can have an obj. or complement: Jn 1²⁹ ὁ αἴρων (the sin-bearer), Ga 1²³ ὁ διώκων ἡμᾶς (our persecutor), Mt 27⁴⁰, BU 388 III 16 ὁ παρὰ Πτολεμαΐδος ἀργυρώματα λαβών.

Anarthrous: Mt 2⁶ OT ἡγούμενος prince, Mk 1³ OT φωνὴ βοῶντος voice of a herald, Lk 3¹⁴ στρατευόμενοι, Ro 3¹¹ᶠ OT BG(A) (rest art. LXX Ps 13 (14)¹ᶠᶠ usually anarth.), Rev 2¹⁴ ἔχεις ἐκεῖ κρατοῦντας.

With πᾶς, usually articular (unless it means every): Mt 5²² πᾶς ὁ ὀργιζόμενος, ²⁸. ³² πᾶς ὁ ἀπολύων anyone who divorces, 7²⁶ πᾶς ὁ ἀκούων any hearer, ⁸ πᾶς ὁ αἰτῶν λαμβάνει every beggar receives, Lk 6³⁰ ADPR ⁴⁷ etc., Ac 1¹⁹ πᾶσι τοῖς κατοικοῦσιν, 10⁴³ 13³⁹, Ro 1¹⁶ 2¹ etc. Anar-throus: Mt 13¹⁹ παντὸς ἀκούοντος, Lk 11⁴ παντὶ ὀφείλοντι, 6³⁰ SBW, 2 Th 2⁴, Rev 22¹⁵.

(b) Neuter: Mt 1²⁰ τὸ ἐν αὐτῇ γεννηθέν her unborn baby, 2¹⁵ and often τὸ ῥηθέν, Lk 2²⁷ κατὰ τὸ εἰθισμένον (D ἔθος), 12³³. ⁴⁴ τὰ ὑπάρχοντα property (8³), 3¹³ τὸ διατεταγμένον ὑμῖν your assessment, 4¹⁶ τὸ εἰωθὸς αὐτῷ his custom, 8⁵⁶ τὸ γεγονός the occurrence, 9⁷ τὰ γινόμενα happenings, Jn 16¹³ τὰ ἐρχόμενα the future, 1 Co 1²⁸ τὰ ἐξουθενημένα ... τὰ μὴ ὄντα ... τὰ ὄντα, 7³⁵ 10³³ Sᶜ τὸ ... συμφέρον (but rest σύμφορον) your welfare, 10²⁷ πᾶν τὸ παρατιθέμενον, 14⁷· ⁹ τὸ αὐλούμενον, etc., 2 Co 3¹⁰ᶠ τὸ δεδοξασμένον, τὸ καταργούμενον, 2 Th 2⁶ τὸ κατέχον, Heb 12¹⁰ κατὰ τὸ δοκοῦν αὐτοῖς ... ἐπὶ τὸ συμφέρον, 12¹¹ πρὸς τὸ παρόν, P. Fay. 91, 28 κατὰ τὰ προγεγραμμένα, BU 362 V 9 τὰ κελευσθέντα; in Hell. Greek τὸ συνειδός = conscience (but a noun in Paul). Ambiguous is τὰ διαφέροντα (Ro 2¹⁸ Ph 1¹⁰; see ICC in loc.): either different values (= moral distinctions NEB) or superior things (RV, RSV, Lat. utiliora).

§ 2. Attributive Participle

Normally the ptc. ὤν is used with the predicate when further defining words are added to the predicate, e.g. Ac 14¹³ SB ὅ τε ἱερεὺς τοῦ Διὸς τοῦ ὄντος πρὸ τῆς πόλεως, 28¹⁷ τοὺς ὄντας τῶν Ἰουδαίων πρώτους, Ro 8²⁸ τοῖς κατὰ πρόθεσιν κλητοῖς οὖσιν, 2 Co 11³¹ ὁ ὢν εὐλογητὸς εἰς ..., 1 Ti 1¹³ τὸν πρότερον ὄντα βλάσφημον. There is no need for ὤν where the predicate stands alone. The redundant use of ὤν is however characteristic of Ac and the Ptol. papyri: Ac 5¹⁷ ἡ οὖσα αἵρεσις τῶν Σαδδουκαίων, 13¹ τὴν οὖσαν ἐκκλησίαν, 14¹³ D τοῦ ὄντος Διὸς πρὸ πόλεως, Ro 13¹ αἱ δὲ οὖσαι, Eph 1¹ p⁴⁶ D τοῖς ἁγίοις οὖσιν καὶ πιστοῖς (which thus need not be rejected), P. Tebt. 309 (ii/A.D.) ἀπὸ τοῦ ὄντος ἐν κώμῃ [τοῦ ἱεροῦ] θεοῦ . . . , P. Lille 29, 11 (iii/B.C.) τοὺς νόμους τοὺς περὶ τῶν οἰκετῶν ὄντας. It is conclusive from the papyri that the ὤν is somewhat redundant and means little more than *current* or *existent*. Translate *the local Zeus* (14¹³D), *the local church* (13¹), *the local school of the Sadducees* (5¹⁷); see *Beginnings* IV 56, Schwyzer II 409, Mayser II 1, 347f, Moulton Einl. 360.

The attributive ptc. stands both with and without the article and is equivalent to a relative clause: Mt 17²⁷ τὸν ἀναβάντα πρῶτον ἰχθύν, 25³⁴ τὴν ἑτοιμασμένην ὑμῖν βασιλείαν *which has been prepared*, Mk 3²² οἱ γραμματεῖς οἱ ἀπὸ Ἱεροσολύμων καταβάντες, 5²⁵ γυνὴ οὖσα ἐν ῥύσει αἵματος, 14²⁴ τὸ αἷμα . . . τὸ ἐκχυννόμενον (pres.), Lk 6⁴⁸ ὅμοιός ἐστιν ἀνθρώπῳ οἰκοδομοῦντι οἰκίαν (= a rel. clause in the parallel Mt 7²⁴), 10³⁷ ὁ ποιήσας τὸ ἔλεος, 15¹² τὸ ἐπιβάλλον μέρος τῆς οὐσίας, Ro 3⁵ μὴ ἄδικος ὁ θεὸς ὁ ἐπιφέρων τὴν ὀργήν; Ga 3²¹ νόμος ὁ δυνάμενος ζωοποιῆσαι. Anarthrous: Ac 19²⁴ Δημήτριος . . . ποιῶν ναοὺς ἀργυροῦς *Demetrius, a maker of silver shrines* (attrib.) or *because he made* (adverbial), Heb 7⁸ ἀποθνῄσκοντες ἄνθρωποι *mortal men* (attrib.) not adverbial. We must distinguish the attributive ptc. from a simple apposition (e.g. οἱ δὲ Φαρισαῖοι ἀκούσαντες εἶπον Mt 12²⁴, not *the Pharisees who heard*).

Also equivalent to a relative clause is the very frequent apposition ὁ λεγόμενος, (ἐπι)καλούμενος, with proper name following, always with an article after the person or object named: Mt 1¹⁶ Ἰησοῦς ὁ λεγόμενος Χριστός, Jn 5² κολυμβήθρα ἡ ἐπιλεγομένη . . . Βηθεσδά (S* τὸ λεγόμενον; W τῇ ἐπιλεγομένῃ) [the omission of ἡ D is an atticistic correction [1] made by those who were oblivious of NT usage], Ac 1¹² ὄρους τοῦ καλουμένου ἐλαιῶνος, 10¹⁸ Σίμων ὁ ἐπικαλούμενος Πέτρος (rel. clause 10⁵. ³²), Rev 12⁹ ὁ ὄφις . . . ὁ καλούμενος Διάβολος.

Whereas in class. Greek a relative clause would have been more correct after an anarthrous noun, in NT we often find an articular ptc., especially if it imparts some information which is well known, perhaps because of misunderstanding of an underlying Semitic ptc. (Moule 103), although it is not quite peculiar

---

[1] In cl. Attic the art. was not placed before the ptc., but before the proper noun. BU 512, 2 παρὰ Σύρου Συρίωνος ἐπικαλουμένου Πετακᾶ is half-way between class, and NT usage.

to Biblical Greek, viz. BU 416³ καμήλους δύο θηλείας αἱ κεχαραγμέναι = who were . . . .

Mk 15⁴¹ ἄλλαι πολλαὶ αἱ συναναβᾶσαι, Lk 7³² παιδίοις τοῖς ἐν ἀγορᾷ καθημένοις, Jn 12¹² ὄχλος πολὺς (BL add art.) ὁ ἐλθών, Ac 4¹² οὐδὲ γὰρ ὄνομά ἐστιν ἕτερον τὸ δεδομένον = ὃ ἐδόθη, 1 Co 2⁷ θεοῦ σοφίαν . . . τὴν κεκρυμμένην, 1 Pt 1⁷ χρυσίου τοῦ ἀπολλυμένου, 2 Jn⁷ ὅτι πολλοὶ πλάνοι . . . οἱ μὴ ὁμολογοῦντες, Jude⁴ τινες ἄνθρωποι οἱ πάλαι προγεγραμμένοι. Unclassical also is the ellipse of the art. in 1 Pt 3¹⁹. ²⁰ with a ptc. which follows a definite antecedent: τοῖς . . . πνεύμασιν . . . ἀπειθήσασίν ποτε. But after τινες the articular ptc. is classical (Stahl 691, 694): Lk 18⁹ πρός τινας τοὺς πεποιθότας ἐφ᾽ ἑαυτοῖς, Ga 1⁷ εἰ μή τινές εἰσιν οἱ ταράσσοντες ὑμᾶς, Col 2⁸. Mk 14⁴ is not an instance because here we have a periphrastic tense: ἦσάν τινες ἀγανακτοῦντες. Lysias 19, 57 (v–iv/B.C.) εἰσί τινες οἱ προαναλίσκοντες. Also cp. the class. Greek construction οὐδείς (ἐστιν) ὁ with fut. ptc.

We also find in the NT, as in class. Greek, the articular ptc. dependent on a personal pronoun: Jn 1¹² αὐτοῖς . . . τοῖς πιστεύουσιν, Ac 13¹⁶ (sc. ὑμεῖς), Ro 9²⁰ σὺ τίς εἶ ὁ ἀνταποκρινόμενος (Jas 4¹² σὺ τίς εἶ ὁ κρίνων [vl. ὃς κρίνεις]), 14⁴, 1 Co 8¹⁰ (p⁴⁶ B om σε). In some passages we must supply the pronoun, esp. with the imper.: Mt 7²³ OT 27⁴⁰, Lk 6²⁵, Heb 4³ 6¹⁸.

§ 3. Adverbial Participle [1]

This circumstantial ptc. differs from a supplementary ptc. in that the latter cannot without impairing the sense be detached from the main verbal idea, whereas the circumstantial is equivalent to a separate participial clause. Such clauses may be either syntactically " joined " to the construction of the sentence, or they may be " absolute ". Normally the clause will have reference to some noun or pronoun in the sentence agreeing with it in gender and number and case, but it may be syntactically independent in an isolated construction (see below, p. 322).

The relationship of this ptc. to the predicate may be of time, manner, cause, purpose, condition, or concession. This is not expressed by the ptc. itself, unless fut., but it is learned from the context or else from some added particle like καίπερ, ἅμα, εὐθύς, ποτέ, νῦν. The Koine does not on the whole favour this

---

[1] K-G II 77ff. Stahl 681ff. Moulton Einl. 363ff. Mayser II 1, 384ff.

method but prefers a prepositional phrase, a true temporal (etc.) clause, or a further co-ordinate sentence; thus Luke prefers κατὰ ἄγνοιαν ἐπράξατε (Ac 3¹⁷) to ἀγνοῶν ἐποίησα (1 Ti 1¹³).

(a) *Modal-temporal* is the most frequent kind of adverbial participial phrase in NT and Koine, as well as elsewhere. Often there is no stress whatever on the temporal relationship.

Mt 19²² ἀπῆλθεν λυπούμενος *in sorrow*, Mk 11⁵ *what do you mean by loosing?* Mt 27⁴ *by betraying*, 2¹⁶ 13² 6¹⁷ 19²².—Mk 1⁷.—Jn 16⁸.— Ac 21³².—1 Ti 1¹³.—1 Pt 5¹⁰.—BU 467, 15 etc. With ἄμα:—Mk 12³⁸ D Ac 24²⁶ 27⁴⁰ Col 1¹² p⁴⁶B, 4³. With εὐθύς:—Mk 6²⁵. With οὕτως (modal), class., in NT in Ac only: 20¹¹·³⁵ 27¹⁷.

Under this head should be included the large number of pleonastic participles in Biblical Greek (for pleon. ptc. in Ptol. pap., see Mayser II 1, 349). Apart from verbs of speaking (see below) the ptcs are ἄγων (pap.), ἀρξάμενος, ἔχων (pap.), φέρων (pap.), and (most used in NT) λαβών. These often have the meaning of the preposition *with*: Mt 15³⁰ (BU 909, 8) ἔχοντες μεθ' ἑαυτῶν (double pleonasm), LXX Ge 24¹⁵ ἔχουσα τὴν ὑδρίαν ἐπὶ τῶν ὤμων αὐτῆς, 1 Mac 8⁶ ἔχοντα ἑκατὸν εἴκοσι ἐλέφαντας, Mt 25¹ παραλαβών, λαβών, Mk 14³ ἔχουσα ἀλάβαστρον μύρου, Lk 2⁴²D, Ac 21²³ εὐχὴν ἔχοντες ἀφ' ἑαυτῶν, Jn 18³ *with a detachment* = Mt 26⁴⁷ μετ' αὐτοῦ; much of this is paralleled in the Koine. But λαβών and some other merely descriptive ptcs. seem to owe their origin in Bibl. Greek to a Hebraic pattern. In Heb. such a ptc. indicates a movement or an attitude which precedes an action. Usually it is superfluous, but it can have its justification sometimes, perhaps very slightly temporal: Mt 13³¹·³³ 14¹⁹ 21³⁵·³⁹ etc. LXX Jdt 12¹⁹ καὶ λαβοῦσα ἔφαγε καὶ ἔπιε, Nu 7⁶ 1 Esd 3¹³. So ἀναστάς (קוּם) and verbs of "departure": Mt 2²⁰ ἐγερθείς; 26⁶² ἀναστάς, Mk 10¹, Lk 15¹⁸·²⁰ 24¹², Ac 5¹⁷ 8²⁷ 9⁶·¹¹·³⁴·³⁹ 10²⁰ 11⁷ 22¹⁰·¹⁶, LXX Ge 22³ Nu 22²⁰; Mt 13²⁸·⁴⁶ ἀπελθών, 25¹⁸·²⁵; Mt 2⁸ 25¹⁶ 21⁶ Lk 7²² 13³² 14¹⁰ πορευθείς; 15²⁵ ἐρχόμενος; LXX Ge 21¹⁴ Ex 12²¹ ἀπελθόντες; Ge 45²⁸ 1 Mac 7⁷ πορευθείς; all these verbs after Heb. הלך. After Heb. ישׁב is καθίσας: Mt 13⁴⁸ Lk 5³ 14³¹ 16⁶, LXX Nu 11⁴ Dt 1⁴⁵.

Reminiscent of the class. ἀρχόμενος *at the beginning*, ἀρξάμενος occurs with meaning *from ... onwards* (class., and Lucian *somn.* 15 ἀπὸ τῆς ἕω ἀρξάμενος ἀχρὶ πρὸς ἑσπέραν) and pleonastically (perhaps again, through Heb. influence) [1]: LXX Ge 44¹² ἀπὸ τοῦ πρεσβυτέρου ἀρξάμενος (+ ἕως ... unclass.), Mt 20⁸ᶠ, Lk 23⁵, 24²⁷ ἀρξάμενος ἀπὸ Μωϋσεως, ⁴⁷ ἀπὸ Ἰερουσαλήμ, Jn 8⁹ ἀπὸ τῶν πρεσβυτέρων (+ ἕως τῶν ἐσχάτων unclass.), Ac 1²² + ἄχρι, 8³⁵ ἀπὸ τῆς γραφῆς ταύτης, 11⁴ ἀρξάμενος Πέτρος ἐξετίθετο αὐτοῖς καθεξῆς, only slightly pleonastic, as the emph. is on καθεξῆς; cp. LXX Jg 19⁶ ἀρξάμενος (Β ἄγε δή) αὐλίσθητι, Jb 6⁹, Xen. of Eph. 5, 7, 9 ἀρξαμένη κατέχομαι. The Hebraism προσθεὶς ἔφη is similar (see below p. 227). But besides the pleonastic ptc., parataxis with καί is possible, also on the Heb. model; use of the participial phrase is reduced in Biblical Greek through this co-ordination. In LXX the ptc. has yielded to parataxis under Heb. influence: cp. Ge 32²² ἀναστὰς δὲ τὴν νύκτα ἐκείνην ἔλαβε τὰς δύο γυναῖκας ... καὶ διέβη with 32²³ καὶ ἔλαβεν αὐτοὺς καί διέβη. NT authors however usually have recourse to the ptc.; but exx. of parataxis are Lk 22¹⁷ λάβετε τοῦτο καὶ διαμερίσατε, Ac 8²⁶ ἀνάστηθι καὶ πορεύου (but D ἀναστὰς πορεύθητι), 9¹¹ B lat copt ἀνάστα πορεύθητι (rest ἀναστάς), 10²⁰ D* ἀνάστα κατάβηθι (rest ἀναστάς), 3 Km 19⁵· ⁷ T. Abr B 110²⁰.

Very frequent also in NT are the pleonastic participles λέγων, εἰπών, ἀποκριθείς, etc. In both LXX and NT the λέγων which corresponds to לֵאמֹר appears repeatedly after ἀποκρίνομαι, λαλέω, κράζω, παρακαλέω, etc., and often we have the formula ἀποκριθεὶς εἶπεν[2] (but not in Jn): twice in second part of Ac (19¹⁵ 25⁹) LXX Ge 18⁹; it is the LXX tr. of וַיַּעַן וַיֹּאמֶר, whereas the asyndetic ἀπεκρίθη λέγων in Jn may be Aramaic; there never occurs ἀποκρινόμενος εἶπεν (Plato) or ἀπεκρίθη εἰπών.

This was already in slight use in class. Greek (Hdt ἔφη λέγων, εἰρώτα λέγων, ἔλεγε φάς), and can with little effort be paralleled in the Ptol. pap. Although the ptc. here has an obj. it does occur without: UPZ I 6³⁰ (163 B.C.) ἀπεκρίθησαν ἡμῖν φήσαντες, P. Giss. 36¹⁰ (135 B.C.) τάδε λέγει Ἀ. καὶ Ἀ. καὶ ..., αἱ τέτταρες λέγουσαι ἐξ ἑνὸς στόματος (Mayser II 3, 63¹⁴). However, λέγων is not pleonastic if the preceding verb governs an obj.: BU 624¹⁵ πολλὰ γὰρ ἠρώτησε λέγων ὅτι δουλεύσω, P. Par. 51²³ καὶ πάλιν ἠξίωκα τὸν Σάραπιν καὶ τὴν Ἴσιν λέγων· Ἔλθε ... Pleonastic for certain are:—BU 523⁶ καὶ ἀντέγραψας λέγων ... πέμψον, P. Par. 35³⁰ ἀπεκρίθησαν ἡμῖν φήσαντες. There is no doubt, however,

---

[1] On pleonastic ἄρχομαι see J. W. Hunkin, "Pleonastic ἄρχομαι in the NT", *JThS*, 25, 1924, 390–402; G. Delling in Kittel WB I 477; Lagrange *S. Luc* CVI.

[2] Mt 25⁹ (pl.),³⁷· ⁴⁴ (fut.), Mk 15⁹ (D ἀποκριθεὶς λέγει), Jn 12²³ (pres.), Ac 15¹³ (not D). Ἀπεκρίνατο λέγων LXX Ezk 9¹¹B (rare). Note the difference between Synoptists and Jn. The Synoptists follow LXX but are more idiomatic in that they put the Heb. main verb in the ptc. (ἀποκριθείς); but Jn does not favour the ptc. and even prefers asyndeton. He also avoids the other redundant ptcs. of the Synoptists: ἐλθών, ἀφείς, ἀναστάς. He prefers co-ordination.

that such expressions when used on a large scale, as in Bibl. Greek, point away from the popular language to a specialized Semitic background. Cp. the concentration of ἀποκριθείς (ἀπεκρίθη καὶ) εἶπεν in Rec. B of T. Abr.: 106⁴· ¹¹· ¹⁸ 107¹B 108¹· ²¹· ²³ 110⁷· ¹⁶· ²¹ 111¹⁸ 112⁶· ⁹ 113⁹ 114⁶ 118¹⁵.

Λέγων occurs with other verbs too, especially in Luke, John and Paul. Thoroughly Septuagintal is Lk 1⁶³ ἔγραψεν λέγων (*as follows*), LXX 2 Km 11¹⁵ ἔγραψεν ἐν βιβλίῳ λέγων, 4 Km 10⁶, 1 Mac 11⁵⁷ (see Klostermann on the passage in Lk);

Also Lk 5²¹ ἤρξαντο διαλογίζεσθαι . . . λέγοντες (12¹⁷); Mt 15²³ ἠρώτων λέγοντες, 26⁷⁰ ἠρνήσατο λέγων (cp. Ac 7³⁵ εἰπόντες), Lk 12¹⁶ 20² εἶπεν λέγων, Jn 1³² ἐμαρτύρησεν λέγων (S* e om λέγων), 4³¹ 9² (D om) etc. ἠρώτων (-τησαν) λέγοντες, 19¹² ἐκραύγαζον (vl. ἔκραζον) λέγοντες (S* ἔλεγον for ἔκρ. λ.), Mt 8²⁹ ἔκραξαν λέγοντες, 14³⁰ etc. Other participles of *saying* occur with these verbs: Lk 5¹³ ἥψατο εἰπών, 22⁸ ἀπέστειλεν εἰπών, Ac 7³⁵ ἠρνήσαντο εἰπόντες (prob. not pleon.), 21¹⁴ ἡσυχάσαμεν εἰπόντες, 22²⁴ ἐκέλευσεν . . . εἴπας, Jn 11²⁸ ἐφώνησεν τὴν ἀδελφὴν εἰποῦσα (not pleon. = *with the words*); Mt 2⁸ πέμψας εἶπεν *sent with the words*, Mk 5⁷ κράξας λέγει (D εἶπε), 9²⁴ κράξας ἔλεγεν (DΘ λέγει; p⁴⁵ W εἶπεν), Ac 13²² εἶπεν μαρτυρήσας.

Moreover, in Heb. *answered* is followed by ויאמר and so, besides ἀπεκρίθη λέγων, the NT and LXX also have ἀπ. καὶ εἶπεν (often Jn, not Mt, rarely Mk Lk), the participial construction thus giving way in Bibl. Greek to the paratactic: ἀπεκρίθη καὶ εἶπεν Jn 14²³ 18³⁰ 20²⁸ etc. (Jn almost always so, unless ἀπ. stands without addition), Lk 17²⁰, LXX Je 11⁵ ἀπεκρίθην καὶ εἶπα, Mk 7²⁸ ἀπεκρίθη καὶ λέγει. With other verbs (in Jn especially): 1²⁵ ἠρώτησαν αὐτὸν καὶ εἶπαν αὐτῷ, 9²⁸ ἐλοιδόρησαν αὐτὸν καὶ εἶπαν, 13²¹ ἐμαρτύρησαν καὶ εἶπεν, 18²⁵ ἠρνήσατο καὶ εἶπεν, Lk 8²⁸D, Ro 10²⁰ ἀποτολμᾷ καὶ λέγει.

Thoroughly Septuagintal also is the addition of the ptc. of the same verb in order to strengthen the verbal idea. It renders the Hebrew Infinite Absolute [1], being the nearest approach to the infin., since the infin. itself would be too literal. It is very rare indeed in secular Greek; better Greek would render the Inf. Absol. idea by means of the dat. of the verbal substantive, and yet in the LXX it is rendered 171 times by the ptc. (against 123 by the dat., 23 by accus., and 5 through an adverb). E.g. Ge

---

[1] K-G II 99f.   Moulton Einl. 118f.   H. St. John Thackeray, " The Infinitive Absolute in the LXX," *JThS* 9, 1908, 597ff; *OT Grammar* 48f. Johannessohn DGKPS 57.

22¹⁷ εὐλογῶν εὐλογήσω σε, 26²⁸ ἰδόντες ἑωράκαμεν, Ex 3⁷ ἰδὼν
ἴδον, Jb 6¹, 1 Km 20³. In NT, only in LXX-quotations:
Mt 13¹⁴ βλέποντες βλέψετε, Ac 7³⁴ ἰδὼν εἶδον, Heb 6¹⁴ εὐλογῶν
εὐλογήσω σε καὶ πληθύνων πληθύνω σε, Eph 5⁵ ἴστε γινώσκοντες
(uncertain textually), 1 Clem 12⁵ γινώσκουσα γινώσκω,
P. Tebt. II 421¹² (iii/A.D.) ἐρχόμενος δὲ ἔρχου (ε)ἰς Θεογονίδα
(but this may not be an instance: simply *when you come, come
to Th.*).

(b) *Causal use.* This follows the class. pattern in the
Koine, except that in NT we do not find ἅτε, οἷον or οἷα
(papyri). Mt 1¹⁹ δίκαιος ὤν (= ὅτι), Lk 10²⁹ θέλων δικαιῶσαι
ἑαυτόν, Ac 19³⁶ ἀναντιρρήτων . . . ὄντων τούτων, 23¹⁸ ἔχοντά τι
λαλῆσαί σοι *because he has something to say*, 2 Co 12¹⁶ ὑπάρχων
πανοῦργος, 1 Th 5⁸; Phm⁹ is ambiguous (causal or concessive),
so also Ga 2³. The papyri show a hybrid construction, beginning
with διὰ τό c. inf. and ending with the causal ptc.: P. Par. 12²¹
διὰ τὸ χωλὸν ὄντα, P. Leip. 108⁵ διὰ τὸ ἐμὲ μετριῶς ἔχοντα.

(c) *Concessive use.* Not frequent. Koine has καίπερ,
καίτοι, and καὶ ταῦτα, like NT. Mt 7¹¹ πονηροὶ ὄντες, Ac 19³⁷,
17²⁷ καί γε (D* καίτε; S καίτοιγε; A καίτοι), 1 Co 9¹⁹ ἐλεύθερος
ὤν, 2 Co 10³ ἐν σαρκὶ . . . περιπατοῦντες, Ph 3⁴ καίπερ, Phm⁸
πολλὴν . . . παρρησίαν ἔχων, Heb 5⁸ καίπερ ὢν υἱός 4³ καίτοι c.
gen. ptc., 11² καὶ ταῦτα, 7⁵ καίπερ, 12¹⁷ καίπερ (p⁴⁶ καίτοι),
2 Pt 1¹² καίπερ.—P. Par. 8, 16 νυνὶ πλεονάκις ἀπαιτούμενοι οὐκ
ἀποδίδωσι *although they are often asked to do it*.

(d) *Conditional use.* Papyri (Mayser II 1, 351): BU 543¹³
εὐορκοῦντι ἔστω μοι εὖ, ἐφιορκοῦντι δὲ ἐναντία, 596¹¹ τοῦτο
οὖν ποιήσας *if you do that* ἔσῃ μοι μεγάλην χάριταν κατατεθειμένος.

Lk 9²⁵ κερδήσας (Mt 16²⁶ ἐὰν κερδήσῃ), Ac 15²⁹, Heb 11³²,
Jn 15² μὴ φέρον καρπόν *if it does not*, but (same verse) πᾶν τὸ
καρπὸν φέρον (substantival ptc.) = *fruiting branch*; however,
Jn's method is often to have variety of vocabulary and syntax in
close proximity.

(e) *Final use.* Papyri (op. cit. 351f) esp. with ἀποστέλλω,
πέμπω etc., with fut. ptc. (class.); only in Mt Lk. Mt 27⁴⁹
ἔρχεται σώσων (W σώζων, S* σῶσαι, D καὶ σώσει), Ac 8²⁷
ἐληλύθει προσκυνήσων, 22⁵ ἐπορευόμην ἄξων, 24¹¹·¹⁷, 25¹³
ἀσπασόμενοι vl. Usually it is the pres. ptc.: Lk 7⁶ ἔπεμψεν
φίλους ὁ ἑκατοντάρχης λέγων αὐτῷ, 10²⁵ ἀνέστη ἐκπειράζων
αὐτόν.

The addition of ὡς (ὥσπερ, ὡσεί)[1] will express subjective motive: Ac 3¹² ἡμῖν τε ἀτενίζετε ὡς ... πεποιηκόσιν, 28¹⁹, Lk 16¹ 23¹⁴ 1 Co 4¹⁸ ὡς μὴ ἐρχομένου δέ μου, 7²⁵ *in the conviction that*, Heb 13¹⁷ ἀγρυπνοῦσιν ὡς λόγον ἀποδώσοντες *with the thought that they must* (fut. ptc.), 12²⁷, 1 Pt 4¹², Rev 1¹⁵, Ac 23¹⁵. ²⁰ 27³⁰ *under pretence of*, 2 Co 5²⁰ gen. abs. (as well as comparison: Ac 2² Rev 1¹⁵).

N.B. class. Greek was fond of lengthening sentences by accumulating the circumstantial participles. The nearest approach to this form of ugliness in NT is 2 Pt 2¹²⁻¹⁵ βλασφημοῦντες ἀδικούμενοι ἡγούμενοι ἐντρυφῶντες. On the other hand, Luke introduces ptcs. quite effectively and thus presents a flowing style which is refreshing after the jerky epistolary style of Paul; Lk 4²⁰ καὶ πτύξας τὸ βιβλίον ἀποδοὺς τῷ ὑπηρέτῃ ἐκάθισεν; with καί connecting, Ac 14²⁷ παραγενόμενοι δὲ καὶ συναγαγόντες, 18²² κατελθὼν εἰς Καισάρειαν, ἀναβὰς καὶ ἀσπασάμενος τὴν ἐκκλησίαν, κατέβη εἰς 'Αντιόχειαν (asyndeton to avoid ugliness), ²³ ἐξῆλθεν, διερχόμενος τὴν Γαλατικὴν χώραν, στηρίζων τοὺς μαθητάς = ἐξῆλθεν καὶ διήρχετο στηρίζων, 19¹⁶ ἐφαλόμενος ὁ ἄνθρωπος ἐπ αὐτοὺς ..., κατακυριεύσας ἀμφοτέρων ἴσχυσεν = ἐφήλετο καί ... (the vl. καὶ κατακυριεύσας S*HLP gives the second ptc. a weaker connection with the first). Matthew, whose gospel is more stylistic than the others, has a little of the same tendency: 14¹⁹ κελεύσας (SZ ἐκέλευσεν) ... λαβὼν ... ἀναβλέψας, 27⁴⁸ δραμὼν ... καὶ λαβὼν ... πλήσας τε (τε om D) ... καὶ περιθείς.

§ 4. Predicative Participle [2]

In the same way as the ordinary adj., the ptc. may fulfil the rôle of a predicate and answer either to the subject or the direct complement of the proposition. In this way, with εἶναι and γίνεσθαι the ptc. forms a periphrastic tense (see pp. 87–89).

As a predicate answering to the subject the ptc. is found with verbs expressing a manner of existence, like ὑπάρχω, but in NT this is restricted and is found almost only in Luke, Paul and Hebrews. In the Ptol. pap. (Mayser II 1, 352f) the predicating ptc. is apparently still very well attested, though not in comparison with class. Greek. When this kind of verb has an adj. or prepositional phrase as a predicate, strictly there should be introduced the ptc. ὤν, but not so inevitably in NT and Hell. Greek; thus Phrynichus designates φίλος σοι τυγχάνω as " Hellenistic ". The omission of ὤν is to be remarked in the

---

[1] With this ὡς there may be ellipse of the ptc. (class.): Ro 13¹³ ὡς ἐν ἡμέρᾳ, 1 Co 9²⁶ 2 Co 2¹⁷, Ga 3¹⁶ Eph 6⁷ Col 3²³ 2 Th 2², 1 Pt 4¹¹.
[2] K-G II §§ 481–484. Stahl 699ff. Mayser II 1, 352ff. Moulton Einl. 361ff. Radermacher² 208.

following NT passages (as also in Strabo, Appian, and Philostratus):

Mk 1²³, Lk 4¹ Ἰησοῦς δὲ πλήρης πνεύματος ἁγίου ὑπέστρεψεν, Ac 6⁸ πλήρης, 19³⁷ οὔτε ἱεροσύλους οὔτε βλασφημοῦντας (concessive), Heb 7²ᶠ.

(A) The Participle in the Nominative

As in class. Greek, and often in the Koine:—

MODIFYING VERBS:

	NT examples	Parallels, excl. class. Greek
ὑπάρχω	Ac 8¹⁶, Jas 2¹⁵ (Ac 19³⁶ ptc. prob. adjectival)	Koine i/B.C.
προϋπάρχω	Lk 23¹² (not D) (Ac 8⁹ ptc. prob. adverbial)	Josephus
παύομαι	Lk 5⁴, Ac 5⁴², 6¹³ etc., Eph 1¹⁶ Col 1⁹, Heb 10²	Hell., LXX Ge 11⁸, 18³³, Nu 16³¹ etc., Hermas
τελέω	Mt 11¹, Lk 7¹ D	Hermas Josephus
διατελέω	Ac 27³³	LXX 2 Mac 5²⁷, Hom. Clem 14⁸, Pap. Milligan p. 9 διατελῶ εὐχομένη *I pray continually*
ἐπιμένω	Jn 8⁷, Ac 12¹⁶	Koine 2 Cl. 10⁵
διαλείπω	Lk 7⁴⁵, Ac 8²⁴ D, 17¹³ D	LXX Je 17⁸, 51 (44)¹⁸ Lit. Hell. Koine
ἐγκακέω	Ga 6⁹, 2 Th 3¹³	
λανθάνω	Heb 13²	P. Hamb. I 27, 9 (250 B.C.)
φαίνομαι	Mt 6¹⁸	Koine
προφθάνω	Mt 17²⁵	Ep. Arist. 137
καλῶς ποιέω	Ac 10³³, Ph 4¹⁴, 2 Pt 1¹⁹, 3 Jn⁶	Koine

VERBS OF EMOTION:

ἀγαλλιάομαι	Ac 16³⁴	
τρέμω	2 Pt 2¹⁰	
χαίρω	Mt 2¹⁰ (*they were glad to see the star*), Jn 20²⁰, Ph 2²⁸	Koine
εὐχαριστῶ	1 Co 14¹⁸ KL (p⁴⁶ inf; SBD λαλῶ)	

VERBA SENTIENDI:

συνίημι	2 Co 10¹² SB p⁴⁶ αὐτοὶ ἐν ἑαυτοῖς ἑαυτοὺς μετροῦντες . . . οὐ συνιᾶσιν *they do not realise that they are measuring themselves by their own standards* (but D*G vulg. om οὐ συνιᾶσιν ἡμεῖς δέ)	Plut. 3. 231d Lucian D. Deor. 2, 1
μανθάνω	1 Ti 5¹³ ἅμα δὲ καὶ ἀργαὶ μανθάνουσιν περιερχόμεναι or sc. εἶναι?). Cp. class. μανθάνω διαβεβλήμενος. More often inf.: Ph 4¹¹, 1 Ti 5⁴, Ti 3¹⁴, 1 Cl. 8⁴ OT, 57²	

(B) The Participle in Oblique Case

(a) With verbs of sensual or spiritual perceiving and knowing: ἀκούω, βλέπω, γινώσκω, ἐπίσταμαι, εὑρίσκω, θεάομαι, θεωρέω, κατανοέω, οἶδα, ὁράω; all these are found in the Ptol. pap. (Mayser II 1, 354ff). Also in NT are: δοκιμάζω, ἔχω, μανθάνω. This ptc. is quite plentiful in NT, where it is almost always in an oblique case (Lk 8⁴⁶ ἔγνων δύναμιν ἐξεληλυθυῖαν ἀπ᾽ ἐμοῦ *I felt that power had gone out*, not *I felt the power going out*), and we do not find parallels to the class. ὁρῶ ἡμαρτηκώς *I see that I have sinned* (NT has ὅτι, see Mk 5²⁹ 1 Jn 3¹⁴). 'Αγνοέω and αἰσθάνομαι are found with ptc. in the papyri, but not NT.

'Ακούω: in NT, if the content of the hearing is given, usually the accus. c. infin. or else ὅτι or ὡς; it is no longer frequently the ptc. In class. Greek the ptc. tended to denote facts and the infin. mere hearsay; but this distinction has quite disappeared and all we can say is, that with the ptc. the accus. appears to denote what is learned (indirect speech), while the gen. is retained for direct audition or hearing with the ears.

Accus. with ptc.: Mk 5³⁶ παρακούσας τὸν λόγον λαλούμενον exceptional (this is direct audition and one would expect gen. B seeks a remedy by inserting the article: τὸν λόγον τὸν λαλούμενον, since without it the meaning should be *overhearing that the word was being spoken*); Lk 4²³ ὅσα ἠκούσαμεν γενόμενα; Ac 7¹² ἀκούσας ὄντα σιτία; 2 Th 3¹¹ ἀκούομεν γάρ τινας περιπατοῦντας *we hear that*; 3 Jn⁴ ἀκούω τὰ ἐμὰ τέκνα... περιπατοῦντα; P. Par. 48¹² ἀκούσαντες δὲ ἐν τῷ μεγάλῳ Σεραπείῳ ὄντα σε *that you were*. Even in Ac sometimes (9⁴ 26¹⁴) the accus. stands for class. gen.; indeed, the gen. is rare in NT outside Ac.

Gen. with ptc.: Mk 12²⁸ ἀκούσας αὐτῶν συνζητούντων, 14⁵⁸, Lk 18³⁶ ὄχλου διαπορευομένου, Jn 1³⁷ ἤκουσαν... αὐτοῦ λαλοῦντος, Ac 2⁶ 6¹¹ etc. Note in Ac 11⁷ 22⁷ ἤκουσα φωνῆς λεγούσης μοι (but accus. in 9⁴ 26¹⁴ [E gen]); if this pointless variation can occur in a writer like Luke, the class. distinction between accus. and gen. has now broken down.

Βλέπω, θεωρέω, θεάομαι, κατανοέω, ὁράω: ptc. Mt 24³⁰ ὄψονται τὸν υἱὸν... ἐρχόμενον, 15³¹, Mk 5³¹ βλέπεις τὸν ὄχλον συνθλίβοντά σε, Jn 1³² τεθέαμαι τὸ Πν. καταβαῖνον, ³⁸. Papyri. LXX To 11¹⁶ Su³⁷. Use of ὄντα is class.: Heb 3¹ᶠ κατανοήσατε τὸν ἀπόστολον... πιστὸν ὄντα; Ac 8²³ ὁρῶ σε ὄντα. 17¹⁶ θεώρ. κατείδωλον οὖσαν τὴν πόλιν. But the ptc. of the verb *to be* may be omitted: Mt 25³⁸ᶠ σε εἴδομεν ξένον, ἀσθενῆ (BD corr. to ptc. ἀσθενοῦντα), Jn 1⁵⁰ εἶδόν σε ὑποκάτω τῆς συκῆς; the use of ὡς occurs instead in Ac 17²² ὡς δεισιδαιμονεστέρους ὑμᾶς θεωρῶ, of which the sense must be *from what I see, it appears as if*, when we compare 2 Th 3¹⁵ ὡς ἐχθρὸν ἡγεῖσθε *as if he were an enemy*.

Sometimes with *to see*, as with other verbs, this kind of ptc. (especially in the pf.) is more plainly separated from the obj. of the main verb, and becomes in effect a distinctive complement, leaving the obj. and its main verb still very closely linked together: Mt 22¹¹ εἶδεν ἄνθρωπον οὐκ ἐνδεδυμένον, etc. (relative clause) = *he saw a man and he had not on*, Mk 11¹³ ἰδὼν συκῆν ἀπὸ μακρόθεν ἔχουσαν φύλλα (*which had*), LXX To 1¹⁷ εἴ τινα... ἐθεώρουν τεθνηκότα *who was dead*, P. Leip. 40²⁰ καὶ εἶδεν τὰς θύρας χαμαὶ ἐρριμένας *which were*. On ὅτι after *to see*, (see pp. 136f). In Mark the accus. c. ptc. construction occurs after ἰδεῖν 15 times, and ὅτι occurs 6 times.

Γινώσκω: in the Ptol. pap. usually with accus. c. ptc., but quite often also with infin. or ὅτι, διότι or ὡς—without much difference of meaning (Mayser II 1, 354f). Infin. or ὅτι also in NT. Lk 8⁴⁶ (Luke has altered Mk 5³⁰ which is not a case in point, since Mk uses the ptc. attributively: ἐπιγνοὺς τὴν ἐξ αὐτοῦ δύναμιν ἐξελθοῦσαν), Ac 19³⁵, Heb 13²³, BU 1078² γείνωσκέ με (this stereotyped letter-formula is very common in Ptol. pap.) πεπρακότα πρὸς τὸν καιρόν, 1078¹⁰ γείνωσκε δὲ ἡγεμόνα εἰσεληλυθότα τῇ τρίτῃ καὶ εἰκάδι.

Δοκιμάζω: 2 Co 8²² ὃν ἐδοκιμάσαμεν *we have proved* σπουδαῖον ὄντα (for inf. see p. 147). With ptc., absent from LXX and papyri.

'Επίσταμαι: Ac 24¹⁰ ὄντα σε κριτὴν ἐπιστάμενος, 26³ γνώστην ὄντα σε ... ἐπιστάμενος AC 614 (S* BEH om ἐπιστ.), 1 Clem 55² ἐπιστάμεθα πολλοὺς παραδεδωκότας ἑαυτούς, Ptol. pap., but more often with ὅτι or διότι. With ὅτι Ac 15⁷ etc.

Εὑρίσκω as a rule with ptc. (class.). Very often in Ptol. pap.: P. Leip. 40¹⁰ εὑρήκασι τοῦτον ... τυπτόμενον ὑπὸ γαλλιαρίων. Mt 12⁴⁴ εὑρίσκει (sc. τὸν οἶκον) σχολάζοντα, 24⁴⁶ ὃν ... εὑρίσκει οὕτως ποιοῦντα etc., LXX Ge 26¹² καὶ εὗρεν ... ἑκατοστεύουσαν κριθήν. Away from the obj.: Ac 9² τινας εὕρῃ τῆς ὁδοῦ ὄντας *who were*. Passive with nom. of ptc. like class. φαίνομαι: Mt 1¹⁸ εὑρέθη ἐν γαστρὶ ἔχουσα.

Οἶδα: only 2 Co 12² οἶδα ... ἁρπαγέντα τὸν τοιοῦτον (but ὅτι in ³ᶠ). Ptol. pap. dates: 254 253 145. With adj. without ptc. Mk 6²⁰. Elsewhere infin. or (usually) ὅτι, as in LXX and often in papyri.

(*b*) With verba dicendi et putandi (Mayser II 1, 312ff, 356):

'Έχω: Lk 14¹⁸ ἔχε με παρῃτημένον. P. Oxy. 292, 6 διὸ παρακαλῶ σε ... ἔχειν αὐτὸν συνεσταμένον.

'Ηγέομαι: Ph 3² ἀλλήλους ἡγούμενοι ὑπερέχοντας ἑαυτῶν.

'Ομολογέω: 1 Jn 4² 'I.X. ἐν σαρκὶ ἐληλυθότα (B inf.), ³ S, 2 Jn⁷. Without ὄντα: Jn 9²², Ro 10⁹.

(*c*) With verba declarandi (Mayser II 1, 355) never in NT, but Ign. Rom. 10² δηλώσατε ἐγγύς με ὄντα.

PART II

WORD-GROUPS DEFINING A NOUN OR ADJECTIVE

CHAPTER TWELVE

THE ADJECTIVAL AND PREDICATIVE DEFINITE ARTICLE

THE NEW TESTAMENT USE of the article comes well up to class. Attic standards on the whole [1]. In later papyri the art. is used as a relative pronoun, but never in NT; nor is it a demonstrative pronoun except in the poetic quotations in Ac 17²⁸ and except with μέν and δέ. In Ionic (Herodotus) and later vernacular Greek the art. is sometimes omitted between the preposition and infin., but never in NT.

We have already considered the art. in its substantival use (see pp. 36f). In its adjectival, it particularizes an individual member of a group or class.

§ 1. The Individual Article with Proper Nouns [2]

(a) Names of persons

In class. Greek, names of persons without attribute or apposition have no art. at their first mention. This appertains

---

[1] T. F. Middleton, *The Doctrine of the Greek Article*, 1808, rev. by H. J. Rose, 1858 last ed. K-G I 598–640. Schwyzer II 19–27. Jannaris, index. Mayser II 1, 56ff; II 2, 1–117, 171 (lit); III 3, index. Winer-Schmiedel §§ 17ff. Wackernagel II 125–152. Moulton Einl. 128ff. Radermacher² 112–118. Abel §§ 28–32. E. C. Colwell, "The Definite Article," *JBL* 52, 1933, 12–21. A. Svensson, *Der Gebrauch des bestimmen Artikel in d. nachklass. Epik.* 1937 Lund. Humbert §§ 59–77. D. M. Nelson, *The Articular and Anarthrous Predicate Nominative in the Greek NT*, unpubl. diss. of S. Baptist Theol. Seminary, 1945. R. H. Poss, *The Articular and Anarthrous Construction in the Epistle of James*, diss. of S-W. Baptist Theol. Seminary, 1948. J. Gwyn Griffiths, "A Note on the Anarthrous Predicate in Hellenistic Greek," *Exp. T.* 62, July 1951, 314. B. M. Metzger, reply to Griffiths, *Exp. T.* 63, Jan. 1952, 125. H. G. Meecham, "The Anarthrous θεός in John i.1 and 1 Cor. iii.16 ", *Exp. T.* 63, Jan. 1952, 126. Moule 106–117. R. W. Funk, *The Syntax of the Greek Article: Its Importance for Critical Pauline Problems* (Diss., Vanderbilt Univ.) 1953.

[2] Carolus Schmidt, *De articulo in nominibus propriis apud Atticos scriptores pedestres*, Kiel 1890. H. Kallenberg, *Philologus* 49, 1890, 515–547; *Studien über den gr. Artikel*, Berlin 1891. F. Völker, *Syntax der griechischen Papyri*: I Der Artikel, Münster 1903. Gildersleeve II §§ 536ff. *AJP* 11, 1890, 483ff; 24, 1913, 482 (articles by Gildersleeve); 27, 1916, 333–340 (F. Eakin, for i–ii/A.D. pap.); 341ff (C. W. E. Miller). A. Deissmann, " Die Artikel bei Eigennamen in der späteren griech. Umgangssprache," *Berliner philol. Wochenschr.* 22, 1902, 1467f. B. Weiss, " Der Gebrauch des Artikel bei den Eigennamen ", *Th. Stud. u. Krit.* 86, 1913, 349–389.

also in Hellenistic : the art. is used after the person has already
been pointed out (*anaphoric*, or pointing back) or when he is
often referred to, as in letters in the papyri, giving a familiar
tone proper to the colloquial language. A father's or a mother's
name, appearing in the gen., usually has the art., although there
are many exceptions. Moreover, names of slaves and animals
have the art. even when mentioned for the first time, whereas
the names of more important persons are anarthrous. The NT
formula Σαῦλος ὁ καὶ Παῦλος has many parallels in the Koine.
The final development of the popular tendency to use the art. is
seen in MGr where proper names almost always have it. It is a
mark of familiar style, like pointing with the finger, but despite
the pundits it was largely a matter of individual caprice even
in class. Greek, for some writers, like Plato, are extremely
partial to articular personal names [1]. No rule will account for
τὸν Ἰησοῦν ὃν Παῦλος κηρύσσει in Ac 19¹³ and τὸν Ἰησοῦν
γινώσκω καὶ τὸν Παῦλον ἐπίσταμαι in ¹⁵. Moreover, the MSS
are frequently divided. In other places, Luke abides by the
rule : thus in Ac 8³ we are introduced to Σαῦλος (anarth.) but are
referred back (anaphoric) in 9¹ to ὁ δὲ Σαῦλος, and meanwhile
Δαμασκόν (anarth.) has been introduced, to be referred to anaphorically in 9³ as τῇ Δαμασκῷ.

Ἰησοῦς

In the Gospels, except perhaps Jn, Jesus takes the art. as
a matter of course except where an articular appositional phrase
is introduced (Mt 26⁶⁹· ⁷¹ μετὰ Ἰ. τοῦ Γαλιλαίου [Ναζωραίου],
27¹⁷· ²² Ἰ. τὸν λεγόμενον Χρ.—Lk 2⁴³ Ἰ. ὁ παῖς, 24¹⁹ περὶ Ἰησοῦ
τοῦ Ναζαρηνοῦ). The rule is almost invariable in Mk, even
with the gen. (5²¹· ²⁷ 14⁵⁵· ⁶⁷ 15⁴³) ; the exceptions are Ἰησοῦ
Χριστοῦ (1¹) and the vocative (1²⁴ 5⁷ 10⁴⁷). This would indicate
that in 1⁹ the anarthrous Ἰησοῦς is to be taken closely with the
phrase which follows, i.e. *Jesus of Nazareth in Galilee*. The

---

[1] As the following statistics for the art. with proper names will indicate :
In the first thousand verses of

Aesch. *Prom. V*   the art. occurs 210 times
Soph. *Oed. T.*   ,, ,, ,, 303 ,,
Eurip. *Med.*   ,, ,, ,, 159 ,,
Aristoph. *Vespae* ,, ,, ,, 562 ,,
    (where the speech is much less elevated)
Plato *Phaed.*   ,, ,, ,, 768 ,, ·
    (Gildersleeve, *AJP* 11; 486n.).

article does not occur before the prepositional phrase, it is true, but in any case this is not usual in Mark (except for scribal insertions). If it were *Jesus came from N. in Galilee*, it would have to be ὁ Ἰησοῦς to accord with Mark's practice. In Mt there is rather more latitude (anarthrous in the gen.: 14¹ 26⁵¹, and nom. 20³⁰; Ἰησοῦ Χριστοῦ 1¹).

In view of this it is over subtle to explain the anarthrous Jesus in some MSS of Mt 28⁹ Lk 24¹⁵ on the ground that it is his first appearance as the risen Christ; rather accept the reading ὁ Ἰησοῦς of DL, which accords with Gospel usage.

Even in Ac, the first mention of Jesus is articular (1¹ SAE; but anarth. in BD).

Jn however normally follows the class. idiom by introducing proper names without the art., and adding it subsequently. This is usual also in the Koine and the rest of NT. E.g. the risen Christ is now τὸν Ἰησοῦν 20¹⁴ on his first appearance. However, ἀπεκρίθη Ἰησοῦς appears to be a set phrase (1⁴⁸· ⁵⁰ etc.). The MSS are particularly divided in Jn 21.

In the Epistles and Rev., however, Jesus stands without the art., except for: 2 Co 4¹⁰ᶠ (D*FG om art.), Eph 4²¹, 1 Th 4¹⁴, 1 Jn 4³; and then there is strong anaphora. The Epistles also usually omit the article with Χριστός; it is here regarded as a proper name rather than = Messiah, probably reflecting a development in Christology. But in Col 2⁶ the author reverts to the earlier designation of Χριστός as a title = Messiah. See H. J. Rose's appendix to his ed. of Middleton, 486–496, for the art. with Ἰησοῦς, κύριος, Χριστός.

Indeclinables

The art. without its proper force has occasionally to serve to determine the case: Mt 1²ᶠᶠ ἐγέννησεν τὸν Ἰσαάκ . . . τὸν Ἰακώβ etc. (But the same form is also used in the case of declinable nouns, such as τὸν Ἰούδαν² and τοῦ Οὐρίου.⁶) It is superfluous with names which have a clause in apposition. Mt 1⁶ τὸν Δαυὶδ τὸν βασιλέα (700 om τὸν β.), in ¹⁶ τὸν Ἰωσὴφ τὸν ἄνδρα Μαρίας (P. Oxy. I 2 B 6 prob. rightly om the first τόν), Jn 4⁵ Ἰωσὴφ τῷ υἱῷ αὐτοῦ (SB add τῷ), Lk 3²³⁻³⁸ ὢν υἱός, ὡς ἐνομίζετο, Ἰωσὴφ τοῦ Ἡλεὶ τοῦ Ματθὰτ . . . τοῦ Ἀδὰμ τοῦ θεοῦ. N.B. no art. with the first in the list of genitives, as in the ii/A.D.

inscriptions (Moulton Proleg. 236), Ac 7⁸ ἐγέννησεν τὸν Ἰσαάκ, 13²¹ ἔδωκεν . . . τὸν Σαούλ.

THE DECLENSION OF Αβρααμ IN NT IS AS FOLLOWS:

Nom	Αβρααμ	—18 times
Voc	Αβρααμ	—Lk 16²⁴⁻³⁰
Acc	⌠τὸν Αβρααμ	—Mt. 3⁹ Lk 3⁸ 16²³ Heb 7⁶·
	⌡Αβρααμ	—Lk 13²⁸ Jn 8⁵⁷ᶠ Ro 4¹
Gen	⌠τοῦ Αβρααμ	—rare (and then anaph.): Jn 8³⁹ Ga 3¹⁴· ²⁹
	⌡Αβρααμ	—19 times
Dat	⌠τῷ Αβρααμ	—11 times
	⌡Αβρααμ	—Heb 7¹
with prepn.	Αβρααμ	—always, exc. Ga 3⁹

The genitive of proper nouns

In the papyri a parent's name is added in the gen. with the nominative art. normally. In the more official papyrus texts however the parental gen. has the nom. art. before it only when the name of the son or daughter is in the gen. Thus Mt 10² is thoroughly vernacular (Mayser II 2, 7. 22ff. 118): Ἰάκωβος ὁ τοῦ Ζεβεδαίου. Also in the accus. Δαυὶδ τὸν τοῦ Ἰεσσαί Ac 13²² OT, but sometimes as in class. Greek without the art.: Ἰούδαν Σίμωνος Ἰσκαριώτου Jn 6⁷¹ etc., Σώπατρος Πύρρου Βεροιαῖος Ac 20⁴ (pap. exx. in Abel § 44a). However, with the gen. case it is not usual to repeat the art., and τοῦ τοῦ (*of the son of*) is avoided (exc. 1 Clem 12² ὑπὸ Ἰησοῦ τοῦ τοῦ Ναυή): e.g. in class. Greek Περικλέους τοῦ Ξανθίππου, where τοῦ belongs to the first name since in the nom. we have Περικλ. ὁ Ξανθίππου; in NT Ἰωσὴφ τοῦ Ἡλὶ τοῦ . . . Lk 3²³ᶠᶠ (see Klostermann p. 419 on this passage for parallels); papyri Βερενίκης τῆς Νικάνορος (254 B.C.) Mayser II 2, 7f.

It is not clear whether we are to supply υἱός with the apostle Ἰούδας Ἰακώβου (Lk 6¹⁶ Ac 1¹³) or ἀδελφός following Jude¹ .

To identify a mother by her son we have (as class.) Μαρία ἡ Ἰωσῆτος Mk 15⁴⁷ (mother, not wife, because this follows Μαρία ἡ Ἰακώβου τοῦ μικροῦ καὶ Ἰωσῆτος μήτηρ⁴⁰), Μαρία ἡ Ἰακώβου Mk 16¹ Lk 24¹⁰. The art. is omitted except for Mt 27⁵⁶ ἡ τοῦ Ἰακ. μήτηρ.   And to identify a wife by her husband (class. also) : P. Ryl. II 1407 Ἀντωνίας Δρούσου *the estate of A., wife of D.*, Mt 1⁶ τῆς τοῦ Οὐρίου, Jn 19²⁵ Μαριὰμ ἡ τοῦ Κλωπᾶ.   The possession of slaves by a family may be indicated by this construction : τοὺς (scil. brothers, Christians) ἐκ τῶν (scil. slaves) Ἀριστοβούλου, Ναρκίσσου Ro 16¹⁰. ¹¹, τῶν (scil. slaves?) Χλόης 1 Co 1¹¹.

(*b*) *Geographical names*

(1) *Names of peoples.*   These do not require the art. any more than personal names.   (a) Anarthrous Ἰουδαῖοι in Paul's defences against the Jews : Ac 26². ³. ⁴. ⁷. ²¹ 25¹⁰ ; πάντες Ἰουδαῖοι 26⁴ BC*E* (+ οἱ SAC² therefore wrong), the exception being 25⁸ (τὸν νόμον τῶν Ἰουδαίων).   Anarthrous Ἰουδαῖοι also in Paul, exc. in 1 Co 9²⁰ (ἐγενόμην τοῖς Ἰουδαίοις ὡς Ἰουδαῖος) where he must have some special occasion in mind like Timothy's circumcision ; τοῖς ἀνόμοις etc. (the Galatians?) in the following clauses, with τοῖς virtually demonstrative.   (b) Anarthrous Ἕλληνες, although in class. Greek regularly with the art. (K-G I 599 ; Gildersleeve II § 538), and also in the Ptol. pap. (Mayser II 2, 13) ; the point with Paul is never the totality of a nation, but its characteristic (*the Greek way of life*) ; consequently Ro 1¹⁴ (Ἕλλησίν τε καὶ βαρβάροις) is, like σοφοῖς τε καὶ ἀνοήτοις which follows it, quite class.[1] : Demosth. 8, 67 (πᾶσιν Ἕλλησι καὶ βαρβάροις = all, whether Greeks or barbarians).   (c) Correctly class. : Ἀθηναῖοι πάντες Ac 17²¹.   (d) But in the Gospel narrative (and to some extent in Ac) we usually find the art. with Ἰουδαῖοι and other names of nations : however, Mt 28¹⁵ παρὰ Ἰουδαίοις (D adds τοῖς), 10⁵ Lk 9⁵² εἰς πόλιν (κώμην) Σαμαριτῶν, Jn 4⁹ οὐ γὰρ συγχρῶνται Ἰουδαῖοι Σαμαρίταις (vl.).   (e) An instance of a national name in masc. sing. is ὁ Ἰσραήλ (prob. because Jacob is thought of).   The art. is wanting in Hebraic phrases like γῆ Ἰσραήλ, ὁ λαὸς Ἰσραήλ, etc.   To conclude, class. Greek has art. only if it is anaphoric or the people is well known (K-G I 598f) ; there is no art. in the Attic inscriptions (Meisterhans-Schwyzer 225, 14) ; in the Ptol. pap. there is very little conformity with any rule (Mayser II 2, 12f).

---

[1] Blass-Debr. § 262, 1.

(2) *Lands and islands* [1]. Like personal names, place names
have the art. only if there is some special reason. But ἡ 'Ασία
and ἡ Εὐρώπη take the art. regularly from early times, and in the
Ptol. papyri (ἡ 'Ασία only), as the two grand divisions of the
earth that are naturally opposed to each other; [2] but 'Ασία is
articular even when it is used to denote the Roman province
(in Ac 2⁹ᶠ Μεσοποταμία, 'Ασία and ἡ Λιβύη ἡ κατὰ Κυρήνην are
the only places with an art., because they seem like adjectives
and one can supply γῆ). The only exceptions are Ac 6⁹ (ἀπὸ
Κιλικίας καὶ 'Ασ.) and 1 Pt 1¹ (where the names of all the
countries are without the art. and there is no art. at all in the
whole address [3]. Beginnings of letters are formula-like:
ἐκλεκτοῖς παρεπιδήμοις διασπορᾶς Πόντου etc.). Many other
names of countries also, being originally adjectives (sc. γῆ, χώρα)
are never anarthrous. Cp. ἡ 'Ιουδαία γῆ in Jn 3²² and also according to D in 4³. (The anarthrous 'Ιουδ. Ac 2⁹ therefore is corrupt;
there are several emendations proposed). 'Η Γαλιλαία (except
Lk 17¹¹ μέσον Σαμαρείας καὶ Γαλιλαίας, where the omission
with Σ. has caused omission with Γ. for balance). 'Η 'Ελλάς
Ac 20² (so MGr). 'Η 'Ιουδαία (for which the Hebraic γῆ 'Ιούδα is
also used Mt 2⁶). 'Η Μεσοποταμία. 'Η Μυσία (adj.). But names
of countries in -ία that are identical with the feminines of
related adjectives fluctuate (Gildersleeve II § 547): e.g. in one
section of Xenophon (Anab. 1, 2, 21) we have εἰς τὴν Κιλικίαν
and ἐν Κιλικίᾳ and εἰς Κιλικίαν; NT anarthrous Ac 6⁹.
'Αραβία also fluctuates in Xen. and Hdt. Φρυγία fluctuates in
Dem., Isocr., Xen., and Hdt. NT Φρυγίαν καὶ Παμφυλίαν
Ac 2¹⁰ (although strictly adjs.), but τῆς Παμφυλίας Ac 13¹³.
The NT always has art. with 'Ιταλία, generally with 'Αχατα
(exc. Ro 15²⁶ 2 Co 9²). If χώρα or γῆ accompany the proper
names, as frequently in Hdt., then those proper names are
frankly adjectival, and we find the art. Gildersleeve II § 548).
The preposition makes a difference; thus εἰς Συρίαν (although

---

[1] K-G I 598f. Meisterhans-Schwyzer 225, 15 (anarthrous except for
Attica, Greece, and Asia, in Attic inscriptions). Gildersleeve II § 547ff.
Radermacher² 116 (articular, if the adjectival nature of the name is still
obvious, i.e. scil. γῆ. Thus ἡ Μεσοποταμία, ἡ 'Ασία, but Αἴγυπτος).
Mayser II 2, 13f.

[2] K-G I 599. Gildersleeve 239ff.

[3] See pp. 221f. Winer-Schmiedel § 18, 14. See also Mayser II 2, 14
for parallels in the abbreviated style of memorials, etc., where there is a
long list as in 1 Pt 1¹.

strictly an adj.), Ac 21³, but Σ. does not have the art. in Isoc.,
Plato or Xen. (Gildersleeve II § 547); also εἰς 'Αραβίαν Ga 1¹⁷.
Not being an adj., Αἴγυπτος never takes the art. in NT if we can
except the reading of SBDAC p⁴⁵ in Ac 7¹¹ (where in any case
the adj. ὅλος appears) and that of BC in 7³⁶.   In the Ptol. pap.
however, it has the art. always, except after a preposition and
in the subordinate genitive (Mayser II 2, 13f).   However, the
geographical genitive does require the art. and so does the post-
positive partitive genitive of the name of a country.   This was
in fact a rule of class. Greek, well observed by Thucydides
(Gildersleeve II § 553).   See Ac 13¹⁴ 'Αντιόχειαν τῆς Πισιδίας
DEHLP (rest accus.), 21³⁹ Ταρσεύς, τῆς Κιλικίας, 22³ 27⁵.

(3) *Names of towns and cities.* In MGr they always have the
art. unless the town is preceded by a preposition (e.g. ἐξ 'Αμβούρ-
γου εἰς Νέαν 'Υόρκην); there was always, even in class. Greek, a
tendency to resist the art. with common or proper nouns in
prepositional phrases.   But in class. Greek names of towns do
not require the art. and even the anaphoric use is sometimes
merely a device to avoid a hiatus; NT follows the rule, and has
the art. only for a special reason.   The art. is present only
because it is anaphoric in Ac 9³. ³⁸. ⁴² (τῆς 'Ιόππης), 17¹³
(ἐν τῇ B, because εἰς B. in ¹⁰), ¹⁶ (ἐν ταῖς 'Α., because ἕως 'Α. in
¹⁵); in 18² τῆς 'Ρώμης is due to attraction to τῆς 'Ιταλίας; in 28¹⁴
the art. denotes Rome as the goal of the journey (demonstrative).
Even Τρῴας, although subject to an art. because it is 'Αλεξάνδ-
ρεια ἡ Τρῴας, is anarthrous in Ac 16⁸ 20⁵ 2 Ti 4¹³ (as in Xen. Hdt),
and is articular only anaphorically in Ac 16¹¹ 20⁶ 2 Co 2¹²
(referring to 1²³ where Troas was in mind).   Yet there is no apparent reason for the art. with towns mentioned as halting-
places: Ac 17¹ τὴν 'Αμφίπολην καὶ τὴν 'Απολλωνίαν (εἰς Θεσσ.
because of the preposition).   Note further ἤλθομεν εἰς Μίλητον
(Ac 20¹⁵), but on leaving and so anaphoric ἀπὸ δὲ τῆς Μιλήτου
⁽¹⁷⁾, both with preposition; also παραπλεῦσαι τὴν "Εφεσον ⁽¹⁶⁾,
but πέμψας εἰς "Εφεσον (because preposition). Yet there is a
preposition with articular place-names in 20¹³ 21¹ (in spite of
εἰς Πάταρα, etc.), 23³¹.   Thus there is a rule, but it is not
unbroken.

Unless an adj. is present (Rev 3¹²) 'Ιεροσόλυμα, 'Ιερουσαλήμ
rarely take the art.   If they do, it is anaphoric: Jn 2²³ 5². In Jn
10²² the art. is absent (but added by ABWL).   The exceptions

to this rule are Jn 11¹⁸ Ac 5²⁸. Josephus usually observes it.

(4) *Names of rivers and seas* [1]. They are generally articular in NT and Ptol. pap. (except sometimes with a preposition). In class. Greek rivers usually take ὁ ποταμός, like Mk 1⁵ ὁ 'Ιορδάνης ποταμός (elsewhere ὁ 'Ιορδάνης) and Her. V. I 1, 2 τὸν ποταμὸν τὸν Τίβεριν. Cp. Jn 18¹ τοῦ χειμάρρου Κεδρών (SBCD corrupt). Ac 27²⁷ ὁ 'Αδρίας (class.).

(c) *Astronomical names and natural phenomena*

Winds. Always without art. in NT. Νότος *south wind* Lk 12⁵⁵ Ac 27¹³ 28¹³. With and without in the papyri (Mayser II 2, 18).

Points of the compass. With prepositions, they never have art. in NT : Mt 2¹ 8¹¹ etc. (ἀπὸ ἀνατολῶν), 12⁴² (βασίλισσα νότου), 24²⁷ (ἕως δυσμῶν), Lk 12⁵⁴ (ἀπὸ δυσμῶν), 13²⁹ (ἀπὸ βορρᾶ καὶ νότου), Rev 7² 16¹² (ἀπὸ ἀνατολῆς ἡλίου). The NT exception is Mt 2²· ⁹ ἐν τῇ ἀνατολῇ; therefore perhaps not a compass-point but *in its rising*.

῞Ηλιος and σελήνη. The art. prevails, as in papyri (Mayser II 2, 18f), but we do find Mt 13⁶ ἡλίου δὲ ἀνατείλαντος (D adds τοῦ), Lk 21²⁵ ἐν ἡλίῳ καὶ σελήνῃ καὶ ἄστροις (yet foll. by ἐπὶ τῆς γῆς), Ac 27²⁰ μήτε δὲ ἡλίου μήτε ἄστρων ἐπιφαινόντων, 1 Co 15⁴¹ ἄλλη δόξα ἡλίου . . . σελήνης . . . ἀστέρων, Rev 7² 16¹² ἀπὸ ἀνατολῆς ἡλίου, 22⁵ φωτὸς ἡλίου.

§ 2. The Individual Article with Common Nouns [2]

(a) *Individual anaphoric use: Introduction*

Used with nouns, the art. has the same double import in Hell. Greek as in class. Greek: it is either individualizing or generic. It either calls special attention to one definite member of a class so that ὁ = οὗτος ὁ (e.g. πλείονες = *more*, but οἱ πλείονες = *the majority*), or else it makes the contrast between the whole class, as such, and other classes, so that οἱ ἄνθρωποι = *mankind*, as opposed to οἱ θεοί. The generic use is considered below, pp. 180f. The necessity for using the art. is not dispensed

---

[1] K-G I 599f. Gildersleeve II §§ 558-561. Mayser II 2, 16.
[2] K-G I 589ff. Gildersleeve II §§ 565-567, 569, 571-572.

with·by the addition of οὗτος or ἐκεῖνος, or a possessive. But the art. is often omitted where we expect it by the rules, especially in set phrases, titles, salutations, letter headings, pairs, lists (e.g. Ro 8³⁵· ³⁸ᶠ), definitions (e.g. Ro 1¹⁶ᶠ 8²⁴). The Heb. construct state had an influence here (see pp. 179f). Sometimes the absence is almost inexplicable : Jas 2⁸ νόμον τελεῖτε βασιλικόν ; we must understand it predicatively *the law as a royal commandment* (Radermacher² 117). Codex Bezae will often omit the art. in an arbitrary way, perhaps through Latin influence.

The individualizing use of the art. was described by Apollonius Dyscolus, an early grammarian, as *anaphoric*, in that it refers back to what is already familiar. Thus ὁ ἀδελφὸς αὐτοῦ is anaphoric, *that brother of his*; while ἀδελφὸς αὐτοῦ is *a brother of his*. It means that the art. will not normally be used when a person or object is first introduced, or when only an undefined part of a group or class is referred to, or when a person or object is thought of only predicatively (and therefore not individually and definitely). In such cases there is no anaphora to particular or well-known specimens or to a class considered as a whole. So it is usual to express a predicate without the art. (see exceptions, pp. 182–184).

It is not difficult to find instances where NT writers conform to this rule ; we have seen it already with the proper names. We see it again in Lk 4¹⁷ βιβλίον and afterwards τὸ βιβλίον ; Ro 5³· ⁵ ὑπομονὴν κατεργάζεται, ἡ δὲ ὑπομονὴ δοκιμήν, ἡ δὲ δοκιμὴ ἐλπίδα· ἡ δὲ ἐλπίς ... , ⁷ (although he is not previously mentioned, *your good man* τοῦ ἀγαθοῦ is very definite) ; Jas 2¹⁴ πίστιν and then ἡ πίστις ; LXX Bel et Drac.³· ⁴ Βήλ and then τῷ Βήλ. Therefore when we find τῷ ἁμαρτωλῷ Lk 18¹³ it must be the *sinner of sinners* ; in Ro 12¹⁹ we must think of it as *the well-known wrath* ; in 1 Co 10¹⁴ that *worship of idols which you know so well* ; in Rev 3¹⁷ ὁ ταλαίπωρος is *that wretched man* ; Mt 5¹ τὸ ὄρος = that great hill which stood like a throne behind the sea (Zerwick § 124), Lk 14¹⁷ τὸν δοῦλον is the servant whose particular task it was to do this ; Mt 8¹² ὁ κλαυθμὸς καὶ ὁ βρυγμὸς τῶν ὀδόντων *that memorable* or *greatest of all*.

The art. was commonly used in class. Attic prose to mark a proper or usual connection of an obj. with its subject : τὴν χεῖρα is *his hand* Jn 7³⁰, τὸν ἀδελφόν *his brother* 2 Co 12¹⁸, just as in the papyri ἡ γυνὴ καὶ οἱ υἱοί is *his wife and children* (Mayser II 2,

23), and Ac 21⁵ σὺν γ. καὶ τέκνοις = *with their wives and children* (art. omitted because a formula, like Ac 1¹⁴ σὺν γυναιξίν, Ro 1⁷ ἀπὸ θεοῦ πατρὸς ἡμῶν), Heb 12⁷ τίς γὰρ υἱός, ὃν οὐ παιδεύει πατήρ (not ὁ πατήρ *his father*) *a father*.

(b) Articular Use with certain nouns

1. θεός and κύριος [1].

Since these words come near to being proper nouns in NT, it is not surprising that the art. is so often omitted. Κύριος even more than θεός seems to have assumed this rôle, for we have Mt 21⁹ ὀνόματι κυρίου, Ac 2²⁰ vl. τὴν ἡμέραν κυρίου, 5⁹ τὸ πνεῦμα κυρίου, 2 Co 3¹⁷ᶠ τὸ πνεῦμα κυρίου, τὴν δόξαν κυρίου, Jas 5¹¹ τὸ τέλος κυρίου [2]. These names are especially anarthrous after a preposition, e.g. ἐν κυρίῳ *passim*, ἀπὸ θεοῦ Jn 3², or when they depend in the gen. on another anarthrous noun : Mt 27⁴³ θεοῦ εἰμι υἱός, Lk 3² ἐγένετο ῥῆμα θεοῦ. Another near-proper name is θεὸς πατήρ 2 Pt 1¹⁷ Jude [1]. In the LXX the anarthrous יהוה is rendered by the more slavish translators by means of anarthrous κύριος ; but the addition of ל, אל, and את causes the art. to be used, hence : τῷ κυρίῳ, τὸν κύριον. But in NT we have both ἄγγελος κυρίου and ἐν κυρίῳ. Like the LXX is κύριος ὁ θεός, with and without gen. : Lk 1⁶⁸ OT κύριος ὁ θεὸς τοῦ Ἰσραήλ, Rev 1⁸ etc. κύριος ὁ θεός. As a general rule it may be said that for Paul ὁ κύριος = Christ, and κύριος = Yahweh (Zerwick § 125ª) ; in which case, we must understand ὁ δὲ Κύριος τὸ πν. ἐστιν (2 Co 3¹⁷) as = Yahweh but anaphoric.

2. οὐρανός, γῆ, θάλασσα, κόσμος.

These words are frequently anarthrous, especially after a preposition. But οὐρανός is anarthrous where there is no preposition : Ac 3²¹ 17²⁴ 2 Pt 3¹⁰ (ABC add οἱ). Papyri : Mayser II 2, 29. Γῆ prefers the art., even sometimes with a

---

[1] B. Weiss, *Theol. Stud. u. Krit.* 84, 1911, 319–392, 503–538. Bauer s.v. κύριος II 2. W. W. Graf Baudissin, *Kyrios als Gottesname im Judentum* ... , I Teil, Giessen 1929 ; *Der Gebrauch des Gottesnamens Kyrios in Sept.*

[2] This flatly contravenes the canon of Apollonius to the effect that an anarthrous noun may not be governed by a noun having the art. ; but κύριος must be taken as a proper name = Yahweh.

preposition; however, we have it anarthrous: Mk 13²⁷ ἀπὸ ἄκρου γῆς ἕως ἄκρου οὐρανοῦ, Ac 17²⁴ οὐρανοῦ καὶ γῆς κύριος, 2 Pt 3⁵ οὐρανοὶ . . . καὶ γῆ, ¹⁰ οὐρανοί (ABC add οἱ) . . . στοιχεῖα . . . γῆ (CP add ἡ). With the preposition, anarthrous: Mt 28¹⁸ (BD add τῆς), Lk 2¹⁵ 1 Co 8⁵ 15⁴⁷ Eph 3¹⁵ Heb 12²⁵ 8¹. Θάλασσα too is anarthrous after a preposition or in gen. after another noun: Mt 4¹⁵ OT ὁδὸν θαλάσσης, Lk 21²⁵ ἤχους θαλάσσης, Jas 1⁶ κλύδωνι θαλάσσης, Jude¹³ κύματα ἄγρια θαλ. The same is true of κόσμος: anarth. predicate Ro 4¹³ 11¹². ¹⁵, and in prepositional formulae: ἐν κόσμῳ 1 Co 8⁴ 14¹⁰ Ph 2¹⁵ etc. 2 Pt 1⁴ vl., ἀπὸ [καταβολῆς] κόσμου Mt 25³⁴ etc. Also anarthrous: 2 Co 5¹⁹ Ga 6¹⁴.

3. θάνατος.

It frequently appears without an art., especially in certain phrases like ἕως θανάτου (Mt 26³⁸), ἔνοχος θανάτου, ἄξιον θανάτου, παραδιδόναι εἰς θάνατον, γεύεσθαι θανάτου. Apart from the anaphoric use (e.g. ἡ πληγὴ τοῦ θ. Rev 13³. ¹²), the art. is used (a) either of the actual death of a definite person (1 Co 11²⁶), or (b) of death in the abstract: Jn 5²⁴ καταβέβηκεν ἐκ τοῦ θ. εἰς τὴν ζωήν, or (c) where Death is half personified (Rev 13³. ¹²), or (d) where assimilation to a noun in connection with it causes a borrowing of the art.: τὸ ἀπόκριμα τοῦ θ. (2 Co 1⁹).

4. πνεῦμα.

It is urged sometimes (e.g. A. M. Perry, JBL 68, 1949, 329ff) that the omission of the art. is important theologically, but the usage is often arbitrary. Τὸ ἅγιον πνεῦμα (rather more often τὸ πν. τὸ ἅγ.) is sometimes personal. When it is anarthrous it is a divine spirit inspiring man (1 Th 1⁵), but the matter is complicated threefold by the question of the non-use of the art. with proper nouns, and in prepositional expressions (increased in Hell. Greek), and even (in Biblical Greek through influence of the Heb. construct state) before a genitive. In none of these situations need the lack of the art. indicate any indefiniteness of reference, and with πνεῦμα the reference could still be to the Pentecostal Spirit. Nevertheless in Luke τὸ πν. τὸ ἅγ. tends to be the Pentecostal Spirit while ἅγιον πνεῦμα is an unknown power, God's spirit as opposed to that of men or demons (Procksch in Kittel WB I 105). Doubtless also anaphora complicates the matter, as in Luke 2²⁶· ²⁷ Ac 2⁴ 8¹⁸. In 10⁴⁴ ἔπεσεν τὸ πν. τὸ ἅγ. ἐπὶ πάντας, there is reference to the well-known fact of the out-pouring. Omission, even when the reference is the Holy Spirit, is also occasioned by the presence of a preposition or by assimilation to an anarthrous noun : Ro 14¹⁷ after a list of anarthrous abstract nouns and after ἐν, Mt 1¹⁸ ἐκ πνεύματος ἁγίου. Without a preposition (Lk 1¹⁵· ³⁵· ⁴¹· ⁶⁷ 2²⁵ 3¹⁶ 4¹ 11¹³ Ac 1² 4²⁵ 6⁵ 7⁵⁵ 8¹⁵· ¹⁷· ¹⁹ 10³⁸ 11²⁴ 19²) it is not the personal Holy Spirit, but the influence of a divine spirit which is intended, if St. Luke omits the article.

5. γράμματα :

2 Ti 3¹⁵ ἱερὰ γράμματα SCᵇD*FG 33 Clem Epiph (AC* corr. to τά) is a technical formula (see Schrenk in Kittel WB I 765¹¹ff), Est 6¹, Jos. Ant. 16, 168.

6. ἐκκλησία :

1 Co 14⁴ ἐκκλησίαν οἰκοδομεῖ, 3 Jn⁶ ἐνώπιον ἐκκλησίας. Is it a *congregation* or *the Church?* (see K. L. Schmidt in Kittel WB III 508¹⁸ff).

7. *Abstract nouns* ¹.

They may be articular or anarthrous in all periods down to MGr. They tend to be anarthrous if there is greater emphasis on the abstract quality, but no vital difference was felt in class. Greek; the passage is too easy from articular to anarthrous. Thus Plato *Meno* 99A ἡ ἀρετή, 99E ἀρετή, 100B ἡ ἀρετή . . . ἀρετή. So Paul, Ro 3³⁰ ὃς δικαιώσει περιτομὴν ἐκ πίστεως καὶ ἀκροβυστίαν διὰ τῆς πίστεως (prob. no significance for exegesis, but the art. is anaphoric : *by that same faith*). Translators do not trouble to distinguish τῇ χάριτι in Eph 2⁸ from χάριτι in 2⁵ (NEB *by his grace* both times) ; it may be that τῇ is merely anaphoric, looking back to ⁵, but there is another point of view : omission of the art. tends to emphasize the inherent qualities of abstract nouns while the art. makes them more concrete, unified and individual. In 2⁸ then the reference is to God's historical act of saving grace ; in 2⁵, to grace as such, in contrast to other means of redemption (Zerwick § 131). The difficulty therefore is to account for the presence of the art.,

---

¹ K-G I 606 i.   Gildersleeve II §§ 565–567.   Mayser II 2, 30f.

just as with concrete nouns the problem is rather to account for its absence.

E.g. Mt 5⁶ τὴν δικαιοσύνην (contrast 5¹⁰), 7²³ τὴν ἀνομίαν (difficult), Ro 12⁷ εἴτε διακονίαν, ἐν τῇ διακονίᾳ· εἴτε ὁ διδάσκων, ἐν τῇ διδασκαλίᾳ; Ro 12⁹ᶠ ἡ ἀγάπη ἀνυπόκριτος, τῇ φιλαδελφίᾳ φιλόστοργοι, τῇ τιμῇ ἀλλήλους προηγούμενοι, τῇ σπουδῇ μὴ ὀκνηροί, because they are virtues assumed to be well known; 1 Co 13¹³ νυνὶ δὲ μένει πίστις ἐλπὶς ἀγάπη ... μείζων δὲ τούτων ἡ ἀγάπη (anaph.), 14²⁰ μὴ παιδία γίνεσθε ταῖς φρεσίν, ἀλλὰ τῇ κακίᾳ νηπιάζετε (art. by attraction to the concrete ταῖς φρεσίν your mind), Col 3⁵ πορνείαν ἀκαθαρσίαν πάθος ἐπιθυμίαν ... καὶ τὴν πλεονεξίαν, ἥτις ἐστιν εἰδωλολατρία and that principal vice, covetousness (the added clause individualizes the noun, as in Ac 19³ 26²⁷ 2 Co 8¹⁸), Heb 1¹⁴ εἰς διακονίαν, κληρονομεῖν σωτηρίαν (2³ 5⁹ 6⁹ 9²⁸ 11⁷), but τῆς σωτηρίας 2¹⁰.

Νόμος.

Paul is fond of anarthrous νόμος, but on no easily intelligible principle. Thus, in Ga, ὁ νόμος 10 times, νόμος 21. Ro 2¹³ is especially difficult: οὐ γὰρ οἱ ἀκροαταὶ νόμου (+ τοῦ KLP) δίκαιοι παρὰ τῷ (BD* om) θεῷ, ἀλλ' οἱ ποιηταὶ νόμου (+ τοῦ DᶜEKL) δικαιωθήσονται; it may not be the total Mosaic Law which Paul has in mind, but law as such (yet we still expect anaphoric τοῦ on the second mention). See also anarthr. νόμος in Jas 1²⁵ 4¹¹ 2¹¹ (but artic. in ¹⁰), ¹² νόμος ἐλευθερίας (not Mosaic). Attempts have been made, from Origen onwards, to establish a principle [1] that the articular form indicates the Mosaic Law, but the context is a surer guide. See also Ro 3²⁰ διὰ γὰρ νόμου ἐπίγνωσις ἁμαρτίας (epigrammatic: to know any sin there must be some law), 5¹³ ἄχρι γὰρ νόμου (till a law came), 6¹⁴ ἁμαρτία (not no sin, but " sin as power ", as usual in Paul; see Lohmeyer Zschr. f. nt. Wiss. 29, 1930, 2ff; J. Jeremias, Die Abendmahlsworte Jesu, 1935, 72f) ὑμῶν οὐ κυριεύσει· οὐ γάρ ἐστε ὑπὸ νόμον (under any law).

Σάρξ being virtually an abstract noun is anarthrous: the natural state of man; frequent ἐν σαρκί and κατὰ σάρκα (+ τήν as vl. 2 Co 11¹⁸ Jn 8¹⁵).

ἀλήθεια.

Altogether inexplicable by the rules of anaphora are Jn 8⁴⁴ (καὶ ἐν τῇ ἀληθείᾳ οὐκ ἔστηκεν, ὅτι οὐκ ἔστιν ἀλήθεια ἐν αὐτῷ), 17¹⁷ (ἁγίασον αὐτοὺς ἐν τῇ ἀληθείᾳ· ὁ λόγος ὁ σὸς ἀλήθειά ἐστιν),

---

[1] Sanday-Headlam ICC Ro on 2¹³ᶠ, p. 58; Burton ICC Ga 447–460.

3 Jn³ (μαρτυρούντων σου τῇ ἀληθείᾳ, καθὼς σὺ ἐν ἀληθείᾳ περιπα-
τεῖς). But Colwell's rule (see below, pp. 183f) may be relevant
(Moule 112). Zerwick's suggestion is (§ 132) that the definite
reference with the art. is to Christ as the real truth, life, light, etc.;
all other truths, lives, lights, being transitory. So he explains the
repeated art. in Jn 14⁶ ἡ ὁδὸς καὶ ἡ ἀλήθεια καὶ ἡ ζωή, which
otherwise is inexplicable, not being anaphoric. Therefore 2 Jn¹
(οὓς ἐγὼ ἀγαπῶ ἐν ἀληθείᾳ, καὶ οὐκ ἐγὼ μόνος ἀλλὰ καὶ πάντες
οἱ ἐγνωκότες τὴν ἀλήθειαν) whom I sincerely love, and . . . all who
have sincere standards (anaphora?), ⁴ (περιπατοῦντες ἐν ἀληθείᾳ)
behaving with sincerity, ³ sincerity, 3 Jn¹ whom I sincerely love,
2 Ti 2²⁵ 3⁷ Ti 1¹ ἐπίγνωσις ἀληθείας, Heb 10²⁶ ἡ ἐπίγνωσις τῆς
ἀληθείας (not Christ, but articular by attraction), Eph 4²¹ (καθώς
ἐστιν ἀλήθεια ἐν τῷ 'Ιησοῦ), 2 Co 11¹⁰ (ἐστιν ἀλήθεια Χριστοῦ ἐν
ἐμοί), 3 Jn⁴ (cp. above) ἵνα ἀκούω τὰ ἐμὰ τέκνα ἐν τῇ ἀληθείᾳ
περιπατοῦντα in the Truth (Christ), ⁸ ἵνα συνεργοὶ γινώμεθα τῇ
ἀληθείᾳ (Christ), ¹² Δημητρίῳ μεμαρτύρηται ὑπὸ πάντων καὶ ὑπὸ
αὐτῆς τῆς ἀληθείας Christ himself. This distinction is a peculiarity of Biblical Greek; the papyri have the art. each time,
P. Par 46; 47 (152 B.C.); 63. 16 (165 B.C.).

In the Ptol. pap. the following other abstract nouns are articular:
φιλοτιμία, ἀηδία, τολμηρία, μέγεθος, ὕψος, πλῆθος, λογεία. The following
are anarthrous: φιλανθρωπία, ἀντίλημψις, ἐπισημασία, εὐγνωμοσύνη,
ἀμνησία, ἡγεμονία μέγεθος (usually), φύσις, βάθος, μῆκος (usually), κρίσις,
ἀναμέτρησις. These vary: πλάτος, γνῶσις (Mayser II 2, 31).

8. Numerals.

Usually with cardinal numerals there is no art., but if the
art. stands it indicates (as in class. Greek) a certain fraction, as
in the scribal correction of Mt 25² αἱ (Z) πέντε . . . αἱ (E fam¹³ 543
28) πέντε, after δέκα, the first five of them . . . the other five of
them; Lk 17¹⁷ οἱ ἐννέα the nine of them; Rev. 17¹⁰ ἑπτά . . . οἱ
πέντε . . . ὁ εἷς . . . ὁ ἄλλος. Or else the art. marks a contrast
of one fraction from another. Thus in Mt 20²⁴ = Mk 10⁴¹ the
ten are the remaining ten disciples, not a fixed group of disciples
(Wackernagel II 318).

The ordinary numeral also commonly lacks the art. as in
class. Greek (e.g. ὀγδόῳ ἔτει), especially after a preposition, and
specially with ὥρα. Mt 27⁴⁵ ἀπὸ ἕκτης ὥρας, Mk 15³³, Ac 12¹⁰
16¹² (vl. -τη prob. corrupt), 2 Co 12². But there is anaphora

with ὥρα in Mt 20⁹ 27⁴⁶. In Mt 20⁶ there is the art. because of
ellipse of ὥρα, and in Ac 3¹ because further defining words are
introduced (τὴν ὥραν τῆς προσευχῆς τὴν ἐνάτην). Cp. papyri:
P. Petr. II 10 (2) 5 (240 B.C.), P. Hib. 110, 65. 100 (253 B.C.) ὥρας
πρώτης; P. Hib. 75, 79 (255 B.C.) ὥρα ‾ια; 106 (255 B.C.) ὥρας ‾ιβ.
With ἡμέρα the art. tends to be used, e.g. τῇ τρίτῃ ἡμέρᾳ always,
and Jn 6³⁹ff ἐν τῇ ἐσχάτῃ ἡμέρᾳ (but 2 Ti 3¹ Jas 5³ ἐν ἐσχάταις
ἡμέραις); but a preposition may cause its omission: Ac 20¹⁸
Ph 1⁵ (+ τῆς p⁴⁶ SBAP) ἀπὸ πρώτης ἡμέρας, like 1 Pt. 1⁵
ἐν καιρῷ ἐσχάτῳ.

(c) *Absence of Article after Prepositions* [1]

Such phrases may be formulae inherited from a pre-articular
age of Greek. In class. Greek they are often anarthrous, like
proverbs and enumerations, although anaphora or contrast may
restore the art.: e.g. Lys. 12, 16 εἰς ἄστυ *to town*, but 54 εἰς τὸ
ἄστυ; Demosth. 19, 30 ἐν ἀγορᾷ but 27, 58 ἐν τῇ ἀγορᾷ. In
NT: Mk 7⁴ ἀπ' ἀγορᾶς, 15²⁷ ἐκ δεξιῶν . . . ἐξ εὐωνύμων, Mt 24³³
ἐπὶ θύραις, Lk 7³² ἐν ἀγορᾷ (but in Mt 11¹⁶ etc. ἐν ταῖς ἀγοραῖς
[CEFW om ταῖς]), Jn 6¹⁷ εἰς πλοῖον *aboard*; papyri ἐπὶ πόταμον
riverwards, κατὰ πόλιν *in town*, κατὰ γῆν καὶ θάλασσαν *by land
and sea* (class.), ἐν δεξιᾷ *on the right* (class.). The omission in
time-designation is class.: e.g. πρὸς ἑσπέραν Lk 24²⁹ (Ac 28²³),
πρὸ καιροῦ Mt 8²⁹ (24⁴⁵ Lk 4¹³ 8¹³ Ac 13¹¹ Ro 5⁶ Heb 11¹¹), διὰ
νυκτός Ac 5¹⁹ (vl. art.), μεχρὶ μεσονυκτίου Ac 20⁷ (but κατὰ τὸ
μεσονύκτιον 16²⁵). For personal anatomy one might expect the
individualizing art., but ἐπὶ πρόσωπον Lk 5¹² etc. (2 Co 10⁷),
and the omission occurs also in profane authors like Polybius;
class. similar κατ' ὀφθαλμούς, ἐν ὀφθαλμοῖς.

Formulae like ἀπ' ἀγροῦ understandably have no art.
because no individual field is in mind; but referring to a definite
field in Mt 13²⁴ ἐν τῷ ἀγρῷ αὐτοῦ. But also ἐν τῷ ἀγρῷ (D Chrys
om τῷ) without indiv. reference (Mt 13⁴⁴) like τὰ κρίνα τοῦ ἀγροῦ
(6²⁸). The excuse for the art. must then be that it is generic,
the country (like τὸ ὄρος *the highlands* Mk 3¹³ etc.).

(d) *Absence of Article before a noun which governs a genitive* [2]

A noun is sometimes made definite by a defining gen. or adj.
In Heb. a noun may be in the construct state or have a suffix

---

[1] K-G I 605f. Gildersleeve II § 569. Eakin 333. Mayser II 2, 14ff.
[2] Radermacher² 116. Zerwick §§ 136–137.

attached to it, and in either case it would be anarthrous. This influenced the LXX and in turn the NT writers in varying degrees. Thus ἄγγελος κυρίου is not *an angel* but *the angel*, δόξα λαοῦ σου is *the glory*. It usually happens that the second noun is also anarthrous; this balance is a Greek characteristic, not Heb. The canon of Apollonius Dyscolus asserts that, of nouns in regimen, either both have the art. (like ἐν τῷ λόγῳ τῆς ἀληθείας Col 1⁵), or neither (like ἐν λόγῳ ἀληθείας 2 Co 6⁷). Philo tends to violate the canon, Plato to keep it (exx. in Radermacher[2] 116). But the canon must be modified to this extent, that the governing noun may be anarthrous while the governed is articular (Ro 3²⁵ εἰς ἔνδειξιν τῆς δικαιοσύνης αὐτοῦ; Eph 1⁶ εἰς ἔπαινον δόξης τῆς χάριτος αὐτοῦ); this through Heb. influence. It is obvious that this omission occurs chiefly in prepositional phrases, to which secular writers normally do not add a gen. after the Semitic way: ἀπὸ προσώπου, διὰ χειρός, διὰ στόματος, ἀπὸ ὀφθαλμῶν σου Lk 19⁴²; ἐκ κοιλίας μητρός (Mt 19¹² Lk 1¹⁵ Ac 3² 14⁸), ἐν βίβλῳ ζωῆς Ph 4³ (cp. Rev, Mk 12²⁶), ἐν δακτύλῳ θεοῦ (Lk 11²⁰). A further complication is that proper nouns and geogr. names in the gen. may be anarthrous even when subordinate to an articular noun: ἡ Ἄρτεμις Ἐφεσίων, τὴν Ἐφεσίων πόλιν, ἐν τῷ βίβλῳ Μωϋσέως.

(e) Generic Article [1]

The principle of the generic art. is to select a normal or representative individual. When all is said, the whole question is affected by personal taste; we have in one sentence both ὑπὲρ δικαίου and ὑπὲρ τοῦ ἀγαθοῦ Ro 5⁷ (*ICC Ro* 128). Almost all the exx. in poetry have been explained on other principles, sometimes by anaphora, sometimes on the principle of contrast (Gildersleeve II § 563). Contrary to our own usage, the art. is put before nouns denoting a species, family or class of any of the kingdoms of nature; and before abstract nouns of virtues, vices, sciences, etc. (Jannaris § 1201), e.g. ὁ ἄνθρωπος *mankind*, ὁ σῖτος *corn*, ἡ ἀρετή *virtue*, ὁ κλέπτης (Jn 10¹⁰) *thieves*.

A generic art. also accompanies plurals like ἄνθρωποι, ἔθνη, νεκροί (exc. after a preposition): Mt 14² ἠγέρθη ἀπὸ τῶν νεκρῶν, 22³¹, 1 Co 15⁴² τῆς ἀναστάσεως τῶν νεκρῶν, Eph 5¹⁴ OT ἐκ τῶν νεκρῶν, Col 2¹² BDEFG (rest om τῶν), 1 Th 1¹⁰ (ACK om τῶν). But Mt 17⁹ etc. ἐκ νεκρῶν

---

[1] K-G I 589, 1.   Mayser II 2, 41ff.   Gildersleeve II §§ 563f.

ἐγερθῇ, Ac 17³² 23⁶ etc. ἀνάστασιν νεκρῶν (construct state and Apoll. canon), 1 Pt 4⁵ κρῖναι ζῶντας καὶ νεκρούς, Heb 1⁴ B p⁴⁶ Chrys ἀγγέλων. Double art.: τὰ ἔθνη τοῦ κόσμου Lk 12³⁰ (Apoll. canon); but ἔθνη is especially liable to be anarthrous: Ac 4²⁵ OT Ro 11¹²ᶠ 15¹² OT; οὐχὶ καὶ ἐθνῶν Ro 3²⁹ᶠ; esp. with prepositions Ac 4²⁷ 15¹⁴ 2 Co 11²⁶ Ga 2¹⁵.

(f) Repetition of Article with several nouns connected by καί [1]

The art. may be carried over from the first noun to the other(s), especially if they are regarded as a unified whole and the gender and number are the same: Col 1² τοῖς ἐν Κ. ἁγίοις καὶ (sc. τοῖς) πιστοῖς ἀδελφοῖς ἐν Χ. *the saints and the faithful brethren*; Eph 2²⁰ τῶν ἀποστόλων καὶ προφητῶν; Lk 22⁴ τοῖς ἀρχιερεῦσιν καὶ στρατηγοῖς; Ac 15² πρὸς τοὺς ἀποστόλους καὶ πρεσβυτέρους. This is so even occasionally when the gender is different but the number the same, as in P. Tebt. I 14¹⁰ (114 B.C.); Lk 1⁶ ἐν πασαῖς ταῖς ἐντολαῖς καὶ δικαιώμασιν τοῦ κυρίου, 14²³ εἰς τοὺς ὁδοὺς καὶ φραγμούς, Mk 12³³ vl. Ac 15²⁰· ²⁹ 21²⁵ Col 2²² κατὰ τὰ ἐντάλματα καὶ διδασκαλίας τῶν ἀνθρώπων, unless κατὰ τά is due to dittography (but in LXX Isa 29¹³, to which this is an allusion, there is no κατά as well as no τά).

One must look critically at the common view that in Ti 2¹³ we have two clauses in apposition: τοῦ μεγάλου θεοῦ καὶ [sc. τοῦ] σωτῆρος ἡμῶν 'I.X. The same is true of 2 Pt 1¹ τοῦ θεοῦ ἡμῶν καὶ [sc. τοῦ] 'I.X. (S κυρίου for θεοῦ) [2]. In Hell., and indeed for practical purposes in class. Greek the repetition of the art. was not strictly necessary to ensure that the items be considered separately. The relevant consideration on the other side is that the phrase *God and Saviour* in contemporary language referred to only one person, c. A.D. 100. Moreover, the art. could have been repeated to avoid misunderstanding if separate individuals had been intended [3].

Often the repetition, even with nouns of the same gender, does indeed indicate that two distinct subjects are involved. Οἱ Φαρισαῖοι καὶ Σαδδουκαῖοι involves no misunderstanding, but

---

[1] K-G I 611, 2. Gildersleeve II §§ 603–605. Mayser II 2, 47ff. Radermacher² 115. Zerwick §§ 138, 139.

[2] See Lock in *ICC* on Ti 2¹³, Hort on Jas 2¹, Moulton Proleg. 84, A. T. Robertson, " The Greek Article and the Deity of Christ ", *Expositor* VIII, 21 (1921) 182–188, Stauffer in Kittel WB III 107²⁶⁸, Moule 109. Stauffer's plea, based on position of ἡμῶν, is grammatically weak.

[3] *NEB* (text) is probably correct, following previous standard versions except AV which follows Vulgate (comma between, in Sixtine and Clementine).

the repetition of the art. prevents misunderstanding in Lk 11⁵¹ μεταξὺ τοῦ θυσιαστηρίου καὶ τοῦ οἴκου, Jn 19⁶ οἱ ἀρχιερεῖς καὶ οἱ ὑπηρέται (not a unified whole like the chief-priests, elders and scribes of Mt 16²¹ etc.), Ac 26³⁰ ὁ βασιλεὺς καὶ ὁ ἡγεμών, 1 Co 3⁸ ὁ φυτεύων καὶ ὁ ποτίζων ἓν εἰσιν (cp. Jn 4³⁶), 1 Th 1⁷· ⁸ ἐν τῇ Μακεδονίᾳ καὶ ἐν τῇ 'Αχαίᾳ (two separate provinces), then they are grouped together (ἐν τῇ Μακεδονίᾳ καὶ 'Αχαίᾳ) and contrasted with ἀλλ' ἐν παντὶ τόπῳ. Repetition generally takes place with τε καί, and that is probably why D adds τῶν in Ac 14⁶ τῶν ἐθνῶν τε καὶ 'Ιουδαίων. There is frequently a variety of readings, e.g. Ro 4¹² τοῖς οὐκ ἐκ περιτομῆς μόνον ἀλλὰ καὶ τοῖς στοιχοῦσιν (*ICC Ro* in loc.)

(g) *Article with Quotations* [1]

As in class. Greek the neuter art. may be prefixed to quoted words : Mt 19¹⁸ τὸ Οὐ φονεύσεις (DM om τό), Mk 9²³ *so far as the εἰ δύνῃ is concerned*, Ro 13⁹, 1 Co 4⁶ τὸ Μὴ ὑπὲρ ἃ γέγραπται ; unless we emend, it is best taken as a quotation of a slogan (Howard in *Exp. T* 33, 479), Ga 4²⁵ vl., 5¹⁴, 6⁹ τὸ δὲ Καλὸν ποιοῦντες μὴ ἐνκακῶμεν (τό introduces a proverbial phrase ; or τὸ καλόν is generic), Eph 4⁹, Heb 12²⁷.

(h) *Article with Indirect Interrogatives* [2]

Class., but in NT this usage is rarely represented except in Lk-Ac. The meaning is not affected by the addition of the art. : Lk 1⁶² ἐνένευον . . . τὸ τί ἂν θέλοι, 9⁴⁶ 19⁴⁸, Ac 4²¹ 22³⁰, 1 Th 4¹, Ro 8²⁶ (ICC in loc ; Moule 200) ; Mk 9¹⁰ τί ἐστιν τὸ ἐκ νεκρῶν ἀναστῆναι (unless τό . . . is articular infin.).

In conclusion, almost anything in Greek can by the addition of the art. be made substantival, whether adj., ptc., infin., adv., prepositional expression, numeral, or any phrase whatever.

A characteristic of Hell. Greek is an anarthrous noun followed by an articular attribute (Zerwick § 145). See below pp. 185, 206, 221.

§ 3. The Article with a Predicate

An adj. or ptc. or a second noun may refer to a noun either as an attribute or as a predicate. As an attribute it usually

---

[1] K-G I 596f.   Gildersleeve I 265.
[2] Mayser II 1, 80 ; II 3, 52f.

occurs between art. and noun. As a predicate it occurs either
before the art. or after the noun, and the connection between
them will be supplied by a copula, either stated or understood.
Although predicate nouns are usually anarthrous, the art.
thus distinguishing the subject from the complement, the art.
may be inserted if the predicate noun is supposed to be a unique
or notable instance (e.g. Mt 6²² *the eye* alone *is the light of the
body*). A predicate adj. or ptc. and the pronoun ὁ αὐτός (*the
same*) will also have the art.

E. C. Colwell (*JBL*, 52, 1933, 12–21) formulates rules for
the art. with predicate nouns in NT in sentences in which the
verb occurs. He finds that (a) definite predicate nouns take the
art., if (as is usual) they follow the verb; (b) otherwise they
usually lack it; (c) proper nouns lack it; (d) in relative clauses it
does not apply since nouns always follow the verb, anarthrous
or not. Obviously if such a rule stands the test, it is valuable
for textual decisions and translation.[1]

Examples : (a) Mt 5¹³ ὑμεῖς ἐστε τὸ ἄλας τῆς γῆς, 13³⁷, 16¹⁶ σὺ εἶ ὁ
χριστός, 24⁴⁵, 26⁶³, 27¹¹. ³⁷, Mk 3¹¹, 6³ οὐχ οὗτός ἐστιν ὁ τέκτων,
15². ¹² ὃν λέγετε τὸν βασιλέα τῶν Ἰουδ. (not AD), ³⁹, Lk 4⁴¹, 22⁷⁰,
23³. ³⁷, Jn 1⁴. ⁸. ³⁹. ⁴⁹, 5³⁵ ἐκεῖνος ἦν ὁ λύχνος, 8¹² ἐγώ εἰμι τὸ φῶς (cp. 9⁵
φῶς εἰμί), ⁴⁴, 11²⁷, 18³³, 20³¹, Ac 9²⁰, 21³⁸, Jas 3⁶ ὁ κόσμος predicate
(M. Dibelius, *Der Brief des Jakobus*, Gött. 1921, in loc.), 1 Jn. 3⁴ καὶ ἡ
ἁμαρτία ἐστιν ἡ ἀνομία 4¹⁵ 5⁵. With an adj. usually the predicate
adj. is anarthrous, but Mt 19¹⁷ εἷς ἐστιν ὁ ἀγαθός, Rev 3¹⁷.

(b) Mt 4³. ⁶ 14³³ 27⁴⁰. ⁵⁴ *Son of God* precedes the verb and so anarthr.,
⁴² *King of Israel* precedes, 13³⁹.—Mk 15³⁹ Lk 4³. ⁹ Jn 10³⁶ *Son of God*
precedes.—Jn 5³⁷ *Son of man* precedes.—Jn 1¹ θεὸς ἦν ὁ λόγος (there
need be no doctrinal significance in the dropping of the art., for it is
simply a matter of word-order), 9⁵ φῶς εἰμι, 1⁴⁹ βασιλεὺς εἶ τοῦ Ἰσρ.
19²¹ βασιλεὺς τῶν Ἰουδ. εἰμί.

There are three passages in Mt where the author, striving for variety,
has fallen into a definite pattern.

(1) 12⁴⁸ *my mother* (artic.) follows verb, ⁵⁰ *my mother* (anarth.)
precedes verb.   (2) 13³⁷. ³⁹ ὁ σπείρων . . . ἐστιν ὁ υἱός (artic. following)
ὁ δὲ ἀγρός ἐστιν ὁ κόσμος . . . οὗτοί εἰσιν οἱ υἱοί . . . τὰ δὲ ζιζάνιά
εἰσιν οἱ υἱοί . . ., ὁ δὲ ἐχθρὸς . . . ἐστιν ὁ διάβολος, ὁ δὲ θερισμὸς συντέλεια
αἰῶνός ἐστιν (anarthr. preceding), οἱ δὲ θερισταὶ ἄγγελοί εἰσιν. (3) 23⁸. ¹⁰
εἷς γάρ ἐστιν ὑμῶν ὁ διδάσκαλος (artic. following) . . . εἷς γάρ ἐστιν ὑμῶν
ὁ πατήρ (idem) . . . ὅτι καθηγητὴς ὑμῶν ἐστιν εἷς ὁ Χριστός (anarth.
preceding). See also Mt 18¹. ⁴.

---

[1] Thus Colwell's rule tends to prove WH wrong in 2 Pt 1¹⁷ ὁ υἱός μου ὁ
ἀγαπητός μου οὗτός ἐστιν. Then Tischendorf rightly places the predicate
after the verb. (SA, etc.).

Colwell notes that variants in the MSS, as well as the undoubted text, also obey his canon, and from this he infers that not only among the NT authors but also among the scribes of a much later period this articular rule applied. For instance, it is true of S and B which, though they differ, differ according to rule in these passages: Mt 23¹⁰ B καθηγητης υμων εστιν εις (anarthr. preceding), S εις γαρ υμων εστιν ο καθηγητης (artic. following).—Jn 1⁴⁹ B συ βασιλευς ει του Ισραηλ (anarthr. preceding), S συ ει ο βασιλευς του I (artic. following).—Jas 2¹⁹ B εις θεος εστιν (anarthr. preceding), S εις εστιν ο θεος (articular following).

In Colwell's count, which is somewhat arbitrary, only 15 articular predicate nouns precede the verb [1], while 239 follow it, and only 40 anarthrous predicate nouns follow the verb [2] while 99 precede it. Judicious selection among the MS variants may remove some of the exceptions to Colwell's canon but cannot remove all. So that while the canon may reflect a general tendency it is not absolute by any means; after all, it takes no account of relative clauses or proper nouns, and he has also omitted a considerable class of " qualitative " nouns like that in ὁ θεὸς ἀγάπη ἐστίν. Moreover, he is the first to admit the lack of objectivity in his method of counting: he professes to include only *definite* nouns among his anarthrous predicates, and the degree of definiteness is extremely difficult to assess.

---

[1] Lk 4⁴¹, Jn 1²¹ 6⁵¹ 15¹, Ro 4¹³ 1 Co 9¹. ² 11³. ²⁵ 2 Co 1¹² 3². ¹⁷, 2 Pt 1¹⁷, Rev 19⁸ 20¹⁴.

[2] E.g. Mt 20¹⁶, 27⁴³ *Son of God* (anarthr. following; but θεοῦ precedes), Mk 4³² 9³⁵ 12³⁸, Lk 20³³ 22²⁴, Jn 4¹⁸ 18¹³. ³⁷, Ac 10³⁶, Ro 4¹¹. ¹⁸ 7¹³ 8¹⁶. ²⁹ 11⁶, 1 Co 12²⁷ 16¹⁵ 2 Co 5²¹ 6¹⁶, Ga 4³¹, 1 Th 4³, 1 Pt 5¹², Heb 11¹. Paul is the most significant breaker of Colwell's rule.

CHAPTER THIRTEEN

ATTRIBUTIVE RELATIONSHIP: ADJECTIVES AND NUMERALS

§ 1. The Adjectival Attribute [1]

As in class. Greek, nouns appear instead of adjs. in an attributive sense: ἀνήρ Lk 24¹⁹ Ac 1¹⁶ 3¹⁴ ἄνδρα φονέα, 22³; ἄνθρωπος Mt 18²³; πύθων Ac 16¹⁶ SBAC*D* (gen., not adjectival, in p⁴⁵ C³ D² E). Sometimes a noun will assume the form of an adj. by coining a fem. or neuter: δούλη Lk 1³⁸· ⁴⁸ Ac 2¹⁸, δοῦλα neut. pl. Ro 6¹⁹, ὅμηρα neut. pl. LXX 1 Mac 13¹⁶; Rev 4³ λίθῳ ἰάσπιδι καὶ σαρδίῳ.

Three relative positions are possible for the art. and noun with attributive adjs., ptcs., or numerals: I. Classical ὁ ἀγαθὸς ἀνήρ. II. ὁ ἀνὴρ ὁ ἀγαθός (the ptc., especially with additional adjuncts, is liable to be placed in this position). III. Hellenistic ἀνὴρ ὁ ἀγαθός: much more frequent in the pap. than in class. Greek (Mayser II 2, 57f); the adj. is a kind of limiting after-thought [2] to a noun which originally was more vague. E.g. Lk 23⁴⁹ γυναῖκες αἱ συνακολουθοῦσαι women, viz. those who ..., Jn 14²⁷ εἰρήνην ἀφίημι ὑμῖν, εἰρήνην τὴν ἐμὴν δίδωμι ὑμῖν, 2 Ti 1¹³ ἐν πίστει καὶ ἀγάπῃ τῇ ἐν Χ.Ι. This happens especially with the ptc.: Ac 7³⁵ ἐν χειρὶ ἀγγέλου τοῦ ὀφθέντος αὐτῷ, Ro 2¹⁴ ἔθνη τὰ μὴ νόμον ἔχοντα [3].

Thus the attribute participates in the force of the art. either by taking an intermediate position or, if placed in the post-position, by assuming its own art. There are occasions however when the adj. is not in the intermediate position and has has no art. of its own. In these circumstances, it is predicative [4] (see last ch. for *nouns* used predicatively); Mk 7⁵ κοιναῖς ταῖς χερσίν DW (rest om. art.) *with hands unwashed,* 8¹⁷ πεπωρωμένην

---

[1] K-G I §§ 404–405. Gildersleeve II §§ 608–613. Mayser II 2, 51–59.

[2] K-G I 613f. Radermacher² 115. Zerwick § 145.

[3] For the further significance of this word-order, see above (Introduction, p. 8). Cp. BU 46 (A.D. 193) ὄνους τέσσαρες τοὺς καλλίστους, Mk 15⁴¹ Ac 10⁴¹ 19¹¹· ¹⁷ 26²² 1 Pt 1⁷.

[4] But the odd variant τὸ γὰρ πνεῦμα ἅγιον Lk 12¹² must be a slip; also 1 Jn 5²⁰.

ἔχετε τὴν καρδίαν ὑμῶν, Jn 5³⁶ ἔχω τὴν μαρτυρίαν μείζω *I have a witness which is greater*, Ac 14¹⁰ εἶπεν μεγάλῃ τῇ φωνῇ, Lk 6⁸ τῷ ξηρὰν ἔχοντι τὴν χεῖρα, 1 Co 11⁵ ἀκατακαλύπτῳ τῇ κεφαλῇ, Heb 7²⁴ ἀπαράβατον ἔχει τὴν ἱερωσύνην *has a priesthood which is inalienable*, 9¹ τὸ ἅγιον κοσμικόν. More difficult to translate is ὁ ὄχλος πολύς Jn 12⁹ (as scribes found : AB³D om ὁ ; W adds ὁ to πολύς),¹². It ought to mean *the crowd is great*, but evidently = ὁ πολὺς ὄχλος (Mk 12³⁷) ; it is probably done on the analogy of πᾶς and ὅλος. Cp. πολλῇ τῇ ἐμφερείᾳ Plut. etc. in Radermacher² 112 ; ὁ φόνος πολύς Arr. An. I 9, 6. Also Isocr. *Philipp.* 56 τὸ σῶμα θνητὸν ἅπαντες ἔχομεν (Jn 5³⁶).

§ 2. The Article with Several Attributes

Where in class. Greek there are several attributes, the art. may or may not be repeated (Gildersleeve II § 669). Moreover, it often becomes clumsy to insert all the attributes between the art. and noun (as in 1 Pt 3³ ὁ ἔξωθεν ἐμπλοκῆς τριχῶν καὶ περιθέσεως χρυσίων ἢ ἐνδύσεως ἱμάτιον κόσμος), and there is a tendency to divide them so that some stand before the noun and some after it. Clauses placed after the noun do not always require repetition of the art. (e.g. Plato *Rpb* 532c πρὸς δὲ τὰ ἐν ὕδασι φαντάσματα θεῖα) and may be translated predicatively. The art. is repeated where the defining clause implies a contrast or if the meaning would be ambiguous, and also where the defining words are emphatic, as in Rev. 2¹² τὴν ῥομφαίαν τὴν δίστομον τὴν ὀξεῖαν Heb 11¹² ἡ ἄμμος ἡ παρὰ τὸ χεῖλος . . . ἡ ἀναρίθμητος.

There is nothing particularly emphatic about the following, but the numeral is thought of as part of the noun and there is but one real attribute : Jn 6¹³ Jas 1¹ Rev 21⁹. Predicative additions of an adj. etc. in NT :—Mt 24⁴⁵ ὁ πιστὸς δοῦλος καὶ φρόνιμος, 1 Co 10³ τὸ αὐτὸ βρῶμα πνευματικόν SᶜDEFG (p⁴⁶ A om αὐτό ; S*BA πν. βρ.), 16²¹ τῇ ἐμῇ χειρὶ Παύλου, Ga 1⁴ τοῦ ἐνεστῶτος αἰῶνος πονηροῦ SᶜDEFG (p⁴⁶ S*BA τοῦ αἰῶνος τοῦ ἐνεστῶτος πονηροῦ), 1¹³ τὴν ἐμὴν ἀναστροφήν ποτε ἐν τῷ Ἰουδαϊσμῷ, Col 1⁸ τὴν ὑμῶν ἀγάπην ἐν πνεύματι, 1 Pt 1¹⁸ τῆς ματαίας ὑμῶν ἀναστροφῆς πατροπαραδότου (not C).

Moreover, an adj. or ptc. which follows a gen. always takes the art., unless it be understood predicatively : Mt 3¹⁷ ὁ υἱός μου ὁ ἀγαπητός, 2 Co 6⁷ τῶν ὅπλων τῆς δικαιοσύνης τῶν δεξιῶν καὶ ἀριστερῶν, Eph 6¹⁶ τὰ βέλη τοῦ πονηροῦ τὰ (om BD*FG) πεπυρωμένα, Heb 13²⁰ 1 Pt 5¹⁰ ; predicatively Ti 2¹¹ ἐπεφάνη ἡ χάρις

τοῦ θεοῦ (ἡ add Cᶜ) σωτήριος πᾶσιν ἀνθρώποις : see Radermacher[2]
117.   Also Ac 23²⁷ Ro 2²⁷ 8¹ A 16¹ 2 Co 11⁹ Ga 3¹.

It is possible for all the attributes to occur after the noun and yet
for the art. not to be repeated : 1 Co 8⁷ τῇ συνηθείᾳ ἕως ἄρτι τοῦ εἰδώλου,
Eph 3⁴ τὴν σύνεσίν μου ἐν τῷ μυστηρίῳ τοῦ X. (the art. would contrast
this particular σύνεσις of Paul with another), 2 Th 3¹⁴ τῷ λόγῳ ἡμῶν διὰ
τῆς ἐπιστολῆς, Col. 1⁴, Ph 1⁵.   But if there is danger of ambiguity or
confusion, the art. occurs, as in the following : Ro 7⁵ 8³⁹ 2 Co 9³ 1 Th 1⁸
ἡ πίστις ὑμῶν ἡ πρὸς τὸν θεὸν ἐξελήλυθεν.

Instead of additional attributes being placed after the noun they
may, sometimes (but not usually) with the art., be placed before, as in
class. Greek : Lk 1⁷⁰ τῶν ἁγίων τῶν ἀπ' αἰῶνος . . . προφητῶν AC,
1 Pt 4¹⁴ τὸ τῆς δόξης καὶ τὸ τοῦ θεοῦ πνεῦμα (but meaning is : *and
therefore* the Spirit of God).   In NT this position is usually found with
the adjs. ὁ ἄλλος, οἱ λοιποί, as in the papyri (Mayser II 2, 60) : Jn 19³²
τοῦ ἄλλου τοῦ συσταυρωθέντος, Rev 2²⁴ τοῖς λοιποῖς τοῖς ἐν Θυατείροις.

§ 3. Numerals

It is not a class. idiom to use εἷς for *first*, but Heb. (אֶחָד) and
Aram., by way of LXX (Ps 23 (24) tit. τῇ μιᾷ σαββάτου, Ge 8¹³
etc. μιᾷ τοῦ μηνός, Ex 40² Nu 1¹· ¹⁸ Ezra 10¹⁶ᶠ 2 Mac 15³⁶),
Mt 28¹ εἰς μίαν σαββάτων, Lk 24¹, Jn 20¹· ¹⁹ Ac 20⁷ 1 Co 16²,
Rev 6¹ μίαν *first*, 9¹² ἡ οὐαὶ ἡ μία.   Mk 16² τῆς μιᾶς σαββάτων.
But Mk 16⁹ (later ending) is exceptional : πρώτῃ σαββάτου.   Jos.
Ant. 1, 1, 1 αὕτη μὲν ἂν εἴη πρώτη ἡμέρα, Μωϋσῆς δ' αὐτὴν μίαν
εἶπεν.   Ga 4²⁴ δύο διαθῆκαι, μία μέν . . . *the first*.

Also Aramaic is the use of reciprocal εἷς τὸν ἕνα, 1 Th 5¹¹.
But cf. Hdt. 4. 50 ἓν πρὸς ἕν, συμβάλλειν, Lucian *Conscr. Hist.* 2
ἕν . . . ἑνί.

Distributive ἀνά and κατά with a numeral are class. (Mk 6⁷D,
⁴⁰ Lk 9¹⁴ 10¹ Herm. S. IX 2, 3), but the following are less so,
censured by the Atticists and rather Semitic and colloquial
Koine : δυὸ δυό (Mk 6⁷, LXX Ge 7⁹, Si 36¹⁵), συμπόσια συμπόσια,
πρασιαὶ πρασιαί (6³⁹ᶠ), δεσμὰς δεσμάς (Mt 13³⁰ Epiph. Orig. ; see
Lagrange *S. Matth.* 268), τάγματα τάγματα (Herm. S. VIII 2, 8 ;
4, 2), ἑπτὰ ἑπτά Ge 7³, τρία τρία (P. Oxy. I p. 188 iii/A.D.), ἀνὰ
δύο δύο (Gosp. Pet. 35, Lk 10¹ BK II), ἀνὰ ἓν ἕν (P. Columb. no.
318 c. A.D. 100), κατὰ δύο δύο (P. Oxy. VI 886¹⁹ iii/A.D.), κατὰ
ἕνα ἕνα Isa 27¹².   Heb לְאֶחָד אֶחָד, etc.

The multiplicative ἑβδομηκοντάκις ἑπτά, as in LXX Ge 4²⁴,
for שִׁבְעִים וְשִׁבְעָה (77), is *77 times* (Moulton Proleg. 98), i.e. *70 times*

(*and*) *seven*, not *70 times seven* (an error still perpetrated by NEB, without so much as a footnote) Mt 18[22]. D* rightly interprets it as ἑβδομηκοντάκις ἑπτάκις, and Vulg. as *septuagies septies*. The same principle applies with ἑπτάκις ἑπτα *14 times* (not *seven times seven*) T. Benj. 7[4]. So δώδεκα for δωδεκάκις in Rev 22[2], δύο for δίς in 9[12]. Semitic speech has ambiguous numerals.

In Mk 4[8. 20] B reads εἰς . . . ἐν . . . ἐν, S reads εἰς . . . εἰς . . . εἰς (a correction), ADWQ εν . . . εν . . . εν (= ἓν . . . ἓν . . . ἕν) correct. Ἕν is a sign of multiplication = ἑκατονταπλασίονα (an Aramaism).

CHAPTER FOURTEEN

ATTRIBUTIVE RELATIONSHIP: PRONOUNS AND PRONOMINAL ADJECTIVES

§ 1. Attributive Pronouns

1. *Possessive pronouns: unemphatic* [1]

It was a tendency of the NT as well as the Koine to prefer the gen. of the pers. pronoun (μου) to the nom. possessive pronoun (ἐμός). The rule for word-order in the Koine generally seems fairly close to the class. model. The genitives of the pers. pronouns μου, σου, ἡμῶν, ὑμῶν, αὐτοῦ, αὐτῆς, αὐτῶν stand without an art. of their own with an articular noun, either (a) after the noun, or (b) before its art., in the LXX, NT and Hell. generally; (c) where the noun has an attribute the gen. pers. pronoun follows the attribute. But if they are very emphatic, we may expect to find the 1st and 2nd pres. pronouns between the art. and the noun, even without this attribute [2]. (d) The 3rd pers. pronoun in this position is not necessarily emphatic in Hell. Greek. With anarthrous nouns it is immaterial whether the gen. pronoun precedes or follows the noun (Mayser II 2, 66).

Exx.:—

(*a*) Very commonly, e.g. ὁ πατήρ μου Jn 15[1] etc., and abundantly frequent esp. with 3rd p. in the pap.[3]

(*b*) Less commonly, and special attention should be paid to the variant readings: Mt 2[2] αὐτοῦ τὸν ἀστέρα, 7[24], 8[8] ἵνα μου ὑπὸ τὴν στέγην, 16[18] 17[15] 23[8].—Mk 5[30] 9[24].—Lk 6[47] 12[18] 15[30] 16[6] 19[35] etc.—Jn 1[27] 2[23] 3[19. 21. 33] 4[47] 9[11. 21. 26] 11[32. 48] 12[40] 13[1] etc.—Ro 14[16] 1 Co 8[12] Ph 2[2] 4[14] Col 2[5] 4[18] 1 Th 2[16] 3[10. 13] 2 Th 2[17] 3[5] Phm 5 1 Ti 4[15] 2 Ti 1[4].—1 Jn 3[20].—Rev 3[1. 2. 8. 15] 10[9] 14[18] 18[5] etc.—PSI IV 372. 12 (250 B.C.)

---

[1] K-G I 619, 4; 627, 3. Schwyzer II 202ff. Mayser II 2, 64ff. Winer-Schmiedel § 22, 14–17. Radermacher[2] 72f, 111. A. Wifstrand, *A Problem concerning Word Order in the NT*, Studia theol., Lund 1951. *Internat. Zeitschriftenschau f. Bibelwiss.*, 1951–2, 180f. Helbing Kasussyntax 178.

[2] K-G I 619, 2. UPZ 113. 12 (156 B.C.) τῆς ὑμῶν ἀγωγῆς. Moulton Einl. 59, 1. In NT, apparently only Pauline, and almost confined to ὑμῶν.

[3] NT uses ἐμοῦ and σοῦ only in connection with another gen., e.g. Ro 1[12] ὑμῶν τε καὶ ἐμοῦ, 16[13] αὐτοῦ καὶ ἐμοῦ.

ἃ καταβεβόσκηκέ σου τὰ πρόβατα.   Before two nouns to save repetition:
Lk 12³⁵ ὑμῶν αἱ ὀσφύες . . . καὶ οἱ λύχνοι, Jn 11⁴⁸ ἡμῶν καὶ τὸν τόπον καὶ
τὸ ἔθος.—Ac 21¹¹.—1 Th 1³ 2¹⁹ 2 Ti 3¹⁰ Ti 1¹⁵.—Rev 2¹⁹.—Diod. Sic.
11. 16.   The above are unemphatic pronouns, but they may be inserted
in this pre-position for special emphasis: Lk 12³⁰ 22⁵³, 1 Co 9¹¹ εἰ ἡμεῖς
ὑμῶν τὰ σαρκικὰ θερίσομεν, Eph 2¹⁰ αὐτοῦ γάρ ἐσμεν ποίημα, Ph 3²⁰.

(c) Mt 27⁶⁰ ἐν τῷ καινῷ αὐτοῦ μνημείῳ, 2 Co 4¹⁶ ὁ ἔξω ἡμῶν ἄνθρωπος,
5¹ ἡ ἐπίγειος ἡμῶν οἰκία, 1 Pt 1³ 2⁹ 5¹⁰ etc.

(d) The 3rd p. αὐτοῦ = *his* is found in the middle position of the
attributive, not merely when emphatic, as in class. Greek, but in NT
and Koine also when unemphatic (Mayser II 2, 66): Ro 11¹¹ τῷ αὐτῶν
παραπτώματι ἡ σωτηρία τοῖς ἔθνεσιν, 3²⁴ τῇ αὐτοῦ χάριτι, 1 Th 2¹⁹, Ti 3⁵
κατὰ τὸ αὐτοῦ ἔλεος emph. (D*EFG τὸ ἐλ. αὐτοῦ), Heb 2⁴ τὴν αὐτοῦ
θέλησιν, 7¹⁸ διὰ τὸ αὐτῆς ἀσθενὲς καὶ ἀνωφελές (no emph.), 1 Pt 1³
τὸ πόλυ αὐτοῦ ἔλεος, 5¹⁰ τὴν αἰώνιον αὐτοῦ δόξαν, 2 Pt 1⁹ τῶν πάλαι
αὐτοῦ ἁμαρτιῶν, LXX 2 Mac 7⁹, Herm. M. VI 2, 2, Clem. Hom. 1⁷·¹¹ 3⁸
and often.   But emphatic: Ro 3²⁵ τῷ αὐτοῦ αἵματι.   For 3rd p. ἐκείνου,
see Jn 5⁴⁷ 2 Co 8⁹·¹⁴ 2 Ti 2²⁶ etc. (but Ro 6²¹ τὸ τέλος ἐκείνων).   For
3rd p. τούτου: Ro 11³⁰ 2 Pt 1¹⁵ (but contrary to rule: Ac 13²³ Heb 13¹¹
Rev 18¹⁵)

Possessive pronouns: *emphatic.*

On the other hand, the genitives ἐμαυτοῦ, σεαυτοῦ, ἑαυτοῦ,
τούτου, ἐκείνου usually have the position of an attribute, not a
predicate, both in class. and in Hell. Greek (Mayser II 2, 65).
As a possess. gen. with a noun, ἐμαυτοῦ is found in NT only at
1 Co 10³³ τὸ ἐμαυτοῦ συμφέρον, while σεαυτοῦ is never found like
this.   In NT also, esp. in Paul, the emph. ὑμῶν is found in
attributive position (cp. Soph. Oed. Rex 1458 ἡ μὲν ἡμῶν μοῖρα)
thus making ὑμέτερος almost superfluous in all NT writings (not
ten instances, and none in Mt-Mk).   The attributive ὑμῶν: 1 Co
16¹⁷ τὸ ὑμῶν ὑστέρημα (BCD ὑμέτερον), 2 Co 1⁶ 9² (vl. ἐξ ὑμῶν),
12¹⁹ 13⁹, 1 Th 3⁷, Clem. Hom. 10¹⁵ (but the predicative position
in Ph 3²⁰ ἡμῶν γὰρ τὸ πολίτευμα for greater emphasis; and Heb
10²⁵ τὴν ἐπισυναγωγὴν ἑαυτῶν, for ὑμῶν αὐτῶν; reflexives: Lk
19¹³ δέκα δούλους ἑαυτοῦ *of his*, Ac 21¹¹ δήσας ἑαυτοῦ τοὺς πόδας,
Ga 6⁴·⁸ (D*FG αὐτοῦ), Eph 4¹⁶ (SD*G αὐτοῦ), Herm. S. II 5;
S. IV 5 (P. Mich. αὐτῶν); V 4, 3A (P. Mich. αὐτοῦ) (Mayser II 2,
70).   Where the emphatic pronoun occurs in predicative
position, there is often a variant reading created by scribes who
correct it to unemph. pronoun, for which this position would be
normal.

Possessive adjectives [1].

'Εμός, σός, ἡμέτερος, ὑμέτερος had been used in class. Greek
as emph. possessives, but they are out of vogue now, being
replaced by the gen. (or dat.: σοι ἦσαν Jn 17⁶) of the pers.
pronoun or by ἴδιος. Still ἐμός is frequent in Jn, and occurs in
1 Co ten times (e.g. 11²⁴ τὴν ἐμὴν ἀνάμνησιν 16¹⁸), but often there
is no emphasis: Lk 22¹⁹ Ro 10¹ Ga 1¹³ Ph 1²⁶; it = μοῦ. But
ἐμός and σός may be reflexive, as occasionally in class. Greek
(K-G I 568f): Mt 7³ 2 Co 1²³ Phm¹⁹ (ἔγραψα τῇ ἐμῇ χειρί), 3 Jn⁴
τὰ ἐμὰ τέκνα, Herm. S I 11 τὸ σὸν ἔργον ἐργάζου. 'Ἡμέτερος
and ὑμέτερος are rarer: Ro 11³¹ 15⁴ 1 Co 15³¹ 16¹⁷ (ὑμῶν p⁴⁶ SA).

Word-order: in Jn about 30 times in post-position (unemphatic):
ἐμός 3²⁹ (ἡ χαρὰ ἡ ἐμή), 5³⁰· ³⁰ 6³⁸ 7⁶· ⁸ 8¹⁶· ³¹· ³⁷· ⁴³· ⁵¹· ⁵⁶ 10²⁶· ²⁷ 12²⁶
14¹⁵· ²⁷ 15⁹· ¹¹· ¹² 17¹³· ²⁴ 18³⁶ (4); σός 17¹⁷ (ὁ λόγος ὁ σός), 18³⁵; ὑμέτερος
7⁶ 8¹⁷. In pre-position, only three times (emphatic): 4⁴² τὴν σὴν λαλίαν,
5⁴⁷ τοῖς ἐμοῖς ῥήμασιν, 7¹⁶ ἡ ἐμὴ διδαχή.—In Mt Mk Lk only emphatic;
therefore pre-position (e.g. Mt 7²² τῷ σῷ ὀνόματι bis).—With no art.
Ph 3⁹ μὴ ἔχων ἐμὴν δικαιοσύνην τὴν ἐκ νόμου (predicatively: *which is
my own*. In Jn 4³⁴ ἐμὸν βρῶμα, 13³⁵ 15⁸ (attrib.); predicative 14²⁴
16¹⁵ 17⁶· ⁹· ¹⁰· ¹⁰, also Mt 20²³ Mk 10⁴⁰ οὐκ ἔστιν ἐμὸν τοῦτο δοῦναι.

'Ἴδιος as *simple, possess. pronoun, or reflex. adjective* [2].

With the old class. meaning *peculiar, private*: Mk 15²⁰
τὰ ἴδια ἱμάτια αὐτοῦ (Θ om αὐτοῦ; BD om ἴδια), Ac 1¹⁹ τῇ ἰδίᾳ
διαλέκτῳ αὐτῶν (B*SD lat om ἰδίᾳ), 4³², 1 Co 3⁸ 7² (ἕκαστος τὴν
ἑαυτοῦ γυναῖκα ἐχέτω, καὶ ἑκάστη τὸν ἴδιον ἄνδρα ἐχέτω. Is this
simply variety in style? Or is ἴδιος class.?), 7⁷ (certainly the
class. use: *his own private gift*), 12¹¹ ἰδίᾳ ἑκάστῳ, 15³⁸ (*its own
peculiar body*), Ti 1¹² ἴδιος αὐτῶν *their own poet* (i.e. not another
nationality), Heb 7²⁷ (individual sins, as oppos. to the people's;
cp. 4¹⁰). However, in the post-class. period there enters the
meaning = ἑαυτοῦ (class. οἰκεῖος): Pap. Rev. Laws 52, 13, 23
(258 B.C.) εἰς τὴν ἰδίαν χρείαν. Moreover, the LXX, NT,
Josephus, Plutarch, etc. use it not only as a reflexive, but even
as a mere possessive, differing little if at all from αὐτοῦ. Reflexive: Mt 14¹³ etc. κατ' ἰδίαν = class. καθ' ἑαυτόν, Lk 2³ (vl.
ἑαυτοῦ), Jn 1¹¹ εἰς τὰ ἴδια ἦλθεν, ⁴² τὸν ἀδελφὸν τὸν ἴδιον, Ac 24²³

---

[1] Mayser II 2, 67f, 68, 71ff. Moulton Einl. 59. G. D. Kilpatrick,
" The Possessive Pronoun in the NT." *JThS* 42, 1941, 184–186 (for Mk
and Lk). Cuendet 40 (for word-order).

[2] Mayser I² 2, 65; II 2, 73f. Meisterhans-Schwyzer 235. E. L. Green,
" 'Ἴδιος as a possessive in Polybius," *Proc. Amer. Philol. Assoc.* 34, 4.
Schwyzer II 205⁵.

192   A GRAMMAR OF NEW TESTAMENT GREEK   [§ 1

τῶν ἰδίων, 2 Co 5¹⁰ p⁴⁶ lat τὰ ἴδια, 2 Pt 3³·¹⁶ Wi 19¹³ P. Oxy. I 37 τὸ ἴδιόν μου τέκνον. Possessive: Mt 22⁵ τὸν ἴδιον ἀγρόν, 25¹⁴, Ti 2⁹ ἰδίοις δεσπόταις, 1 Pt 3¹·⁵ τοῖς ἰδίοις ἀνδράσιν, 2 Pt 2¹⁶ ἰδίας παρανομίας. *Word-order* (Cuendet 41): in Syn. Gosp. pre-position (e.g. Lk 6⁴¹ ἐν τῷ ἰδίῳ ὀφθαλμῷ, emph.), in Jn usually post-position.

2. Attributive demonstrative pronouns

Ὅδε [1].

It no longer forms part of the living language; it is rare in NT and papyri but occurs attributively in Jas 4¹³ εἰς τήνδε τὴν πόλιν, and hardly correctly even here [2] as it appears to mean τὴν καὶ τήν *such and such*, as in popular Attic and Hell.: LXX Ru 1¹⁷. MGr ὁ τάδε(ς) = ὁ δεῖνα: *Mr So-and-so*; Wackernagel II 107f., and literature.

Οὗτος and ἐκεῖνος [3].

Whereas in the Ptol. pap. we hardly ever find them used attributively but only predicatively, on the the other hand in both the LXX and NT the attributive is by far the greater use. It is only in books like 2–4 Mac and Wi, and the writings of John and Paul that there is any approach to normal contemporary usage in this respect.

The omission of the art.[4] is possible where conceivably the noun is regarded as a predicate of the pronoun, which is quite in accord with class. Greek. In the Ptol. pap. it is frequently omitted where ordinal numerals are concerned: Zen. pap. (258 B.C.) ἤδη δ᾽ ἐστὶν ἔτος τοῦτο δεύτερον, UPZ (163 B.C.) ἔτος τοῦτο δέκατον *this is the tenth year*; cp. Lk 1³⁶ *this is the sixth month*, 2² *this was the first census*, 12 *this shall be a sign to you*, Jn 2¹¹ ταύτην ἐποίησεν ἀρχὴν τῶν σημείων *he did this as a beginning of the miracles*, 2 Pt 3¹ *this is the second letter*. So also Achilles Tatius 7. 11. 2 (iv/A.D.) τρίτην ταύτην ἡμέραν, Menander *Epitr.* 26f (iv/B.C.), Lucian *dial. mort.* 13. 3. But even Hdt 5, 76

---

[1] See above, p. 44. K-G I § 467 pp. 641ff. Gildersleeve II § 665. Meisterhans-Schwyzer 231–232. Τοιᾶσδε only in 2 Pt 1¹⁷.

[2] It is correctly used in 1 Clem 50³ 63².

[3] K-G I 627ff, 645ff. Mayser II 2, 79–82. N. Turner, "The Unique Character of Biblical Greek," *Vet. Test.* 5, 1955, 2, pp. 208–213.

[4] J. E. Harry, "The omission of the article with substantives after οὗτος, ὅδε, ἐκεῖνος in prose," *Trans. Amer. Phil. Assoc.* 29, 1898, 48–64. Bauer⁴ col. 1087. Winer-Schmiedel § 23, 12. L.S.s.v. οὗτος B I 4. Mayser II 2, 81.

τέταρτον δὴ τοῦτο, and LXX Ge 27³⁶ δεύτερον τοῦτο. Nu 14²²
Jg 16¹⁵. However, the real difficulty occurs where there is no
copula, real or understood, but a main verb which excludes the
possibility of supplying the verb *to be* and taking the noun as a
predicate of the demonstrative pronoun. The difficulty is that
in an attributive sense the art. is always present in earlier Greek
(with the negligible exception of the Epic poets and sometimes in
the tragedians). Yet in NT there are clear instances of omission :
Mk 16¹⁷ σημεῖα δὲ τοῖς πιστεύσασιν ταῦτα παρακολουθήσει
these miracles (but ταῦτα may be construed as obj. of the ptc.),
Ac 1⁵ οὐ μετὰ πολλὰς ταύτας ἡμέρας (οὐ reverses the meaning of
πολλάς : thus *after these few days*), 24²¹ περὶ μιᾶς ταύτης φωνῆς
ἧς ἐκέκραξα (*this single utterance*). The def. art. was being
carelessly used, as time went on, in these connections. Radermacher notes its absence, where it would have been inevitable
at an earlier period (πᾶς βίοτος *the whole life* on a Galatian
inscription, and Dionysius of Halicarnassus has καθ' ἕκαστον
ἐνιαυτόν) and there is little doubt of the attributive sense in the
phrases τούτου πράγματος, ταῦτα ἀδικήματα, τοῦτο μνῆμα,
ὀνόματα ταῦτα, τούτῳ δικαίῳ, τόδε σῆμα (p. 113). In the
imperial period therefore the usage was already established and
we should not strive to render the anarthrous demonstrative in
NT in a predicative way unless the copula (actual or understood)
makes this necessary.

The position of the attributive pronoun, like that of the adj.,
is either before the art. or after the noun. The post-positive
position may in part be due to Hebrew influence, for in LXX
Ge 7¹ (and thus in Syn. Gosp. and Heb 3¹⁰) בַּדּוֹר הַזֶּה becomes
ἡ γενεὰ αὕτη, and it was probably the later Hebrew עוֹלָם הַזֶּה
(*this world-time*) that produced ὁ καιρὸς οὗτος (Mk 10³⁰ Lk 12⁵⁶
18³⁰) and ὁ κόσμος οὗτος (Jn, Paul), which Paul more correctly
terms ὁ νῦν καιρός, and עוֹלָם הַבָּא accounts for ὁ αἰὼν ἐκεῖνος
Lk 20³⁵ (in Pastorals ὁ νῦν αἰών 1 Ti 6¹⁷ Ti 2¹²). There are a few
examples of pre-positive position in NT (Mt 12³² 11²⁵ 12¹ 14¹
Ac 12¹) but not usually in the Heb. sense of *world-time*.

Τοιοῦτος and τοσοῦτος ¹.

Τοιοῦτος is occasionally preceded by the art. (when referring

---

¹ K-G I 630, 5. Meisterhans-Schwyzer 232. Gildersleeve II § 586.
Mayser II 2, 82ff.

to individuals or individualizing a class): e.g. Mk 9³⁷ ABDLNW
τῶν τοιούτων παιδίων (SC παιδ. τούτων), 2 Co 12³ τὸν τοιοῦτον
ἄνθρωπον, Jn 4²³ τοιούτους ζητεῖ τοὺς προσκυνοῦντας (predicative). Τοσοῦτος has the art. only Rev 18¹⁷ ὁ τοσοῦτος
πλοῦτος.

Αὐτός = self as attributive ¹.

It is in general agreement with class. and Koine usage.   It
is found in the predicative position, e.g. αὐτὸ τὸ πνεῦμα Ro 8²⁶ =
the Spirit himself; but attributive τὸ αὐτὸ πνεῦμα 2 Co 4¹³ = the
self-same Spirit.   The art. however does not belong to αὐτός
but to the noun, and is therefore sometimes omitted, as in Jn 2²⁴
αὐτὸς Ἰησοῦς.   It is found in connection with the pers. pronoun
(αὐτὸς ἐγώ I myself) where it is to be distinguished from the
reflexive (I do this to myself): Ac 20³⁰ ἐξ ὑμῶν αὐτῶν, 1 Co 5¹³
ἐξάρατε τὸν πονηρὸν ἐξ ὑμῶν αὐτῶν yourselves (not reflexive),
Ga 4¹⁷ ἵνα αὐτοὺς ζηλοῦτε = αὐτοὺς αὐτούς (in 3rd p. αὐτός is
not repeated) the men themselves.

It is a debatable point whether in the Ptol. papyri αὐτός can
stand in demonstrative sense for οὗτος or ἐκεῖνος ²; it is any way
almost restricted to the official style of writing.   If so, it appears
again abundantly in NT in Luke, especially in certain phrases
(and even where Semitic sources are not in question, e.g. Ac 16¹⁸
22¹³) ³.   This significantly affects the exegesis of certain passages,
where the translation is this or that, but not the same, or even
that very, e.g. Lk 10⁷ ἐν αὐτῇ τῇ οἰκίᾳ, Lk 13¹ ἐν αὐτῷ τῷ καιρῷ
(ἐν ἐκείνῳ τῷ κ. Mt 11²⁵) LXX To 3¹⁷; (ἐν) αὐτῇ τῇ ὥρᾳ, ἡμέρᾳ
Lk 2³⁸ (= ἐκείνῳ in 7²¹) 10²¹ 12¹² (ἐκεῖνος Mk 13¹¹) 13³¹ 20¹⁹
24¹³ etc., P. Teb. I 411³ (ii/A.D.) αὐτῇ ὥρᾳ, P. Oxy III 528. 14
(ii/A.D.) αὐτῇ τῇ ὥρᾳ, inscr. Ditt. Syll.² 1173¹ (ii/A.D.) αὐταῖς ταῖς
ἡμέραις, T. Abr. 113²⁹ 116²⁷ (αὐτῇ τῇ ὥρᾳ); αὐτῇ τῇ νυκτί Herm.
V. III 1, 2 S; 10, 7; ἐν αὐτῇ τῇ νυκτί LXX To 2⁹.   It appears to
be synonymous with ἐκεῖνος in the otherwise puzzling sentence,
2 Ti 2²⁶ ἐζωγρημένοι ὑπ' αὐτοῦ εἰς τὸ ἐκείνου θέλημα.

---

¹ K-G I 627, 4.   Gildersleeve II §§ 654–655.   Ljungvik BSSV 8f.
Mayser II 2, 75ff.
    ² Moulton says it can (Proleg. 91), but Black doubts this (AAGA² 72);
the latter prefers the hypothesis of the influence of Aramaic proleptic
pronoun (see p. 41).
    ³ Moulton-Howard, App. p. 432.

3 *Indefinite pronouns in attributive use* [1]

τις.

As to word-order, though they are enclitics, τις and τι occasionally, when used adjectivally, stand before their noun, as long as they are not first word in the sentence (and even first word in Soph. *Trach.* 865, *Oed. Rex* 1471 Plato *Theaet.* 147c., Plutarch *Tranqu.* c. 13): Ac 3² καί τις ἀνήρ, Ro 1¹¹. But τινές [2] may now stand first in the sentence: Mt 27⁴⁷ τινὲς δὲ τῶν, Lk 6² idem, Jn 13²⁹ τινὲς γάρ, 1 Ti 5²⁴ τινῶν ἀνθρώπων. Attributive τις, often with adjs. and numerals (*about*) in class. Greek, is now largely used in the sense of *quidam = so to speak*: Jas 1¹⁸ ἀπαρχήν τινα, Heb 10²⁷ φοβερά τις ἐκδοχή; but τινα in Ac 8⁹ (εἶναί τινα ἑαυτὸν μέγαν) is not an instance, but is *a person of imporance* (like Ga 2⁶ 6³), with μέγαν inserted for emphasis. With numerals also in Lk 7¹⁸ δύο τινάς, Ac 23²³ τινας δύο: not *about two* but *a certain pair*; so also Lk 22⁵⁰ Jn 11⁴⁹ εἴς τις *a certain one*.

As substitutes for τις there are ἄνθρωπος: Mt 12¹⁰, 13²⁸ ἐχθρὸς ἄνθρωπος, ⁴⁵ ἀνθρώπῳ (BS* om) ἐμπόρῳ CDΘ, ⁵² 18²³ Mk 1²³ etc. and ἀνήρ (in Lk, e.g. 9³⁸ Ac 3¹⁴) like Aram. שיא[3] but also = Heb שׁיא *each, anyone* (Thackeray OT Gr. 45). We find ἀνήρ and ἄνθρωπος = τις in Homer and class. Greek (K-G I 272; Svensson op. cit. 136–140). Also γυνή: Mt 15²².

εἷς.

Another post-class. substitute for τις is the numeral εἷς [4], as also in the Ptol. papyri, in the sense of *aliquis* or *quidam*, with analogies in modern languages (*one, ein, un*). In Luke it does not seem to be a Semitism; he always follows εἷς with a gen. (e.g. 15¹⁵ ἑνὶ τῶν πολιτῶν; same phrase in Hyperides *Lycophr.* 13 (iv/B.C.), which makes it conform closely to Greek usage: pap. Mayser II 2, 86 ἀποστείλας τῶν οἰκοδόμων ἕνα. In Mk also in three places (5²² 14¹⁰· ⁶⁶) we have gen.; whereas in Mt 9¹⁸ 26⁶⁹

---

[1] K-G I 662, 663. Mayser II 2, 84ff. On confusion of relative and interrogative pronouns. including their attributive form (i.e. τις and ὅστις, πόσος and ὅσος, πῶς and ὡς) see pp. 4, 49f.

[2] Also τινές (substantivally) stands at the beginning of the sentence Ac 17¹⁸ τινὲς δέ, 19³¹, Jn 7⁴⁴ etc., especially where there is a contrasted clause Ph 1¹⁵ τινὲς μὲν . . . τινὲς δέ (classical).

[3] Wellhausen Einl.² 20. Moulton-Howard 433 (Epict. 3, 23, 15). Black AAGA² 248–52.

[4] Schwyzer II 27. Mayser II 2, 85. Lagrange *S. Matth.* XCVIII. Winer-Schmiedel § 26, 5. Radermacher² 76. Moulton Einl. 154.

there is no gen. after εἷς or μία. Mt (e.g. εἷς γραμματεύς 8¹⁹) thus comes closer to Semitic than do Mk or Lk, and is probably influenced by Heb. אֶחָד or Aram. חַד. In 21¹⁹ he has συκῆν μίαν, where Mk 11¹³ has no μίαν (except SKM for harm.). Mt 18²⁴ 19¹⁶ Mk 10¹⁷ have εἷς for τις, where Lk has τις. Εἷς is more likely to reflect Semitic influence on the rare occasions when it is in post-position Mt 9¹⁸ ἄρχων εἷς SᵇB lat syrᵖᵉ· ʰˡ (S*ᶜ C* DWΘ fam¹ 700 copt om εἷς), Jn 6⁹ παιδάριον ἕν ΑΓ, LXX Da 7⁸ ἄλλο ἓν κέρας ἀνέφύη, 1 Esd 4¹⁸ γυναῖκα μίαν, but even here we have papyrus precedent (PSI IV 571, 15 ἄλλον ἕνα *a further one* παρατρέφω, 252 B.C.). The use with τις is class.: Lk 22⁵⁰ εἷς τις, Mk 14⁴⁷ (SA om τις), Jn 11⁴⁹ (Schwyzer II 215 b. 1).

-ουν and -ποτε [1].

These additions form an indef. pronoun, e.g. ὁστισοῦν, ὅστις δήποτε, but rarely if at all in NT. There is Ga 2⁶ ὁποῖοί ποτε ἦσαν *whatever kind of persons they were* (ποτε is not a separate word, *at one time*.) Ac 19²⁶ D ὁ Παῦλος οὗτος τίς ποτε (not τοτε): gig *hic Paulus nescio quem.*

οὐ ... πᾶς.

This peculiarly Biblical Greek [2] phenomenon should be included among negative indef. pronouns. The Hebraistic οὐ (μὴ) ... πᾶς = כֹּל ... לֹא, as also πᾶς ... οὐ = לֹא ... כֹּל [3]. Mt 24²² Mk 13³⁰ οὐκ ἂν ἐσώθη πᾶσα σάρξ, Lk 1³⁷ οὐκ ... πᾶν ῥῆμα (*nothing*), Jn 12⁴⁶ πᾶς ὁ πιστεύων ... μὴ μείνη, Ac 10¹⁴ οὐδέποτε ἔφαγον πᾶν κοινόν, Ro 3²⁰, 1 Co 1²⁹, Eph 4²⁹ 5⁵ πᾶς πόρνος ... οὐκ ἔχει, 2 Pt 1²⁰, 1 Jn 2²¹ 3¹⁵, Rev 7¹· ¹⁶ 9⁴ 18²² 21²⁷ 22³, LXX Ps 142 (143) ² etc., DaO′ θ 2¹⁰ πᾶς βασιλεὺς ... οὐκ ἐπερωτᾷ, 2¹¹, O′ 5⁹ 6⁵ etc., θ 4⁶ etc., Acta Pionii 11⁴ μὴ σύμπασαν for μηδεμίαν. As in class. Greek, οὐ πᾶς with nothing intervening: Mt 7²¹ 1 Co 15³⁹ *not everyone*. The harshness is mitigated where a positive

---

[1] K-G II 410, 3.   Schmid Attiz. I 184, 426; IV 553.   Wackernagel II 116, 121f, 317.   Mayser I² 2, 70; II 2, 86f.   Radermacher² 76f.

[2] Extra-biblical exx. are rare: Dion. Halic. (*de Plat. ad Pomp.*) 756 οὐκ ἀπὸ τοῦ βελτίστου πάντα περὶ αὐτῶν γράφουν. P. Ryl. II 113¹²ᶠ (A.D. 133) μὴ ἔχοντας πᾶν πρᾶγμα πρὸς ἐμέ. Apoll. Disc. *de Synt.* I 14 πᾶς λόγος ἄνευ τούτων οὐ συγκλείεται (where however one could join οὐ closely with συγκλ., as in the French *toute autre doctrine ne leur plaît pas* = all other ... displeases.

[3] Wackernagel II 273f.   Ljungvik BZSSV 18ff.   Moulton Einl. 126f. Radermacher² 219f.

clause with ἄλλα follows, containing the main point of the sentence: Jn 3¹⁶ ἵνα πᾶς ὁ πιστεύων μὴ ἀπόληται, ἀλλὰ ἔχῃ *that every believer may have* . . . , *and not perish*, 6³⁹.

§ 2. Attributive Pronominal Adjectives

ἄλλος and ἕτερος [1].

For the position of ἄλλος with another attribute see p. 187 and Cuendet 112f.

Ἕτερος is not in wide use in the NT and does not occur in Mk (16¹² only), Jn (19³⁷ only), Peter, Rev. It is chiefly found in Lk, and to some extent in Mt and Paul. It is correctly used in 1 Co 10²⁴ τὸ ἑαυτοῦ . . . τὸ τοῦ ἑτέρου, Ph 2⁴ τὰ τῶν ἑτέρων D*FG. In Lk 19²⁰ ὁ ἕτερος apparently = *the third* (A om ὁ). But in all writers it has largely lost its sense of duality by this time [2]. Mt 16¹⁴ οἱ μὲν . . . ἄλλοι δέ . . . ἕτεροι δέ (in the last two clauses Mk 8²⁸ Lk 9¹⁹ have ἄλλοι twice). Lk 8⁶ff καὶ ἕτερον three times (D ἄλλο, as in Mt 13⁵ff Mk 4⁵ff). 9⁵⁹ πρὸς ἕτερον *to another*. ⁶¹ εἶπεν δὲ καὶ ἕτερος *another said*. 1 Co 12⁸ᶠ ᾧ μὲν . . . ἄλλῳ δὲ . . . ἑτέρῳ—then four times ἄλλῳ δὲ . . . ἑτέρῳ . . . ἄλλῳ δέ. Ἄλλος and ἕτερος are found together for variety, showing there is little difference between them: 2 Co 11⁴ ἄλλον Ἰησοῦν . . . πνεῦμα ἕτερον . . . εὐαγγέλιον ἕτερον, Ga 1⁶· ⁷εἰς ἕτερον εὐαγγέλιον, ὃ οὐκ ἔστιν ἄλλο εἰ μή . . . (but ἄλλο probably serves to introduce the εἰ μή-clause. Papyri, e.g. UPZ I 42³². ³³ (162 B.C.) καὶ ἄλλοι . . . καὶ ἕτεροι. Heb 11³⁶ ἕτεροι = *others*. Mt 15³⁰ καὶ ἑτέρους πόλλους. So also Lk 3¹⁸ πόλλα μὲν οὖν καὶ ἕτερα, Ro 8³⁹ οὔτε τις κτίσις ἑτέρα, 13⁹ εἴ τις ἑτέρα ἐντολή, 1 Ti 1¹⁰ εἴ τι ἕτερον. In class. Greek ὁ ἕτερος is never used for anything but a definite division into two parts, as it is in e.g. Mt 10²³ ἐν τῇ πόλει ταύτῃ . . . εἰς τὴν ἑτέραν SBW (DCE corr. to ἄλλην, leaving the incongrous art.), Lk 4⁴³ ταῖς ἑτέραις πόλεσιν—*the remaining cities*. But ἄλλος too appears to mean *the next*, as in Hom. Clem. 15⁴ 19¹ τῆς ἄλλης ἡμέρας. Thus ὁ ἄλλος will usurp the province of ὁ ἕτερος and denote a division into only two parts: Mt 5³⁹ (Lk 6²⁹) τὴν ἄλλην (of a cheek), 12¹³ ἡ ἄλλη (of a hand), Jn 18¹⁶ 19³² 20³ᶠ etc. There

---

[1] K-G I 635, 275n. Meisterhans-Schwyzer 250, 5. 6. Gildersleeve II 587–593 (ἕτερος); 594–599 (ἄλλος). Mayser II 2, 87ff. Radermacher² 77. Moulton Einl. 125. 128. Winer-Schmiedel § 26, 6.

[2] Hom. Clem. 19⁹ a striking alternation: πολλούς . . . ἄλλους δὲ . . . ἑτέρους δὲ . . . ἄλλους δέ (ἄλλους = ἑτέρους).

were isolated examples of this in class. Greek[1]. Papyri:
Mayser II 1, 57; Corp. Pap. Rain. 22¹⁵ (ii/A.D.) τὸ ἄλλο ἥμισυ.
The concentrated phrasing ἄλλοι ἄλλο is class. (*one one thing . . .
one another*): Ac 19³² 21³⁴.

ἕκαστος [2].

In Attic inscriptions until 318 B.C. without exception,
ἕκαστος with a noun and art. is in the predicative position; the
rule is observed also in Attic writers except in prepositional
expressions and genitive expressions of time. However, popular speech dispenses with the art., and the proportions in the
Ptol. papyri are (with: without) 1 : 3 in iii/B.C. and 1 : 4 in
ii–i/ B.C.; and in popular speech ἕκαστος is used only rarely in an
attributive position; we have intensive εἷς ἕκαστος, and (Heb
3¹³) ἕνα ἑκάστην ἡμέραν, (Rev 22²) μῆνα ἕκαστον. It is added to
a plural subject without affecting the construction (class. and
Koine): Winer § 58, 4, K-G I 286ff, Mayser II 2, 115, II 3, 37³⁷ff.
Jn 16³² (εἷς in same way: 1 Co 4⁶) ἵνα σκορπισθῆτε ἕκαστος . . .
κἀμὲ μόνον ἀφῆτε.

Καθ’ εἷς is a colloquialism which does not occur widely in
NT: Mk 14¹⁹ εἷς κατὰ εἷς (C εἷς ἕκαστος, harm. with Mt 26²²),
Jn 8⁹, Ro 12⁵ τὸ δὲ καθ’ εἷς (pap. Mayser I² 3, 205³⁸ff τὸ καθ’ ἕν;
LXX 3 Mac 5³⁴ ὁ καθεὶς τῶν φίλων), Rev 21²¹ ἀνὰ εἷς ἕκαστος.
Its origin lies in the compression of καθ’ ἕνα ἕκαστον *each one by
one* into καθένα ἕκαστον and the next step was to invent καθ’ εἷς
when a nominative was needed (ἀνὰ εἷς appears by the same
principle: distributive ἀνά). A further step was an addition to
produce the pleonastic *one one by one* εἷς κατὰ εἷς.

In the NT ἑκάτερος does not survive.

ἀμφότεροι.

This is substantival [3] in the NT, as in the papyri, except
for Lk 5⁷ ἀμφότερα τὰ πλοῖα.

---

[1] Eurip. Iph T. 962f: θάτερον . . . τὸ δ’ ἄλλο. Plato Leg. 629D τὸ
μὲν . . . τὸ δ’ ἄλλο, but probably corrupt.
[2] K-G I 634. 7. Meisterhans-Schwyzer 232. 38. Gildersleeve II
660, 661, 662. Mayser II 2, 90ff. Radermacher² 113, 117.
[3] Ac 23⁸ Eph 2¹⁴ τὰ ἀμφότερα. Eph 2¹⁶ τοὺς ἀμφοτέρους, 2¹⁸ οἱ
ἀμφότεροι. See Mayser II 2, 94.

ὅλος [1].

Whole. Usually anarthrous in NT, whereas always articular in Ptol. papyri: Mt 22³⁷ BS*Θ (vl. +art.), Mk 12³⁰. ³³ BD* (vl. + art.), Lk 5⁵ δι' ὅλης νυκτός SABWL (CD + τῆς), 10²⁷ B* (vl. + art.), Jn 7²³ ὅλον ἄνθρωπον *a whole man*, Ac 11²⁶ ἐνιαυτὸν ὅλον. With anarthrous city-names: Ac 21³¹ ὅλη Ἰερουσαλήμ (=πᾶσα Ἱεροσόλυμα Mt 2³). With art., always predicative: Mt 16²⁶ τὸν κόσμον ὅλον, 26¹³ ἐν ὅλῳ τῷ κόσμῳ.

ἅπας.

Only found in Lk-Ac with any frequency, and σύμπας is lacking altogether. Outside Lk: Mt 6³² 24³⁹ (D πάντες) 28¹¹ (A πάντα), Mk 8²⁵ (DW πάντα) 11³² 16¹⁵ (D om), Ga 3²⁸ ASB³; Eph 6¹³, Jas 3². Even Luke does not always observe the not invariable class. rule of πᾶς after a vowel and ἅπας after a consonant (1³ ἄνωθεν πᾶσιν); but ἅπας generally occurs after a consonant, as in papyri (see Mayser I¹ 161f; II 2, 96 n. 3). The MSS vary with πᾶς. Word order, like πᾶς.

πᾶς [2].

(1) In the interests of exegesis it is important to ask how much is involved in the Hellenistic deviation from class. standards as to the def. art. with πᾶς. First of all, πᾶς before an anarthrous noun means *every* in the sense of *any*; not every individual, like ἕκαστος, but any you please [3]. Similarly, the negative is *none, no*, as in Mt 24²² οὐκ ἂν ἐσώθη πᾶσα σάρξ (Semitic, see pp. 7, 196f).

Mt 3¹⁰ πᾶν δένδρον *any tree*, Lk 3⁹ *any tree*, not *every tree*, 2 Ti 3¹⁶ πᾶσα γραφή *whatever is Scripture*.

On the other hand, this anarthrous πᾶς also means *all, the whole of*, just as it does when it has the art. It may be that is

---

[1] K-G I 631. 6. Mayser II 2, 95f, 568. Meisterhans-Schwyzer 234, 45. Winer-Schmiedel § 20, 12.

[2] K-G I 631, 6. Gildersleeve II 642-52. Meisterhans-Schwyzer 233ff. Mayser II 2, 96f. Winer-Schmiedel § 20, 11. Radermacher² 112, 113, 117.

[3] This is important for the correct interpretation of Mt 19³ κατὰ πᾶσαν αἰτίαν, which is not *for every cause*, but *for any cause you like to single out among those in the Law*, i.e. *for any cause at all.* Jesus was not being asked for his opinion on the varying merits of each Mosaic ground for divorce, but whether he rejected all grounds.

due to Hebraic influence: for כָּל־בָּשָׂר becomes πᾶσα σάρξ *all flesh, everything fleshly* (Mt 24²² Lk 3⁶ Ro 3²⁰ 1 Co 1²⁹). Mt 3¹⁵ πᾶσα δικαιοσύνη *the whole of*; Ac 2³⁶ πᾶσα οἶκος Ἰσραήλ *whole*, 4²⁹ μετὰ πάσης παρρησίας *complete*, 23¹ πάσῃ συνειδήσει ἀγαθῇ; Ro 11²⁶ πᾶς Ἰσραήλ *the whole of Israel*; Col 1²³ (SᶜDᶜ add τῇ), 1¹⁵ πρωτότοκος πάσης κτίσεως; Eph 2²¹ πᾶσα οἰκοδομή (but SᵃACP have art.) prob. not here as class. *whatever is built*, but (under Semitic infl.) *the whole building*; 1 Pt 2¹³ πᾶσα κτίσις *the whole creation*.

It is more likely, however, that πᾶς with this meaning will have the art.: Ac 12¹¹ πάσης τῆς προσδοκίας *the whole*, Ro 8²² πᾶσα ἡ κτίσις (cp. 1 Pt 2¹³), 1 Co 13² πᾶσαν τὴν γνῶσιν and πᾶσαν τὴν πίστιν *all that exists*; Eph 2²¹; 4¹⁶ πᾶν τὸ σῶμα; Ph 1³ ἐπὶ πάσῃ τῇ μνείᾳ (DE om τῇ) *the whole*.

But sometimes a distinction can be traced between πᾶς with and without the art. in the same passage: 2 Co 1⁴ ὁ παρακαλῶν ἡμᾶς ἐπὶ πάσῃ τῇ θλίψει ἡμῶν *in all our affliction*, εἰς τὸ δύνασθαι ἡμᾶς παρακαλεῖν τοὺς ἐν πάσῃ θλίψει *in any affliction*.

If πᾶς is placed after a noun with the art., special stress is laid upon the noun, e.g. 1 Co 15⁷ ἔπειτα Ἰακώβῳ, ἔπειτα τοῖς ἀποστόλοις πᾶσιν. A frequent use is that of πᾶς with ptc., even without the art., e.g. Mt 3¹⁰ πᾶν δένδρον μὴ ποιοῦν, 13¹⁹ παντὸς ἀκούοντος, Lk 11⁴.

Nevertheless the distinction of an anarthrous and articular noun with πᾶς is not very clear in NT, even to the extent that πᾶς with an articular noun can approach the meaning of *any*: Mk 4¹³ πάσας τὰς παραβολάς *any parables*, not *all the parables*.

(2) The plural (*all*) does not require the art., any more than οὗτος does at this period, and much depends on the noun itself which accompanies πάντες: Ac 17²¹ πάντες Ἀθηναῖοι and 26⁴ πάντες Ἰουδαῖοι are class., for people-names do not require the art. (see p. 169). With πάντες ἄνθρωποι *everybody* (Ac 22¹⁵ Ro 5¹². ¹⁸ 12¹⁷. ¹⁸ etc.) and πάντες ἄγγελοι (Heb 1⁶ OT) the meaning is weakened and the art. is omitted because no totality is really involved: so also Ga 6⁶ πᾶσιν ἀγαθοῖς, 1 Pt 2¹ πάσας καταλαλιάς (S* sing.). When however totality is involved the art. is still needed: Eph 3⁸ πάντων ἁγίων (P + τῶν; p⁴⁶ om τῶν ἁγίων). Its omission in Lk 4²⁰ is unclassical (πάντων ἐν τῇ συναγωγῇ) and that may have caused the MSS to change the position of ἐν τῇ σ. in various ways.

(3) Sometimes, however, the art. occurs before πᾶς, and then ὁ πᾶς and οἱ πάντες contrast the whole with the part: [1] Ac 19⁷ οἱ πάντες ἄνδρες *the sum total of the men* (which is different from the predicative *men as a whole* πάντες οἱ ἄνδρες, see Zerwick § 142), 20¹⁸ τὸν πάντα χρόνον *all that time*, 27³⁷ αἱ πᾶσαι ψυχαί *we were in all* . . . , Ga 5¹⁴ ὁ πᾶς νόμος = " universa lex " as opposed to πᾶς ὁ νόμος = " integra lex nullo praecepto excepto " (Zerwick § 142), 2 Co 5¹⁰ τοὺς πάντας ἡμᾶς the sum total of us.

The non-attributive substantival use of οἱ πάντες is frequent in Paul: Ro 11³² 1 Co 9²² 10¹⁷ 2 Co 5¹⁵ Eph 4¹³ Ph 2²¹; and τὰ πάντα Mk 4¹¹ vl., Ac 17²⁵ Ro 8³² 11³⁶ 1 Co 12⁶·¹⁹ 15²⁷ᶠ (pap. Mayser II 2, 101f).

(4) In relation to its noun, various positions are possible for πᾶς [2] : 1. πᾶς ἄνθρωπος, 2(a) πᾶς ὁ ἄνθρωπος, 2(b) ὁ ἄνθρωπος πᾶς, 3. ὁ πᾶς ἄνθρωπος, and the plurals respectively. Mayser (II 2, 102) shows that the Koine has developed the emphatic form 2(b), at the expense of 2(a) which incidentally is extremely popular in Biblical Greek (LXX NT). Hebrew influence has brought this about. The entry of a demonstrative pronoun may be between πᾶς and its noun or outside: 2(a) πάντα ταῦτα τὰ πονηρά Mk 7²³, πάντα τὰ ῥήματα ταῦτα Lk 1⁶⁵, 2(b) τὴν ἐξουσίαν ταύτην ἅπασαν Lk 4⁶. Only Lk has the order ταῦτα πάντα.

The following tables prove the essential unity of Biblical Greek against that of the Ptolemaic papyri, especially when the second table (percentage proportion) is examined. Types 2(b) and 3 occur scarcely at all in Biblical Greek, but occur strongly in secular. Type 2(a) is very strong in Biblical Greek, but only average in the papyri.

---

[1] Class. exx. e.g. Thuc. 1, 60, in K-G I 632f, Gildersleeve II 309ff. Papyri: Mayser II 2, 100f.

[2] See N. Turner op. cit. 211f; Cuendet 131f).

ACTUAL OCCURRENCES

	Type 1 s.	Type 1 pl.	Type 2(a) s.	Type 2(a) pl.	Type 2(b) s.	Type 2(b) pl.	Type 3 s.	Type 3 pl.
Papyrus iii/B.C.	17	2	14	40	18	56	22	5
Papyrus ii–i/B.C.	23	11	11	20	5	90	19	13
LXX								
Ge	58	12	69	160	2	1	1	–
Ex	99	1	64	105	1	1	–	–
Le	109	6	57	56	–	–	5	–
Nu	93	21	83	113	–	2	1	–
Dt	80	15	64	154	–	–	2	–
Pentateuch	439	55	337	588	3	4	9	–
Jo 1–12	28	3	43	33	1	–	1	1
Jo 13–24	9	3	16	38	–	–	–	–
Joshua	37	6	59	71	1	–	1	1
Jg Ru B	31	6	36	36	–	1	1	3
Jg Ru A	25	8	42	41	–	–	–	1
E. Kms	104	24	102	162	–	–	3	1
L. Kms	73	18	91	124	–	–	–	–
1 Chr	53	21	24	43	–	1	7	3
2 Chr	79	13	62	100	1	2	1	3
Chronicles	132	34	86	143	1	3	8	6
1 Esd (para- phrase)	18	5	19	46	–	4	1	1
2 Esd-Ne	32	9	33	31	–	–	2	4
Ps 1–77	17	4	22	105	–	–	–	–
Ps 77–151	23	8	20	120	–	–	–	–
Psalms	40	12	42	225	–	–	–	–
Pr	33	10	4	20	–	–	–	–
Eccl	20	2	9	12	–	–	2	–
Ca	–	7	–	1	–	–	1	2
Jb	31	2	3	16	–	2	–	1
Wi	11	2	2	1	–	3	1	–
Si	112	10	11	24	–	2	–	–

	Type 1 s.	Type 1 pl.	Type 2(a) s.	Type 2(a) pl.	Type 2(b) s.	Type 2(b) pl.	Type 3 s.	Type 3 pl.
Est	26	1	10	28	–	1	–	2
Jdt	38	7	57	68	2	–	–	–
To S	12	6	11	50	1	2	1	–
To B	16	2	4	37	–	–	–	–
Min. Proph.	20	9	36	110	–	–	–	–
Isa	67	9	26	75	1	6	–	1
Je α	38	4	35	73	–	–	1	–
Je β	28	5	44	102	–	1	1	–
Je γ	2	–	1	6	–	–	–	2
Ezk α	50	10	20	86	–	–	–	–
Ezk β	21	6	23	59	1	1	–	–
Da O′	35	3	19	56	–	1	–	–
Da θ	32	4	21	43	–	–	–	–
1 Mac	39	30	2	86	3	5	–	–
2–4 Mac	44	12	17	38	3	2	16	2
NT								
Mt. Mk	29	3	21	46	2	5	–	–
Lk	18	2	28	47	–	3	–	–
Ac	26	6	24	45	–	4	1	2
Jn	4	–	15	3	2	2	–	–
Jn. Epp	8	–	16	1	–	–	–	–
Rev	29	1	2	18	1	1	–	–
Ro. Co.	39	8	20	20	–	9	–	1
Ga. Th	12	2	3	9	–	1	1	1
Eph. Col. Ph	45	2	9	13	–	1	–	1
Past	21	5	1	7	–	2	–	–
Heb	13	1	2	7	–	–	–	–
1 Pt	9	–	2	1	–	–	–	–
Jas	7	–	–	1	–	–	–	–
2 Pt	2	1	–	–	–	–	–	–
Jude	1	–	1	3	–	–	–	–
T. Abr. A	17	1	13	18	–	2	–	–
B	4	3	3	3	–	2	–	–
Ps. Sol.	11	2	7	3	–	–	–	–

PERCENTAGE OF TYPE WITHIN EACH BOOK

	Type 1		*Type* 2(a)		*Type* 2(b)		*Type* 3	
	s.	pl.	s.	pl.	s.	pl.	s.	pl.
Papyrus iii/B.C.	10	1	8	23	10	32	13	3
Pap. ii–i/B.C.	12	6	6	10	2	46	10	7
LXX								
Ge	20	4	22	55	½	¼	¼	–
Ex	33	¼	23	39	¼	¼	–	–
Le	46	2	24	24	–	–	2	–
Nu	30	7	26	36	–	¾	¼	–
Dt	25	5	20	49	–	–	1	–
Pentateuch	30	4	25	40	¼	¼	¾	–
Jo 1–12	25	2	39	30	1	–	1	1
Jo 13–24	13	5	24	57	–	–	–	–
Joshua	22	3	33	40	1	–	½	½
Jg. Ru B	27	5	32	32	–	1	1	2
Jg. Ru A	21	7	36	36	–	–	–	1
E. Kms	26	6	26	41	–	–	¾	¼
L. Kms	24	6	30	40	–	–	–	–
1 Chr	35	14	15	28	–	–	5	2
2 Chr	30	5	23	40	½	¾	½	1¼
Chronicles	32	8	21	35	¼	¾	2	1
1 Esd (paraphrase)	19	6	20	47	–	5	1½	1½
2 Esd–Ne	29	8	30	28	–	–	2	4
Ps 1–77	11	3	15	71	–	–	–	–
Ps 77–151	13	5	12	70	–	–	–	–
Psalms	13	3	13	70	–	–	–	–
Pr	49	15	6	30	–	–	–	–
Eccl	44	4	20	27	–	–	4	1
Ca	–	70	–	10	–	–	10	20
Jb	56	4	5	29	–	4	–	2
Wi	55	10	10	5	–	15	5	–

	Type 1		Type 2(a)		Type 2(b)		Type 3	
	s.	pl.	s.	pl.	s.	pl.	s.	pl.
Si	70	6	7	15	–	1	–	–
Est	38	1	15	41	1	1	–	3
Jdt	22	4	33	40	1	–	–	–
To S	14	8	13	60	1	3	1	–
To B	27	4	6	63	–	–	–	–
Min. Proph.	11	5	21	63	–	–	–	–
Isa	37	5	14	40	$\frac{1}{2}$	3	–	$\frac{1}{2}$
Je α	26	3	22	48	–	–	1	–
Je β	15	$2\frac{1}{2}$	24	56	–	$\frac{1}{2}$	$\frac{1}{2}$	–
Je γ	20	–	10	60	–	–	–	20
Ezk α	30	6	12	51	–	–	–	–
Ezk β	20	$5\frac{1}{2}$	21	54	1	1	–	–
Da O′	30	$2\frac{1}{2}$	17	49	–	1	–	–
Da θ	32	4	21	43	–	–	–	–
1 Mac	23	1	18	52	2	3	–	–
2–4 Mac	33	9	13	28	2	2	12	2
NT								
Mt. Mk	27	3	20	43	2	5	–	–
Lk	18	2	28	47	–	3	–	–
Ac	25	5	23	44	–	3	1	1
Jn	15	–	59	11	7	7	–	–
Jn. Epp	32	–	64	4	–	–	–	–
Rev	57	2	3	35	2	2	–	–
Ro. Co	40	8	21	21	–	9	–	1
Ga. Th	41	7	10	31	–	$3\frac{3}{4}$	$3\frac{3}{4}$	$3\frac{3}{4}$
Eph. Col. Ph	63	3	13	18	–	1	–	1
Past	58	14	3	16	–	6	–	–
Heb	56	4	9	30	–	–	–	–
1 Pt	75	–	17	8	–	–	–	–
Jas	87	–	–	12	–	–	–	–
2 Pt. Jude	$37\frac{1}{2}$	$12\frac{1}{2}$	$12\frac{1}{2}$	$37\frac{1}{2}$	–	–	–	–
T. Abr. A	$33\frac{1}{2}$	2	$25\frac{1}{2}$	34	–	4	–	–
B	25	19	19	19	6	12	–	–
Ps. Sol.	48	9	30	13	–	–	–	–

CHAPTER FIFTEEN

ATTRIBUTIVE RELATIONSHIP: SUBSTANTIVES

§ 1. In the same case: Apposition [1]

A substantival attribute placed either before or after another noun, or a pers. pronoun, is said to be in apposition. This will occur with a proper noun, and the apposition then has the art. to distinguish that person from others of the same name: Ἰωάννης ὁ βαπτιστής, Σίμων ὁ Καναναῖος, Ἰάκωβος ὁ τοῦ Ἀλφαίου, Σαῦλος ὁ καὶ Παῦλος, ὁ βασιλεὺς Ἡρῴδης (or Ἡρῴδης ὁ βασιλεύς), Φίλιππος ὁ εὐαγγελιστής, Τιμόθεος ὁ συνεργός μου. The proper noun itself is generally anarthrous; and so the readings τῆς (SABD) Μαρίας τῆς μητρός (Ac 12¹²) and τὸν Ἰωάννην (D*) τὸν ἐπικληθέντα Μάρκον (12²⁵) are probably incorrect. There are some exceptions to the use of the art. with the apposition: Ac 7¹⁰ Φαραὼ βασιλέως Αἰγύπτου, 10⁶ Σίμωνι βυρσεῖ, 13¹ Μαναὴν Ἡρῴδου τοῦ τετραάρχου σύντροφος, 21¹⁶ Μνάσωνί τινι Κυπρίῳ. Col 1³ vl. ¹² vl. 2² 3¹⁷ ὁ θεὸς πατήρ [2], 1 Pt 5⁸ ὁ ἀντίδικος ὑμῶν διάβολος (ἀντιδ. adjectival?). The proper noun usually comes first; hence D corrects ἡ Μαγδαληνὴ Μαρία to Μαρία ἡ Μαγδ. Lk 24¹⁰. Sometimes ὁ (ἐπι)καλούμενος or ὁ καί c. gen. precedes the surname. The latter is rare in the nominative in pre-Christian papyri (Mayser I² 2, 69; II 1, 60ff; II 3, 56); instead ὃς καί. In rather formal wording, as in the opening of an epistle, κύριος or θεός will occur without art., followed by an anarthrous appositional phrase: Ro 1⁷ ἀπὸ θεοῦ πατρὸς ἡμῶν καὶ κύριος ..., Ph 3²⁰ κύριον Ἰησοῦν Χριστόν 1 Th 1¹ ἐν θεῷ πατρὶ καὶ κυρίῳ Ἰ. Χ., 1 Ti 1¹ θεοῦ σωτῆρος ἡμῶν. On Jn 8⁴⁴, see above p. 40, but note that to be predicative (*the devil is your father*) πατρός ought not to have the art.; τοῦ διαβόλου is therefore in apposition or else possessive genitive. A phrase in apposition with a pers. pronoun requires the art. in class. Greek: so Mk 7⁶ ὑμῶν τῶν ὑποκριτῶν, Lk 6²⁴ ὑμῖν τοῖς πλουσίοις, Ac 13³³ C² EHLP τοῖς τέκνοις αὐτῶν ἡμῶν.

---

[1] K-G I § 406, pp. 281ff. Mayser II 2, 103ff. Radermacher² 116.
[2] But variants make it easier; e.g. in Col 1³: τῷ πατρί D*G Chrys, καὶ πατρί SA.

§ 2. In a different case:

1. ADJECTIVAL GENITIVE[1]

I. *True Genitive*

This is a large subject, as the genitive is so hard worked a case in Greek. The adjectival is the commonest way the case is used, and Luke is particularly fond of it. The relationship expressed by the gen. is so vague that it is only by means of the context and wider considerations that it can be made definite. For practical purposes perhaps the only real division among the genitives is that between subjective and objective (Zerwick § 25). The sole question which the translator and exegete need ask is whether the relationship is directed outwards from the noun in the genitive to some other person or from some other person to the noun in the genitive; or, to put it differently, whether or not the action implied by the independent noun is carried out by the noun in the genitive. Obviously, ἡ πτῶσις αὐτῆς Mt 7²⁷ is subjective: the house *falls*; so is Ac 6¹ γογγυσμὸς τῶν Ἑλληνιστῶν: the Hellenists *murmur*; so also 2 Co 6⁷ *the armour of righteousness* is probably that which the divine righteousness provides.[2] Clearly οἱ εὐλογημένοι τοῦ πατρός μου and τὸν ἀγαπητόν μου, like the LXX ἐκλεκτοὺς κυρίου, are subjective. But Ph 1³ is quite ambiguous: ἐπὶ πάσῃ τῇ μνείᾳ ὑμῶν may be (a) subjective: *whenever you remember me*, or (b) objective: *whenever I think of you*.

(a) *Possessive Genitive.* In class. and Koine Greek the relationship of parents to children is expressed in this way, with or without υἱός (see above, pp. 168f): but in the latter case the phrase is ὁ τοῦ δεῖνος, contrary to class. usage which omits the second art. The frequent addition of υἱός is Semitic rather than typically Greek, and even in the papyri this and θυγάτηρ are added only for clarity (Mayser II 2, 9): Lk 3² Ἰωάννην τὸν Ζαχαρίου υἱόν. The only exception to the use of υἱοί with the sons of Zebedee (Mt 26³⁷ 27⁵⁶ Mk 10³⁵ Lk 5¹⁰) is Jn 21² οἱ τοῦ Z. ABL (SD οἱ υἱοὶ Z.). Figuratively υἱός is used with a noun in the genitive in order to express a certain quality. It

---

[1] K-G I § 414–421. Schwyzer II 89–137. Mayser II 2, 118ff. Eakin 335ff.

[2] Kittel WB, English translation, *Righteousness*, 1951, 53.

would seem to be a Semitism; it is rare in pre-Biblical Greek
and is there confined to such phrases as υἱὸς Ἑλλάδος *a son of
Greece*. It is very common in LXX: Ps 88²³ 2 Km 7¹⁰ 1 Mac
2⁴⁷ 4², and Hebrew uses the words *man, son, daughter, mother,
father, lord,* in this sense.[1] In the NT: Mk 3¹⁷ υἱοὶ βροντῆς
thunderbolts, Mt 5⁹· ⁴⁵ *sons of God*, 9¹⁵ בְּנֵי הַחֻפָּה *bridegroom's
friends*, 13³⁸ *men of the kingdom* . . . *of evil*, Lk 10⁶ *man of
peace*, 16⁸ *men of this age*, 20³⁶ *of the resurrection* (= those who
will rise), Jn 17¹² 2 Th 2³ Ap. Pet. 2 τῆς ἀπωλείας, Jn 8³⁹· ⁴⁴
Ga 3⁷ *children of Abraham*, Ac 13¹⁰ *of the Devil*, Eph 2² Col 3⁶
TR *of disobedience* (= disobedient), 1 Th 5⁵ υἱοὶ φωτός ἐστε καὶ
υἱοὶ ἡμέρας (and then without υἱοί), Ap. Pet. 3 Herm V. III 6, 1
υἱοὶ τῆς ἀνομίας, Ac 3²⁵ Ps. Sol. 17¹⁵ τῆς διαθήκης, Ac 4³⁶
υἱὸς παρακλήσεως (Bauer s.v. υἱός 1 c.δ). Vulg. inserts *filii*
in Heb 10³⁹ where Greek has simple gen. In the same sense
as υἱός we have τέκνον in Lk 7³⁵ Ga 4²⁸ Eph 2³ 1 Pt 1¹⁴ 2 Pt 2¹⁴
etc. In ecclesiastical Greek, e.g. Epiph. Haer. 43, 2.

(b) *Partitive Genitive*[2]. This is the gen. of a whole which
is divided. It is still in use in the Koine, but since class. times
it has been more and more displaced by the use of the prepositions ἀπό, ἐκ, ἐν [3]. This ἐν is rare in the papyri (Mayser II 2,
352f), and ἀπό is more frequent than ἐκ. This ἐκ is not
common in class. Greek but we do find μόνος ἐξ ἁπάντων.
Partitive ἀπό is even rarer there; it abounds in LXX and
prevails in MGr (Mayser II 2, 348f.; Johannessohn DGKPS 17).

There is a construction which is not widely acknowledged
in NT: the partitive ἀπό and ἐκ introducing a phrase which
can stand independently of a noun as subject or object of a
verb, with something like τινές suppressed, a substantival
phrase in fact.[4] It may be either subj. or obj.:—(a) subject: Mt
27⁹ ὃν ἐτιμήσαντο ἀπὸ υἱῶν Ἰσραήλ OT, Lk 8³⁵ D παραγενομένων
ἐκ τῆς πόλεως (sc. *some people from*), Jn 3²⁵ ἐγένετο ζήτησις
(sc. ἐν τοῖς) ἐκ τῶν μαθητῶν, 7⁴⁰ ἐκ τοῦ ὄχλου . . . ἔλεγον (vl.

---

[1] Thackeray OT Gr. 41f. Deissmann *Bibelstudien*, 1895, 162–166.
Johannessohn DGKPS 32. Lagrange *S. Matth.* 166.
[2] K-G I § 414, 5. Mayser II 2, 121ff.
[3] Esp. in LXX, through Heb. מִן partitive. E.g. Ex 9⁴· ⁶· ⁷ (οὐκ
ἐτελεύτησεν ἀπὸ πάντων τῶν κτηνῶν οὐδέν), 1 Mac 4¹⁵ ἔπεσαν ἐξ αὐτῶν εἰς
ἄνδρας τρισχιλίους.
[4] K-G I 345. Mayser II 2, 351f, 195f. Johannessohn DGKPS 18f.
Schwyzer II 102.

πολλοί, to improve), 16¹⁷ εἶπον ἐκ τῶν μαθητῶν *some of his disciples*, Ac 19³³ ἐκ δὲ τοῦ ὄχλου συνεβίβασαν (*some of the crowd*), 21¹⁶ συνῆλθον δὲ καὶ τῶν μαθητῶν (*some disciples*), Rev 11⁹ 15⁷ p⁴⁷ ἐκ τῶν τεσσάρων ἔδωκαν (*some of the four*). LXX 1 Km 14⁴⁵ 2 Km 14¹¹ τῆς τριχός, 4 Km 10²³ τῶν δούλων, 1 Mac 7³³ ἐξῆλθον ἀπὸ τῶν ἱερέων, 10³⁷ κατασταθήσεται ἐξ αὐτῶν (*let some of them be stationed*). (b) object : Mt 23³⁴, Mk 2²¹ *some of it*¹, 6⁴³ ἀπὸ τῶν ἰχθύων *some fish*, 12² ἀπὸ τῶν καρπῶν *some fruit*, 14²³ ἐξ αὐτοῦ (drink) *some of it*, Lk 11⁴⁹, 2 Jn⁴, Rev 2¹⁰, Herm. S. VIII 6, 5 ἐξ αὐτῶν, Mk 9³⁷ WΘ ἐκ τῶν τοιούτων παιδίων Lk 21¹⁶ θανατώσουσιν ἐξ ὑμῶν (*some of them*). LXX Ge 27²⁸ δῴη σοι ὁ θεὸς ἀπὸ τῆς δρόσου τοῦ (*may God give you some dew from heaven*), 2 Km 11¹⁷ ἔπεσαν ἐκ τοῦ λαοῦ (*some of the people fell*). This is a Bibl. Greek construction, not unknown but rare in class. Greek, really originating in LXX, and is parallel to similar constructions in Heb., Syriac and Arabic. Scribes felt the need to correct the construction in 1 Mac 6⁴⁸ καὶ ἐκ τῆς παρεμβολῆς τοῦ βασιλέως ἀνέβαινον A (SV οἱ δέ) *some soldiers of the king's army went up*. There is much further evidence : Ge 3¹² 4⁴ 33¹⁵ 45²³ Ex 17⁵ 1 Mac 8⁸.

With τις it is usually the simple genitive; but Ac 7⁵² Heb 1⁵·¹³ are interrogative τίς. Thus Mt 9³ τινες τῶν γραμματέων, Lk 7³⁶ τις τῶν Φαρισαίων. The exceptions are John's Gospel and the LXX (e.g. Ex 16²⁷ τινες ἐκ τοῦ λαοῦ). Partitive gen. without preposition appears to be the rule with ἕκαστος (e.g. Ro 14¹²), and usually so with εἷς (e.g. Mt 5²⁹·³⁰ 10⁴²)². Other exx. are: Mk 2¹⁶ οἱ γραμματεῖς τῶν Φαρισαίων (vl) *among?*, Lk 18¹¹ Rev 9²⁰ οἱ λοιποὶ τῶν ἀνθρώπων, Ro 15²⁶ τοὺς πτωχοὺς τῶν ἁγίων *among*. However, ἐκ is usually found with πᾶς (Lk 14³³, Le 21²¹ πᾶς ἐξ ὑμῶν) in spite of the class. πᾶς Ἑλλήνων, and with τίς ³ : Mt 6²⁷ τίς ἐξ ὑμῶν, 27²¹ τίνα ἀπὸ τῶν δύο (syrˢⁱⁿ only τίνα),

---

¹ The best reading from a syntax point of view in Mk 2²¹ is εἰ δὲ μή, αἴρει ἀπ' αὐτοῦ (*some of it*) τὸ πλήρωμα τὸ καινὸν (*the new fulness*) ἀπὸ τοῦ παλαιοῦ (*namely, some of the old*). The prepositional phrase immediately follows the verb, which is good Bibl. Greek word-order. The MS variants are probably afterthoughts to remove the Aramaic construction of a proleptic pronoun followed by a noun. (For Proleptic Pronouns, see p. 41. See also Black AAGA² 37, 251; Moulton-Howard 461.) The suggestion is given to me verbally by Dr. G. D. Kilpatrick, and adopted by him in the (privately circulated) *Mark: a Greek-English Diglot for the use of Translators*, B. and F.B.S., 1958, 6.

² But ἐκ in LXX Ge 3²² εἷς ἐξ ἡμῶν, etc., Mt 10²⁹ 18¹² etc.

³ But gen. only in Ac 7⁵² Heb 1⁵·¹³. Some texts are uncertain: Mt 22²⁸ τίνος τῶν ἑπτά, Mk 12²³ τίνος αὐτῶν (Δ c k om αὐτῶν), Lk 7⁴² τίς αὐτῶν (D om αὐτῶν), 14⁵ τίνος ὑμῶν (D ἐξ ὑμῶν), 20³³ τίνος αὐτῶν (S* e ff² om αὐτῶν).

Lk 11¹⁵ Jas 2¹⁶. Against the apparent Semitism (בְּ or לְ, as in Le 11³·²⁶) we must set the class. precedent for a partitive ἐν, as in Ac 5³⁴ τις ἐν τῷ συνεδρίῳ (D ἐκ), 1 Co 15¹², Jas 5¹³·¹⁴·¹⁹ τις (τινες) ἐν ὑμῖν. Probably we have a true Semitism from the Hebrew superlative in Rev 5¹¹ μυριάδες μυριάδων καὶ χιλιάδες χιλιάδων (from 1 Enoch: Rev ICC in loc.). The partitive gen. may be used predicatively as well as attributively: Lk 22⁵⁸ Jn 18¹⁷ 1 Co 12¹⁵·¹⁶ ἐκ, Ac 21¹⁶ 1 Ti 1²⁰ (ὧν ἐστιν 'Υμέναιος). It is debatable whether we have partitive gen. in Col 1¹⁵ (πρωτότοκος πάσης κτίσεως) and Rev 3¹⁴ (ἡ ἀρχὴ τῆς κτίσεως) = among, or whether the idea is not rather that of rule and supremacy.

We have πάντων in Mk 12²⁸ without preposition: ποία ἐστὶν ἐντολὴ πρώτη πάντων (only πασῶν M*; om πάντων DW lat etc.); πάντων however may belong to the next verse: πάντων πρῶτον. ῎Ακουε Ἰσραήλ (Euseb. minusc.). Without preposition are also the Hebraic superlative constructions τὰ ἅγια τῶν ἁγίων and εἰς τοὺς αἰῶνας τῶν αἰώνων.

After an indication of quality we have one NT example of a phenomenon which has class. precedent, namely the assimilation of gender and number of a neuter substantival adj. to that of its dependent gen.; this occurs in Lk 19⁸ τὰ ἡμίσεια τῶν ὑπαρχόντων (for ἥμισυ, sc. μέρος), which reminds us of the class. ἡ ἡμίσεια τῆς γῆς (K–G I 279; Mayser II 2, 123; Abel § 44 d). Otherwise the neuter adj. is properly used: Mk 6²³ ἕως ἡμίσους τῆς βασιλείας, LXX Est 5³, Rev 11¹³ τὸ δέκατον τῆς πόλεως, 12¹⁴ ἥμισυ καιροῦ.

The geographic gen. is partitive. It indicates the country within which a town lies and is class. and Koine. We may translate *in*. Mt 21¹¹ Mk 1⁹ Ναζαρὲθ τῆς Γαλιλαίας, Jn 2¹ Κανᾶ τῆς Γαλιλαίας, Ac 16¹² ἥτις ἐστιν πρώτη μερίδος τῆς Μακεδονίας πόλις = *a city in*, Ac 22³, ἐν Ταρσῷ τῆς Κιλικίας (Mayser II 2, 126; K–G I, 334).

(c) *Objective and subjective genitive.*[1] A noun in the gen. may be the object of the action implied in the noun on which it depends. There is much ambiguity here in NT interpretation. Often a gen. might equally well be subjective or objective: it is moreover important not to sacrifice fullness of interpretation to an over precise analysis of syntax. There is no reason why a gen. in the author's mind may not have been both subjective and objective. *The love of Christ constrains us* is not to be so strictly analysed, if the author thought of Christ's love to us and our love to him as a compelling force.[2] But it is always an

---

[1] K-G I 335ff.   Mayser II 129.   [2] Zerwick § 25.

objective gen. which depends on *gospel* in the following instances :
the good news *about* τῆς βασιλείας Mt 4²³ etc. (which is the same
thing as the dir. obj. in Lk 8¹ εὐαγγελίζεσθαι τὴν βασιλείαν),
about ᾽Ιησοῦ Χριστοῦ Mk 1¹, *about* τοῦ Χριστοῦ 1 Co 9¹² (= dir.
obj. in Ac 5⁴²). It may be indirect object : Ga 2⁷ τὸ εὐαγγέλιον
τῆς ἀκροβυστίας, *good news for the uncircumcised* (like the indir.
obj. in Ac 14²¹ εὐαγγελίζεσθαι τὴν πόλιν). Also indirectly
objective are the following expressions : Ro 3²² Jas 2¹ etc.
πίστις ᾽Ιησοῦ Χ. (but πίστις εἰς τὸν κύριον ᾽Ι. Χ. Ac 20²¹ 24²⁴
etc., and ἐν Χ. ᾽Ι Col 1⁴, especially where there is close proximity
with a subjective genitive, e.g. 1 Th 1⁸ ἡ πίστις ὑμῶν ἡ πρὸς τὸν
θεόν, Col 2⁵ ἡ εἰς Χριστὸν πίστις ὑμῶν), ὑπακοὴ τοῦ Χριστοῦ or
τῆς πίστεως or τῆς ἀληθείας (Ro 1⁵ 2 Co 10⁵ 1 Pt 1²² etc.),
which are parallel to the indir. obj. with the verb in Ac 6⁷
ὑπήκοον τῇ πίστει. But 2 Co 7¹⁵ πάντων ὑμῶν is subjective.
Lk 4¹⁹ LXX ἐνιαυτὸν κυρίου δεκτόν possessive? But Moule, 40,
suggests that it is tinged with the subjective idea : *the year when
the Lord will accept* (man).

Either subjective or objective or both may be phrases like πίστις
᾽Ιησοῦ Χριστοῦ Ro 3²², ἀγάπη τοῦ θεοῦ (Χριστοῦ) Ro 8³⁵ 2 Co 5¹⁴ (subj.)
Lk 11⁴² 2 Th 3⁵ (obj.).   But δικαιοσύνη τοῦ θεοῦ Ro 1¹⁷ 3²², τῆς πίστεως
4¹¹·¹³, indicates the source, and is therefore subjective, as shown by the
phrases ἡ ἐκ θεοῦ δικαιοσύνη Ph 3⁹, ἡ ἐκ πίστεως Ro 9³⁰ and ἡ διὰ
πίστεως δικαιοσύνη Ph 3⁹.   Actually Ro 3⁵ (Ps 97 (98)²) is more like a
possessive gen. : *the justice which God dispenses.*   Other instances of a
subjective gen. of origin or cause are Ro 1¹ 15¹⁶ εὐαγγέλιον τοῦ θεοῦ
(since the obj. is said to be περὶ τοῦ υἱοῦ αὐτοῦ ³), and the phrase τὸ
εὐαγγέλιόν μου (ἡμῶν) where the gen. is the preacher, although κατά
also occurs for this in the titles (Ro 2¹⁶ 16²⁵ 2 Co 4³ 1 Th 1⁵ 2 Th 2¹⁴
2 Ti 2⁸).   That is doubtless the way to regard Mk 1⁴ βάπτισμα μετανοίας ;
it does not lead to, but springs from, repentance. So also Col 2²
πληροφορία τῆς συνέσεως : *conviction which is the result of insight* (or
intelligence) ; 1 Th 1³ τῆς ὑπομονῆς τῆς ἐλπίδος : *the sustaining patience
which hope brings* ; it is parallel to τοῦ ἔργου τῆς πίστεως and τοῦ κόπου
τῆς ἀγάπης, *work done from faith and love.*
        It is not easy to decide in 2 Co 13¹³ (ἡ κοινωνία τοῦ ἁγίου πνεύματος)
between subjective and objective (Hauck in Kittel WB, s.v. κοινωνία).
In 1 Co 2¹³ οὐκ ἐν διδακτοῖς ἀνθρωπίνης σοφίας λόγοις ἀλλ᾽ ἐν διδακτοῖς
πνεύματος the context requires subjective genitive : *which human wisdom
teaches* (cp. Jn 6⁴⁵ Isa 54¹³) ; but in 1 Mac 4⁷ διδακτοὶ πολέμου is the
very reverse, *masters of warfare*, unless it means *taught by war.*
        The following are objective genitive : Mt 13¹⁸·³⁶ *the parable about*,
24⁶ ἀκοὰς πολέμων *about wars* (Lk 21⁹ ἀκούσητε πολέμους), Mk 6⁷ etc.
ἐξουσία c. gen. = *authority over* (Foerster in Kittel WB II 563), Jn 7¹³

20¹⁹ *for fear of*, Ac 4⁹ εὐεργεσία ἀνθρώπου *help given to a sick man* (NEB), Ro 2⁷ ὑπομονὴ ἔργου ἀγαθοῦ *perseverence in* (2 Th 3⁵ ὑπομονὴ τοῦ Χριστοῦ *steadfast loyalty to Christ*? or subjective?), 7² νόμος τοῦ ἀνδρός *the law about the husband* (Le 14² ὁ νόμος τοῦ λεπροῦ *the law about the leper*; class. ὁ νόμος τῆς βλαπῆς; Abel § 44 g), 1 Co 1¹⁸ ὁ λόγος τοῦ σταύρου, 1 Pt 3¹⁴ φόβον αὐτῶν (context decides for objective: *fear of them*), Col. 3¹⁴ σύνδεσμος τῆς τελειότητος *the bond producing perfection*, Heb 9⁸ τὴν τῶν ἁγίων ὁδον, 10¹⁹ εἰς τὴν εἴσοδον τῶν ἁγίων *for entering the Holy Place* (Michaelis in Kittel WB V 109. 54ff.)   This is perhaps the explanation of ὁδος ἐθνῶν (*a way leading to*) Mt 10⁵; ὁδον θαλάσσης Mt 4¹⁵; ἡ θύρα τῶν προβάτων Jn 10⁷ (or subjective: *where the sheep enter*?); ἡ θύρα πίστεως Ac 14²⁷ (*leading to faith*? obj., or *where faith enters*? subj.); ἡ θύρα τοῦ λόγου Col 4³ (same); μετοικεσία Βαβυλῶνος Mt 1¹¹· ¹² *leading to*; ἡ διασπορὰ τῶν Ἑλλήνων Jn 7³⁵; κῶμαι Καισαρίας Mk 8²⁷ (or possessive).   The question of Semitism may be raised in view of LXX Ge 3²⁴ ἡ ὁδος τοῦ ξύλου τῆς ζωῆς *leading to*, Ps 44 (43)²² πρόβατα σφαγῆς = צֹאן טִבְחָה *destined for* (Ro 8³⁶), Am 8¹⁰ πένθος ἀγαπητοῦ אֵבֶל יָחִיד *towards, concerning*.   Moreover, there seems to be a gen. of place—where: Col 1²⁰ αἵματος σταυροῦ (blood) *shed on the cross*, 2 Co 11²⁶ κινδύνοις ποτάμων, ληστῶν *in rivers, among robbers*; and a gen. of time duration: Lk 2⁴⁴ ἦλθον ἡμέρας ὁδόν *a day's journey* (class.).

(*d*) *Genitive of relationship.* Often θεοῦ and Χριστοῦ in Paul are used to express an ill-defined relationship which may be called " mystical " (Deissmann *Paulus*, 1925, 126f), especially after ἐκκλησία, since it seems to be interchangeable with Deissmann's " in "-formula: see especially 1 Th 2¹⁴ *the churches OF God which are in Judea IN Christ Jesus*, Ga 1²² *IN Christ*, Ro 16¹⁶ αἱ ἐκκλησίαι πᾶσαι τοῦ Χριστοῦ *OF Christ*.   Indeed, so rich is Paul's compression of language with genitives that the attempt to define too narrowly the various types of genitive is vain; they all denote a relationship which is amplified by the context.   We might even be tempted to borrow Paul's own comprehensive way of speech and render δικαιοσύνη θεοῦ simply *divine grace*.¹   Perhaps some genitives which we have taken as subjective or objective may come under this " mystical" genitive: 2 Th 3⁵ τὴν ὑπομονὴν τοῦ Χριστοῦ *steadfast loyalty in the Body of Christ*; Ro 3²²· ²⁶ *faith exercised within the Body*.

(*e*) *Genitive of quality.*²   This is a feature of Biblical Greek which has been handed down to MGr, e.g. καράβι τοῦ πολέμου

---

¹ Zerwick § 28: genetivus " generaliter " determinans.
² Schwyzer II 122. Mayser II 2, 135f; II 3, 168. Johannessohn DGKPS 27f. Radermacher² 108f. Nachmanson, Eranos 9, 63ff. Wackernagel, *Mélanges de Saussure* 135.

battleship. With the help of Heb. influence the Bibl. Greek gen. often provides an attribute which normally would be supplied by an adj. The adj. was nearly non-existent in Heb., and so the LXX introduces such phenomena as πύργος ἰσχύος Ps 60 (61)⁴ (from מִגְדַּל־עֹז) and ἡ στολὴ τοῦ ἁγίου Ex 29²⁹ (from בִּגְדֵי הַקֹּדֶשׁ). There may be class. parallels, but they are poetic (Eurip. *Bacch*. 389 ὁ τᾶς ἡσυχίας βίοτος = ἥσυχος βίοτος: Jebb's note. Soph. *Ajax* 464f. K–G I 264). There may be Koine parallels, but they are few.¹

Combinations with σῶμα are especially common in Paul: Ro 6⁶ 7²⁴ τοῦ θανάτου (= adj. θνητός in 6¹² 8¹¹), Ph 3²¹ Col 1²² 2¹¹; with ἡμέρα Ro 2⁵ 2 Co 6² 1 Pt 2¹². Other exx. Mt 5²² etc. γέεννα τοῦ πυρός, Mk 1⁴ etc. βάπτισμα μετανοίας (?), Lk 2¹⁴ ἐν ἀνθρώποις εὐδοκίας S*AB*DW *among approval-men* (i.e. "among men of whom God approves"); the Heb. would be בְּנֵי רְצוֹנוֹ (εὐδοκία = רְצוֹנוֹ, as in Si 15¹⁵ 39¹⁸); supply αὐτοῦ as in the opposite instance in Eph. 2³ (τέκνα ὀργῆς).² Lk 4²² οἱ λόγοι τῆς χάριτος, 16⁸ οἰκονόμος τῆς ἀδικίας, ⁹ ὁ μαμωνᾶς τῆς ἀδικίας (= ὁ ἄδικος μαμωνᾶς 16¹¹), 18⁶ κριτὴς τῆς ἀδικίας, Ac 1¹⁸ 2 Pt 2¹⁵ μισθὸς (τῆς) ἀδικίας, Ac 6¹¹ ῥήματα βλασφημίας S*D (Rev 13¹ 17³ ὀνόματα βλασφημίας), 7³⁰ ἐν φλογὶ πυρός (2 Th 1⁸ ἐν πυρὶ φλογός) = LXX Ex 3² ἐν πυρὶ φλογός, 8²³ χολὴ πικρίας, 9¹⁵ σκεῦος ἐκλογῆς (Ro 9²²· ²³ σκεύη ὀργῆς . . . ἐλέους), Ro 1²⁶ πάθη ἀτιμίας, 6⁴ ἐν καινότητι ζωῆς *new life*, 7⁶ ἐν καινότητι πνεύματος καὶ οὐ παλαιότητι γράμματος *in a new spirit and not according to an out-of-date literalness*, 8²¹ δουλείας τῆς φθορᾶς, Col 1⁵ λόγῳ τῆς ἀληθείας τοῦ εὐαγγελίου *of the true Gospel* (or apposition: *the Truth which is the Gospel*?), 2 Ti 4⁸ ὁ τῆς δικαιοσύνης στέφανος (or apposition?), 1 Pt 1⁴ τέκνα ὑπακοῆς, 5⁴ τῆς δόξης στέφανον, Heb 3¹² καρδία πονηρὰ ἀπιστίας, 5¹³ ἄπειρος λόγου δικαιοσύνης *incapable of understanding correct speech* (Schrenk in Kittel WB II 200⁵ᶠ), 12¹⁵ ῥίζα πικρίας, Jas 1¹² Rev 2¹⁰ στέφανον τῆς ζωῆς (or appositive: *that crown which is life*), Jas 1²⁵ ἀκροατὴς ἐπιλησμονῆς, 2⁴ κριταὶ διαλογισμῶν πονηρῶν *judge by false standards* (*NEB*) (better than Schrenk op. cit. II 98; Büchsel in Kittel WB III 944 n. 3), 1 Jn 2¹⁶ ἡ ἐπιθυμία τῆς σαρκός (or subjective?), Rev 14¹⁰ etc. ὁ οἶνος τοῦ θυμοῦ LXX Ezk 14⁴ 44¹² κόλασις (τῆς) ἀδικίας. On the Heb. pattern, ἡμέρα is used in this connection: Mt 10¹⁵ κρίσεως, Lk 1⁸⁰ ἀναδείξεως, Ro 2⁵ ὀργῆς, 1 Pt 2¹² ἐπισκοπῆς, LXX Ezk 22²⁴ (= בְּיוֹם זַעַם), Soph 2³.

---

¹ P. Tebt. 105 (ii/в.с.) ἀκίνδυνος παντὸς κινδύνου ἀνυπόλογον πάσης φθορᾶς, and ἀνυπεύθονοι παντὸς ἐπιτίμου. Etc. See Moulton Einl. 113 n. 1. The gen. of quality may be used predicatively however, as in normal Greek: ἦν ἐτῶν δώδεκα Mk 5⁴² Lk 2⁴² (not D). See Preisigke, s.v. ἔτος.

² See the discussion by Schrenk in Kittel WB II 245–8; C. H. Huntzinger, *ZNW* 44, 85ff.

A further Semitism [1] is the addition of the personal (or demonstrative) pronoun to the gen. of quality when properly it belongs to the first noun, e.g. his throne of glory (= *his glorious throne*) becomes " the throne of his glory " (Mt 19²⁸); this body of death (= *this dead body*) becomes " the body of this death " (Ro 7²⁴), our body of humiliation (= *our humble body*) becomes " the body of our humiliation " (Ph 3²¹); his son of love (= *his beloved son*) becomes ὁ υἱὸς τῆς ἀγάπης αὐτοῦ (Col 1¹³);[2] his word of power (= *his powerful word*) becomes " the word of his power " (Heb 1³); his plague of death (= *his mortal wound*) becomes " the plague of his death " (Rev 13³). This is because the Semitic rule adds the suffix in composite expressions to the second member, although the suffix pertains to the whole phrase.

(*f*) *Genitivus materiae, and epexegeticus.*[3] The appositive genitive. This gen. represents more than an adj.; it represents a second noun in apposition to the first, or indicates the material of which the first noun consists. It conforms to class. and Koine usage but is incidentally Hebraic: cp. class. πλοῖα σίτου, papyri οἴνου κεράμια and Heb. נֵבֶל־יַיִן (ἀσκὸς οἴνου) Ge 40¹⁶ 1 Sam 10³.

Mt 12³⁹ Lk 11²⁹ τὸ σημεῖον Ἰωνᾶ *the sign which was Jonah*, Mt 24³⁰ ambiguous, either *the sign which is the S.M.* (appos.), or *the sign which the S.M. will give* (possess.), see Feuillet in Rev. Bibl. 56, 1946, 354; very prevalent in Mark:—1⁴ *baptism involving repentance?*, ²⁸ *the region Galilee*, 4³¹ *a grain consisting of mustard seed*, ³⁷ *a storm involving wind*, 5¹¹ *a herd consisting of swine*, ²⁵·²⁹ *a fount containing blood*, 8⁸·²⁰ *an abundance consisting of broken pieces*, ¹⁵ *leaven consisting of the Pharisees*, 9⁴¹ *a cup containing water*, 10¹⁴ τῶν γὰρ τοιούτων ἐστὶν ἡ βασιλεία τοῦ θεοῦ not necessarily possessive (as Mt 18³ and Jn 3³·⁵ understood it); but *consists of such*; children are the very nature of the kingdom.   14³ ἀλάβαστρον μύρου, ¹³ κεράμιον ὕδατος, 15²⁶ *an inscription consisting of his accusation*, Jn 2²¹ τοῦ ναοῦ τοῦ σώματος αὐτοῦ, Ac 2³⁸ the gift which *is* the Spirit, Ro 4¹¹ σημεῖον περιτομῆς (-μήν is a correction by AC*) which *is* circumcision, 5¹⁸ justification which *is* life (Zerwick § 33), 2 Co 3³ ἐν πλαξὶν καρδίας σαρκίναις FK lat syrᵖ arm Iren Orig Eus (rest καρδίαις), 5¹ ἡ οἰκία τοῦ σκήνους, ⁵ τὸν ἀρραβῶνα τοῦ πνεύματος *the guarantee consisting of the Spirit* (cp. 1²²), Ga 5⁵ either (appos.) *the*

---

[1] Zerwick § 30.

[2] Which makes it more likely that ὁ υἱὸς ὁ ἀγαπητός is *beloved son*, not *only son*, being a parallel phrase.

[3] K-G I 333. Mayser II 2, 122f. NT examples in U. Holzmeister, *Verb. Dom.* 25, 1947, 112–117.

thing hoped for, which is righteousness (as ICC Ga p. 279) or (subj. gen.)
the thing which the righteous hope for, Eph 1¹⁴ εἰς ἀπολύτρωσιν τῆς
περιποιήσεως: either (appos.) *till our redemption which is our purchase
by God* (or *which is our possession,* if active), or (obj. gen.) *till the redemption
of those whom God has acquired* (interpreting abstract noun by concrete),
2¹⁴ τὸ μεσότοιχον τοῦ φραγμοῦ, 4⁹ τὰ κατώτερα τῆς γῆς: may be partitive,
or appositive (Zerwick § 33) *the lower regions, that is, the earth* (it might
also be comparative gen.: regions lower *than* the earth; Büchsel in Kittel
WB III 641f), Col 2² πλοῦτος τῆς πληροφορίας *a wealth consisting of
conviction,* Heb 6¹ θεμέλιον ... μετανοίας, Jas 3¹⁸ καρπὸς δικαιοσύνης
the harvest of a life devoted to the will of God (Kittel WB II 203, ET), cp.
Pr 3⁹ 11³⁰ Am 6¹², Rev 14¹⁸ the grapes *which are* the earth (Zerwick § 33).
LXX Isa 38¹⁴ τὸ ὕψος τοῦ οὐρανοῦ.

The gen. with πόλις, of city-names, which is like Latin, occurs almost
only in poetry in class. Greek; it has one example in Ptol. papyri (Mayser
II 2, 117) but appears more frequently in later Greek, and is attested
only at 2 Pt 2⁶ for certain: πόλεις Σοδόμων καὶ Γομόρρας, because
πόλεως Θυατείρων may be gen. of πόλις Θυάτειρα (Ac 16¹⁴). However,
names of festivals with gen.: Jn 13¹ (Ex 34²⁵) τῆς ἑορτῆς τοῦ πάσχα,
7² (Dt 31¹¹) τῆς σκηνοπηγίας, Lk 22¹ (Dt 16¹⁶) τῶν ἀζύμων, class. Greek.

II. *Ablatival Genitive* (" Genitivus separationis ").

For replacing of this by means of ἀπό and ἐκ, see below
pp. 235f.

(*a*) *With adjectives and adverbs* (much rarer now than in
class. Greek, and κοινός and ἴδιος are never used with gen.):

(i) with adjectives having the idea of sharing: Mt 23³⁰ 1 Co 10¹⁸. ²⁰
Heb 10³³ substantival κοινωνός c. gen. of person (*an associate of*). 1 Pt
5¹ 2 Pt 1⁴ Paul: (συγ-)κοινωνός c. gen. of thing. Eph 3⁶ συνκληρονόμα
... συμμέτοχα τῆς εὐαγγελίας. Ro 8²⁹ σύμμορφος τῆς εἰκόνος. Heb 1⁹
OT μέτοχος.

(ii) adjectives of fullness and emptiness: Mt 23²⁸ etc. μεστός,
Lk 4¹ etc. πλήρης (κενός and ἐνδεής c. gen. never, although κένος ἀπό
in Herm.) LXX Johannessohn DGKPS 43.

(iii) adjectives of worthiness and guilt: Mt 3⁸ 1 Co 6² etc. (ἀν-)
ἄξιος. With ἔνοχος LXX has gen. and dat. (Johannessohn DGKPS 43).
Mt 26⁶⁶ etc. Ge 26¹¹ Isa 54¹⁷ Si prol⁹ (dat. Jb 15⁵).

(iv) adjectives of strangeness (class.): Eph 2¹² ξένος. Jas 1¹³
ἀπείραστος *inexperienced in* (class. ἀπείρατος; for pap. Moulton Einl.
113 n.); but this may not be its meaning here. 2 Pt 2¹⁴ ἀκατάπαυστος
ἁμαρτίας *not ceasing from sin* (but vl.-παστος perhaps *unfed*). Paul
has created the phrase ἄνομος θεοῦ—ἔννομος Χριστοῦ (1 Co 9²¹) [1].
The following always have ἀπό: Mt 27²⁴ ἀθῷος, Ac 20²⁶ καθαρός (Bauer
s.v., Mayser II 2, 353, 570), Ro 7³ ἐλεύθερος *independent of* (pap. in
Preisigke Arch. f. P. III 419³¹ vi/A.D. (ἐκ in 1 Co 9¹⁹), Jas 1²⁷ (CP ἐκ)

---

[1] The nearest parallels are Soph. Ant. 369, Eurip. Med. 737, and MGr
ἄφοβος τοῦ θεοῦ (Thumb² § 45, 3).

ἄσπιλος. For LXX see Johannessohn DGPS 282. Very rare is ὅμοιος ὑμῶν Jn 8⁵⁵ SCLX (ὑμῖν ABDW); it is invariably the dat. (9⁹, 1 Jn 3² etc.); Barn 10³ ὅμοιοι χοίρων, Did. 3¹ ὁμοίους ἐκείνου, Aelian Hist. An VIII 1 (K–G I 413). Latin infl?. The gen. with ὅμοιος in LXX Isa 13⁴ may not be an instance: φωνή ... ὁμοία ἐθνῶν πολλῶν *a voice like [the voice] of a great multitude.*

(v) adverbs. Unlike LXX (Ge 45¹⁰ and often), ἐγγύς ¹ never has gen. (Johann. DGKPS 43): dat. Ac 9³⁸ 27⁸? Mt 4²⁵ etc. πέραν, 5⁴³ etc. ὁ πλησίον, 21³⁹ etc. ἔξω, 23²⁵ τὸ ἔξωθεν τοῦ ποτηρίου, Mk 15¹⁶ ἔσω τῆς αὐλῆς *further into the palace* (DP ἔσω εἰς τὴν αὐλήν), Lk 7⁶ SD μακράν (ABCL μ. ἀπό), 8²⁶ ἀντιπέρα, 17²¹ ἐντός, Jn 4⁵ πλησίον, 1 Co 6¹⁸ etc. ἐκτός, 2 Co 10¹⁶ ὑπερέκεινα, Ph 2²⁷ παραπλήσιον (vl. dat.). Also see pp. 276ff.

(b) *Genitive of comparison.* In the latter part of the class. period it was still being used much more often then ἤ. But as in class. Greek and pap. (Mayser II 2, 140ff), ἤ is used chiefly in instances where the gen. would not have been sufficiently clear: Mt 10¹⁵ 19²⁴ Ac 4¹⁹ ὑμῶν μᾶλλον ἤ τοῦ θεοῦ, 5²⁹ 20³⁵ Ro 13¹¹ 1 Ti 1⁴ ἐκζητήσεις παρέχουσιν μᾶλλον ἤ οἰκοδομίαν θεοῦ, 2 Ti 3⁴ φιλήδονοι μᾶλλον ἤ φιλόθεοι. But sometimes there is ἤ without such good reason: Jn 3¹⁹ 4¹ 1 Co 14⁵ 1 Jn 4⁴.

The class. gen. of comparison ² occurs still in e.g. Mt 3¹¹ ἰσχυρότερός μου, Lk 12⁷ πολλῶν στρουθίων διαφέρετε, Ac 23¹³. ²¹ 24¹¹ 25⁶ πλείων c. gen., Mk 14⁵ 1 Co 15⁶ ἐπάνω (= πλείων in colloqu. Greek) c. gen., 1 Ti 5⁹ ἔλαττον c. gen. There is an abbreviated comparison, omitting a gen. art (Mt 5²⁰ ἐὰν μὴ περισσεύσῃ ἡ δικαιοσύνη ὑμῶν πλεῖον τῶν γραμματέων, Ac 4²² ἐτῶν ... ἦν πλειόνων τεσσεράκοντα: *of more years* (gen. of definition) *than forty* (gen. of comp., indeclinable), see Moule 42), which can cause ambiguity at times: Jn 5³⁶ ἐγὼ ἔχω τὴν μαρτυρίαν μείζω τοῦ Ἰωάννου (*greater than John had* or *greater than John*), 21¹⁵ ἀγαπᾷς με πλέον τούτων (*more than these* or *more than these do*). The NT uses παρά and ὑπέρ in place of both gen. and ἤ. There are a few class. exx. (ὑπέρ rarer than παρά), and in MGr παρά or ἀπό is the regular substitute for gen. of comp. Lk 3¹³ πλέον παρὰ τὸ διατεταγμένον, 16⁸ φρονιμώτερον ὑπέρ, 18¹⁴ D μᾶλλον παρ' ἐκεῖνον (SBL om μ.; W ἤ ἐκεῖνος), Jn 12⁴³ μᾶλλον ὑπέρ (ABD ἤπερ), Heb 4¹² Barn 5⁹ ὑπέρ. LXX Ge 49¹² ὑπέρ and ἤ together (Johannessohn DGKPS 45).

---

¹ K-G I 352, 5. Meisterhans-Schwyzer 213, 11. Mayser II 2, 528. Radermacher² 144.

² What is not class. is πρῶτός μου, πρῶτον ὑμῶν Jn 1¹⁵. ³⁰, because πρότερος would occur here.

III. *Position of Attributive and Partitive Genitive.*[1]

The attributive gen. very rarely stands first either in class. or Koine Greek, but it does so, e.g. in Mt 1[18] τοῦ 'Ιησοῦ Χ. ἡ γένεσις, obviously for emphasis on Jesus. The usual order in class. Greek was either (a) οἱ τῆς χώρας νόμοι, or (b) οἱ νόμοι οἱ τῆς χώρας. But increasingly more common in Hell. Greek, especially in NT, was (c) οἱ νόμοι τῆς χώρας. Mayser's figures for the pre-Christian papyri [2] are:

	(a)	(c)	Proportion		(a)	(c)	Proportion
iii/B.C.	32	44	3 : 4	ii–i/B.C.	45	94	1 : 2

It is doubtful whether any LXX books have a large proportion of (a) and (b), whereas in the first two chapters of Ge (c) occurs at 1[10. 14. 17. 26. 28. 30] 2[9. 12. 18. 18. 19. 19. 20]. In the pap. (b) is extremely rare except in the attribute of proper nouns (e.g. Μαρία ἡ τοῦ 'Ιακώβου in NT). In Mk the relative position of the articular noun and its gen. is striking: it is almost invariably position (c), never (a) as is regular in the papyri; and (b) occurs twice with personal relationship and once (11[30]) τὸ βάπτισμα τὸ 'Ιωάννου. Thus, possessive: 2 (b): 35 (c), objective 0 (b): 5 (c), subjective 1 (b): 4 (c), content 0 (b): 5 (c), partitive 0 (b): 7 (c). In any case, the partitive gen. (as in class. Greek) must take this position, outside the art. and noun, either before or after, without repetition of the art. In the rest of NT, although (b) is still infrequent, (a) is more common than in Mark: e.g.

(a)	Jn 18[10] BAC 2 Co 8[8. 19] (ten in Paul), 1 Pt 3[1] 4[17] 5[1. 1] 2 Pt 1[8] 2[7] 3[2]
(b)	Jn 6[33] SD ὁ ἄρτος ὁ τοῦ θεοῦ, 7[23] S ὁ νόμος ὁ Μ., Ac 15[1] τῷ ἔθει τῷ Μωϋσέως (DEHLP om 2nd τῷ)[3], 1 Co 1[18] ὁ λόγος ὁ τοῦ σταυροῦ, 2 Co 4[11] ἡ ζωὴ ἡ (p[46]) τοῦ (but 4[10] ἡ ζ. τοῦ), Ti 2[10] τὴν διδασκαλίαν τὴν τοῦ σωτῆρος . . .

---

[1] K-G I 617. 3.   Mayser II 2, 143ff.

[2] This is based on the following for iii/B.C.: P. Hib. nos. 27–121; Zen. P. I and II, nos. 59001–59297; ii–i/B.C. UPZ I; P. Teb. nos. 5–124.

[3] But with Μωϋσέως the position is that of (c), i.e. anarthrous: Mk 12[26] Lk 2[22] 24[44] Ac 13[39] 15[5] 28[23].

A frequent construction is the appearance, as a kind of after-thought, of the art. with an attribute after an anarthrous noun: Ac 1¹² ἀπὸ ὄρους τοῦ καλουμένου ἐλαιῶνος, 26¹² καὶ ἐπιτροπῆς τῶν ἀρχιερέων, Jas 1²⁵ εἰς νόμον τέλειον τὸν τῆς ἐλευθερίας.

IV. *The Joining together of several different Genitives*

Characteristic of Paul and often ambiguous or obscure. Rather rarely two genitives depend on the same noun, which then usually stands between them: Ac 5³² αὐτοῦ μάρτυρες τῶν ῥημάτων τούτων *his witnesses for these things*, 2 Co 5¹ ἡ ἐπίγειος ἡμῶν οἰκία τοῦ σκήνους (possess. and appos.), Ph 2³⁰ τὸ ὑμῶν (subj.) ὑστέρημα τῆς πρός με λειτουργίας (obj.), 2 Pt 3² τῆς τῶν ἀποστόλων ὑμῶν ἐντολῆς τοῦ κυρίου καὶ σωτῆρος perhaps *of the commandment of the Lord and Saviour transmitted by the apostles to you*, Rev 7¹⁷ ἐπὶ ζωῆς πηγὰς ὑδάτων (scribes attempted to remove the obscurity: ζώσας).

More commonly, especially in Paul, but also in the papyri [1] one gen. is dependent on the other, the result being sometimes a clumsy accumulation. We can usually assume in such circumstances that the governing gen. will precede the dependent one [2]:

LXX Wi 13⁵ ἐκ γὰρ μεγέθους καλλονῆς κτισμάτων, 2 Co 4⁴ τὸν φωτισμὸν τοῦ εὐαγγελίου (gen. of origin: *light from the Gospel*) τῆς δόξης τοῦ Χριστοῦ (obj.). Note that the last of the genitives is usually a possessive. Eph 1⁶ εἰς ἔπαινον δόξης [3] τῆς χάριτος αὐτοῦ *for the praise of his grace* (DE τῆς δόξης, which would be *praise of the glory of his grace*; cp. Eph 1¹². ¹⁴), 1¹⁸ ὁ πλοῦτος τῆς δόξης τῆς κληρονομίας αὐτοῦ, 1¹⁹ κατὰ τὴν ἐνέργειαν τοῦ κράτους τῆς ἰσχύος αὐτοῦ, 4¹³ εἰς μέτρον ἡλικίας τοῦ πληρώματος τοῦ Χριστοῦ, Col 2¹² διὰ τῆς πίστεως τῆς ἐνεργείας τοῦ θεοῦ, 1 Th 1³, Rev 14⁸ 16¹⁹ 19¹⁵. Note the order of words in 1 Pt 3⁸ ὁ . . . ἐμπλοκῆς τριχῶν . . . κόσμος.

---

[1] Abel § 44,   Mayser II 2, 143, 144.
[2] There are exceptions: Mt 24³¹B μετὰ σάλπιγγος φωνῆς μεγάλης, 2 Co 3¹⁸ ἀπὸ κυρίου πνεύματος (assuming it = *the Sp. of the Lord*), Heb 6² βαπτισμῶν διδαχῆς (p⁴⁶B prob. rightly: διδαχήν) *teaching concerning baptisms*.
[3] To be taken very closely together, as in Ph 1¹¹ εἰς δόξαν καὶ ἔπαινον.

V. *Attributive and Partitive Genitives in Mark*

TRUE GENITIVE

Possessive	Partitive	Objective Subjective	Quality	Content	Price
1[6]. 7. 15. 16. 16	1[9]. 28 2[6]	1[1]. 4. 14. 17	1[4] 2[29]	1[4]. 28 4[11]	6[37] 8[37]
1[9]. 24. 29. 30	16. 21 3[22]	2[28] 4[19] 6[7].	4[4]. 19	31. 37 5[11]	
2[10]. 18. 26. 28	5[1]. 22 6[15]	43 7[4]. 35	5[1]. 42	25. 29 7[24].	
3[5]. 17. 27. 28. 34	23 7[1]. 2	9[35] 10[44]	6[21]. 48	31 8[8]. 15.	
5[37]. 38. 40. 41	8[10]. 27. 28	11[3]. 22 12[9].	8[33] 11[13]	20 9[41] 10[1].	
6[3]. 17. 24. 56	9[1]. 37 11[1].	27 13[7]. 8	15[38]	14 12[16]	
7[3]. 5. 27. 28. 31	5 12[13]. 28	14[4]. 9 15[2]. 9		14[2]. 3. 13	
8[23]. 38 9[24]. 31. 41	14[10]. 12.			15[26]	
10[25]. 35. 46. 47. 48	43. 47. 66	subj.			
11[10]. 15	15[35]	7[8]. 9. 13			
12[14]. 17. 26. 35. 40		11[30] 12[24]			
13[35] 14[3]. 47. 54					
15[21]. 40. 43. 46					

ABLATIVAL GENITIVE

With adjectives	Comparison
3[29] 6[47] 8[19] 9[36] 14[64]	1[7] 4[31] 9[35] 12[22]. 28. 31. 33. 43 14[5]. 12 16[2]

One gospel has been chosen in order to illustrate the variety and difficulty f interpreting the genitive.

2. ADJECTIVAL DATIVE [1]

(a) *With nouns.* It occurs in class. and Koine Greek with a verbal noun, but in NT only 2 Co 9[11. 12] εὐχαριστία τῷ θεῷ. With other nouns : 1 Co 7[28] θλίψις τῇ σαρκί, 2 Co 2[13] ἄνεσις τῷ πνεύματι, 12[7] σκόλοψ τῇ σαρκί. Many apparent instances display not an attributive, but a predicative, use of the dat. (ATR, 536f). However, Col 2[14] may be an example of a noun with a dat. attribute : τὸ ... χειρόγραφον τοῖς δόγμασιν *subscription to the ordinances.*

---

[1] K-G I § 424. Meisterhans-Schwyzer 209ff. 26–31. Schwyzer II 137–173. Radermacher[2] 110. J. Humbert, *La Disparition du Datif (du Ier au Xe siècle)*, Paris 1930. Mayser II 2, 145–151.

(b) *With adjectives.* Mk 6⁴⁸ etc. ἐναντίος (πρός Ac 26⁹) Ac 4¹⁶ 7¹³ 1 Ti 4¹⁵ (vl. ἐν) ἀρκετός, ἱκανός, φανερός, Ac 7³⁹ ὑπήκοος, 10⁴⁰ Ro 10²⁰ ἐμφανής, Ac 16¹⁵ πιστός, 26¹⁹ etc. ἀπειθής, Ti 2¹¹ σωτήριος, 3⁸ ὠφέλιμος. These correspond to a cognate verb which has the dat. Then there are adjectives of likeness : ὅμοιος frequent (in the " abbreviated " construction : Rev 9¹⁰ ἔχουσιν οὐρὰς ὁμοίας σκορπίοις, 13¹¹ εἶχεν κέρατα δύο ὅμοια ἀρνίῳ), Mt 20¹² ἴσους . . . ἡμῖν, 1 Co 11⁵ ἓν καὶ τὸ αὐτὸ τῇ ἐξυρημένῃ, Ph 3²¹ σύμμορφος, Ro 6⁵ σύμφυτοι τῷ ὁμοιώματι τοῦ θανάτου αὐτοῦ (unless instr. dat., in which case the gen. goes with συμφ., but this is unnatural), 2 Pt 1¹ (Jude ⁷) τοῖς ἰσότιμον ἡμῖν λαχοῦσιν πίστιν (" abbreviated "), Heb 11¹¹ αὐτῇ Σάρρᾳ = class. *together with Sarah* (better sense than αὐτὴ Σάρρα).

(c) *Dative of respect.* The dat. of respect (e.g. ὀνόματι by name) in NT has almost displaced the class. accus. of respect, and as in the papyri (Mayser II 2, 149f, 285) it becomes almost an adverb, and is especially used when contrast is involved, e.g. φύσει . . . νόμῳ, λόγῳ μὲν . . . ἔργῳ δέ.

Mt 5³ πτωχὸς τῷ πνεύματι, ⁸ καθαρὸς τῇ καρδίᾳ, 11²⁹ ταπεινὸς τῇ καρδίᾳ, Ac 4³⁶ etc. τῷ γένει *by birth* (and pap.), 7⁵¹, 14⁸, 16⁵ τῷ ἀριθμῷ (BU II 388 III⁸ ii–iii/A.D.), 18⁵· ²⁵, Ro 5¹⁷ πολλῷ μᾶλλον, 12¹⁰⁻²² (several), 1 Co 7³⁴, 14²⁰, 2 Co 7¹¹ difficult : συνεστήσατε ἑαυτοὺς ἁγνοὺς εἶναι τῷ πράγματι (ἐν would make better sense than εἶναι; DᵇEKLP read εἶναι ἐν), Ga 2⁵ εἴξαμεν τῇ ὑποταγῇ *yield submissively*, ¹⁵ Ph 2⁷ (Philo Byz. σχήματι or σχήμασι 69¹²), 3⁵ *with respect to circumcision*, Heb 5¹¹ νωθροὶ γεγόνατε ταῖς ἀκοαῖς, 10²⁹ πόσῳ . . . χείρονος *by how much . . . worse.* Diod. 12¹⁸ 13⁸⁹ προβεβηκὼς τῇ ἡλικίᾳ, UPZ II 161⁶¹ (119 B.C.), 162 VII 29 (117 B.C.) τοῖς ἔτεσιν. With this dat., ἐν is often used : Lk 1⁷ προβεβηκότες ἐν ταῖς ἡμέραις αὐτῶν (1¹⁸ 2³⁶), but προβεβηκὼς (ταῖς) ἡμέραις LXX Jo 23¹· ² 3 Km 1¹ (accus. τὴν ἡλικίαν is atticistic 2 Mac 4⁴⁰ 6¹⁸), Ditt. Syll ³ 647¹⁷ (ii/B.C.). There is both dat. and accus. of respect in LXX : 2 Mac 5¹¹ τεθηριωμένος τῇ ψυχῇ (accus. in Lucian : atticistic), Johannessohn DGKPS 69–71.

3. ADJECTIVAL ACCUSATIVE.¹

During the Hell. period the accus. of respect (or specification, or general reference) yields to the dat. of respect, as we have just seen, or to a prepositional phrase, as in the pre-Christian papyri and LXX, as well as in NT. Sometimes the two cases appear side by side : Mt 27³² (τῷ) ὀνόματι, 27⁵⁷ τοὔνομα.

---

¹ K-G I 315ff.   Mayser II 2, 151.   Schwyzer II 67–88 (part).

But NT uses τῷ γένει for the class. τὸ γένος (Mk 7²⁶ Ac 4³⁶), and where Diod. Sic. (20, 1) has τὴν ψυχήν, Heb 12³ has τῇ ψυχῇ.

Jn 6¹⁰ τὸν ἀριθμὸν *as to number*. But in Ac 17²⁸ ἐκ τοῦ γὰρ γένος ἐσμέν the translation is *we are his offspring* (because of v. 29), although in Aratus Phaenom. 5 γένος is an accus. of general reference. Ac 18³ vl. σκηνοποιὸς τὴν τέχνην (but better reading is τῇ τέχνῃ), cp. P. Oxy. I 40 (ii–iii/A.D.) ἰατρὸς ὑπάρχων τὴν τέχνην, Heb 2¹⁷ 5¹ πιστὸς ἀρχιερεὺς τὰ πρὸς τὸν θεόν (same phrase is adv. accus. in Ro 15¹⁷). For δεδεμένος τοὺς πόδας see p. 247. For τὸ λοιπόν see p. 336.

§ 3. Attributive Prepositional Phrases [1]

In the same way that adjectives, pronouns, pronominal adjectives, and nouns in gen. or dat. or accus., may be employed as attributive phrases defining a noun, so also may a prepositional expression be used. The class. arrangement is still found: Ac 26³ τῶν κατὰ Ἰουδαίους ἐθῶν, Ro 11²¹ τῶν κατὰ φύσιν κλάδων, ²⁷ ἡ παρ' ἐμοῦ διαθήκη, 16¹⁵. If this prepositional expression stands in post-position, the repetition of the art. is necessary for the sake of clarity, e.g. Ac 3¹⁶ ἡ πίστις ἡ δι' αὐτοῦ, Ro 3²⁴ τῆς ἀπολυτρώσεως τῆς ἐν Χριστῷ Ἰησοῦ, Ga 1²² ταῖς ἐκκλησίαις ταῖς Ἰουδαίαις ταῖς ἐν Χριστῷ, Ph 3¹¹ τὴν ἐξανάστασιν τὴν ἐκ νεκρῶν, 1 Th 1⁸ ἡ πίστις ὑμῶν ἡ πρὸς τὸν θεόν. For this very reason we hardly ever find a prepositional clause used as attribute to an anarthrous noun: in 1 Co 12³¹ εἴ τι for ἔτι is read by p⁴⁶ D*F, making καθ' ὑπερβολήν no longer an attribute of the anarthrous ὁδόν. The only real exceptions appear to be: Mk 1²³ ἄνθρωπος ἐν πνεύματι ἀκαθάρτῳ, Ro 14¹⁷ χαρὰ ἐν πνεύματι ἁγίῳ, 2 Co 12² ἄνθρωπον ἐν Χριστῷ, and with the art. before the attribute: Ac 16²³ ἀδελφοῖς τοῖς κατὰ τὴν Ἀντιόχειαν (an address), 26¹⁸ πίστει τῇ εἰς ἐμέ, ²² ἐπικουρίας ... τῆς ἀπὸ τοῦ θεοῦ, Ro 9³⁰, Ph 3⁹, 1 Ti 1⁴, 2 Ti 1¹³.

In NT, as opposed to class. Greek, a considerable number of instances of omission of the second art. appear to exist, apart from those cases where the noun has additional defining clauses: Mk 6⁶ τὰς κώμας κύκλῳ (but κύκλῳ may define the verb περιῆγεν; it is used with a verb in Ro 15¹⁹; Swete takes it so), Lk 16¹⁰ ὁ πιστὸς ἐν ἐλαχίστῳ = ὁ ὤν ..., Ro 6⁴ διὰ τοῦ βαπτίσματος

---

[1] K-G I 594. 6.   Schwyzer II 417ff.   Mayser II 2, 152ff.   Winer-Schmiedel § 20, 1–6.   Radermacher² 112. 117.   Johannessohn DGPS 365.

εἰς τὸν θάνατον, 10¹, 1 Co 10¹⁸, 11²⁴ 12¹², 2 Co 1¹¹, 9¹³ Ph 1¹⁴
(unless ἐν κυρίῳ is taken with πεποιθότας), Col 1², 1 Th 4¹⁶,
Eph 2¹¹, 4¹, 6⁵ SAB, Col 3²² p⁴⁶ S, 1 Ti 6¹⁷.

It is not surprising that we find the types δικαιοσύνη ἡ ἐκ
πίστεως and τὸ χάρισμα διὰ πολλῶν fairly frequently in NT,
and there is no need to explain away the construction or adopt
a more orthodox variant reading, for these types appear (less
regularly than the other two) in the Koine. Thus, for pre-
Christian papyri:—

		iii/B.C.	ii–i/B.C.
1.	ἡ ἐκ πίστεως δικαιοσύνη	98	210
2.	ἡ δικαιοσύνη ἡ ἐκ πίστεως	74	6
3.	δικαιοσύνη ἡ ἐκ πίστεως	16	66
4.	ἡ δικαιοσύνη ἐκ πίστεως	10	5

See Mayser II 2, 161.

In conclusion we may note that attributive adverbs[1],
though found already in class. Greek, occur much less frequently
in NT than other attributives. Nevertheless they do occur
sometimes, e.g. Ro 3²⁶ ἐν τῷ νῦν καιρῷ, cp. PSI IV 402, 7,
ἐν τῶι νῦν καιρῶι (iii/B.C.); Ac 20²⁶ ἡ σήμερον ἡμέρα (Ro 11⁸
2 Co 3¹⁴); 2 Pt 3⁶ ὁ τότε κόσμος.

---

[1] K-G I 594, 6; 609.   Mayser II 2, 168–171.   Winer-Schmiedel § 20, 7.

PART III

WORD-MATERIAL WHICH DEFINES A VERB

CHAPTER SIXTEEN

PREDICATIVE USE OF ADJECTIVES AND ADVERBS

§ 1. Adjectives

The predicative use of adjectives, participles and pronouns has already been discussed in connection with the definite article. When the predicate occurs before the articular noun it tends to be emphatic. For papyrus examples, see Mayser II 2, 172f. For class. Greek, K–G I 273, 2.

Μέσος and ἄκρος were used in this predicative way in class. Greek, but more rarely now: Mt 25⁶ μέσης δὲ νυκτός Lk 23⁴⁵ ἐσχίσθη δὲ τὸ καταπέτασμα τοῦ ναοῦ μέσον, Jn 19¹⁸ μέσον δὲ τὸν Ἰησοῦν, Ac 26¹³ ἡμέρας μέσης. But elsewhere τὸ μέσον with partitive gen. We never have the class. περὶ μέσας νύκτας, but κατὰ μέσον τῆς νυκτός (Ac 27²⁷) or κατὰ τὸ μεσονύκτιον (16²⁵); for class. τὸ δάκτυλον ἄκρον we have τὸ ἄκρον τοῦ δακτύλου (Lk 16²⁴), like τὸ ἄκρον τῆς ῥάβδου αὐτοῦ (Heb 11²¹). We may take Mt 24³¹ (ἀπ’ ἄκρων οὐρανῶν) and Mk 13²⁷ (ἀπ’ ἄκρου γῆς) in the class. predicative sense, but they may equally well be intended for the gen. of τὰ ἄκρα and τὸ ἄκρον.

In class. Greek a predicative adj., especially a temporal numeral ending in -αῖος, may correspond to an adverb, since it defines a verb. Although this idiom is rare in NT, yet in the neuter gender it became increasingly popular in post-classical Greek and eventually became the regular way of forming adverbs in MGr.

Mk 4²⁸ αὐτομάτη ἡ γῆ καρποφορεῖ, Lk 21³⁴ αἰφνίδιος, 24²² γενόμεναι ὀρθριναὶ ἐπὶ τὸ μνημεῖον (cp. Herm. S.V 1, 1 ὀρθρινὸς ἐλήλυθας), Jn 4¹⁸ τοῦτο ἀληθὲς εἴρηκας (SE ἀληθῶς) class., 13³⁴ καινὴν δίδωμι *I give you it anew*, Ac 12¹⁰ αὐτομάτη, 14¹⁰, 20⁶ D πεμπταῖοι, 28¹³ δευτεραῖοι ἤλθομεν *on the second day*, Ro 10¹⁹, 1 Co 9¹⁷, Heb 11²³ p⁴⁶ ἐκρύβη τρίμηνος, 2 Mac 10³³ V ἄσμενοι περιεκάθισαν.

There is therefore not surprisingly some confusion of μόνος with the adv. μόνον: Mk 6⁸ μηδὲν εἰ μὴ ῥάβδον μόνον (D μόνην), Ac 11¹⁹ μηδενὶ εἰ μὴ μόνον (D μόνοις) Ἰουδαίοις, Heb 12²⁶ OT

σείσω οὐ μόνον τὴν γῆν, ἀλλὰ καί ..., 2 Ti 4⁸, 1 Jn 5⁶ οὐκ ἐν τῷ
ὕδατι μόνον (B μόνῳ). In Jn 5⁴⁴ μόνου is best taken adverbial;
not *from him who alone is God*, but *only from God* (Jewish
monotheism was unimpeachable; Jesus was referring to their
love of human praise), in spite of the word order. Lk 5²¹ adv.
μόνος.

§ 2. Adverbs[1]

Already in class. Greek adverbs are used predicatively, e.g.
ἐγγύς, πόρρω : Eph 2¹³ οἵ ποτε ὄντες μακρὰν ἐγενήθητε ἐγγύς,
Ph 2⁶ τὸ εἶναι ἴσα (adv) θεῷ, 4⁵ ὁ κύριος ἐγγύς. But οὕτως is
not good class. : Mt 1¹⁸ ἡ γένεσις οὕτως ἦν (class. = τοιαύτη ἦν
or οὕτως ἔσχεν, as Ac 7¹ etc.), 19¹⁰, Mk 2¹², Ro 4¹⁸, 9²⁰, 1 Pt 2¹⁵,
LXX Ge 1⁶·⁹·¹¹.   In spite of PSI IV 442, 14f (iii/B.C.) οὐ δίκαιον
οὖν ἐστιν οὕτως εἶναι *so to behave oneself*, the construction may
correspond to Aramaic כדנה (Lagrange, *S. Matth.* XCVIII).
More class. are Mk 11¹⁹ ὀψὲ ἐγένετο, Jn 18²⁸ ἦν δὲ πρωΐ.   Fairly
frequent in NT is ἔχω with predicative adv. : Jn 4⁵² κομψότερον,
Ac 21¹³ 2 Co 12¹⁴ 1 Pt 4⁵ ἑτοίμως.   Also γίνομαι: Ac 20¹⁸
πῶς ... ἐγενόμην (D ποταπῶς ἦν), 1 Th 2¹⁰ ὡς ὁσίως καὶ
δικαίως καὶ ἀμέμπτως ὑμῖν τοῖς πιστεύουσιν ἐγενήθημεν.

Proleptic attraction (*whither* for *where*) is found once in NT: Lk 16²⁶
μηδὲ οἱ (S*BD om οἱ) ἐκεῖθεν πρὸς ἡμᾶς διαπερῶσιν (unless we supply
θέλοντες διαβῆναι from the foregoing); *whence* for *where* Mt 25²⁴·²⁶
συνάγων ὅθεν; *thither* for *thence* Mt 2²² ἐφοβήθη ἐκεῖ ἀπελθεῖν (reverse
Ac 22⁵); ποῦ for ποῖ Jn 7³⁵.
Very rarely ἐκεῖ may be temporal: Mt 24⁵¹ Lk 13²⁸.

§ 3. Adverbial Verbs

Some verbs came to express certain adverbial ideas; they
were used as main verbs, but the main verbal idea was transferred to an infin. or ptc.   E.g. λανθάνω c. ptc. *unconsciously,
secretly* Heb 13² (elsewhere adv. λάθρᾳ, Mt 1¹⁹ etc.), LXX To
12¹³ B, Jos. BJ 3, 7, 3; διατελέω, ἐπιμένω, οὐ διαλείπω c.
ptc. = *permanently, incessantly* Jn 8⁷ (ἐπέμενον ἐρωτῶντες),
Ac 12¹⁶ (*he knocked persistently*), 27³⁴ (ἄσιτοι διατελεῖτε),
Lk 7⁴⁵ οὐ διέλειπεν καταφιλοῦσα, P. Oxy. 658⁸ θύων καὶ σπένδων
τοῖς θεοῖς διετέλεσα; φιλέω c. infin. Mt 6⁵ *gladly*, Ael. 14, 37

---

[1] K-G I 38, 4; 43 n. 1.   Schwyzer II 414.   Mayser II 2, 175ff.

(φιλῶ τὰ ἀγάλματα . . . ὁρᾶν). We mention here [1] the Hebraistic προστίθεμαι c. infin.: in Hebrew the verb which represents the adv. may be joined syntactically with the verb which represents the main verbal idea (לְשֵׁלּחַ יֹסֶף *he sent again*) but sometimes both verbs are finite (Ge 25[1]); the first method is more common and is imitated in Lk 20[11f] (not D) προσέθετο πέμψαι, Mk 14[25] D οὐ μὴ προσθῶ πεῖν. The question for the translator is whether the meaning is *he did something AGAIN* or *he ALSO did something*. Lk 20[11f], by the parallel Mk 12[4, 5] (πάλιν), would mean *he sent again*. But Ac 12[3] appears to mean *he also arrested Peter*. It is one of the very few Hebraisms in the atticistic Josephus (Ant. 6, 287; 19, 48), but here the meaning must be *to attach oneself to, acquiesce in* (Thackeray *JThS* 30, 1929, 161–370). 1 Clem 12[7] καὶ προσέθεντο αὐτῇ δοῦναι σημεῖα *also gave*, P. Grenf. I 53[29] (iv/A.D.) (see Moulton-Howard 445). LXX Ge 4[2] προσέθηκεν τεκεῖν *also bore*, Ex 10[28] προσθεῖναι ἰδεῖν *see again* 14[13] Dt 3[26] 18[16] Jo 7[12] etc. Similarly there is προσθεὶς εἶπεν: LXX Ge 25[1] προσθέμενος Ἀβραὰμ ἔλαβε γυναῖκα *took another*, 38[5] προσθεῖσα ἔτι ἔτεκεν *bore again*, Jb 27[1] 29[1] 36[1] προσθεὶς εἶπεν *again spoke*, Lk 19[11] προσθεὶς εἶπεν παραβολήν *another parable?* or *he also told a parable?* Polyc. 31, 7, 4, Apoc. Pet. 4, Acta Phil. 10.

For *beforehand*, προλαμβάνω c. inf. Mk 14[8], προυπάρχω c. ptc. Lk 23[12]. For *willingly* θέλω (fin. and ptc.), unless it involves a definite act of will, Mk 12[38] Lk 20[46] τῶν θελόντων περιπατεῖν *who love to*, Jn 6[21] ἤθελον οὖν λαβεῖν αὐτὸν εἰς τὸ πλοῖον, 8[44] *you gladly do his will* (so in class. Greek with ἐθέλω; Origen contra Marc., ed. Wetst. 35, with βούλομαι). For *from the beginning* ἄρχομαι Ac 1[1] ὧν ἤρξατο (= ἃ ἐποίησεν ἀπ᾽ ἀρχῆς). So also the adverbial use of τυγχάνω, φθάνω, φανερός εἰμι.

§ 4. Position of the Adverb

An adverb usually follows the adj. or verb which it determines, in NT. Mt 2[16] ἐθυμώθη λίαν, 4[8] ὑψηλὸν λίαν, Lk 12[28] ἐν τῷ ἀγρῷ τὸν χόρτον ὄντα σήμερον *which exists to-day* not *which is in the field to-day*. Exceptions: Mk 16[2] λίαν πρωΐ (D om λίαν), 2 Ti 4[15] λίαν γὰρ ἀντέστη, P. Par. 42[3] λίαν σοι χάριν μεγάλην

---

[1] W-M § 54, 5. Thackeray OT Gr. 52f. Lightfoot on Clem. 1 Co. 12. Moulton Proleg. 67, 233. Deissmann BS 67. MM Vocab. s.v. Moulton-Howard 445.

ἐσχήκαμεν. Therefore, in Col 1³ it will be more natural to take παντότε with the former verb εὐχαριστοῦμεν than with the subsequent ptc. προσευχόμενοι. Occasionally the adv. is given great emphasis by its divorce from its verb: e.g. Lk 7⁶ at the beginning of the clause. But in Lk 1⁵¹ the adverbial phrase διανοίᾳ καρδίας goes closely with ὑπερηφάνους (i.e. *haughty in heart*) and not with διεσκόρπισεν which is furthest from it.

To what does μόνον refer in 1 Co 15¹⁹ εἰ ἐν τῇ ζωῇ ταύτῃ ἐν Χριστῷ ἠλπικότες ἐσμὲν μόνον? Not to *this life*, but *we have done no more than hope in Christ*.

Mt has the peculiar habit, in the imperative, of giving second place to adverbs which in other moods he puts first:

Imperative	Other moods
3¹⁵ ἄφες ἄρτι	9¹⁸ ἄρτι ἐτελεύτησεν 26⁵³ ἄρτι παρακαλέσαι ADCW
18¹⁶ παράλαβε . . . ἔτι	19²⁰ ἔτι ὑστερῶ 26⁶⁵ τί ἔτι χρείαν ἔχομεν;
27⁴² καταβάτω νῦν, ⁴³ ῥυσάσθω νῦν	26⁶⁵ νῦν ἠκούσατε

In the exception, 5¹³ ἰσχύει ἔτι, it should be observed that DW omit ἔτι.

However, in the Ptol. pap. the normal position of adverbs in the simple sentence increasingly tends to be before the verb to which they belong. Even in the class. period a considerable flexibility obtained, under the influence of rhythm or emphasis, and the conversational style differed markedly from the rhetorical.

	Conversational style		Rhetorical		Ptol. pap.	
	Plato: Apol	Xen. Hell. I	Thuc. II	Demosth. I	iii/ B.C.	ii–i/ B.C.
Pre	171 (5)	77 (3·5)	2·5	2·1	30	40
Post	35 (1)	22 (1)	1	1	28	25

(Mayser II 2, 181f.)

In the language of Ptol. documents the normal pre-positive adverbs and those which for a rhetorical purpose are post-positive are fairly evenly distributed. In many documents, such as official acts, the tendency to emphasize the adverb in post-position is very strong. Conversely certain adverbs are always pre-positive, others always post-positive; others again are both.

In Mark πάλιν is used both as an adv. and as a conjunction. When, like εὐθύς, it occurs at the beginning of its phrase, it may be reasonable to take it as a mere conjunction.[1] Usually, however, it occurs either just before or just after its verb: i.e. 23 out of 29 instances. This close proximity with the verb suggests that here we should treat it as a true adverb (before verb 4[1], 7[31] 8[25] 10[1. 24] 12[4] 14[39. 40] vl. 70 15[4. 12. 13]; after verb 2[1. 13] 3[1. 20] 7[14] vl. 8[13] 10[1. 32] 11[27] 14[69]). But the text is doubtful at 5[21] where we have both πάλιν εἰς τὸ πέραν and εἰς τὸ πέραν πάλιν, and perhaps the fact that Mark usually has πάλιν near its verb sways the balance in favour of the latter.

Nevertheless Mark uses εὐθύς only five times near the verb, i.e. as an adverb (viz. 1[28] 5[13] vl. [36. 42] 6[25] 7[25] 1[31] vl. 3[6] vl.); elsewhere it is probably merely a connective conjunction, occurring at the beginning of its clause (viz. 1[10. 12. 18. 20. 21. 23. 29. 30. 31] vl. [42. 43] 2[2] vl. [8. 12] 3[6] 4[5. 15. 16. 17. 29] 5[2. 29. 30. 42] 6[25. 27. 45. 50. 54] 7[25. 35] 8[10] 9[8] vl. [15. 20. 24] 10[52] 11[2. 3] 14[43. 45. 72] 15[1]). Some thirty of these instances are καὶ εὐθύς: *and so* (consecutive, like the Heb.), like καὶ ἰδού in Matthew. But it must be said that sometimes, as at 6[25], εὐθύς has rather stronger adverbial force: *she went in immediately.*[2]

---

[1] 5[21] 8[1] vl. 10[10] 11[3] vl. 12[5] vl. 14[61].

[2] For πάλιν and εὐθύς I owe much to private communications from Dr. G. D. Kilpatrick.

CHAPTER SEVENTEEN

CASE ADDITIONS TO THE VERB:
WITHOUT A PREPOSITION [1]

§ 1. Nominative [2]

(a) *The nominative " ad sensum "*: Eph 3¹⁷ κατοικῆσαι
τὸν Χριστὸν . . . ἐν ταῖς καρδίαις ὑμῶν, ἐν ἀγάπῃ ἐρριζωμένοι,
4¹· ² παρακαλῶ οὖν ὑμᾶς . . . ἀξίως περιπατῆσαι . . ., ἀνεχόμενοι,
Col 2² ἵνα παρακληθῶσιν αἱ καρδίαι αὐτῶν, συνβιβασθέντες, 3¹⁶
ὁ λόγος τοῦ Χριστοῦ ἐνοικείτω . . ., διδάσκοντες.

(b) *Proper nouns without syntax* [3]. Proper nouns usually fit
syntactically into the construction (e.g. Mt 1²¹· ²⁵ τὸ ὄνομα αὐτοῦ
Ἰησοῦν, Mk 3¹⁶ Πέτρον, vl. Πέτρος, Ac 18² εὑρών τινα . . . ὀνόματι
Ἀκύλαν, 27¹ ἑκατοντάρχῃ ὀνόματι Ἰουλίῳ), but sometimes
they are introduced independently in the nominative: Lk 19²⁹
21³⁷ τὸ ὄρος τὸ καλούμενον Ἐλαιών (unless this is ἐλαιῶν, like
19³⁷), Jn 13¹³ φωνεῖτέ με ὁ κύριος . . . Rev 9¹¹ ὄνομα ἔχει
Ἀπολλύων, P. Par. 18. 3 (Abel § 42 (a)).

The divine name (ὁ ὢν καὶ ὁ ἦν καὶ ὁ ἐρχόμενος Rev 1⁸) is used in
nom. after ἀπό: Rev 1⁴. There is some LXX history behind this name,
which is based on Ex 3¹⁴ ἐγώ εἰμι ὁ ὤν . . . ὁ ὢν ἀπέσταλκέ με.
Jeremiah has ὁ ὢν δέσποτα κύριε (4) and Hos 1⁹ οὐκ εἰμὶ ὑμῶν (Ziegler
Duodecim Prophetae, Göttingen 1943, in loc., and *Beitr. z. Ieremias-
LXX*, 1958, 40). It may have been regarded as indeclinable in Greek.

(c) *Nom. is found in parenthesis (class.)*: ὄνομα αὐτῷ (=שְׁמוֹ),
LXX Jg 13², Jn 1⁶ (but S*D*W add ἦν); 3¹ (but S* ὀνόματι)
adds ἦν, however. More common are the phrases ᾧ (ῇ, οὗ) ὄνομα,
and ὀνόματι. Zen. pap. 59037, 7 (258 B.C.) ὄνομα δ᾽ ἐστὶ αὐτῶι
Ἡδύλος, 59148, 2 (256 B.C.) ὧι ὄνομα Ὀνήσιμος.

---

[1] K-G I 44–51 (nom. voc.), 250–448 (acc. gen. dat.). Schwyzer II 52ff.
Gildersleeve I §§ 3–25 (nom. voc.). Johannessohn DGKPS. R. Helbing,
Die Kasussyntax der Verba bei den LXX, Göttingen 1928. A. Jannaris
§ 1242ff (MGr). L. D. Brown, *A Study of the Case Construction of Words
of Time*, New York, 1904. Wackernagel I 14f, 17–20, 294–312.

[2] K-G I 44ff. Meisterhans-Schwyzer § 84, 1–5. Gildersleeve I
§§ 3–13. Radermacher² 21, 111, 219, 223. Mayser II 2, 185–187.

[3] Thackeray OT Gr 23. Johannessohn DGKPS 7. Abel § 42 a.
Mayser II 2, 185ff. Moulton-Howard 154. Kittel WB II 342f.

. (d) *The nom. with time-designation.*   Here we expect accus.
It may be an instance of ellipse and we are to supply a main
verb(e.g. εἰσιν) with καί.   Class.: ὅσαι ἡμέραι *daily.*   LXX Jo
1¹¹ A ἔτι τρεῖς ἡμέραι ὑμεῖς διαβήσεσθε (true text has καί before
ὑμεῖς), Eccl. 2¹⁶ ἤδη αἱ ἡμέραι ἐρχόμεναι τὰ πάντα ἐπελήσθη,
Mt 15³² ὅτι ἤδη ἡμέραι (S accus.) τρεῖς (D adds εἰσιν καί)
προσμένουσίν μοι, Lk 9²⁸ 13¹⁶(?), Ac 5⁷ Acta Paul. Thecl. 8
(P. Oxy. I 6. 3) ἡμέραι γὰρ ἤδη τρεῖς καὶ νύκτες Θέκλα καὶ
ἐγήγερται, and fairly often in post-Ptolemaic papyri.   Adverbial
nom.: Mk 6³⁹ᶠ συμπόσια συμπόσια, πρασιαὶ πρασιαί.

Nom. pendens is a nom. standing at the head of a clause without
construction.   See p. 316.

Ἴδε with nom. as object is explained by the fact that, like ἰδού, ἴδε
has become a stereotyped particle of exclamation.   So have ἄγε and
φέρε: Jn 1²⁹ ἴδε ὁ ἀμνὸς τοῦ θεοῦ, 19²⁶· ²⁷ ἴδε ὁ υἱός σου . . . ἴδε ἡ μήτηρ
σου.

§ 2. Genitive [1]

(a) *True Genitive*

1. *A possessive* [2] *gen.* may be used predicatively with εἶναι
to belong to, e.g. Jn 17⁶ W σοῦ ἦσαν (rest dat.), Ac 27²³, 1 Co 1¹²
3⁴ 6¹⁹, 3⁹ *fellow-workers belonging to* (not *with*) God, 3²¹, 14³⁷
DFG κυρίου ἐστιν (but p⁴⁶ S*BA add ἐντολή), Heb 5¹⁴ 12¹¹.
With γίνεσθαι, e.g. Ac 20³ ἐγένετο γνώμης.

2. *With verbs and verbal adjectives.*   The gen. with verbs
like *accuse* denotes the ground of accusation: only Ac 19⁴⁰
ἐγκαλεῖσθαι στάσεως.   The construction is so rare [3] that one is
tempted to take the gen. closely with σήμερον, and thus construe
in the usual way περὶ τῆς σήμερον στάσεως.   Elsewhere in Ac
we have the class. περί after ἐγκαλεῖσθαι and κρίνεσθαι, 23⁶· ²⁹
26⁷.

Gen. with μεταδίδωμι (Helbing 252, Mayser II 2, 197) is not
found in the NT; instead we have accus. (Ro 1¹¹ 1 Th 2⁸) and
elsewhere the dative.   With μεταλαμβάνω (Helbing 136, Mayser
II 2, 197f) *to receive a share of* always the gen., e.g. Ac 2⁴⁶ 27³³
Heb 6⁷.   With μετέχω (Helbing 136, Mayser II 2, 198) ἐκ is
found only 1 Co 10¹⁷, elsewhere gen. (1 Co 9¹² Heb 2¹⁴).   But

---

[1] Schwyzer II 89–137.   Mayser II 2, 118–145, 187–240.
[2] K-G I 372, 1 b.   Mayser II 2, 188f.   Radermacher² 124.
[3] But see Dio Cass. 58. 4. 5. ἀσεβείας.

with the last two verbs, the gen. is limited to Luke, Paul and Hebrews. With κοινωνέω gen. occurs only [1] at Heb 2¹⁴.

To *touch* still has gen., never accus. in NT (Mayser II 2, 199, Helbing 123), but ψηλαφάω has accus. (Lk 24³⁹ Ac 17²⁷ 1 Jn 1¹) and in passive Heb 12¹⁸. To *take hold of* (ἐπι-) λαμβάνομαι regularly has gen., especially the part grasped, in LXX, NT and papyri (Mayser II 2, 202, Helbing 127): in Lk 14⁴ Ac 9²⁷ 16¹⁹ 18¹⁷ ἐπιλαβόμενος ἰάσατο αὐτόν the accus. goes with the main verb (but see Delling in Kittel WB IV 9, n. 3), in Lk 23²⁶ SBCDL have accus. but WA have gen., Mk 8²³ D λαβόμενος τὴν χεῖρα τοῦ τυφλοῦ (unusual Greek), in LXX Ezk 16⁴⁹ χεῖρα . . . οὐκ ἀντελαμβάνοντο (but accus. is rare in class. and Hell. Greek). But κρατέω has surrendered to the accus., as in Hell. Greek, only the part grasped being in the gen.: Mt 9²⁵ Mk 1³¹ 5⁴¹ Lk 8⁵⁴ Mk 9²⁷ SBD. But if it means to *hold fast to* (Ac 27¹³ Heb 4¹⁴ 6¹⁸), or like ἔχομαι *hold sway over*, more literary works have gen. (Ac 27¹³ Heb 4¹⁴ 6¹⁸) but Rev 2¹⁴. ¹⁵ accus. If it means to *arrest*, NT has accus. (but Luke avoids). Gen. with αἴρω Mt 22¹³ D lat syr, and with the figurative uses of (ἀντ-) ἔχομαι (Helbing 128f, Mayser II 2, 200, Nägeli 54).

Gen. (class.) is still used with *desire, reach, obtain* (Helbing 136–144, Mayser II 2, 203ff), but there is a tendency towards the accus. in Hell. Greek. Thus ἐπιθυμέω c. gen. Ac 20³³ 1 Ti 3¹ LXX Ex 34²⁴ Pr 21²⁶; c. accus. often in LXX (Helbing 138; Johannessohn 40) Ex 20¹⁷ Dt 5²¹, Mt 5²⁸ BDWE (S* gen.). Accus. δικαιοσύνην after πεινάω and διψάω Mt 5⁶ (class. gen.; LXX Ex 17³ διψάω ὕδατι). But with the following verbs of *reaching, obtaining*, there are relics of the gen. in the more cultured authors: τυγχάνω Lk 20³⁵ Ac 24³ 2 Ti 2¹⁰ Heb 8⁶, ἐπιτυγχάνω Heb 6¹⁵ 11³³ (but accus. Ro 11⁷, and pap. 161 B.C. UPZ I 41²⁵). Phrynichus protests against the Hell. accus. with κληρονομέω *inherit*, but it occurs Mt 5⁵ 19²⁹ Lk 10²⁵ Heb 6¹² LXX Si 4¹³ 6¹.

While the gen. with to *fill, be full of*, is still apparent, the accus. is encroaching on the gen. already in LXX (Ex 31³; Johannessohn DGKPS 37, Helbing 144–150) and Koine (K-G I 354, Mayser II 2, 205, Völker *Pap. gr. synt. spec.* 14): Ph 1¹¹

---

[1] Dative: Ro 12¹³ 15²⁷·¹ Ti 5²² 1 Pt 4¹³ 2 Jn ¹¹; ἐν Ga 6⁶ Barn 19⁸ and papyri; εἰς Ph 4¹⁵.

πεπληρωμένοι καρπὸν δικαιοσύνης, Rev 17³ γέμοντα ὀνόματα βλασφημίας.

We may include here the difficult gen. in 2 Pt 2¹⁴ καρδίαν γεγυμνασμένην πλεονεξίας (vl. dat.) *trained in extortion?* (it may be gen. of quality, giving further definition: *a heart trained and greedy*).

Although *to eat, drink, of* (= מִן LXX) have partitive preposition or the accus.[1], nevertheless gen. is found in NT with the meaning *satiate, eat one's fill*, chiefly where we may suspect the influence of literary style (class. authors would have used the gen. often where accus. is found in NT): Ac 27³⁸. With γεύομαι occurs θανάτου and other genitives, on the Aram. model: Mt 16²⁸ Mk 9¹ Lk 9²⁷ 14²⁴ Jn 8⁵² Ac 23¹⁴ Heb 6⁴ᶠ; the accus. is not class. (e.g. Jn 2⁹ τὸ ὕδωρ, Heb 6⁵ ²) and is a Hebraism [3], perhaps influenced by the construction with טָעַם (sifre Num. on 11⁴ טַעֲמוּ אֹתוֹ), and it is fairly common in LXX: 1 Km 14⁴³ 2 Km 19³⁵ Jb 12¹¹ 34³ Si 36²⁴ To BA 7¹¹ Jon 3⁷.

The partitive gen. occurs in NT with verbs of perception [4], especially with a personal object. For ἀκούω, the class. rule is that the person whose words are heard is in the gen. (sometimes with παρά) but the thing (or person) about which one hears is in the accus., and ἀκούω c. accus. may mean *to understand*. In NT, ἀπό is also found with the person (Ac 9¹³ 1 Jn 1⁵) as in Heb. (see especially ἀπὸ τοῦ στόματός τινος Lk 22⁷¹ Ac 1⁴D 22¹⁴). NT breaks the class. rule with τὴν βλασφημίαν Mt 26⁶⁵ Mk 14⁶⁴ DWAG, τὸν ἀσπασμόν Lk 1⁴¹, λαλοῦντας Ac 2⁶D. We have to ask whether the class. distinction between gen. and accus. has significance for exegesis in NT. There may be something in the difference between the gen. in Ac 9⁷ (the men with Paul heard *the sound*) and the accus. in Ac 22⁹ (they did not *understand* the *voice*): Zerwick § 50. On the whole, the accus. is used of the hearing of speech in NT (except Lk 6⁴⁷, which corrects Mt 7²⁴,

---

[1] ἀπό Mt 15²⁷ Mk 7²⁸ Lk 22¹⁸ LXX Le 11⁸ 22⁶; ἐκ Jn 4¹⁴ 6²⁶ 1 Co 11²⁸ Rev 14¹⁰ LXX Ge 9²¹.   Accus.: Mt 15² Mk 1⁶ 1 Co 8¹⁰ 10¹⁸. ²⁵. ²⁷.

[2] But Moule (36) suggests that καλὸν θεοῦ ῥῆμα is virtually a substantival clause = καλὸν εἶναι θεοῦ ῥῆμα (cp. the ὅτι-clause 1 Pt 2³). Moulton (Proleg. 66) however had found the variation from gen. in 6⁴ to accus. in 6⁵ "subtle and suggestive."

[3] Behm in Kittel WB I 675 n. 7.   There are one or two secular parallels: see Mayser II 2, 206 (οἱ συμπόσιον γευόμενοι) but the Aristotelian instance to which Mayser refers is conjectural.

[4] Helbing 150–159.   Mayser II 2, 207ff.

Jn 7⁴⁰ 12⁴⁷ 19¹³ vl.), whereas the gen. would be class. (unless it means *understand*). In Jn it seems possible to trace a distinction between the gen. (*obey* 5²⁵· ²⁸ 10³· ¹⁶ etc.) and accus. (mere perception 3⁸ 5³⁷) with ἀκούω and φωνή, but there is no such discrimination in Ac or Rev or LXX (Ac 9⁴· ¹¹ 11⁷ (p⁴⁵ D accus.) 22⁷· ⁹· ¹⁴ (E gen.) Rev 1¹⁰ 4¹ 10⁴ (p⁴⁷ SCP) 14¹³ 16¹ 21³ : Johannessohn DGKPS 36, Mayser II 2, 207). In class. Greek αἰσθάνομαι = *understand* if it has accus. as Lk 9⁴⁵ (NT = συνίημι elsewhere).

So also with *remember* and *forget* the accus. is now encroaching on the gen. Gen. with μιμνήσκω Heb 2⁶ 13³ (as usually LXX : Johannessohn DGKPS 37, Helbing 108). But gen. (usually e.g. Lk 17³²) and accus. (e.g. Mt 16⁹, Jn 15²⁰ SD (rest gen.), 1 Th 2⁵, 2 Th 2⁸, 2 Ti 2⁸, Rev 18⁵) with μνημονεύω.

Gen. with ἐπιλανθάνομαι, only Heb 6¹⁰ 13²· ¹⁶, accus. Ph 3¹³ Heb 13² S*, and papyri. Gen. with ὑπομιμνήσκω Lk 22⁶¹, accus. Jn 14²⁶ 3 Jn¹⁰, but he may have had ὄζω in mind, and Hom. Clem. 13¹⁶ has μύρου δὲ πνέει, τῆς ἀγαθῆς φήμης, and Stobaeus (v/A.D.) ἐμπνεῖν Ἀραβίης ὀδμῆς (Schwyzer II 2, 128).

The verbs of emotion ὀργίζομαι, θαυμάζω, ἐλεέω, no longer have gen. of cause, but ἀνέχομαι *bear with* retains it : Mt 17¹⁷ Col 3¹³ (not gen. in Mt 18²⁷ with σπλαγχνίζομαι, but with δοῦλος). The gen. has survived in LXX and NT with verbs meaning *to care for*, but ἐντρέπομαι has only accus. in NT and nothing of the former gen. survives. Verbs meaning *to rule* or *surpass* also still have gen., but καταβραβεύω has accus.

The gen. of price occurs with *to buy, sell*, and *agree on* (συμφωνέω), in addition to ἐκ. Moule (39) suggests classifying Jude¹¹ here : μισθοῦ ἐξεχύθησαν *they went headlong for a reward*.

The substantivized verbal adjective, as a passive, has the gen. to designate the agent, e.g. Mt 11¹¹ Lk 7²⁸ γεννητοὶ γυναικῶν, Mt 24³¹ ἐκλεκτοὶ θεοῦ *chosen by God*, Ro 1⁷ ἀγαπητοὶ θεοῦ *beloved of God*, Jn 6⁴⁵ διδακτοὶ θεοῦ, 1 Co 2¹³ οὐκ ἐν διδακτοῖς ἀνθρωπίνης σοφίας λόγοις *words dictated by wordly wisdom*. Hebrew influence is apparent here. The θεο- in θεοστυγεῖς (Ro 1³⁰) may be a gen. (= θεοῦ), and so we should take the word passively in a subjective, not an objective sense : *out of favour with God*. With a passive ptc.: Mt 25³⁴ οἱ εὐλογημένοι τοῦ πατρός, Lk 2²⁷ τὸ εἰθισμένον τοῦ νόμου (D ἔθος).

. 3. *Local and temporal*. Very little trace of local gen. remains, and it was rare and poetical in Attic [1]. It survives in ποῦ, αὐτοῦ, etc. LXX To B 10[7] οἵας ἀπῆλθεν, Lk 5[19] ποίας εἰσενέγκωσι, 19[4], Ac 19[26]?, 1 Pt 1[1] *sojourners in the Diaspora* (E. G. Selwyn, *The First Epistle of St. Peter*, London 1955, 118). The class. gen. of time-within-which still occurs: Mt 2[14] νυκτός *during the night*, Mk 5[5] Lk 18[7] Ac 9[24] ἡμέρας καὶ νυκτός, Mt 24[20] Mk 13[18] χειμῶνος, Mt 24[20] D σαββάτου, Lk 2[8] 9[37] p[45] Rev 21[25]. Class. is τοῦ λοιποῦ (like τὸ λοιπόν) *henceforth*: Ga 6[17] Eph 6[10] p[46] S*BA. A distributive gen. occurs with numerals, e.g. class. δὶς τῆς ἡμέρας *twice a day*, Lk 18 [12] δὶς τοῦ σαββάτου, Heb 9[7] ἅπαξ τοῦ ἐνιαυτοῦ. But the gen. of point of time is not class.: Mt 25[6] μέσης νυκτός *at midnight*, Mk 13[35] μεσονυκτίου and ἀλεκτοροφωνίας (SBC μεσονύκτιον), Lk 24[1] ὄρθου βαθέως, Jn 11[49. 51] 18[13] τοῦ ἐνιαυτοῦ ἐκείνου *that year*, Ac 26[13] ἡμέρας μέσης; it occurs in the Ptol. pap. ὥρας ἑωθινῆς and the like (Mayser II 2, 225), and in MGr τοῦ χρόνου *next year*.

(b) *Ablatival Genitive* [2]

The gen. (or ablative) of separation has been largely replaced by ἀπό or ἐκ which, in addition to the regular gen., were both found in class. Greek; LXX and Koine also often use ἀπό (Johannessohn DGKPS 38f, Helbing 159–181, Mayser II 2, 227ff, 234ff), as well as later Greek. The verbs concerned are ἐλευθερόω, καθαρίζω, λούω, λυτρόω, λύω, ῥύομαι, σῴζω, χωρίζω. In NT, also with gen. ἀπαλλοτριόω *separate* Eph 2[12] 4[18], ἀποστερέομαι 1 Ti 6[5], μεθίστημι Lk 16[4] AW (SBD ἐκ; L ἀπό), καθαιρέομαι Ac 19[27] SBAE (HLP accus.), κωλύω τινά τινος Ac 27[43] (as normally), but τι ἀπό τινος *to refuse someone something* (Semitism, LXX Ge 23[6]) Lk 6[29], φείδομαι (class. always gen.: as in Ac 20[29] Ro 8[32] 2 Pt 2[4. 5]) LXX has prepositions (Abel § 44k); also ἀπέχομαι, ὑστερέω, βραδύνω, παύομαι (ἀνα-, κατα-), ἀφίσταμαι, λείπομαι, ἀστοχέω 1 Ti 1[6] (but περί τι, 1 Ti 6[21] 2 Ti 2[18]).

The gen. may also depend to some extent on prepositions in compounds; here it is mainly κατά (*against* or *down upon*) which concerns

---

[1] K-G I 384. 2.   Meisterhans-Schwyzer 205. 14.   Mayser II 2, 223ff.
[2] K-G I §§ 420f.   Meisterhans-Schwyzer 207, 18. 19.   Mayser II 2, 227ff.   Radermacher[2] 123ff.   Helbing 159–178.

us, and the more usual compounds, which in class. Greek had gen., have now tended to go over to accus. (e.g. καταδικάζω Mt 12⁷ Jas 5⁶; κατακρίνω): Helbing 182ff., Mayser II 2, 237ff.

§ 3. Dative [1]

The case tended to disappear in later Greek, but the process has scarcely begun yet; in the NT there is not much to choose between the comparative frequency of accus., gen., or dat., but the special popularity of ἐν makes the dat. more frequent than it would normally be. Besides this encroachment of ἐν, there is the growth of διά, σύν and μετά in the post-classical period at the expense of the simple dat. There are in NT already traces of the process which ended in the complete disappearance of the simple dat. in MGr; Zerwick (§ 36) points to Mk 8¹⁹ (εἰς = for), Ac 24¹⁷ (εἰς = for the benefit of), 1 Pt 1⁴ (εἰς = for). It is the more remarkable, therefore, that in Hell. Greek the dat. does sometimes oust the class. accus. (e.g. Rev 2¹⁴ ἐδίδασκεν c. dat.), and in NT the dat. is still retained in a large range of meanings, notwithstanding the constant tendency to add ἐν (even with instrumental dat.).

The dat. indicates the person more remotely concerned:

(a) *As indirect object.*

To give: dat. as well as εἰς c. accus., (ἐπι-)χορηγέω, ἐπαγγέλλομαι *promise* Jas 2⁵ dat. *To serve*: διακονέω, δουλεύω, λατρεύω, ὑπηρετέω always dat., but προσκυνέω has dat., accus., and (Hebraistic) ἐνώπιον c. gen.; and ἀρέσκω has dat. and (Ac 6⁵) ἐνώπιον c. gen. *To show, reveal, appear*: always dat. (verb *to be* in this sense 1 Co 14¹¹ ἔσομαι τῷ λαλοῦντι βάρβαρος).

Verbs of *speaking, writing*, etc. The following have dat.: ᾄδω and ψάλλω Eph 5¹⁹ Col 3¹⁶ (LXX Je 20¹³), αἰνέω Rev 19⁵, ἀπολογέομαι *make a defence before* Ac 19³³ 2 Co 12¹⁹ Hell., ἀποτάσσομαι *say farewell to* Mk 6⁴⁶ etc. Hell., ἐξ-, ἀνθ- ομολογέομαι Mt 11²⁵ Lk 2³⁸ 10²¹ Ro 14¹¹ 15⁹, εὔχομαι Ac 26²⁹ (but πρός 2 Co 13⁷), καυχάομαι *boast to* 2 Co 7¹⁴ 9², ὁμολογέω *praise* Heb 13¹⁵, *confess before* Mt 7²³ Ac 24¹⁴ (+ ἐν also), *promise* Mt 14⁷ Ac 7¹⁷ vl., προσεύχομαι dat. only, ψεύδομαι c. accus. Ac 5³ *deceive by lying* (class.), 5⁴ c. dat. *lie to*. In class. Greek κελεύω usually has accus., as in NT (but dat. Mt 15³⁵ EFG); class. dat. = *summon*. Other verbs for *censure and command*: dat. (but ἐγκαλέω κατά c. gen. Ro 8³³).

[1] K-G I 406–448. Meisterhans-Schwyzer 208ff. 23–40. Mayser II 2, 240–297. Radermacher² 126ff. Helbing 191–319. Schwyzer II 137–173 (part). J. Humbert, *La Disparition du Datif en Grec*, Paris 1930. A. Green, *The Dative of Agency. A Chapter of Indo-European Case-Syntax*, Diss. New York, 1913.

Λέγω πρός, which is common in Luke (Gosp. 99, Ac 52), absent in Mt, Mk 5, Jn 19 times, Paul twice, is part of the Hellenistic tendency to use prepositions in place of the simple case.

	λέγω	εἶπον	κατηγορέω	ἀποκρίνομαι	λαλέω
John	2³, 3⁴ 4¹⁵. ³³. ⁴⁹ 6⁵, 7⁵⁰	4⁴⁸, 6²⁸ vl. ³⁴ 7³. ³⁵, 8⁵⁷ vl. 11²¹, 12¹⁹ 16¹⁷, 19²⁴	5⁴⁵	8³³ vl. Otherwise always dative	Always dative

It is mainly with the reflexive that πρός occurs after verbs of *saying* in Mk and Jn. Representative figures from other books written in Biblical Greek show a large proportion of πρός c. accus.

	πρός or dat. after verbs of speaking: λαλέω, λέγω, εἶπον									
	Lk	Ac	Heb	Rev	Gen. 1–25	26–50	4 Mac	T. Abr. A	B	Ep. Barn
πρός	99	45	4	–	27	31	–	31	32	10
dat.	187	48	4	28	75	154	4	30	36	15
μετά				6						

But the reversal of technique half way through LXX Genesis is remarkable; either different translators divided the LXX books between them, or the books were subsequently revised piecemeal.

Besides the dat., πέποιθα and πιστεύω have also ἐν, ἐπί (dat., acc), εἰς; and πειθάρχω has accus. (class.). Dat. occurs with πείθομαι, ὑπακούω, ἀπιστέω, ἀπειθέω. When πιστεύω has dat., it may mean *believe in*: Ac 5¹⁴ 16³⁴ (D ἐπί c. accus.) 18⁸ (D εἰς); same meaning with εἰς (e.g. εἰς τὸ ὄνομα) and ἐπί c. accus. (Mt 27⁴² SBL Ac 9⁴² 11¹⁷ 16³¹ 22¹⁹ Ro 4²⁴), ἐπί c. dat. only with ref. to LXX (according to J. Jeremias in Kittel WB IV 275f): Ro 9³³ 10¹¹ 1 Pt 2⁶ ὁ πιστεύων ἐπ᾽ αὐτῷ, but this is not true, because of 1 Ti 1¹⁶ and Lk 24²⁵ *slow of heart* τοῦ πιστεύειν ἐπὶ πᾶσιν οἷς ἐλάλησαν (but this might mean *on the basis of*, not *in* [1]), and Mt 27⁴² WEF (SBL ἐπί c. accus.; DΘ αὐτῷ). When πιστεύω is followed by ἐν, the meaning may be *believe* absolute, and the prepositional phrase taken separately, viz. in Mk 1¹⁵ *believe, in the sphere of the Gospel*, in Jn 3¹⁵ B ἐν αὐτῷ to be taken closely with ἔχῃ ζωήν (Bauer s.v.).

---

[1] A. Schlatter, *Der Glaube im NT*⁴, 1927, 591f.

But LXX has ἐν: Ps 77²² 105¹². ²⁴ Si 35²¹. ²³ Je 12⁶, Johannessohn DGKPS 60f. According to Bultmann in Kittel WB VI 204, πιστεύω εἰς = to believe that Jesus is the Christ, or that J. died and rose, etc. The dat. with ἐλπίζω to hope in (instead of ἐπί c. gen. or dat., or εἰς) occurs only in Mt 12²¹ (D + ἐν) = Isa 42⁴ (ἐπί c. dat). Jude¹¹ τῇ πλάνῃ τοῦ Βαλαάμ ... ἐξεχύθησαν abandon themselves to?

(b) The dat. of advantage and disadvantage ¹ (or " dativus commodi ") marks out a person whose interests are much less remotely concerned than in the previous section.

Mt 13¹⁴ ἀναπληροῦνται αὐτοῖς (D + ἐπί) ἡ προφητεία, 23³¹ Lk 4²² Jn 3²⁶ Ro 10² etc. μαρτυρέω bear witness to someone, Mt 27⁷ εἰς ταφὴν τοῖς ξένοις, Lk 18³¹ τελεσθήσεται πάντα τὰ γράμματα ... τῷ υἱῷ (D περί c. gen), 1 Pt 5⁹ τῇ ἀδελφότητι ἐπιτελεῖσθαι, 2 Co 2¹ ἔκρινα ἐμαυτῷ τοῦτο, also Mt 6²⁵ Lk 12²² μεριμνάω, Lk 1⁵⁵ ἐλάλησεν πρὸς τοὺς πατέρας ἡμῶν, τῷ 'Αβραὰμ καὶ τῷ σπέρματι ... (dat. can hardly be in appos. to accus., and may be dat. commodi: he spoke to our fathers in favour of Abraham; Zerwick § 40), LXX 1 Esd 4⁴⁹ ἔγραψεν πᾶσι τοῖς 'Ιουδαίοις. The dat. commodi is probably " the curious dative " (Moule, 43) in Rev 8⁴ ἀνέβη ὁ καπνὸς ταῖς προσευχαῖς in favour of their prayers, although it may be temporal dat. (BGU 69, A.D. 120, ἃς καὶ ἀποδώσω σοι τῷ ἔγγιστα δοθησομένῳ ὀψωνίῳ which I will pay you with the next wages that are paid). For dat. of disadvantage see Rev 2⁵. ¹⁶ ἔρχομαί σοι; advantage 21² κεκοσμημένην τῷ ἀνδρὶ αὐτῆς. See also: Mk 10¹² 1 Co 7³⁹ γαμέομαι, Ro 14⁴ τῷ ἰδίῳ κυρίῳ στήκει ἢ πίπτει, 14⁶ κυρίῳ φρονεῖ ... κυρίῳ ἐσθίει in honour of, 11²⁵ ἑαυτοῖς φρόνιμοι p⁴⁶ FG (AB + ἐν, SCD + παρ'), 6²⁰ ἐλεύθεροι ... τῇ δικαιοσύνῃ, 8¹² ὀφειλέται ... τῇ σαρκί, 1 Co 7²⁸ θλῖψιν τῇ σαρκί (D*FG + ἐν), 2 Co 10⁴ δυνατὰ τῷ θεῷ, 2¹³ ἄνεσιν τῷ πνεύματί μου, Jas 3¹⁸ καρπὸς ... σπείρεται τοῖς ποιοῦσιν εἰρήνην.

(c) Reference. Paul has various loose combinations: Ro 6¹⁰ τῇ ἁμαρτίᾳ ἀπέθανεν ... ζῇ τῷ θεῷ, 2 Co 5¹³ εἴτε γὰρ ἐξέστημεν, θεῷ· εἴτε σωφρονοῦμεν, ὑμῖν, for God's sake ... in your interest. This is aptly named a dat. of reference, in so far as the idea of personal interest is so diminished as to be no more than a vague reference. Jas 2⁵ τοὺς πτωχοὺς τῷ κόσμῳ, Jude¹⁴ ἐπροφήτευσεν ... τούτοις (J. B. Mayor in loc. he prophesied for these, but better sense in the context is provided if this is the dat. of vaguer reference: as to these, although περί c. gen. would be more natural, like Mt 15⁷ Mk 7⁶).

(d) " Dativus relationis " is very similar (see p. 220). Where class. Greek tended to have accus. (even in NT at Mt 27⁵⁷

---

¹ K-G I 417, 17.   Mayser II 2, 270ff.

ἄνθρωπος . . . τοὔνομα 'Ιωσήφ), the dat. now occurs in an adverbial sense:

Mt 5³· ⁸ πτωχὸς τῷ πνεύματι, καθαρὸς τῇ καρδίᾳ, Mk 5²² Lk 1⁶¹ Ac 18²⁴ etc. ὀνόματι, Mk 7²⁶ Ac 4³⁶ 18²⁴ τῷ γένει, Ac 16⁵ στερεοῦσθαι τῇ πίστει περισσεύειν τῷ ἀριθμῷ, Ro 12¹⁰ τῇ φιλαδελφίᾳ . . . φιλόστοργοι, 1 Co 14²⁰ νηπιάζειν τῇ κακίᾳ, 2 Co 7¹¹ ἁγνὸς τῷ πράγματι (if text is sound), Ph 2³⁰ παραβολευσάμενος τῇ ψυχῇ, 3³ οἱ πνεύματι θεοῦ λατρεύοντες, Col 2⁵ τῇ σαρκί *physically*.

(e) *Ethical dative.* Perhaps Mt 21⁵ OT ἔρχεταί σοι and Rev 2⁵· ¹⁶ (Hebraisms) (see under (b)), 2 Pt 3¹⁴ ἄσπιλοι καὶ ἀμώμητοι αὐτῷ (God) εὑρεθῆναι. The ethical dat. in Ac 7²⁰ ἀστεῖος τῷ θεῷ (*in God's eyes*) is a Hebraism, reminding us of LXX Jon 3³ πόλις μεγάλη τῷ θεῷ לֵאלֹהִים (an elative; i.e. *very big* according to D. W. Thomas in *Vet. Test.* III, 1953, 15ff, as the LXX fail to appreciate that אלהים or אל sometimes express a superlative).   The dat. in Lk 2¹¹ ἐτέχθη ὑμῖν σήμερον σωτήρ may be described as " sympatheticus "; see SIG 1240. 25 (ii/A.D.) πληθύοι αὐτῷ οἶκος παίδων γοναῖς (Schwyzer II 147f; J. Weber, *Der sympathetische Dativ bei Herodot*, diss. Münster 1915).

(f) Where εἶναι with dat. forms part of the predicate it usually carries the idea of credit (or discredit) in the person's eyes:

Mt 18¹⁷ ἔστω σοι ὥσπερ ὁ ἐθνικός, Lk 5¹⁰ κοινωνοὶ τῷ Σίμωνι (D gen.) *Simon had in them partners,* Ac 9¹⁵ σκεῦος ἐκλογῆς ἐστίν μοι οὗτος *I have in him,* 19³¹ ὄντες αὐτῷ φίλοι (but gen. Jn 19¹² etc.), Ro 1¹⁴ ἀνοήτοις ὀφειλέτης εἰμί, 8¹² (but 15²⁷ gen.), 1 Co 1¹⁸ τοῖς μὲν ἀπολλυμένοις μωρία ἐστίν *serves as folly,* 2¹⁴, 11¹⁴· ¹⁵ ἀτιμία αὐτῷ, 15³² τί (μοι) τὸ ὄφελος, 2 Co 2¹⁵ Χριστοῦ εὐωδία ἐσμὲν τῷ θεῷ, Ga 5¹³ μὴ τὴν ἐλευθερίαν εἰς ἀφορμὴν τῇ σαρκί (ellipse of verb), 1 Th 2¹⁰ ὁσίως . . . ὑμῖν ἐγενήθημεν (but adverbs are rare in this construction), LXX To 3¹⁵ μονογενής εἰμι τῷ πατρί μου.

(g) There is also more obviously a dat. of possession (K-G I 416, 15; Mayser II 2, 269f), in which the personal interest, which is always latent in the dat. is strengthened to the point of ownership, and the class. distinction between the gen. for emphasis on the possessor and dat. for emphasis on the object possessed is often preserved: Mt 19²⁷ 18¹² Ac 21²³.   Exceptions: Lk 12²⁰ ἃ ἡτοίμασας, τίνι ἔσται; (D corrects to τίνος), Ac 2³⁹ ὑμῖν ἐστιν ἡ ἐπαγγελία, Ro 7³, 7⁴ (cp. Heb. הָיָה לְאִישׁ).   Besides εἰμι and γίνομαι, ὑπάρχω is used like this (Lk 8³ Ac 28⁷ 2 Pt 1⁸).

(h) In addition, εἰμί c. dat. occurs with the meaning to *happen to* : Mt 16²² οὐ μὴ ἔσται σοι τοῦτο, and with ellipse of the verb : Mk 1²⁴ τί ἡμῖν καὶ σοί, Lk 1⁴³ πόθεν μοι τοῦτο ; 1 Co 5¹² etc. τί γάρ μοι ; Epict. 1, 22, 15 τί μοι καὶ αὐτῷ, εἰ οὐ δύναταί μοι βοηθῆσαι (see 1, 27, 13).

(i) *Dat. of Agent* [1]. In NT there are very few exx. of dat. with passive = ὑπό c. gen. Lk 23¹⁵ ἐστὶν πεπραγμένον αὐτῷ (D + ἐν, c in) ; however, it could be taken as *in his case*, Ro 8¹⁴ πνεύματι θεοῦ ἄγονται, Ga 5¹⁸ πνεύματι ἄγεσθε, LXX Ge 14¹⁹, Jos. Ant. 11, 206 ἡμῖν δεδήλωται, Gosp. Pet. 11 τοῖς ἀγαπωμένοις αὐταῖς, Clem. Hom. (atticistic) 3⁶⁸ 9²¹ 19²³.

(j) *Instrumental dat.* Jas 3⁷ δαμάζεται καὶ δεδάμασται τῇ φύσει τῇ ἀνθρωπίνῃ, 2 Pt 2¹⁹ ᾧ τις ἥττηται, Jude ¹ τοῖς . . . Ἰησοῦ Χριστῷ τετηρημένοις κλητοῖς. It is the instrumental ἐν which is more used than plain dat. in Biblical Greek ; it occurs only occasionally in secular Greek (see pp. 252f). Without the preposition : Lk 21²⁴ στόματι μαχαίρης, Ac 12² μαχαίρῃ. There are phrases like *to season with* Mk 9⁴⁹ Col 4⁶, *to burn with* Mt 3¹² Lk 3¹⁷ Rev 8⁸ 17¹⁶ (SBP) 21⁸ (with ἐν 14¹⁰ 16⁸ 17¹⁶ vl. 18⁸), LXX with and without ἐν, *to baptise with* usually ἐν but ὕδατι Lk 3¹⁶ (D + ἐν) Ac 1⁵ 11¹⁶, χρίω πνεύματι 10³⁸, *to vindicate by* Ro 3²⁸ (also ἐν and ἐκ), *to mix with* Rev 15² (also ἐν and μετά), *to measure with* Lk 6³⁸ Rev 21¹⁶ (also ἐν).

This instrumental dat. is sometimes used where the class. rule expects the gen. construction : Eph 5¹⁸ LXX Pr 4¹⁷ μεθύσκομαι οἴνῳ, Mt 20¹⁸ Mk 10³³ κατακρινοῦσιν αὐτοῦ θανάτῳ, (Hellenistic : Büchsel in Kittel WB III 953 n. 1) 2 Pt 2⁶ καταστροφῇ κατέκρινεν.

Other exx. of instrumental dat. are probably : Ro 1²⁰ τοῖς ποιήμασιν νοούμενα *perceived by means of his works*, 5¹⁵. ¹⁷ τῷ . . . παραπτώματι *by the transgression*, 8¹³ πνεύματι . . . θανατοῦτε *by the Spirit*, 8¹⁴, Ga 5⁵. ¹⁶. ¹⁸. ²⁵, Ro 12² μεταμορφοῦσθε τῇ ἀνακαινώσει τοῦ νοός *transformed by*, Eph 2⁵ χαριτί ἐστε σεσωσμένοι *by grace*.

(k) *Associative dat.* which, when used with verbs is often known as " dativus sociativus " or " comitativus ", expresses the " means by which ", but with strong emphasis on physical

---

[1] Moulton-Howard 459.

accompaniment or nearness.   E.g. ἀκολουθέω often has dat., but also μετά and the Biblical ὀπίσω; συνέπομαι Ac 20⁴; ἐγγίζω Lk 7¹²; κολλάομαι Lk 15¹⁵ etc.; κοινωνέω Ro 12¹³ etc.; ὁμιλέω Ac 24²⁶; and other verbs of this kind.   However, μάχομαι (class. dat.) has only πρός (Jn 6⁵²), πολεμέω (class. dat.) only μετά (Rev 2¹⁶ 12⁷ 13⁴ 17¹⁴).

But this dat. may be more loosely connected with the verb to describe accompanying circumstances or manner, and it is then often designated " dativus modi ".   NT adds ἐν with the former:

Mt 16²⁸ ἐρχόμενον ἐν τῇ βασιλείᾳ αὐτοῦ, Mk 1²³ 7²⁵ p⁴⁵ ἐν πνεύματι ἀκαθάρτῳ, Lk 14³¹ ἐν δέκα χιλίασιν ὑπαντᾶν, 23⁴² ὅταν ἔλθῃς ἐν τῇ βασιλείᾳ σου (BL correct to εἰς), Ac 7¹⁴ πᾶσαν τὴν συγγένειαν ἐν ψυχαῖς ἐβδ. πέντε, 1 Co 4²¹ ἐν ῥάβδῳ ἔλθω, Heb 9²⁵ εἰσέρχομαι ἐν αἵματι, Jude¹⁴ ἦλθεν ... ἐν ἁγίαις μυριάσιν αὐτοῦ. Of clothing: Lk 4³² 24⁴, Ac 1¹⁰ ἐν ἐσθήσεσι λευκαῖς, Col 2¹⁵, LXX 1 Mac 11⁵⁸ 3 Mac 1¹⁶. Of manner (dat. alone): Mt 8¹⁶ ἐξέβαλεν τὰ πνεύματα λόγῳ, Mk 5⁴ πέδαις καὶ ἁλύσεσιν δεδέσθαι, 14⁶⁵ ῥαπίσμασιν αὐτὸν ἔλαβον (a Latinism? see Cicero Tusc. 2, 34 verberibus accipere. But Acta Joan. 90 τί εἰ ῥαπίσμασίν με ἔλαβες; pap. c. A.D. 100, Blass-Debr. § 198 κονδύλοις ἔλαβεν), Lk 2³⁷ νηστείαις καὶ δεήσεσιν λατρεύουσα, Ac 2⁸·¹¹·⁴⁰ τῇ ἰδίᾳ διαλέκτῳ, 16³⁷ δημοσίᾳ, 24⁴ ἀκοῦσαι... τῇ σῇ ἐπιεικείᾳ with your clemency, Ro 8²⁴ τῇ ἐλπίδι ... ἐσώθημεν in hope but not actually, 1 Co 10³⁰ χάριτι with thankfulness, 11⁵, 14¹⁵ προσεύξομαι τῷ πνεύματι... τῷ νοΐ (or local dat.?), Ph 4⁶ τῇ προσευχῇ καὶ τῇ δεήσει μετὰ εὐχαριστίας (NB. both dat. and μετά), Col 3¹⁶ ψαλμοῖς etc., Heb 6¹⁷ ἐμεσίτευσεν ὅρκῳ (but μετά in Mt 26⁷² and pap.).

Then there are various stereotyped phrases (e.g. παρρησίᾳ): Ph 1¹⁸ παντὶ τρόπῳ.   But μετά and ἐν are found in such phrases in both LXX (Johannessohn DGPS 209ff) and NT, and papyri (e.g. μετὰ βίας).   Some are almost peculiar to Biblical Greek, e.g. ὁδῷ, ἴχνεσιν, with πορεύομαι, περιπατέω, στοιχέω: Lk 10³¹ B, Jas 2²⁵ ἑτέρᾳ ὁδῷ ἐκβαλοῦσα, but usually figuratively in NT: Ac 9³¹ πορεύομαι τῷ φόβῳ τοῦ κυρίου, 14¹⁶ ταῖς ὁδοῖς αὐτῶν, 21²¹ τοῖς ἔθεσιν περιπατέω, Ro 4¹², 13¹³ Ga 5¹⁶ Jude¹¹ Hom. Clem. 10¹⁵ τῷ ὑμῶν στοιχεῖτε παραδείγματι.

(l) The Hebrew infinite absolute shows its influence in the use of the cognate dat. of verbal nouns in LXX and NT (Thackeray OT Gr 48f, Johannessohn DGKPS 56f), e.g. Ge 2¹⁷ Mt 15⁴. There was already some class. precedent (Schwyzer II 166), but Biblical Greek has a wealth of exx: Lk 22¹⁵ ἐπιθυμίᾳ ἐπεθύμησα, Ac 2¹⁷ ἐνυπνίοις ἐνυπνιάζεσθαι, 4¹⁷ ἀπειλῇ ἀπειλησώμεθα vl., 5²⁸

παραγγελία παρηγγείλαμεν, 23¹⁴, 28²⁶ LXX, Ga 5¹ τῇ ἐλευθερίᾳ...
ἠλευθέρωσεν, Jas 5¹⁷. However, the addition of an attribute
almost always results in the substitution of the accus.
of content : so Jn 3²⁹ χαρᾷ χαίρει becomes Mt 2¹⁰ ἐχάρησεν χαρὰν μεγάλην ;
but not always, because we find Mk 5⁴² ἐξέστησαν ἐκστάσει
μεγάλῃ 1 Mac 14²⁹ δόξῃ μεγάλῃ ἐδόξασαν.

(m) *Cause.* This dat. is extraordinary [1]. Ac 15¹ περιτμη-
θῆτε τῷ ἔθει τῷ Μωϋσέως (not D) may be *because of the Law* (for
according to we would expect κατά). Most exx. are in Paul:
Ro 4²⁰ οὐ διεκρίθη τῇ ἀπιστίᾳ, ἀλλ' ἐνεδυναμώθη τῇ πίστει, 11²⁰
τῇ ἀπιστίᾳ ἐξεκλάσθησαν, 30. 31, 14¹⁵ μὴ τῷ βρώματί σου ἐκεῖνον
ἀπόλλυε, 2 Co 2⁷ τῇ περισσοτέρᾳ λύπῃ καταποθῇ (or local?), 2¹³
τῷ με εὑρεῖν με *because I did not find*, Ga 6¹² ἵνα τῷ σταύρῳ τοῦ Χρ.
μὴ διώκωνται, Col 2¹⁴ (transposing τοῖς δόγμασιν after ὃ ἦν)
which was against us because of the decrees (but Eph 2¹⁴ adds ἐν,
suggesting that this is a dat. of attendant circumstances, even
instrumental; i.e. take the phrase closely with the verb implied
in χειρόγραφον *written in* . . .), Ph 1¹⁴ πεποιθότας τοῖς δεσμοῖς μου
confident because of my imprisonment, Heb 13¹⁶ τοιαύταις
εὐαριστεῖται, 1 Pt 4¹² μὴ ξενίζεσθε τῇ, Jude¹¹ τῇ ἀντιλογίᾳ τοῦ
Κόρε ἀπώλοντο *because of the contradicting of.* More commonly
a preposition takes the place of dat. at this period.

(n) *With compound verbs* [2]. Here the dat. is frequent, but is
often supplemented by a preposition, and increasingly so in
Hell. Greek. The construction with the dat. is often figurative
e.g. ἀνατίθεμαι Ac 25¹⁴ etc. The dat. predominates with verbs
compounded with ἀντι-, and πρός is rare. But compounds with
εἰσ- always take a preposition. Compounds with ἐν- in a
literal sense always have a preposition ; but these figurative
meanings always have a plain dat. : ἐγκαλέω, ἐμμαίνομαι, ἐμπαίζω,
ἐνέχω, ἐντυγχάνω (Ro 11², Wi 8²¹, BUI 2461² ii–iii/A.D.). With
ἐπι- the practice fluctuates, but usually the plain dat. is
figurative. With παρα- it is almost only the dat., and Ac 15¹⁹
has dat. where Hell. Greek has usually accus. (Mayser II 2,
299f) ; the same is true of περι- and προσ- and συν-.

(o) *Locative* [3]. This is the " in- " case, the case of position.
The predominant use is now with prepositions, e.g. ἐν Ἀθήναις, not

---

[1] K-G I 438, 11. Mayser II 2, 284.
[2] K-G I 431 n. 1 ; 443 n. 1. Helbing 268–319. Mayser II 2, 285ff.
[3] K-G I 441ff. Schwyzer II 154ff. Mayser II 2, 295f.

'Αθήναζε, and even in the class. period the plain dat. was extremely limited. It is doubtful whether there are any more than these exx. in NT: πάντη, πανταχῆ; Jn 21⁸ οἱ μαθηταὶ τῷ πλοιαρίῳ ἦλθον; Ac 2³³ 5³¹ τῇ δεξιᾷ τοῦ θεοῦ ὑψωθείς. For pap. see Mayser, and also Vettius Valens 181, 22, and Herm. V. IV 3, 7.

(p) *Temporal.* (i) Of time-when[1]. Still in NT, but ἐν often enters to clarify the meaning, as class. The dat. is used for only point of time, strictly speaking, but p⁴⁶ in Ro 13¹³ has ἡμέρᾳ for *in the day* (the rest add ἐν). Normally, the dat. alone (or with ἐν) indicates a specific day or night, e.g. Mk 14³⁰ ταύτῃ τῇ νυκτί; it is useless to multiply examples. There is the Hebraism ἡμέρᾳ καὶ ἡμέρᾳ *every day* 2 Co 4¹⁶. It is usual to add ἐν when ἐκείνη and ταύτη are used. Φυλακή *night watch* and ὥρα are used like ἡμέρα, but ἔτει only has ἐν (Lk 3¹). The temporal dat. is still used with names of festivals: Mt 14⁶ γενεσίοις δὲ γενομένοις SBDL is apparently a dat. absolute[2], Mk 6²¹ (p⁴⁵ + ἐν), Mt 12¹ etc. τοῖς σάββασιν *on the sabbath*, Lk 2⁴¹ τῇ ἑορτῇ τοῦ πάσχα (D + ἐν). Other instances: Ac 13³⁶ ἰδίᾳ γενεᾷ, Ro 11³⁰ᶠ τῇ τούτων ἀπειθείᾳ *at the time of their disbelief*, Eph 2¹² τῷ καιρῷ ἐκείνῳ p⁴⁶ (2nd hand) SBAD*FG (p⁴⁶ DᶜEKLP + ἐν), 3⁵ ἑτέραις γενεαῖς *in other generations*, 1 Ti 6¹⁵ καιροῖς ἰδίοις.

(ii) Of duration of time. Class. usage has accus.; Hell. Greek uses dat. (even Josephus) mainly with transitive verbs: Lk 1⁷⁵ πάσαις ταῖς ἡμέραις ἡμῶν (cp. Mt 28²⁰ πάσας τὰς ἡμέρας), 8²⁹ πολλοῖς χρόνοις συνηρπάκει αὐτόν (unless it means *on many occasions*), Ac 8¹¹ ἱκανῷ χρόνῳ, 13²⁰ ὡς ἔτεσιν . . . ἔδωκεν *for 450 years*, Ro 16²⁵ χρ. αἰωνίοις σεσιγημένου. Examples abound in Hellenistic sources; and since they are usually with transitive verbs, it may be that there was some reticence felt at placing a second accus. alongside a verb which already had an accus. of dir. object. Textual variants in NT illustrate the uneasiness of scribes about the use of the dat.: Mk 8² ἤδη ἡμέραις τρισίν B

---

[1] K-G I 445, 2.   Schwyzer II 158f.   Moulton Einl. 116f.   Mayser II 2, 296f.

[2] There may be instances in Greek of dat. absolute. See C. C. Tarelli on Plutarch (Moule 45). In the NT: Mk 9²⁸ p⁴⁵ (SBCDLWΘ fam¹ fam¹³ 700 have gen. absol) εἰσελθόντι αὐτῷ, Ac 28¹¹ παρασήμῳ Διοσκούροις *with the Dioscuri as ship's insignia* (inscriptional precedent, W. M. Ramsay, *St. Luke the Physician*, London 1908, 36f).

(some have nom.; some accus.), Lk 8²⁷ χρόνῳ ἱκανῷ (some have gen.), Jn 14⁹ τοσούτῳ χρόνῳ SDLWQ (BA corr. to accus.), Ac 28¹² B ἡμέραις τρισίν (some nom.; some accus., as Mk 8²).

§ 4. Accusative [1]

(a) *The simple accus.* of external object occurs also with verbs which were originally intransitive, as a characteristic of Hell. Greek. The absol. ἐνεργέω *to be at work* is increased to *to be at work at something* in literary Koine (1 Co 12⁶ Ph 2¹³ etc.), by the simple addition of an accusative.[2]

Similar words in NT are: ἐμπορεύομαι *defraud* 2 Pt 2³ (Bauer s.v.), ἐνεδρεύω Lk 11⁵⁴ Ac 23²¹, εὐσεβέω Ac 17²³ 1 Ti 5⁴, θριαμβεύω 2 Co 2¹⁴ Col 2¹⁵ (Kittel WB III 160, n. 2), ἱερουργέω Ro 15¹⁶, καρτερέω Heb 11²⁷ (Bauer s.v.), πλεονεκτέω Paul, συνεργέω Ro 8²⁸ BA, τρίζω Mk 9¹⁸, ὑβρίζω, χορηγέω 2 Co 9¹⁰ 1 Pt 4¹¹. The same process has occurred with verbs of emotion: ἀπορέομαι Ac 25²⁰ SBAHP; ἐλεέω Mt 9²⁷ etc. Ptol. pap. (Mayser II 2, 308); εὐδοκέω Mt 12¹⁸ (OT) S*B, Heb 10⁶· ⁸, LXX Ps 50¹⁸ etc.; θέλω with same meaning Mt 27⁴³ ῥυσάσθω νῦν εἰ θέλει αὐτόν, LXX Ps 21⁹ 40¹² To 13⁸; θαυμάζω Lk 7⁹ (D om αὐτόν) Jn 5²⁸ Ac 7³¹ Jude¹⁶; ἱλάσκομαι *propitiate* Lk 18¹³ (pass.), *expiate* Heb 2¹⁷, LXX, Philo; κλαίω Mt 2¹⁸ (not LXX) Lk 23²⁸ D; κόπτομαι class. Lk 8⁵²; πενθέω 2 Co 12²¹, LXX (only dat. in Ptol. pap.). The same tendency to accus. in Hell. Greek appears with verbs which (in class. Greek) would have governed the (partit.) gen.: Mt 5⁵ κληρονομέω τὴν γῆν, ⁶ πεινάω διψάω, ²⁸ ἐπιθυμέω γυναῖκα, Jn 6⁵³ ἐσθίω πίνω; if the writer wishes to emphasize the *part* he often uses prepositions (Mt 15²⁷ 1 Co 11²⁸). Hellenistic addition of an object sometimes changes the entire meaning, as appears in μαθητεύω: cp. Mt 27⁵⁷ B with 28¹⁹ Ac 14²¹.

The accus. also accompanies verbs of fearing, fleeing, swearing, guarding from; but NT does have ἀπό c. gen. in addition, under strong Semitic influence (occasionally class.). Thus φοβέομαι has accus. except at Mt 10²⁸ = Lk 12⁴ (ἀπό), LXX has accus. and ἀπό c. gen., whereas Ptol. pap. has only accus. Jas 5¹² ὄμνυμι c. accus., while elsewhere there is a preposition as in LXX; but (ἐν-) ὀρκίζω *adjure* still has accus. Φεύγω ἀπό *shun* 1 Co 10¹⁴, *flee from* Mt 3⁷ = Lk 3⁷, Mt 23³³, Rev 9⁶ (in class. Greek ἀπό was only local, as in Jn 10⁵ᶠ Jas 4⁷), ἀπὸ προσώπου

---

[1] K-G I 293–331. Schwyzer II 67ff. Meisterhans-Schwyzer 204-6–12. Mayser II 2, 151, 297–336. Johannessohn DGKPS 67. Rader, macher² 120–122.

[2] F, Krebs *Zur Rection der Kasus*, 1887–90, *passim.* Moulton Proleg. 63ff.

(לְפָנֵי נוּס) Rev 20¹¹. Before Plutarch, ἐντρέπομαι usually has gen., but accus. in Mt 21³⁷ Lk 18² Heb 12⁹.

On the other hand, the dat. is sometimes used instead of, or besides, the class. accus.: καλῶς ποιέω (class. accus.) has the Hellenistic dat. Lk 6²⁷, and so does εὖ ποιέω Mk 14⁷ (A corrects to accus.), but accus. still in LXX (Schwyzer II 144; Mayser II 2, 263f). In addition to class. accus. προσκυνέω has dat. about 150 times in LXX (against about ten times with accus.), also in Dio Cassius, Jos., Aristeas, Lucian, 2 Clem. 3¹; so NT e.g. Mt 2². ¹¹ Jn 4²¹ Ac 7⁴³ 1 Co 14²⁵ Heb 1⁶ Rev 4¹⁰ 7¹¹ 13⁴. ¹⁵ 14⁷ 16² 19⁴. ¹⁰. ²⁰ 22⁸. ⁹; with acc., only Mt 4¹⁰ = Lk 4⁸, Lk24⁵² (D om), Jn 4²². ²². ²³ (S* dat.) ²⁴ 9³⁸ D. Rev several times (9²⁰ 13⁴. ⁸. ¹² 14⁹. ¹¹ 20⁴) in addition to dat. The dat. in LXX is due to influence of לְ, and in order to avoid the interpretation kiss¹. Of human superiors: c. dat. Mt 2². ⁸ 8² 9¹⁸ 14³³ 15²⁵ 18²⁶ 28⁹ Mk 15¹⁹ Jn 9³⁸: c. accus. Mk 5⁶ vl.

The accus. has usurped the place of class. dat. with verbs meaning censure, revile, blaspheme, curse (Helbing 1–23): ἐπηρεάζω (Lk 6²⁸ 1 Pt 3¹⁶; not in LXX); ὀνειδίζω (Wi 2¹² is only ex. of dat. in LXX); καταράομαι (the dat. in Mt 5⁴⁴ D* and Lk 6²⁸ EHL is an atticistic correction; the rare dat. in LXX is also probably atticistic: 4 Km 2²⁴ Ep. Je⁶⁵); φθονέω Ga 5²⁶ p⁴⁶ BG (SACD dat.). As well as class. εἰς NT (Hell. Greek) has plain accus. with βλασφημέω like LXX (4 Km 19⁴. ⁶. ²²), Jos., Vett. Val., Babrius (ii/A.D.): Lk 23³⁹ Ac 19³⁷ Rev 13⁶. Whereas class. Greek has dat. of person with εὐαγγελίζομαι, NT has accus. as well. With ἐγκόπτω hinder (class. dat.), NT has accus.: Ac 24⁴ Ga 5⁷ 1 Th 2¹⁸ (Stählin in Kittel WB III 855). Some NT exx. of accus. gaining over gen.: Mt 1²⁰ 9⁴ ἐνθυμέομαι (gen. in P. Par. 63 vii 9, ii/B.C.), Mt 12⁷ Jas 5⁶ καταδικάζω, Ro 2¹⁰ προηγέομαι Ph 1¹¹ πληρόομαι.

(b) Content, or internal object ("cognate accusative"). This follows a Semitic principle, and may consist of a noun with an attribute: Mt 2¹⁰, 2 Co 6¹³ τὴν δὲ αὐτὴν ἀντιμισθίαν πλατύνθητε, perhaps pregnant for τὸν αὐτὸν πλατυσμὸν ὡς ἀντιμισθίαν (or adverbial: with the same reward, or accus. in apposition to a sentence, Moule 35f), 1 Pt 3¹⁴ τὸν φόβον αὐτῶν (of them) μὴ φοβηθῆτε, Rev 16⁹ ἐκαυματίσθησαν καῦμα μέγα, Jn 7²⁴ κρίνω with τὴν δικαίαν κρίσιν, Mk 10³⁸ τὸ βάπτισμα, ὃ ἐγὼ βαπτίζομαι, βαπτισθῆναι, Jn 17²⁶ ἡ ἀγάπη ἣν ἠγάπησάς με (D ᾗ), Eph 24. No attribute: Lk 2⁸ φυλάσσω φυλακάς, Jas 5¹⁸. It may consist of

---

¹ Kittel WB VI 762f.

an adj. or pronoun: Lk 12⁴⁷ᵗ δαρήσεται πολλάς, ὀλίγας; the neuters of certain pronouns (τοῦτο, τί, οὐδέν, πάντα) are less frequent than in class. Greek but they still appear: Lk 4³⁵ μηδὲν βλάψας (or accus. of respect?), Mt 19²⁰ τί ὑστερῶ, Mk 7³⁶ ὅσον *as much as* (W 700 dat.), Ac 10²⁰, Ro 6¹⁰, 1 Co 9²⁵, 10³³, 11², 2 Co 12¹¹, 12¹³, 12¹⁴ˑ¹³¹ τρίτον, Ga 2²⁰ ὃ νῦν ζῶ, 5² ὑμᾶς οὐδὲν ὠφελήσει, Ph 1⁶ πεποιθὼς αὐτὸ τοῦτο *in just this confidence* (= *I am sure*), 2¹⁸ Mt 27⁴⁴ τὸ δ' αὐτό *in the same way.* We might take ἅ like this in Col 2¹⁸ ἃ ἑώρακεν ἐμβατεύων, εἰκῆ φυσιούμενος *upon what he vainly imagined in the vision of his initiation* (making the conjectural emendations unnecessary). Papyri of 145 and 118 B.C.: πολλὰ χαῖρε and χαίρειν (Mayser II 2, 319).

(c) *Double accusative* [1]. The NT conforms mainly to class. usage, with certain verbs: e.g. *teach* and *remind* Mk 6³⁴, Jn 14²⁶, Ac 21²¹, 1 Co 4¹⁷, Heb 5¹² τοῦ διδάσκειν ὑμᾶς τινα τὰ στοιχεία (but διδάσκω c. dat. Rev 2¹⁴); *enquire* and *entreat* Mk 6²². ²³ Lk 12⁴⁸ Mt 21²⁴ Mk 4¹⁰, LXX has both single and double accus.; *dress* and *undress* Mt 27³¹ Mk 15¹⁷· ²⁰ (ἐγδύω τινά τι in pap.), Lk 19⁴³, LXX περιβάλλω τινά τι, τί τινι, ἔν τινι. Causatives are more popular than in class. Greek and have double accus.: ποτίζω Mk 9⁴¹ 1 Co 3², φορτίζω Lk 11⁴⁶ τοὺς ἀνθρώπους φορτία. We find the double accus. of both external and internal object: Lk 4³⁵, Jn 17²⁶, Ac 13³² ἡμεῖς ὑμᾶς εὐαγγελιζόμεθα τὴν ... ἐπαγγελίαν, Ga 4¹², 5², Eph 2⁴, Rev 14⁷ p⁴⁷ δοξάσατε αὐτὸν δόξαν An accus. of object and a predicative accus. (without the help of a ptc. or a particle like ὡς, such as would be needed with other cases) occurs in the class. manner: *to reckon as* Ac 13⁵ (but with ὡς Mt 21²⁶, with εἰς 21⁴⁶ vl.); *to receive as* Jas 5¹⁰; *to make to be* Lk 19⁴⁶ ὑμεῖς δὲ αὐτὸν ἐποιήσατε σπηλαῖον, Jn 6¹⁵, Ro 4¹⁷ LXX πατέρα ... τέθεικά σε, Lk 12¹⁴ Heb 1²; *to do something to* Mt 27²² τί οὖν ποιήσω 'Ιησοῦν, Herm. S. I 4 τί ποιήσεις τὸν ἀγρόν, LXX Nu 24¹⁴ τί ποιήσεις ... τὸν λαόν σου; *to designate as*, Mk 10¹⁸, Lk 1⁵⁹, Jn 9²² (D + εἶναί), 10³⁵, Ro 10⁹, 1 Jn 4² (B accus. c. inf.), 2 Jn⁷, and Semitism καλέσεις τὸ ὄνομα αὐτοῦ 'Ιωάννην etc. Mt 1²¹. ²³. ²⁵ Lk 1¹³. ³¹ 2²¹; *to consider as* Lk 14¹⁸· ¹⁹ ἔχω, Ac 20²⁴ ποιοῦμαι, Ro 6¹¹ p⁴⁶ DAEFG λογίζομαι, Ph 3⁷ ἥγημαι (cp. Lat. *habeo*); *to prove to be* 2 Co 6⁴ Ga 2¹⁸. To this predicative accus. we may add 1 Co 9⁵ ἀδελφὴν γυναῖκα after περιάγω (it is not attributive:

---

[1] K-G I 318ff. Mayser II 2, 320–323. Helbing 38–68. Radermacher[2] 121.

a wife who is a sister, but predicative: *a sister as a wife*); Lk 11¹¹ *which of you shall the son ask as the father* (τὸν πατέρα predicative of τίνα); 1 Pt 1¹⁷ *if you invoke as father the one who judges* (πατέρα a predicate of τὸν ... κρίνοντα). In a Semitic way, εἰς (like normal Greek ὡς) may be added to this predicate: Mt 21⁴⁶ εἰς προφήτην (vl. ὡς), Ac 13²² εἰς βασιλέα, ⁴⁷ (= Isa. 49⁶), 7²¹, 1 Clem. 42⁴ εἰς ἐπισκόπους, BGU 1103¹¹ (13 b.c.) ὃ εἶχεν εἰς φερνάριον *which he has received for dowry*.

(d) *Accus. with passive*. This occurs with the passive of verbs which have double accus. in the active, and is classical: e.g. μουσικὴν διδαχθείς. 1 Co 12¹³ ἓν πνεῦμα ἐποτίσθημεν, 2 Th 2¹⁵, Heb 6⁹, Lk 16¹⁹ ἐνεδιδύσκετο πορφύραν. In the Koine, and actually already in LXX, occurs accus. instead of gen. with *fill*, *be full*: Ph 1¹¹ πεπληρωμένοι καρπὸν δικαιοσύνης, Col 1⁹ πληρωθῆτε τὴν ἐπίγνωσιν *filled with knowledge*. The person which appears in dat. with active voice may become the subject with the passive, and therefore such a passive will have accus. of the thing (as in English: " I am given a book "): Lk 12⁴⁷ δαρήσεται πολλάς, Ga 2⁷ πεπίστευμαι τὸ εὐαγγέλιον, 1 Th 2⁴, 1 Co 9¹⁷.

(e) *Adverbial accus*. (i) Manner: for τὸ λοιπόν see p. 336. Also δωρεάν *gratuitously* and μακράν have become simple adverbs. Mt 15¹⁶, Heb 5¹³ D* E* ἀκμήν (Hellenistic, not LXX). This accus. is often formed by a superfluous article: Lk 11³ 19⁴⁷ Ac 17¹¹· ²⁸ D 19⁹ D τὸ καθ' ἡμέραν *daily* (class.); Ac 5²¹ D τὸ πρωΐ, Ro 1¹⁵ τὸ κατ' ἐμέ, 9⁵, 12⁵· ¹⁸, 15²², 16¹⁹, 1 Co 14²⁷, 1 Pt 3⁸. For Jn 8²⁵ τὴν ἀρχήν see pp. 49f. Lk 11⁴¹ τὰ ἔνοντα may be attributive accus. (*alms relating to what is within*) or accus. of respect (*as for what is inside, give alms*), but neither makes as good sense as adverbial accus. (*give alms from the heart*). Other instances: ὃν τρόπον Mt 23³⁷ 2 Ti 3⁸ etc. (LXX often) (pap. Mayser II 2, 329), τὸν ὅμοιον τρόπον Jude⁷, Mt 13³⁰ LXΔ δήσατε αὐτὰ δεσμάς (SBCEF add εἰς; D om αὐτά), Lk 9¹⁴ κατακλίνατε αὐτοὺς κλισίας. Cp. adverbial nom., p. 231.

(ii) *Extent*. In Mt 4¹⁵ ὁδὸν θαλάσσης (in LXX Isa 8²³ perhaps a harmonization with the NT) is a literal translation of Heb. יָם דֶּרֶךְ = *seawards*, rather than a ref. to some road leading to the sea. Lk 22⁴¹ ὡσεὶ λίθου βολήν, 2³⁶ ζήσασα ... ἔτη ἑπτά, Mt 28²⁰, Mk 4²⁷ Ac 26⁷ 2 Th 3⁸ ADE (SB gen.). Distributive: Mt 20² τὴν ἡμέραν *per day* (Mayser II 2. 333), Mk 9²⁶ πολλὰ

σπαράξας *fit after fit.*   There is a Hell. Greek idiom for indicating
duration of time by placing the preposition with the inappropriate noun : e.g. instead of *six days before the passover* Jn 12¹
reads *before six days of the passover* [1].

(iii) Point of time.   This is not unclass. (e.g. Demosth. 54,
10 ἐκείνην τὴν ἑσπέραν *on that evening*), and is found in the Koine
(Moulton Proleg. 63), LXX (e.g. Ge 43¹⁶ Ex 9¹⁸), and Church
writers (e.g. Justin M. Apol. 1, 67, 8 τὴν δὲ τοῦ ἡλίου ἡμέραν ; but
67, 3 dative).   In NT Jn 4⁵² ἐχθὲς ὥραν ἑβδόμην, Ac 10³ ὥραν
ἐνάτην, 10³⁰ (unless τὴν ἐνάτην = *the ninth-hour prayer,* cogn.
accus.), 20¹⁶ τὴν ἡμέραν τῆς πεντηκοστῆς (D + εἰς), Rev 3³
ποίαν ὥραν.

(iv) For the accus. in apposition to a clause, see pp. 220f.

---

[1] Moulton Proleg. 100f.

CHAPTER EIGHTEEN

CASE ADDITIONS TO THE VERB: WITH A PREPOSITION [1]

§ 1 Preparatory Note on Prepositions in NT

This study is important for the exegete, provided he is aware that class. niceties must not be pressed too far. In the search for a theology of prepositions it is straining credulity for instance to adopt a distinction between ἐκ and διά in Ro 3³⁰ (ICC Ro in loc.; Moule 195). In Hell. Greek there is a strong preference for the preposition against the simple case, and also a growing laxity which entails closer examination of the context. Thus the meanings of εἰς and ἐν tend to approximate to each other in Hell. Greek.

Although the NT has kept most of the old "proper" prepositions the number was decreasing until only seven were left in MGr, and ἀμφί and ὡς have been discarded as in LXX and pap.[2], while ἀνά and ἀντί have been much curtailed. The variety in the use of each preposition has also diminished. On the other hand, ἐν εἰς ἐκ are much more widely used. The dat. is beginning to wane at this period with all prepositions (except ἐν in NT) and has disappeared entirely with ἀνά μετά περί ὑπό, bringing to a close a development already present in the class.

---

[1] K-G I 448–555. Schwyzer II 417ff. Jannaris 365–399. Wacker-nagel II 153–248. Mayser II 2, 337–543. F. Krebs, *Die Präpositionen bei Polybius*, Würzburg 1882; *Die Präpositionsadverbia in der späteren historischen Gräcitat*, 2 Teile, Munich 1884–5; *Zur Rection der Kasus in der späteren histor. Gräcitat*, 1887–90. R. Helbing, *Die Präpositionen bei Herodot und andern Historiken* (B.z.h.S.dgr.Spr. 16), 1904. W. Kuhring. *De praepositionum Graecarum in chartis Aegypt. usu quaestiones selectae*, Bonn 1906. C. Rossberg, *De praepositionum Graecarum in chartis Aegypt. Ptolemaeum aetate usu*, Jena 1909. P. F. Regard, *Contributions à l'étude des prépositions dans la langue du NT*, Paris 1919. J. Waldis, *Die Präpositions-Adverbien mit der Bedeutung "vor" in der Septuaginta*, Lucerne 1921–2. M. Johannessohn, DGPS, Berlin 1926. R. F. Rickel-son, *The Ablative after* διά, Diss. S-W. Bapt. Sem., 1944. P. Southern, *The NT Use of the Preposition KATA*, ibid. 1949. B. Blackwelder, *Causal Use of Prepositions in the Greek NT*, ibid. 1951. Kittel WB VI 11, 1958, 683ff. (πρό); VI 12, 1958, 720–725 (πρός).

[2] Rossberg 11. Regard Prép. 683f. Mayser II 2, 338.

period. There is now a preference for the accus.. In the LXX
the dative is used with περί four times only, and with ὑπό in
Job 12⁵ A only. In NT the only prepositions which still have
all three cases are ἐπί and παρά ¹. In MGr only the accus. is
used with prepositions.

The niceties of class. Greek in the precise use of cases after
prepositions are obliterated in Hellenistic; the distinctions in the
cases after διά ἐπί πρός, for example, are becoming less clear.

Because of the tendency of the language towards fuller
forms, the "improper" prepositions begin to gain ground in
Hell. Greek: in the NT there are 42, against 18 "proper".
These are adverbs or nouns in various cases which assumed the
character of prepositions, but are not compounded with verbs.
They now supplement the old stock of prepositions.

No distinct line of demarcation between adverbs and
prepositions can easily be drawn and the combination of a
preposition and adverb is common in the Koine; ² e.g. in NT
ἀπὸ τότε for ἀφ' οὗ Mk 8² D (popular), ἐκ πάλαι etc. ³.

The old adverbial meaning of the prepositions is not well attested
in Hell. Greek, except of course when compounded with verbs, and it is
doubtful whether all the instances suggested for the NT can be accepted,
viz. ὑπέρ (accent?) 2 Co 11²³ ὑπὲρ ἐγώ I more (Wackernagel II 167),
11⁵ 12¹¹ ὑπὲρ λίαν (but perhaps a compound ὑπερλίαν, like ὑπερεκπερισσοῦ
Eph 3²⁰ 1 Th 3¹⁰ 5¹³), Lk 16⁸ φρονιμώτεροι ὑπέρ; ἐν Mk 1²³ ἐν πνεύματι
ἀκαθάρτῳ with an unclean spirit in him; Ph 3¹³ ἐν δέ but thereby, for
ἓν δέ. The Ptol. pap. have παρά thus apparently only once (Mayser
II 2, 339) and ἐπὶ δέ moreover, ἒξ καὶ πρός six and more (Pap. Oxy. I
68²⁴ A.D. 131). The LXX has τὸ πρὸς πρωί right early Ps. 45⁶, πρὸς ἐπὶ
τούτοις moreover besides this Sir 29²⁵, and Cant 1¹⁶ has πρός moreover,
and Aquila Deut 33³ has the same; Aquila Eccles. 1¹⁷ 7²³ ⁽²²⁾ πρός (adv.).
Symmachus in Eccles 9² has πρός τε (adv.).

In brief, the LXX and NT share the following innovations
of the Hellenistic period in the use of prepositions: (a) the tendency to discard one of the cases where formerly a preposition
was used with more than one. (b) Adverbs and adverbial
prepositions now supplement the old stock of prepositions: thus

---

¹ On the other hand. the accus. is declining with ὑπό ὑπέρ περί, while
μετά περί ὑπό have ceased to take the dat., and κατά has lost its hold
of the gen.

² Schmid, Der Attizismus IV 625. Hatzid. 213.

³ See also ἀφ' ὅτε Hermas, and μέχρι ὅτε (Blass-Debr. §§ 241, 2;
455, 3).

ἐναντίον, ἐνώπιον etc. for πρό; ἐπάνω for ἐπί; ἀπάνωθεν, ἐπάνωθεν, ὑπεράνω for ὑπέρ; ὑποκάτω for ὑπό; ἀνὰ μέσον for μεταξύ; κύκλῳ, περικύκλῳ for περί; ἐχόμενος etc. for παρά. (c) There is a new use of ὑπέρ and περί. (d) εἰς and ἐν are now confused in two ways: 1. ἐν is used after verbs of motion (= בְּ), 2. εἰς is used for ἐν after expressions denoting rest. (e) There is a change in the relative frequence of prepositions: e.g. ἀπό encroaches on ἐκ and ὑπό.

§ 2. Prepositional Periphrases for the simple cases

This usage is greatly extended in Hell. Greek; e.g. εἰς and πρός c. accus. serve for the simple dat., ἐν c. dat. for the simple dat., and παρά is used after a comparative in place of the simple gen. In place of the simple gen., Polybius can write ἡ κατὰ τὸν ἥλιον πορεία.

(a) For Genitive: see pp. 207ff, 231ff. For partitive ἀπό, see pp. 208f; for gen. of separation, see pp. 258f; for ἀπό instead of accus. after verbs of fleeing, fearing, etc., see p. 244. Besides these, there is the Pauline use of ἀπό in the sense of alienation, where older Greek would have the simple case, e.g. Ro 9[3] ἀνάθεμα ... ἀπὸ τοῦ X., Col 2[20] ἀποθνήσκω ἀπό (for dat.). The following verbs are followed by ἀπό in the same way: παρέρχομαι Mt 26[39] = Mk 14[35], παραφέρω Mk 14[36] = Lk 22[42] (cp. MGr θὰ περάσω ἀπὸ τὴ Σμύρνη; we must not interpret ἀπό as far from), μετανοέω Ac 8[22] (ἐκ in Rev 2[21] etc.; noun in Heb 6[1]), ἄφαντος γίνομαι Semitism Lk 24[31], καταργέομαι Ro 7[6] Ga 5[4], φθείρω 2 Co 11[3], εἰσακούω Heb 5[7] (but the meaning is difficult; perhaps on account of).

(b) For Dative[1]. For διά c. gen. in instrumental or modal use see p. 267. As a circumlocution for the simple case ἐνώπιον c. gen. Ac 6[5] appears to render לִפְנֵי, בְּעֵינֵי, or נֶגֶד; to a less extent also ἔμπροσθεν, ἐναντίον (Heb 13[21] 1 Jn 3[22]). Lk 15[18. 21] ἁμαρτάνω ἐνώπιον, Mt 7[6] βάλλω ἔμπροσθεν, Heb 4[13] ἐμφανὴς ἐνώπιον.

The preposition ἐν, too, takes the place of plain dat. in instances where in is quite unsuitable as a translation.

---

[1] K-G I 436, n. 7; 483. Mayser II 2, 354ff. Johannessohn DGPS 239f. Radermacher[2] 127.

(i) In an adverbial sense, quite briefly stated. Thus in Ro we have: *powerfully* 1⁴, *openly* 2²⁸, *secretly* ²⁹, *patiently* 9²², *in this way* 14¹⁸, *in carnal things* 15²⁷, *joyfully* ³², *quickly* 16²⁰. Perhaps we may also include the six exx. in 12⁷· ⁸: *liberally, zealously, cheerfully*, etc. In 1 Co we have *weakly, fearfully, tremblingly* 2³, 15⁴²· ⁴²· ⁴³ quat., ἐν πρώτοις 15³, *peacefully* 16¹¹, and perhaps *in love* 16¹⁴. Other NT exx. come to mind: the class. ἐν τάχει *quickly* Lk 18⁸, ἐν δικαιοσύνη = δικαίως Ac 17³¹ Rev 19¹¹), ἐν πάση ἀσφαλεία = ἀσφαλέστατα (Ac 5²³), *boldly* (Col 2¹⁵). The ἐν δόλῳ of Mk 14¹ shows how close we are to the instrumental sense: *by means of guile* or *guilefully*.

(ii) An ἐν of accompaniment is apparently the equivalent of μετά or σύν or simple dat. (= *with*), as in class. Greek. The idea of manner is often implied. There is in Mk 1²³ 5² the man *with* the unclean spirit, unless we may take this as *in the power of*; but in 5²⁵ the woman must be *with*, not *in the power of*ₓ a flow of blood. *With* is also the way to translate Lk 14³¹ *with ten thousand* (especially as μετά occurs in the adjacent parallel phrase), Ro 1²⁷ relations *with* women, 15²⁹ to come *with* a blessing, 1 Co 4²¹· ²¹ come *with* a rod ... *with* love (but this may be instrumental rather than of accompaniment), Heb 9²²· ²⁵ *with* blood, Jude¹⁴ *with* his saints. The method is classical enough and belongs to the Koine, but its use in the LXX to render ב seems to have suggested an increase of use in NT. Col 1⁵ ἐν τῷ λόγῳ τῆς ἀληθείας τοῦ εὐαγγελίου *by means of the Gospel* (or perhaps temporal ἐν: *when the true Gospel was preached*.

(iii) There is the relatively frequent instrumental use,[1] in the stricter sense : e.g. nineteen times in Mt 1–14, twenty-five in Ro, twenty-eight in 1 Co, and very common in Rev. It is least common in the second part of Ac. It is as old as Homer, who uses this preposition for seeing *with* the eyes, but it is comparatively rare before the LXX,[2] in which it is extremely common (on the model of ב)—much more so proportionately than in the NT. Moreover, it is not very common in the Koine,[3] where many apparent instances, as in NT, may be accepted satisfactorily in the strictly locative sense. We cannot rule out the possibility [4] of *in water* Mt 3¹¹, nor of *in one mouth* Ro 15⁶, since words are certainly formed here, as thoughts were considered to be formed in the heart. Our own idiom is often *in* in these phrases: *in* God's will (Ro 1¹⁰), *in* the likeness (8³), to sum up *in* one word (13⁹), but usually we shall employ *with*. Semitic influence may be behind *swear by* (Mt 5³⁴),

---

[1] K-G I § 431, 3a. Kuhring § 30. Rossberg 28, 2. Mayser II 2, 357f. Deissmann BS 115f (against Hebraism). Johannessohn DGKPS 52ff. N. Turner, " The Preposition EN in the NT," *Bible Translator*, vol. 10, no. 3, 1959. Lagrange *S. Matth.* XCIX.

[2] K-G I 464f. Helbing 146f. Radermacher[2] 130, n. 4.

[3] ἐν μαχαίρη in the pap., but not combined with *kill*, etc. (Moulton Einl. 15f., Kuhring 43f, Rossberg 28, Mayser II 2, 358, 393). NT has ἐν μαχαίρη. ἐν ῥομφαία Mt 26⁵² Lk 22⁴⁹ Rev 2¹⁶ 6⁸ 13¹⁰ 19²¹.

[4] Many readers will prefer a stronger word, even " certainty ". But I hesitate because of the imminent parallel ἐν πνεύματι ἁγίῳ καὶ πυρί.

with his arm (Lk 1⁵¹), *ransom by* (Rev 5⁹), *call with a loud voice* (14¹⁵);
and Semitic influence was probably at work in Mt 7² ἐν τῷ μέτρῳ
(because Lk 6³⁸ avoids it), 7⁶ ἐν τοῖς ποσὶν αὐτῶν, 22¹⁶ ἐν ἀληθείᾳ
(because Mk 12¹⁴ Lk 20²¹ have ἐπ’ ἀληθείας), 24⁴¹ ἐν τῷ μύλῳ (Lk 17³⁵
ἐπὶ τὸ αὐτό). But Greek usage sufficiently accounts for *salted with*
(Mt 5¹³), *to be known by means of* (Lk 24³⁵), *mingle with* (Rev 8³), *burn
with fire* (18⁸). So also Mt 9³⁴ Ac 17³¹ Col 1¹⁶.

A causal sense is probably best included here. We must render
because of at Mt 6⁷ 11⁶ 13⁵⁷ Jn 16³⁰ (= *propterea*) Ac 7²⁹ 24¹⁶ Ro 2¹⁷· ²³
5³· ¹¹ 14²¹ 1 Co 2⁵· ⁵ 4⁴ 10⁵ Col 1¹⁶, and *because* (ἐν ᾧ) at Ro 2¹ 8³ Heb
2¹⁸ 6¹⁷.

A curious instrumental dat. of price is found with ἐν, a distinctly
Semitic construction literally rendering the *beth pretii* [1]: Ro 3²⁵ 5⁹ Rev 5⁹
(*at the cost of his blood*).

Then there is a semi-forensic sense, suggested by 1 Co 6² 11¹³ and
found in the Koine: *in your judgment.*

Probably εἰς, as in MGr, also occurs as a substitute for
the dat. (or gen.): Ga 3¹⁴ ἵνα εἰς τὰ ἔθνη ἡ εὐλογία τοῦ
Ἀβραὰμ γένηται, unless we understand εἰς = *among*. Cp.
γίνομαι εἰς in papyri (Mayser II 2, 406) *to fall to someone* as a
possession.

(c) *The accus.* occasionally appears in place of the predicative nominative owing to the Hellenistic tendency towards
greater expressiveness and this is assisted by the Semitic εἰς
(= ל) [2], although there are occasionally parallels outside
Biblical Greek (Jannaris § 1552, Radermacher[2] 20f). (i) with
γίνομαι and εἰμί: Mt 19⁵ = Ge 2²⁴, 1 Co 6¹⁶ ἔσονται εἰς σάρκα
μίαν (but Mt 19⁶ has truer Greek predicative nom.), Mt 21⁴² =
Ps 118²² ἐγενήθη εἰς κεφαλήν, Lk 3⁵, 1 Co 15⁴⁵ = Ge 2⁷
ἐγένετο . . . εἰς ψυχὴν ζῶσαν, 2 Co 6¹⁸ Heb 8¹⁰ LXX, and (outside
of quotations) Lk 13¹⁹ ἐγένετο εἰς δένδρον, Jn 16²⁰ ἡ λύπη ὑμῶν
εἰς χαρὰν γενήσεται, Ac 5³⁶ ἐγένετο εἰς οὐδέν, 8²³ εἰς γὰρ χολὴν
. . . ὁρῶ σε ὄντα, 1 Th 3⁵, 1 Jn 5⁸, Rev 8¹¹, 16¹⁹. (ii) with
λογίζομαι: [3] Ac 19²⁷, Ro 4³ = Ge 15⁶, 9⁸, 2²⁶, LXX Isa 40¹⁷
1 Mac 2⁵² (A corrects to nom.).

(d) *For Accusative*: on εἰς for predicative accus. see pp. 246f.

---

[1] *Hebrew and English Lexicon*, ed. Brown, Driver, Briggs, Oxford 1906,
s.v. ב, III. 3.
[2] Zerwick § 20.   Johannessohn DGKPS 4f.   Psichari 201f.   Jannaris
§ 1552.   Helbing 60–67.   Moulton Proleg. 71f.   Moulton-Howard 462f.
[3] Helbing 66f.   Bonaccorsi 603f.   Mayser II 2, 362ff; 416ff.   Heid-
land in Kittel WB IV 287, 288 n. 4.

§ 3. Anomalies in the use of Prepositions

(a) For ἀπό with nom. see p. 230.

(b) Εἰς for local ἐν [1].

Etymologically these two prepositions are related, and at this period, from c. 150 B.C., εἰς is used instead of ἐν in a local sense, for the distinction between motion and rest becomes obscured in Hell. Greek. The same approximation occurs between πρός c. accus. and παρά c. dat. In the Koine εἰς and ἐν are freely interchanged, until in MGr εἰς has absorbed ἐν completely, consistently with the disappearance of the dat. However, under Hebraic influence ἐν appears almost twice as often as εἰς in NT, and confusion between the two prepositions has already begun, εἰς often appearing for ἐν and more rarely ἐν for εἰς (see p. 257).

Even in the class. period we sometimes find εἰς for ἐν in a compressed or pregnant construction,[2] but no NT writer except Mt [3] is entirely innocent of the replacing of ἐν by εἰς in a local sense; in Lk–Ac most of the exx. are found. Mk 1⁹ ἐβαπτίσθη εἰς τὸν Ἰορδάνην (possibly pregnant, implying the notion of coming), Lk 9⁶¹ τοῖς εἰς τὸν οἶκόν μου (no idea of motion), 11⁷ (D ἐν), Jn 1¹⁸ εἰς τὸν κόλπον (Syrᶜᵘʳ gen.): there is therefore nothing very profound here concerning mutual motion between Father and Son; nevertheless John (including Rev) does not usually blur the distinction between εἰς and ἐν, and except for Mt he has fewer exx. of εἰς = ἐν than any NT author. Mk 1³⁹ (EF ἐν) 2¹ (SBD ἐν), 8²⁶ μηδενὶ εἴπῃς εἰς τὴν κώμην, 10¹⁰ (AC ἐν), 13³·⁹ εἰς συναγωγὰς δαρήσεσθε (= Mt 10¹⁷ ἐν, D εἰς), ¹⁶ (= Mt 24¹⁸ Lk 17³¹ ἐν), Lk 4²³ (vl. ἐν), 9⁶¹, Jn 20⁷ τὸ σουδάριον ... ἐντετυλιγμένον εἰς ἕνα τόπον (pregn?), Ac 2⁵ (SᶜBDCE ἐν) ²⁷ OT (motion impossible), ³⁹ τοῖς εἰς μακράν (a Semitism; not in LXX of Isa 57¹⁹), 4⁵ S (pregn?), 7⁴ (but perhaps by attraction), ¹² (but LXX Ge 42², which is cited, has ἐν), 8²³ (or destined for the gall of bitterness), 9²¹SA (rest ἐν), 9²⁸, 11²⁵ D, 12²⁵ SB (pregn.?), 14²⁵ (BCD ἐν), 17¹³ D, 18²¹ D, 19²² (D ἐν), 21¹³, 23¹¹·¹¹, 25⁴, 26²⁰, 1 Pt 5¹² (a post-script?) τὴν χάριν ... εἰς ἣν ἑστήκατε KLP. Especially Semitic are the following: Lk 1⁴⁴ ἐγένετο ἡ φωνὴ εἰς τὰ ὦτά μου, Ac 20¹⁶ 21¹⁷ 25¹⁵, Jn 17²³ 1 Jn 5⁸ εἰς (τὸ) ἕν. But εἰς = ἐν occurs in the secular Koine: P. Oxy VI 929¹² ταῦτα δὲ πάντα συνενῆι εἰς τὸν χιτῶνα καροῖνον inside the brown tunic, see also Bauer s.v. εἰς.

---

[1] Mayser II 2, 371ff. Moulton Einl. 93. Rossberg 54. Radermacher[2] 140, 145. Johannessohn DGPS 330ff.

[2] As in NT Jn 9⁷ ὕπαγε νίψαι εἰς τὴν κολυμβήθραν, 20¹⁹· ²⁶ ἔστη εἰς τὸ μέσον, 1 Pt 3²⁰ εἰς ἣν ὀλίγοι διεσώθησαν by entering which (pregn.).

[3] C. H. Turner examined the use of εἰς for ἐν in Mk and pointed out that Matthew and Luke disliked the confusion, especially Matthew. See JThS 26, p. 14.

The Pauline and Johannine epistles and Rev (in spite of its Semitic character) do not often confuse local ἐν and εἰς. This is important for the exegete, because in Mt, the epistles, and Rev we can always presume that εἰς has its full sense even where one might suspect that it stood for ἐν (e.g. Mt 28¹⁹ baptism *into* the name, i.e. a relationship as the goal of baptism ; also Mt 10⁴¹ receiving a righteous man εἰς ὄνομα of a righteous man, which is not the same as ἐν ὀνόματι, for it has the Semitic causal sense, εἰς being ל. See לְשֵׁם Jo 9⁹ Ezk 36²² : *because of* or *for the sake of* a righteous man's name. Cp. Mt 12⁴¹ they repented *because of* the preaching of Jonah. See Zerwick § 70a, 76. But in Mt 5³⁵ μὴ ὀμόσαι . . . εἰς Ἱεροσόλυμα, *by*).

In the LXX (e.g. Ge 31³³ Nu 35³³), Diodorus (e.g. 3, 44), and in Hermas (e.g. V, I 2, 2 ; II 4, 3 ; S. I 2), εἰς = ἐν is common. Note especially κρύπτω εἰς Jb 40⁸ (¹³), Pr 1¹¹ Isa 2¹⁰ Je 4²⁹ Ps 88⁴⁰ (Johannessohn DGPS 331f, Jannaris § 1548, Oepke in Kittel WB II 418f. n). There do not seem to be any papyrus exx. earlier than the Imperial period, e.g. P. Fay. 111¹¹ b (A.D. 95–100) ἐνετιλάμην συ εἰς Διονυσιάδα μῖναι *I have bid you remain at Dionysias*. The earlier examples are pregnant with the idea of motion (Mayser II 2, 371ff), but while it is true that some of the instances in NT (especially Lk 21³⁷ Jn 19¹³) may be the " pregnant " construction, the real explanation at this date lies not so much here as in the inevitable progress of the absorption of ἐν by εἰς [1].

(c) Interchange of εἰς and ἐν in a metaphorical (non-local) sense.

Polyb. V 13, 8 εἰς δὲ τὴν ὑστέραιον *on the next day*, Lk 1²⁰ εἰς τὸν καιρὸν αὐτῶν *at their proper time* (ἐν correctly Mt 21⁴¹ 2 Th 2⁶), 13⁹ εἰς τὸ μέλλον *in the future* (P. Oxy. I 36, iii 3), class. ἐς αὔριον, Ac 13⁴² εἰς τὸ μεταξὺ σάββατον *on the next Sabbath*, 2 Co 13² Ph 1¹⁰ εἰς ἡμέραν Χριστοῦ, 1 Th 4¹⁵ εἰς τὴν παρουσίαν (P. Oxy. XIV. 1764. 9). In Ac 7⁵³ εἰς διαταγὰς ἀγγέλων may be a Hebraism (A. T. Robertson 482) or an Aramaism (*Beginnings* II 148). Also εἰς varies with ἐν in the formula which renders לְּךָ לְשָׁלוֹם (1 Km 1¹⁷ etc., Mk 5³⁴ Lk 7⁵⁰ 8⁴⁸ εἰς; LXX Jg 18⁶B Jas 2¹⁶ Lk 7⁵⁰D 8⁴⁸D ἐν). We have εἰς in the baptismal formula Ac 19³ εἰς τὸ Ἰωάννου βάπτισμα. Corresponding to Heb ב, εἰς or ἐν occurs where the dat. would suffice, with πιστεύω, ὄμνυμι, εὐδοκέω (e.g. with βαπτίζω: Ac 8¹⁶ 19⁵ εἰς τὸ ὄνομα, as well

---

[1] For this reason alone the argument of J. H. Greenlee seems mistaken in his article in *The Bible Translator*, vol. 3, Jan. 1952.

as Ac 10⁴⁸ ἐν τῷ ὀνόματι). Variation occurs too with ποιέω and ἐργάζομαι (see pp. 236f.). In Jn 15²¹ ποιήσουσιν εἰς ὑμᾶς and Mt 26¹⁰ ἠργάσατο εἰς ἐμέ, εἰς occurs where one expects ἐν. With ἵστημι: Ro 5² ἐν ᾗ ἑστήκαμεν, but 1 Pt 5¹² εἰς ἣν στῆτε. But variation was possible in class. Greek also with verbs of public speaking; so in NT κηρύσσω Mk 13¹⁰ εἰς (D ἐν), 14⁹ εἰς (Mt has ἐν), Lk 24⁴⁷ 1 Th 2⁹ (S* dat.), and εὐαγγελίζομαι Ga 1¹⁶ ἐν, 1 Pt 1²⁵ εἰς; Ac 17¹⁵ D; "it is an Aramaic construction" (Black AAGA² 71).

But a distinction between the two prepositions may sometimes, especially in Paul, be intended. Ph 1⁵ κοινωνία εἰς τὸ εὐαγγέλιον: Jerome (Vulg.) and other translators may have failed to appreciate that Paul is not prone to confuse εἰς and ἐν. A process may be envisaged therefore (Zerwick § 77). The Vulg. etc. may also be wrong at Ph 2¹¹: not *confiteatur quia dominus Iesus Christus in gloria est Dei Patris*, but *in gloriam* (confess *to* the glory of . . .), Zerwick § 78. Even more important theologically, the distinction between εἰς and ἐν has been missed in Col 1¹⁶: *omnia per ipsum et ipso* (εἰς αὐτόν) *creata sunt*; but to Paul Christ is the *efficient and* the *final* cause (§ 79). Probably the only instance where Paul does confuse them is Eph 3¹⁶ κραταιωθῆναι... εἰς τὸν ἔσω ἄνθρωπον (strangely, Vulg. has *in* c. accus.: §80).

(*d*) Sometimes also εἰς appears to stand for ἐπί and πρός. Except for mere stylistic variation there is no point in the change in Phm⁵ πρὸς τὸν κύριον Ἰ. καὶ εἰς πάντας τοὺς ἁγίους (so also 2 Ti 2²¹ 3¹⁷). In Mk 5³⁸ καὶ ἔρχονται εἰς τὸν οἶκον, the sequel εἰσελθὼν λέγει αὐτοῖς makes it clear that εἰς = πρός. In Mk the instances of πρός are limited and εἰς assumes much of the sphere of πρός and ἐν; the full meaning of εἰς and ἐν cannot be insisted on. So also Mt 12⁴¹ *repent* c. εἰς (class. πρός), 21¹, Mk 11¹, ⁸ (= ἐπί), Lk 9¹⁰ 18³⁵ 19²⁹, Jn 4⁵ εἰς πόλιν *to*, not *into*, 11³¹· ³⁸ ὑπάγει (ἔρχεται) εἰς (D in ³⁸ corrects to ἐπί) τὸ μνημεῖον *towards*, and in 20³ εἰς cannot be *into* (from the context). Ἁμαρτάνω c. εἰς: Mt 18²¹ Lk 15¹⁸ (cp. P. Eleph. 1, 9 κακοτεχνεῖν μηδὲν . . . εἰς Δημητρίαν); βλασφημέω εἰς Lk 12¹⁰. There is the Hebraism (or Aramaism) in Lk 15²² δότε δακτύλιον εἰς τὴν χεῖρα (for class. περί), and εἰς often directs to a part of the body to, or on, which an act is done: Mk 8²³ Mt 27³⁰ ἔτυπτον εἰς τὴν κεφαλήν, 2 Co 11²⁰, cp. P. Tebt. III 798¹⁶ λακτίσαντες εἰς τὴν κοιλίαν, Acta Petr. et Paul. 187¹ δραμὼν τῇ ἑξῆς ἡμέρᾳ Ἰουβενάλιος ἔρριψεν ἑαυτὸν εἰς τὰ ἴχνη τοῦ Πέτρου. With verbs of seeing:

Mt 22¹⁶ βλέπω εἰς, cp. P. Oxy XIV 1680¹¹ βλέπων εἰς τὸ ἀσύστατον. With verbs of speaking: Jn 8²⁶ λαλῶ εἰς τὸν κόσμον.

It may be that πρός tends to be used with a personal object, εἰς with an impersonal: 2 Co 1¹⁵ᶠ πρὸς ὑμᾶς, then εἰς Μακεδονίαν, εἰς τὴν Ἰουδαίαν; Mk 2¹³ πρὸς αὐτόν but 3⁷ a vl. gives εἰς τὴν θάλασσαν. Nevertheless εἰς αὐτόν Ro 11³⁶.

(e) Confusion of διά τινος and τινα. See pp. 267f.

(f) Confusion of παρά τινος and τινι. See p. 273.

(g) Use of ἐν for εἰς. This occurs often enough in the LXX and even in Imperial and later papyri (Johannessohn DGPS 330ff; Mayser II 2, 372f).

Since there are 2,698 exx. of ἐν in NT it is not surprising that sometimes it bears the meaning of *into* or *into a state of* (especially ἐν μέσῳ). Mt 26²³ after *dip* (but Mk 14²⁰ εἰς), Lk 1¹⁷ ἐπιστρέψαι . . . ἐν φρονήσει δικαίων (or instrumental ἐν?), 4¹ (SBDLW have ἐν after *was led*) but the parallel has εἰς (Mt 4¹); Ro 1²³· ²⁵ have ἐν after *change*, but 1°⁶ has εἰς. After ἱστάναι (tr.) and τιθέναι the use of ἐν is class.: Ac 5²⁷; Mt 27⁶⁰ (Mk 4³⁰ is instrumental), Mk 6²⁹· ⁵⁶ 15⁴⁶ Lk 1⁶⁶ 21¹⁴ 23⁵³ Jn 19⁴¹ Ac 1⁷ 5⁴· ¹⁸· ²⁵ 7¹⁶ 9³⁷ Ro 9³³ 1 Co 12²⁸ 2 Co 5¹⁹ 1 Pt 2⁶. Sometimes after δίδωμαι the preposition is pleonastic and means no more than *to*, but not always: Lk 12⁵¹ (*bring into*), Jn 3⁵³ (*committed into*), 2 Co 1²², 8¹⁶ (*put into the heart*). After other verbs of motion of course the usage is more extensive in later Greek than in class., especially so in LXX. The usage is not class. after verbs of coming and going (e.g. Rev 11¹¹ A), but it is literary and non-literary Hellenistic.

However, ἐν, is not likely to be *to* or *into* after ἔρχομαι in Mk. Except for ἐπὶ c. accus. in two instances, Mark's rule is invariable for expressing motion after this verb: εἰς (22 times) or πρός (12 times); and so in 5²⁷ 8³⁸ 13²⁶ the prepositional phrase will not express motion from place to place, but rather the accompanying circumstances or the sphere in which motion occurs. Nor is there any support at all for the rendering *into* after πίπτω in Heb 4¹¹; never, except in the compound ἐν μέσῳ, does ἐν occur in NT in a pregnant sense after this verb, even in the more Semitic parts. In a work like Hebrews it is even less likely to occur in the LXX sense of a literal rendering of ב. Nor is Lk 7¹⁷ a case of constructio praegnans: the Word spread abroad *in* . . . . (Nain is certainly away from Judaea, but the addition of " surrounding districts " makes *in* more natural than *to*.)

§ 4. True Prepositions[1]

I. WITH ONE CASE

Hellenistic Greek tends to limit prepositions to one case each, preferably accus.

(a) Genitive

'Αντί is represented by 318 exx. in LXX, but only 22 in NT. The class. ἀνθ' ὧν remains, and coincides with Heb. תַּחַת אֲשֶׁר etc.: *because* Lk 1²⁰ 19⁴⁴ Ac 12²³ 2 Th 2¹⁰; *therefore* Lk 12³. It alternates with ὅτι and διότι in Biblical Greek, and sometimes the two are combined: ἀνθ' ὧν ὅτι. For *therefore* there is also ἀντὶ τούτου. The class. ἀντί with a kind of gen. of price also remains: Mt 17²⁷ δὸς αὐτοῖς ἀντί ἐμοῦ καὶ σοῦ (class. ὑπέρ), 20²⁸ = Mk 10⁴⁵ λύτρον ἀντὶ πολλῶν (1 Ti 2⁶ ἀντίλυτρον ὑπέρ), Ro 12¹⁷ κακὸν ἀντὶ κακοῦ. Clearly in a substitutionary sense: Lk 11¹¹ ἀντὶ ἰχθύος ὄφιν, 1 Co 11¹⁵ κόμη ἀντὶ περιβολαίου (*instead of a wrap*), Jas 4¹⁵ ἀντὶ τοῦ λέγειν ὑμᾶς (*instead of saying*). It is more difficult to decide in the case of the atonement passages and of Jn 1¹⁶ χάριν ἀντὶ χάριτος ἐλάβομεν (substitutionary? i.e. the Spirit *in place of* Jesus' presence; or does it imply *a succession of* graces?) [2].

'Από takes the place of ὑπό in a causal sense [3]. Mt 13⁴⁴ etc. ἀπὸ τῆς χαρᾶς, Lk 12⁵⁷ ἀφ' ἑαυτῶν κρίνετε *because of yourselves? for your own sake?*, 22⁴⁵ *for grief* (class. ὑπὸ), Ac 20⁹ κατενεχθεὶς ἀπὸ τοῦ ὕπνου, 2 Pt 1²¹ ὑπὸ πνεύματος ἁγίου φερόμενοι ἐλάλησαν ἀπὸ θεοῦ ἄνθρωποι (or perhaps for τὰ ἀπὸ θεοῦ?). The MSS vary greatly between ἀπό and ὑπό with the agent after passive verbs: Lk 1²⁶ angel sent ἀπὸ τοῦ θεοῦ, Lk 6¹⁸ 7³⁵ 8⁴³ Ac 10³³ 15⁴. 2 Co 7¹³ Jas 1¹³ 5⁴ Rev 12⁶ (all pregnant: *prepared and derived from?*). Note the variants: Mt 11¹⁹ B² CDEF ἀπὸ τῶν τέκνων, 16²¹ (D ὑπό), Mk 8³¹ AXW (1st hand), Ac 4⁹D ³⁶B (D ὑπό) 15⁴ BC (yet ὑπό in previous verse) 1 Pt 2⁴ C. Variants for ὑπό in LXX: Isa 11¹¹ (AQ ἀπό) etc.

'Από stands for παρά c. gen. (rare in class. Greek): after ἀκούω

---

[1] K-G I § 428ff. Krebs, D. P. Polyb. Radermacher² 137ff. Moulton Einl. 158ff. Johannessohn DGKPS; DGPS. Mayser II 2, 373ff.

[2] J. M. Bover, "Χάριν ἀντὶ χάριτος", *Biblica* 6, 1925, 454–460. M. Black, *JThS* 42, 1941, 69f (*grace instead of disgrace*).

[3] Imperial papyri, see Kuhring 35. See also Johannessohn DGPS 281f. Also MGr.

(see pp. 233f), μανθάνω (Ga 3² Col 1⁷), παραλαμβάνω (1 Co 11²³ etc.). After *coming* from a person: Jn 3² 16³⁰ ἀπὸ θεοῦ (Jn 8⁴² ἐκ, 16²⁷ παρά, ²⁸ ἐκ), Ga 2¹².

The confusion of ἀπό and ἐκ is common enough in Hell. Greek, and the process of incorporating ἐκ in ἀπό has begun already in NT; nevertheless ἐκ still outnumbers ἀπό: thus Rev has proportion 100 : 20. In a local sense the usage is still fairly accurate, except e.g. in Mk 16⁹ (C*DWL correct to παρά), Ac 13⁵⁰ 16³⁹ (E corrects to ἐκ, since they went *out of*, not *from*, the city), Heb 11¹⁵. But particularly in Lk, ἀπό is used with ἐξέρχομαι (*going out of*): 13 times, and never with ἐκ, in contrast to Mk who only once has ἀπό with ἐξέρχομαι (11¹²), but ἐκ 10 times (Zerwick § 62a). Nevertheless ἐξέρχομαι does have the sense of going *away from* in Lk 5⁸ (ἔξελθε ἀπ' ἐμοῦ). Similarly Ac 12⁷ has ἐκ where one expects ἀπό (ἐξέπεσαν αὐτοῦ αἱ ἁλύσεις ἐκ τῶν χειρῶν).

But to mark the place of origin, ἀπό appears as well as ἐκ: Mt 21¹¹, Jn 1⁴⁴ has both (ἦν ὁ Φ. ἀπὸ Βηθσαιδά, ἐκ τῆς πόλεως 'Ανδρέου), ⁴⁵ (but ⁴⁶ 4²² ἐκ), 11¹ has both (ἀπὸ Βηθανίας, ἐκ τῆς κώμης Μαρίας), Ac 10³⁸; ἀπό apparently occurs where πόλις or κώμη is not included. Always ἀπό for the country of origin (except in Jn): Ac 6⁹ 21²⁷ 23³⁴ 24¹⁸, papyri (Mayser II 1, 14ff; II 2, 377, 383.).

In the sense of *after* (class. ἐκ): Mk 7⁴ ἀπ' ἀγορᾶς *on return from market*, Heb 11³⁴ ἀπὸ ἀσθενείας *after weakness*. Temporal sense: ἀπὸ τότε Mt 16²¹ 26¹⁶ Lk 16¹⁶ (never ἐκ), ἀπ' ἄρτι Jn 13¹⁹ etc. (never ἐξ), but ἐκ τούτου Jn 6⁶⁶ 19¹² etc. (unless causal), ἀπὸ δὲ τῶν ἡμερῶν 'Ιωάνου Mt 11¹², ἀπὸ καταβολῆς κόσμου Mt 25³⁴ Lk 11⁵⁰ Heb 4³ 9²⁶ Rev 13⁸ 17⁸, ἀπὸ κτίσεως κόσμου Ro 1²⁰; but ἐκ παιδιόθεν Mk 9²¹, ἐκ γενετῆς Jn 9¹, ἐκ κοιλίας μητρός μου Ga 1¹⁵ (cp. LXX Isa 49¹), ἐκ πολλῶν ἐτῶν Ac 24¹⁰, ἐκ τοῦ αἰῶνος Jn 9³².

There cannot be much significance in the change in 1 Th 2⁶ οὔτε ζητοῦντες ἐξ ἀνθρώπων οὔτε ἀφ' ὑμῶν οὔτε ἀπ' ἄλλων. Vulg. ignores the distinction; in Mt 3¹⁶ ἀνέβη ἀπὸ τοῦ ὕδατος (after standing on the bank?) surely nothing different is intended from Mk's ἀναβαίνων ἐκ τοῦ ὕδατος (Mk 1¹⁰).

'Εκ: for partitive use, see pp. 208ff. As subjective gen. 2 Co 8⁷ τῇ ἐξ ὑμῶν ἐν ἡμῖν ἀγάπῃ, 9² (p⁴⁶ SBCP om ἐξ). One or two peculiarities confront us: it is used in a causal sense ¹ (= ὑπό):

---

¹ Mayser II 2, 388f. Abel § 46 b. MGr: Thumb² § 161, 5.

Mt 23²⁵ *they are full because of greed*, but perhaps *full of greed*,
Jn 4⁶ *because of the journey*, 2 Co 7⁹ ζημιωθῆτε ἐξ ἡμῶν, 13⁴ ἐξ
ἀσθενείας, 1 Pt 2¹² *because of good deeds*, 1 Jn 4⁶ ἐκ τούτου
γινώσκομεν (or instr.), Rev 8¹³ οὐαί . . . ἐκ, 16¹⁰. ¹¹. ¹² *because of.*
The instrumental use is similar : class. σωτηρία ἔκ τινος, θνήσκω
ἔκ τινος, and τὰ ἐξ Ἑλλήνων τείχεα; Lk 16⁹ *make friends* ἐκ τοῦ
μαμωνᾶ, Jn 6⁶⁵ Rev 2¹¹ (like the class. δωρηθὲν ἐκ θεῶν, Ac 26²³
(or local?), Ga 3⁸ ἐκ πίστεως *by means of?*, 1 Jn 4⁶ (see causal),
Rev 18³ ἐκ . . . ἐπλούτησαν; papyri in Abel § 46 b.   Rev 15²
τοὺς νικῶντας ἐκ τοῦ θηρίου is probably a compressed phrase
(sc. *by separating themselves from* or *and delivered themselves from*).
It is difficult to decide in Ro 1⁴ ὁρισθέντος υἱοῦ θεοῦ . . . ἐξ
ἀναστάσεως whether ἐκ is causal or temporal.   A frequent use
in Paul is the sense *belonging to* (-*ists*, of a sect or school): ὁ ἐκ
or οἱ ἐκ Ro 3²⁶ οἱ ἐκ πίστεως Ἰησοῦ *believers in Jesus* (the noun
after ἐκ expresses the character or standards of these men), 4¹⁴
οἱ ἐκ νόμου *nomistae*, ¹⁶ *who share Abraham's faith*, Ga 3⁷· ⁹, 3¹⁰
believers in justification by works.   Outside Paul (without def.
art.): Jn 8²³ etc. 1 Jn 3¹⁹ *God-ists, devil-ists, world-ists*, also
Jn 8⁴⁴· ⁴⁷ 15¹⁹ 17¹⁴ 1 Jn 3⁸· ¹⁰· ¹². Indeed ἐκ in general is very
common in the Johannine writings.

Πρό has 48 instances, mainly temporal, e.g. Mt 5¹² 8²⁹ Lk 2²¹
Jn 11⁵⁵ (D has πρὶν τὸ πάσχα in accordance with the general
preference for accus. with prepositions in Hell. Greek), 1 Co 2⁷.
It is local : Ac 5²³ vl., 12⁶ (vl. πρός c. dat.),¹⁴, Jas 5⁹.   Preference :
Jas 5¹² 1 Pt 4⁸, perhaps Col 1¹⁷ (or temporal).   For the Hellenistic construction πρὸ ἓξ ἡμερῶν τοῦ πάσχα (Jn 12¹), πρὸ ἐτῶν
δεκατεσσάρων (2 Co 12²) etc., see Wackernagel II 194f : like the
Latin means of dating with *ante*, e.g. *ante diem tertium Nonas
Maias* (the second day before the nones of May).   But the
earliest exx. are before the date of Latin influence : LXX Am 1¹
πρὸ δύο ἐτῶν τοῦ σεισμοῦ, Herm S. VI 5, 3, Hom. Clem. 9¹,
13¹¹, Did. 7⁴ (see also Jannaris § 1651, K-G I 391, Johannessohn
DGPS 188f, Moulton Proleg. 100ff. See previous chapter,
p. 248).

(b) Dative

Ἐν.   See pp. 254–7 for εἰς and ἐν confused.   In spite of the
substitution of εἰς by some authors, ἐν is the most popular

preposition in NT. J. H. Moulton described it as " a maid of
all work " in late Greek and thought the increasing vagueness of
its meaning contributed to its ultimate disappearance; in MGr
it no longer survives in the spoken language. In the Koine all
the prepositions become increasingly elastic and their sense has
to be determined more often by the context than was earlier the
case. This is notably so with εἰς, ἐν and ἐκ. Such elasticity
makes it dangerous to press doctrinal distinctions as though our
authors were writing class. Greek. For idiomatic translation,
either the immediate context or else parallel usage of the
prepositional expression in other contexts will be decisive. But
in or *among* is still the primary meaning in Hell. Greek, even
NT Greek.

Three factors contributed to the popularity and extension
of usage in NT: first, the growing lack of clarity in the dat. case;
then, the influence of the LXX, wherein ἐν had been widely
employed to render the much-used ב; but equally important is
the influence of Christian ideas, especially in phrases peculiar
and vital to the Christian religion, like *in Christ*.

The meanings in NT may be classified: (1) Local: (a) *in*
etc., actual and metaphorical, (b) *into* etc. (praegnans); see
p. 257. (2) Temporal: *in, at, within, during*. (3) Peculiarly
Christian usages, especially *in the Lord, in Christ*. After this we
reach controversial meanings, where the idea of *within* is seldom
satisfactory, and these together represent about one-third of all
the NT instances: (4) Circumstance and instrument. (5) As a
dat. of advantage or disadvantage. (6) Various occasional
uses: reference, rate, etc.

(1) *Local*: (a) The meaning which still predominates in NT
is *within, inside, on, at, among*, but a distinction must be made
between those in a material sense and those in a metaphorical
sense. Among the former are quotation-formulae: *in the book*
(ἐν τῷ ʽΩσηέ Ro 9²⁵), *in the Law, in David* (Heb 4⁷), ἐν ʽΗλίᾳ *in
the story of Elijah* Ro 11², of which there are class. exx. (K-G I
431, 462–6): as well as *among* and *in the house of* (ἐν τοῖς τοῦ
Lk 2⁴⁹), and *at home* (Mk 2¹ 1 Co 11³⁴ 14³⁵), and the class. ἐν
μέσῳ; there is also the notion of being *inside* clothing or equip-
ment (Mk 12³⁸ Jn 20¹² Jas 2²) which is class. Among the metaphorical are phrases like *in the heart, in secret, in prayers, in
thoughts, in the mortal body, on the right hand, in the mouth, in*

glory, in the vine, in a race, in the church. There are some border-line cases: 1 Co 7¹⁷ may be *in* or *to* the churches. Ac 17³¹ ἐν ἀνδρί may be *in the person of* or may be instrumental. There may be a causal ἐν in Ro 1²⁴ (*because of the lusts of their hearts*); [1] so also 1²¹.

The local sense is slightly extended to denote *in the sphere of*, especially of God, Christ, and the gospel, and probably also of the Spirit's sanctification (1 Pt 1²) and the Name. The following are some spheres *in* which individuals, Christians or not, are mentioned⁻: the gospel, the Law, darkness, circumcision, uncircumcision, grace (but in Ro 5² it may be instrum.), new life, death, sin, the flesh, the spirit, a calling, Adam (for in 1 Co 15²² it is not instrumental; Adam is a representative man *in* whom all mankind is viewed), the Christian wife or husband (1 Co 7¹⁴ also representative). 1 Co 7¹⁵ might be *in the sphere of* (Christian) peace, or probably *into* peace. Ro has 23 exx. of this use, and 1 Co has 14.

(*b*) *into*: see p. 257.

(2) *Temporal meanings*: ἐν often reinforces the dat. of time, both point of time and duration. The first may be rendered *in*, *at*, or *on*; the second by *within* or *during*, e.g. *in one day* (1 Co 10⁸), and this may be the way to take ἐν ὀλίγῳ in Ac 26²⁸ (*in a short time*), although *by a short argument* (scil. λόγῳ) is not impossible. Note here also ἐν with the articular infin., especially with Luke; most NT exx. have the temporal significance, and sometimes it is the class. meaning: e.g. *in rowing* Mk 6⁴⁸, *in the abounding* Lk 12¹⁵, *in turning* Ac 3²⁶, and also Mt 13⁴ Mk 6⁴⁸ Ro 3⁴ 15¹³ Ga 4¹⁸. All these are present infin. and the meaning is usually *while*, but with aor. infin. *when* or *after* (e.g. Lk 9³⁶). However, this is not invariable, because the aor. construction in 1 Co 11²¹ must mean *while you are eating* or *in eating*.

(3) *Peculiarly Christian usages*: the phrases *in Christ*, *in the Lord*, difficult to define, occur in Ro, for instance, 21 times and in 1 Co 21 times. The inventiveness of Christian usage is seen also in their frequent resort to similar expressions, such as *in the truth, in the Spirit, in the Name*. Sometimes Paul says we are in Christ (or the Spirit), and sometimes that Christ (or the Spirit) is in us: once indeed he says both in the same sentence,

---

[1] H. A. A. Kennedy, *Exp. T.* xxviii, 322, argues for this.

Ro 8⁹ *you are not in the flesh but in the Spirit, if the Spirit of God
dwells in you.* Such ideas seem to be mutually exclusive and it
is tempting in view of contemporary Greek to translate the
preposition simply *belongs to* or *with.* However, full weight
must be given to the mystical conception of being *in Christ* [1],
inside a new sphere of experience and spiritual existence, so
that the early Christian could define it illogically and experien-
tially as Christ being *in me.* In no other way is the ἐν of the
Johannine epistle to be explained : *in* (not *with*) God is no darkness; men walk *in the sphere of* either darkness or light, truth
or lies, love or hate; his word is *in* us, his love is made perfect
in us, we abide *in* God and he abides *in* us (*with* is inadequate).
It would be misleading to explain this as God *with* us or *for* us,
and we *with* him; it is more profound. This applies to all other
Christian experiences : hope, consecration, peace. It would
not be safe to ignore the primary force of the preposition in any
of these. They are states in which the believer moves. It is
legitimate to take Eph 4⁴ 1 Th 4⁷ 1 Co 7¹⁵ as instances of
constructio praegnans ; but then the translation is *into*, not simply
to. Paul carefully distinguishes ἐπί from ἐν in 1 Th 4⁷ and has
a reason for the change from one preposition to the other. It is
misleading in Col 3²⁰ to render *pleasing TO the Lord*; Paul means
that obedience to parents is fit and proper *in that state* of grace
in which the Christian now lives. In Paul, *to* after εὐάρεστος is
simple dat., not ἐν, and we would expect only the dat. here if *to*
is meant; moreover, the parallel with ἐν κυρίῳ, in the command
to women just above, would be lost; for just above it can only
mean *in the Lord.* We perceive then that it is from theology
and Biblical syntax, and not from comparative syntax, that
light is shed on this peculiar relationship expressed by ἐν; to
compare non-Biblical parallels is largely irrelevant. Internal
syntax-study reveals for the NT that πιστεύω is followed by εἰς
or ἐπί or simple dat. when it means *believe in* someone or something; when the meaning is *believe* someone, it has the simple
dat. The instances with ἐν are predicated of Christ or the gospel
and mean *in the sphere of* Mk 1¹⁵ Jn 3¹⁵ vl. [2].

---

[1] A. Deissmann, *Die nt. Formel " in Christo Jesu "*, Marburg, 1892.
Oepke in Kittel WB II 534 n.   Zerwick § 88.

[2] The same is probably true of πίστις ἐν: Ro 3²⁵ Col 1². ⁴ Eph 1¹. ¹⁵
1 Ti 3¹³ 2 Ti 3¹⁵ either *the belief of those who are in Christ*, or *Christ's personal
faith.* (In Eph 3¹² the object after πίστις is expressed by a gen.)

With καλέω in 1 Co 7¹⁸ the phrase does not mean *to* un-circumcision but *while he was uncircumcised*; and 7²⁴ *let each remain in the state he was in when he was called*. Therefore in 7²² (ἐν κυρίῳ κληθείς) it is the less likely that the meaning is *called to* or *by* the Lord. Moreover, the presence of another preposition besides ἐν in Col 3¹⁵ indicates that here ἐν cannot mean *to* but must denote membership *within* the Body. Elsewhere in NT εἰς is used with καλέω for inviting *to* weddings, fellowship, eternal life, and glory; and ἐπί with dat. for inviting to liberty and impurity (nine times in all). In Ro 6¹¹ there is the simple dat. as well as ἐν: ζῶντας δὲ τῷ θεῷ ἐν Χριστῷ 'Ιησοῦ. When Paul means *to live to*, and not *in the sphere of*, he uses the simple dat.: Ga 2¹⁹, Ro 6¹⁰, 14⁷·⁸, 2 Co 5¹⁵; and when he means *to live by* he uses ἐκ: 1 Co 9¹⁴ 2 Co 13⁴·⁴ and OT quotations. There can be no question about the meaning of ἐν with ζάω in Ga 2²⁰ Ph 1²² *in the flesh*, Col 2²⁰ *in this world*, Ti 2¹² *in the present age*. For *to* with φανερόω the dat. is used; ἐν means *in, in the sphere of*. So with παρρησιάζομαι.

(4) *Circumstance and instrument*: see pp. 241, 252f.

(5) *Advantage or disadvantage*. No doubt occasionally ἐν c. dat. stands pleonastically for the normal dat., *to* or *for*[1] (sometimes in Attic poetry): *did to him* Mt 17¹², *done to me* Mk 14⁶, *speak to the perfect* 1 Co 2⁶, *veiled to those* 2 Co 4³, *to me* (perhaps *through me*) Ga 1¹⁶. *To the churches* is possible in 1 Co 7¹⁷ 2 Co 8¹ 2 Th 1⁴, but *within* is not impossible; *among* is possible Lk 2¹⁴ Ac 4¹² (the sphere of activity is emphasized). *Among* is possible Ro 10²⁰, where the presence of the preposition depends on the variant readings; 1st time p⁴⁷ BDFG; 2nd time BD). It may well be that in 1 Co 14¹¹ ἐν (SBA) was inserted by Paul in order to prevent λαλῶν being taken closely with ἐμοῖ, but it is omitted by some good authorities (p⁴⁶ DFG Clem. Alx. Chrys.). Jas 5³·⁵ ἐν not equivalent to a plain dat. (*treasure for the last days, for a day of slaughter*) but εἰς of Greek OT is deliberately altered to ἐν, since we are now *in* the last days. Jude 1 (difficult): the preposition may be displaced, but *beloved in God* in the Christian mystical sense is reasonable. Ac 20³² not simply a general statement that God's grace gives an inheritance *to* those who are sanctified, but that he will give to these

[1] Zerwick § 90.

particular saints at Ephesus, whose pastors Paul is addressing, an inheritance *among* all the sanctified, emphasizing the corporate nature of the Church *within* which these believers have their place [1].

(6) *Various occasional usages.* There are still a few phrases which elude classification. There is the ἐν which, as in the papyri, seems to mean *amounting to, at the rate of,* in the parable of the Sower: *sixtyfold, a hundredfold* Mk 4[8. 20], and the quotation at Ac 7[14]. A meaning *consisting in ordinances* Eph 2[15] can be supported from the papyri, and this seems right at 1 Co 4[20]: RSV *the kingdom . . . does not consist in talk.* For ἐν = occupied in (1 Ti 4[15] Col 4[2]) we have papyrus support. It is permissible to classify a number of phrases as dat. of reference: *concerning* or *with reference to.* In Ro 8[37] we are said to be conquerors *with regard to* all these things: 11[2] *about Elijah.* So also 14[22] 15[13] 16[2] 1 Co 1[5. 5. 7. 10] 3[21] 4[2] 7[15] 9[15] 12[6] 15[28. 41. 58]. A variety of interpretations is possible at Col 2[15] (1) local *in him,* or *on it* (the cross), (2) instrum. *by means of him* or *by means of it* (the cross; cp. Eph 2[16]).

Σύν: *including* in Attic Greek (μετά *with*). Ionic and Hellenistic *with,* synom. for μετά. In NT, most frequent in Lk-Ac (but Ac 14[4] οἱ μὲν ἦσαν σὺν τοῖς Ἰουδαίοις, οἱ δὲ σὺν τοῖς ἀποστόλοις has something of the inclusive meaning of *on the side of*). It is absent from Heb, 1 Pt, 2 Th, Phm, Past, Johann. Epistles, Rev [2], and almost absent from Jn (12[2] 18[1]; without vl. only 21[3]; μετά very common). Only in Col does Paul make much use of it. It appears to be a synonym of μετά, e.g. Mt 26[35] σὺν σοὶ ἀποθνῄσκω *in your company,* Lk 9[32] Πέτρος καὶ οἱ σὺν αὐτῷ, 1 Th 4[17] 5[10] Ph 1[23] Jas 1[11].

(c) *Accusative*

This becomes the popular case with prepositions in Hellenistic Greek.

Ἀνά: [3] rare in class. Greek, only 13 times in NT and only in ἀνὰ μέσον, ἀνὰ μέρος *in turn,* and in distributive sense as a

---

[1] Luke does not in fact use δίδωμι with ἐν for *give to.* Out of 81 occasions when he uses this verb with a possible indirect object, 74 have simple dat., and of the seven others it is very doubtful whether the preposition means *to* in any instance: it more naturally introduces an adverbial expression and is not an indirect object.

[2] See Wackernagel II 154, who notes the fact that the " stylistic " Hebrews and the " vulgar " Rev. shares this aversion to σύν.

[3] K-G I 473f. Tycho Mommsen, *Beitr. z. Lehre von den griech. Präp.,* Berlin 1895, 381. Mayser II 2, 401ff. Krebs Polyb. 33f. Preisigke s.v. Moulton Einl. 170. Radermacher[2] 20, 72, 138, 140, 143, 145.

particle, *each*: ἔχων ἀνὰ πτέρυγας ἕξ Rev 4⁸, and as a distributive preposition: Mk 6⁴⁰ AL (but SBD κατά) Lk 9¹⁴ 10¹ Jn 2⁶ (Hellenistic).

Εἰς:¹ " une des prépositions les plus riches en surprises " (Psichari 178). See pp. 253–256.

Its use is very extensive and it is encroaching on the functions of other prepositions, especially ἐν.

(1) In its normal local sense it is used with a variety of verbs of *coming, going*, etc., when the verb indicates direction, and so is used of motion into a place or state. Mk 14⁵⁴ ἕως ἔσω εἰς τὴν αὐλήν. It occurs also with verbs like πέμπω ἀποστέλλω παραβάλλω ἀποδημέω καταλύω ἄγω (and compounds): so Lk 21¹² παραδιδόντες εἰς τὰς συναγωγάς, 2 Ti 4¹⁸ σώσει εἰς τὴν βασιλείαν αὐτοῦ, 1 Pt 3²⁰ εἰς ἣν ὀλίγοι... διεσώθησαν.

(2) Distributive εἰς with numbers = *-fold, up to*: Mk 4⁸ εἰς τριάκοντα (vl. ἐν or τὸ ἕν).

(3) Purposive εἰς, with τέλος² (*with a view to the end, fully*) Lk 18⁵ Jn 13¹ LXX Barn Herm, P. Tebt. III 793 xi 8 τὸν (sic) Δωρίωνος δεξιὸν εἰς τέλος ἐξέτεμεν; with τὸ παντελές Lk 13¹¹; with κενόν Paul (class. διὰ κενῆς, as in LXX Jb and Ps) 1 Th 3⁵ Diodorus, LXX Pr; with μάτην (on analogy of εἰς κενόν). Otherwise purposive εἰς Mt 8³⁴ (εἰς ὑπάντησιν), 27⁷, Mk 1⁴ Ac 2³⁸ etc. εἰς ἄφεσιν ἁμαρτιῶν, Mk 14⁸, Lk 2³² LXX, 21¹³, Jn 9³⁹ εἰς κρίμα, Ro 5¹⁸ εἰς κατάκριμα... εἰς δικαίωσιν, 10¹, ⁴·¹⁰, 13⁴ εἰς τὸ ἀγαθόν *for your good*, 1 Co 14²², Ph 1¹⁹ εἰς σωτηρίαν (LXX Jb 13¹⁶), Col 3¹⁰ εἰς ἐπίγνωσιν, ¹⁵ εἰρήνην... εἰς ἥν, Ti 3¹⁴, Heb 6⁶ εἰς μετανοίαν, 9²⁶, Jas 5³ εἰς μαρτύριον ὑμῖν, 1 Pt 1⁵, 2²¹, 3⁹; P. Ryl. II 174¹⁵ εἰς ἀθέτησιν καὶ ἀκύρωσιν *to be annulled and cancelled*; NB εἰς τοῦτο completed by ἵνα or ὅπως, or infin. clause: Jn 18³⁷ Ac 26¹⁶ Ro 9¹⁷.

(4) εἰς for Heb. לְ Mt 21⁴⁶, εἰς τί = לְמָה Mt 14³¹.

(5) Some contexts would certainly suit a causal sense:³ Mt 3¹¹ *because of repentance* (so some modern translators); 10⁴¹; 12⁴¹ = Lk 11³² μετενόησαν εἰς τὸ κήρυγμα Ἰωνᾶ: they repented *because of* the preaching of Jonah (but *at* is sufficient); Ac 2³⁸ *be baptized* εἰς ἄφεσιν τῶν ἁμαρτιῶν *on the basis of* (but *with a view to* is sufficient, if your theology is satisfied), Ac 7⁵³; Ro 4²⁰ *on account of* the promises of God, Abraham did not waver (but *looking to* is sufficient); 11³² God has imprisoned all *because of disobedience*; 2 Ti 2²⁶ God gave them repentance *because they knew the truth* (but purposive εἰς is better); Ti 3¹⁴ to maintain good works,

¹ K-G I 468ff. Krebs Polyb. 106. Rossberg 30ff. Johannessohn DGPS 293–305. Moulton Einl. 93ff. Radermacher² 20f, 122, 128, 135f, 140, 145.
² Bauer s.v. εἰς 3. Mayser II 2, 419, 570. Preisigke s.v. τέλος.
³ On the possibility of causal εἰς in NT, see J. R. Mantey in *JBL* 70, 1951, 45ff, 309ff, and Zorell's Lexicon s.v.

because of the compelling need of them; Heb 12[7] you are enduring *because of discipline* (but *as a discipline* is sufficient); 1 Jn 5[10]. Mantey brought forward examples from Hellenistic Greek in support of a *causal* sense for εἰς, but some of them can be taken in a purposive way.   By way of reply, R. Marcus observed that if Mantey is right to interpret these NT passages causally his support must come from theology rather than linguistics.[1] In Mt 14[31] Mk 15[34] εἰς τί is not strictly = διὰ τί (Mt 9[14] Mk 2[18]) but is *in order to what* rather than *because of what*.   Hardly any of the Hellenistic parallels brought forward by Mantey are convincing, as Marcus has shown.

II. WITH TWO CASES : GEN. AND ACCUS.

Διά : [2] c. gen.

Through, place Mk 9[30] διὰ τῆς Γαλιλαίας, time Lk 5[5] δι' ὅλης νυκτός, Heb 2[15] διὰ παντὸς τοῦ ζῆν, 1 Mac 12[27] 2. Mac 13[10] 4 Mac 3[7]; unclass. is the meaning the period of time within which something takes place: Mt 26[61] Mk 14[58] διὰ τριῶν ἡμερῶν *within three days*, Lk 9[37] D διὰ τῆς ἡμέρας *in the course of the day*, Ac 1[3] *during forty days* (not continuously, but *now and then*).   Of agency:[3] Ro 11[36] δι' αὐτοῦ (creation), 1 Co 1[9] 12[8] Ga 1[1] Phm[7] Heb 2[10] 13[11] 1 Pt 2[14].   Of manner: 1 Ti 2[15] σωθήσεται δὲ διὰ τῆς τεκνογονίας *shall be kept safe throughout childbirth* (temp.) or *shall be saved by means of* (Moule 56), 1 Pt 3[20] διεσώθησαν δι' ὕδατος (attendant circumstances or environment), Heb 3[16] οἱ ἐξελθόντες ἐξ Αἰγύπτου διὰ Μωϋσεως, Ac 15[27] διὰ λόγου *openly* (as opp. to *by letter*, [32] διὰ λόγου πολλοῦ *at length, with much talk*, Ro 2[27] *with all your scripture and circumcision*, 4[11] (Schrenk in Kittel WB I 765) *believers for all their uncircumcision*, 14[20] *with offence*, Ac 24[2], Ro 8[25], 1 Co 16[3], 2 Co 2[4], 3[11], 5[7], 6[8], 10[9], Ga 3[19], but not 4[13] (not as vulg. *per*, but *propter*), Col 1[22], Eph 6[18] *with all possible*, 1 Ti 2[10] 4[5. 14] 2 Ti 2[2] *in the presence of*, Heb 9[12], 13[22], 1 Jn 5[6] 2 Jn 12, 1 Th 4[14] τοὺς κοιμηθέντας διὰ τοῦ Ἰησοῦ *with Jesus*.   In an urgent petition = *by* (Latin *per*, Attic πρός c. gen.): Ro 12[1] παρακαλῶ ὑμᾶς διὰ τῶν οἰκτιρμῶν τοῦ θεοῦ, 15[30], 1 Co 1[10] 2 Co 10[1] διὰ τῆς πραΰτητος καὶ ἐπιεικείας τοῦ Χριστοῦ.   Uncertain meaning: Ac 3[16] ἡ πίστις ἡ δι' αὐτοῦ *faith which is caused by him* (author) or *faith in him* (circumstantial), 2 Pt 3[5].

c. accus.

Through (local), only poetical in class. Greek, but Hellenistic prose: Lk 17[11] only, SBL, διήρχετο διὰ μέσον ...: never Polyb. (Krebs 68f) or LXX (Johannessohn DGPS 241, n. 1).   Elsewhere consecutive *on account of*, e.g. Mk 6[26] Ac 18[2] 28[2] Rev 12[11] 13[14]; but sometimes there

---

[1] *JBL* 71, 1952, 44.

[2] K-G I 480ff. Krebs Polyb. 65.   Rossberg 37f.   Mayser II 2, 419ff. Johannessohn DGPS 235.   Radermacher[2] 135 (instrum.), 138 (διά ~ ἕνεκα), 142 (accus. instrum.).   145 (διά ~ ἐν).   Moulton Einl. 169ff.   Moule 54–58.

[3] Mayser II 2, 421ff.   Ljungvik BSSVS 29ff.   Johannessohn 237.

are indications of a later final sense, denoting purpose (ἕνεκα in class. Greek)[1] = γιά MGr *for*: Mt 24²², Mk 2²⁷ τὸ σάββατον διὰ τὸν ἄνθρωπον ἐγένετο, Jn 11⁴² 12³⁰, Ro 3²⁵ διὰ τὴν πάρεσιν τῶν προγεγονότων ἁμαρτημάτων *with a view to*, 4²⁵ ὃς παρεδόθη διὰ τὰ παραπτώματα ἡμῶν (*because of*) καὶ ἠγέρθη διὰ τὴν δικαίωσιν ἡμῶν (*with a view to*), 11²⁸ etc.

Κατά : [2] more frequent c. accus. than gen.

c. gen.

Against (hostile) Mt 12³⁰, Mk 9⁴⁰, 14⁵⁵ κατὰ τοῦ Ἰησοῦ, Lk 11²³ Ro 8³¹. Local, *down from* Mt 8³², Ac 27¹⁴ ἔβαλεν κατ' αὐτῆς ἄνεμος τυφωνικός (*down from Crete?* or *against the ship?* The first may be better topographically), 1 Co 11⁴ etc.; *throughout* (Hellenistic) Lk 4¹⁴ καθ' ὅλης τῆς περιχώρου, 23⁵, Ac 9³¹· ⁴² 10³⁷. Special uses: 2 Co 8² ἡ κατὰ βάθους πτωχεία *profound poverty* (*from the depths* or *down to the depths*) Mt 26⁶³ Heb 6¹³· ¹⁶ with ὄμνυμι.

c. accus., various senses (generally as class.) :

1. For possessive or subjective gen. (from local sense *spectans ad* to metaph. *pertinans ad*), frequ. in Hell. Greek: Ac 17²⁸ οἱ καθ' ὑμᾶς ποιηταί *your poets*, 18¹⁵ νόμου τοῦ καθ' ὑμᾶς *your law*, 16³⁹ D, 25¹⁴ τὰ κατὰ Παῦλον *Paul's case*, Ro 1¹⁵ τὸ κατ' ἐμὲ πρόθυμον *as far as I am concerned*), 9¹¹ ἡ κατ' ἐκλογὴν πρόθεσις τοῦ θεοῦ *God's purpose of choosing*. Perhaps the Gospel headings come under this category: i.e. *of Matthew*; this is found with the authorship of books (2 Mac 2¹³ κατὰ Νεεμίαν). 2. But more probably *in accordance with*: Ro 8²⁶· ²⁷ 2 Co 7⁹· ¹¹ κατὰ θεόν *in a godly way*, 11²¹ κατὰ φύσιν *in accordance with nature*, 1 Co 15³ κατὰ τὰς γραφάς 2 Co 10³ κατὰ σάρκα *in accordance with material standards*, Ga 3¹⁵ *in human fashion*, Eph 4²⁴ *in God's image*, Heb 9⁹. 3. Distributive: Mt 27¹⁵ Mk 15⁶ καθ' ἑορτήν *at each feast*, Heb 7²⁷ *daily*, 9²⁵ *yearly*, Mk 6⁴⁰ κατὰ ἑκατὸν καὶ κατὰ πεντήκοντα SBD *one hundred each*, 1 Co 14³¹ καθ' ἕνα *one by one*, Eph 5³³ οἱ καθ' ἕνα *individually*, Heb 9⁵ κατὰ μέρος *in detail*. The phrase κατὰ εἷς or καθεῖς (Mk 14¹⁹ Jn 8⁹ Ro 12⁵) has now become stereotyped as an adverb. More difficult to assess are: Mt 19³ κατὰ πᾶσαν αἰτίαν (causal), Mk 13⁸ κατὰ τόπους *in places*, Lk 1¹⁸ κατὰ τί *in view of what?* whereby (or causal?), 15¹⁴ κατὰ τὴν χώραν ἐκείνην *throughout that land*, Ac 12¹ *at* (temporal), 25²³ τοῖς κατ' ἐξοχήν *eminent men* (a stock phrase for *par excellence*), 1 Co 7⁶ *as a concession*, 2 Co 8³ κατὰ δύναμιν *according to their power*, 8¹² *in proportion to what one has*, 10⁷ τὰ κατὰ πρόσωπον *what is in front of you*, Heb 7¹⁶ κατὰ νόμον . . . κατὰ δύναμιν *by virtue of.*

Μετά : [3] c. gen. :

Its frequence relative to that of σύν:

────────────

[1] H. G. Meecham, *Exp. T.* L. no. 12, Sept. 1939, 564.
[2] K-G I 475ff.   Krebs Polyb. 128.   Mayser II 2, 427ff.   Johannessohn DGPS 245ff.   Radermacher² 139ff.   Moulton Einl. 158 (frequence), 169f.
[3] K-G I 505ff.   Tycho Mommsen, *Beitr. z. Lehre von d. griech. Pap.* 256f.   Krebs 58ff.   Rossberg 8f. (frequence), 49–50 (use).   Mayser II 2, 440ff.   Johannessohn DGPS 202–216.   Moulton Einl. 158 (frequence), 170. 172.   Radermacher² 128, 138, 140f 145, 146.

	Ptol. texts (Rossberg)	Polyb. (Krebs)	Lucian	NT (Moulton)
μετά	1·5	6·7	7	3·5
σύν	1	1	1	1

Ionic influence accounts for the greater relative frequence of σύν in Ptol. pap. and NT. On the whole, μετά far outweighs σύν in NT, but in some individual books σύν holds its own (e.g. Ac). The accus. is on the decline: thus in Ptol. pap. gen.: accus. is 2·5:1 (iii/B.C.), 3: 1 (ii/B.C.), 10+: 1 (i/B.C.). The NT has 3·6:1 (361:100), LXX Ezek β 14·5:1, Ps 16:1.

(1) *amongst* Mk 1¹³ ἦν μετὰ τῶν θηρίων, 10³⁰ μετὰ διωγμῶν, Lk 22³⁷ μετὰ ἀνόμων ἐλογίσθη, 24⁵ μετὰ τῶν νεκρῶν, Jn 11⁵⁶, 1 Ti 4¹⁴ μετὰ ἐπιθέσεως τῶν χειρῶν (impersonal for person: *among those who laid on their hands*), but perhaps (2), Heb 12¹⁴ 2 Ti 2²² εἰρήνην διωκέω μετά not *peace with*, but *in company with* (Foerster in Kittel WB II 412, 415), 1 Jn 4¹⁷ τετελείωται ἡ ἀγάπη μεθ᾿ ἡμῶν.

(2) *with*, of mutual participation (e.g. κρίνομαι 1 Co 6⁶, λαλέω Jn 4²⁷; also πολεμέω, εἰρηνεύω, συμφωνέω, etc.) or accompanying circumstances (e.g. μεθ᾿ ὅρκου Mt 14⁷) or instrument (e.g. Lk 22⁵² ἐξήλθατε μετὰ μαχαιρῶν). In contrast to σύν, the meaning of μετά is never *in addition to*. In composition with a verb, when the meaning is *with*, συν- or ὁμο- is used, and not μετα- (except with μετέχω, μεταδίδωμι and μεταλαμβάνω).

c. accus., only *after* (temporal): an exception may be Heb 9³ μετὰ τὸ δεύτερον καταπέτασμα. Ac 1⁵ etc.

Περί : ¹—*about*, literal or metaph.
c. gen. extremely common.

Esp. metaph. with such verbs as *think, care*, etc.: Mt 9³⁶ ἐσπλαγχνίσθη περὶ αὐτῶν, Mt 20²⁴ Mk 10⁴¹ ἠγανάκτησαν περί, Lk 2¹⁸ θαυμάζω, Jn 7¹³, 9¹⁷, 1 Th 5²⁵ προσεύχεσθε περὶ ἡμῶν, 1 Pt 5⁷ αὐτῷ μέλει περὶ ὑμῶν, Lk 24²⁷ τὰ περὶ ἑαυτοῦ, Ac 18²⁵ Ph 2²⁰. Absolutely, at the beginning of the sentence: 1 Co 7¹· ²⁵ 8¹ 12¹ 16¹. Also *on behalf of, on account of* (= ὑπέρ) class. and Hell., in the debatable phrase Mt 26²⁸ τὸ αἷμά μου τῆς διαθήκης τὸ περί (D ὑπέρ) πολλῶν ἐκχυννόμενον (ὑπέρ in parallels of Mk, Lk, Paul), Heb 10²⁶ περὶ ἁμαρτιῶν (same sense 10¹²

---

¹ K-G I 491ff. Krebs 98ff. Rossberg 8f (frequ.), 41ff (use). Kuhring 15. Mayser II 2, 445ff. Johannessohn DGPS 219ff. Radermacher² 118, 125, 135, 139, 140, 141, 143, 145, 146. Moulton Einl. 158. 170. Moule 62f.

270   A GRAMMAR OF NEW TESTAMENT GREEK   [§ 4

ὑπὲρ ἁμαρτιῶν); Heb 5¹·³ ὑπέρ ... ὑπέρ ...: then περί ... περί ...
περί ..., Jn 17⁹, Ac 26¹ (B ὑπέρ), 1 Co 1¹³ D*B p⁴⁶ ἐσταυρώθη περὶ
ὑμῶν, Ga 1⁴ (SᶜB ὑπέρ). Perhaps with περισσός in mind, AV has
above all things in 3 Jn² περὶ πάντων ... εὐοδοῦσθαι (*in every respect*),
but it may correspond to the salutation which occurs in papyrus letters:
πρὸ μὲν πάντων εὔχομαί σε ὑγιαίνειν *before all*.

c. accus. rarer :

About literally (local and temporal), Mk 4¹⁰ Lk 22⁴⁹ οἱ περὶ αὐτόν
his disciples or *those who were round him*, but οἱ περὶ Παῦλον (Ac 13¹³)
includes Paul, as in class. idiom.   But πρὸς τὰς περὶ Μάρθαν καὶ Μαρίαν
(Jn 11¹⁹ p⁴⁵ Θ AC² Γ) denotes Martha and Mary only (as in later Greek;
see Bauer s.v. 2 δ).   Temporal: Mt 20³ etc. περὶ τρίτην ὥραν *about
the third hour*.   Also *concerning* with ἐπιθυμίαι (Mk 4¹⁹), περισπάομαι,
θορυβάζομαι (Lk 10⁴⁰ᶠ), τοὺς περὶ τοιαῦτα ἐργάτας (Ac 19²⁵); the
general tendency, culminating in MGr, was for the prepositions to be
followed only by the accus., and already in Aristotle there are instances
where περί c. accus. is used for the Attic περί c. gen. (Wackernagel II
215); so Paul, Ph 2²³ τὰ περὶ ἐμέ *my affairs*, exactly as 2²⁰ τὰ περὶ ὑμῶν
your affairs, 1 Ti 1¹⁹ περὶ τὴν πίστιν ἐναυάγησαν, 6⁴·²¹, 2 Ti 2¹⁸ 3⁸,
Ti 2⁷ περὶ πάντα *in all respects*.

Πρίν :

= πρό, c. acc. Mk 15⁴² D πρὶν σάββατον, Jn 11⁵⁵ D πρὶν τὸ πάσχα;
c. gen. (as Hell. Greek) Mt 26³⁴ p³⁷·⁴⁵ L fam¹ πρὶν (ἢ) ἀλεκτοροφωνίας;
acc. or gen.? Jn 8⁵⁸ D lat πρὶν Ἀβραάμ.

Ὑπέρ : [1] = *over*, but not locally in NT (except Heb 9⁵ D* E*
for ὑπεράνω); locally in papyri (Mayser II 2, 461).   Comparatively rare in Ptol. pap. (13th place among true prepositions)
and Herodotus (16th place) and NT (12th place).   The accus. is
comparatively rare : Ptol. 20 : 1, LXX 239 : 211 (1 : 1), NT 6 : 1.

c. gen.

For, on behalf of (Mk 9⁴⁰ 1 Co 4⁶), often oppos. to κατά in the same
passages; περί is often substituted, but there is also the reverse change
of περί to ὑπέρ for *concerning* (e.g. λέγω ὑπέρ)[2], which is almost confined
to Paul in NT: Jn 1³⁰ ὑπὲρ οὗ ἐγὼ εἶπον (corrected to περί SᶜAC³L),
Ac 8²⁴ *pray* ὑπὲρ ἐμοῦ, 2 Co 1⁸ ἀγνοεῖν ... ὑπὲρ τῆς θλίψεως, 8²³ ὑπὲρ Τίτου
as for Titus, 12⁸ *about this*, 1 Th 3² παρακαλέσαι ὑπὲρ τῆς πίστεως ὑμῶν
to encourage you concerning your faith, 2 Th 2¹ ἐρωτάω ὑπέρ, Ph 4¹⁰ φρονέω
ὑπέρ *think upon*; note the two prepositions together in the same sense
Eph 6¹⁸ᶠ προσευχόμενοι περὶ πάντων τῶν ἁγίων καὶ ὑπὲρ ἐμοῦ. Etc.

---

[1] K-G I 486ff. Schwyzer II 518f. Krebs 40ff. Rossberg 8f, 40f.
Kuhring §§ 19. 20. Johannessohn DGPS 216ff. Radermacher² 139
(ὑπέρ = ἀντί), 140, 143 (frequence). Moulton Einl. 158 (relative frequ.)
170f. Mayser II 2, 456ff.
[2] Mayser II 2, 457ff. Johannessohn DGPS 217f.

in Paul. The boundary between ἀντί and ὑπέρ c. gen. is very narrow (substitution), necessarily so because what is done *on behalf of one* is often done *in one's stead*; the compound of ἀντί occurs closely with ὑπέρ in 1 Ti 2[6] ἀντίλυτρον ὑπὲρ πάντων; Mk 14[24] *blood is shed* ὑπέρ (but ἀντί in 10[45]), Jn 11[50], Ac 21[26], Ro 5[7. 8], 1 Co 15[29], 2 Co 5[14. 15. 21], Ga 3[13], Phm[13], 1 Ti 2[6], Ti 2[14]. Adverbial ὑπερ: 1 Co 4[6](?) 2 Co 11[23].

III. With three cases

'Επί : [1]

	Polyb.	Ptol. pap.	NT	LXX Pent.	Isa.	LXX total	
gen.	1·5	4·5	1·2	2·5	1	1730	1·4
dat.	1	1	1	1	1	1219	1
acc.	3	2·5	2	3·7	2	4629	3·8

Even in class. Greek the distinctions between the cases with this preposition are difficult to define; all attempts to be dogmatic in Biblical Greek are doomed. Although all cases are largely represented, there is a tendency for the accus. to prevail, as is seen in Mk 4[38] (Wackernagel II 215) where D has an atticistic correction to the gen. ἐπὶ προσκεφαλαίου.

c. gen.

(1) Local, usually = *upon*: Mk 2[10] etc. ἐπὶ τῆς γῆς; but also place to which: Mk 4[26] βάλῃ τὸν σπορόν ἐπὶ τῆς γῆς; Rev 14[19] S (p[47] ἐπί c. acc.; ACP εἰς) etc.; *at, by* Mt 21[19] ἐπὶ τῆς ὁδοῦ, etc.; *in the presence of* Mt 28[14], Mk 13[9] etc. (2) Metaph., *over* (authority, oversight), with καθίστημι and βασιλεύω, but ἐξουσία ἐπί c. gen. is exclusively Biblical. (3) Temporal:[2] Mk 2[26] ἐπὶ 'Αβιάθαρ ἀρχιερέως, Mt 1[11], Ac 11[19] AE τῆς θλίψεως τῆς γενομένης ἐπὶ Στεφάνου *at the time of Stephen's death* (but vl. ἐπί c. dat. *on account of*), Heb 1[2] etc. ἐπ' ἐσχάτου τῶν ἡμέρων (Semitism). Mk 12[26] Lk 20[37] *in the passage where*.

c. dat.

(1) Local, not easy to distinguish from ἐπί c. accus. or gen.: *before, upon* Eph 1[10] τὰ ἐπὶ τοῖς οὐρανοῖς καὶ τὰ ἐπὶ τῆς γῆς (interchangeable;

---

[1] K-G I 495ff. Meisterhans-Schwyzer 211, 36; 217, 29. Krebs 76. Rossberg 44f. Kuhring § 29. Johannessohn DGPS 305ff. Radermacher[2] 125, 126, 128, 136. Moulton Einl. 173f. Moule 49f. Mayser II 2, 462ff.

[2] C. H. Turner, "'Επὶ Ποντίου Πειλάτου (1 Tim. vi. 12, 13) ", *JThS* 28, 1927, 270ff.

as also Ac 27⁴⁴ ἐπὶ σανίσιν and ἐπί τινων τῶν ἀπὸ τοῦ πλοίου), Mt 24³³, Jn 4⁶, Mt 16¹⁸ (D acc.), Ac 8¹⁶ (D* acc.) etc.   (2) More often to denote cause, especially with verbs expressing motion, and also Mt 4⁴ Lk 1⁵⁹ etc.; Ro 5¹² 2 Co 5⁴ ἐφ' ᾧ *because*,[1] Lk 5⁵ ἐπὶ δὲ τῷ ῥήματί σου.   (3) Addition, Lk 3²⁰ 16²⁶ (SBL ἐν), Col 3¹⁴, Heb 8¹.   (4) Condition Ro 8²⁰, 1 Co 9¹⁰, Ga 5¹³, 1 Th 4⁷, Ti 1².   (5) Final Ga 5¹³ ἐπ' ἐλευθερίᾳ ἐκλήθητε, Eph 2¹⁰, Ph 3¹², 1 Th 4⁷.   (6) Consecutive 2 Ti 2¹⁴.   (7) Temporal Jn 4²⁷ ἐπὶ τούτῳ (S*D ἐν) *at this juncture*, 1 Co 14¹⁶, Ph 1³ ἐπὶ πάσῃ τῇ μνείᾳ ὑμῶν, 2¹⁷, 4¹⁰ ἐφ' ᾧ *whereon*, Eph 4²⁶, 1 Th 3⁷, Heb 9²⁶ *at the close of the ages*, 11⁴.

c. ¯accus. :

(1) In class. Greek it answers to question " whither ", but also in Hellenistic it is interchangeable with gen. and dat.: Mk 4³⁸ (DW gen.), Mt 14²⁵ περιπατῶν ἐπὶ τὴν θάλασσαν SBW (CD gen.), but gen. in Mk 6⁴⁸ Jn 6¹⁹; Mt 14²⁶ WEFG (SBDC gen.); Rev 13¹ ἐπὶ τῶν κεράτων . . . καὶ ἐπὶ τὰς κεφαλάς; 13¹⁶, 14⁹ ἐπὶ τοῦ μετώπου . . . ἢ ἐπὶ τήν χεῖρα (p⁴⁷ corrects to gen). Κάθημαι ἐπί c. accus. Rev 4², c. dat. 21⁵, c. gen 14¹⁶. (2) In metaph. sense: Lk 1³³ βασιλεύσει ἐπί; same interchange, e.g. Mt 25²¹ ἐπὶ ὀλίγα ἧς πιστός, ἐπὶ πολλῶν σε καταστήσω; it is used with σπλαγχνίζομαι *upon* (Mt 15³²), μοιχάομαι *with* (Mk 10¹¹, cp. LXX Je 5⁹ χρεμετίζω ἐπί) etc.   (3) Temporal: Ac 16¹⁸ ἐπὶ πολλὰς ἡμέρας *for many days*; Mt 25⁴⁰? ἐφ' ὅσον ἐποιήσατε (vulg. *quamdiu*), etc.; Ac 4⁵ ἐπὶ τὴν αὔριον (Hell. Greek: Krebs 17, Mayser II 2, 540).

Παρά [2]

The most frequent after ἐν, εἰς, ἐπί in Ptol. pap. but in 12th place in NT.

The relative frequency of the cases reveals a sharp contrast between the NT and contemporary Koine.

	Hdt.	Ptol. pap.	Mk	Lk–Ac	Ro Co Ga	NT	Pent	Isa	Ps.	LXX
gen.	1·8	22·5	6	1·6	0·2	1·6	2	8	1·6	501	2·
dat.	1	1	1	1	1	1	1	1	1·	191	1
acc.	3·5	2·5	7	1·5	1·3	1·2	2	1·3	1	293	1·

---

[1] ICC Ro.⁵ p. 349. But cf. S. Lyonnet, " Le sens de ἐφ' ᾧ en Rom 5 : 12 et l'exégèse des pères grecs ", *Biblica* 36, 1955, 436–456.
[2] K-G I 509ff.   Meisterhans-Schwyzer 207, 17; 219, 40. Krebs 51ff. Rossberg 51ff. Mayser II 2, 482ff. Radermacher² 126, 136, 139, 141f, 225. Moulton Einl. 158, 173. Johannessohn DGPS 226–35.

c. gen. :

In class. Greek *from the side of* (so Lk 1⁴⁵) ; unclass. with κατηγορέομαι Ac 22³⁰ HLP (rest ὑπό), and Mk 3²¹ οἱ παρ' αὐτοῦ *his kinsfolk.*

c. dat. :

In all NT writers except Heb and Jude (but Mt 13⁵⁶ has αἱ ἀδελφαὶ πρὸς ἡμᾶς εἰσι, instead of class. Attic παρ' ἡμῖν, marking the Hellenistic preference for accus. : Wackernagel II 215) ; rarest of the cases : *by, beside* (nearly always personal), not of immediate neighbourhood : Jn 19²⁵ ; *in the house of* Lk 19⁷ Jn 1⁴⁰ Ac 10⁶, *amongst* Rev 2¹³. Figurative : Lk 1³⁰ *with*, etc. The local παρά c. dat. has almost disappeared in NT.

c. accus. (never occurs in Johannine writings, incl. Rev, or in Cath. epistles) :

Beside, in answer to questions where? and whither? But not, as frequently in class. Greek, with personal names (πρός instead), oppos. of κατά (metaph.) *contrary to, beyond* Ro 1²⁶ 11²⁴ 1 Co 3¹¹ 2 Co 8³ ; *more than* Lk 13². ⁴ παρὰ πάντας, Ro 1²⁵ 12³ 14⁵ ; *minus* or *except* Lk 5⁷ D παρά τι *almost*, 2 Co 11²⁴ *40 minus one*, Herm. S VIII 1, 14 ; IX 19, 3 ; *because* 1 Co 12¹⁵ᶠ οὐ παρὰ τοῦτο οὐκ ἔστιν ἐκ τοῦ σώματος *that is no reason for its not being.* Mt Mk have παρά c. accus. only in local sense.

Πρός [1]

In 8th place of frequency in the Ptol. papyri. With regard to the use of the cases, NT and LXX are decidedly *sui generis*.

	Hdt.	Polyb.	Ptol. pap.	NT	LXX
gen.	2	0·2	0·02	0·16	23 (0·2)
dat.	1	1	1	1	104 (1)
acc.	6	15	4	116	*passim*

c. gen. :

In class. Attic πρός, like ὑπό, was used with all three oblique cases. But πρός c. gen. is found only three times in Polyb., rarely in inscriptions and in the Ptol. pap. (Mayser II 2, 493f). It occurs only 23 times in LXX

---

[1] K-G I 515ff. Meisterhans-Schwyzer 220. 43; 45. Wackernagel II 208. Mayser II 2, 492ff. Krebs 113ff. Rossberg 54ff. Kuhring 17, 29, 31. Johannessohn DGPS 259–71. Radermacher² 135, 136, 141, 145, 146. Moulton Einl. 173.

(Moulton Proleg. 106); in NT, only at Ac 27³⁴ τοῦτο πρὸς τῆς ὑμετερας σωτηρίας ὑπάρχει *advantageous to* (very close to Thuc. 3, 59, 1 οὐ πρὸς τῆς ὑμετέρας δόξης τάδε).

c. dat. :

By, at (class.). Six times in NT (accus. instead): Mk 5¹¹ πρὸς τῷ ὄρει, Lk 19³⁷ (D acc.), Jn 18¹⁶ 20¹¹ (vl. acc.) ¹² Rev 1¹³.

c. accus. : abundantly used.

In accordance with (class.): Mt 19⁸ Mk 10⁵ Lk 12⁴⁷ 1 Co 12⁷ 2 Co 5¹⁰. With verbs of saying, it illustrates the Hellenistic tendency to use prepositions in place of the simple case (pp. 236f, 251). So with verbs of coming, sending, etc. Also taking the place of παρά after εἰμι etc.: e.g. Mt 13⁵⁶ πρὸς ὑμᾶς εἰσιν, 26¹⁸. ⁵⁵ vl, Mk 6³ Jn 1¹, especially Mk 9¹⁰ ἐκράτησαν πρὸς ἑαυτούς, 11³¹ διελογίζοντο πρὸς ἑαυτούς (cp. Mt 21²⁵ παρ᾽ ἑαυτοῖς), Mt 21¹ πρὸς τὸ ὄρος (vl. εἰς), Mk 1³³, 2², 11¹· ⁴. Temporal: *about,* such phrases as πρὸς ἑσπέραν, καιρόν, ὥραν, ὀλίγας ἡμέρας, Lk 8¹³ 24²⁹ Jn 5³⁵ Heb 12¹⁰ᶠ etc. Relationship, hostile or friendly: Mt 27⁴ Jn 21²². ²³ Mk 12¹² Lk 20¹⁹, Ac 28²⁵ ἀσύμφωνος, 1 Co 6¹ πρᾶγμα ἔχω πρός, Heb 4¹³. Purpose, result: 2 Co 10⁴ Eph 4²⁹ 1 Ti 4⁸.

Ὑπό ¹

In the Ptol. papyri, 12th place : in NT 10th place.

PROPORTIONS :

	Hdt.	Polyb.	Ptol. pap.	NT	Pent	Mi. Pr.	2–4 Mac	1 Mac	Isa	LXX
gen.	10·8	61	60·4	3·3	0·5	4	5	3	6	(291) 1·4
dat.	1	1	1	0	0	0	0	0	0	*
acc.	1	25	10·6	1	1	1	1	1	1	(203) 1

* Only Jb 12⁵ A.

Whereas ὑπό still occurs with dat. about eleven times in Polyb., it never (ex. Jb 12⁵ A) occurs so in LXX or NT and there is the same tendency as with πρός.

---

¹ K-G I 521ff. Meisterhans-Schwyzer 222, 50. Mayser II 2, 509ff. Krebs 47ff. Rossberg 58ff. Kuhring § 25. Johannessohn DGPS 174ff. Radermacher² 139, 142, 145. Moulton Einl. 170.

c. gen.: *by* (agent), after passive and virtually passive verbs.
c. accus.:

Under (combining the old local use of ὑπό c. gen. and dat.: Mayser II 2, 371); never in Jn (except 1⁴⁸ ὑπὸ τὴν συκῆν) or Rev (which has ὑποκάτω). In class. temporal sense (*circa*), only Ac 5²¹ ὑπὸ τὸν ὄρθρον.

§ 5. Repetition or Omission of the Preposition [1]

Both repetition and omission of the preposition before two or more phrases connected by καί is found in Ptol. pap. and NT. Polyb. is fond of repeating the preposition, especially in quotations, sometimes three or four times. The omission can sometimes be rather harsh in NT: Mt 4²⁵ ἀπὸ τῆς Γαλιλαίας . . . καὶ Ἰουδαίας καὶ πέραν τοῦ Ἰορδάνου.

Actually, repetition is more usual when each of the united ideas has to be brought into emphatic prominence; but in by far the greater majority of instances in the Ptol. papyri, especially in the unofficial style of writing, the preposition is not repeated. Repetition in any large degree is a peculiar feature of Biblical Greek [2]. In Thucyd. book 1 there are only six instances of repetition, out of 25 opportunities for its occurrence, and in these six instances there is an emphasis which makes repetition necessary. Let us compare this with Biblical Greek.

	Ezek. (B-text) *	Mk	Mt	Lk	Ac	Jn	Ro 1 Co	Eph	Past	Rev
opportunities	93	26	35	55	56	15	24	16	24	38
repetitions	78	10	11	9	16	8	14	6	4	24

* The result is even more remarkable, assuming the AQ readings.

§ 6. Improper Prepositions

Ἄνευ [3]

Only three examples in NT: Mt 10²⁹ ἄνευ τοῦ πατρὸς ὑμῶν

---

[1] K-G I 548. Mayser II 2, 515f. Krebs 10f. Black AAGA² 83. See also above, Introduction, p. 4, n.7.
[2] See N. Turner, "An Alleged Semitism", *Exp. T.* LXVI 8, 1955, 252–254.
[3] K-G I 402, 4. Kuhring 46f. Mayser II 2, 518ff. Johannessohn DGPS 337–339. Radermacher² 140.

without the knowledge of or *without the permission of*, like ἄνευ θεῶν
in Ptol. pap. (Mayser II 2, 519f) 1 Pt 3¹ 4⁹. Usually ἄνευ has
post-positive position only after interrog. and rel. pronouns, but
3 Mac 4⁵ and Aristot. *Metaph.* 1071ᵃ 2 are among the exceptions
(Wackernagel II 199).

῎Ενεκα, ἕνεκεν [1]

= *propter* and διά c. accus. Position nearly always
pre-positive in NT, following Semitic model; but post-positive
in Ptol. pap. and Polyb. more than twice as often as pre-positive.

῞Εως and μέχρι (ἄχρι) [2].

In the Ptol. pap., although these prepositions will appear
with the same meaning in the same phrase, ἕως is much more
frequent than μέχρι both in its temporal and local meaning.
Whereas the relationship in the Ptol. papyri is 1 : 8, in Polyb.
it is only 1 : 1·7. Originally ἕως was a conjunction (see pp. 110f),
becoming a preposition in the Hell. period. It is often combined
with an adverb : πότε, κάτω, ἄρτι, σήμερον; and sometimes it
receives strengthening from another preposition : ἕως πρός
Lk 24⁵⁰, ἕως ἐπί Ac 17¹⁴, ἕως ἔξω Ac 21⁵, ἕως καὶ εἰς 26¹¹, ἕως
ἔσω εἰς τὴν αὐλήν Mk 14⁵⁴.

῎Αχρι(ς) occurs in Mt 24³⁸, and Lk-Ac, Paul, Heb, Rev;
μέχρι(ς) in Mt, and occasionally in Lk, Ac, Paul, Heb; they are
also conjunctions (e.g. ἄχρις οὗ Ro 11²⁵, μέχρις οὗ Mk 13³⁰).
All absent in Jn, except 8⁹ S.

§ 7. Prepositional Adverbs

῎Αμα [3]

This adv. has the dat. only at Mt 13²⁹ ἄμα αὐτοῖς τὸν σῖτον (D
ἄμα καὶ τ.σ. σὺν αὐτοῖς); elsewhere ἄμα σύν 1 Th 4¹⁷ 5¹⁰. Cp. ἄμα μετ'
αὐτῶν Ditt. Syll.³ 705 ⁵⁷ (112 B.C.).

'Εγγύς

Very frequent in NT. See p. 216.

῎Εσω [4]

Mk 15¹⁶ ἔσω τῆς αὐλῆς (vl. ἔσω εἰς τὴν αὐλήν). Only used as
an adv. in the Ptol. papyri (Mayser II 2, 528).

---

[1] K-G I 462c. Meisterhans-Schwyzer 213, 12; 215, 23–27. Mayser II
2, 520ff. N. Turner, *Vet. Test.* 5, 1955, 210f.
[2] K-G I 346, 2. Meisterhans-Schwyzer 217, 30. Schwyzer II 549f.
Mayser II 2, 522ff. Johannessohn DGPS 304f. Radermacher² 140.
[3] K-G I 432, 2; II 82 n. 3. Mayser II 2. 526ff. Johannessohn DGPS
212, 322. Radermacher² 142.
[4] Radermacher² 66, 224.

Ἐκτός [1]

Except: as a preposition in Ptol. pap. 30, in NT 9 (e.g. Ac 26²²
1 Co 15²⁷), in LXX 20, in Polyb. 43. See p. 216.

Ἐνάντιον [2]

In NT the meaning is weakened from *opposite* (class.) to *before*
(a mere substitute for πρό). Never as adv. in NT. Mk 2¹² ACD (vl.
ἔμπροσθεν), Lk 1⁸ SAC, 20²⁶, 24¹⁹ (D ἐνώπιον), Ac 7¹⁰ 8³² OT. Ἀντικρύς
opposite: Ac 20¹⁵ ἀντικρὺς Χίου. ἀπ- and κατ- ἀντικρύ(ς) do not
appear at all. The β-text has κατὰ Χίον at Ac 20¹⁵.

Ἐντός [3]

See p. 216. Rare in LXX, only twice in NT, but 37 times in
Polyb., and about 20 times in Ptol. pap. (Mayser II 2, 530).

Ἐνώπιον [4]

Hellenistic, earliest in LXX. Frequent in Lk and 1st part of Ac
and Rev. In Jn, only at 20³⁰ 1 Jn 3²² 3 Jn⁶. Never in Mt Mk.
κατενώπιον Eph 1⁴ Col 1²² Jude ²⁴ (Biblical Greek word).

Ἔξω [5]

See p. 216. In class., Polyb., Ptol. pap. and NT, used as a
preposition.

Κυκλόθεν

LXX Je 17²⁶, NT (Rev), Ptol. pap. (Mayser II 2, 532).

Λάθρα

K-G I 402, 4. Mt, Mk, Jn, Ac.

Μεταξύ [6]

Rare in NT and LXX (only Ge² Jg¹, Km⁴, Wi³), which prefer
ἀνὰ μέσον and ἐν μέσῳ. Μεταξύ is the literary and even atticizing
form, and occurs in three insertions from Aquila: Jg 5²⁷ (in same
verse ἀνὰ μέσον), 3 Km 15⁶· ³². NT: Mt 18¹⁵ etc. Adverbial: Jn 4³¹
Ac 13⁴².

Ὄπισθεν

As a preposition only at Mt 15²³ Lk 23²⁶. But ὀπίσω occurs 26
times (300 in LXX); twice as an adv. The prepositional use belongs to
Bibl. Greek and arises from LXX rendering of אַחֲרֵי. It does occur, but
extremely rarely, in the Koine (Mayser II 2, 533: " lässt sich als Präposition nur im Kanop. Dekr. 62 und in post postiver Form nach-
weissen." But see also P. Oxy. 43B IV 3 (iii/A.D.) ὀπίσω Καπιτολείου).
Ac 5³⁷ Rev 13³.

---

[1] K-G I 402, 4. Mayser II 2, 529. Kurhing § 51. Johannessohn
DGPS 336. Radermacher² 140, 144.

[2] K-G I 353. Meisterhans-Schwyzer 215, 22. Mayser II 2, 529f.
Johannessohn DGPS 190 (365 times in LXX). Radermacher² 144.

[3] K-G I 385 n. 3. Meisterhans-Schwyzer 205, 14. Johnnessohn
DGPS 336.

[4] Mayser I² 3, 120; II 2, 530ff. Johannessohn DGPS 194–196, 359–
361. Radermacher² 140, 143, 145. Moulton Einl. 159 n. 2.

[5] K-G I 402, 4. Mayser II 2, 531ff. Radermacher² 144.

[6] K-G I 348 n. 4. Mayser II 2, 532f. Johannessohn DGPS 173f.
Radermacher² 138, 144. P. Katz, *Vetus Test.* 8, 1958, 267.

'Oψέ
Literature in Bauer s.v. Mt 28¹ Mk 16¹ ὀψὲ σαββάτων. A
Latinism? *Just after.*

Πέραν ¹
In pap. of 258 B.C. πέρα Μέμφεως. See p. 216.

Πλήν
Except: Mk 12³² Jn 8¹⁰ EGHK Ac 8¹ 15²⁸ 27²²; also as adv. and
conjunction.

Χάριν ²
Lk, Jn, Past. Cp. ἕνεκα. With one exception, post-positive.
Hell. Greek favours the pre-positive position (but οὗ χάριν etc. in pap.).

	Polyb.	Ptol. pap.	LXX	NT
post-positive	76	18	8	8
pre-positive	100	32	13	1

Χωρίς ³
Without. Hellenistic.

§ 8. Proper Prepositions combined with Adverbs

The tendency of the later language is towards fuller forms,
and these are Hellenistic ⁴. Ἔναντι Lk 1⁸ BD Ac 7¹⁰ S 8²¹ (vl.
ἐνώπιον). Ἀπέναντι occurs three times only in Polyb., four or
five times only in all the Ptol. pap. examined by Mayser (II 2,
538), but six times in NT alone and 80–90 in LXX: Mt 27²⁴
(vl. κατέναντι) ⁶¹ Mk 12⁴¹ (vl. κατέναντι) Ac 3¹⁶ 17⁷ Ro 3¹⁸ OT.
Κατέναντι occurs only once in the Ptol. papyri as a preposition,
but 83 in LXX, 9 in NT (e.g. Mt 27²⁴ κατέναντι τοῦ ὄχλου
in the sight of); see Mayser II 2, 541.

Ἔμπροσθεν ⁵ is in NT the normal word for *before* in the spatial
sense, as alternative to πρό which is seldom used in a local sense.
In class. Greek and Ptol. pap. (Mayser II 2, 539) it is used more
often as an adv. than with the gen.   It is extremely rare outside

---

¹ K-G I 402, 4.   Mayser II 2, 533.
² K-G I 461 n.   Meisterhans-Schwyzer 222, 52.   Mayser II 2, 535.
Johannessohn DGPS 244.   Radermacher² 144.
³ K-G I 402, 4.   Mayser II 2, 536ff.   Kuhring § 34.   Johannessohn
DGPS 337, 339.   Radermacher² 140–144.
⁴ Mayser II 2, 538.   Johannessohn DGPS 193, d.   Radermacher²
140, 143, 144.
⁵ Johannessohn DGPS 189–198.   Radermacher² 144, 145.

Bibl. Greek, and Semitic influence is obvious.   Mt Mk Lk Jn Ac
Past Rev; more frequent in Mt (e.g. 10³², 27¹¹).   Rev 19¹⁰
(B ἐνώπιον) 22⁸ (A πρό).   Temporal = πρό (also class.) perhaps
Jn 1¹⁵· ³⁰ (or = *ranks before me*).   Adverbial: only Lk 19⁴· ²⁸
Ph 3¹³ Rev 4⁶.   Adjectivally: ἔμπροσθέν μου γέγονεν Jn
1¹⁵· ³⁰.

'Ἐπάνω ¹.   *On top of.*   In place of simple ἐπί.   Hell. Greek
also uses ὑπεράνω: only Eph 1²¹ 4¹⁰ Heb 9⁵.   Such compounds
are already found in Attic, but the meaning is weakened by this
time.   The later language prefers the longer forms.   Ἄνω and
κάτω are always adverbs.   Βάλλω ἔξω and βάλλω κάτω are always
preferred to ἐκβάλλω and καταβάλλω (Mt 4⁶ 5¹³).   Mt 5¹⁴ ἐπάνω
ὄρους (for older ἐπ' ὄρους), 21⁷ ἐπάνω αὐτῶν.   Adverbial:
Mt 2⁹.

Ὑποκάτω: an adv. and preposition from Plato on; still more
frequent in Koine (Diodorus, Plutarch); only twice in Polyb.
About 90 times in LXX as substitute for ὑπό (Johannessohn
DGPS 183): very prevalent in Kms (19 against 17 ὑπό c. acc.)
and MiPr (8 against 4) and Ezek (13 against 6), Isa (8 : 4); but
Pent only 16 against 42.   Never in Est, 1 Esd, To, Wisdom
literature or Mac (exc. Si once).   In NT eleven times and only
as a preposition.   Lk 8¹⁶ ὑποκάτω κλίνης (for older ὑπὸ κλίνην).
Rarely as adv. in Ptol. papyri.

§ 9. Biblical Circumlocutions by means of Nouns with Gen.

Πρόσωπον:² for Heb. מְפְּנֵי the LXX bequeathes ἀπὸ
προσώπου c. gen. to Bibl. Greek (Thackeray OT Gr. 44) in place
of the normal ἀπό or παρά.   It occurs in Ac 3²⁰ 5⁴¹ (with *come, go*),
7⁴⁵ Rev 6¹⁶ 12¹⁴ 20¹¹ (with *drive, hide, flee*).   So from לִפְנֵי πρὸ
προσώπου Mt 11¹⁰ Lk 1⁷⁶ (SB ἐνώπιον) Ac 13²⁴.   So κατὰ
πρόσωπον: Lk 2³¹ Ac 3¹³ 25¹⁶ 2 Co 10¹ (= בִּפְנֵי).   So εἰς πρ.
2 Co 8²⁴ and Aquila Ge 17¹.   Prepositional compounds of
πρόσωπον are undoubtedly a Semitism in spite of their occurrence
in the papyri of ii/A.D. and one of iv/A.D. (MM Vocab. 553).

---

¹ Mayser II 2, 539ff.   Radermacher² 144.   G. D. Kilpatrick, " Mark
xiv. 5 'Ἐπάνω," *JThS* 42, 1941, 181ff.

² Johannessohn DGPS, 184–186, etc.   Cf. also 1 Clem 4⁸· ¹⁰ 18¹¹ 28³
Barn. 6⁹ 11⁷ ἀπὸ προσώπου.   Ign Pol 2² εἰς πρόσωπον.   1 Clem 35¹⁰
κατὰ πρόσωπον.   1 Clem 34³ Ign Eph 15³ πρὸ προσώπου.   Aqu. 1 Km 22⁴
2 Km 6¹⁴ πρὸ προσώπου, Aqu. Isa 7² ἀπὸ (ἐκ Q) προσώπου.

Χείρ : Heb. בְּיַד becomes εἰς χεῖρας *in the power of* Mt 26⁴⁵ Lk 23⁴⁶ Jn 13³ Heb 10³¹ etc., or ἐν (τῇ) χειρί Jn 3³⁵ Ac 7³⁵ (vl. σύν), or διὰ χειρός, χειρῶν (Ge 39⁴ etc.) Mk 6² Ac 2²³ 5¹² and oft. Heb. מְיַד becomes ἐκ χειρός Lk 1⁷¹ Ac 12¹¹. (Johannessohn DGPS *passim.*)

Στόμα although Heb. influence has increased the usage, στόμα is used in many similar ways in class. Greek : διά (Lk 1⁷⁰ Ac 1¹⁶ etc.), ἐκ, ἐπί. (Johannessohn DGPS *passim.*)

CHAPTER NINETEEN

NEGATIVES

(especially the encroachment of MH upon the
province of Oϒ)

§ 1. General[1]

The distinction between οὐ and μή is now far less subtle
than in class. Greek. Broadly, in the LXX οὐ renders לֹא
and μή אַל, and οὐχί הֲלֹא (e.g. Ge 40⁸).

In his examination of the Ptol. pap., Mayser observes that
the use of the two negative particles (οὐ as objective, μή as
subjective), as handed down from the classical period, managed
to hold its own in the Koine of the Hellenistic period as far as
finite verbs are concerned. There are of course many deviations
from classical standards. The infin. and ptc. play a special role
in so far as here μή has won from οὐ the major part of its use
(Mayser II 2, 543).

In post-classical prose, appreciation of the nice differences
between οὐ and μή, which broadly speaking are like those
between *non* and *ne*, has partially disappeared. It is not good
to bring the difference between οὐ and μή under a definite rule,
but doubtless there is a large increase in the use of μή in the
later language. The same observations apply to the NT.
There is sometimes no valid reason in favour of one particle
against the other, and either may be used according to the
author's own way of looking at things. There can be no
difference between ἁμαρτίαν μὴ πρὸς θάνατον and ἁμαρτία οὐ πρὸς
θάνατον 1 Jn 5¹⁶. Blass [2] made the rule that, in the NT, οὐ
negatives the indicative (facts) and μή the remaining moods
(ideas): this applies also to οὐδείς μηδείς, οὐδέ μηδέ, οὔτε μήτε,

---

[1] K-G II 178–223. Gildersleeve *AJP* 3, 202. O. Birke, *De particularum* μή *et* οὐ *usu Polybiano, Dionysiaeo, Diodoreo, Straboneo*, Diss.
Leipzig 1897. E. L. Greene, " Μή and οὐ before Lucian," in *Studies in Honor of Gildersleeve*, 1902. Mayser II 2, 543–567. Radermacher[2] 210
(with literature).

[2] Blass-Debr. § 426.

οὔπω μήπω, οὐκέτι μηκέτι, οὐδαμῶς μηδαμῶς, οὐδέποτε μηδέποτε.
There are exceptions where μή negatives the indic., and οὐ is
used with infin. and ptc. With a few exceptions, Blass's rule
applies to the Ptol. papyri (Mayser II 2, 552) for the infin., but
with the ptc. οὐ maintains its position fairly constantly, although even here also μή finally prevailed.

In general it seems that οὐ stands its ground where a clause
with ἀλλά follows it, and for the major part where the negative
expressions form a single idea, like οὐκ ὀλίγοι, οὐ πολλοί, etc.
(Mayser II 2, 550). Mt 9¹³ οὐ θυσίαν, Mk 9³⁷ οὐκ ἐμέ, Ro 9²⁵
τὸν οὐ λαόν μου, 10¹⁹ (LXX Dt 32²¹) ἐπ' οὐκ ἔθνει לֹא עָם.
Like οὐ βούλομαι (refuse to) in Ptol. pap., we find in NT οὐ θέλω
Mk 9³⁰ (I am averse to), οὐκ ἔχω Mt 13¹², οὐκ ἐάω Ac 16⁷
(forbid), οὐκ ἀγνοέω 2 Co 2¹¹ (know well). So also Lk 15¹³ Ac 1⁵
μετ' οὐ πολλὰς ἡμέρας, Jn 3³⁴ οὐκ ἐκ μέτρου, Ac 17⁴ οὐκ ὀλίγα,
20¹² οὐ μετρίως, 21³⁹ οὐκ ἀσήμου, 27¹⁴ μετ' οὐ πολύ, 1 Co 1²⁶
οὐ πολλοί, Eph 5⁴ τὰ οὐκ ἀνήκοντα. In LXX: 2 Mac 4¹³ οὐκ
ἀρχιερεύς. In the Ptol. pap. οὐκ ὀλίγοι = πολλοί, οὐκ εὖ
ὤν = κάκος, and οὐχ ὁ τυχών = unusual. It should be observed that οὐ πᾶς is capable of two meanings, limiting and
denying: (1) not all, i.e. some,[1] and (2) not any, i.e. none at all
(οὐδείς).[2] Both senses appear in Jn. The similar use of μή in
class. Greek [3] does not appear in NT; in each instance the μή
has another explanation.

§ 2. Main clauses

The prohibitive future has μή in NT (and οὐ μή Mt 16²²),
whereas class. Greek sometimes has μή (as in Hom. Clem. 3⁶⁹
μηδένα μισήσετε). Mt 5²¹ 6⁵ 20²⁶ οὐχ οὕτως ἔσται ἐν ὑμῖν.

Both οὐ and μή are both found in questions: [4] οὐ or οὐχί
or οὐδέ or οὐκοῦν [5] if a positive answer is expected (= nonne)

---

[1] E.g. Mt 7²¹ 19¹¹ 1 Co 15³⁹.

[2] E.g. Mt 24²² οὐ ... πᾶσα σάρξ = Heb, לֹא כֹּל or כֹּל לֹא; Ac 10¹⁴
οὐδέποτε ἔφαγον πᾶν κοινόν.

[3] Plato Gorg. 459, ὁ μὴ ἰατρός, Ant. 5, 82 οἱ μὴ καθαροί, Thuc. 2,
45, 1 τὸ μὴ ἐμποδῶν.

[4] K-G II 524. F. C. Babbitt, " Questions with μή," Proc. Amer.
Philol. Assocn. 32, 43.

[5] Jn 18³⁷ is difficult, because a neg. answer is expected; οὐκοῦν appears
to be merely inferential (the stress on the οὖν). In Ac 2⁷ οὐχὶ ἰδοὺ is a
Koine idiom, like the class. ἆρ' οὐ: Beg. in loc.

Mt 7²² 13²⁷· ⁵⁵ Mk 14⁶⁰ Lk 12⁶ 17¹⁷ Ac 13¹⁰ 21³⁸ Ro 2²⁶ 1 Co 9¹ (οὐχί alongside οὐ) 14²³; μή or μήτι if a negative answer (*num, surely not*): Mt 7¹⁶ 26²⁵ (Judas's μήτι ἐγώ εἰμι *expects* a negative answer but *receives* a positive), Jn 5³⁸ (may be a question: *do you marvel at this?*), 7⁵¹ (Nicodemus is rather subtle in using μή), 21⁵, 6⁶⁷, 7³¹· ⁴⁷, Ro 11¹ (μὴ ἀπώσατο is expressly answered in 11² with οὐκ ἀπώσατο), 1 Co 6³ (elliptical μήτιγε, as Demosth. 2, 23). Sometimes the difference is illustrated in a single verse: Lk 6³⁹ μήτι δύναται τυφλὸς τυφλὸν ὁδηγεῖν (answer no); οὐχὶ ἀμφότεροι εἰς βόθυνον ἐμπεσοῦνται (answer yes); 1 Co 9⁸ μὴ κατὰ ἄνθρωπον ταῦτα λαλῶ, ἢ καὶ ὁ νόμος ταῦτα οὐ λέγει; 2 Co 12¹⁸ μήτι ἐπλεονέκτησεν ὑμᾶς Τίτος (no); οὐ τῷ αὐτῷ πνεύματι περιεπατήσαμεν (yes); Jn 4³³⁻³⁵, Ro 9²⁰ᶠ.

A positive answer will be expected if οὐ μή (= *nonne*) is found in questions: Lk 18⁷ Jn 18¹¹ Rev 15⁴.

Where μή negatives the whole sentence the verb alone may already be negatived by οὐ (Paul, as class.), and so μή . . . οὐ stands with a sentence which expects a positive answer: Ro 10¹⁷ᶠᶠ μὴ οὐκ ἤκουσαν *surely you haven't not-heard it* (missed hearing it), 1 Co 9⁴ᶠ μὴ οὐκ ἔχομεν: 11²², 2 Co 12²⁰ μήπως . . . οὐχ . . . εὕρω.

In some passages the strength of μή is somewhat modified: Jn 4²⁹ μήτι οὗτός ἐστιν ὁ Χριστός *he must be* (or *perhaps he is*) *the Messiah*; hardly *num* here; it is more like οὐ; the distinction is sometimes difficult to draw for much depends on the tone of the speaker; it is here rather hesitant, as in 4³³. On the later μήτι = *perhaps*, see Abbott Joh. Gr. 2702 b 1. See also A. T. Robertson, "The NT Use of μή with hesitant question in the Indicative Mood," Expos. Series VIII No. 152, 1923.

In main clauses μή occurs with subjunctive (Mk 12¹⁴ Ga 6⁹), optative (only wish-opt. in NT., viz. Mk 11¹⁴ Ro 3⁴· ⁶· ³¹ Ga 6¹⁴ etc.), and imperative (Mt 6³ μὴ γνώτω, 24¹⁸ μὴ ἐπιστρεψάτω ὀπίσω, LXX Ex 34³ Ps 6²). But see 1 Co 5¹⁰, 1 Pt 2¹⁸ (οὐ μόνον), 3³ (ὧν ἔστω οὐχ ὁ . . . κόσμος), and we find οὐ and ἔστω in Ptol. pap. and οὐδενὶ ἐξέστω in inscr. cited by Radermacher (171).

§ 3. Dependent Clauses

The indicative with εἰ has οὐ in the NT and Koine, if the condition is "real", seldom the μή which was normal in classical;[1] sometimes even class. Greek had οὐ if εἰ = ἐπεί or = *if, as you hope* (K-G II 189f), in which case always οὐ in NT and Koine. Lk 11[8] εἰ καὶ οὐ δώσει, 16[31] εἰ Μωϋσέως ... οὐκ ἀκούουσιν, Jn 10[37] εἰ οὐ ποιῶ τὰ ἔργα ... εἰ δὲ ποιῶ. So also Lk 14[26] 16[11] Jn 1[25] 3[12] Ro 11[21] 1 Co 7[11] 15[13] 1 Ti 3[5] 5[8] Jas 2[11] Rev 20[15]. Contrary to normal Greek usage, οὐ enters once with " unreal " indicative: Mt 26[24] Mk 14[21] καλὸν αὐτῷ εἰ οὐκ ἐγενήθη. But μή is always found when εἰ = *nisi* (e.g. Mt 5[13] Ac 26[32] Ga 1[7]).

Relative clauses regularly have οὐ with indic., and μή on very rare occasions: Lk 8[18] ὃς ἂν μὴ ἔχῃ (conditional), Ac 15[29] D, Col 2[18] ἃ μὴ ἑώρακεν C vulg syr[p] (p[46] S*ABD om μή), Ti 1[11] διδάσκοντες ἃ μὴ δεῖ (= 1 Ti 5[13] τὰ μὴ δέοντα), 2 Pt 1[9] ᾧ γὰρ μὴ πάρεστιν ταῦτα (correct according to literary style, as the speech is not about definite things: K-G II 185f), 1 Jn 4[3] ὃ μὴ ὁμολογεῖ, Rev 14[4] p[47] οἳ μὴ μετὰ γυναικῶν ἐμολύνθησαν (rest: οὐκ). See also Ac 3[23] Rev 13[15], LXX Le 23[29] (πᾶσα ψυχὴ ἥτις μὴ ταπεινωθήσεται), Si 13[24].

In statement clauses with ὅτι and ὡς, and temporal and causal clauses with indic., although οὐ largely remains, μή is encroaching in the Koine.[2] Jn 3[18] ὅτι μὴ πεπίστευκεν *because (such a person) would not have believed* (but οὐ in 1 Jn 5[10]), Heb 9[17] ἐπεὶ μή ποτε ἰσχύει, B.U. 530[35] ἐπὶ μὴ ἀντέγραψας αὐτῇ (i/A.D.), Jos. c. Ap. 1, 217, Hom. Clem. 8[14] etc. Blass-Debr. § 428, 5.

§ 4. Participles [3]

The post-classical language strongly tends towards μή (MGr only μή) with participles, whereas in class. Attic the decision to use μή depended on the meaning of the ptc. in each instance. NT follows the Hellenistic tendency and μή is the rule, especially with articular ptc., and even where the ptc. has

---

[1] Classical μή: Lk 6[4]D εἰ δὲ μὴ οἶδας; 1 Ti 6[3] εἴ τις ἑτεροδιδασκαλεῖ καὶ μὴ προσέχεται (yet οὐ in 3[5] 5[8]).
[2] K-G II 188. Jannaris § 1818. Mayser II 2, 551. Moulton Einl. 271n. Radermacher[2] 211.
[3] K-G II 198ff. Jannaris §§ 1815f. Mayser II 2, 556ff. G. E. Howes, " The Use of μή with the Participle, where the negation is influenced by the construction upon which the Participle depends," *Harvard Studies* 12, 1901, 277ff, A. G. Laird, " When is generic μή particular? " *AJP* 43, 1922, 124–45.

an "indicative" sense: 2 Co 6³ μηδεμίαν ἐν μηδενὶ διδόντες προσκοπήν, Ti 1⁶· ⁷ τέκνα ἔχων πιστά, μὴ ἐν κατηγορίᾳ ἀσωτίας. Indeed the use of μή in NT is wider than in the Ptol. papyri. The proportions for the latter are: iii/B.C. οὐ: μή = 4 : 1, ii–i/ B.C. οὐ: μή = 2 : 3 (Mayser II 2, 556, 562). However, the use of individual NT authors does vary to some extent. Thus in Mt and Jn οὐ is scarcely found at all apart from Mt 22¹¹ εἶδεν ἄνθρωπον οὐκ ἐνδεδυμένον ἔνδυμα γάμου (C³D μή), Jn 10¹² ὁ μισθωτὸς καὶ οὐκ ὢν ποιμήν (μή more correct as it refers to no definite person; but καὶ μή is not liked in the Koine). But Lk–Ac is more classical in this respect: Lk 6⁴² αὐτὸς ... οὐ βλέπων (not D), Ac 7⁵ οὐκ ὄντος αὐτῷ τέκνου, 19¹¹ 28² οὐχ ὁ τυχών (no ordinary; in Ptol. pap. with same meaning: BU 436⁹ καὶ ὕβριν οὐ τὴν τυχοῦσαν συνετελέσαντο committed a more than ordinary outrage ¹), 26²² οὐδὲν ἐκτὸς λέγων, 28¹⁷ οὐδὲν ... ποιήσας, ¹⁹ οὐχ ὡς ἔχων.

But Paul, Heb. and 1 Pt (with few exceptions) prefer the Hellenistic μή. The exceptions are Ro 9²⁵, 1 Co 9²⁶ ὡς οὐκ (but 2 Co 10¹⁴ ὡς μή where it is a conception only and not a fact), 2 Co 4⁸ᶠ (p⁴⁶ μή), 5¹² CDEFG (p⁴⁶ SB μή). The fact that Paul almost invariably uses μή with participles does lead to ambiguity ²: Ga 6⁹ μὴ ἐκλυόμενοι (which in class. Greek must be if we do not faint; but by Paul it is intended as a fact), Ro 8⁴ ἐν ἡμῖν τοῖς μὴ κατὰ σάρκα περιπατοῦσιν (it would be IF we do not walk ... in class. Greek, but Paul probably means us who DO not ...).

§ 5. Infinitive ³

Here in general is μή, but there are traces of an older use of οὐ. It is simplifying too much to say that μή stands throughout; it occurs indeed even after verbs of feeling (Ac 25²⁵ 2 Co 11⁵), but there is Ac 19²⁷ εἰς οὐθὲν λογισθῆναι and 2 Ti 2¹⁴ μὴ λογομαχεῖν ἐπ' οὐδὲν χρήσιμον, even if with Blass in Mk 7²⁴ Jn 21²⁵ Ac 26²⁶ we rather perversely take the οὐ more closely with the main verb than with the infin. (Blass-Debr. § 429). A redundant μή appears with infin. sometimes depending on a

---

¹ Mayser II 2, 518, 546. Preisigke s.v. τυγχάνω 4. Bauer s.v. 2d.
² Zerwick § 307a.
³ Mayser II 2, 552ff, 564f. Jannaris § 1815. Moulton Einl. 271 n.

negative main verb (class. and Hell.), e.g. Lk 4⁴², 17¹ ἀνένδεκτόν
ἐστιν τοῦ τὰ σκάνδαλα μὴ ἐλθεῖν, 20²⁷ WA (SBD etc. avoid it by
harmonizing with Mt Mk), 22³⁴ (SB om μή), Ac 4²⁰ οὐ δυνάμεθα
. . . μὴ λαλεῖν, Ga 5⁷, 1 Pt 3¹⁰, 1 Jn 2²².

§ 6. Double Negatives

These are of two types, self-cancelling and pleonastic.
The self-cancelling is classical and appears rarely in NT : Lk 8¹⁷
οὐ γάρ ἐστιν κρυπτὸν ὃ οὐ φανερὸν γενήσεται ; also Mt 24² Ac 4²⁰
1 Co 9⁶ 12¹⁵.   Sometimes however it is not so much that the
negatives are self-cancelling as that both have their full force :
Mt 10²⁶ Lk 12² οὐδὲν δὲ συγκεκαλυμμένον ἐστὶν ὃ οὐκ ἀποκαλυφ-
θήσεται, Mt 24² etc. οὐ . . . ὃς οὐ, Ac 19³⁵ τίς ἐστιν . . . ὃς οὐ.

Pleonastic negatives, which were frequent in class. Attic and well
suited to the lively Greek temperament, are not as plentiful now.   The
negative was strengthened by sequences like οὐ (μή) . . . οὐδείς (μηδείς),
e.g. Mk 5³ καὶ οὐδὲ ἁλύσει οὐκέτι οὐδεὶς ἐδύνατο αὐτὸν δῆσαι, 11² vl.
οὐδεὶς . . . οὔπω, ¹⁴ μηκέτι . . . μηδείς, 15⁴· ⁵ (οὐ . . . οὐδέν often in Ptol.
pap.), Lk 4² 23⁵³ Jn 15⁵ 19⁴¹Ac 8³⁹ (οὐκ . . . οὐκέτι in Ptol. pap.) Ro 13⁸
2 Co 11⁹ 1 Ti 1⁷ μὴ . . . μηδέ . . . μηδέ is frequent in Ptol. pap.) Heb 13⁵.
But two constructions are not classical : (1) the use of τις with the negative
in the Koine (for οὐδείς), e.g. Mt 11²⁷ οὐδὲ τὸν πατέρα τις ἐπιγνώσκει,
12¹⁹, Jn 10²⁸ οὐχ ἁρπάσει τις, 1 Co 6¹², 1 Th 1⁸ μὴ . . . τι (in Ptol. pap.
μηθὲν . . . τι, οὔτε . . . τι, and μηδὲ . . . τινάς (Mayser II 2, 567) ; (2) the
amalgam of οὐδέ and οὐ μή to form a very strong but pleonastic οὐδ'
οὐ μή, e.g. Mt 24²¹ (D οὐδὲ μή), Mk 14²⁵ οὐκέτι οὐ μὴ πίω (SDWCL
om οὐκέτι), Heb 13⁵ from LXX Dt 31⁶ where only A has οὐδ' οὐ μή
(p⁴⁶ οὐδὲ μή), Mt 25⁹BDC Did 4¹⁰ μήποτε οὐ μή, LXX Am 2¹⁵ Jb 32²¹,
pap. Wilcken Chr. no. 122⁴ (A.D. 6) οὐδ' οὐ μὴ γένηται.   On μὴ οὐ
see p. 98.   On οὐ μή see pp. 95–98.

§ 7. Yes and No

Yes ναί Mt 5³⁷ Lk 7²⁶ 2 Co 1¹⁷ Jas 5¹² and *no* οὔ or οὐχί
(MGr ὄχι) Mt 13²⁹ Lk 1⁶⁰ etc.   Note the contrast of objective
and subjective negative in Mk 12¹⁴ ἔξεστι . . . δοῦναι ἢ οὔ ;
δῶμεν ἢ μὴ δῶμεν ;

§ 8. Position of the Negative

As a rule the negative precedes what is negatived, except
that it may also (as in class. Greek) precede the preposition or ὡς
if such occurs before a ptc. or adj. : Ac 1⁵ Lk 15¹³ D οὐ μετὰ

πολλὰς ἡμέρας, 2 Co 10¹⁴ p⁴⁶ μὴ ὡς (the rest correct to ὡς μή),
Heb 11³ τὸ μὴ ἐκ φαινομένων. Often negative and verb are
blended in one idea: οὐκ ἐάω (and more popular οὐκ ἀφίω)
prevent Ac 19³⁰ etc. This may be altered to achieve emphasis,
and in Ac 7⁴⁸ the position of οὐχ puts *the Most High* in relief,
as μή in Jas 3¹ puts πολλοί in relief (also οὐδέν emphatic, away
from λανθάνειν in Ac 26²⁶, and οὐ before the inappropriate verb
in 1 Co 2²). So LXX Nu 16²⁹ᵇ. But a negative which is
separated from its verb may affect the complement: Mk 9³⁷
οὐκ ἐμὲ δέχεται *it is not me that he receives*, 2 Co 3³ ἐνγεγραμμένη
οὐ μέλανι *written not with ink*. The rule is several times broken
with πᾶς: Ro 3²⁰ πᾶσα σάρξ . . . οὐ, Eph 5⁵ 1 Jn 2²¹ πᾶς . . . οὐ,
Eph 4²⁹ πᾶς . . . μή, 1 Co 15⁵¹ πάντες οὐ κοιμηθησόμεθα (*must*=οὐ
πάντες). On the other hand, οὐ πάντως (Ro 3⁹) must be
reversed or taken separately: *no! absolutely* or *certainly not* (*not
in all cases* is scarcely possible); scribes felt the difficulty, too.

BOOK TWO

THE SENTENCE COMPLETE:

SYNTHETIC SYNTAX

PART I

THE ORDINARY SIMPLE SENTENCE

CHAPTER TWENTY

SUBJECT AND PREDICATE:
APPARENT ABSENCE OF SUBJECT[1]

§ 1. Impersonal Verbs[2]

Hellenistic (Polyb.) βρέχει Jas 5¹⁷ for class. ὕει (Mayser II 3, 2; Abel § 39a); but personal at Mt 5⁴⁵ (as class., and LXX Ge 19²⁴). For βροντῆσαι Jn 12²⁹ has βροντὴν γεγονέναι. The problematic ἀπέχει Mk 14⁴¹ may be impersonal, for class. ἀρκεῖ: *it is receipted, the account is settled* (consistent with the meaning of the variant in DW ἀπέχει τὸ τέλος *it has its end, the matter is settled*); so in P. Lond. IV 1343³⁸ (709 A.D.), etc.[3] Lk 24²¹ may not be impers., τρίτην ταύτην ἡμέραν ἄγει, but the subject is Jesus: *he has ʽalready allowed three days to pass* (see Bauer s.v., ἄγω, 4). In Mk 2² ὥστε μηκέτι χωρεῖν μηδὲ τὰ πρὸς τὴν θύραν, the last four words may be the subject of χωρεῖν (Moule 27). Impers. μέλει Mt 22¹⁶ Mk 12¹⁴ Jn 10¹³ 1 Co 9⁹ 1 Pt 5⁷. But in Mk 4³⁸ Lk 10⁴⁰ 1 Co 7²¹ a clause is the subject.

The impers. passive, quite common in Latin, is fairly so in NT but on the whole is very rare in Greek apart from some exx. of the perfect παρεσκεύασται *preparations are made*. The desire to avoid God's name enters into the picture in NT. Mt 7² μετρηθήσεται ὑμῖν (but a cognate noun μέτρον may be understood), Lk 6³⁸ δίδοτε καὶ δοθήσεται ὑμῖν (but further on μέτρον ... δώσουσιν), 1 Pt 4⁶ νεκροῖς εὐηγγελίσθη; a cognate noun may be supplied here, but not in Ro 10¹⁰ πιστεύεται ... ὁμολογεῖται, 1 Co 15⁴²f σπείρεται ... ἐγείρεται.

Certain verbs are only apparently impersonal, since the clause which follows can be taken as subject, e.g. ἐρρέθη in Mt 5³¹ Ro 9¹²; and so also δεῖ, ἔξεστιν, ἐξόν, ἐγένετο, ἐνδέχεται,

---

[1] K-G I § 352, pp. 32ff. Gildersleeve I 68–82. Meisterhans-Schwyzer 195. Wackernagel I 113f. Mayser II 3, 1ff. Zerwick §§ 1–4.

[2] For δέον, χρή, ἔδει see pp. 88, 90, 148, 322; for δοκεῖ p. 147.

[3] Alternative suggestions: A. Pallis, *Notes on St. Mark*, new ed., Oxford 1932, 47ff; G. H. Boobyer *NTS* 2, 1955–6, 44ff.

γέγραπται, πρέπει, ὠφελεῖ, which have a following infin. as
subject (e.g. Ac 7²³ ἀνέβη ἐπὶ τὴν καρδίαν, Semitic). Lk 17¹
has as subject τοῦ τὰ σκάνδαλα μὴ ἐλθεῖν (Moule 27); so with
λυσιτελεῖ (only Lk 17²), πρέπον ἐστιν, συμφέρει, συνέβη. In
1 Pt 2⁶ περιέχει ἐν γραφῇ, the quotation may be the subject.
But in Mt 13¹² περισσευθήσεται is probably passive and impers.,
because of the parallel (not *he shall be made to abound*).

§ 2. Impersonal "they"

Much more usual than the impers. passive, and a characteristic feature of Mk's style, is the 3rd plural without subject,
meaning *one* or *they*. Languages which lack any special indeterminate subject like *man* (German) or *on* (French) tend to
display this finite plural in verbs of speaking and narrating.
The tendency of Aramaic to avoid the passive has exercised an influence extending to other verbs in NT, e.g. Lk 12²⁰ (ἀπαιτοῦσιν),
and the same Aramaic tendency appears in words like ἀναβαίνω,
said of the fish which *is taken up* Mt 17²⁷, or ἐξέρχομαι in place
of ἐκβάλλομαι Lk 4⁴¹ 8²; see also ἀπελθεῖν εἰς τὴν γέενναν in
place of βληθῆναι Mk 9⁴⁴; so Mt 5¹⁵ οὐδὲ καίουσιν λύχνον, 9²
ἰδοὺ προσέφερον αὐτῷ παραλυτικόν, ¹⁷ οὐδὲ βάλλουσιν οἶνον.
Dan 4²² Ο' and θ, 4²⁸ σοί λέγουσιν (Ο' λέγεται), 4²⁹ ἀπὸ τῶν
ἀνθρώπων σε ἐκδιώκουσιν ... χόρτον ὡς βοῦν ψωμιοῦσίν σε.
In Mk 2¹⁸ the undefined plural may be impers. or it may refer
to the subject of the preceding sentence; but ἔλεγον in 3²¹ is
an example of the impers. pl. which C. H. Turner showed to
be a special feature of Mark (*JThS* 25, 1924, 377–386). In at
least two places this is of some importance to the exegete, for
(1) at Mk 3²¹ we read *when his own people heard, they went out
to take him, for THEY said* ... ἔλεγον γὰρ ὅτι ἐξέστη. It is
wrong to assume that his mother and brothers think that Jesus
is mad, for the verb ἔλεγον can be considered an indef. plural:
rumour had it, that he was mad. (2) Also Mk 14² becomes
more intelligible if ἔλεγον is taken as an indefinite plural: the
chief priests and scribes were plotting the death of Jesus with
subtilty, *for* (true text of Mark) *THEY said, Not during the
feast* .... This γάρ gives a reason for their decision, and *they*
is therefore someone else, not the chief priests and scribes
(C. H. Turner, op. cit. 384f).

Aramaic influence has enlarged the class of verbs which may be so used, since Aramaic avoids the passive, but Moulton and Milligan (Vocab. 52) cite a iii/A.D. papyrus with ἀπαιτοῦσιν, like Lk 12²⁰; so also P. Fay. III 14 λέγουσιν, P. Hib. 27. 167 κάουσιν. In class. Greek the construction was used primarily with verbs of saying, φασί, λέγουσι, καλοῦσι, ἔρχονται, but in NT we have also τεθνήκασιν (Mt 2²⁰), συλλέγουσιν (Mt 7¹⁶ Lk 6⁴⁴), προσέφερον (Mk 10¹³). In Heb 10¹ προσφέρουσιν and δύνανται may be in this class. The subject οἱ ἄνθρωποι is actually present in Mk 8²⁷ Lk 6³¹, and this may be the intermediate stage towards the impers. verb. The suppression of the subject seems to bring emphasis on the action. At times the 3rd pl. may be used circumspectly for God's own action, and so his name rather than οἱ ἄνθρωποι is to be understood: Lk 6³⁸ δώσουσιν, 12²⁰. ⁴⁸ (ἀπ-)αἰτοῦσιν, 16⁹ (*that God may receive you into eternal dwellings*), 23³¹ (?). See Moulton-Howard 447.

§ 3. Scil. "the Scripture"

In the quotation formula λέγει, etc. a subject θεός or γραφή is understood: Ro 10⁸ λέγει p⁴⁶ SAB (DFG insert ἡ γραφή); λέγει also in 2 Co 6² Ga 3¹⁶ etc., φησίν in 1 Co 6¹⁶ Heb 8⁵, εἴρηκε Heb 4⁴. We have something like a diatribe in 2 Co 10¹⁰ φησίν *says my opponent*. See also Wackernagel I 113.

CHAPTER TWENTY-ONE

SUBJECT AND PREDICATE:
ABSENCE OF THE VERB " TO BE "

§ 1. The Copula[1]

From the standpoint of class. Attic there is nothing remarkable about the extensive absence of the copula in NT, for this was the most common form of ellipse and, except where ambiguity threatened, was almost the rule. The NT is indeed nearer to Ionic Greek where " en dehors de quelques expressions consacrées, [Herodotus] n'exprime plus, dans la langue courante, un jugement en juxtaposant simplement le sujet et l'attribut. Il ajoute une copule." (Barbelenet 103). The pure nominal phrase is still a living thing in Herodotus, but very seriously limited (ibid. 18); it is commoner in the Ionic poets (ibid. 19). In NT the ellipse is not so general as in the earlier Attic Greek and is almost confined to ἐστιν and to these " expressions consacrées ", viz. dead phrases of either an impersonal or stereotyped and epigrammatic character (incl. ὄνομα) or else very live phrases of a rhetorical and dramatic sort. It was the post-classical tendency to view the pure nominal phrase as an ellipse and to reserve it for poetic archaism, stylistic expressions and set formulae (Schwyzer II 623). The NT has gone further than class. Attic or contemporary literary Hellenistic in inserting the copula, but not so far as Herodotus, except in Mk and Jn. Semitic influence may have assisted the NT, but more probably

---

[1] K-G I § 354, pp. 40ff. Gildersleeve I 83–86. Meisterhans-Schwyzer § 80, pp. 195ff. Mayser II 3, 16ff. J. E. Harry, " On the omission of the copula in certain combinations in Greek," *Proc. Amer. Philol. Assocn.* 34, p. viii ff. J. Kinzel, *Die Kopula bei Homer und Hesiod*, Progr. Mährisch-Ostrau 1908, 1909. C. G. Wilke, *De ellipsi copulae verbi* εἶναι *in fabulis Euripideis*, Breslau 1877. D. Barbelenet, *De la Phrase à Verbe être dans l'Ionien d'Hérodote*, Paris 1913. E. Ekman, *Der reine Nominalsatze bei Xenophon*, 1938. P. F. Regard, *La Phrase nominale dans la Langue du NT*, Paris 1919. A. W. Milden, " The possessive in the predicate in Greek ", *Proc. Amer. Philol. Assocn.* 37, 24 ; " The article in the predicate in Greek," ibid. 40, 63.

it is a matter of literary standards.[1] Luke and Paul resort
much less to the copula than Mark or John. In MGr it is not
usual to omit the appropriate part of εἶναι unless oratorical
effect is deliberately sought.

So side by side in Biblical Greek there are the Attic pure
nominal phrase and the Ionic nominal phrase with the copula,
both used by each Biblical writer with equal spontaneity; but
the writers vary considerably in their preferences. In common
with the Indo-Germanic languages in general, Greek was tending
to replace the pure nominal phrase by the phrase with a copula,
and some writers have taken the process further than others.

(a) Fixed phrases

In detail, the part of the verb which most usually is to be
supplied is 3rd sing. pres. ind., as in class. Greek. This is seen
in certain impers. phrases introduced by the neuter of an adj.
(αἰσχρόν, ἀρκετόν, ἀδύνατον, δῶρον, δῆλον, εἰ δέον, εἰ δυνατόν,
ἐξόν, κακόν, καλόν, μέγα, ὄφελον, (ἔτι) μικρόν (καί), οὐ μόνον, οὐχ
οἷον, πρόδηλον, συμφέρον, φάνερον), or by a noun expressing possibility or necessity (ἀνάγκη, χρή, ὥρα). This is so occasionally,
even in Ionic (Hdt). It is true that πρέπον is never found
without ἐστιν in NT (unlike 1 Mac 12[11]; but ἦν in 3 Mac 7[13]),
and neither are the impers. ἄξιον or δίκαιον found without ἐστιν,
as they are in contemporary Hellenistic writers. But ellipse is
frequent with the other words. There is however no regular
pattern within the NT.

A similar archaic usage is the Ionic ἔνι (= ἐν) as a kind of
adverbial predicate without the copula. It is always negative
in NT, not in Hdt. (Barbelenet 13).

A more frequent NT example of the survival of a lifeless
formula is the pure nominal phrase containing ὄνομα, whether
as a parenthesis or as a main or subordinate clause. The
formula may be Hebraistic, through the influence of שְׁמוֹ and
וּשְׁמָהּ (LXX 1 Km 1[1] etc.), but it is not absent from class. and
Hell. Greek and the papyri. The papyri and NT even here

---

[1] In the nearly exhaustive references at the close of this chapter not
enough notice or discussion of text variants could be given. The student
of the text will, however, gather the general principles behind each author's
usage, and the exceptions, and ought thereby to be able to come nearer
to a decision between the text variants.

sometimes insert a copula: Jn 18¹⁰ Lk 8³⁰, Zen. pap. 59037, 7 (258 B.C.).

Another antique survival of the pure nominal phrase is the stereotyped phrase at the beginning and end of letters. We may supply either the optative or imperative or fut. indic. (Mayser II 3, 19). The formulae are less stereotyped at the end than at the beginning of letters. No doubt Semitic influence assisted their survival in NT (cf. שָׁלוֹם לָכֶם Ge 43²³). See Büchsel in Kittel WB III 300f.

The survival of the pure nominal phrase is seen above all, as in class. Greek (even in Hdt.), in proverbial saws which abound in the NT. When we do occasionally find the copula it may be that special emphasis is intended.

(b) Spontaneous or live expressions

These on the contrary are not verbally the same phrases as in earlier Greek, which testifies to the originality and spontaneity of the method of using the pure nominal phrase in NT. Attic influence may explain it, since the corresponding phrase in Ionic Greek usually has the copula (Regard 45).

On the Semitic model, and occurring in an OT atmosphere, is ἰδού (scil. pres. or impf. or even aor. or fut. of εἰμί and of πάρειμι and (παρα)γίνομαι), although there are secular parallels. Besides, interjections do not need a verbal predicate in normal Greek, as οὐά in Mk 15²⁹. Yet the copula does occur with ἰδού in NT. On the Semitic model is οὐαί (אוֹי הוֹי, etc.) and yet the copula appears here too.

Free of any suspicion of archaism are pure nominal phrases in the form of exclamations. They are very common in NT, even when we exclude direct LXX quotations, e.g. ἅγιον τὸ ὄνομα αὐτοῦ Lk 1⁴⁹, εὐλογήμενος ὁ ἐρχόμενος Mt 21⁹ 23³⁹ = Lk 13³⁵ 19³⁸ = Jn 12¹³, εὐλογητὸς κύριος Lk 1⁶⁸, εὐλογητὸς ὁ θεός 2 Co 1³, and μακάριοι ὤν, μακάριος ἀνὴρ ὅς Ro 4⁷ᶠ Jas 1¹². Usually the order is attribute-subject. Again we are reminded of Semitic influence, but we should remember the class. and Hell. parallels. Moreover, there are many instances where the copula creeps in, even in the μακάριος phrase. In the doxologies, indic., imper., or optative might equally well be supplied. However, in spite of LXX precedent,[1] it is not the optative

---

[1] 3 Km 10⁹ γένοιτο εὐλ., Jb 1²¹ εἴη εὐλ.

idea which is in mind, for God is thought of as being *already* blessed and glorious. Since there is no need to pray for it, the phrase is simply an exclamation.

Akin to this is the pure nominal phrase in a series of graphic clauses. The most outstanding instance is the series of exclamations in 1 Co 15[39-56] and Ph 1[21-24]. It is typically Pauline but it is found in the LXX and in contemporary Hell. authors. The statements are usually brief and vivid and abound in passages which rise to heights of oratory. One frequently finds it in the apodosis and protasis of conditional sentences. Yet sometimes in NT the copula is found in this kind of phrase, especially if the identity of the subject would otherwise be obscure. This literary tendency also appears when there is a striving after rhetoric in epigrammatic phrases and those which express general or abstract truths, especially in connection with the demonstrative pronoun; again there are exceptions. Some of these questions are stereotyped, but the majority are spontaneous. In the NT it is equally common to find the copula as the pure nominal phrase in questions.

The pure nominal phrase is found sometimes in indirect questions in Lk and Paul, as in literary Hell. Greek; also after ὅπου, ὡς, ὥσπερ, καθώς. Pernot (p. 53) notes the rather frequent absence of the copula in Jn after ὅτι (although it is far more often inserted) and we find this ellipse all over the NT (Mt Mk Lk 1 2 Co Ph Ro Rev), as well as in class. and Hell. writers, and papyri.

(c) *Ellipse of other parts besides ἐστιν*

This is more rare, and the pers. pronoun is usually added to avoid ambiguity—though not always in Paul. Almost universally in NT, εἰμί is inserted. If there is ellipse of εἶ, there is usually a pronoun, but ellipse is rare. Only in Paul is both pronoun and ἐσμεν absent. The ellipse of ἐστε is also rare: Lk 6[20] has neither pronoun nor copula. Ellipse of εἰσιν is much more frequent, especially when it closely follows that of ἐστιν. The fut. indic. never suffers ellipse in NT except for rare instances of ἔσται. Almost the only kind of phrase in which ἦν might be supplied is that with ὄνομα; there are a few other instances, especially in vivid and interrogative phrases and the stereotyped εἰ δυνατόν. It is all but impossible to

decide whether ἦν is a copula or something stronger.   Other
persons of impf. indic. are to be supplied very occasionally:
ἦσαν or ἐγένοντο, and ἤμην.

There are but two or three places in NT (nearly all in Paul)
where subjunctive ᾖ and ὦσιν may be supplied.   The ellipse
after ὅς ἄν etc. is classical (K–G § 354e, n. 2c; Gildersleeve I
§ 86).   As well as epistolary formulae and formal wishes, there
is the spontaneous use of the pure nominal phrase where optative
is expected, as with εἰρήνη (Hebraic).   There is no ellipse of
ἔστω except in χάρις τῷ θεῷ (class. and early papyri).   There
are some further exx. in NT and Koine vernacular.   Imper.
ἐστέ may be supplied with some participles in Peter and Paul.
But the ptc. is perhaps in itself imperatival; the phenomenon,
which may be a peculiarity of the " eastern " Koine, is frequent
in the vernacular and in Malalas.   Something like ἴσθι is presumably to be supplied with δεῦρο.   There is never need to
supply ἔσεσθε.

Some phrases have only an apparent ellipse, because they
follow immediately upon a previous clause which has the copula,
and the copula is to be understood of both phrases: Mt 22[14]
25[35f] 28[3] Lk 19[2] Jn 15[5] 20[26] 1 Co 14[10. 22] 11[3] 2 Co 10[11] 1 Jn 3[12]
Rev 10[1] etc.

§ 2. Stronger or Essential meaning of ἐστιν or εἰσιν

On occasion, when emphasis or feeling is more than normal,
there is even ellipse where the meaning is *there is* (*are*) or *it is*,
and stronger than a mere copula.   This happens also in both
class. and literary Hell. Greek, and even sometimes in the papyri.
Something like ἐστιν is to be supplied *before* ἵνα at times in Jn,
and to some extent in Mk, Lk, and Paul.   We may compare
the ellipse before οὐχ ὅτι in Jn and Paul.

§ 3. Individual writers

The books of Biblical and certain secular writers may be
laid side by side and in a general way the relative tendency to
introduce or omit the copula will be discovered.   It will be seen
that in the Gospels there is some considerable difference from
secular usage.   (The copula infin. and ptc. have been excluded.)

	Mt	Mk	Lk	Ac	Jn
Verb *to be*	257	174	318	213	395
Ellipse	81	37	91	27	47
Proportion	3:1	5:1	3:1	8:1	8:1

	Ro	1 Co	2 Co	Ga	Eph	Ph	Col	1 Th	2 Th	1 Ti	2 Ti	Ti	Ph
To be	67	133	48	48	38	11	24	9	6	20	13	8	2
Ellipse	105	90	72	19	19	29	5	10	7	16	7	5	2
Propn.	$\frac{3}{4}$:1	1:1	$\frac{3}{4}$:1	$2\frac{1}{2}$:1	2:1	$\frac{1}{2}$:1	5:1	1:1	1:1	1:1	2:1	$1\frac{1}{2}$:1	1:1

	Paul (non-Past)	Past	Heb	Jas	2 Pt Jude	Joh. Epp.	Rev 1–4, 21f	Rev 5–20	Rev tot	1 Pt
To be	386	41	35	27	15	105	48	44	92	8
Ellipse	358	28	60	16	4	2	39	52	91	28
Propn.	1:1	$1\frac{1}{2}$:1	$\frac{1}{2}$:1	2:1	5:1	50:1			1:1	$\frac{1}{4}$:1

	Strabo I 1 64 B.C.–A.D. 21	Diod. Sic. pt. 1 (c. 50 B.C.)	Dio Chrys. *Kingship* I, II (A.D. 40–120)	Philostr. *Vit. Apoll.* I (ii–iii/A.D.)	Hdt I–IV approx. *
To be	37	48 (some are essential)	51	70	381
Ellipse	54	27	55	83	70
Propn.	$\frac{3}{4}$:1	2:1	1:1	1:1	5:1

* For Hdt, the figures are based on Barbelenet; I take responsibility for the others.

Individual writers: Paul [1].

(a) *Fixed phrases:* δῆλον ὅτι 1 Co 15²⁷ 1 Ti 6⁷ DᶜKLP; αἰσχρόν
c. infin. 1 Co 11⁶ (but 14³⁵ Eph 5¹² copula), δίκαιον 2 Th 1⁶, εἰ δυνατόν
Ro 12¹⁸ Ga 4¹⁵, ἐξόν c. infin. 2 Co 12⁴, μέγα εἰ 1 Co 9¹¹ 2 Co 11¹⁵, συμφέρον
2 Co 12¹, ὄφελον c. ind. 1 Co 4⁸ 2 Co 11¹ Ga 5¹², ἀνάγκη c. inf. Ro 13⁵ SBA
(but p⁴⁶ᶜ DEFG Irenˡᵃᵗ have imper. without ἀνάγκη; p⁴⁶* imper. and
καί without ἀνάγκη), ὥρα c. infin. Ro 13¹¹, οὐχ οἷον 9⁶, etc.   (Exceptions:
Ph 1⁷ καθώς ἐστιν δίκαιον, 1 Co 4³ 7⁹ 11²⁰ etc.).   Epistolary formulae:
χάρις (ὑμῖν) καὶ εἰρήνη Ro 1⁷ etc., χάρις ἔλεος εἰρήνη 1 Ti 1² 2 Ti 1²,
ἡ χάρις . . . μετά Ro 16²⁰; and Ro 15³³ 1 Co 16²¹ Eph 6²³ Col 4¹⁸ 2 Th 3¹⁶
2 Ti 4²² (Exception: with ἔσται 2 Co 13¹¹).   Proverbial expressions:
1 Ti 2⁵ εἷς γὰρ ὁ θεός, Ti 1¹⁵ πάντα καθαρὰ τοῖς καθαροῖς; 1 Co 6¹³
τὰ βρώματα τῇ κοιλίᾳ . . .; note πιστὸς ὁ θεός 1 Co 1⁹ etc., with the
exception πιστὸς δέ ἐστιν ὁ κύριος 2 Th 3². Strangely, the copula
does appear with οὐαί 1 Co 9¹⁷ (unlike Syn. Gospels).

(b) *Spontaneous phrases:* exclamations (we are reminded of Heb.
infl. in the Semitism μακάριος ὁ Ro 14²², but there are Greek parallels;
another Hebraism, not from the LXX, is ὡς ὡραῖοι Ro 10¹⁵). Ro 11³³
ὡς ἀνεξεραύνητα, 1 Co 12³ ἀνάθεμα Ἰησοῦς, κύριος Ἰησοῦς, 15¹⁴ κενὸν
ἄρα τὸ κήρυγμα ἡμῶν, ¹⁷· ²⁴· ⁵⁷, 2 Co 2¹⁴, χάρις τῷ θεῷ Ro 6¹⁷ etc.,
Ro 7²⁴ ταλαίπωρος ἐγὼ ἄνθρωπος, Ph 4⁵ ὁ κύριος ἐγγύς, etc. There are
phrases with μάρτυς, as 1 Th 2⁵· ¹⁰ Ph 1⁸ (but ἐστιν is retained Ro 1⁹).
Then there is the negative phrase οὐ θαῦμα 2 Co 11¹⁴ (see Bertram in
Kittel WB III 40). Doxologies: εὐλογητὸς ὁ θεός (בָּרוּךְ אֱלֹהִים)
2 Co 1³ Eph 1³, ᾧ ἡ δόξα Ga 1⁵ etc. (but ἐστιν added 1 Pt 4¹¹). (Exceptions: ὅς ἐστιν εὐλ. Ro 1²⁵, ὁ ὢν εὐλ. 2 Co 11³¹.)   Graphic sentences
(typical of Pauline style): ἄρα ἡ πίστις ἐξ ἀκοῆς, ἡ δὲ ἀκοὴ διὰ ῥήματος
Χριστοῦ Ro 10¹⁷, οὐ δὲ τὸ πνεῦμα κυρίου, ἐλευθερία (sc. essential ἐστιν)
2 Co 3¹⁷, τὰ γὰρ βλεπόμενα πρόσκαιρα, τὰ δὲ μὴ βλεπόμενα αἰώνια
4¹⁸; 7⁴· ⁵ (sc. essential ἐστιν), Ph 3¹, Ga 3¹⁸, Ro 2²⁸ᶠ, 5¹⁶· ¹⁸, 6²³ 7¹²
8⁶· ¹⁰ 1 Co 1²⁶ 3²²ᶠ 4¹⁰ 2 Co 10¹⁰ Ph 1²¹· ²²· ²⁴ 3¹⁹, 4⁸.

Conditional sentences: with ellipse in both apodosis and protasis
Ro 11⁶· ¹²· ¹⁵ᶠ. (Exceptions: the copula is sometimes found in these
graphic sentences, especially if the identity of the subject would otherwise be obscure: ὁ γὰρ ἐν κυρίῳ κληθεὶς δοῦλος ἀπελεύθερος κυρίου
ἐστιν· ὁμοίως ὁ ἐλεύθερος κληθεὶς δοῦλός ἐστιν Χριστοῦ 1 Co 7²².)

Other expressions, mainly rhetorical or epigrammatic: 1 Co 5⁶
οὐ καλὸν τὸ καύχημα ὑμῶν, Ro 9⁷ (οὐδὲ) πάντες τέκνα, 13¹⁰ πλήρωμα
οὖν νόμου (ἡ) ἀγάπη, 1 Co 1²⁴ p⁴⁶ Clem Alx Χριστὸς θεοῦ δύναμις καὶ
θεοῦ σοφία ²; Ro 3²⁰· ²² 4¹³ 5¹⁶ 6²¹ 7⁸ 8⁷ 10⁴ 13¹¹ 14¹⁸ 2 Co 4¹⁵ 5¹⁷· ¹⁸
8²³· ²⁴ Ro 10¹· ¹² 12¹⁹ Ga 5⁸ 1 Co 11¹¹· ¹² 13¹³ 15²¹· ³⁹ (and so throughout

---

[1] I have drawn up a complete list of every occurrence in the NT, but
there is room only for representative instances in this volume, and the
rest must be left over for a separate monograph. The word " etc."
indicates that there are further examples. See also footnote above, p. 295.

[2] The source from which Paul may have derived the phrase, i.e. Danθ
2²⁰, has the copula: ἡ σοφία καὶ ἡ δύναμις αὐτοῦ ἐστι.

this eloquent chapter: [40. 41. 46. 47. 48. 56. 56]) 2 Co 1[7. 21] 2[6] 5[5] 10[4] Eph
5[9. 23] Col 2[17] 1 Th 2[3] 4[6] 2 Th 3[2] 1 Ti 4[4] 5[25] 2 Ti 3[16] Ti 1[15] (Exceptions:
Ro 1[19] 1 Co 6[18] 7[29] (periph. pf.) 1[18] 2[14] 3[19] 4[4] 6[17. 19] 9[16] 11[7. 8. 15. 25]
(Lk's parallel 22[20] omits the copula; Cadbury remarks on the strangeness
of this [1], in view of Luke's regular practice of inserting the copula, esp.
if he found it in his sources. It is probably not a Pauline phrase, but
one which he inherited) 12[14. 22] 3[7] 6[7] 7[14. 14] 14[15], Col 1[18] καὶ αὐτός ἐστιν ἡ
κεφαλὴ τοῦ σώματος, 1 Ti 1[5] τὸ δὲ τέλος τῆς παραγγελίας ἐστὶν ἀγάπη.)

Much emphasis (= is certainly) appears to be achieved by the
insertion of ἐστιν in πιστὸς δέ ἐστιν ὁ κύριος 2 Th 3[3] (better text);
so also Ro 1[16] 2[28] 11[23] 1 Co 1[25] 3[17. 21] 11[7t] 14[33] 2 Co 3[17] Ga 3[12] 4[2. 26]
5[19] Eph 5[13. 32] 6[12] 1 Ti 3[16] 4[8. 8] 6[10] 2 Ti 4[11. 11] Ti 1[10]. There is no subject
expressed in ἐστιν ἀπίστου χείρων 1 Ti 5[8], ἐλευθέρα ἐστιν Ro 7[3] 1 Co
7[39], Ro 13[4. 6] 1 Co 7[40] Ga 5[3], and therefore the verb to be is inserted
for clarity's sake.

Demonstratives: there is sometimes ellipse when the attribute is a
demonstrative adj. or adv. (οὕτως καὶ τὸ χάρισμα, etc.) Ro 5[15] 9[6. 8. 9]
1 Co 12[12] 14[12] 2 Co 10[7] Eph 2[8] 1 Th 5[18] 1 Ti 2[3]. (Exceptions: Ro 8[9. 14]
1 Co 9[3] 10[28] 11[24] 2 Co 1[12] 10[18], Ga 3[7] (emphatic however), 4[24] (εἰσιν =
represent), Eph 4[10] 6[1] Col 3[20] 1 Ti 5[4] Ti 3[8]; and τοῦτ' ἔστιν is a frequent
idiom: Ro 1[12] 7[18] 9[8] 10[6. 8] Phm[12].)

Interrogatives: τί γάρ μοι; 1 Co 5[12] etc., τί (μοι) τὸ ὄφελος 15[32],
τί οὖν: Ro 3[9] 6[15] 11[7], τί γάρ; Ro 3[3] Ph 1[18]. Questions introduced by
τίς or τί: Ro 3[1] 8[31] 1 Co 5[12] 2 Co 2[2. 16] 6[14] (sc. essential ἐστιν) [14. 15. 16]
Ga 3[19] 1 Th 2[19]. By ποῦ: Ro 3[27] 1 Co 1[20] ter 12[17. 17] 15[55. 55] OT, 12[19]
(sc. ἦν), Ga 4[15]. By πόθεν: 1 Co 13[54. 56] 15[33]. Simple interrogative:
ἢ 'Ιουδαίων ὁ θεὸς μόνον; ... Ro 3[29]; also 4[9] 7[7] Ga 3[21] 1 Th 2[19] (sc.
ἐστε). By μή: Ro 3[5] 9[14], in a series of five rhetorical questions 1 Co
12[29. 30]. (Exceptions: τί οὖν ἐστιν 'Απολλῶς; 1 Co 3[5] 9[18] 14[15] Ro 9[20]
14[4] 2 Co 3[8], 1 Co 10[16. 16] (but = represent; stronger than copula),
2 Co 12[13].)

Subordinate clauses: indir. questions: τί Ro 8[27] 12[2], τίς, τί Eph 1[18]
(but after ἐστιν in the previous clause), τί τὸ πλοῦτος Col 1[27]. (Exceptions: ὁποῖόν ἐστιν 1 Co 3[13], τίς ἐστιν Eph 1[18], τί ἐστιν 5[10].) After
ὅπου sc. ἐστιν 1 Co 3[3]. In protasis of conditions: sc. ἐστιν 1 Co 11[6];
sc. ἦν 1 Co 12[17. 17]; sc. essential ἐστιν, there is Ro 3[30] 13[9]; sc. ἐστιν or
ἦν Ro 4[14]; sc. ἐστιν 8[31] 11[6] 2 Co 3[9] 5[17] Eph 4[29]; sc. ἦν? 2 Co 3[11]. This
is Lukan and Pauline practice, which accords with class. and Hell.
usage. (Exceptions: ἐὰν ᾖς Ro 2[25], εἴπερ εἰσιν 1 Co 8[5], ἦν 1 Co 12[19],
ἐστε 2 Co 2[9], ἐστιν (periph. pf.) 4[3], εἰμι 2 Co 12[11], εἴ τις ἐστιν Ti 1[6].)
In relative clauses (see under Graphic, above): also Ro 9[4] ὧν ἡ υἱοθεσία
(sc. essential ἐστιν), 14[23], 1 Co 5[1] (sc. ess. ἐστιν), 8[6] (do.), 2 Co 1[20], 8[18]
(do.); Ph 3[15] 4[3]; confined to Luke, Paul, Heb. in NT, but more general
in class. and Hell. (Exceptions: ἐστιν Ro 1[25] 3[8] 4[16] 5[14] 8[34] 16[5] 1 Co 3[11]
4[17] 2 Co 4[4] Ga 1[7] 4[1] 4[24] constitutes ... represents, 4[26] difficult, as ἐστιν
is merely copula, 5[19] consists of, Eph 1[14. 23] 3[13]; 4[16] 5[5] constitutes; 6[2. 17],

---

[1] Style and Literary Methods of Luke, 149.

Ph 4⁸, Col 1⁷· ¹⁵· ¹⁸· ²⁴· ²⁷ 2¹⁰· ¹⁷· ²²· ²³ 3⁵· ¹⁴ 4⁹ 2 Th 2⁹ 3¹⁷; 1 Ti 1²⁰ 2 Ti 1¹⁵ 2¹⁷ *se trouve*; 1 Ti 3¹⁵ 4¹⁰ 2 Ti 1⁶ ess. ἐστιν; Ro 9⁴ 16⁷ 1 Ti 6¹ εἰσι; Ga 3¹⁰ εἰσι *se trouvent*; Ro 1⁶ ἐστε, 2 Co 11¹⁵ ἔσται.) After ὡς: Ro 5¹⁵ ὡς τὸ παράπτωμα, 2 Co 10⁷, Col 1⁶ (but ἐστιν in previous clause), Eph 5²³. (Exceptions: copula after ὥσπερ 1 Co 8⁵; after καθώς Eph 4²¹ (essential) Ph 1⁷ Col 1⁶ (periphr. pres.) 1 Th 2¹³ (ess. ἐστιν).) After καθάπερ: sc. essential ἦν 2 Co 8¹¹ (exception: 1 Co 12¹²). After ὅτι: Ro 7¹⁶ 8¹⁸ 11³⁶ 14¹⁴· ²³ 1 Co 8⁴· ⁴ 2 Co 10⁷ 13⁵ Ph 2¹¹ (ὅτι κύριος Ἰησοῦς Χριστός). Regard (p. 55) thinks that this emphasizes κύριος, since this type of phrase has the copula elsewhere, e.g. 1 Jn 4¹⁵. 1 Ti 1⁸ Eph 2¹¹ (sc. ἐστε). (Exceptions: Ro 1³² εἰσιν, 2² 4²¹ 7¹⁴ 8¹⁶ ἐσμεν 15¹⁴ ἐστε 1 Co 1¹¹ 6¹⁵· ¹⁶ 10¹⁹· ¹⁹ 11³ 15⁵⁸ (but emph.) 14³⁷ 16¹⁵ 2 Co 1¹⁸ 2³ 9¹² 13⁶ ἐσμεν Eph 4²⁵ ἐσμεν 5³⁰ (do.) 5¹⁶ εἰσιν ²³ ἐστιν 2 Th 2⁴ (do.) 2 Ti 1¹² (do.).)

(c) *Ellipse of other parts besides* ἐστιν: Scil. εἰμι: Ro 7²⁴ (exclam.), κἀγώ 2 Co 11²² ter. Not even the pronoun is present with πρόθυμος Ro 1¹⁵ *d e* vulg (2) Orig. Ambst. Ambr., and εἰ δὲ καὶ ἰδιώτης τῷ λόγῳ 2 Co 11⁶ (D*E add εἰμι), ἀλλ' οὐ τῇ γνώσει 11⁶, ὃς κατὰ πρόσωπον μὲν ταπεινός 10¹. (Exceptions: more often εἰμι, whether essential or copula, is present: Ro 1¹⁴ 7¹⁴ 11¹· ¹³ 1 Co 1¹² 3⁴ 9¹· ² 12¹⁵· ¹⁵· ¹⁶· ¹⁶ 13² 15⁹· ⁹· ¹⁰ 2 Co 12¹⁰ Ph 4¹¹ Col 2⁵ 1 Ti 1¹⁵.)

Scil. εἶ even without pronoun: εἰ δὲ υἱός, καὶ κληρόνομος Ga 4⁷ (but the sense is made clear by εἶ in previous clause). See further under Interrogatives. (Exception: Ga 4⁷.)

Scil. ἐσμεν: with pronoun 2 Co 10⁷. No pronoun: εἰ δὲ τέκνα, καὶ κληρονόμοι Ro 8¹⁷ (but ἐσμεν in previous sentence), Ph 3¹⁵ 2 Co 4⁸ 7⁵ 11⁶; see also Graphic. (Exceptions: Ro 6¹⁵ 8¹² 14⁸ 12⁵ vl. etc.)

Scil. ἐστε: see Graphic. 2 Co 1¹⁴ Eph 2¹¹ (after ὅτι) 2¹³ (= *vous trouvez*). (Exceptions: Ro 6¹⁴· ¹⁶ 8⁹ 1 Co 1³⁰ 3³ 1 Th 2²⁰ 4⁹ 5⁴· ⁵ etc.)

Scil. εἰσιν: in connection with ellipse of ἐστιν 2 Co 8²³. But not always: Ro 2¹³ 4¹⁴ 11¹⁶· ²⁸· ²⁸ 1 Co 16⁹ 2 Co 8⁴ (ptc. as main verb) 10¹⁰. (Exceptions : Ro 2¹⁴ (cp. previous verse) 13¹ (periphr. pf.)³ 15²⁷ 1 Co 14¹⁰· ²² 10¹⁸ 3⁸ 2 Co 11²² (question: Ἑβραῖοί εἰσιν; essential εἰσιν) Eph 5¹⁶ (ὅτι) 1 Ti 5²⁴ 6²· ² (ὅτι) 2 Ti 3⁶ (ess.) Ti 1¹⁰ (ess.) 3¹⁰ (ess.).)

Scil. fut. indic.: doubtful are 1 Co 15²¹ 2 Co 3¹¹. Apart from these possible instances of ἔσται the fut. never suffers ellipse in Paul (or indeed in NT). Scil. imperf. indic.: very rare; there is the stereotyped εἰ δυνατόν Ga 4¹⁵, also 1 Co 2⁴ Ph 2⁵ Ro 4¹³. There is ellipse of ἦσαν in καθώς τινες αὐτῶν 1 Co 10⁷. Otherwise the impf. is always expressed.

Scil. subjunctive: this ellipse occurs only in Paul (and Heb 12¹⁶?). 2 Co 8¹¹ ὅπως ... καὶ τὸ ἐπιτελέσθαι, ¹³ οὐ γὰρ ἵνα ἄλλοις ἄνεσις, ὑμῖν θλίψις (sc. ess. ᾖ), 12²⁰ μή πως ἔρις (do.). It is probably subjunctive which has to be supplied in 2 Co 5¹⁰ (εἴτε ... εἴτε ...), and we may supply ὦσιν before ἐν τῇ διακονίᾳ Ro 12⁷; another instance is 2 Co 12²⁰ where ὦσιν is preferable to εὑρεθῶσιν. Also scil. the essential verb Ro 4¹⁶. In this respect Paul is nearer to class. practice than any other NT writer. However, the insertion of subjunctive is much more regular.

. Scil. optative: see epistolary formulae, above.   Other wishes are: ἐπικατάρατος πᾶς ὅς ... (ὁ ...) Ga 3¹⁰. ¹³, εἰρήνη ἐπ᾽ αὐτοὺς καὶ ἔλεος 6¹⁶. Paul does not use opt. of εἰμι.

Scil. imperative: ἔστω is rarely omitted except in the formula χάρις τῷ θεῷ (see Exclamations), which is class. too (K-G § 354 n. 2e; Abel § 157) and occurs in the early papyri.   There are also ἡ ἀγάπη ἀνυπόκριτος Ro 12⁹, ὁ λόγος ὑμῶν πάντοτε ἐν χάριτι Col 4⁶, and perhaps before κατὰ τὴν ἀναλογίαν Ro 12⁶.   (Exceptions: ἤτω 1 Co 16²², ἔστω 2 Co 12¹⁶ Ga 1⁸.)   Ἐστέ may be supplied with the ptcs. in Ro 12⁹ᶠ. ¹⁶ᵗᵉʳ Col 3¹⁶ 2 Co 9¹¹. ¹³ 8²⁴ BD*G (against S) Eph 4², and Regard includes the ptcs. at Eph 5¹⁵⁻²³ 6¹⁶. ¹⁸. ¹⁸ (pp. 211f).   But the ptc. itself may be imperatival; in fact, ἐστέ imper. does not occur at all in NT (but there is ἴστε with γινώσκοντες Eph 5⁵, which may be intended for ἐστέ), 1 Ti 4¹⁵ ἴσθι.

(d) *Stronger meanings of ἐστιν and εἰσιν*: even here there is ellipse in Paul, which is not confined to the copula; there is the meaning *there is* (are), or *it is*; e.g. 1 Th 5³ εἰρήνη καὶ ἀσφάλεια, 2 Ti 1⁵ ὅτι καὶ ἐν σοί, Ro 2⁸. ⁹. ¹⁰ 4¹⁶. ¹⁶ 8¹ 9¹⁶. ³² 11¹¹ 1 Co 8⁶ 11³⁰ 13⁸ 15⁴⁰ 2 Co 1²⁰ 3¹⁷ 4⁶ 6² Ga 2²¹ 3⁴. ⁵ Eph 2⁸. ⁹ 4⁴. ⁵. ⁹, a series of four in the vehement passage Ph 2¹, 1 Ti 2⁵.   Something like ἐστιν is to be supplied before ἵνα 1 Co 7²⁹ 1 Ti 3¹⁵, and οὐχ ὅτι 2 Co 1²⁴ 3⁵ Ph 4¹¹. ¹⁷ 2 Th 3⁹.   Normally of course the verb *to be* is not absent.

It may be that we are to supply ἐστιν in 1 Co 10¹⁷ ὅτι εἷς ἄρτος (sc. ἐστιν), ἓν σῶμα οἱ πολλοὶ ἔσμεν: *because there is one bread, we the many are one body*, instead of the usual interpretation which is less intelligible.

Individual writers: the Fourth Gospel.

We find here almost the very opposite of Pauline usage: the pure nominal phrase and ellipse of the copula is the exception rather than the rule.

(a) *Fixed phrases:* (ἔτι) μικρὸν καί 14¹⁹ 16¹⁶. ¹⁷. ¹⁹.   (Exceptions: (τὸ) θαύμαστόν ἐστιν ὅτι 9³⁰.)   Parenthetical ὄνομα αὐτῷ 1⁶ (ἦν S*D*W), 3¹ (ὀνόματι S*).   (Exception: ἦν δὲ ὄνομα 18¹⁰.)   Proverbial: πνεῦμα ὁ θεός 4²⁴.   (Exc. 13¹⁶ 15²⁰.)

(b) *Spontaneous phrases:* ἰδού 19⁵, ἴδε 1²⁹. ³⁶. ⁴⁸ 19¹⁴. ²⁶ᶠ, μακάριοι οἱ 20²⁹ (Hebr. infl.?), but ἐστε 13¹⁷.   In Jn even exclamations may retain ἐστιν: as σκληρός ἐστιν ὁ λόγος 6⁶⁰.   Οὕτως with ἐστιν 3⁸, οὗτος with ἐστιν 1¹⁹. ³⁰ etc. (22 times), ἐκεῖνος 5³⁹ etc. (5 times).   But the copula is absent in the interrogative idiom τί ἐμοὶ (ἡμῖν) καὶ σοί Jn 2⁴ which has a parallel in Hebrew besides affinities with class. speech (K-G I 417).   Another idiomatic phrase is τί πρός σε (ἡμᾶς) Jn 21²²ᶠ; there is the Latin *quid hoc ad te*, which has a class. Greek parallel in the proverb-like οὐδὲν πρὸς Διόνυσον, although normally there is ἐστι (cf. οὐδέν ἐστι δήπου πρὸς ἐμέ Demosth. 18, 21) and parallels later in Epictetus (see Schenkl's Index, under πρός): τί (οὐδὲν)

πρὸς ἐμέ (σέ) and in a papyrus of 9 B.C. (BU IV 1158¹⁷). There is also
the conversational formula τί οὖν 1²¹ (sc εἴ) and the interrogatives
οὗτος δὲ τί 21²¹ (note the ch.) and τί πρός σε 21²²ᶠ (do.). But much
more, frequently ἐστιν appears in questions: 21²⁰ 6⁹ 7³⁶ etc.; this is
true also of indir. questions 2⁹ 9²⁹· ³⁰ 7²⁷ etc., of the protasis of a condition 9²⁵, of relative clauses 1⁴¹ etc., after καθώς 19⁴⁰ etc., after ἕως 9⁴.
Ellipse is rather frequent after ὅτι: 4⁵³ (sc. ἦν), 10³⁸ (sc. ἐστιν and εἰμί)
14¹⁰ (sc. εἰμί), ¹¹ (sc. εἰμι and ἐστιν), ²⁰ (sc. εἰμι bis and ἐστε). But
this is only nine instances, compared with sixty where the copula is
inserted: 2¹⁷ 3²¹ etc. including ὅτι = *because* 1³⁰ 3²³· ³³ etc.

(c) *Ellipse of other parts besides* ἐστιν: see above. There is also
ellipse of εἰμι at 1²³ ἐγὼ φωνὴ βοῶντος, and of εἴ at 17²¹ (but σὺ appears),
and of ἐσμεν at 17¹¹ (καθὼς ἡμεῖς), and of ἐστέ 15⁵ (ὑμεῖς τὰ κλάσματα),
and of ἦν 19⁴¹ (καὶ ἐν τῷ κήπῳ μνημεῖον καινόν). The subjunctive ὦ
may be understood at 17²⁶, but the ellipse occurs immediately after the
insertion of ᾖ. The opt. probably has to be supplied in the formal wish
εἰρήνη (σοι) at 20¹⁹· ²¹· ²⁶. Presumably ἴσθι is to be supplied with δεῦρο
ἔξω 11⁴³. Against these ten instances of ellipse there are some 202
instances without it.

(d) *Stronger meanings:* there is no instance of ellipse here, but
something like ἐστιν is to be supplied *before* ἵνα at 12³⁸ 18⁹· ³² 19²⁴
and ἀλλ' ἵνα 9³ 13¹⁸ 15²⁵, and before οὐχ ὅτι 6⁴⁶ 7²². With ἵνα this
may be a kind of imperative, as in the phrases which begin with γιὰ νά
in good MGr. (Pernot 69). The presence of ἐστιν or εἰσιν is the rule
with stronger meanings: 1⁴⁷ 4³⁵ etc. (12 times).

Individual writers: the Johannine Epistles.

(a) *Fixed phrases:* εἰρήνη σοι 3 Jn ¹⁵. But an exception
to the NT practice is the presence of ἔσται in the formula at
2 Jn³. Regard ascribes this to inherited Ionic influence (p. 42).
Proverbial expressions: ὁ θεὸς ἀγάπη ἐστιν 4⁸· ¹⁶ is an instance
which in other parts of NT would be a pure nominal phrase,
even in Jn, e.g. πνεῦμα ὁ θεός. So also ὁ θεὸς φῶς ἐστιν 1⁵,
καὶ ἡ ἁμαρτία ἐστιν ἡ ἀνομία 3⁴, πᾶσα ἀδικία ἁμαρτία ἐστιν 5¹⁷.

(b) *Spontaneous:* ellipse 1³ καὶ ἡ κοινωνία δὲ ἡ ἡμετέρα
μετὰ τοῦ πατρός. (Exceptions: copula ἐστιν 42 times, other parts
26 times.)

Individual writers: Luke–Acts.

Luke prefers the copula on every possible occasion, apart
from set phrases, titles, and a few exclamations and questions.

(a) *Set phrases:* φάνερον ὅτι Ac 4¹⁶, ἐξόν 2²⁹, σκληρόν 26¹⁴. Proverbial: Lk 10² (= Mt 9³⁷) ὁ μὲν θερισμὸς πολύς, οἱ δὲ ἐργάται ὀλίγοι,
14³⁴ (= Mk 9⁵⁰) καλὸν τὸ ἅλας, 10⁷ (= Mt 10¹⁰ 1 Ti 5¹⁸), 18¹⁹ (= Mk 10¹⁸,
as opp. to Mt 19¹⁷), 16¹⁵· ¹⁶. Also Lk 1²⁶ᶠ 2²⁵ 8⁴¹ 24¹³ ᾧ (ᾖ) ὄνομα (D

ὀνόματι, as elsewhere in Lk and almost always in Ac and class.) 24¹⁸ (SB ὀνόματι) Ac 13⁶ (p⁴⁵ ὀνόματι, D ὀνόματι καλούμενον). Lk 1⁵· ²⁷ καὶ τὸ ὄνομα. Epistolary formulae: χαίρειν Ac 15²³ 23²⁶. (Exceptions: δέον with ἐστιν Ac 19³⁶, ὄνομα with ἐστιν Lk 1⁶³ 8³⁰ (as opp. to Mk 5⁹), εἰ δυνατόν with εἴη Ac 20¹⁶; also ἐστιν with μακάριον Ac 20³⁵, καλόν Lk 9³³, ἀνενδεκτόν 17¹, ἱκανόν 22³⁸, εὐκοπώτερον 16¹⁷ 18²⁵ (= Mk 10²⁵ Mt 19²⁴), and so on Ac 2²⁴ 4¹⁹ 6² 12³ 10²⁸ 13⁴⁶ 25¹⁶ 28²². Proverbial: τὰ ἀδύνατα παρὰ ἀνθρώποις δυνατὰ παρὰ τῷ θεῷ ἐστιν Lk 18²⁷ (as opp. to Mt Mk).)

(b) *Spontaneous:* (καὶ) ἰδού Lk 1³⁸ 5¹⁸ etc. (Exceptions Lk 2²⁵ 17²¹ etc.) οὐαί Lk 6²⁴ᶠ 10¹³ etc. Exclamations: εὐλογήμενος ὁ ἐρχόμενος Lk 13³⁵ 19³⁸ (= Mt Jn); so also Lk 10²³ 12⁴³ (as Mt) etc., μακάριος 1⁴⁵ 11²⁷ 14¹⁵, ὑμεῖς μάρτυρες Lk 24⁴⁸, οὐκ εὐθέως τὸ τέλος 21⁹ (sc. ἔσται?), ὑμεῖς δὲ οὐχ οὕτως 22²⁶ (sc. ἐστε), εὐλογημένη σύ 1⁴²· ⁴², τὸ σκότος πόσον 11³⁶ D, μεγάλη ἡ Ἄρτεμις Ac 19²⁸· ³⁴. Doxology: δόξα ἐν ὑψίστοις (sc. ἔστω or εἴη) Lk 2¹⁴. Verbal adj.: οἶνον νέον εἰς ἀσκοὺς καινοὺς βλητεόν Lk 5³⁸ (only instance in NT, but class. and Hell.). Other phrases (esp. rhetorical or declarative), e.g. οὗ τὸ πτύον ἐν τῇ χειρὶ αὐτοῦ Lk 3¹⁷; also 11³⁴ 22²⁰. Demonstrative: ὁ βασιλεὺς τῶν Ἰουδαίων οὗτος Lk 23³⁸ (Mt-parall. has copula), οὕτως 12²¹, οὗτοι 24⁴⁴. Interrogatives: Lk 4³⁴ (Mk Mt Jn), ³⁶· ⁸²⁸· ⁴⁵, 21⁷, 22²⁷, 24¹⁷, Ac 10²¹ etc. Indir. questions: Lk 7³⁹ 13²³ Ac 26²³ 17¹⁹. After ὅπου Lk 17³⁷ (but parall. Mt 24²⁸ adds ἐὰν ᾖ). In protasis of conditional (Lucan and Pauline habit): Lk 11³⁵D ³⁶. In a rel. clause there is ellipse after καθότι Lk 19⁹ S*. After ὅτι Lk 16¹⁵ (Lk sometimes avoids Mk's ellipse, by adding ἀνέστη 9⁸· ¹⁹). But under this heading there are a very great many exceptions, and with spontaneous phrases in Lk–Ac the copula is the general rule.

(c) *Other parts besides* ἐστιν.

See above. Scil. ptc. ὄντα in WH of Ac 26²¹ (rest have it). Scil. εἰμι Ac 7³² OT (but not LXX, which adds εἰμι: Ex 3⁶) 10³⁹ 18⁶. But εἰμι inserted 28 times. Sc. ptc. ὄντες in WH of Lk 6³ (rest have it). Sc. εἶ: see Exclamations (usually inserted). Ἐσμεν always inserted (ten times). Sc. ἐστε indic.: ὑμεῖς μάρτυρες τούτων Lk 24²⁸, and see above (otherwise inserted). Sc. εἰσιν Lk 24¹⁷ and see above (but usually inserted). Sc. ἔσται: Lk 21⁷ καὶ τί τὸ σημεῖον (no other ellipse of fut. indic.: inserted 48 times). Sc. ἦν Lk 1⁵ (*there was*) γυνὴ αὐτῷ 2²⁵· ³⁶· ³⁷; see also above. (But ἦν inserted 113 times; ἦσαν 43 times; ἤμην 5; ἦμεν 2; ἤμεθα Ac 27³⁷). Scil. optative: Lk 10⁵ 24³⁶ εἰρήνη τῷ οἴκῳ τούτῳ, 1²⁸ ὁ κύριος μετὰ σοῦ; see also Subordinate Clauses. There is ellipse of either opt. or imper. in ἐν οὐρανῷ εἰρήνη καὶ δόξα ἐν ὑψίστοις Lk 19³⁸, τὸ αἷμα ὑμῶν ἐπὶ τὴν κεφαλὴν ὑμῶν Ac 18⁶. Sc. ἐστε imper. Lk 12³⁶ ὑμεῖς ὅμοιοι, 24⁴⁷ with ptc. Sc ἴσθι: Ac 7³ δεῦρο εἰς . . . .

(d) *Stronger meanings.*

Ellipse before ἵνα: Lk 18⁴¹ (but prob. imperatival ἵνα). Ellipse of ἐστιν *it is*: Ac 12²² θεοῦ φωνὴ καὶ οὐκ ἀνθρώπου (inserted 37 times).

Individual writers: Mark.

The ellipse here is usually confined to fixed phrases.

(a) *Fixed phrases:* ὄνομα 14³², 5⁹ (parall. Lk 8³⁰ adds ἐστιν). εἰ δὲ μή 2²¹ᶠ. ἀδύνατον 10²⁷ (Mt adds ἐστιν). εἰ δυνατόν 13²² = Mt 24²⁴ (but ἐστιν is retained at Mk 14³⁵ Mt 26³⁹). καλόν 14²¹ BWL (others add ἦν; Mt's parall. has ἦν, also Lk 9³³; even in Mk the copula is retained at 7²⁷ 9⁵·⁴²·⁴³·⁴⁵·⁴⁷). (Exceptions 2⁹ 10²⁵·⁴⁰.) Proverbial expressions: καλὸν τὸ ἅλας Mk 9⁵⁰ = Lk 14³⁴, τὸ μὲν πνεῦμα πρόθυμον, ἡ δὲ σὰρξ ἀσθενής 14³⁸ = Mt 26⁴¹, οὐδεὶς ἀγαθός 10¹⁸ = Lk 18¹⁹ (Mt. 19¹⁷ adds the copula in εἷς ἐστιν ὁ ἀγαθός), παρὰ θεῷ πάντα δυνατά 10²⁷ = Mt 19²⁶.

(b) *Spontaneous expressions:* ellipse with ἴδε 3³⁴ 13¹·²¹, οὐαί 13¹⁷ 14²¹, τί ἐμοὶ (ἡμῖν) καὶ σοί 1²⁴ 5⁷. In other less stereotyped forms of questions, the copula has also to be supplied: τίς ἡ σοφία 6², τίνος ἡ εἰκὼν αὕτη 12¹⁶ (parall. Lk 20²⁴ avoids the ellipse), πόθεν τούτῳ ταῦτα 6², simple interr. οὐ 4²¹. But there are exceptions: τί ἐστιν τοῦτο 1²⁷, τί ἐστιν εὐκοπώτερον 2⁹ = Lk 5²³, τίς ἐστιν ἡ μήτηρ μου 3³³, τίς ἄρα οὗτός ἐστιν 4⁴¹, ποῦ 14¹⁴ = Lk 22¹¹, πόθεν 12³⁷, ποῖος 12²⁸, πόσος 9²¹. Exclamations or simple declarations: 13⁷ (where Mt 24⁶ adds ἐστιν) οὔπω τὸ τέλος, 14³⁶ πάντα δυνατά σοι. But even these have ἐστιν: οὐχ οὕτως δέ ἐστιν ἐν ὑμῖν 10⁴³ = Mt 20²⁶, even when impersonal: πῶς δύσκολόν ἐστιν 10²⁴. Other non-ellipses: ἐνοχός ἐστιν = 3²⁹, but here we have no subject expressed and the verb must be there to supply it (*he is*). The same applies to οὐκ ἔστιν θεὸς νεκρῶν 12²⁷ = Lk 20³⁸ (*he is*), and to οὐκ ἔστιν ὧδε 16⁶ = Mt 28⁶ = Lk 24⁶. Ἔρημός ἐστιν ὁ τόπος 6³⁵ = Mt 14¹⁵ (emph.?). Κύριός ἐστιν ὁ Ὑιὸς ... καὶ τοῦ σαββάτου 2²⁸ = Lk 6⁵ = Mt 12⁸. In οὐ γάρ ἐστίν τι κρυπτὸν ἐάν 4²², it is the essential ἐστιν *there is*, as also most probably in 6⁴ = Mt 13⁵⁷, 9⁴⁰ = Mt 12³⁰ = Lk 9⁵⁰, 12³³. The copula is not omitted with οὕτως 4²⁶ 10⁴², nor with demonstratives 3³⁵ etc. (13 times). The copula is inserted in indir. questions: 5¹⁴ 9¹⁰ 13³³, and after ὅπου 5⁴⁰ (ἦν); in relat. clauses 2¹⁹ etc. (10 times). With two exceptions (6¹⁵) where the parall. Lk 9⁸ inserts ἀνέστη, 8²⁸ where the parall. Lk 9¹⁹ adds ἀνέστη, the copula occurs in clauses beginning with ὅτι: 2¹ 6⁴⁹·⁵⁵ 12³⁵ 13²⁸ᶠ; of these exceptions, it looks as if προφήτης is direct speech, with ὅτι introducing a mere exclamation of the people, in 6¹⁵, and in the same way there is no need for ἐστιν in 8²⁸ if ὅτι is thought of as introducing the dir. speech εἷς τῶν προφητῶν. When Mark intends ὅτι to introduce indir. speech he has the copula, as ἀκούσας ὅτι Ἰησοῦς ὁ N. ἐστιν 10⁴⁷ (parall. Lk 18³⁷ has παρέρχεται). Thus the proportion in this section is striking: ellipse 15 or less, copula 56.

(c) *Other parts.*

Strangely enough there is sometimes the ellipse of εἰμι in Mk: ἐγὼ ὁ θεὸς Ἀβραάμ 12²⁶ = Ac 7³² (the LXX of Ex 3⁶ adds εἰμι), μήτι ἐγώ 14¹⁹. There is ellipse of ἦν with καλόν 14²¹ and at 1¹¹ (καὶ φωνὴ ἐκ τῶν οὐρανῶν), although BWA add ἐγένετο (and Lk's parall. 3²² adds γενέσθαι), and 1⁴⁵ vl. The apparent ellipse of ἦν in καὶ αὐτὸς μόνος 6⁴⁷ is covered by ἦν in the previous clause. There is one instance of ellipse of ἦσαν, 15⁴⁰ ἐν αἷς καὶ Μαρία ... There is ellipse of ἔστω at 14³⁶ = Mt 26⁴⁰ (οὐ τί ἐγὼ θέλω), where the parallel Lk 22⁴² avoids it, and perhaps at 14² (μὴ ἐν τῇ ἑορτῇ). Elsewhere the appropriate part of εἶναι fails to be inserted: again the proportion is striking, ellipse 7, verb 88.

(d) Stronger meanings.

Even here, when drama is present, there is ellipse: εἷς τῶν δώδεκα (it is) 14²⁰. It is probably also so before ἀλλ᾽ ἵνα 14⁴⁹ (imperatival) 2¹⁰. Some read the opening of the gospel like this: scil. ἐστιν before καθώς (the beginning of the gospel is as it is written ...). But Mark's fondness for the verb to be is against this interpretation. The insertion of ἐστιν = consists in 7¹⁵ 10¹⁴ (or belongs to) 12²⁹, 1²⁷ means.

Individual writers: Hebrews.

In avoidance of the copula Heb. is even more class. and literary in tendency than Paul; there is always good reason for the insertion of ἐστιν where it occurs.

(a) Fixed phrases. Ellipse with πρόδηλον 7¹⁴ (but κατάδηλον has ἐστιν 7¹⁵, emphatic), ἀδύνατον 6⁴·¹⁸ 10⁴ 11⁶, λόγος 5¹¹, ἔτι μικρὸν ὅσον ὅσον 10³⁷ (but LXX Isa 26²⁰ has ἀποκρύβηθι μικρὸν ὅσον ὅσον), ὡς ἔπος εἰπεῖν 7⁹, ἀναγκαῖον 8³, ἀνάγκη 9¹⁶·²³, ἔθος 10²⁵, φοβερόν 10³¹, καλόν 13⁹. Epistolary formula ἡ χάρις μετά 13²⁵.

(b) Spontaneous phrases. Ellipse: 13⁸ Ἰησοῦς Χ. ... ὁ αὐτός, 5¹³ 8¹ 9¹⁶ᶠ 4¹²·¹³·¹³ 5⁴ 2¹⁰·¹¹ 6⁸·⁸·¹⁰ 9¹⁷ 10²³·³⁰. Ellipse after ὡς 3² (sc. ἦν), πηλίκος 7⁴ (do.), τίς 7¹¹ (sc. ἐστιν), in relative sentences (unlike Paul) 9⁹ 11¹⁰, after ὅτι 11¹⁹, with demonstratives 9²⁰ (τοῦτο τὸ αἷμα, where LXX has ἰδοὺ τὸ αἷμα) 13¹⁷. In doxology ᾧ ἡ δόξα 13²¹. (Presence of εἰσιν in a question 1¹⁴, ἐστιν with demonstratives 2¹⁴ 7⁵ 9¹¹ 10²⁰ 11¹⁶ 13¹⁵, ἐστιν = he is 5¹³ 8⁶ 9¹⁵, = belongs to 5¹⁴, after relative 7²; presence of εἰσιν in periphr. pf. 7²⁰·²³. Therefore the presence of ἐστιν at 11¹ (ἔστιν δὲ πίστις ἐλπιζομένων ὑπόστασις) is either very exceptional or is not a copula (= represents)).

(c) Other parts.

Th. Nissen (in Philologus 92, 1937, 248) conjectures at 12¹⁶ μή τις πόρνος ⟨ἢ⟩ ἢ βέβηλος. Otherwise ellipse of subjunctive in 12¹⁵ (the only other place in NT is Paul). 13⁴ τίμιος ὁ γάμος (sc. ἔστω), ⁵ ἀφιλάργυρος ὁ τρόπος Scil. ἐστε imperatival with ptc. 13⁵ (as Paul, Peter, Luke). Ellipse of ἦν 3⁵·⁶ (and see stronger meanings); of εἰ 7²¹ (σὺ ἱερεύς, even when LXX inserts εἰ). (Exceptions: insertion of ἦσαν 2¹⁵, of ἐσμεν 3⁶ 4² 10¹⁰·³⁹, of ἔσται (after μήποτε) 3¹², of ἦν 7¹⁰·¹¹ 8⁴·⁴·⁷ 11³⁸ 12²¹, of εἰσιν 11¹³ (but = they are), of ἐστε 12⁸·⁸.)

(d) *Stronger meanings.*

Ellipse of ἐστιν *there is* or ἦν *there was* 9². ⁴· ⁵.   Scil. ἐστιν before οὐχ ἵνα 9²⁵; scil. ἐστιν *there is* 9¹⁶ ὅπου γὰρ διαθήκη, ²⁷ μετὰ δὲ τοῦτο κρίσις, 10³, 10¹⁸ ὅπου δὲ ἄφεσις τούτων, ¹⁸, 12⁷.   (No ellipse: 4¹³ 9⁵ (οὐκ ἐστιν *it is impossible*), 11⁶ *exists.*)

Individual writers: James.

On the contrary, Jas is not very fond of the pure nominal phrase, outside stereotyped expressions.

(a) *Fixed phrases.* χρή 3¹⁰, ἔνι 1¹⁷.   Epistol. formulae χαίρειν 1¹. Proverbial ἡ γὰρ κρίσις ἀνέλεος τῷ μὴ ποιήσαντι ἔλεος 2¹³.

(b) *Spontaneous.* Proportion of ellipse 9: copula 15.   The idiomatic question τί τὸ ὄφελος 2¹⁴· ¹⁶, ἰδού 3⁴.   Exclamations 1¹²· ²⁶ 3²· ⁶. Interrogative 3¹³ 4¹, 4¹⁴ ποία ἡ ζωή AKLP lat copt.   Indir. question 4¹⁴ S*B 614 syrh arm.   (No ellipse 15 times.)

(c) *Other parts.* No ellipse (12 times).

(d) *Stronger meanings.* Ellipse *it is* 3⁸ ἀκατάστατον κακόν, *there is* 3¹⁶ ὅπου γὰρ ζῆλος καὶ ἐριθεία, ἐκεῖ ἀκαταστασία, *it is* 4¹ οὐκ ἐντεῦθεν. (No ellipse 4¹²· ¹⁴ L vulg ¹⁷.)

Individual writers: 1 Peter.

He tends towards the ellipse.

(a) *Fixed phrases.* εἰ δέον 1⁶, κρεῖττον 3¹⁷.   Epistol. formula εἰρήνη ὑμῖν 5¹⁴.

(b) *Spontaneous.* Doxology εὐλογητὸς ὁ θεός 1³, αὐτῷ τὸ κράτος 5¹¹ (but ᾧ ἐστιν [A om. ἐστιν] ἡ δόξα 4¹¹).   Demonstrative 2¹⁹ᶠ.   Interrog. 2²⁰ 3¹³.   (Exceptions: 1²⁵ 2¹⁵ 3⁴· ²⁰· ²².)

(c) *Other parts.* We may supply the imper. (2nd pl.) with adjs. and ptcs.: 1¹⁴· ²² 2¹⁸ 3¹· ⁷· ⁸ᶠ 4⁸ᶠᶠ (but Moulton Proleg. 182f); ἐστε (pres. ind.) is absent: ὑμεῖς δὲ γένος ἐκλεκτόν 2⁹, οἵ ποτε οὐ λαός ¹⁰, μακάριοι 3¹⁴ 4¹⁴. Impf. ἦν (perhaps ἐστιν) is to be understood in ἀρκετὸς γὰρ ὁ παρεληλυθὼς χρόνος 4³; soil. εἰμι in ὅτι ἐγὼ ἅγιος 1¹⁶ (LXX inserts εἰμι). (Exceptions: ἦτε inserted 2²⁵, ἔστω 3³.)

(d) *Stronger meanings.* Ellipse 4¹⁷ ὅτι ὁ καιρὸς τοῦ ἄρξασθαι, ¹⁷ εἰ δὲ πρῶτον ἀφ' ἡμῶν, τί τὸ τέλος.

Individual writers: 2 Pt. and Jude.

Strangely the ellipse is never found except in the stereotyped doxology and with the Hebraic οὐαί.   The ptc. is probably imperatival in itself, without the need to supply ἐστε.   There is thus no instance of a spontaneous phrase containing the ellipse.   Doxology 2 Pt 3¹⁸ Jude ²⁵; οὐαί Jude ¹¹.

Individual writers: Matthew.

It is almost only in stereotyped phrases, proverbs, and exclamations that Matthew omits the copula, and even here (as with πρέπον, ἀδύνατον, ἐξόν, καλόν) he inserts the copula sometimes. The only exceptions are the Semitic ἰδοῦ and οὐαί, and the interesting case of ὅτι (ellipse with which is characteristic of Mt.).

(a) *Fixed phrases.* With ἀρκετόν 6³⁴ 10²⁵, εἰ δυνατόν 24²⁴ (= Mk 13²²), although ἐστιν is inserted at 26³⁹ (= Mk 14³⁵), ἀνάγκη 18⁷ BL 33 (but SDW insert ἐστιν). Semitic influence may explain δῶρον 15⁵, ἵλεώς σοι (scil. ὁ θεὸς εἴη or more prob. a homonym for חָלִילָה) 16²². Proverbial expressions: ὁ μὲν θερισμὸς πολύς 9³⁷ = Lk 10², so also 10¹⁰ = Lk 10⁷, 11⁸ (parall. Lk 7²⁵ has εἰσιν), 19²⁶ = Mk 10²⁷ (Lk 18²⁷ adds ἐστιν), 26⁴¹ = Mk 14³⁸. No ellipse: Mt adds ἐστιν in εἷς ἐστιν ὁ ἀγαθός 19¹⁷ (against Mk 10¹⁸ Lk 18¹⁹). (Exceptions: πρέπον has ἐστιν 3¹⁵, and so has ἀδύνατον 19²⁶ (against the parall. Mk 10²⁷); ἦν is inserted with ἐξόν 12⁴ and with καλόν 26²⁴ (against Mk 14²¹), ἐστιν with καλόν 15²⁶ 17⁴ 18⁸· ⁹, with οὐδέν 23¹⁶· ¹⁸, εὐκοπώτερον 19²⁴ = Mk 10²⁵ Lk 16¹⁷ 18²⁵; also οὐκ ἔστιν θέλημα ἵνα 18¹⁴.)

(b) *Spontaneous.* With ἰδού 3¹⁷ 7⁴ 9¹⁰ 11¹⁹ 12¹⁰· ¹⁸· ⁴²· ⁴⁹ 17⁵ 24²³· ²⁶ 25⁶ (but copula 24²⁶). With οὐαί 18⁷· ⁷ 23¹³· ¹⁶· ²³· ²⁵· ²⁷· ²⁹ 24¹⁹ 26²⁴. Exclamations: μακάριοι οἱ 5³⁻¹⁰ 13¹⁶ = Lk 10²³, 24⁴⁶ (sing.) = Lk 12⁴³ (but the copula does occur in the same formula 5¹¹, 11⁶ = Lk 7²³, 16¹⁷), τὸ σκότος πόσον 6²³ = Lk 11³⁶ D, μεγάλη σου ἡ πίστις 15²⁸, εὐδία 16², σήμερον χειμών 16³, δευτέρα ὁμοία αὐτῇ 22³⁹ (but Mt adds ἐστιν to οὔπω τὸ τέλος 24⁶, against Mk 13⁷, and retains ἐστιν in οὐχ οὕτως δέ ἐστιν ἐν ὑμῖν 20²⁶ = Mk 10⁴³, οὐχὶ ἡ ψυχὴ πλεῖόν ἐστι 6²⁵). Graphic sentences: οἱ ταῦροί μου καὶ τὰ σιτιστὰ τεθυμένα καὶ πάντα ἕτοιμα 22⁴ (the only place where there is ellipse with ἕτοιμος in NT [1]). Rhetorical: ἐχθροὶ τοῦ ἀνθρώπου οἱ οἰκιακοὶ αὐτοῦ 10³⁶. Demonstrative: 24⁷ (but the copula is not normally omitted with demonstratives: 33 times). Interrogatives: the idiom τί ἐμοὶ (ἡμῖν) καὶ σοί 8²⁹, and τί πρός σε (ἡμᾶς) 27⁴; questions with τίς or τί 23¹⁹ 24³ 26⁸, ποῖος 22³⁶ (but more often the copula is inserted: 16 times). After ὅτι Mt often prefers the ellipse: 5¹² 7¹³· ¹⁴ 24³² (but 33 and the Mk-parall. insert ἐστιν). Relative: 3¹². There is no ellipse where ἐστιν = *he is* (i.e. no subject expressed): 28⁶ = Mk 16⁶ = Lk 26⁶, 27⁴², 26⁶⁶. The verb is also inserted in emphatic phrases beginning with οὐκ ἐστιν: 13⁵⁷ = Mk 6⁴, 10²⁴ = Lk 6⁴⁰ = Jn 13¹⁶ 15²⁰. The position of the predicate and insertion of ἐστιν add emphasis in κύριός ἐστιν ὁ υἱὸς ... καὶ τοῦ σαββάτου 12⁸ = Mk 2²⁸ = Lk 6⁵, εἷς γάρ ἐστιν ὑμῶν ὁ διδάσκαλος 23⁸· ⁹· ¹⁰, ἔρημός ἐστιν ὁ τόπος 14¹⁵. But this does not explain ὁ καιρός μου ἐγγύς ἐστιν 26¹⁸, and there are 30 other instances where the copula is inserted for no apparent reason.

---

[1] In class. Greek also it is only in elevated language that there is an ellipse with this word.—J. E. Harry, *Proc. Amer. Philol. Assocn.*, 1903, xxxiv, pp. viiiff.

(c) *Other parts* (*except as included above*). Ellipse of εἰμι 22³² (but inserted 13 times); of εἰσιν 1¹⁷ 10³⁶ (but inserted 12 times); of ἔσονται 24⁴¹ (but added in parall. Lk 17³⁵) (but fut. indic. is inserted 35 times); of ἦσαν or ἐγένετο in 24³⁷ ὥσπερ γὰρ αἱ ἡμέραι (but impf. indic. is inserted 26 times, subjunctive 6 times, imperat. 4 times). Ellipse of imperative: 27¹⁹. ²⁵ 26⁵. ³⁹.

(d) *Stronger meanings*. No ellipse (10 times).

Individual writers: Revelation.

The occurrence of the copula is about half and half, the apparent lack of preference being due perhaps largely to the use of various sources.

(a) *Fixed phrases*. Ellipse in epistolary formulae: χάρις ὑμῖν καὶ εἰρήνη 1⁴, ἡ χάρις μετὰ πάντων 22²¹; ὄφελον with finite verb 3¹⁵; εἰ δὲ μή 2⁵. ¹⁶; ὄνομα αὐτῷ 6⁸ 9¹¹.

(b) *Spontaneous phrases*. Ellipse in exclamations: μακάριος 1³ 16¹⁵ 20⁶ 22⁷, plur. 14¹³ 19⁹ 22¹⁴; ὁ γὰρ καιρὸς ἐγγύς 1³ (but cp. 22¹¹), ἅγιος κύριος 4⁸ (not LXX), μεγάλα καὶ θαυμαστὰ τὰ ἔργα σου 15³, δίκαιαι καὶ ἀληθιναὶ αἱ ὁδοί σου 15³, ὅτι ἰσχυρὸς κύριος 18⁸, ὅτι ἀληθιναὶ καὶ δίκαιαι αἱ κρίσεις αὐτοῦ 19², οὗτοι οἱ λόγοι πιστοὶ καὶ ἀληθινοί 22⁶, καὶ ὁ μισθός μου μετ' ἐμοῦ ¹² (Exceptions 5¹² 16²¹ 22¹¹). Doxologies: αὐτῷ ἡ δόξα 1⁶, τῷ ἀρνίῳ ἡ εὐλογία 5¹³, similarly 7¹², ἡ σωτηρία τῷ θεῷ 7¹⁰, similarly 19¹. Relative: 1⁴ 20¹⁰ (exceptions 2⁷ 5¹³ 20². ¹² 21⁸. ¹⁷ 22¹²). Demonstratives: 17⁹ 20⁵ (exceptions 13¹⁰. ¹⁸ 14¹² 17¹¹ 20¹⁴). Interrog. 5² 13⁴ 18¹⁸. Indir. quest. 2¹³. Καὶ ἰδού 4¹ 6². ⁵. ⁸ 7⁹ 12³ 14¹. ¹⁴ 19¹¹, ἰδού 21³, οὐαί 8¹³ 18¹⁰. ¹⁶. ¹⁹. Other ellipses: 2¹⁹ 19¹² 21¹⁸. ¹⁹. ²¹. ²³. Other copulae 21¹⁶. ²² (but cp. next verse).

(c) *Other parts*. Scil. εἰσιν 1¹⁴. ¹⁵ff 14⁴ 16⁷ 17¹⁴ 21¹⁹. Scil. ἦν 1¹⁶ 4⁷ 10¹. ². ⁸ 9⁵. ⁹. ¹⁶ 13¹⁸ 14² 20⁸ 21¹¹. ¹⁴. Scil. ἦσαν 7⁵ 9⁷. ¹⁷. ¹⁹. Scil. εἰμι 21⁶ (A adds εἰμι) 22¹³, εἶ 15⁴, ἔσται 22⁴. (No ellipse: εἰμι 1⁸. ¹⁷ 3¹⁷ 2²³ 18⁷ 19¹⁰ 22⁹. ¹⁶, εἶ 2⁹ 3¹. ¹⁵. ¹⁶. ¹⁷ 4¹¹ 5⁹, εἰσιν 1¹⁹. ²⁰ 2². ⁹ 3⁴. ⁹ 4⁵ 5⁶. ⁹ 7¹³. ¹⁴. ¹⁵ 11⁴ 14⁴. ⁵ 16⁶ 17⁹. ⁹. ¹². ¹⁵ 19¹⁰ 21⁵, ἔσομαι 21⁷, ἔσται 10⁶. ⁹ 21 ³. ⁴. ⁷, ἔσονται 20⁶ 21³, ἦν 3¹⁵ 4⁸. ¹¹ 5¹¹ 10¹⁰ 13² 21²¹, ἦσαν 9⁸ 18²³.

(d) *Stronger meanings*. Sc. ἦν there was 4⁶ 9¹⁰ 10¹, se trouve 11⁸; ἦσαν there were 9⁷; εἰσιν there are 22¹⁵ (No ellipse 9¹⁹ 13¹⁸ 16¹⁴ 17⁸. ⁸. ¹⁰. ¹¹. ¹⁴. ¹⁸ 19⁸. ¹⁰ 21¹¹. ¹². ²⁵ 22². ³. ⁵. ¹⁴.)

CHAPTER TWENTY-TWO

CONGRUENCE OF GENDER AND NUMBER

§ 1. Incongruence in Gender

Whereas in class. Greek a discordant neuter of the *pro-nominal* predicate (τί, οὐδέν, ὅ, ἕν, πλεῖον, etc.) will appear (e.g. Plato *Civ.* 341e), as in Mt 6²⁵ Lk 12²³ (ἡ ψυχὴ πλεῖον ἐστι), Ac 12¹⁸ 1 Co 6¹¹ 11⁵ 13² 15¹⁰ Ga 6³, Hell. Greek exceeds classical usage by extending the practice to neuter *adjectival* predicates even where the subject is not abstract and does not represent a class, e.g. P. Rei. 11. 25 ἡ χεὶρ ἥδε κύριον ἔστω, Mt 6³⁴ ἀρκετὸν ... ἡ κακία, Ac 12³ D ἀρεστὸν ... ἡ ἐπιχείρησις, 2 Co 2⁶ ἱκανὸν ... ἡ ἐπιτιμία. Like the Koine, NT follows Latin (quod est, id est, hoc est) with the discordant explanatory neuter pronoun in ὅ ἐστιν and τουτ' ἔστιν (Mayser shows that ὅ ἐστιν is vernacular, τουτέστιν literary: II 1, 75, 77): e.g. Mt 27³³ (exc. A) ⁴⁶ Mk 3¹⁷ 12⁴² 15¹⁶. ²² Jn 1⁴¹ Eph 5⁵ 6¹⁷ Col 1²⁷ p⁴⁶ BAFGIP 2¹⁰ p⁴⁶ BDEFG 2¹⁷ BFG 3¹⁴ vl. Heb 2¹⁴ 7⁵ 9¹¹ 1 Pt 2¹⁹ (exceptions: Ac 16¹² 1 Co 3¹⁷ Eph 3¹³ Ph 1²⁸ Col 2¹⁰ vl. ¹⁷ vl.). We find assimilation of the gender of the pronoun to that of the antecedent, and not to that of the subject, in Col 3⁵ Rev 4⁵ 5⁶. ⁸. When an adj. agrees with two or more nouns differing in gender it is usually repeated, or else, if it precedes the first noun, it agrees with it (Lk 10¹ εἰς πᾶσαν πόλιν καὶ τόπον) and, if it follows, it takes the gender of the nearer noun (Heb 9⁹ δῶρά τε καὶ θυσίαι ... μὴ δυνάμεναι); in Heb 3⁶ βεβαίαν (om. p¹³ p⁴⁶ B) is interpolated from 3¹⁴.

§ 2. " Constructio ad sensum " [1]

These good Greek constructions [2] take the form of:—

(*a*) Collective noun with plural verb. In the Ptol. papyri, LXX, and NT, especially with ὄχλος, λαός, στρατία, οἰκία,

---

[1] K-G I § 359, pp. 52ff. Gildersleeve I 119–122. Wackernagel I 103. Mayser II 3, 25.

[2] There is in the NT nothing so blatant as LXX Ex 9⁷ where a subordinate clause is not syntactically connected with its main clause: ἰδὼν δὲ Φαραώ ... ἐβαρύνθη ἡ καρδία Φαραώ.

πλῆθος, σπέρμα. This is not too harsh if the verb occurs in a
fresh clause (Jn 6² 1 Co 16¹⁵) but more noticeable when the
collective noun is followed by a plural circumstantial ptc.
(Lk 2¹³, Ac 21³⁶ where DHLP have corrected the ptc. to sing.)
and when the plural verb follows in the same clause: Mt 21⁸
Jn 7⁴⁹ Ac 6⁷ (AE corr. to sing.) 25²⁴ (BHΨ' corr. to sing.)
Rev 8⁹ 9¹⁸ (p⁴⁷ corr. to sing.), Herm. S IX 1. 8 (pap. Mich.
corr. to sing.), Evang. Thom. 15² ὄχλος δὲ πολὺς παρειστήκεισαν
ἀκούοντες. In Mk at any rate the tendency is that if ὄχλος
comes first the verb is plur.: if the verb comes first it is sing.
The same tendency occurs in the Koine: PSI IV 402. 4 (mid.
iii/B.C.) ὁ λαὸς ὁ ἐν τῆι πόλι τὰς κολοκύνθας ὀπτῶσιν, IV 380. 4
(249 B.C.) ἐπέθετο (sing. verb. first) ἡμῖν ὁ λαὸς καὶ τὰς χεῖρας
ἐπενηνόχασιν (plur. verb follows) τοῖς ποιμέσιν.

(b) A masc. ptc. may follow a fem. or neut. personal collective noun like ἐκκλησία, ἔθνος or πλῆθος: Lk 10¹³ (p⁴⁵ DEG
corr. to fem.), Ac 5¹⁶, Ga 1²³, Eph 4¹⁷ᶠ. In the same way a
masc. pronoun may follow a noun in another gender: Mt 28¹⁹
ἔθνη ... αὐτούς, Jn 6⁹ παιδάριον ὅς (vl. ὅ), Ga 4¹⁹ τέκνα οὕς,
Ph 2¹⁵ γενεᾶς ... ἐν οἷς, Co 2¹⁵ ἀρχαί ... αὐτούς, ¹⁹ κεφαλή
... ἐξ οὗ.

(c) A masc. ptc. may follow a neut. personal noun like
πνεῦμα, βδέλυγμα: Mt 9²⁶ (AC³NX corr. to neut.), Mk 1²⁶ D,
9²⁰ 13¹⁴ (DAEF corr. to neut.), Lk 9⁴⁰ p⁴⁵, 11²⁴ p⁴⁵ minusc.

(d) ἕκαστος with plur. verb occurs eleven times in NT
(Mt 2, Lk 1, Jn 2, Ac 2, Eph 1, Heb 1, Rev 2), the correct sing.
25 times (Lk 1, Jn 1, Ac 2, Ro 3, 1 & 2 Co 13, Ga 1, Eph 2,
Jas 1, 1 Pt 1), which presents a contrast to the LXX where the
plur. verb occurs 89 times (sing. 56). See Mayser II 3, 37.

§ 3. The "Schema Atticum" ¹

On many occasions the NT (and Hermas), LXX, and Koine
break the classical rule of the "schema Atticum", whereby a
neut. plur. subject has a sing. verb. MGr does not follow it
at all. However, it is not quite true to say with Jannaris
(§ 1171) that among the post-classical authors only Atticists
keep the sing. verb, because like Biblical Greek the Ptol. papyri
hold a middle course between the Attic and the later use
(Mayser II 3, § 151).

---

¹ K-G I § 364, p. 64.   Gildersleeve I 97–102.   Mayser II 3, 28ff.

The NT usually keeps the rule when the subject is used in a non-personal sense (πρόβατα, σώματα), especially with abstracts, or unless the subject is a pronoun: Mt 10[2] 18[12] Lk 12[27] Jn 10[3]. [4]. [8] p[45] L 10. 12 p[45] SBA [27] vl. [28] vl. 17[7] vl. 19[31] Ac 5[12] 1 Ti 5[25] vl. Rev 15[4] p[47]. But the following exceptions break the class. rule and conform to Koine standards: Mt 6[28] (as opp. to Lk 12[27]), Lk 24[11], Jn 19[31] (sing. immediately before), Rev 1[19]; there has been an attempt sometimes on the part of scribes to atticize, e.g. Jn 10[8] p[45], [12]. [27]. [28] 17[7], Ac 5[12] (note the parchment fragment of iv/A.D. init.: *ZNW* 26, 1927, 118), 1 Ti 5[25], Rev 15[4] p[47]. The NT usually breaks the class. rule with words used in a personal sense (ἔθνη, τέκνα, δαιμόνια) but there is a good deal of fluctuation with πνεύματα, and the Atticists have been at work on the MSS :– τέκνα Mt 10[21] (exc. BΔ) = Mk 13[12] (exc. B); ἔθνη Mt 6[32] (exc. EG) 12[21] 25[32] (exc. AE), Lk 12[30] (exc. p[45] AD), Ac 4[25] 11[1] (exc. D*) 13[48], Ro 2[14] (exc. D[c]E) 15[12]. [27], 1 Co 10[20] vl., Ga 3[8], 2 Ti 4[17] (exc. KL), Rev 11[18] p[47] S* 15[4] 18[3]. [23] 21[24] δαιμόνια Lk 4[41] SC 8[30] CF [35]S[c] [33](exc. SU), Jas 2[19]; πνεύματα Mk 1[27] 3[11] vl. 5[13] (exc. B), Ac 8[7], Rev 4[5] 16[14] vl. The following instances thus approach more nearly the class. style, and the variants may well be scribal atticisms, except perhaps in Paul :— τέκνα Mt 10[21] BΔ = Mk 13[12] B, 1 Jn 3[10], 2 Jn[13], Ro 9[8], 1 Co 7[14]; ἔθνη Mt 6[32]EG 25[32]AE, Lk 12[30]p[45]AD, Ac 11[1] D*, Ro 2[14] D[c]E 9[30], 1 Co 10[20] KL, Eph 4[17], 2 Ti 4[17] KL, Rev 11[18] vl.; δαιμόνια Lk 4[41] vl. 8[2]. [30] vl. [35] vl. [38] [33] SU 10[17]; πνεύματα Mk 3[11] vl. 5[13] B, Lk 11[26] 10[20] vl., 1 Co 14[32] (vl. πνεῦμα), Rev 16[13] S [14] vl.

§ 4. Number of the Verb when there are several subjects [1]

The rules as to sing. or plur. verb where several co-ordinate words form the subject were as lax in class. Greek as they are in the NT.

(i) The verb, if it stands first, usually agrees with the first subject: Mt 5[18] Mk 2[25] Jn 2[2] 18[15] 20[3] Ac 11[14] 16[30]. [31] Ro 16[21] 1 Co 13[13] 2 Ti 1[15] (variants: Lk 8[19] Ac 17[14] Ro 15[26] p[46] B). The exception is when the group which forms the subject has already been conceived as a whole (i.e. when all the subjects partake in the action expressed by the verb): Mk 10[35] Lk 23[12] Ac 5[24].

---

[1] K-G I § 370, pp. 77f.   Gildersleeve II 468ff.   Mayser II 3, 30ff.

(ii) The verb, if it stands between the subjects, agrees with the first subject: Lk 8²² Jn 4³⁶ etc.

(iii) If there are verbs on either side of the subject, the rule seems to be that the first verb (finite or ptc.) agrees with the first noun and the second verb with both (i.e. it is plural): Mt 17³ ὤφθη (SBD plur.) ... Μωϋσῆς καὶ 'Ηλίας συλλαλοῦντες, Lk 2³³, Jn 12²², Ac 5²¹· ²⁹ 13⁴⁶D 14¹⁴D.

(iv) If one of the subjects is 1st pers., the verb is 1st pers. plur. and modifying ptcs. are masc. plur.: Lk 2⁴⁸ Jn 10³⁰ 1 Co 9⁶.

(v) Attributive adjectives and ptcs. agree with the noun which is nearer: Lk 10¹ 1 Th 5²³ Heb 9⁹ (in Heb 3⁶ the adj. is interpolated from 3¹⁴).

(vi) When sing. words in the subject are connected by ἤ or οὔτε the verb, or an attribute, is usually sing.: Mt 5¹⁸ 12²⁵ 18⁸ 1 Co 14²⁴ Ga 1⁸ Eph 5⁵ (Jas 2¹⁵ is an understandable exception).

(vii) When the verb comes last, after two subjects Mk has plural verb (13³¹), which is altered by Mt to sing. (24³⁵); cf. LXX Da 3³³. But Mk has sing. verb. in 4⁴¹. Jn also (1¹⁷), and Mt (6¹⁹), and Paul (1 Co 15⁵⁰), have sing. verb.

§ 5. Solecisms in the New Testament

There are two varieties: those found only in Rev, which are severe, and those in the Johannine books and the rest of NT, which are largely excusable.

(a) Revelation

(i) Circumstantial ptcs. and appositional phrases tend to be in the nom. instead of the necessary oblique case (see Allo, *Apocalypse* p. cxlv f): 1⁵ (but the nom. phrase is probably intended as a quotation or else as an indecl. divine title; in the next verse the appositional τῷ ἀγαπῶντι agrees with its antecedent αὐτῷ), 2¹³ ἐν ταῖς ἡμέραις 'Αντιπᾶς ὁ μάρτυς μου ὁ πιστός μου, ²⁰, 3¹², 7⁴, 8⁹, 9¹⁴, 14¹², 20². 17⁴ is extraordinary: ποτήριον ... γέμων βδελυγμάτων καὶ τὰ ἀκάθαρτα. Some of the OT translators also do this: 3 Km 1²⁰ καί σύ, ... οἱ ὀφθαλμοὶ πάντος 'Ισραὴλ πρός σε; for papyri examples see Abel § 40 m.

(ii) Less often it is the accus. or gen. which is *pendens*: 1¹¹? 1¹⁵ ὅμοιοι χαλκολιβάνῳ ὡς ἐν καμίνῳ πεπυρωμένης (why fem. and why gen.? There are scribal corrections), 7⁹ (accus. following nom.), 21⁹ (gen. following accus.).

(iii) Quite often masc. is found mistakenly for fem. or neut.: 4⁸A (but S has indic., and 046 neut.), 5⁶S (BAP have neut.), 5⁶ (P neut.), 11⁴ (SᶜᶜP have fem.), 14¹⁹ (S has fem),

17³ γυναῖκα ... γέμοντα, ⁴ γέμων S*, 13¹⁴ (S neut.), ¹¹ p⁴⁷, 14¹, 9¹⁴ SA. On the reading ἄρσεν or ἄρρενα 12⁵, see Blass-Debr. § 136, 3. Examples of this solecism from late Greek in Jannaris § 1181 b; from a papyrus, Abel § 40 m.

(iv) λέγων, λέγοντες, appear as if they were indeclinable: 4¹ 5¹² 11¹ vl. ¹⁵ (p⁴⁷ SCP have fem.) 14⁷ (exc. p⁴⁷) 19⁶ vl. This results from a literal rendering of לֵאמֹר in the LXX, and appears also Ac 6¹¹ SD*A ¹³ S. Extended to ἔχων: 10² 21¹⁴.

(v) Plur. (not neut.) subject with sing. verb: 9¹² ἔρχεται ἔτι δύο Οὐαί (but it may be a Semitic solecism of gender, and therefore neut. plur. Alternatively, δύο = second).

(vi) τέσσαρες for τέσσαρας Rev 4⁴ vl.; frequent in MSS of LXX and the papyri.

In all these types of solecism it is usually the ptc. which is involved (esp. the ptc. of λέγω), and this is interesting because in later Greek the use of ptcs. developed along the same lines; the masc., especially in the nom. sing., is preferred—until in MGr the ptc. has but one indecl. form. An uneducated writer, like the author of Rev, is foreshadowing the language of the future. The tendency, reflected in the least educated writers of the NT, to neglect congruence of gender and case in appositions, is seen in the Koine: P. Ryl. II 112¹³ (A.D. 250) εἴδαμέν σε θυσιάζοντα (of a woman) and BU 1078⁵ (A.D. 39) εἰδότος σοῦ (a woman)—gender; P. Par. 51²⁵ (Milligan p. 21) ἐμὲ λέλυκας πολιὰς ἔχων—case; P. Amh. II 111–113 (A.D. 128) ἀπέχω παρ' αὐτοῦ τὸν ὁμολογοῦντα—case. Moulton (Proleg. 60) gives instances from the papyri of breach of concord in gender and case, usually the ptc. being concerned.

(b) *Rest of NT*

For papyri, see Mayser II 3, 22.

(i) The indecl. πλήρης,[1] which is indecl. only when followed by the gen., appears several times, but always with variants. It was commonly used in the Koine from i/A.D. onwards, and is found also in LXX (e.g. Jb 21²⁴): Jn 1¹⁴ (declinable in D) is important for exegesis because, if πλ is indecl. we may take it either with δόξαν or with αὐτοῦ; Ac 6⁵ (decl. in BC²) 6³ (decl. in

---

[1] Mayser I¹ 63f; I² 2, 58.   Thackeray *OT Gr.* 177.   Moulton-Howard 162.   Deissmann *LO*⁴, 99f.

SBCD) 19²⁸ AEL (decl. in the rest), Mk 8¹⁹ (decl. in SBCL).
When πλήρης is not followed by the gen. it is declinable, but
there are indecl. variants to Mk 4²⁸.

(ii) No doubt εἴ τι might have been written throughout in
Ph 2¹, instead of εἴ τις σπλάγχνα καὶ οἰκτιρμοί (Moulton
Proleg. 59). In the papyri we find indecl. τι, and it is no cause
for surprise if we find also indecl. τις (Zerwick § 5).

(iii) As in Rev, sometimes appositional phrases and circumstantial ptcs. are found in the nom. instead of oblique cases:
Mt 10¹¹ D, Lk 20²⁷ 21⁶ Jas 3⁸ (unless we punctuate with a
semicolon before ἀκατάσχετον), Lk 24⁴⁷ (corr. in D), Ac 10³⁷
(p⁴⁵ LP corr. to ἀρξάμενον), Ac 7⁴⁰, 2 Th 1⁸ D*FG. Sometimes the nom. ptc. is without construction: Mt 4¹⁶D 5⁴⁰D
17²D ⁹D ¹⁴D Mk 7¹⁹ (D indic.). This is the only instance
which is important for exegesis: πᾶν τὸ ἔξωθεν εἰσπορευόμενον
... εἰς τὸν ἀφεδρῶνα ἐκπορεύεται, καθαρίζων πάντα τὰ
βρώματα. Some refer καθ. to Jesus, of course (Origen, Jülicher,
A. Schlatter: see Zerwick § 8). Others however take it as false
concord, meant to agree with ἀφεδρῶνα, and translate: *the
latrine which removes filth* (Zorell, Knabenbauer, Klostermann,
Blass-Debr. §§ 126, 3; 137, 3.). Mk 9²⁰ 16¹⁴ W ὁ μὴ ἐῶν,
Jn 7³⁸ (or place a stop after ἐμέ; see p. 320n), Ac 19³⁴. An
accus. ptc. without construction: Ac 26³ (SᶜAC corr. it)—which
shows that lack of congruence in ptcs. is not confined to the
least educated writers of the NT. For frequent papyri examples,
see Mayser II 3, 190ff, and for i and ii/A.D. see Blass-Debr.
§ 137, 3; § 466; Radermacher² 219; Ljungvik BSSVS 6ff. The
use of πᾶς with art. and ptc. which in itself is normal popular
Greek is so frequent in Mt that it raises the question of Semitic
influence (the phrase beginning with כל or, as in Da 6⁸,
די כל) in a legislative kind of style: 3¹⁰ 5²². ²⁸. ³² 7¹⁹. The
same observation holds good of πᾶς ὅς and ὅστις: 7²⁴ 10³² 12³⁶
19²⁹ 21²² 23³ (Lagrange S. Matth. XCVIIf). Luke is guilty too:
Lk 12⁴⁸ παντὶ δὲ ᾧ ..., παρ' αὐτοῦ, and John: 6³⁹ 15².

(iv) Masc. πάντων for fem. πασῶν: Mk 12²⁸, P. Giss. 23, 4
(early ii/A.D.). But Abel (§ 41 a) quotes Thucyd. 4, 52, 2.
Acta Thomae 41³⁹ πάντων τῶν ἐπιθυμιῶν, 66¹⁷ πάντων
γυναικῶν, 70³⁰ πάντων τῶν ἡδονῶν.

(v) Nom. for accus. (a slip): Ro 2⁸ ὀργὴ καὶ θυμός, obj. of
ἀποδώσει! Cp. LXX 3 Km 5¹⁴ ⁽²⁸⁾ καὶ ἀπέστειλεν αὐτοὺς εἰς

τὸν Λίβανον, δέκα χιλιάδες, ἐν τῷ μηνί, ἀλλασσόμενοι.

(vi) Remarkable changes in person and number, in : Lk 13³⁴ Ἰερουσαλήμ . . . ἡ . . . λιθοβολοῦσα τοὺς ἀπεσταλμένους πρὸς αὐτήν, ποσάκις ἠθέλησα ἐπισυνάξαι τὰ τέκνα σου . . . καὶ οὐκ ἠθελήσατε Semitic? Cf. Moule 180.

(vii) Since, of the numerals 1–100, only the first four are declinable, it is not surprising to find a tendency even for these to be indecl., e.g. Mk 14¹⁹ Jn 8⁹ εἷς καθ' εἷς.

(viii) πᾶσα indecl. at Mt 2³; and πᾶν also seems to be indecl., as it is used of persons in Jn 17² πᾶν ὃ δέδωκας αὐτῷ, δώσει αὐτοῖς . . .

(ix) Grammatically we expect the nom., instead of ὑποδεδεμένους Mk 6⁹ and at 12⁴⁰ οἱ κατεσθίοντες . . . καὶ . . . προσευχόμενοι refers perhaps to the distant genitive ἀπὸ τῶν γραμματέων (12³⁸).

(x) πᾶς πόρνος . . . ὅ ἐστιν Eph 5⁵, τὴν ἀγάπην, ὅ ἐστιν Col 3¹⁴ (vl. ἥτις ἐστίν). Such a solecism appears nowhere else in the Paulines. Is this important for authorship? See Moffatt *ILNT* 153ff.

CHAPTER TWENTY-THREE

THE SUBORDINATION OF CLAUSES

§ 1. Substantival Clauses [1]

They include clauses with infinitive, participle, ὅτι, ὡς, etc., and indirect questions. See pp. 134–149 (for verb and infin.), and pp. 325f (for problems of the Relative).

§ 2. Adjectival Clauses

See under Relative Pronouns, pp. 47f, 106–110.

§ 3. Adverbial Clauses

(a) *Causal clauses* [2]

Subordination by ὅτι and διότι is often so loose that only the feeble translation *for* is possible (e.g. Ac 18¹⁰ διότι ἐγώ εἰμι μετά σοῦ, Ro 1¹⁹· ²¹ 3²⁰ 8⁷ 1 Co 1²⁵ 4⁹ 10¹⁷ 2 Co 4⁶ 8⁸· ¹⁴). Strictly the meaning is *because, quoniam*, and διότι = διὰ τοῦτο ὅτι: e.g. Mt 5³⁻¹² Ac 22¹⁸ Jas 4³ 1 Pt 1²⁴. Correspondence with כִּי has influenced the meaning of ὅτι somewhat in Biblical Greek, to an almost consecutive sense, *so that*: Mt 8²⁷ ποταπός ἐστιν οὗτος ὅτι..., Mk 4⁴¹ Lk 4³⁶ 8²⁵ Jn 2¹⁸, Heb 2⁶ τί ἐστιν ἄνθρωπος ὅτι. So in Hebrew 1 Sam 11⁵ מַה־לָּעָם כִּי יִבְכּוּ.

᾽Επεί has a causal sense, but it too is weakened in Biblical Greek to *for otherwise*: Ro 3⁶ 11⁶· ²² 1 Co 5¹⁰ 7¹⁴ Heb 10². Purely causal Jn 13²⁹ ἐπεὶ τὸ γλωσσόκομον εἶχεν, Lk 1¹ ἐπειδήπερ. ᾽Επειδή appears in the Ptol. papyri (BU 844¹⁵ ἐπιδή χρίαν αὐτοῦ ἔχω *because I need it*) but it is retreating gradually before ἐπεί (Mayser II 3, 82). Καθότι too in Hell. Greek may be little more than *for* (e.g. Lk 1⁷ καθότι ἦν ᾽Ελισαβὲτ στεῖρα, 19⁹ Ac 2²⁴ 17³¹, P. Par. 27, 23). Δι᾽ ἣν αἰτίαν 2 Ti

---

[1] See also K-G II pp. 354ff. Mayser II 1, 306ff. Moulton Einl. 335f.
[2] K-G II, § 569, pp. 460–463. Mayser II 3, 82ff. Martin P. Nilsson, "Die Kausalsätze im Griechischen bis Aristoteles," (*Beiträge zur histoischen Syntax der griechischen Sprache*, 18, ed. M. v. Schanz, Würzburg), 1907. Zerwick §§ 297–299.

1⁶· ¹² etc., ἐφ' ᾧ (see p. 272), ἀνθ' ὧν (see p. 258), ὡς, καθώς (see pp. 158, 320(2)), οὖ χάριν Lk 7⁴⁷—are also causal conjunctions.

(b) Conditional Clauses

There are four chief kinds of conditional clauses, and we have discussed them all under various heads in the chapters on the Mood of Verbs. For (i) εἰ with indic., representing the simple assumption, see pp. 92, 115. For (ii) εἰ with opt., representing the "potential" conception, see pp. 125ff. For (ii) εἰ with aor. or impf. indic., representing an assumption as not corresponding with reality, see pp. 91f. For (iv) ἐάν with subjunctive, indicating an expected result based on the present general or particular circumstances, see pp. 113f.

This is the class. norm. but in fact the opt. is now greatly reduced and in NT scarcely occurs at all in conditions, and never (as in class.) to express repetitions in past time. Moreover there is, according to classical standards, a misuse of εἰ with indic., and there is a liberal mixing in the various categories of conditional sentences. Whereas class. Greek had μή for negative in all conditions, the NT often has εἰ οὐ (but always ἐὰν μή).

Besides the more orthodox method of a subordinate clause with εἰ or ἐάν, a plain statement in the form of a ptc. (see p. 157) or independent clause will serve as the protasis of a condition. Thus in Mt 12⁴⁴ καὶ ἐλθὸν εὑρίσκει is if he comes and finds; it has always been obscure why the spirit necessarily returns. In 24⁴⁰ᶠ τότε ἔσονται δύο ἐν τῷ ἀγρῷ ... δύο ἀλήθουσαι is if there are two in the field ..., if there are two women grinding. In Ro 13³ θέλεις δὲ μὴ φοβεῖσθαι τὴν ἐξουσίαν is if you wish to be fearless of. Such interpretation lends point to the context and is good Greek.

Under this head note the strong Hebraism, εἰ in oaths and protestations.[1]

(c) Comparative Clauses [2]

The atticistic καθάπερ is found in Paul and Hebrews, but often as a possible scribal correction, e.g. Ro 10¹⁵ B (rest καθώς),

---

[1] Also in questions, in the Pauline εἴπερ if indeed and εἴγε si tamen, in εἴτε ... εἴτε (LXX for סִﬦ ... סִﬦ) whether ... or. See ch. 25.

[2] K-G II 490ff. Mayser II 2, 440; II 3, 92ff. See also, for ὡς, Index.

11⁸ SB (rest καθώς), 12⁴ p⁴⁶ SBA (D*EFG ὥσπερ). Phrynichus (425) condemns the Hellenistic καθώς, which occurs frequently in the ii/в.с. papyri (Mayser II 2, 440; II 3, 92, n. 4), and prefers καθό (Ro 8²⁶ 2 Co 8¹² 1 Pt 4¹³) or καθά (Mt 27¹⁰ Lk 1² D Eus).

1. As correlatives we find ὡς, ὥσπερ, καθώς, καθάπερ, alongside οὕτως or καί or οὕτως καί. Some authors prefer ὥσπερ (Mt 10 ὥσπερ: 4 καθώς, Jas, Rev), some καθώς (Mk, Eph, Past, 1 & 2 Pt, 1, 2, 3 Jn; Lk 17:1, Jn 32:1, Ac 12:3, Paul 81:15, Heb 9:3). Some authors make the ὥσπερ-clause follow the main clause (Ac 2² 3¹⁷ 11¹⁵ Heb 4¹⁰ 7²⁷ 9²⁵ Rev 10³); but in Paul it nearly always precedes (Ro 5¹². ¹⁹. ²¹ 6⁴. ¹⁹ 11³⁰ 12⁴ vl. 1 Co 11¹² 15²² 16¹ Ga 4²⁹; ὥσπερ ... ἀλλά 1 Co 8⁵, ὥσπερ ἵνα 2 Co 8⁷), the two exceptions being 1 Th 5³ and the introduction to a quotation in 1 Co 10⁷ (where however ὡς, in CD*KP 81 181 Marcion, is prob. correct as it accounts for the omission by haplography of τινες αὐτῶν ὥσπερ (ὡς) in FG f g, the eye travelling from ως to ως in καθως τινες αυτων ως γεγραπται). The ὥσπερ-clause precedes also in Lk 17²⁴ 18¹¹ (vl. ὡς) Jn 5²¹ (S ὡς) ²⁶ (S*DW Eus¹ ὡς), whereas Mt has both orders: ὥσπερ ... οὕτως 12⁴⁰ 13⁴⁰ 24²⁷. ³⁷, ὥσπερ following 6². ⁷ 18¹⁷ 20²⁸ 25¹⁴. ³². Where καθώς introduces a following quotation in NT it almost invariably follows its main clause. Mk 1² would seem to be an exception, as it is usual to take ἐγένετο in 1⁴ as the main verb; however, the exception can be negatived if the καθώς-clause be taken with the preceding verse and the verb ἐστιν is supplied, although it is not at all like Mark to omit the copula in such circumstances. If we accept the necessary variants, the καθώς-clause introducing a quotation does precede in all other instances: Lk 2²³ Jn 6³¹ 12¹⁴ Ac 7⁴² Ro 1¹⁷ 3⁴ AD (but SB καθάπερ) ¹⁰ 4⁶ DG (rest καθάπερ) ¹⁷ 8³⁶ 9¹³ (B corr. to καθάπερ) ²⁹. ³³ 10¹⁵ vl. 11⁸ vl. ²⁶ 15³. ⁹. ²¹ 1 Co 1³¹ 2⁹ 2 Co 6¹⁶ 8¹⁵ Ga 3⁶ Heb 4³. ⁷ 5⁶. ¹

2. As *quandoquidem* = *even so as*, especially καθώς: Ro 1²⁸ 1 Co 1⁶ 5⁷ Eph 1⁴ Ph 1⁷, Mt 6¹² ὡς.

3. In Mk 4²⁶ ὡς = *as if* (ὡς ἄνθρωπος βάλῃ) SBD (others add ἐάν or ὅταν; so LXX Isa 7² 17¹¹ 31⁴); similar Lk 11⁵. ⁶, where ἐάν appears to be omitted before εἴπῃ.

4. In Bibl. Greek, through influence of כְּ, ὡς may serve to soften a statement: *as it were, perhaps, approximately*, Mk 6¹⁵ Lk 15¹⁹, T. Abr. 82¹¹ 118²⁶ ὡς ἐν ὀνείροις *in a sort of dream*, 118²² τινες ἐν ῥομφαίᾳ τελευτῶσιν ὡς (*or perhaps*) ἐπὶ τόξοις, 107⁵ ἤγγισεν τῇ πόλει ὡς (*approx.*) ἀπὸ σταδίων τριῶν. Perhaps Heb. 11²⁷.

---

¹ On the strength of this evidence of clause-order, G. D. Kilpatrick argues in *JThS* XI, 2, 1960, 340ff., that at Jn 7³⁸ the main clause ends with εἰς ἐμέ, and the dependent clause begins at καθώς (so *he that believes* is subject of *let him drink*). Among other things, this depends on whether it is feasible for τις to be resumed in the same sentence by such a phrase as ὁ πιστεύων εἰς ἐμέ. Besides the note in *JThS*, I owe much to Dr Kilpatrick for private communications on this point of word order.

5. The predicative use of ὡς is very common: Mt 22³⁰ ὡς ἄγγελοι
θεοῦ εἰσιν, 18³ Lk 15¹⁹ 1 Co 7⁸. Class. writers would have preferred
the adj. ἴσος.

6. Sometimes ὡς may be confused with ἕως, e.g. Ac 17¹⁴ ὡς ἐπί
(SBAE corr. to ἕως), for in Hell. Greek ὡς ἐπί = against, versus (Polyb.
1, 29, 1), as also do ἕως ἐπί and ἕως εἰς (cp. 1 Mac 5²⁹ ἕως ἐπὶ τὸ
ὀχύρωμα, where V reads ὡς).

7. ὡσεί (and rarely ὡσπερεί or ὡσάν) may stand for ὡς: Lk 3²³
ὡσεὶ ἐτῶν τριάκοντα (but 8⁴² ὡς ἐτῶν δώδεκα), Mt 14²¹ (D ὡς), etc.
Ὡσάν 2 Co 10⁹ (Hellenistic), ὡσπερεί 1 Co 4¹³ vl. 15⁸ vl. (Mayser II 3,
167. Radermacher² 203. Moulton Einl. 261, n. 2).

(d) Concessive Clauses

For καίπερ and καίτοι see pp. 153, 157.

When one cannot render the particles κἄν and εἰ καί by
although, they keep their proper sense as conditional, e.g.
2 Co 11¹⁵ οὐ μέγα οὖν εἰ καὶ οἱ διάκονοι αὐτοῦ μετασχηματίζονται
ὡς διάκονοι δικαιοσύνης, Jn 8⁵⁵ κἄν εἴπω ὅτι, Lk 12³⁸. Concessive clauses with εἰ or ἐάν are essentially conditional clauses
and follow the rules of class. Greek. When it does not mean
even if or *and if* (καὶ ἐάν), κἄν is equivalent to ἐὰν καί (e.g.
Mk 5²⁸ *if only*, 6⁵⁶, Heb 10² p⁴⁶, etc.). See Harsing 46, Jannaris
§ 598.

In the sense of *except if* Hell. Greek places ἐκτός (1 Co 14⁵
15², 1 Ti 5¹⁹) before the class. εἰ μή (Mk 6⁵ 2 Co 13⁵ Ga 1⁷ etc.).
Hell. Greek, from i/A.D. onwards, is also fond of considering
εἴ τις as equivalent of ὅστις ὅ τι (as Mt 18²⁸ ἀπόδος εἴ τι ὀφείλης)
and of adding ἄν (as 1 Co 7⁵ εἰ μή τι ἂν ἐκ συμφώνου, Hist.
Lausiaca p. 70, 14 Butl. εἴ τι ἄν με διδάξῃς, ἐκεῖνο ποιῶ).
See Radermacher ² 199, Ljungvik BSSVS 9ff.

(e) Temporal Clauses

There is a preference in Biblical Greek for temporal conjunctions, as against the genitive absolute, which is due perhaps
to the frequency with which temporal clauses are introduced by
כְּדִי or כַּד in Aramaic. For ὅταν, etc., see pp. 112f, 124f. There
are also ὅτε (indic.), ἡνίκα (Paul), ὁπότε (only Lk 6³ AEHK;
rest ὅτε), ἐπειδή (temporal only Lk 7¹ vl.), ἵνα (Jn 16²), ὡς
(Ionic influence: Lk 1²³ 12⁵⁸ 24³² Jn 2⁹ Ga 6¹⁰; Mk 4³⁶ either
when he was in the boat or *as he was, in the boat*), ὡς ἄν (see
pp. 112f), ἕως *while* (Jn 9⁴), *until* (Mk 6⁴⁵ Jn 21²²ᶠ 1 Ti 4¹³),
πρίν and πρὸ τοῦ (see pp. 78, 113, 140, 144).

(*f*) *Participle Absolute: accusative.*

'Εξόν occurs in NT only as a predicate to a missing ἐστιν, and altogether lacking are ὑπάρχον (PSI IV 340, 9, 257 B.C.), πρέπον, etc., which are also very rare indeed in the Ptol. papyri. The obscure τυχόν (*perhaps, without doubt*) occurs Lk 20¹³ D Ac 12¹⁵D 1 Co 16⁶; δέον Ac 19³⁶ 1 Ti 5¹³ 1 Pt 1⁶.

Participle Absolute: genitive

The correct use is becoming rarer in Hell. Greek and it is misused more often; that is to say, the gen. is not truly absolute but is used even where the ptc. might have agreed with the subject or object of the sentence. This is one of the marks of the Koine (Mayser II 3, 66ff. Moulton Einl. 114. Radermacher² 208f) and of Biblical Greek (Johannessohn DGKPS 46).

Mark's usage is fairly regular: it is only a temporal use and always precedes the main clause, except for ὀψίας γενομένης 4³⁵ (unless we take this closely with the next sentence) and ἀνατείλαντος τοῦ ἡλίου 16². Nevertheless there are falls from class. grace in Mark, as in many NT authors, which scribes have often corrected: he should have placed the ptc. in the dat. at 13¹ (so also Mt at 1²⁰ 5¹ (B corr) 8¹ (S* corr) 8⁵ vl. 28 vl. 9¹⁰·¹⁸ 17⁹ 18²⁴ 21²³ vl. 24³ 27¹⁷; Lk at 12³⁶ 14²⁹ (p⁴⁵ corr.) 17¹² (BL corr.) 22¹⁰; Jn 4⁵¹ vl. Ac 4¹, LXX Gen 18¹). But Mayser quotes the same thing in papyri of 255, 249, 218, 221, iii/B.C. ter, 161, 156, ii/B.C. (II 3, 67f), and Thucyd. 1, 114, 1 has διαβεβηκότος ἤδη Περικλέους στρατιᾳ 'Αθηναίων ἠγγέλθη αὐτῷ, ὅτι (and Xen. Anab. 5, 2, 24). Mark should have made the ptc. agree with the accus. at 5¹⁸ ἐμβαίνοντος αὐτοῦ εἰς τὸ πλοῖον παρεκαλεῖ αὐτὸν ὁ δαιμονισθείς, 9²⁸ vl., 10¹⁷, 13³; so should Luke at 9⁴² 15²⁰ 18⁴⁰ and Ac 7²¹ 19³⁰ 21¹⁷ vl. 25⁷; and Mt 18²⁵ Jn 8³⁰ and Paul at 2 Co 12²¹ vl.; papyri of 258, 254, iii/B.C., 168, 176, 114, 51. More irregular still, Mark has a gen. absol. agreeing with the subject at 6²² SBC* (corr. by p⁴⁵ C³DWΘ), and so has Mt at 1¹⁸ (but a clause lies in between), Luke at Ac 21³⁴, and the LXX at Ex 4²¹, 1 Km 3¹¹ παντὸς ἀκούοντος αὐτά, ἠχήσει ἀμφότερα τὰ ὦτα αὐτοῦ. Instances in the Ptol. pap. are so plentiful that Mayser gives only a selection (II 3, 68ff). When these " mistakes " are made in the NT it is very rarely that the gen. absol. takes up a word which has preceded (but 2 Co 4¹⁸). There is no instance of gen. absol. without a finite verb, as often occurs in the Ptol. pap., e.g. βασιλέως προστάξαντος (= *in the King's name*) followed by a command.

(*g*) *Final Clauses.*   See pp. 95, 100–6, 111, 128f 141–6.

(*h*) *Consecutive Clauses.*   See pp. 102, 106, 136, 141f, 272.

CHAPTER TWENTY-FOUR

INCONSISTENCIES BETWEEN MAIN AND DEPENDENT CLAUSES

§ 1. Attraction of Relative Pronoun to case of antecedent [1]

Little need be noted, as this phenomenon is well known to students of class. Greek, the LXX, and the papyri (Mayser II 3, 102). It may not occur if the relative clause is sharply divided from the rest, as in Heb 8[2], but often the scribes have corrected by bringing in the relative attraction, e.g. Mk 13[19] (ἧς AWC[2]), Jn 4[5] (οὗ DWC*) [50] (ᾧ AW) 7[39] (οὗ SDW) Ti 3[5] (ὧν D[c] C[b]) Rev 1[20] (ὧν 046).

The Greek relative, unlike the English, includes in itself the demonstrative idea, so that we find compressions like Mk 10[40] ἀλλ' οἷς ἑτοίμασται (= τούτοις οἷς) and Lk 9[36] οὐδὲν ὧν (= οὐδὲν τούτων ἅ).

Equally classical is the attraction of the noun into the relative clause sometimes (the art. omitted), e.g. Jn 9[14] ἐν ᾖ ἡμέρᾳ (for papyri, Mayser II 3, 98ff), and not necessarily immediately after the relative, e.g. Jn 11[6] ἐν ᾧ ἦν τόπῳ, 17[3] ὃν ἀπέστειλας Ἰησοῦν, 2 Co 10[13] κατὰ τὸ μέτρον τοῦ κανόνος, οὗ ἐμέρισεν ἡμῖν ὁ θεὸς μέτρου (οὗ incidentally attracted to κανόνος).

§ 2. Inverse attraction of the antecedent to the relative [2]

This attraction of the case of the antecedent to that of the relative pronoun may occur even when the antecedent is not drawn into the relative clause, and even when it precedes the relative (as class.): Mk 6[11. 16] 12[10] OT (= Mt 21[42]) λίθον ὃν ἀπεδοκίμασαν . . . , οὗτος ἐγενήθη, Lk 1[73] 12[48] Ac 10[36] 1 Co 10[16] LXX Ge 31[16] etc.

---

[1] K-G II 406ff. Meisterhans-Schwyzer 237ff 18–30. Mayser II 3, 98ff. Moulton Einl. 148. Radermacher[2] 220, 222.
[2] K-G II 413. Meisterhans-Schwyzer 239, 25. Mayser II 3, 107ff. Radermacher[2] 222. Wackernagel I 49f.

§ 3. Pleonastic insertion of Personal Pronoun [1]

It is a Semitism in the sense that the Heb. אֲשֶׁר לוֹ is reflected through LXX usage, helped by a parallel Aramaic idiom; but non-Biblical Greek, and indeed many languages, reveal the same pleonasm. LXX Gen 41¹⁹ βόες οἵας οὐκ εἶδον τοιαύτας, cp. Mk 13¹⁹ οἵα οὐ γέγονεν τοιαύτη, Mt 3¹² (= Lk 3¹⁷) οὗ τὸ πτύον ἐν τῇ χειρὶ αὐτοῦ, Mt 3¹¹ corrects Mk 1⁷ by omitting αὐτοῦ. Other exx.: Jn 1³³ ἐφ' ὃν . . . ἐπ' αὐτοῦ, 18⁹, Ac 15¹⁷ OT 1 Co 8⁶ 2 Pt 2³ Rev 2². ¹⁷ 3⁸ 7². ⁹ 13⁸ 17² 20⁸. Nevertheless scribes have endeavoured to remove the feature: e.g. Mk 7²⁵ (SDW om αὐτῆς). Papyri: e.g. PSI IV 433, 7 ὅσα ποτὲ ὑπῆρχεν ἐν ταμιείωι (ἦν δ' ὀλίγα), ἐγὼ αὐτὰ ἐφύτευσα (261 b.c.).

§ 4. Prolepsis [2]

Prolepsis (anticipation) occurs when the subject (object) of the dependent clause is brought forward into the main clause. Such interlacing was frequent in class. Greek but is relatively rare in the Koine. In the NT the subject is brought forward in Mt 6²⁸ Mk 1²⁴ 7² 11³² 12³⁴ Lk 13²⁵ Ac 9²⁰ 19⁴ 1 Co 16¹⁵ Rev 3⁹; and the object (less often) in Lk 24⁷ Ac 13³² Ga 4¹¹ 5²¹.

§ 5. Anacoloutha after relative clauses [3]

In class. Greek there sometimes occurred a false grammatical connection when to a relative clause a second relative clause was joined by καί, to which clause the rel. pronoun was not appropriate in its existing form: e.g. Rev 17² μεθ' ἧς ἐπόρνευσαν . . ., καὶ ἐμεθύσθησαν, Mk 6¹¹ (scribes have corrected), Lk 17³¹ 1 Co 7¹³ (p⁴⁶ SD* εἴ τις) Ti 1²ᶠ. But Semitic rather than class. is the anacolouthon in Mt 7⁹ᶠ τίς ἐστιν ἐξ ὑμῶν, ὃν αἰτήσει ὁ υἱὸς αὐτοῦ ἄρτον, μὴ λίθον ἐπιδώσει αὐτῷ; ἢ καὶ ἰχθὺν αἰτήσει, μὴ ὄφιν ἐπιδώσει αὐτῷ.

§ 6. Mingling of direct and indirect speech: recitative ὅτι [4]

The Koine found it much more difficult than the class. Greek and Latin languages to sustain indirect speech for very

---

[1] K-G II 432f, 443f.   Jannaris § 1439.   Ljungvik SSAA, 27f.   Psichari 182f.   Abel § 134.   Pernot Études 152.   Winer-Schmiedel § 22, 7. Thackeray OT Gr 46.   Moulton-Howard 434f.

[2] K-G II 577f.   Jannaris § 1937.   Mayser II 3, 111.

[3] K-G II 431ff.   Mayser II 3, 112.

[4] K-G II 431ff, 557.   Mayser II 3, 46f, 112ff.   P. Winter, " Hoti recitativum in Lc 1, 25. 61, 2, 23," HTR 48, 1955, 213–216.

long, and in the NT direct speech is preferred in narrative wherever possible, especially in Mk and Jn (but not so much in Lk, and even less in Mt [1]). The equivalent of inverted commas is " ὅτι recitativum ". The lattter, and even the mingling of direct and indirect speech, is not unknown in class. Greek. The Hebrew כִּי and Aramaic דִּי helped to commend such an idiom to NT writers. It is the regular usage in Coptic. Note the peculiar positions of ὅτι in Jn 3[28] and the way some writers will attempt *oratio obliqua*, reverting to *recta* in a very short time (Mk 6[8f] Lk 5[14] Ac 1[4] 23[22] 25[4f]), although sometimes they will repent also of direct speech in mid-stream and change to indirect (Mk 11[31f], but D[2] W and Mt 21[26] keep this in *oratio recta*), Jn 13[29] Ac 23[23f].

---

[1] See C. H. Turner, *JThS* 28, 1927, 9–15.

PART II

CONNECTIONS BETWEEN SENTENCES

CHAPTER TWENTY-FIVE

CO-ORDINATING PARTICLES [1]

IN THE widest sense, prepositions and adverbs as well as conjunctions may be classed as particles, but in this chapter the study is confined to co-ordinating conjunctions. Nothing like a complete thesaurus will be attempted, attention being restricted to correct classification and observation of new tendencies, unusual instances, and instances with an interest for exegesis or textual criticism. The Koine and NT are more careless than the older Greek regarding the position of particles and, as in syntax generally, display the popular love of over-emphasis. The use of post-positive particles is declining and emphasis is achieved by forming more compound particles.

The double influence of later Greek usage and Jewish background worked upon NT writers and combined to achieve a considerable reduction in the number of particles as compared with more refined Greek; thus τοι and μήν (by themselves) and γοῦν are too subtle to be needed in the NT. Fascinating problems arise for the meticulous student. Why does οὖν occur so often in the fourth Gospel and what does it signify? Why is Paul so fond of οὐχί? Has Mark, who loves καί, any reason for changing to δέ at times? What NT writers use τε . . . καί, and is καί . . . καί the same thing?

§ 1. Simple Particles [2]

'Αλλά.

Paul is particularly fond of it [3]. It is a stronger adversative particle than δέ but is often weakened in the clause where it most frequently occurs, that is, after a preceding οὐ or οὐ μόνον:

---

[1] K-G II 116–339. Jannaris §§ 1700–1728. Mayser II 3, 114–174. J. D. Denniston, *The Greek Particles*[2], Oxford 1954.

[2] K-G II §§ 515ff. Mayser II 3, 116ff.

[3] Ro 67, 1 Co 71, 2 Co 66, Ga 23; cp. with Lk only 32, Ac 29, Mt 37, Heb 16, Rev 13, LXX Ge 20, Ex 13.

thus in Mt 10²⁰ Mk 5³⁹ 9³⁷ 14³⁶ Jn 12⁴⁴ 1 Co 15¹⁰ etc. the meaning
is simply *not so much . . . as*.   The preceding negative may easily
be supplied in Mt 11⁷⁻⁹ Ac 19² Ga 2³, or an interrogative may
be the equivalent of a negative in Jn 7⁴⁸ Ac 15¹¹.   Thus the
meaning is *sed etiam*.   It also occurs simply as *however, nevertheless*, at the beginning of a sentence, but stronger than δέ,
e.g. Ro 5¹⁴ *sin is not imputed when there is no law; nevertheless . . . .*
In Mk 14³⁶ it reverses a previous command.   Sometimes before
a command it is not so much adversative as consecutive, and is
best translated as an interjection, *Well!* : Mk 16⁷ *See the place
where they laid him.   Well, go to his disciples . . . .* Ac 9⁶ *I am
Jesus . . . .   Well, rise and . . .* , Mt 9¹⁸ Mk 9²² Ac 10²⁰ 26¹⁶.
After a conditional protasis, we must translate *at least*, e.g.
Mk 14²⁹ 1 Co 4¹⁵.   Introducing a strong addition, ἀλλά or
ἀλλὰ καί may be *yes, indeed*, as in Jn 16² 1 Co 3² 2 Co 7¹¹ 11¹
Ph 1¹⁸.   There is an ellipse (e.g. scil. *this has happened*) with
ἀλλ' ἵνα in Mk 14⁴⁹ Jn 1⁸ 9³ 13¹⁸ 15²⁵ 1 Jn 2¹⁹.   It is clear from
Mk 4²² that ἀλλά must sometimes have the meaning of εἰ μή
except (so Mt 20²³, and ἀλλ' ἤ in Lk 12⁵¹ 2 Co 1¹³), just as εἰ μή
serves for ἀλλά (Lk 4²⁶. ²⁷)—a confusion which may be traceable
to Aramaic influence.

Ἄρα ¹

Even Paul, who makes good use of it, sometimes breaks the
classical rule by giving it first position (Ro 10¹⁷ 1 Co 15¹⁸ etc.).
It is often combined with other particles : οὖν, γε, εἴπερ, ἐπεί, μήτι.
Its use in the Ptol. papyri is rare and literary.   It is not in itself
an interrogative particle, like ἆρα, although it may be introduced
into an interrog. sentence.

Ἆρα and ἆραγε.

Also particles of literary style, = οὖν, *num igitur, ergone*.
Interrogative.   Luke and Paul.   There are four exx. in LXX,
three of them in Ge (e.g. 18¹³), but it is more frequent in
Symmachus.   Lk 18⁸ Ac 8³⁰ Ga 2¹⁷ (it would be ἄρα here, since
μὴ γένοιτο in Paul always answers a question ; it may however
be ἄρα. if the clause is not interrogative but an argumentative
statement posed for an imaginary opponent to answer).

---

¹K.-G II 317ff.   Mayser II 3, 119ff.

Γάρ [1].

The usage is classical. Paul uses it even more than he does ἀλλά, and Matthew and Luke are fond of it [2]. It is very rare in the Johannine writings, which makes the οὖν of D more likely than γάρ at Jn 9³⁰.

Γε [3].

A modal particle which lends emphasis to another word. It is very elusive in NT and is almost always merged with another particle as a meaningless appendage: with ἀλλά, αρα, εἰ, εἰ δὲ μή, καίτοι, μήτι. Nevertheless it may have some significance in καί γε since, through the LXX, we can trace the influence of the Heb. וְגַם: Ac 2¹⁸ 1 Co 4⁸ (D*FG om γε) *and indeed*, Lk 19⁴² *at least*. Occasionally without another particle: Lk 11⁸ διά γε *at least because of*, 18⁵, Ro 8³² (DFG om) ὅς γε *he who even*.

Δέ and μὲν ... δέ [4].

Sometimes δέ will have the strong adversative force of ἀλλά after a foregoing negative (Ac 12⁹. ¹⁴ Heb 4¹³ 6¹²) but usually it is weaker and indistinguishable from καί. Indeed the proportion of this δέ to καί raises interesting problems in Biblical Greek since it varies considerably in and between different books; in the NT the proportion of δέ : καί varies from 1 : 0·6 in Paul to 1 : 73 in Rev (4-21). The variety is still greater in the LXX, from 1 : 1 in 4 Mac to 1 : 188 in Jer β.

At times δέ will introduce a parenthesis (Ac 1¹⁵ (SBA τε) 4¹³D 12³) and that is how νυνὶ δέ is best explained in the middle of a sentence (Col 1²²). One of the most characteristic departures from class. style is the rarity of the correlation of μέν and δέ in Biblical Greek; it occurs with any frequency only in some Paulines, Ac and Heb. Matthew has 20 instances, and this, together with his comparatively wide use of δέ (491 against Mk's 150), make the translation hypothesis for his gospel the less certain. Mark has only two or three instances, and Luke only

---

[1] K-G II 330ff. Mayser II 3, 121ff.

[2] Mt 125, Lk 96, Ac 80, Heb 91, Rev 16, Ro 143, 1 Co 108, 2 Co 74, Ga 35. LXX Ge 107, Ex (1–24) 70, Ex (25–40) 21, Isa 181, MiPr 3, 4 Mac 87. Didache 31, Ep. Barn. 47.

[3] K-G II 171–178. Mayser II 3. 123ff. T. K. Abbott, *ICC* on Eph and Col, pp. ivf.

[4] K-G II 261–278. Meisterhans-Schwyzer 250. 6. Mayser II 3, 125ff.

Proportion of δέ : καί

LXX	NT	Apost. Fathers, etc.
4 Macc 123:141 (1:1)	Paul	Didache 66:31
Ex (1–24) 369:800	Ga 58:21 (1:0·4)	(1:0·5)
(1:2·1)	Ro 145:77 (1:0·5)	Ep. Barn. 66:84
Ge 840:2023 (1:2·4)	1 Co 208:129 (1:0·6)	(1:1·3)
Isa (40–66) 81:672	2 Co 74:58 (1:0·8)	T. Abr. A 157:305
(1:8·3)	Ac 556:522 (1:1)	(1:2)
Isa (1–39) 82:882	Mt. 491:762 (1:1·5)	T. Abr. B 43:210
(1:10·7)	Lk (3–24) 511:853	(1:5)
Ex (25–40) 35:605	(1:1·6)	
(1:17)	Lk (1–2) 26:132	
Mi Pr 59:1548 (1:26)	(1:5)	
Jer α 22:917 (1:42)	Mk. 150:785 (1:5)	
Ezk α 26:1642 (1:63)	Rev (1–3) 4:69 (1:17)	
Jg A 17:1588 (1:93)	Rev (4–21) 8:586	
Ezk β 6:592 (1:99)	(1:73)	
Jer β 4:754 (1:188)		

The books are arranged in reverse order of Semitic style.

seven (to Luke, asyndeton often seems more effective, e.g. 7²²);
the whole of the Pent. (LXX) has only about 20 exx. of μέν . . .
δέ, Dan O' has μέν 8 times, but the more slavish θ has none.
Mt's exx. are all in the part usually assigned to Q, which fact,
unless a translator took great liberties, is against Q having been
originally Aramaic.

	Mt	Mk	Lk	Jn	Ac	Past	Heb	Jas	1 Pt	Jude
μέν only	–	2	3	4	34	–	5	1	–	–
μέν .. δέ	20	3	7	4	14	3	14	–	4	3

	Ro	Cor	Ga	Eph	Ph	Col	Thes	Tot Paul	NT	Pap. iii/B.C.	ii–i/ B.C.
μέν only	7	10	1	–	2	1	1	22	71	4	8
μέν . . . δέ	12	19	2	1	4	–	–	38	110	18	47

The MSS differ considerably over the omission of μέν.

Δή [1].

An invitatory particle (class.), as Lk 2¹⁵ *come, let us go,* Ac 13² 15³⁶ 1 Co 6²⁰ 15⁴⁹ p⁴⁶. But ὅς δή *who ever,* in Mt 13²³.

Διό, διόπερ [2].

Properly subordinating, but not necessarily so in NT. Διό occurs most often in Ac and Paul, and is confused with διότι by scribes (e.g. A*W in Lk 1³⁵). The context favours διό (*and so*) in Ac 20²⁶, but the MSS appear to favour διότι.

Εἰ.

For conditions, see pp. 113ff. In direct questions, as opposed to indirect, it is a Bibl. Greek usage (Mt 12¹⁰ 19³ Lk 13²³ Ac 1⁶, LXX Ge 17¹⁷ 1 Km 10²⁴ 2 Mac 7⁷ 15³, nineteen times in Luke), probably a Hebraism from ־ה or אִם, which also may stand in both direct and indirect questions. In the Vulgate *si* renders this εἰ and as a result *si* in later Latin became a direct interrogative. Note that the interrog. ἦ is absent from Bibl. Greek (exc. in Jb 25⁵ B); like ἆρα, it is a mark of literary style.

In oaths [3], εἰ renders Heb. אִם (Mk 8¹² Heb 3¹¹ 4³. [5] LXX) and is the equivalent of a strong negative. Conversely, εἰ μή is a strong positive in Ro 14¹¹ D*FG (LXX Isa 45²³ S*B) ζῶ ἐγώ, . . ., εἰ μὴ κάμψει πᾶν γόνυ.

Ἔτι [4].

In NT = *still* Mt 12⁴⁶ 17⁵ (and parall.) 26⁴⁷; not *further.*

Εἴτε . . . εἴτε.

Properly with subordinate clauses, but also with ellipse of the verb, either disjunctive or copulative: Ro 12⁶⁻⁸ 2 Co 5¹⁰ Eph 6⁸ Ph 1¹⁸.

---

[1] K-G II 122–131. Mayser II 3, 133f.

[2] K-G II 462. Meisterhans-Schwyzer 253, 25. Mayser II 3, 134f.

[3] Moulton-Howard 469. N. D. Coleman, " Some noteworthy uses of εἰ or εἶ in Hellenistic Greek—with a note on Mark viii. 12 " *JThS* 28, 1927, 159ff. F. C. Burkitt, " Εἰ in Hellenistic Greek. Mark viii. 12 " (reply to Coleman), *JThS* ib. 274ff.

[4] Mayser II 3, 136f. Radermacher² 69.

"H and ἤ καί [1].

Disjunctive particles (or), especially when introducing a question: Mt 12²⁹ Ro 3²⁹ 9²¹ 1 Co 10²²; but (esp. in questions or negative sentences and with synonyms) almost copulative: Mt 5¹⁷ Jn 8¹⁴ (S corr. to καί) Ac 1⁷ 11⁸ Ro 9¹¹ FG Ga 3²⁸ D* 1 Co 11²⁷ 1 Th 2¹⁹. As a correlation, ἤ . . . ἤ either . . . or (ἤτοι . . . ἤ Ro 6¹⁶).

Καί [2].

1. *The copula*: a. καί.   b. καὶ . . . καί.

2. *The adverb* (*also, even*).

1. (*a*) Καί joins together nouns, adjs., numerals, adverbs, or joins a part with the whole (Ac 5²⁹). Its excessive use in the narrative of many NT writers, esp. Mark, would appear vulgar to the normal reader; Luke and John to some extent mitigate this fault by the use occasionally of asyndeton, and of δέ, οὖν, or τε. The nuance may really be *and yet* (*et tamen*), as in Mt 3¹⁴ *and yet you come to me!* where we expect καὶ μήν or καίτοι. Or the nuance may be consecutive (Mt 5¹⁵ 2 Co 11⁹ Heb 3¹⁹ 2 Pt 1¹⁹) and even final (Mt 8²¹ ἀπελθεῖν καὶ θάψαι, 26¹⁵ Jn 14³ Rev 14¹⁵). This admittedly belongs to the uncultivated Koine, but note also the possibility of Aramaic influence [3], by which the waw of apodosis might well be rendered by καί: Dan θ 4² ἐνύπνιον ἴδον καὶ ἐφοβέρισέν με (καί = rel. pronoun [4]), θ' 7¹⁶ (καί purposive). The same appears in Mt: 6⁴ καὶ ὁ πατήρ (*for*, cp. Dan 10¹⁷) 18²¹ 21²³ etc. Καί in place of temporal subordination: Mt 26⁴⁵ Mk 15²⁵ Lk 19⁴³ 23⁴⁴ Jn 2¹³ Ac 5⁷ Heb 8⁸. Καί with fut. may also resume a final clause to express further result (Mt 26⁵³ Heb 12⁹). Although the papyri provide ample evidence that popular speech favours parataxis, we must remember as a

---

[1] K-G II 296ff.   Mayser II 3, 138ff.   Radermacher² 33f, 201, 207. H. Margolis in *Amer. Journ. Sem. Lang.*, 25, 1908–9, 257–275 (for LXX).
[2] K-G II § 521ff.   Meisterhans-Schwyzer 161. 16; 162. 2; 249; 250. Mayser II 3, 140ff.   S. Trenkner, *Le Style* KAI *dans le recit oral attique* (Institut d'Études Polonaises en Belgique) Brussels 1948.   Abel § 78. Radermacher² 28, 37, 218, 222.   Ljungvik BSSVS 55ff.
[3] Lagrange *S. Matth.* XCI.
[4] Cp. Lk 1⁴⁹ καὶ ἅγιον τὸ ὄνομα αὐτοῦ, for οὗ τὸ ὄνομα ἅγιον ἔστιν; esp. in Rev.

contributory influence that the Heb. waw introduced propositions of a temporal, conditional, causal and consecutive kind. Obviously Hebraic (not Aramaic) is the use of καί after (καὶ) ἐγένετο(δέ) in place of accus. and infin.[1]: Lk 5¹ 9²⁸ 19¹⁵ Ac 5⁷. The translation of καὶ ἰδού constitutes a problem: R. A. Knox renders it in Lk with a variety of English. It is often as redundant as the ἐγένετο construction (Lk 7¹² D implies that it is equivalent); at least the καί, if not the ἰδού, is often pleonastic, which is why p⁴⁵ SBA omit καί in Ac 10¹⁷ (CD καὶ ἰδού): Lk 7¹² Ac 1¹⁰ Rev 3²⁰ (AP om καί).

(b) καὶ . . . καί. The probability is that this is the Bibl. Greek equivalent of τε . . . καί, which is there extremely rare. Thus Mk 4⁴¹ ὅτι καὶ ὁ ἄνεμος καὶ ἡ θάλασσα ὑπακούει αὐτῷ = both wind and sea (but RSV, NEB, etc. take the first καί as even); so Mk 9¹³ Lk 5³⁶ Jn 6³⁶ 7²⁸ 11⁴⁸ 12²⁸ 15²⁴ 17²⁵ (both the world and these) Ac 26²⁹ Ro 14⁹ 11³³ etc., LXX Nu 9¹⁴ᵇ, Pap. BU 417¹⁷ ὅτι καὶ σοὶ τοῦτο ἀνήκει καὶ συμφέρει. The scribes have corrected this in Mt 10²⁸ and Jn 4³⁶.

2. The adverbial or epexegetical καί (that is, even): Mk 1¹⁹ Lk 3¹⁸ Jn 1¹⁶ (that is, to receive grace upon grace) 20³⁰, Ac 22²⁵, καὶ ἀκατάκριτον and uncondemned at that), Ro 1⁵ (that is, apostleship, or hendiadys?: grace of apostleship), 13¹¹ idque, 1 Co 2² et quidem, 6⁶⁻⁸, Eph 2⁸. It is pleonastic before a second adj., esp. after πολύς: Lk 3¹⁸ Jn 20³⁰ Ac 25⁷ Ti 1¹⁰ vl. The original meaning of καί, before it became also merely a coordinating particle, was also, as in Ro 8¹⁷ εἰ δὲ τέκνα, καὶ κληρόνομοι, Ph 4³. This appears with pronouns frequently: Mt 2⁸ κἀγώ I too, Lk 14¹² Jn 7⁴⁷; Ro 8²⁴ S ὃ γὰρ βλέπει, τίς καὶ ὑπομένει who needs also to wait for that which he sees? (p⁴⁶ B*DFG misunderstood and omitted καί). And with adverbs of comparison: Ac 11¹⁷ ὡς καί, Ro 15⁷ καθὼς καί. And after other particles: Lk 24²² ἀλλὰ καί sed etiam.

The idoms καὶ νῦν (וְעַתָּה) and καὶ τίς (classical) are fairly common, where καί is best rendered emphatically well, then: Mk 10²⁶ Lk 10²⁹ Jn 9³⁶ 14²² SW Ac 3¹⁷ 7³⁴ 10⁵ 13¹¹ 20²². ²⁵ 22¹⁶ Ro 3⁷ 2 Co 2² Ph 1²² 2 Th 2⁶ 1 Jn 2²⁸.

A chain of dependent genitives, which is not liked by NT writers, is avoided by the use of hendiadys: Mk 6²⁶ (not oaths

---

[1] Thackeray OT Gr 50ff. Pernot Études 189–199. M. Johannessohn, Das biblische KAI EΓENETO und seine Geschichte, Göttingen, 1926.

and guests, but *oaths sworn before the guests*), Lk 2⁴⁷ (not *his intelligence and answers*, but *the intelligence of his answers*), 21¹⁵ Ac 1²⁵ 14¹⁷ 23⁶ (*hope of the resurrection*), Ro 1⁵ 2 Ti 4¹ Ti 2¹³ Jas 5¹⁰ 1 Pt 4¹⁴ 2 Pt 1¹⁶.

(Τὸ) λοιπόν [1].

Essentially the meaning is *from now, henceforth*, as Eph 6¹⁰ DG (τοῦ λοιποῦ p⁴⁶ S*AB), and λοιπόν 1 Th 4¹ (cp. BGU IV 1079. 6, A.D. 41). Although it is weakened in Hell. Greek to a mere *so*, it cannot mean its opposite, *still*, as in so many modern translations of Mk 14⁴¹ (Moffatt, Goodspeed, RSV, NEB), for *still* means *until now*. Jesus means *from now*. He says, "Are you going to *continue* sleeping? " To introduce *still* is to throw emphasis on the past, but the point is that they must not be asleep when the betrayer arrives (future). Ἀπέχει will then have a direct ref. to Judas. He has been paid; he is here. *Henceforth*, it is no time for sleep.

Μήν and ναί [2].

Particles of solemn affirmation or corroboration. In class. Greek ἦ μήν, but Hell. Greek (esp. LXX and pap.) since ii/B.C. substitutes εἶ μήν: Heb 6¹⁴ εἶ μὴν εὐλογῶ εὐλογήσω σε (KL* corr. to ἦ) *yes, certainly I will bless*. But elsewhere in NT the corroborating and recapitulating particle is ναί (still current in MGr): Mt 11⁹. ²⁵ᶠ 15²⁷ Lk 11⁵¹ 12⁵ Jn 11²⁷ Ro 3²⁹ Ph 4³ Phm²⁰ Rev 1⁷ 14¹³ 16⁷, LXX Ge 17¹⁹ Jdt 9¹².

Νή.

With accus., (scil. ὄμνυμι) 1 Co 15³¹ LXX Ge 42¹⁵ᶠ *I swear by* (class.). K-G. II 147, 2. Mayser II 3, 147f.

Ὅθεν.

Consecutive co-ordinating particle (class.): Mt 14⁷ Ac 26¹⁹ Heb 2¹⁷ and often. Mayser II 3, 148. Meisterhans-Schwyzer 253, 25 (i/B.C. inscr.).

---

[1] K-G I 315 n. 15. Mayser II 3, 145f. Moule 161f. A. Cavallin, " (Τὸ) λοιπόν: Eine bedeutungsgeschichtliche Untersuchung," *Eranos* 39, 1941 [21-144.
[2] R.G II 135ff; 147, 2. Mayser II 3, 146f.

"Ὅμως.

K-G II 85 n. 1; 95f. Mayser II 3, 148. Jn 12⁴² ὅμως μέντοι *but yet*. Displaced by hyperbaton in 1 Co 14⁷ *lifeless things may give a sound, nevertheless if* . . . (transfer ὅμως after διδόντα), Ga 3¹⁵ *it may be only a man's will, nevertheless no one* . . . (transfer before οὐδείς). Conceivably in these two passages we could accent it perispomenon, as adv. from ὁμός (Homer, class. poet.), and translate *likewise*. But ὅμως (sic) is much more frequent in Bibl. Greek (Wi 13⁶ 2 Mac 2²⁷ 14¹⁸ 15⁵ 4 Mac 13²⁷ SR 15¹¹ SR).

Οὖν.

The interrogative οὐκοῦν (only Jn 18³⁷) may be Pilate's ipsissimum verbum.

This interesting particle is the most widely used of the consecutive co-ordinating conjunctions and its use enters widely into the idiosyncratic style of the various Bibl. authors [1]. John is very fond of it (but not in the epistles); in Rev it occurs only in 1–3 (one of several distinguishing features in the syntax of this part of Rev). It occurs most frequently in narrative. It is characteristic of Luke to place it after a ptc.: Lk 5⁷ D 23¹⁶. ²² Ac 10²³ 15² vl. 16¹¹ 25¹⁷. He also invariably adds μέν if the opening word is a noun or pronoun. Its use sharply divides the work of the translators in LXX Ge and Ex; in Ge it occurs almost only in the second half, in Ex almost only in the first half: Ge (1–25) 3, (26–50) 27, Ex (1–24) 26, (25–40) 3.

It is not always strictly causative, but sometimes temporal (= *then*), esp. in Jn. Moreover μὲν οὖν (μενοῦν) is no longer the class. affirmation *indeed* (παντάπασι μὲν οὖν), but is usually resumptive (= *so then*); it occurs most frequently in Ac (merely resumptive: 1⁶. ¹⁸ 2⁴¹ 5⁴¹ 8⁴. ²⁵ 9³¹ 13⁴ 15³. ³⁰ 17¹². ³⁰ 19³⁸ 23¹⁸. ³¹ 26⁴, 26⁹ ἐγὼ μὲν οὖν ἔδοξα *why, I myself thought*, Moule 163). Also resumptive: Lk 3¹⁸ (μὲν οὖν nowhere else in Lk) Jn 19²⁴ Ph 2²³. Nevertheless μὲν οὖν has the class. use of modifying a previous statement by introducing a new one: *nay rather* Jn 20³⁰ Ac 12⁵ 14³ (see *Beg.* in loc., where it is suggested

---

[1] K-G 154; 163ff; 336. Mayser II 3, 148ff, W. Nauck, "Das οὖν Paräneticum," *ZNW* 49, 1958, 134. J. R. Mantey, "Newly discovered meanings for οὖν," *Expositor* ser. VIII 22, 1921, 205–214: contending that in Lk 14³⁴ Ac 8²⁵ Jn 20³⁰ (and papyri) οὖν = *nevertheless*.

to transpose ² and ³, to give οὖν its usual meaning in Ac) 17¹⁷ 25⁴ 28⁵ Heb 7¹¹ 9¹.   What is not classical is the use of μεν οὖν (γε) to open a sentence : Lk 11²⁸ Ro 9²⁰ (p⁴⁶ corrects) 10¹⁸ (corr. by FG), Ph 3⁸ : *much more, in fact.*

Οὐ, etc.

For negative particles, see ch. 19.   For οὐ, μή, and οὐ μή in questions, see ch. 19 § 2 ; for οὐ μή otherwise, see ch. 8 § 2.2.

Πλήν ¹.

In class. Greek, a preposition (as in Mk, Ac) or a conjunction in πλὴν ὅτι *except* (as Lk 22²² Ac 20²³ Ph 1¹⁸).   In Hell. Greek it becomes an adversative particle.   D corrects to δέ in Lk 12³¹ and to ἀλλά in 23²⁸.   Lk 17¹ corrects Mt 18⁷ to οὐαὶ δέ (but SBDL harmonize it back again to πλὴν οὐαί).   Matthew is fond of it ; he changes Mk 14³⁶ ἀλλ᾿ οὐχ into πλὴν οὐχ (26³⁹).   Paul's use is peculiar and like that of LXX, a pleonastic *only* 1 Co 11¹¹ Eph 5³³ Ph 1¹⁸ (om B) 3¹⁶ 4¹⁴, LXX e.g. Ge 41⁴⁰ Ex 9⁹· ¹¹ 9²⁶ 4 Km 14⁴ 15³⁵ (= Heb. רק).

Πότερον . . . ἤ.

Only Jn 7¹⁷ in NT and rarely in LXX (e.g. Jb 7¹· ²).

Τε ².

This copulative enclitic particle, declining in use in the Koine and later revived as an atticism, occurs in NT in all forms and compounds, but not very frequently (except in Ac), and it is an indication of stylistic pretension, its place being taken by καί or οὐδέ.   In their use of τε we may group the books as follows : (1) Mk Jn Rev : 14 times, (2) Johannines : 1, (3) Mt : 9, (4) Pastorals : 1, (5) Lk : 11, (6) Paul : 32, (7) Heb : 23, (8) Ac : approx. 170.   It is not surprising that in textual transmission scribes and editors were unable to resist introducing τε, sometimes at the expense of δέ : Ac 1¹⁵ (SAB ἦν τε, wrongly in parenthesis) Lk 4³⁵ D 23³⁶ D 24²⁰ Mt 28¹² Ro 7⁷.   Although the

---

¹ Mayser II 2, 534.   Schmid Attizismus I 133.
² K-G II §§ 517–520 ; 522. 2.   Meisterhans—Schwyzer 249f.   Mayser II 3, 155ff.   Radermacher² 5f.   J. A. Brown, *An Exegetical Study of* τε (Diss of Southern Baptist Theol. Sem.) 1948.

simple form almost disappeared οὔτε and μήτε lingered on awhile.   But the single τε (without καί) occurs in Ac 2³³ 1 Co 4²¹ Heb 6⁵ 9¹ (only poet. in class. Greek).   At times τε before γάρ appears to be a superfluous affectation: Ro 7⁷ 2 Co 10⁸ (see K-G II 245, Radermacher² 5).

The correlation τε . . . τε (class. especially in poetry) occurs only in Ac 26¹⁶ and elsewhere in οὔτε . . . οὔτε, εἴτε . . . εἴτε, etc.   In Ro 1²⁶ᶠ (τε . . . ὁμοίως τε καί) the variant which reads δέ for the second τε has support from BU 417¹⁶ (ὁμοίως δὲ καὶ περὶ τῶν τοῦ . . . Abel § 78).   Ac 2⁴⁶ is not an instance of correlation.

The distribution of the correlation τε . . καί is instructive (* τε καί):—Mt 22¹⁰* 27⁴⁸ Lk 2¹⁶ 12⁴⁵ 15² 21¹¹. ¹¹ 22⁶⁶* 23¹² 24²⁰, Ac 60 times, Ro 1¹²* ¹⁴. ¹⁴. ¹⁶ vl. ²⁰. ²⁷ v. 2⁹. ¹⁰ 3⁹ 10¹² vl. 1 Co 1² vl. ²⁴. ³⁰ Ph 1⁷ Heb 2⁴. ¹¹ 4¹² vl. 5⁷. ¹⁴ 6². ⁴ ¹⁹* 8³ 9². ⁹. ¹⁹ 10³³ 11³². ³² Jas 3⁷. ⁷ Rev 19⁸ vl.   It joins more closely than simple καί and joins words which have between themselves a close or logical affinity (non solum . . . sed etiam).   "Jews and Greeks" is the kind of phrase which demands τε . . . καί or τε καί (Ac 14¹ 19¹⁰ vl. ¹⁷ vl. 20²¹ etc.).   Other combinations occur: τε . . . καὶ . . . τε (Ac 9¹⁵ vl. 26¹⁰ᶠ ²⁰ vl.), τε . . . τε . . . καί (Heb 6² 11³²), τε καὶ . . . καὶ . . . καί (Ac 5²⁴ 21³⁰ Heb 2⁴).   The correlative τε will usually stand after the first word of the phrase in correlation, but τε is misplaced in Ac 26²²: it should follow and not precede οἱ. When a preposition (or article) joins two ideas together, τε may be placed after the preposition (Ac 10³⁹ 25²³ 28²³).

In ascertaining the true text we should remember the strong tendency of atticizing editors and scribes to add τε, but this may not always be so in the case of Ac where τε occurs so often that it must be a stylistic feature of the author.

§ 2. Compound Particles

Δήπου ¹.

An ironical particle (class. and literary Hell.), partly confirmatory and partly hesitant, appealing to mutual knowledge: Heb 2¹⁶ οὐ γάρ δήπου.

Καί(τοιγε).

Parenthetical particle, although: Jn 4² Ac 14¹⁷ 17²⁷ᶠ.

---

¹ K-G II 131.   Mayser II 3, 169.

Μέντοι.

A rare adversative particle, and very weak (*but*) in Jas 2⁸ Jude⁸. Stronger in 2 Ti 2¹⁹ and in Jn where it is most found: οὐ(δείς) μέντοι 4²⁷ 7¹³ 20⁵ 21⁴ ὅμως μέντοι 12⁴².

Οὐδέ, μηδέ.

See ch. 19. Besides beginning a sentence (Mk 8²⁶ Lk 7⁹), it may resume and emphasize a previous negative: Mt 6¹⁵ Mk 3²⁰ Lk 16³¹ Ro 4¹⁵.

Οὔτε and μήτε.

Fairly evenly distributed in all parts of the NT, but in many of these instances the endings -δε and -τε are confused in the MSS (cp. δέ and τε): e.g. Lk 20³⁶ οὐδὲ γάρ (corr. to οὔτε γάρ by SW), Mk 5³ 12²⁵ 14⁶⁸ Lk 7³³ Ac 2³¹ 23⁸ (SBACE corr. to μήτε) 1 Co 6⁹· ¹⁰ Ga 1¹² Jas 3¹². This is not surprising in view of the general confusion, e.g. Pap. Rei. 13¹⁰ᶠ καὶ μήτ' αὐτὸν "Ανδρωνα μηδ' ἄλλον . . . μηδ'. . . μηδέ . . ., BU 388 II 36f πῶς οὔτε ὁ αὐτὸς χρόνος ἐν αὐταῖς πρόσκειται, ἀλλ' οὐδέ . . . .

In class. Greek οὔτε . . . καί is very rare. In NT Jn 4¹¹ (D syrˡᵉʷ corr. to οὐδέ), 3 Jn¹⁰. See Jn 5³⁷ᶠ οὔτε . . . οὔτε . . . καὶ . . . οὐ.

Τοιγαροῦν.

Class. but not Thucyd. Not Koine, and only 13 times in Polyb. I Th 4⁸ Heb 12¹ (p⁴⁶ τοίγαρ). First word.

Τοινῦν.

Only 5 times in Thucyd. Not Koine, and only 3 times Polyb. Second word (class.): Lk 20²⁵ ACW 1 Co 9²⁶. First word (Hell.): Lk 20²⁵ SBL Heb 13¹³.

§ 3. Unconnected words and sentences: Asyndeton [1]

Except occasionally for effect, this is contrary to the genius of Greek, but Paul and Hebrews are full of it (e.g. 1 Co 7²⁷ Heb 11³²ᶠᶠ). It increases in the Ptol. pap. between iii and i/B.C. Yet in NT scribes frequently introduced connecting particles (see Jn, for variants between asyndeton, δέ, καί and οὖν). Matthew is fond of asyndeton with ἔφη and λέγει (see Lagrange *S. Matth.* XCII) and John has λέγει, λέγουσιν 70 times

---

[1] K-G II § 546. Meisterhans-Schwyzer 161; 250, 4. Schwyzer II 632ff. , Mayser II 3, 179–183.

with asyndeton (against 31 with particle—but there are variants); Aramaic influence is probable (Lagrange *S. Jean* CIVf). On Mark see Zerwick, *Untersuchungen* 22f.

The use of τότε [1] to link sentences is not class. Mt has it 90 times, Mk 6, Lk 15, Ac 21, Jn 10, rest 18; LXX canonical books 156, Dan O′ 43, θ′ 30. Its extreme use in Mt must be explained ultimately as a rendering of Aramaic אדין or באדין, so frequent in Daniel, and rendered by τότε 30 times in LXX. The Heb. אז is less frequent. It is significant that LXX has τότε five or six times in 2 Esd 5, against only four times in the whole of Genesis (Lagrange *S. Matth.* CX). Scribes have sought to reduce the exuberance of τότε in Mt.

Because of his elementary knowledge of popular Greek, the author of Rev confines his transition-formulae to the very simplest kind, most often μετὰ ταῦτα (εἶδον), varying with καὶ (εἶδον) καὶ ἰδού. There is a poverty of particles and continual parataxis (Allo, *Apoc.* CLI).

Asyndeton makes the beginning of new long sections conspicuous, e.g. Ro 9¹ 10¹ 13¹ 1 Pt 5¹ 2 Pt 3¹.

---

[1] A. H. McNeile, " Τότε in St. Matthew," *JThS* 12, 1911, 127ff.

CHAPTER TWENTY-SIX

IRREGULARITY OF SUBORDINATION

§ 1. Parataxis instead of hypotaxis [1]

We have seen how prevalent parataxis is in popular speech (ch. 25, καί), and it goes even further in MGr. We find direct in place of indirect speech (Lk 14[18] 1 Co 7[40] FG), and καί is often used in place of subordination (Mt 18[21] 26[53] Lk 14[5]) on the Semitic model which happens to coincide with popular Greek, and even without καί there is parataxis where we expect conditional hypotaxis (Jn 7[34] 10[12] Ro 13[3]). Parataxis is too much for D in Mk 2[15] (οἵ for καί). The imperatives ὁρᾶτε and βλέπετε are common in NT, as in the Koine (Mt 9[30] 24[6] Mk 13[33]) and are probably asyndetic additions to the normal imperative; so also ὕπαγε, ἔγειρε, θέλεις. Again, popular Greek coincides with a strong Hebraic idiom: e.g. LXX Ex 19[24] βάδιζε κατάβηθι (לֶךְ־רֵד), 3 Km 19[7] ἀνάστα φάγε (קוּם אֱכֹל). For ἐγένετο with finite verb see p. 335; Moulton-Howard 425–428.

§ 2. Interpolation of sentences: Parenthesis [2]

The NT parentheses are harsher than would be permitted to a Greek stylist, especially those in Paul (Ro 1[13] 2[15f]), which may be due to dictation of the letters, but also those in Ac (1[15] 4[13] 5[14] 12[3f]). Short parentheses, such as those with οἶδα, μαρτυρῶ, ὁρᾷς, are found in class. Greek. Punctuation in Mark is often clarified if more parentheses than usual are recognized (Zerwick, *Untersuchungen* 130–138. C. H. Turner in *JThS* 26, 145). E.g. transpose 12[12], as [a] [c] [b].

§ 3. Anacoloutha

(a) For *casus pendens* see ch. 22 § 5.

(b) For gen. absol. improperly used, see pp. 322f.

---

[1] K-G II § 516. Wackernagel I 62f. Mayser II 3, 184ff. Ljungvik BSSVS 76ff, 87ff. Radermacher[2] 213, 222.

[2] K-G II § 548. Schwyzer II 705. Mayser II 3, 186ff. Radermacher[2] 221. C. Grünewald, *Die Satzparenthese bei den zehn attischen Rednern* (B.z.h.Sd.gr.Spr.19) 1912.

(c) Chiefly in Paul's letters there occurs the anacolouthon whereby the original sentence construction is forgotten after an insertion: Ro 2[17] (but read ἴδε for εἰ δέ?), 16[27] (B improves by omitting ᾧ), Ga 2[4f] (D* improves by omitting οἷς), 2[6], 1 Ti 1[3ff].

(d) Paul also tends to make a ptc. co-ordinate with a finite verb: 2 Co 5[12] 6[3] 7[5] 8[18ff] (χειροτονηθείς and also στελλόμενοι. But if [19] is a parenthesis, the ptc. depends on συνεπέμψαμεν and there is no anacolouthon), 9[11. 13] 10[4. 15. 15] 11[6].

(e) The imperatival ptc. is a well known phenomenon [1] in Peter and Paul, and it is common in the Koine. However, as ἐστέ (imperat.) never occurs in NT we must presume that it is understood as a copula with all these ptcs., which therefore do not constitute an anacolouthon.   Note the durative sense of the ptcs.: *always* Ro 12[9ff] 2 Co 6[3-10] (the ptcs. skip over [2] and carry on the construction of [1], which is resumed in [9]) 8[24] B δ-text (SC correct to imperat.) Eph 3[17. 18] 4[1] (the ptc. may depend on the verb immediately before it) 5[15-22] Ph 1[29f] (but WH. make a long parenthesis and try to connect ἔχοντες with στήκετε) Col 2[2] 3[16f] 4[11] 1 Pt 2[12. 18] 3[1. 7] 4[8ff] 2 Pt 3[3].

The only example outside Peter and Paul is Heb 13[5] (but Moulton would add Lk 24[47]: Proleg. 182).

(f) Very frequent is the use of a finite verb co-ordinate with a ptc. and strengthening it unnecessarily. This is class., but not in the same profusion as in NT.   It may be that there is ellipse of the verb *to be* with the ptcs. (Regard, *Phrase nom.* 186-216): Mt 13[22. 23] Lk 8[12. 14] Jn 1[32] (for emphasis) 5[44] (vl. corrects to ptc.) 15[5] 2 Co 5[6ff] 6[9] Eph 1[20] (not WH.) Col 1[26] (D corr. to ptc.) 2 Jn [2] Rev 1[5f] 2[2. 9] 3[7. 9].   LXX Ps 17[33-35].

---

[1] Moulton Einl. 284-288, 353f.   Joüon, *Grammaire de l'Hébreu Biblique* § 121 e, n. 2.   Zerwick § 265f.   H. G. Meecham, " The Use of the Participle for the Imperative in the New Testament," *Exp. T.* 58, 1947, 207ff.   C. K. Barrett, " The Imperatival Participle," *Exp. T.* 59, 1948, 165ff.   Mayser II 1, 340f.

CHAPTER TWENTY-SEVEN

WORD ORDER

THE DETAILS of clause order and of word order within the clause ought to be more closely examined than is possible in the strict compass of this syntax volume and will be reserved for a separate publication on style as distinct from syntax. Certain ways in which the study may benefit textual and exegetical research will however be indicated. The matter has also been separately discussed in part at various points in this volume: the position of adverbs (pp. 227ff), of demonstratives (pp. 193f), the combinations with πᾶς (pp. 201–5), the position of adjs. relative to their noun with special reference to πολύς (pp. 185f), the position of the dependent genitive (pp. 217f), of comparative clauses (p. 320), and the difference between εἰ καί and καὶ εἰ (or κἄν) (p. 321).

§ 1. Clause Order

(a) Normally the dependent clause follows the main clause.

1. FINAL clauses with ἵνα precede in a very few instances, and mainly in the gospels: Mt 9⁶ (and parallels) 17²⁷ (Jn 14²¹?) Jn 19²⁸· ³¹ Ac 24⁴ (Ro 7¹³?) Eph 6²¹ Ὅπως-clauses never precede.

2. LOCAL clauses: ὅθεν-clauses (15 times in post-position) never precede. Οὗ-clauses (21 post-position) precede only at Mt 18²⁰ (2⁹ 28¹⁶ post-position) Ro 4¹⁵ 5²⁰ (9²⁶ post-position) 2 Co 3¹⁷ (1 Co 16⁶ post).

3. TEMPORAL clauses: here alone the pre-position is as much in favour as the post-position. But as ἕως-clauses are invariably post-positive, we must alter our punctuation of 1 Ti 4¹³ and take the clause with what precedes [1]. We find however that ὅτι-, ὅταν-, and ὡς (temp.)-clauses precede much more often than they follow, especially in the gospels; while ἐπεί(δη)-, ἐπάν-, and ἡνίκα-clauses invariably precede, and

---

[1] " Make yourself an example, until I come."

ὁπότε-, ἄχρι (οὗ)-, μέχρις οὗ-, and μέχρι-clauses invariably
follow.   But πρίν- and πρὸ τοῦ-clauses are about equally divided.

4. CAUSAL clauses: the majority have post-position, but
ἐπεί and ἐπειδή are equally divided, and ἐπεὶ ἄν (1 Co 14¹⁶) has
only pre-position.   Ὅτι (causal) is post-positive 397 times, and
the only exceptions are as follows: Lk 19¹⁷ Jn 1⁵⁰ (a question)
8⁴⁵ (14¹⁹?) 15¹⁹ 16⁶ 20²⁹ (a question) Ro 9⁷ Ga 4⁶ Rev 3¹⁰· ¹⁶ 18⁷.
Invariably post-positive are ἀνθ' ὧν, ἐφ'ᾧ, καθότι, διότι.   But
διὰ τό c. infin. (post-positive 23 times) has pre-position in Mt 13⁶
24¹² Mk 4⁶ Ac 18³ 27⁹.

5. COMPARATIVE clauses: see also ch. 23 § 3. c. 1.
Καθώς (with καθάπερ and καθά as variants)—clauses follow the
main clause invariably in Mt, in Mk (except for Mk 1²ᶠ, which is
not an exception if punctuated with a stop after 1³), in Lk
(except for 6³¹ 11³⁰ 17²⁶· ²⁸).   But in Jn the distribution is
more even (19 post: 13 pre), like the Joh. epp. (8:5).   In Ac
there are 10 post: 2 pre.   In Ro 15 (+5 vl.) post: 1 pre.   1 and
2 Co 24 (+2 vl.): 7.   Ga 3:0.   Ph 2:1.   Eph 10:0.   Col 4:1.
1 and 2 Th 12:3.   Past 0:1.   Heb 7:2.   1 Pt 0:1.   2 Pt 2:0.

(b) Chiasmus [1].

Lund argues that chiasmus is largely Semitic: hence, in the
material common to Mt and Lk, it occurs rather in Mt.   The
instances outside Biblical Greek are not extensive chiastic
systems but usually the simpler kind of chiasmus of four terms
only.   The chiasmus in the MT of Ps 7¹⁶ 58⁶ is well preserved
in LXX, but the remarkable ten-fold instance in Ps 3⁷ᶠ is not
preserved quite so obviously, and in Ps 6³⁽⁴⁾ the LXX spoils
the chiasmus by using ἐταράχθη in both members.   Before
Lund, a chiasmus of four or six members had already been
pointed out by J. Weiss in Ro 14⁷ᶠᶠ 1 Co 7¹⁻⁷ 9¹⁹⁻²² Ph 4¹¹⁻¹³,
but most writers had applied class. standards to the NT and
failed to appreciate any influence of ancient Semitic culture
or of contemporary Aramaic literature.   Greek rhetorical forms
do not explain everything in NT style, where the writers were
Jews accustomed to the sound of a Hebrew liturgy.   Lund

---

[1] N. W. Lund, *Chiasmus in the New Testament*, N. Carolina 1942.
W. Milligan, *Lectures on the Apocalypse*³, 1892, pp. 94f, noticed chiasmus
in Rev, using it to counter the source hypotheses of Vischer and Völter.
J. Jeremias, ZNW 49, 1958, 145–156.

argues that although J. Weiss may correctly contend that the Paulines were written for the *ear*, the influence of the OT and the synagogue was paramount. Of this literary influence, Lund is concerned with one particular expression, chiasmus or inverted order. Discovering certain laws governing these structures in the OT, he makes tests for their occurrence in the NT. A point to which he might have given more attention is the important question whether the Semitic influence was direct from the Hebrew OT or whether it was by way of the LXX.

Instances of chiasmus are as follows—
(a) Mt 9[17] old—burst—skins—skins—lost—new (ABC CBA)
(b) 1 Co 7[3] to woman—man—woman—to man (AB—BA)
(c) 1 Co 11[8-12]

A		B		C		B		A	
man	A	man	A			woman	B	woman	B
woman	B	woman	B	angels		man	A	man	A
woman	B	woman	B			man	A	man	A
man	A	man	A			woman	B	woman	B

Ps 89[30-34] may have been the (unconscious?) model for Paul here, if he knew the psalms in Hebrew form.

(d) Col 3[3f] death—life—hidden—Christ—Christ—manifested—life—glory.

(e) 1 Co 5[2-6] is the kind of sentence which seems interminable to the Greek student and on which Semitic culture throws light, with a ABCBA arrangement and chiasmus within chiasmus:

A		B		C		B		A	
puffed up		misconduct	A	Lord		Satan	A	boast-ing	
		presence	B	Jesus	A	destruction	B		
		presence	B	you	B	flesh	C		
		misconduct	A	me	B	spirit	C		
				Lord		salvation	B		
				Jesus	A	Day of Lord	A		

In this instance the study of chiasmus helps the textual critic. The first reference to " Lord Jesus " in member C has the addition ἡμῶν in p[46] BKL 0142 DG lat syr[pesh], and as this addition balances the fourth member of the chiasmus-within-chiasmus, there is a good reason for accepting it.

(f) Not only does this study help with the text, but also in interpretation, e.g.: Mt 7[6]

" Give not what is holy to the *dogs* (A),
Neither cast your pearls before *swine* (B),
Lest they [B must be *swine*] trample them under foot (B),
And they [A must be the *dogs*, not swine] turn and rend you (A)."
The last line is different from the usual interpretation.

Probably much longer passages than these, even whole epistles, among Paul's writings, may be planned (unconsciously?) on the chiasmic pattern.

§ 2. Word Order within the Clause [1]

(*a*) Idiosyncrasies of Biblical Greek through Semitic influence.

1. Co-ordinating particles as first word.   Semitic languages avoid second-place conjunctions, and this tendency was inherited by Biblical Greek, which either placed the conjunction first or else avoided altogether the second-place conjunctions like γάρ, γε, μέν, δέ, οὖν, τε.   Thus ἄρα is first word in Mt 12²⁸, τοίνυν in Lk 20²⁵ Heb 13¹³, μενοῦνγε in Ro 10¹⁸, τοιγαροῦν in Heb 12¹.

2. The verb (contrary to contemporary secular Greek, where mainly it has middle position) occurs as near the beginning as possible [2], followed by pers. pronoun, subject, obj., supplementary

---

[1] T. D. Goodell, " The Order of Words in Greek," *Trans. and Proc. Amer. Phil. Assn.* XXI. 5 (21. 24).   W. Rhys Roberts, "A Point of Greek and Latin Word-Order," *Class. Rev.*, 1912, 177–9.   G. Cuendet, *L'ordre des mots dans le texte grec et dans les versions gotique . . . des Évangiles, I. Les groupes nominaux*, Paris 1929.   M. Frisk, *Studien zur griechische Worstellung*, Göteborg 1932.   J. M. Rife, " The Mechanics of Translation Greek," *JBL* 52, 1933, 244ff.   D. J. Wieand, *Subject-Verb-Object Relationship in Independent Clauses in the Gospels and Acts* (Diss. Univ. Chicago) 1946.   Moulton-Howard 416–418.   E. Norden, *Agnostos Theos*, Leipzig 1913, 365f " Stellung des Verbums in NT Griechischen."   He makes the prominence of the verb in first-place a sign of Semitism, and on this he quotes Wellhausen with approval.

[2] The normal order in the ancient Greek was Subj.-Obj.-Verb (SOV) and the nearest books to this ideal in Bibl. Greek literature are 2–4 Mac.

	VSO	SVO	SOV	VOS	OSV	OVS
2 Mac	1	4	4	–	–	–
3 Mac	1	2	5	–	2	–
4 Mac	–	2	5	2	1	–
Plato	–	1	7	1	1	–

ptc. E.g. Lk 1¹¹ ὤφθη δὲ αὐτῷ ἄγγελος κυρίου ἑστὼς ἐκ δεξιῶν. In Mk the copula occurs in this position in 24 out of 29 instances (the exceptions: 5⁵ 7¹⁵ 13²⁵ 14⁴⁹). The predicative ptc. immediately follows the subject in Bibl. Greek: Mk 1⁶ καὶ ἦν ὁ Ἰωάννης ἐνδεδυμένος, 14⁴· ⁴⁰ Lk 2³² Ac 12⁶. This is Hebraic word-order, for in Aramaic the verb tends to end the clause. In periphrastic tenses the subject comes between the copula and the ptc., e.g. Mk 1⁶· ³³ 2⁴· ⁶· ¹⁸ 3¹ 4³⁸ 5¹¹· ⁴⁰ 6⁵² 14⁴· ⁴⁰ 15⁷· ²⁶· ⁴⁰· ⁴³ (exceptions 7¹⁵ 10³² 13²⁵). In Hebrew the subject follows the verb directly, but occasionally the object intervenes between the verb and subject (e.g. Ge 1¹⁷), and the personal pronoun always does so (see 8 below).[1]

3. Article and noun adhere closely together, and in Hebrew they are actually one. That is why in LXX only 4 per cent of the def. articles stand apart from their nouns in books translated from the canonical literature, whereas in the books having no MT as *Vorlage* the percentage is as high as 11 per cent. For the NT epistles the figure is 18 per cent. It is still higher (25 per cent) when seven non-Biblical works of class., Koine, and MGr are chosen for a count (Rife, *JBL* 52, 248).

Some NT books approach this standard, but on the whole NT is closer to the Hebraic order (VSO) and towards the subsequent tendency of MGr (SVO)

	VSO	SVO	SOV	VOS	OSV	OVS
Synoptic parallels:						
Mk	3	9	4	–	1	1
Mt	1	5	1	–	–	1
Lk	1	4	2	–	–	1
Luke entire	9	19	8	2	–	1
John	–	4	3	1	2	–
Acts	6	31	1	1	1	5
Ro	–	4	5	–	–	1

The figures are those of Rife who restricted himself to main declarative clauses where both subj. and obj. were nouns, his method being to read from the beginning of each book until ten exx. were collected (*JBL* 52, 250f). But requirements of emphasis will everywhere upset rules of word-order. See also Zerwick *Untersuchungen* 75–108; P.–L. Couchoud, "La Place du Verbe dans Marc," *JThS* 30, 1929, 47ff.

[1] Therefore in Mk 2¹⁵ᶠ punctuate (not as NEB, etc.): "For they were many. There followed him some scribes of the Pharisees. They noticed him eating . . . ."

4. Again, Hebrew word-order supports the after-position of the adj., because nothing can come between art. and noun. Although the NT epistles display a very high proportion of non-Semitic word-order in this respect, the gospels more closely conform. The tendency in the Koine is for the adj. to precede the noun. A significant comparison is that between the papyri of ii–i/B.C. examined by Mayser and the first nineteen chapters of the LXX. The papyri have 140 exx. of the type ὁ ἀγαθὸς ἀνήρ and only four or five of ὁ ἀνὴρ ὁ ἀγαθός; whereas the Biblical chapters have ὁ ἀγαθὸς ἀνήρ 17 times, but ὁ ἀνὴρ ὁ ἀγαθός 56 times (the proportion in 1 Km 1–6 is 1 : 16). See Mayser II 2, 52ff and see also, pp. 189f.

5. As in the Heb. construct state, the genitive in translation Greek follows immediately upon its governing noun. The tendency in the literary style was, however, for the gen. to precede, and we find this much more frequently in the free Greek books of the LXX. In the NT it is consciously stylistic, as 2 Co 1¹⁹ ὁ τοῦ θεοῦ . . . υἱός, 2 Pt 3² τῆς τῶν ἀποστόλων ὑμῶν ἐντολῆς. The need to follow the Hebrew construction closely may result in the dissociation of analogous nouns, as in Ge 41⁸ *the magicians of Egypt and their wise men.*

6. Unemphatic direct or indirect personal pronouns (αὐτῷ, αὐτῇ, αὐτοῖς) come closely after the verb in Bibl. Greek on the model of the Heb. pronominal suffix which is one with the verb : Lk 1¹¹ ὤφθη δὲ αὐτῷ, Ac 27² ὄντος σὺν ἡμῖν Ἀριστάρχου. There are exceptions, e.g. : the pronoun αὐτῷ precedes the verb in Jn 7²⁶ 10⁴ 12²⁹ (but it follows the verb 145 times in Jn), and αὐτοῖς has an intruding word (other than δέ or οὖν) between it and the verb in 2²⁴ (ἑαυτόν p⁶⁶ WΘ), 8²¹ (οὖν πάλιν, but S omits πάλιν, and some minusc. have πάλιν *after* αὐτοῖς), 10⁷ (οὖν πάλιν, but p⁴⁵ p⁶⁶ SW om πάλιν, and SB om αὐτοῖς).

7. In Semitic word-order the demonstrative adj. always follows the noun, and this is usual in Bibl. Greek. See p. 193. Some displacements are difficult to understand, e.g. Lk 24³¹ αὐτῶν δὲ διηνοίχθησαν οἱ ὀφθαλμοί.

8. (i) As in Hebrew the prepositional phrase comes immediately after the verb if the Heb. preposition would have a pronominal suffix (e.g. Ge 24⁶), but the prepositional phrase comes after the subject (which itself is after the verb) if the Hebrew preposition would have a noun after it (e.g. Ge 24²).

This makes it certain that, against RSV, NEB, etc., in Mk 6²⁶ we interpret *he was grieved because of his oaths and guests* (not *he was unwilling . . . because of his oaths and guests*); and in Lk 11¹³ it is *your heavenly Father*, not *your Father will give from heaven*.

(ii) So also the prepositional phrase occurs immediately after its noun, following the Heb. phrase with אשׁר or the Heb. genitive of quality. The LXX books written in free Greek, especially 2–4 Mac, tend to place the prepositional phrase between article and noun (Johannessohn DGPS 362ff). The translation books tend to place the prep. phrase after the noun, usually with repetition of the article.

(*b*) Oratory and word-order. Interruption of the normal order to give oratorical effect may result in ambiguity : Ac 4³³ AE μεγάλη δυνάμει ἀπεδίδουν οἱ ἀπόστολοι τὸ μαρτύριον τῆς ἀναστάσεως Ἰησοῦ Χρ. τοῦ κυρίου (p⁴⁵SB τὸ μαρτύριον οἱ ἀπόστολοι ; B τοῦ κυρίου Ἰ. τῆς ἀναστάσεως) ; either *the apostles of the Lord Jesus witnessed to the resurrection*, or *the apostles witnessed to the resurrection of the Lord Jesus* ; the order is rather unnatural, whatever reading we adopt (see *Beg.* III, cclix n. 2). Ac 19²⁰ οὕτως κατὰ κράτος τοῦ κυρίου ὁ λόγος ηὔξανεν (τοῦ κυρίου must refer to ὁ λόγος). Ac 1² ἐντειλάμενος τοῖς ἀποστόλοις διὰ πνεύματος ἁγίου οὓς ἐξελέξατο (unnatural order). Heb 12²³ κριτῇ θεῷ πάντων *God of all* or *judge of all*? All this reveals a weakness inherent in the flexibility of the Greek language.

(*c*) Stereotyped phrases. A customary word-order is observed, e.g. ἄνδρες καὶ γυναῖκες, γυν. καὶ παιδία (but παιδία first in Mt 14²¹ D), ἐσθίειν καὶ πίνειν, βρῶσις καὶ πόσις, πόδες καὶ χεῖρες (reversed at Lk 24³⁹ but not in S), ζῶντες καὶ νεκροί, νυκτὸς καὶ ἡμέρας, etc. The suggestion that there is a stereotyped phrase may account for the peculiar order in Ro 8¹⁸ πρὸς τὴν μέλλουσαν δόξαν ἀποκαλυφθῆναι, and Ga 3²³ εἰς τὴν μέλλουσαν πίστιν ἀποκαλυφθῆναι (ἡ μέλλουσα δόξα being a set phrase).

INDEX TO REFERENCES

(a) New Testament.

Thick type represents more important discussion.

MATTHEW		MATTHEW—*continued*		MATTHEW—*continued*	
	PAGE		PAGE		PAGE
1. 1 . .	167	4. 3 . .	183	5. 48 . .	86
1. 2 f.	**167, 345**	4. 6 . .	183	6. 1 . .	**144**
1. 6 .	167, 169	4. 8 . .	227	6. 2 .	42, **77**, 112
1. 11 f. . .	212	4. 11 . .	67	6. 3 .	17, 39
1. 16 .	152, 167	4. 15	175, **212, 247**	6. 4 .	39, 334
1. 18	78, 140, 162,	4. 16 .	39, 316	6. 5·	86, 112, **226**
	176, **226**, 322	4. 23 .	51, 211	6. 6 .	77, 112
1. 19 . .	157	4. 25 . .	**275**	6. 7 . .	253
1. 20	**77, 151**, 322	5. 1 .	**173**, 322	6. 8 .	49, 144
1. 21 .	**40**, 40, 246	5. 3	220, 239	6. 9 . .	35
1. 22 . .	70	5. 5 . .	232	6. 10 .	**75**, 77
2. 1 .	26, 172	5. 6 .	177, 232	6. 12 . .	37
2. 2	**26**, 134, 172, 189	5. 8	220, 239	6. 13 .	**14**, 77
2. 3 . .	317	5. 9 . .	208	6. 16 .	76, 112
2. 4 .	63, 65	5. 10 . .	85	6. 17	37, 54, 154
2. 6	31, 48, 151, 170	5. 12 . .	**76**	6. 18 .	106, 159
2. 8	112, 154, 156, 335	5. 13 . .	183	6. 19 .	**42, 76**
2. 9	**26**, 172, 279	5. 14 . .	279	6. 22 . .	**183**
2. 10 .	**160, 242**	5. 15 .	**150**, 292	6. 24 . .	36
2. 12 . .	52	5. 16 .	72, **150**	6. 25	24, 76, 99, **117**
2. 13 .	141, 142	5. 17 .	**77**, 134	6. 27 . .	209
2. 14 . .	235	5. 18 . .	96	6. 28	76, 179, **313**, 325
2. 15 . .	151	5. 19 .	31, 45, **107**	6. 30 . .	**115**
2. 16	72, 154, 227	5. 20 .	96, **216**	6. 32 . .	313
2. 20	**25**, 75, **81**, 154,	5. 21 . .	86	6. 34	72, **76, 77**, 311
	293	5. 22 . .	151	7. 2 . .	**291**
2. 22 .	26, **64**, 226	5. 24 . .	75	7. 3 . .	191
2. 23 .	. 7, 26	5. 25 .	88, 89, **110**	7. 4 . .	94
3. 3 .	. 44	5. 25 . .	96	7. 5 . .	139
3. 4 .	**41, 66**	5. 28	73, **144**, 151, 232	7. 6 .	77, **346**
3. 5 .	**16, 66**	5. 29 f.	32, 42, 115,	7. 8 . .	151
3. 6 . .	**66**		139	7. 9 .	55, 325
3. 7 . .	**66**	5. 32 .	**107**, 151	7. 11 . .	157
3. 9 .	42, 168	5. 34 . .	149	7. 12	**107, 108, 138**
3. 10	62, **199, 200**	5. 35 . .	255	7. 15 . .	48
3. 11 .	**252, 266**	5. 36 . .	75	7. 16 . .	293
3. 12 . .	325	5. 39	48, 77, 149, **197**	7. 17 . .	63
3. 13 . .	141	5. 40 .	39, 316	7. 21 . .	196
3. 14	39, 65, 139, **334**	5. 41 . .	48	7. 23 .	153, 177
3. 15	88, 149, 200	5. 42 . .	76	7. 24	48, 189, **233**, 316
3. 16 .	25, **259**	5. 43 . .	86	7. 26 .	151, 221
3. 17 .	25, 44, 186	5. 44 . .	86	7. 27 . .	207
4. 1 . .	134	5. 45	52, 53, 208, 291	7. 28 . .	66

351

(b) Septuagint.

(c) Other Versions of Old Testament.

(d) Pseudepigrapha of Old Testament.

(e) Early Christian Writings.

Clement of Rome (i/a.d.)

Epistle of Barnabas (i/ii a.d.)

Shepherd of Hermas (i/ii A.D.)

V *Visions* M *Mandates* S *Similitudes*

Ignatius, bp. of Antioch (ii/A.D.)

Martyrdom of Polycarp (ii/A.D.)

Didache (ii/A.D.)

Epistle to Diognetus (c. A.D. 150)

(f) INSCRIPTIONS AND PAPYRI

Please see vol. II pp. 503–12 for abbreviations not explained here.

(g) GREEK LITERATURE.

i. Classical.

ii. *Hellenistic.*

INDEX OF SUBJECTS

wish opt. 121—ὅταν w. ind. 125—εἰ w. fut. ind. (wish) 127—M. Zerwick and 137, 341, 342—ἄρχομαι 138—artic. inf. 141—ἰδεῖν w. ptc. or ὅτι 161—art. w. Ἰησοῦς 166 f.—ἕτερος absent 197—word-order w. gen. 217—attrib. and partit. gen. 219—word-order of εὐθύς and πάλιν 229— G. D. Kilpatrick and 229, 320—constr. w. ἔρχομαι 257—παρά 272— παρά w. acc. only local 273—repet. of prep. 275—ἐνώπιον absent 277— impers. " they " 292 f.—insertion of copula 294—ellipse of copula 299, 306—pl. vb. w. ὄχλος 312—καθώς 320—gen. abs. 322 f.—ὅτι recit. 326—δέ or καί 329, 332, 334—μέν . . . δέ 331 f.—τότε 341—position of verb 348.

Mary of Bethany, identification 80.

Masculine : f. fem. or neut. 21—masculinizing of πέτρα 22—pl. incl. masc. and fem. components 22.

Matthew, gospel of : πρωΐα and ὀψία unclass. 17—meaning of πολλοί 26— pl. of ὄχλος 26—oblique αὐτός 38—avoids refl. pron. 42—anaphora : prefers οὗτος to ἐκεῖνος 46—ὅς and ὅστις confused 47, 48—ὅ ἐστιν 48—λέγει 61, 340—style 66, 158—γέγονεν f. pf. 70—Chantraine and pf. 71—tenses and Lk. 77 f.—periphr. f. pres., impf. 88, 89—imperat. ἵνα 94—οὐ μή 96 f.—epexeg. ἵνα 103—non-fin. ἵνα 104—rel. clauses 107, 108—and LXX 108—ἕως 111—ὅταν w. subj. 112—ἐάν w. subj. 114 f.—artic. inf. 135, 141—fin. inf. (cp. Mk) 135—ἄρχομαι 138—τοῦ w. 2nd fin. inf. 142—Semit. εἷς 196—ἕτερος 197—position of adv. 228—καὶ ἰδού 229—εἰς and ἐν correctly distinct 254—παρά w. accus. only local 273—repet. of prep. 275—ἕως, ἄχρι, μέχρι 276—ἐνώπιον absent 277—οὐ 285—ellipse of εἶναι 299, 309 f.— ὁ πᾶς w. ptc. 316— ὥσπερ 320—gen. abs. 322—ὅτι recit. 326—μέν . . . δέ 331 f.—γάρ 331— πλήν 338—asyndeton 340—τότε 341.

Mayser, E. passim.

Meecham, H. G. v, 81, 268, 343.

Meisterhans, K. 122, 128.

Menander 18—s. Index of Ref.

Michaelis, W. 212.

Middle voice 53–7—in class. Gk. 54—rarely refl. in NT 54—mid. f. act. 54–6—forms tend to merge w. pass. 54—not recipr. in NT 54—pass. f. mid. 56 f.—act. f. mid. 56 f.—not very significant 56—disappearing 56–7.

Milligan, G. 25, 293.

Milligan, W. 345.

Minor Prophets (LXX) 203 f., 274, 279, 332—s. Index of Ref.

Modern Greek 3, 17, 18, 26, 31, 32, 36, 40, 51, 52, 53, 58, 60, 68, 69, 74, 75, 91, 94, 95, 99, 103, 107, 138, 166, 171, 192, 212, 216, 225, 235, 236, 249, 250, 251, 253, 254, 261, 270, 284, 286, 295, 304, 312, 315, 336, 342, 347.

Moffatt, J. 317, 336.

Moule, C. F. D. 73, 86, 152, 178, 211, 233, 234, 245, 249, 267, 269, 271, 291, 292, 317, 337.

Moulton, J. H. v, 1, 9, 16, 34, 63, 70, 77 f., 86, 96, 143, 147, 168, 194, 233, 248, 261, 269, 293, 308, 315, 316, 343.

Multiplicatives 187.

N.E.B. (New English Bible) 95, 102, 137, 143, 143, 145, 146, 151, 176, 181, 187, 212, 335, 336, 348, 350.

Nauck, W. 337.

Negatives 94, 95, 281–7, 286 (double).

Neuter : substantival expressions 13 f.—neut. adj. w. sing. or pl. of persons (collective) 14, 150—plur. adverbially 21—masc. f. 21, 312, 314 f.—fem. f. (Heb.) 21—ὅ ἐστιν 48—pronom. pred. in neut. (τι, οὐδέν, ὅ, etc.) 311—predic. adj. in neut. 311—sg. and pl. vb. w. neut. pl. 312 f.—Οὐαί 315.

Nissen, Th. 307.

of ὅς and ὅστις, ὅσος and ὁπόσος 47—rules 47 f.—general rel. 47,
107—ὅσπερ 48—ὅ ἐστιν (i.e.) 48—ὅ interrog.? 50—ὅς ἄν f. ἐάν τις
107 f.—constr. ad sens. 312—rel. attract. and inverse 324.
Repetition : of prep. 275—distrib. doubling 187.
Revelation : usage and style like Jn 25—αἰῶνες eternity 25—repet. of
pers. pron. 39—τάδε λέγει 44—ὅ ἐστιν 48—pf. f. aor. 69, 70—periphr.
tenses 88 f.—fut. f. Heb. impf. 86—imperat. ἵνα 95, 102—οὐ μή 96 f.—
ἵνα w. fut. ind. 100—ἵνα w. subj. 101—epexeg. ἵνα 104—τοῦ w. inf.
(imper.) 141—anarthr. Ἰησοῦς 167—ἕτερος absent 197—position of
πᾶς 203, 205—προσκυνέω w. accus. 245—εἰς and ἐν not confused 255—
ἐκ against ἀπό 259—σύν absent 265—παρά w. acc. absent 273—ὑπό w.
acc. absent 275—repet. of prep. 275—ἄχρις 276—ἐνώπιον frequ. in
Ist part 277—ellipse of εἶναι 299, 310—solecisms 314 f.—ὥσπερ 320—
γάρ 331—μέν lacking 332—δέ or καί 332—οὖν 337—few particles
341—parataxis 341—μετὰ τοῦτο (ταῦτα) 341.
Rhetoric 39.
Rhythm 39.
Rife, J. M. 347, 348.
Robertson, A. T. 80, 255, 283.

Schema Atticum 312 f.
Schlatter, A. 316.
Schmid, W. 135.
Schmidt, K. L. 27, 176.
Schneider, J. 26.
Schrenk, G. 213, 267.
Schwyzer, E. 33.
Scribes' corrections 25, 26, 27, 35, 38, 39, 43, 44, 52, 56, 68, 70, 71, 76, 77,
82, 83, 87, 91, 96, 97, 98, 100, 109, 116, 129, 132, 135, 136, 138, 140,
142, 152, 167, 178, 184, 190, 200, 209, 218, 228, 243, 245, 264, 286, 287,
312, 314, 319, 321, 322, 324, 325, 333, 335, 338, 340, 341, 342, 343.
Selwyn, E. G. 235.
Semitic influence 4, 8, 23, 88, 96 and *passim*—in MGr 32.
Semitisms 4—interchange of εἰς and ἐν 2, 249, 251, 254–6, 257—pers.
pron. : unemph. nom. 3, 37 f. ; oblique cases frequ. and unemph. 3,
38 ; f. refl. 42—pos. f. superl. (Heb.) 3, 31—proleptic pron. (Aram.) 3,
9, 41, 209—reduced number and use of particles 4—hist. pres. 5, 61,
61—perf. aor. (Heb. stative pf.) 5, 72, 73—periphrasis 5, 85, 87–9—
partit. expression as subj. or obj. (Heb.) 7, 207 f.—αὐτός demonstr. 7,
41—gen. of qual. f. adj. 7, 212 f.—ἀπὸ μιᾶς (Aram.) 7, 18, 21—ψυχή
refl. pron. 7, 43—οὐ . . . πᾶς 7, 196 f.—πᾶς . . . οὐ, εἰς . . . οὐ 196 f.—
anarthr. πᾶς 199 f.—case w. vbs. 7—distrib. sing. 7, 23, 25, 187—τοῦ
w. inf. 8, 141, 142—ἐν τῷ w. inf. 8, 144 f.—εἰς τό w. inf. 8, 143—
position of adj. 8—pleon. pers. pron. after rel. pron. 9, 325—word-order
9, 193—parataxis 9, 155, 334 f., 342—asyndeton (Aram.) 9, 341—fem.
f. neut. (Heb.) 21—εἰς κρυπτήν (Aram.) 21—pl. f. sing. (αἰῶνες,
οὐρανοί) 25—true superl. almost dead 31—ἀπὸ προσώπου 25, 279—pl.
of ἡμέρα (Heb.) 27—periphr. w. πρόσωπον, στόμα, χείρ 25, 279, 280—
pos. f. compar. (Heb.) 29, 31, 32—compar. expressing exclusion (ἤ or
παρά f. μᾶλλον ἤ) 32—vocat. 33, 34 f.—Aram. emph. state 34—Heb.
constr. state 34, 169, 170, 173, 179 f.—uses of εἰς 36, 187, 195 f.—ὅδε
f. οὗτος 44—causatives in -εύειν 52 f.—act. form w. pass. meaning
(Aram.) 53—ποιέομαι ἔλεος (Heb.) 56—fut. ind. for Heb. impf. (Rev)
86 ; f. imper. 86—pres. ptc. f. fut. ptc. 87—imperat. ἵνα 95, 102, 129,
305—compar. opt. 132—τίθημι ἐν τῇ καρδίᾳ, etc. 139—use of inf.
(without ὥστε) to express result 134–6—artic. inf. 134—pleon. ἄρχομαι
138, 154 f.—complem. inf. 138 f.—ἐγένετο constrs. 139, 145, 148 f.,
291, 335—πρὸς τό w. inf 144—artic. ptc. as proper noun (Heb.) 150 f.—
ptc. f. rel. clause 152 f.—pleon. λαβών, λέγων 154, 155—ἔγραψεν λέγων
156—ὁδόν as prep. 175, 212, 247—ptc. f. Heb. inf. abs. 156—ἐν in

multiplic. 188—distrib. doubling 187—ἄνθρωπος f. τις 195—εἷς in post-pos. 196—πᾶς ὁ frequ. 201, 316—υἱός 207 f.—μυρίαδες μυριάδων 210—partit. ἐν 210—obj. gen. 212—appos. gen. or gen. of content 214— pron. added to gen. of qual. properly belonging to 1st noun 214—οὕτως predic. 226—fill w. accus. 232 f.—γεύομαι w. accus. 233—σπλαγχνίζομαι 234, 272—gen. w. verbal adj. 234—κωλ ύω ἀπό 235—eth. dat. 239— ἔρχεταί σοι 239—ἀστεῖος τῷ θεῷ 239—γίνομαι w. dat. 239 f.—dat. of agent w. pass. 240—dat. f. Heb. inf. abs. 241 f.—ἡμέρᾳ καὶ ἡμέρᾳ 243— φοβέομαι ἀπό 244—ὄμνυμι ἐν 244, 252, 255—accus. of content 245— καλέω τὸ ὄνομα w. accus. 246—εἰς predic. 247—ἄφαντος ἐγένετο ἀπό 251—ἐν instr. 252 f.—τοῖς εἰς μακράν 254—εἰς ὄνομα 255—δίδωμι εἰς place on 256—δὸς ἀντὶ ἐμοῦ καὶ σοῦ 258—ἐπ' ἐσχάτου τῶν ἡμερῶν 271— pre-position of ἕνεκα 276—ἐν μέσῳ etc. w. gen. 277—ὀπίσω as prep. 277—ἔμπροσθεν, ἐναντίον, ἐνώπιον 277 f.—impers. " they " (Aram.) 292 f.—ὄνομα without copula 295—οὐαί 296—ellipse of εἶναι 300— τί ἐμοὶ καὶ σοί; 303, 309—τί πρός σε; 303, 309—indecl. λέγων, λέγοντες 315—πᾶς ὅς 316—ὁ πᾶς w. ptc. 316—consec. ὅτι 318— weakening of ἐπεί 318—εἰ f. οὐ in oaths 319, 333—εἰ w. dir. qu. 319, 333—ὡς to soften 320—tempor. conj. instead of gen. abs. 321— anacolouthon after rel. clause 325—ὅτι recit. 326—εἰ μή interchanged w. ἀλλά (Aram.) 330—καί introd. subord. clause 334—τότε (Aram.) 341—chiasmus 345-7—particle 1st word 347—vb's position in sentence 347 f.—art. close to noun 348 f.

Sentence building 11, book I—sentence complete book II.

Septuagint : ὅδε more common than in NT 44—τῇδε 44—ὅστις confined to nom. and acc. 47—hist. pres. 61—aor. pf. 70—pf. 82 f., 84—periphr. tenses 89—ὄφελον 91—imperat. ἵνα 95—οὐ μή 96 f.—fin. ἵνα 102— non-fin. ἵνα 104—ἐάν w. impf. 116—opt. 120 f., 122, 123, 125, 126, 127, 130, 131, 133—inf. of purpose 135—τοῦ w. inf. 141—ἐν τῷ w. inf. 145 f.—ptc. 156—rendering of Yhvh 174—position of πᾶς 202 ff.— piecemeal transl. 237, 337—and passim.

Septuagintisms 8, 142, 145, 156.

Sibylline Oracles 25, 26, 27.

Singular 22-5—distrib. sing. 7, 23, 25—w. collectives (generic) 22 f.— ἕκαστος w. pl. 312—vb. w. neut. pl. subj. 312 f.—w. cmpd. subj. 313 f.— w. fem. pl. 315.

Sirach (LXX) : πρίν 140—πᾶς 202 ff.

Slavery (Paul's advice) 76.

Slotty, F. 95.

Soffray, M. 35.

Solecisms 93, 314-7.

Solomon, Psalms of 96, 203 ff.

Sophocles 49, 96, 97—s. Index of Ref.

Sophocles, E. A. (lexicographer) 58.

Souter, A. 22.

Stählin, G. 245.

Stauffer, E. 40.

Strabo 13, 14, 71, 118, 159, 299.

Style 137—desire f. variety 67, 105, 109 f., 113, 135, 142, 157.

Subject 11—absence of 291-3, change of, marked by ὁ (οἱ) δέ 37.

Subjunctive 93-117—more often without ἄν in Hell. Gk. 2—Aktionsart 74-8, 107—periphrastic 88-9—confused w. opt. in wishes 94, 120— πρίν 113, 140—as substitute for opt. 119.

Use in main clauses 93-9—prohib. subj. 74, 76-8, 94. 95—as substit. f. imperat. 93-8 ; f. fut. 98—jussive 94—hortat. 94—imperat. ἵνα 94 f.—οὐ μή w. aor. subj. (prohib. and denials) 96 f., 97 ; w. pres. subj. 97—w. μή f. cautious statements 98—in dubit. or delib. qu. 98 f.—οὐ μή in qu. 283.

Subord. clauses 99-117—fearing 99—after μή 99 f.—after ἵνα 100-5— neg. μή 100, 105, 106—fin. clause 100-6—w. ὅπως, ὡς 105 f.—w. ὥστε

INDEX OF GREEK WORDS

δύο second 315
δυσμαί anarthr. 26, 172
δωρεάν 247
δῶρον 295, 309

ἐάν 109, 113 f., 115 f.—instead of εἰ
(w. indic.) 107, 115 f.—ὅς ἐάν
107 f.—ἐὰν καί 321—f. ἄν 2
ἐάω: οὐκ ἐῶ 287
ἑαυτός f. 1st or 2nd p. 42
ἑαυτοῦ: f. ἀλλήλων 43 f.—and αὐτοῦ
41—indir. refl. 43—in Lk 42—
position 190
ἑβδόμη, ἡ 17
ἑβδομηκοντάκις ἑπτά 187
ἐγγίζω: pf. 5, 82—ingress. aor. 72—
constr. 241
ἐγγύς: case 216—as predic. 226
ἐγείρω: intrans. 52—pass. w. act.
meanings 57—futur. pres. 63—
ἐγήγερται he is risen 69—pres.
imper. 75—ἐγρήγορα 82—ἐγερθείς
154
ἐγκαίνια 27
ἐγκακέω w. ptc. 159
ἐγκαλέω: pass. 57—constr. 236, 242
ἐγκαταλείπω perf. aor. 72
ἐγκόπτω constr. 245
ἐγώ: μου f. ἐμός 4—literary pl. 28—
use of nom. 37 f.—μου and ἐμοῦ
38, 189—emph. obl. cases 39—
ἐμοῦ f. ἐμαυτοῦ 42—possess. gen.
189—position of μου 189
ἔθνη: anarthr. 180—schema Atticum
313
ἔθος ἐστίν constr. 149
εἰ 115 f.—wish-clause 91—f. ἐάν (w.
subj.) 107, 116—εἰ καί 115, 321—
w. opt. (final) 127—εἴ γε 319—
whether 319, 333—oaths, etc. 319,
333—εἰ οὐ 319—dir. quest. 319,
333—εἰ μή 333—εἰ μή f. ἀλλά
330—εἰ δὲ μή (γε) 331
εἰδέναι: constr. 160, 162—οἶδα perf.
pres. 62, 82
εἴθε w. ind. 91
εἰθισμένον, τό w. gen. 234
εἰμι, εἶναι: perf. pres. 62—imperat.
fut. 86—fut. ptc. 86—in periphr.
5, 85, 88 f., 153—ὁ ὢν καὶ ὁ ἦν
230—ptc. redund. 151 f. — ellipse
231, 294-310—w. dat. 240
εἴπερ 319, 330

εἶπεν: and ἔλεγεν 64—εἰπών 155 f.
—w. ἵνα 103— πρός 237
εἴπως 127
εἰρήνη w. dat. 304, 308
εἰς: εἰς κρυπτήν 6—εἰς τό w. inf.
8, 85, 106, 135, 141, 142, 143—
ὁ (οἱ) εἰς 15—εἰς χεῖρας 24, 280
— encroaches on simple case 236,
251, 253— w. λογίζομαι 246—w.
ἔχω, etc. (predic.) 246, 247—
γίνομαι, εἰμι 253—f. ἐπί, πρός 256
local 266 — distrib. 266— final
266 —causal 266 f.— confused w.
ἐν, see ἐν
εἷς: indef. art. 4, 195 f.—ἀπὸ μιᾶς
7, 18, 21—μία f. πρώτη 17, 187—
ἕν fem. 21—ὁ εἷς . . . ὁ ἕτερος 36
—εἷς τὸν ἕνα 187—ἓν τριάκοντα
188— w. partit. gen. 195—εἷς τις
196—καθείς 197—εἷς ἕκαστος 198
—cmpd. vbs. constr. 242
εἰσάγω aor. 69
εἰσακούω 251
εἰσέρχομαι linear aor. 71
εἰσφέρω aor. imper. 77
εἴτε . . . εἴτε 302, 319, 333
εἴωθα 82
ἕκαστος 198—anarthr. 198— diff.
from πᾶς 199—w. pl. vb. 312
ἐκβάλλω futur. pres. 63
ἐκδίδομαι mid. 55
ἐκεῖ: redund. after ὅπου 46—f. ἐκεῖθεν 226—temp. 226
ἐκεῖθεν: οἱ ἐ. 14—f. ἐκεῖ 226
ἐκεῖνος 5, 45 f., 192 f.—ἐκείνης
(scil. τῆς ὁδοῦ) 16—anaph. 46—
simply he 46—meaning 45 f.—
ἐκείνου possess. 190—art. 192
ἐκκλησία: anarthr. 176—constr. ad
sens. 312
ἐκκλίνω intr. 52
ἐκκόπτομαι 63
ἐκλέγομαι mid. 55
ἐκλεκτός w. gen. 234
ἐκπίπτω: f. ἐκβάλλομαι 53—gnom.
aor. 73
ἐκπλήσσομαι impf. 66
ἐκτός: w. gen. 216, 277—ἐ. εἰ μή 321
ἐκχέω: w. gen. 234—w. dat. 238
ἐλαία ellipse 18
'Ελλαιῶν ὄρος 230
ἔλαττον, τό f. persons 14, 21
ἐλαύνω impf. 67

οὐδέ 340
οὐκοῦν 282, 337
οὖν 329, 337 f.—ἄρα οὖν 330—
position 347— -ουν 196
οὐρανός: sg. and pl. 25—anarthr.
174 f.
οὔτε . . . οὔτε 340
οὗτος 192 f.—αὕτη f. τοῦτο 21—
αὐτή and αὕτη confused 40—deictic
44—w. anaphora 44 f., 46—pronominal 44 f.—αὐτὸ τοῦτο 45—
pointing forward to ὅτι, ἵνα, ἐάν,
infin. 45, 139—τοῦτο μὲν . . . τ.
δέ 45—elliptical τοῦτο δέ 45—
τούτου possess. 190—art. 192—
asyndetic μετὰ τοῦτο (ταῦτα) 341
οὕτω(ς): w. ptc. 154—as predic. 226,
303—ὡς . . . οὕτως 320
οὐχί 96, 282, 286, 329
ὀφείλω: intr. 51—ὤφειλον 90—ὄφελον 91, 295, 300—constr. 141
ὀφειλέτης constr. 238
ὀφθαλμός anarthr. 179
ὄχλος: constr. ad sens. 311—ὄχλοι
πολλοί 7, ?6
ὀψέ: ἐγένετο 226—ο. σαββάτων 278
ὀψία 17
ὄψιμον scil. ὑετός 18
ὀψώνιον pl. 27

παῖς, ἡ (voc.) 34—οἱ παῖδες 22
πάλαι, ἐκ 250
πάλιν in Mk 229
Παμφυλία art. 170
παντότε position 228
πάντως οὐ (οὐ πάντως) 287
παρά 6, 250, 272—w. acc. 273—
w. pos. and comp. 3, 7, 29, 31,
216, 251—w. inf. 144—w. gen.
273—οἱ π. 16—τὰ π. 15—ἀπό f.
233 f. 258 f.—w. dat. 273—
cmpd. vbs. constr. 242
παραβιάζομαι 65
παραγγέλλω : punctil. pres. 64—impf.
65, 67
παράγω intr. 51
παραδίδομαι : futur. pres. 63—aor. pf.
83—fut. ptc. 86, 151
παραινέω constr. 149
παρακαλέω: impf., aor. 65—constr.
142, 149
παραλαμβάνω Aktionsart 79
παραπλήσιον case 216

παρατηρέομαι 55
πάρειμι perfective 62
παρέχομαι 56
παριστάνω pres. and aor. imper.
76, 77
παρρησία constr. 241
πᾶς: position 5, 201-5—πᾶς . . . οὐ
(οὐ . . . πᾶς) 7, 196 f., 287—πᾶς
ὅστις (ὅς) 21, 316—ὁ πᾶς and pl.
21, 201—πᾶς ὁ w. ptc. 151, 197,
316—anarthr. 199 f.—w. art.
200 f.—πάντων f. fem. 316—
anacolouthon w. 316
πάσχα, τά 27
πάσχω: pres. imper. 76—aor. pf. 82
—w. ὑπό 53
Πάταρα 27
πατήρ: voc. 34, 35—art. 174
παύομαι mid. constr. 159, 235
πειθαρχέω constr. 7, 237
πείθω, -ομαι: constr. 137, 138, 237
—perf. pres. 62—πέπεισμαι 82,
137—s. πέποιθα
πεινάω w. acc. 232, 244
πέμπω epistol. aor. 73
πενθέω: trans. and intr. 244—aor.
imper. 76
πενθεροί, οἱ 22
πέποιθα: constr. 237, 242—pres.
sense 5, 82
πέραν w. gen. 216, 278
περί 6—not w. dat. 249—w. acc. 270
—οἱ π., τὰ π. 15, 16, 270—w.
gen. 269 f.—w. σπλαγχνίζομαι,
μεριμνάω, μέλει 269—w. ἐγκαλέομαι 231—w. θαυμάζω 269—
interch. w. ὑπέρ 270—τὰ π. w.
gen. 15, 269
περιάγω: intr. 51—w. double acc.
246
περιβάλλω: aor. imper. 77—w.
double acc. 246
περιβλέπομαι mid. 55—impf. 66
περιέχω 52, 292
περικύκλῳ f. περί 251
περίοδος ellipse 17
περιπατέω: pres. imper. 75, 77—
aor. imper. 76
περίχωρος, ἡ 16
πέτρα, πέτρος 22
πηλίκος exclam. 50
πίνω constr. 244
πίπτω: impf. 66—fut. f. impf. 86

πρότερον, τό 30
προϋπάρχω w. ptc. 159
προφθάνω w. ptc. 159
πρωΐ: τὸ π. adv. 14, 247—ἦν π. 226
πρωΐα, ἡ 17
πρῶτος f. πρότερος 32
πτωχεύω ingress. aor. 71, 72
πτωχός, ὁ 13, 23
πυκνότερον 3, 30
πύλη: ellipse 18—sing. and pl. 27
πυνθάνομαι impf. 65—aor. 65
πῦρ: w. φλόξ 213—(ἐν) πυρί 240, 252, 253
πῶς 117, 123, 137—f. ὡς, ὅτι 137

ῥαβδίζω constat. aor. 72
ῥάβδος: ellipse 18—ἐν 241
ῥίπτω intr. 52
ῥομφαία, ἐν 252
ῥύομαι: pass. 58—constr. 235
Ῥώμη, ἡ 171

σάββατον: sing., pl. 27—(δὶς τοῦ) σαββάτου 235—(ἐν) τῷ σ., τοῖς σ. 243—ὀψὲ σ. 278
σαλπίζω: aor. imper. 77
Σαμαρίτης art. 169
σαπρά, τά 14
σάρξ: anarthr. 177—τῇ σ. 239—(τὸ) κατὰ σ. 268
σεαυτοῦ 41—position 190
σελήνη art. 172
σημεῖον 26, 214
σήμερον, ἡ 17
σιγάω ingress. aor. 71 f.
σιωπάω impf. 66
σός disappearing 42, 191
σπάω 55
σπέρμα constr. ad sens. 312
σπλαγχνίζομαι constr. 234, 269, 272
σπουδαῖος comp. 30
σταυρόω aor. and pf. ptc. 85
στήκω 82
στηρίζω w. πρόσωπον τοῦ w. inf. 142
στοιχέω: imperat. inf. 78—pres. imper. 75
στολή distrib. sing. 25
στόμα Hebraism 25, 280
στρατεία constr. ad sens. 311 f.
στρ φω: intr. 2, 51, 52—aor. imper.

σύ: nom. 37—possess. gen. 38 f.
189—σου f. σεαυτοῦ 42 f.—
position of μου, σου, ἐμοῦ 189
συγκαλέομαι 55
συγκληρονόμος w. gen. 215
συλλαμβάνω pf. 84
συλλέγω impers. pl. 293
συμβαίνω: aor. pf. 82—συνέβη 139, 148, 292
συμβουλεύω, -ομαι constr. 149
συμπόσια 231
συμφέρει: constr. 103, 139, 149, 292
—συμφέρον scil. ἐστιν 88, 295, 300
σύμφυτος w. dat. 220
συμφωνέω constr. 149, 234
σύν: encroaches on simple dat. 236
—and μετά 265, 269—οἱ σὺν αὐτῷ 265
συνάγω intr. 51
συναίρω λόγον 56
συναντάω fut. ptc. 86
συναρπάζω pf. 84
συνέπομαι constr. 241
συνεργέω 244
συνέρχομαι linear aor. 71
συνίημι constr. 160
συντίθεμαι constr. 142
Συρία art. 170
σύρω 66
συσχηματίζομαι to conform 57
σῴζω constr. 235, 240—pf. 69, 83, 84—aor. 69—fut. ptc. 87
σῶμα: distrib. sing. 7, 23, 24—
w. gen. of qual. 213—schema Attic. 313
σωτήριος constr. 220—τὸ σωτ-ήριον 14

ταπεινόω aor. imper. 77
τάσσω constr. 149
ταχύς: τάχιον 30—ἐν τάχει 252
τε . . . καί, τε . . . τε, etc. 329, 338
f., 347—τε γάρ 339
τέκνον ellipse 21—τὰ τ. voc. 34
τελειόω: futur. pres. 63—w. ἵνα 102
τελέω: pf. 85—w. ptc. 159
τελευτάω aor. pf. 82
τέλος, εἰς 266
-τεος 91
τέταρτον, τό 17
τηρέω pf. 84
τίθημι: act. and mid. 55—ἔθετο 56
—impf. 67—pf. 84—constr. 246

χειμῶνος gen. of time within which 235
χείρ: ellipse 17—distrib. sing. 24—πόδες καὶ χεῖρες 350—Hebraism 24, 280
χειρόγραφον 219
χερουβείν gender 21
χιτῶνες 27
χορηγέω constr. 244
χρεία constr. 103, 104, 139
χρή 295, 308
χρηματίζω: pass. 57—gnom. fut. 86 —constr. 149
χρῆσαι aor. imper. 76
χρηστόν, τό 14—χρηστός comp. 31
χρίω constr. 240
Χριστός 212—art. 167
χρόνος: pl. 27—w. ἵνα 104—τοῦ w. inf. 141
χώρα ellipse 16
χωρίζω constr. 235
χωρίς w. gen. 278

ψάλλω constr. 236
ψεύδομαι: pres. imper. 76—constr. 236

ψηλαφάω w. acc. 232
ψυχή reflex. pron. 43—τῇ ψυχῇ 221

ὤ, ὦ 3, 33
ὧδε 44
ὥρα 243—ellipse 17—w. ἵνα 103—constr. 139—art. 179—acc. for time-when 248—scil. ἐστιν 295, 300
ὡς 135, 137, 161—w. superl. 31 (ὡς τάχιστα)—final 105, 136—consec. 136—w. inf. abs. 136—declarative 137—w. ptc 158—w. predic. 246, 321—no longer prep. 249—position w. neg. 286 f.—scil. ἐστιν 297 —to soften a statement 320—causal 320—as if 320—correlative 320—temp. 321—f. ἕως 321—clause-order 344
ὡσάν, ὡς ἐάν 112 f., 321
ὡσεί 158, 321
ὥσπερ 158—scil. ἐστιν 297, 310—correlative 320—ὡσπερεί 321
ὥστε 106, 134, 135, 136, 137 f., 139 —final 106, 136
ὠφελέω constr. 246, 292
ὠφέλιμος constr. 220